CONTENTS

Boxes

Tables

Figures

ASSUMPTIONS AND CONVENTIONS

A number of assumptions have been adopted for the projections presented in the *World Economic Outlook*. It has been assumed that real effective exchange rates will remain constant at their average levels during July 23–August 17, 2001, except for the currencies participating in the European exchange rate mechanism II (ERM II), which are assumed to remain constant in nominal terms relative to the euro; that established policies of national authorities will be maintained (for specific assumptions about fiscal and monetary polices in industrial countries, see Box A1); that the average price of oil will be $26.80 a barrel in 2001 and $24.50 a barrel in 2002, and remain unchanged in real terms over the medium term; and that the six-month London interbank offered rate (LIBOR) on U.S. dollar deposits will average 4.1 percent in 2001 and 3.7 percent in 2002. These are, of course, working hypotheses rather than forecasts, and the uncertainties surrounding them add to the margin of error that would in any event be involved in the projections. The estimates and projections are based on statistical information available through early September, 2001.

The following conventions have been used throughout the *World Economic Outlook*:

. . . to indicate that data are not available or not applicable;

— to indicate that the figure is zero or negligible;

– between years or months (for example, 1997–98 or January–June) to indicate the years or months covered, including the beginning and ending years or months;

/ between years or months (for example, 1997/98) to indicate a fiscal or financial year.

"Billion" means a thousand million; "trillion" means a thousand billion.

"Basis points" refer to hundredths of 1 percentage point (for example, 25 basis points are equivalent to ¼ of 1 percentage point).

In figures and tables, shaded areas indicate IMF staff projections.

Minor discrepancies between sums of constituent figures and totals shown are due to rounding.

As used in this report, the term "country" does not in all cases refer to a territorial entity that is a state as understood by international law and practice. As used here, the term also covers some territorial entities that are not states but for which statistical data are maintained on a separate and independent basis.

This report on the *World Economic Outlook* is available in full on the IMF's Internet site, *www.imf.org*. Accompanying it on the website is a larger compilation of data from the WEO database than in the report itself, consisting of files containing the series most frequently requested by readers. These files may be downloaded for use in a variety of software packages.

Inquiries about the content of the *World Economic Outlook* and the WEO database should be sent by mail, electronic mail, or telefax (telephone inquiries cannot be accepted) to:

World Economic Studies Division
Research Department
International Monetary Fund
700 19th Street, N.W.
Washington, D.C. 20431, U.S.A.
E-mail: weo@imf.org   Telefax: (202) 623-6343

PREFACE

The projections and analysis contained in the *World Economic Outlook* are an integral element of the IMF's ongoing surveillance of economic developments and policies in its member countries and of the global economic system. The IMF has published the *World Economic Outlook* annually from 1980 through 1983 and biannually since 1984.

The survey of prospects and policies is the product of a comprehensive interdepartmental review of world economic developments, which draws primarily on information the IMF staff gathers through its consultations with member countries. These consultations are carried out in particular by the IMF's area departments together with various support departments.

The country projections are prepared by the IMF's area departments on the basis of internationally consistent assumptions about world activity, exchange rates, and conditions in international financial and commodity markets. For approximately 50 of the largest economies—accounting for 90 percent of world output—the projections are updated for each *World Economic Outlook* exercise. For smaller countries, the projections are based on those prepared at the time of the IMF's regular Article IV consultations with those countries and updated during the WEO exercise.

The analysis in the *World Economic Outlook* draws extensively on the ongoing work of the IMF's area and specialized departments, and has been coordinated in the Research Department under the general direction of Michael Mussa and Kenneth Rogoff, former and current Economic Counsellors and Directors of Research. The *World Economic Outlook* project is directed by David Robinson, Senior Advisor in the Research Department, together with Tamim Bayoumi, Chief of the World Economic Studies Division.

Primary contributors to the current issue include Hali Edison, Thomas Helbling, Maitland MacFarlan, James Morsink, Cathy Wright, Marc Auboin, Geoffrey Bannister, Luis Catão, Markus Haacker, Luca Ricci, Torsten Sløk, and Marco Terrones. Other contributors include Jahangir Aziz, Taimur Baig, Robin Brooks, Ximena Cheetham, Susan Collins, Karl Habermeier, Ayhan Kose, Manmohan Kumar, Il Houng Lee, Anne McGuirk, Guy Meredith, Ashoka Mody, Gary Moser, Eswar Prasad, Blair Rourke, Scott Roger, Kevin Ross, and Stephen Tokarick. Several consultants were also involved in background work, namely Michael Artis, Nicholas Crafts, Michael Klein, and Ross Levine. Nese Erbil, Mandy Hemmati, Yutong Li, and Bennett Sutton provided research assistance. Gretchen Byrne, Nicholas Dopuch, Toh Kuan, Olga Plagie, Di Rao, and Anthony G. Turner processed the data and managed the computer systems. Sylvia Brescia, Dawn Heaney, and Laura Leon were responsible for word processing. Jeff Hayden of the External Relations Department edited the manuscript and coordinated production of the publication.

The analysis has benefited from comments and suggestions by staff from other IMF departments, as well as by Executive Directors following their discussion of the *World Economic Outlook* on September 5 and 7, 2001. However, both projections and policy considerations are those of the IMF staff and should not be attributed to Executive Directors or to their national authorities.

CHAPTER I

PROSPECTS AND POLICY CHALLENGES

Since the May 2001 World Economic Outlook, *prospects for 2001–02 have weakened further, and downside risks have been further exacerbated by the recent terrorist attack in the United States (see Box 1.1). Growth projections for almost all regions have been reduced, reflecting a variety of factors, including the greater-than-expected impact of the global slowdown in a number of regions; a delayed recovery in the United States; weakening domestic demand growth and confidence in Europe; the prospect of a period of slower growth in Japan as it presses ahead with structural reforms (although this will have substantial medium-term benefits); the continued decline in information technology spending, which affects Asia in particular; and deteriorating financing conditions for emerging markets, especially in Latin America. GDP growth is now slowing in almost all regions of the globe, accompanied by a sharp decline in trade growth. In response, many countries—especially the United States—have eased macroeconomic policies, most recently in mid-September in the aftermath of the terrorist attack. This easing, along with the gradual abatement of oil prices and of other shocks that have contributed to the slowdown, should help support activity and confidence in the period ahead. But substantial uncertainties and risks persist, as the downturn makes the world more vulnerable to further unexpected developments, and a significant danger of a deeper and more prolonged slowdown remains. The recent terrorist attack has also increased uncertainty. The challenge facing policymakers is how best to limit these downside risks while promoting an orderly resolution of the imbalances in the global economy over the medium term.*

Global growth is now projected at 2.6 percent in 2001,[1] 0.6 percentage points lower than expected in the May 2001 *World Economic Outlook*, and a decline of over 2 percentage points from the unusually rapid pace in 2000 (Table 1.1 and Figure 1.1). Among the advanced economies, growth in the *United States* is projected at 1.3 percent, 0.2 percentage points lower than in the May 2001 *World Economic Outlook*, with activity expected to begin to pick up modestly in the period ahead as the effects of previous policy easing take hold. The outlook for other industrial countries has weakened more significantly. In the *euro area*, growth has been marked down by 0.6 percentage points

to 1.8 percent, driven by a sharp weakening in domestic demand growth, particularly in *Germany*, and the greater-than-expected impact of the global slowdown. Of most concern, the prospects for *Japan* have become increasingly somber. With GDP now projected to decline by 0.5 percent in 2001, over 1 percentage point worse than earlier projected, Japan is now likely experiencing its fourth recession of the past decade.[2]

Prospects for most developing and transition countries have also deteriorated. Growth has been marked down sharply in the *Western Hemisphere*, where activity has been adversely affected by the renewed financial difficulties in Argentina,

---

[1]In the *World Economic Outlook*, global growth is calculated using purchasing power parity weights. Global growth rates using market exchange rate based weights—which yield lower figures, mainly due to the relatively smaller weights given to China and other faster growing developing countries—are presented in Table 1 of the Statistical Appendix.

[2]Defining a recession as two quarters of negative real GDP growth.

Table 1.1. Overview of the *World Economic Outlook* Projections

(Annual percent change unless otherwise noted)

	1999	2000	Current Projections 2001	Current Projections 2002	Difference from May 2001 Projections[1] 2001	Difference from May 2001 Projections[1] 2002
World output	**3.6**	**4.7**	**2.6**	**3.5**	**−0.6**	**−0.4**
Advanced economies	3.4	3.8	1.3	2.1	−0.6	−0.6
Major advanced economies	3.0	3.4	1.1	1.8	−0.5	−0.6
United States	4.1	4.1	1.3	2.2	−0.2	−0.3
Japan	0.8	1.5	−0.5	0.2	−1.1	−1.3
Germany	1.8	3.0	0.8	1.8	−1.1	−0.8
France	3.0	3.4	2.0	2.1	−0.6	−0.5
Italy	1.6	2.9	1.8	2.0	−0.2	−0.5
United Kingdom	2.3	3.1	2.0	2.4	−0.6	−0.4
Canada	5.1	4.4	2.0	2.2	−0.3	−0.2
Other advanced economies	4.9	5.3	1.9	3.3	−1.1	−0.5
Memorandum						
European Union	2.7	3.4	1.8	2.2	−0.6	−0.6
Euro area	2.7	3.5	1.8	2.2	−0.6	−0.6
Newly industrialized Asian economies	7.9	8.2	1.0	4.3	−2.8	−1.2
Developing countries	3.9	5.8	4.3	5.3	−0.7	−0.3
Africa	2.5	2.8	3.8	4.4	−0.4	—
Developing Asia	6.1	6.8	5.8	6.2	−0.1	−0.1
China	7.1	8.0	7.5	7.1	0.5	—
India	6.8	6.0	4.5	5.7	−1.1	−0.4
ASEAN–4[2]	2.8	5.0	2.4	4.1	−1.0	−0.6
Middle East, Malta, and Turkey	1.0	6.0	2.3	4.8	−0.6	0.2
Western Hemisphere	0.2	4.2	1.7	3.6	−2.0	−0.8
Brazil	0.8	4.5	2.2	3.5	−2.3	−1.0
Countries in transition	3.6	6.3	4.0	4.1	—	−0.1
Central and eastern Europe	2.0	3.8	3.5	4.2	−0.4	−0.2
Commonwealth of Independent States and Mongolia	4.6	7.8	4.4	4.0	0.3	−0.1
Russia	5.4	8.3	4.0	4.0	—	—
Excluding Russia	2.8	6.8	5.4	4.1	1.2	−0.3
World trade volume (goods and services)	**5.3**	**12.4**	**2.7**	**5.2**	**−4.0**	**−1.3**
Imports						
Advanced economies	7.6	11.5	1.7	4.7	−5.0	−1.8
Developing countries	2.1	16.6	6.4	8.0	−2.4	0.1
Countries in transition	−7.8	12.9	10.1	7.9	1.5	1.0
Exports						
Advanced economies	5.0	11.5	1.7	4.5	−4.5	−1.7
Developing countries	4.6	15.1	5.0	6.6	−2.1	−0.4
Countries in transition	0.2	16.5	7.1	6.5	2.5	1.4
Commodity prices						
Oil[3]						
In SDRs	36.5	62.6	−1.4	−8.8	6.3	3.1
In U.S. dollars	37.5	56.9	−5.0	−8.6	4.6	3.2
Nonfuel (average based on world commodity export weights)						
In SDRs	−7.7	6.4	1.0	4.2	−1.6	−0.2
In U.S. dollars	−7.0	2.6	−2.6	4.5	−3.1	—
Consumer prices						
Advanced economies	1.4	2.3	2.4	1.7	0.3	−0.1
Developing countries	6.8	6.0	5.9	5.1	0.2	0.3
Countries in transition	43.9	20.0	16.4	10.7	1.1	0.7
Six-month London interbank offered rate (LIBOR, percent)						
On U.S. dollar deposits	5.5	6.6	4.1	3.7	−0.4	−0.6
On Japanese yen deposits	0.2	0.3	0.2	0.1	−0.2	−0.4
On euro deposits	3.0	4.6	4.3	3.9	−0.1	−0.2

Note: (a) These projections were finalized before the September 11 terrorist attack in the United States and subsequent economic policy actions; (b) real effective exchange rates are assumed to remain constant at the levels prevailing during July 23–August 17, 2001.

[1]Using updated purchasing-power-parity (PPP) weights, summarized in the Statistical Appendix, Table A.

[2]Includes Indonesia, Malaysia, the Philippines, and Thailand.

[3]Simple average of spot prices of U.K. Brent, Dubai, and West Texas Intermediate crude oil. The average price of oil in U.S. dollars a barrel was $28.21 in 2000, the assumed price is $26.80 in 2001, and $24.50 in 2002.

as well as political uncertainties and other shocks, including the energy crisis in *Brazil*. Capital inflows to most countries—except *Mexico*—have also slowed, a concern given the region's large external financing requirement. In *emerging Asia*, growth in *China* remains resilient, but many countries have been hard hit by slowing global growth and the downturn in the electronics cycle, with the impact exacerbated by intraregional trade linkages and developments in Japan. Growth prospects have also weakened moderately in the *Middle East* owing to lower oil prices and cuts in production and the ongoing crisis in *Turkey*. Projected growth in *Africa* has also been reduced, although it is still expected to be higher than in 2000, aided by improved weather and an easing of security problems in several countries. In contrast, the outlook for the transition economies has remained broadly unchanged, with the impact of slowing growth in Europe offset by stronger-than-expected rebounds in a number of countries in the Commonwealth of Independent States, notably Ukraine.

This forecast has not been adjusted for the September 11 terrorist attack on the United States. Clearly, recent events will have an impact on activity in the short term, and add to the already significant downside risks both in the United States and elsewhere. The attack has taken a terrible toll in human lives and resulted in substantial property damage, but its direct impact on U.S. activity is likely to be moderate (as was the case, for example, with the Kobe earthquake in Japan on January 11, 1995, where the damage was, if anything, somewhat larger); moreover, indications are that the financial infrastructure around the world has held up well. However, the indirect effects may be more substantial, including the possibility of a sustained deterioration in consumer, corporate, and financial confidence, of a flight to quality in financial markets that could exacerbate existing weaknesses associated with financial stability or funding, and of oil price volatility. While it is as yet too early to make a full assessment of such risks, the recent cuts in interest rates in the United States, Canada, and Europe, accompanied by

Figure 1.1. Global Indicators[1]
(Annual percent change unless otherwise noted)

Global growth is projected to slow markedly in 2001, while inflation remains subdued.

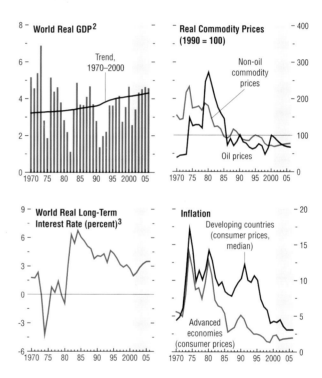

[1]Shaded areas indicate IMF staff projections. Aggregates are computed on the basis of purchasing-power-parity weights unless otherwise indicated.
[2]Average growth rates for individual countries, aggregated using purchasing-power-parity weights; these shift over time in favor of faster growing countries, giving the line an upward trend.
[3]GDP-weighted average of the 10-year (or nearest maturity) government bond yields less inflation rates for the United States, Japan, Germany, France, Italy, the United Kingdom, and Canada. Excluding Italy prior to 1972.

Box 1.1. The Terrorist Attack: Impact on the Global Outlook

The latest round of quantitative projections presented in this *World Economic Outlook* were completed just before the tragic events of September 11. A central question is how these projections might be interpreted in light of the terrorist attack and its aftermath. At press time, there was no doubt that the attack was having a negative effect on activity in many regions of the globe, and that it had increased what were already significant downside risks to the short-term global outlook, including for emerging market economies. However, it is important to put the current economic situation in perspective. While there are clearly substantial uncertainties about unfolding events, one should not overlook that the economic fundamentals in many countries and in many respects have improved in recent years and, from an economic perspective, this leaves the world somewhat less vulnerable than it might otherwise be. These improvements, together with the aggressive response by central banks across the globe, should help reduce the risk of sustained reductions in consumer and business confidence, a key concern in the months ahead.

The attack has certainly had a substantial initial impact in financial markets, although experience suggests that financial markets can overreact to such shocks initially. In the two weeks following the attack, major stock market indices in the United States, Europe, and Japan have fallen by 5 to 15 percent. Many emerging stock markets have fared even worse, particularly in Latin America and East Asia. There has also been a broad-based flight to quality, reflected in a sharp rise in spreads for both high-yield and emerging-market bonds. Oil prices, after rising immediately after the attack, have since fallen back sharply to levels significantly below those prevailing on September 10. Movements in the major currencies have been relatively moderate, with the U.S. dollar weakening slightly against the euro and the yen.

National regulators, financial authorities, and market participants have shown that the global financial system can continue to function smoothly even under a difficult and totally unanticipated form of extreme duress. Monetary policy in the major economies has responded aggressively to support the global payments system and to strengthen confidence and activity. The monetary authorities in the United States, the euro area, Japan, Switzerland, Canada, and the United Kingdom directly injected large amounts of liquidity. The Federal Reserve also entered into temporary swap arrangements with the European Central Bank (ECB), the Bank of England, and the Bank of Canada to facilitate the functioning of financial markets and to provide liquidity in U.S. dollars. In addition, the Federal Reserve moved to cut interest rates by 50 basis points on September 17, quickly followed by cuts of the same magnitude by the Bank of Canada, and then the ECB and the Swiss National Bank. Subsequently, the Bank of England and the Bank of Japan also cut rates, as did the monetary authorities in a number of other economies, including Denmark, Sweden, New Zealand, Hong Kong SAR, and Korea. In the United States, additional fiscal appropriations for defense, reconstruction, and the airlines will also provide support to activity.

Abstracting from uncertainties surrounding the possibility of further conflict, what is the likely direct economic impact of the events of September 11? The attack has taken a terrible toll in human lives, but the *direct* economic damage—in relation to the overall United States economy—is still relatively moderate, even though certain industries have been hard hit, particularly airlines, insurance, and tourism. While it is difficult to find close parallels in recent history, the direct damage is much smaller than that resulting from the Kobe earthquake of January 1995, which, as it turned out, had only a very limited impact on output growth in Japan (Box 1.3). The potential *indirect* effects of the attacks—on consumer sentiment and spending, on business confidence, and on risk aversion—are likely to be significantly more important. These are much more difficult to assess, and will depend importantly on how non-economic events evolve in the aftermath of the attack.

On the economic front, there are a number of reasons for cautious optimism. First, there is now a sizable amount of policy stimulus in the pipeline in most major economies, even more than had been anticipated before the attack. Second, economic fundamentals across the globe are considerably stronger than they were a few years ago, reflected in lower inflation; stronger fiscal positions; greater monetary policy credibility; and, in many emerging markets, more flexible exchange rate regimes and lower external vulnerabilities. And third, the terrorist attack should not substantially affect underlying productivity growth in the U.S. economy and elsewhere, on which economic prosperity ultimately depends (see Chapter III).

At press time, the situation was fluid, making it premature to try to quantify the implications of the attack for growth in the United States and elsewhere. There will clearly be a short-term effect on activity, particularly in the last part of this year, both in the United States and in other countries. However, there is still a reasonable prospect that a recovery will begin in the first half of next year. In terms of the projections in the *World Economic Outlook*, the effect on projected global growth in 2001 is likely to be moderate, since developments in the third and fourth quarters of the year have a limited impact on the average growth rate for the year as a whole. In 2002, however, global growth is likely to be lower than the 3.5 percent projected here.

In sum, the downside risks identified in the main text of this *World Economic Outlook* have now increased, even if the economic channels are largely the same. The task for policymakers has correspondingly become more challenging, both in industrial and in developing countries. The basic requirements remain those set out in the *World Economic Outlook*; in particular:

- The aggressive monetary policy response following the attack has been appropriate, and there remains room for maneuver, to varying extents, if additional action is needed. In particular, there remains room for a more aggressive monetary easing in Japan, even following the welcome steps after the September 11 attack. On the fiscal side, the automatic stabilizers should be allowed to operate. Beyond that, it is probably best to wait a little to see how events develop.
- Given the uncertainties in the United States, other countries—notably in Europe and Japan—will have to rely more on internally generated growth. This makes it even more important to press ahead with structural reforms.
- The weaker global outlook has clearly added to the difficulties facing emerging market countries. With markets increasingly differentiating according to policy performance, the central requirement remains to stay the course of prudent macroeconomic policies and structural reforms.

Figure 1.2. Selected European Union Countries, Japan, and United States: Indicators of Consumer and Business Confidence[1]

After falling sharply from late 2000, confidence in the United States has begun to stabilize. In Europe, business confidence has weakened, and recently consumer confidence has turned down.

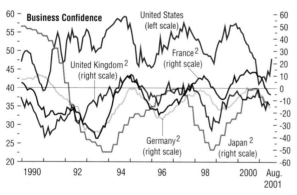

Sources: Consumer confidence for the United States, the Conference Board; for European countries, the European Commission. Business confidence for the United States, the U.S. Department of Commerce, Purchasing Managers Composite Diffusion Index; for European countries, the European Commission; and for Japan, Bank of Japan.
[1]Indicators are not comparable across countries.
[2]Percent of respondents expecting an improvement in their situation minus percent expecting a deterioration.

moderate additional easing in Japan, will be helpful in sustaining confidence and activity.

The global slowdown since early 2000 has been driven by a variety of interlinked factors, including a reassessment of corporate profitability and the associated adjustment in equity prices; the rise in energy prices in 2000, which proved more enduring than initially expected; and the tightening of monetary policy in late 1999 and 2000, particularly in the United States and the euro area, in response to rising demand pressures. Weakening global activity has been accompanied by a downturn in business and consumer confidence, starting in the United States but then spreading to Europe (Figure 1.2), a tightening of credit conditions for some key emerging markets, and heightened risk aversion. Among these factors, the boom and bust in the stock prices of information technology (IT) firms, and the associated sharp fall in IT investment and output, have played a particularly important role. As discussed in Chapter III, unsustainable financial booms have been a common feature of past technological revolutions, and have typically been associated with a significant degree of over investment in the sector concerned, and an ensuing correction. However, the latest episode has been distinguished by the globalization of IT production, so that the decline in IT spending—which as yet shows little sign of abating—has had a particularly widespread impact.

In response, policymakers have generally moved promptly to ease macroeconomic policies; nonetheless, given the size of the shocks, the impact has inevitably been substantial. Moreover, given the global nature of these shocks, as well as the increased trade and financial linkages among countries, their impact has been more rapid and widespread than many expected (and in a number of cases has been exacerbated by country specific factors). The net result is that growth has slowed in almost all major regions of the world, accompanied by a sharp decline in trade growth (Figure 1.3). While the latter has been evident in all regions, the falloff has been particularly steep for many Asian emerging markets, reflecting their heavy dependence on IT trade.

Financial markets have remained volatile, partly reflecting rapidly changing expectations about the duration and depth of the slowdown and recently rising risk aversion and broad-based flight to quality following the terrorist attack. In mature markets, equity prices rallied temporarily in April and May, but have since fallen significantly as incoming news on corporate profitability remained weak and growth prospects deteriorated, with equity markets in all major industrial countries falling sharply following the events of September 11 (Figure 1.4); yields on government bonds broadly mirrored these developments, but have risen lately at long maturities. With short-term rates declining in response to cuts in official rates in most industrial countries, yield curves have generally steepened, albeit to varying extents. In currency markets, the U.S. dollar continued to appreciate in nominal effective terms through July, apparently reflecting continued confidence in the relative strength of the U.S. economy, while the yen and the euro remained relatively weak.[3] In August and September, however, as concerns about U.S. growth prospects increased, the dollar depreciated moderately against most major currencies, with the euro returning close to its level against the dollar at the beginning of the year.

In emerging markets, financial developments have been influenced by mature markets, but also by country-specific factors. During the first half of 2001, the EMBI+ spread remained volatile, with the positive effect of lower U.S. interest rates offset by rising risk aversion and in some cases deteriorating economic fundamentals. While spreads for most emerging market countries declined through June, there were substantial increases in *Argentina*—which also affected *Brazil*—and *Turkey*. As difficulties in Argentina and Turkey intensified in July, their spreads widened sharply, with spillovers to other emerging markets, particularly in Latin America. But overall, contagion effects have so far proved

[3]See "What Is Driving the Weakness of the Euro and the Strength of the Dollar," Chapter II, *World Economic Outlook*, May 2001.

Figure 1.3. Global Output, Industrial Production, and Trade Growth
(Percent change from four quarters earlier)

Growth in output and industrial production has weakened in almost every region of the globe, accompanied by a sharp slowdown in the growth of trade flows.

Global GDP Growth

Global Industrial Production Growth

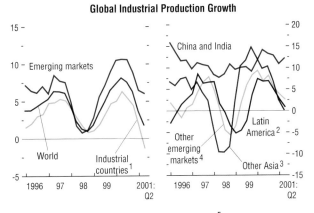

Global Trade Growth (SDRs)[5]

Sources: Central banks and ministries of finance; and European Central Bank, *Monthly Bulletin*.
[1]Canada, euro area, Japan, United Kingdom, and United States.
[2]Argentina, Brazil, Chile, Colombia, Mexico, Peru, and Venezuela.
[3]Hong Kong SAR, Indonesia, Korea, Malaysia, Philippines, Singapore, Taiwan Province of China, and Thailand.
[4]Czech Republic, Hungary, Israel, Poland, Russia, Turkey, Pakistan, and South Africa.
[5]Defined as exports plus imports of the relevant region.

Figure 1.4. Financial Market Developments

Equity markets and interest rates have fallen significantly since 2000, including in the aftermath of the terrorist attack on September 11, 2001. Despite some recent strengthening, the euro and the yen remain relatively weak against the U.S. dollar.

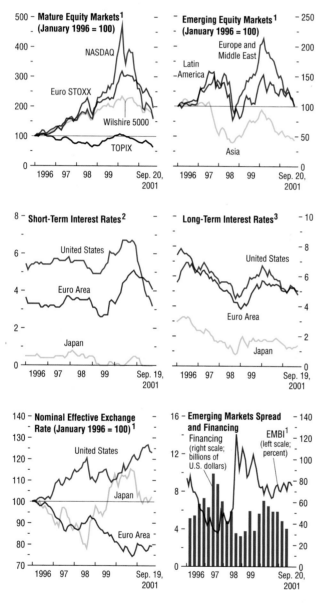

Sources: Bloomberg Financial Markets, LP; European Central Bank; IMF Treasurer's Department, Nikkei Telecom; and WEFA, Inc.
[1] Average of the month.
[2] Three-month deposit rate; euro area data prior to January 1999 reflect Germany.
[3] Ten-year government bond rate. To December 1998, euro area yields are calculated on the basis of harmonized national government bond yields weighted by GDP. Therefore, the weights are nominal outstanding amounts of government bonds in each maturity band.

moderate, in part because increasingly risk averse investors had already tended to diversify away from all but the highest quality emerging market credits, and also because of the relatively low level of leverage in financial markets. As the *World Economic Outlook* went to press, high yield and emerging market spreads had risen markedly following the terrorist attack, reflecting a broad-based flight to quality, accompanied by significant declines in emerging equity markets. After a weak first quarter, gross financing flows held up relatively well in the second quarter, but have subsequently fallen again. For 2001 as a whole, net capital flows to emerging markets are projected to turn negative for the first time since the mid-1980s (Table 1.2).[4] Moreover, given the sharp deterioration in financing conditions since June and rising global risk aversion, there are downside risks to this outlook.

During the first five months of 2001, headline inflation continued to rise in most advanced economies (with the important exception of Japan), driven by the earlier sharp increase in energy prices, and—particularly in Europe—rising food prices due to animal diseases and bad weather. Core inflation also rose, but in most countries is still moderate. During the rest of the year, oil and food prices are expected to fall back (Appendix I) while underlying inflationary pressures are expected to remain modest, reflecting weak demand, increasingly competitive product markets, and the improved anti-inflation credibility of central banks in the past decade (see Box 1.2 on page 13). As a result, headline inflation in almost all advanced economies is projected to decline significantly by 2002 (Table 1.3), and recent inflation data for most advanced countries appear consistent with this expectation. Inflation could in some circumstances become more worrisome—for instance, if in the euro area higher headline inflation fed through into 2002 wage rounds, or if in the

---

[4] It should be noted, however, that this partly reflects the substantial current account surpluses in oil producing countries, and the corresponding net private capital outflows.

Table 1.2. Emerging Market Economies: Net Capital Flows[1]

(Billions of U.S. dollars)

	1993	1994	1995	1996	1997	1998	1999	2000	2001	2002
Total										
Private capital flows, net[2]	139.1	147.5	205.5	234.4	119.1	69.1	58.6	0.5	−1.4	71.0
Private direct investment, net	57.6	81.4	97.5	120.0	145.8	155.9	153.1	147.3	162.7	158.2
Private portfolio investment, net	87.6	112.8	43.8	87.8	48.1	−2.0	31.7	1.5	−0.2	24.0
Other private capital flows, net	−6.1	−46.8	64.2	26.7	−74.8	−84.9	−126.2	−148.3	−163.9	−111.2
Official flows, net	50.3	5.5	24.1	0.1	62.2	55.4	9.5	1.4	19.6	−3.5
Change in reserves[3]	−64.3	−69.8	−117.7	−109.1	−61.9	−44.4	−87.6	−112.7	−81.5	−83.8
Memorandum										
Current account[4]	−117.3	−72.7	−91.6	−95.7	−70.0	−52.6	39.1	128.1	69.6	14.5
Africa										
Private capital flows, net[2]	2.9	13.4	12.2	12.7	8.8	9.8	10.8	3.5	10.8	12.0
Private direct investment, net	3.2	3.3	2.9	4.8	8.4	6.9	8.4	7.6	11.8	11.4
Private portfolio investment, net	0.9	3.5	3.1	2.8	6.9	3.7	8.7	−1.7	3.1	3.8
Other private capital flows, net	−1.3	6.6	6.2	5.0	−6.5	−0.8	−6.2	−2.4	−4.1	−3.3
Official flows, net	4.4	3.2	4.1	−2.5	2.1	3.6	1.8	−0.3	−0.1	−7.1
Change in reserves[3]	2.8	−5.7	−1.9	−9.1	−10.6	1.9	−3.6	−13.3	−10.5	−9.3
Memorandum										
Current account[4]	−11.3	−11.8	−16.6	−6.0	−7.8	−20.6	−15.5	2.1	−3.9	−6.4
Developing Asia[5]										
Crisis countries[6]										
Private capital flows, net[2]	30.8	35.0	54.9	74.1	−5.9	−31.9	−18.3	−19.8	−28.9	−15.1
Private direct investment, net	6.7	6.5	10.3	11.7	10.2	11.4	8.9	5.1	6.6	6.0
Private portfolio investment, net	25.0	13.3	18.6	27.6	8.8	−9.0	13.1	6.9	−4.5	0.3
Other private capital flows, net	−0.8	15.2	26.0	34.7	−25.0	−34.3	−40.3	−31.9	−31.0	−21.5
Official flows, net	3.2	1.1	8.6	−4.4	14.1	17.3	−3.3	1.8	1.0	−2.7
Change in reserves[3]	−20.0	−6.5	−18.0	−5.3	39.4	−46.9	−39.3	−23.9	−0.2	−8.1
Memorandum										
Current account[4]	−13.5	−23.2	−39.1	−53.0	−25.5	69.7	62.9	46.0	31.6	28.6
Other Asian emerging markets										
Private capital flows, net[2]	21.6	34.1	36.5	49.8	22.3	−14.1	8.9	4.3	6.6	11.6
Private direct investment, net	26.4	38.2	39.6	45.6	49.6	48.5	43.0	41.8	44.5	43.8
Private portfolio investment, net	0.9	7.5	2.1	3.5	−0.1	−6.3	0.7	−3.3	−6.2	1.9
Other private capital flows, net	−5.7	−11.6	−5.2	0.6	−27.2	−56.2	−34.8	−34.2	−31.6	−34.1
Official flows, net	8.2	2.5	−3.7	−7.9	−7.2	0.2	2.1	−9.3	−2.5	1.6
Change in reserves[3]	−16.8	−51.6	−25.4	−41.6	−46.8	−16.8	−38.7	−25.8	−28.4	−27.2
Memorandum										
Current account[4]	−7.2	18.3	8.0	14.9	51.1	41.5	37.9	41.5	27.2	16.0
Memorandum										
Hong Kong SAR										
Private capital flows, net[2]	—	—	—	—	11.6	−8.5	1.0	3.8	1.6	−2.6

United States the economy were to rebound significantly more rapidly than expected, or if underlying productivity growth were to slow. Nonetheless, at the present juncture, the balance of risks still lies clearly on the side of weaker activity rather than higher inflation.

Overall, the current conjuncture is characterized by unusually large uncertainties and risks, both in advanced and emerging market economies. First, with the broadening of the eco-

nomic slowdown, there is now no major region providing support to global activity. This has increased the vulnerability of the global economy to shocks, and heightened the risk of a self-reinforcing downturn whose consequences could prove difficult to predict, given the progressively stronger and more complex linkages across economies (Chapter II). Second, slowing growth will put increasing pressure on financial and corporate sectors in a number of countries, notably

Table 1.2 *(concluded)*

	1993	1994	1995	1996	1997	1998	1999	2000	2001	2002
Middle East, Malta, and Turkey[7]										
Private capital flows, net[2]	26.7	16.8	8.1	11.8	22.4	11.9	−1.1	−26.0	−34.0	−1.8
Private direct investment, net	3.2	4.9	6.6	4.9	5.6	6.8	5.8	7.3	5.7	11.2
Private portfolio investment, net	6.7	7.7	2.0	0.7	−0.9	−12.1	−4.4	−9.7	−4.2	1.8
Other private capital flows, net	16.9	4.2	−0.5	6.2	17.7	17.2	−2.4	−23.6	−35.5	−14.7
Official flows, net	5.1	3.1	4.3	6.5	4.3	1.9	1.4	1.5	8.8	−4.6
Change in reserves[3]	1.2	−4.7	−11.3	−22.0	−20.8	10.6	−6.3	−25.0	−26.5	−21.7
Memorandum										
Current account[4]	−31.4	−6.2	−5.2	5.0	3.0	−24.4	11.9	59.5	58.8	33.9
Western Hemisphere										
Private capital flows, net[2]	37.4	42.4	41.6	63.8	68.3	72.7	44.6	36.7	39.0	57.8
Private direct investment, net	12.2	23.2	24.9	40.5	56.5	60.8	63.4	62.8	67.2	54.5
Private portfolio investment, net	45.5	63.7	3.4	39.7	25.4	17.7	10.8	5.1	6.7	11.8
Other private capital flows, net	−20.3	−44.4	13.2	−16.4	−13.6	−5.8	−29.6	−31.2	−34.9	−8.5
Official flows, net	30.4	7.8	17.8	5.8	16.0	15.1	7.0	8.1	11.2	6.2
Change in reserves[3]	−20.7	4.0	−23.3	−29.0	−13.8	8.7	7.6	−3.1	6.0	−2.9
Memorandum										
Current account[4]	−45.9	−52.0	−37.1	−39.8	−66.8	−90.4	−56.3	−48.6	−57.9	−62.4
Countries in transition										
Private capital flows, net[2]	19.7	5.7	52.1	22.3	3.2	20.7	13.6	2.0	5.1	6.4
Private direct investment, net	6.0	5.3	13.1	12.4	15.6	21.6	23.6	22.7	26.9	31.3
Private portfolio investment, net	8.7	17.1	14.6	13.4	8.0	4.0	2.8	4.3	5.0	4.3
Other private capital flows, net	5.0	−16.8	24.5	−3.6	−20.3	−4.9	−12.8	−25.0	−26.7	−29.1
Official flows, net	−1.1	−12.2	−7.1	2.6	32.9	17.2	0.5	−0.4	1.3	3.1
Change in reserves[3]	−10.9	−5.3	−37.8	−2.1	−9.4	−1.9	−7.2	−21.6	−21.9	−14.6
Memorandum										
Current account[4]	−7.9	2.3	−1.7	−16.7	−24.0	−28.5	−1.9	27.5	13.9	4.8

[1]Net capital flows comprise net direct investment, net portfolio investment, and other long- and short-term net investment flows, including official and private borrowing. Emerging markets include developing countries, countries in transition, Korea, Singapore, Taiwan Province of China, and Israel.

[2]Because of data limitations, "other net investment" may include some official flows.

[3]A minus sign indicates an increase.

[4]The sum of the current account balance, net private capital flows, net official flows, and the change in reserves equals, with the opposite sign, the sum of the capital account and errors and omissions.

[5]Includes Korea, Singapore, and Taiwan Province of China.

[6]Includes Indonesia, Korea, Malaysia, the Philippines, and Thailand.

[7]Includes Israel.

Japan where banks remain exposed to equity and bond markets. Third, while emerging markets benefit from lower global interest rates, financing conditions remain volatile, partly reflecting continued uncertainties in Argentina and Turkey. The implications of a serious slowdown in industrial countries for emerging market financing, whose structure has increasingly shifted from bank finance to equity and bond markets during the 1990s, have also yet to be seen. Finally, as already mentioned, the terrorist attack on the United States on September 11 exacerbates all of these risks and adds a further one, namely uncertainty and volatility in oil prices.

The outlook needs also to be viewed against the backdrop of the substantial imbalances that have developed in the global economy during the recent expansion, including the large U.S. current account deficit matched by relatively strong current account positions in a number of other major countries (Table 1.4); the apparent overvaluation of the U.S. dollar, particularly vis-à-vis the euro; low U.S. personal savings rates; and equity markets that—at least prior to the terrorist attack—still appeared richly valued by historical standards. In particular, the question arises whether short-term developments and policies are likely to be consistent with an orderly resolution of these imbalances, or whether they could actually make them worse, increasing the risk of a larger and more disorderly adjustment later on. Such concerns are heightened by

Table 1.3. Advanced Economies: Real GDP, Consumer Prices, and Unemployment

(Annual percent change and percent of labor force)

	Real GDP				Consumer Prices				Unemployment			
	1999	2000	2001	2002	1999	2000	2001	2002	1999	2000	2001	2002
Advanced economies	**3.4**	**3.8**	**1.3**	**2.1**	**1.4**	**2.3**	**2.4**	**1.7**	**6.4**	**5.8**	**6.0**	**6.2**
Major advanced economies	3.0	3.4	1.1	1.8	1.4	2.3	2.3	1.6	6.1	5.7	5.9	6.3
United States	4.1	4.1	1.3	2.2	2.2	3.4	3.2	2.2	4.2	4.0	4.7	5.3
Japan	0.8	1.5	-0.5	0.2	-0.3	-0.6	-0.7	-0.7	4.7	4.7	5.0	5.6
Germany	1.8	3.0	0.8	1.8	0.7	2.1	2.5	1.3	8.2	7.5	7.5	7.9
France	3.0	3.4	2.0	2.1	0.6	1.8	1.8	1.1	11.2	9.5	8.7	8.5
Italy	1.6	2.9	1.8	2.0	1.7	2.6	2.6	1.6	11.4	10.6	9.5	9.1
United Kingdom[1]	2.3	3.1	2.0	2.4	2.3	2.1	2.2	2.4	6.0	5.6	5.2	5.3
Canada	5.1	4.4	2.0	2.2	1.7	2.7	3.1	2.3	7.6	6.8	7.4	7.3
Other advanced economies	4.9	5.3	1.9	3.3	1.3	2.4	3.0	2.2	7.3	6.2	6.3	6.1
Spain	4.0	4.1	2.7	2.8	2.2	3.4	3.6	2.5	15.9	14.1	13.0	12.6
Netherlands	3.7	3.5	1.4	2.2	2.0	2.3	4.9	2.5	3.2	2.8	3.6	3.9
Belgium	2.7	4.0	1.7	2.0	1.1	2.7	2.5	1.7	8.8	7.0	7.1	7.3
Sweden	4.1	3.6	1.7	2.5	0.5	1.0	2.5	2.2	5.6	4.7	4.1	4.1
Austria	2.8	3.3	1.6	2.6	0.5	2.0	2.3	2.0	3.9	3.7	3.7	3.6
Denmark	2.1	3.2	1.4	2.0	2.5	3.0	2.4	2.3	5.6	5.2	5.2	5.4
Finland	4.0	5.7	2.0	2.6	1.3	3.0	2.6	1.9	10.3	9.8	9.9	10.4
Greece	3.4	4.3	4.3	3.8	2.2	2.9	3.5	3.1	12.0	11.3	10.9	10.7
Portugal	3.4	3.4	1.6	1.7	2.2	2.8	4.3	2.5	4.4	4.0	3.9	4.1
Ireland	10.9	11.5	6.3	4.9	2.5	5.2	4.0	3.2	5.6	4.3	3.7	4.0
Luxembourg	7.3	8.5	4.2	4.3	1.0	3.2	1.5	1.3	2.9	2.6	2.7	2.6
Switzerland	1.5	3.5	1.6	1.7	0.8	1.6	1.4	1.5	2.7	1.9	1.8	1.9
Norway	1.1	2.3	1.9	2.2	2.3	3.1	3.5	2.9	3.2	3.4	3.3	3.3
Israel	2.6	6.2	0.7	5.4	5.2	1.1	1.0	2.0	8.9	8.8	9.0	8.6
Iceland	4.1	3.6	1.7	0.7	3.4	5.1	6.3	5.7	1.9	1.4	1.4	2.0
Cyprus	4.5	5.1	4.2	4.0	1.8	4.1	2.2	2.5	3.6	3.5	3.6	3.8
Korea	10.9	8.8	2.5	4.5	0.8	2.3	4.4	3.4	6.3	4.1	4.0	3.5
Australia[2]	4.7	3.8	2.3	3.8	1.5	4.5	4.2	2.0	7.0	6.3	6.8	6.7
Taiwan Province of China	5.4	6.0	-1.0	4.0	0.2	1.3	0.1	0.8	2.9	3.0	4.6	4.8
Hong Kong SAR	3.0	10.5	0.6	4.0	-4.0	-3.7	-1.4	0.6	6.3	5.0	5.6	5.3
Singapore	5.9	9.9	-0.2	4.0	0.1	1.4	1.5	1.7	3.5	3.1	3.2	3.1
New Zealand[2]	3.8	3.7	1.8	2.9	1.1	2.7	2.7	2.2	6.8	6.0	5.5	5.7
Memorandum												
European Union	2.7	3.4	1.8	2.2	1.4	2.3	2.6	1.8	9.1	8.1	7.7	7.7
Euro area	2.7	3.5	1.8	2.2	1.2	2.4	2.7	1.7	9.9	8.8	8.4	8.4

[1]Consumer prices are based on the retail price index excluding mortgage interest.
[2]Consumer prices excluding interest rate components; for Australia, also excluding other volatile items.

the weakening of growth outside the United States and—partly associated with that—the present constellation of exchange rates. Notwithstanding recent developments, the continued strength of the U.S. dollar against the euro may inhibit recovery in the United States while reducing the scope for monetary policy easing in the euro area, constraining a desirable rebalancing of external and domestic sources of growth in both areas and making an orderly resolution of global imbalances more difficult.

As discussed in several recent issues of the *World Economic Outlook*, an important factor un-derlying these imbalances appears to have been a belief that the underlying rate of productivity growth in the United States has increased relative to other countries, making the United States a relatively more attractive environment for new investment. This, in turn, contributed to larger capital inflows, rising equity prices, and an appreciation of the U.S. dollar, which led to a widening U.S. current account deficit and a drop in U.S. personal saving. To the extent that these imbalances have been driven by such factors, their evolution in the period ahead—and the risks associated with them—will depend importantly on how

Table 1.4. Selected Economies: Current Account Positions
(Percent of GDP)

	1999	2000	2001	2002
Advanced economies	**−0.5**	**−1.0**	**−0.9**	**−0.8**
Major advanced economies	−1.0	−1.6	−1.5	−1.4
United States	−3.5	−4.5	−4.0	−3.8
Japan	2.4	2.5	2.2	2.6
Germany	−0.9	−1.0	−0.8	−0.5
France	2.6	1.8	2.5	2.6
Italy	0.5	−0.5	−0.1	0.1
United Kingdom	−1.1	−1.7	−1.7	−2.0
Canada	0.2	2.5	1.9	0.9
Other advanced economies	2.0	2.1	2.1	2.1
Spain	−2.1	−3.2	−2.3	−2.1
Netherlands	4.1	4.4	4.8	4.6
Belgium-Luxembourg	5.0	4.8	4.6	4.8
Sweden	3.5	2.6	2.2	2.1
Austria	−3.2	−2.9	−2.9	−2.6
Denmark	1.5	1.7	2.2	2.5
Finland	6.0	7.4	5.9	5.3
Greece	−4.1	−6.8	−6.5	−6.4
Portugal	−8.8	−10.1	−9.4	−8.7
Ireland	0.4	−0.7	−1.2	−2.2
Switzerland	11.6	12.9	10.7	10.9
Norway	4.0	14.3	15.0	14.4
Israel	−3.0	−1.3	−3.1	−2.7
Iceland	−7.0	−10.3	−9.6	−6.5
Cyprus	−2.4	−5.0	−3.6	−3.0
Korea	6.0	2.4	2.6	2.1
Australia	−5.8	−4.0	−3.0	−2.8
Taiwan Province of China	2.9	2.9	2.5	2.6
Hong Kong SAR	7.3	5.4	6.6	7.5
Singapore	25.9	23.7	21.0	19.8
New Zealand	−6.7	−5.6	−4.0	−3.8
Memorandum				
European Union	0.3	−0.3	—	0.1
Euro area[1]	0.4	−0.1	0.3	0.4

[1]Calculated as the sum of the balances of individual euro area countries.

expected and *actual* productivity growth unfolds in the United States and elsewhere. Clearly, this issue is—and will no doubt remain—subject to debate and considerable uncertainty. In the United States, some part of the recent increase in actual productivity has likely been cyclical, but a portion may well be more enduring in nature, reflecting the benefits of the information technology revolution (Chapter III). In most other advanced countries—with *Australia* being an important exception—there is much less evidence of an underlying increase in productivity, suggesting that developments in the future will depend importantly on progress with structural reform.

Despite these risks and uncertainties, there remains a reasonable prospect of a pickup in global growth in the coming period, although more slowly than earlier envisaged, especially following the terrorist attack. Most importantly, since the beginning of the year macroeconomic policies have been eased in most advanced countries, and in the United States in particular there is now substantial stimulus in the pipeline. At the same time, activity is likely to be bolstered by the abatement of oil and food price shocks, which appear to have had a particularly important effect in the euro area; the completion of ongoing inventory adjustments; and, as past overinvestment is worked off, a recovery in the IT sector (although the timing of this remains very uncertain). Against this background, in the IMF's baseline scenario, GDP growth in the United States and the euro area is projected to begin to strengthen mildly in the coming period, although the pace will be dampened by the lagged impact of past wealth losses on consumption, as well as by the continued unwinding of IT overinvestment, particularly in the United States, and the impact of the terrorist attack. Stronger demand in industrial countries, along with the pickup in the IT sector, would support improved growth in emerging market economies and a gradual improvement in external financing conditions. As a result, global growth in 2002 is projected to increase to 3.5 percent, although—especially if the timing of recoveries in major countries is delayed or confidence weakens sharply as a result of the terrorist attack—there are downside risks to this projection.

In this baseline scenario, the moderation in global imbalances in the short-term would be limited, with the U.S. current account deficit falling only modestly in 2001–02. Provided that the future growth outlook in the United States was still perceived as solid, there would be a reasonable prospect that capital inflows would be sustained. Thereafter, provided structural reforms to boost potential growth and productivity in Japan and the euro area are put in place, investment opportunities outside the United States are likely to become increasingly attractive.

Box 1.2. How Much of a Concern Is Higher Headline Inflation?

With global growth weakening, how far should monetary policy be eased to support activity? The scope for such monetary easing must be weighed against both near-term inflation prospects and longer-term concerns about anti-inflationary credibility. A current complication is that inflation developments have been obscured by price shocks that have boosted "headline" (or overall) inflation rates in many countries (including the euro area and United States), despite slowing real growth. Abstracting from these shocks, inflationary pressures appear to have remained subdued. Should policymakers be concerned about rising headline inflation, or instead focus on underlying price measures?

The argument for focusing on core as opposed to overall inflation is based on what drives prices across markets.[1] In some markets, especially for commodities, sharp price movements tend to be associated with supply and demand developments that are specific to those markets without reflecting generalized inflationary pressures. Labor markets, in contrast, tend to adjust sluggishly in response to broader-based imbalances between aggregate supply and demand. Hence, shocks specific to commodity markets will tend to generate one-off changes in the price level, while labor market imbalances may be associated with much longer-lived changes in prices.

There are also arguments for looking at overall inflation. Firstly, price *level* shocks can lead to higher wage *growth* if the inflation expectations of wage-setters are affected. Secondly, what appear to be isolated price shocks may instead reflect general conditions of excess demand that show up first in markets where prices are flexible. These phenomena were apparent in the 1970s, when price shocks in specific markets were accompanied by an acceleration in underlying inflation that persisted until the 1980s.

[1]Core inflation is defined here as the overall CPI less food and energy prices to abstract from temporary supply shocks in these markets. This measure can still be influenced by price shocks. For instance, the weak euro has boosted import prices in the euro area, while the reverse has been true in the United States.

Regression Results for Overall and Core CPI Inflation

Dependent variable	Parameter on 12-month lagged inflation[1]	
	Overall	Core
	1965M1–1982M12	
U.S. overall	1.51 (6.7)	−0.94 (3.6)
U.S. core	1.22 (7.9)	−0.54 (3.1)
	1983M1–2001M4	
U.S. overall	0.14 (0.5)	0.15 (0.6)
U.S. core	0.14 (0.6)	0.40 (1.6)
	1997M1–2001M2	
Euro area overall	0.30 (1.0)	−1.40 (2.0)
Euro area core	0.26 (0.4)	−0.37 (2.3)

[1]Absolute values of t-statistics in parentheses, adjusted for MA (12) error terms. Constant terms in the regressions have been suppressed.

Since then, the anti-inflationary credibility of monetary policymakers has become better established, as they have responded firmly to forestall any signs of emerging pressures. With the enhanced credibility of policy, specific price shocks, such as the oil price surge during the Gulf War, have not triggered generalized inflation. Indeed, during the 1990s, industrial countries have enjoyed the lowest sustained inflation rates since the 1950s. Such anecdotal evidence suggests that price shocks should be of less concern now than at times in the past.

Statistical evidence on the relationship between overall and core inflation also supports the view that price shocks are now of less concern. During 1965–82, the dominant factor explaining U.S. inflation (either overall or core) was past *overall* inflation, while the effect of lagged core inflation was actually negative (see the Table). In other words, price shocks that drove a wedge between overall and core inflation tended to cause long-lived increases in both measures of inflation. The results for 1983–2001 are quite different—the parameters on both lagged inflation rates are small and statistically insignificant, with the borderline exception of that on lagged core inflation in its own equation. While data limitations for the euro area preclude a comparison over the same time peri-

Box 1.2 *(concluded)*

ods, over a relatively short 1997–2001 sample, lagged overall inflation in the euro area again plays a much smaller role than during the 1965–82 period for the United States.

What lessons can be drawn for monetary policy from these results? The apparent change in the behavior of inflation since the early 1980s supports downplaying shocks to headline prices. Moreover, indicators of inflation expectations suggest that recent price shocks will have temporary effects: consensus forecasts point to significant declines in U.S. and euro-area inflation next year; market forecasts of longer-term inflation implicit in index-linked bond yields remain subdued (see the Figure); and other traditional inflation indicators, such as gold and commodity prices, have not suggested inflationary pressures. At the same time, the change in the behavior of inflation since the early 1980s also reflects changes to the policymaking process, in particular the determination of central banks to contain inflation by resisting any second-round impacts of temporary price shocks. The continued credibility of such policies depends on the willingness to tighten policies given any signs that price shocks are fuelling underlying inflationary pressures.

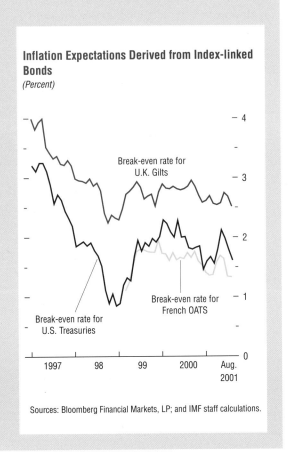

Inflation Expectations Derived from Index-linked Bonds
(Percent)

Sources: Bloomberg Financial Markets, LP; and IMF staff calculations.

Capital flows to the United States, and the U.S. dollar, would then fall back, ideally in a gradual fashion, consistent with an orderly resolution of global imbalances.[5]

However, given the risks already described, there remains a significant danger of a worse outcome. For instance, if U.S. productivity growth were to disappoint, and overinvestment during the recent boom turned out to have been more extensive and widespread than presently believed, equity markets in the United States could weaken markedly, accompanied by a sharp fall in fixed investment and in private consumption (which has so far remained relatively resilient). As discussed

in Appendix II, this could result in a much deeper and more protracted global downturn—similar to that experienced in the early 1980s and early 1990s—especially if also accompanied by continuing structural weaknesses and consequently weaker-than-projected productivity growth in Europe and Japan. There would also be a possibility of substantial financial market turbulence, including in some circumstances a possible abrupt decline in the value of the U.S. dollar. The impact on developing countries would be substantial, including through a further deterioration in external financing conditions; this could both aggravate and be aggravated by country-specific risks.

[5]Since the baseline projections in the *World Economic Outlook*, like those of a number of other forecasters, assume constant real exchange rates, there is only a small reduction in imbalances in the baseline scenario. See Appendix II for a more detailed discussion.

In this environment, policymakers across the globe face a particularly challenging task. With the slowdown becoming increasingly synchronized, and significant downside risks, short-term macroeconomic policies need to remain supportive of activity and confidence, and in some cases a more proactive stance would be desirable:

- In the *United States*, recent tax cuts and monetary policy easing—along with the higher expenditures in the wake of the terrorist attack—should provide support to activity in the second half of 2001 and beyond, but this has been partly offset by the strength of the U.S. dollar. The U.S. monetary authorities have already cut rates substantially, although some limited room for further reductions remains were the outlook to weaken significantly further.
- In *Japan*, the scope for further macroeconomic policy stimulus remains limited. Recent monetary easing is welcome, but there remains room to exploit the flexibility afforded by the new monetary framework more aggressively, even if this results in some depreciation of the yen. On the fiscal side, a modest supplementary budget is appropriately being considered, as the authorities should avoid too rapid a withdrawal of stimulus (Table 1.5).
- In the *euro area*, the recent cuts in interest rates were appropriate. If the outlook were to weaken materially further, provided that inflation developments remain favorable, there would be scope for additional easing. Tax cuts in some countries are providing modest support to activity, and automatic stabilizers should be allowed to operate fully to buffer weaker activity.

At the same time, it will be important that policies are consistent with an orderly resolution of the global imbalances over the medium term. While these imbalances have been largest and perhaps of most concern in the United States, it does not follow that it is the sole responsibility of the United States to correct them. Indeed, as suggested above, they are a reflection not just of strong growth in the United States—and some

excesses associated with it—but also of relatively weak growth elsewhere, in turn partly the result of delays in addressing long standing structural problems. Therefore, from both a national and global perspective, policymakers—particularly, but not only, in the euro area and Japan—must move quickly to implement the structural reforms necessary to achieve sustainably higher potential growth rates. The announcement by the new Japanese government of a timetable for the reform process is therefore particularly encouraging, even if such reforms were to involve some short-term cost in output growth.

In emerging market economies, the outlook inevitably remains heavily dependent on developments in the major industrial countries, underscoring the need for the latter to implement policies along the lines described above. At the present conjuncture, emerging market policymakers face a difficult balance between seeking to offset—to the extent possible—the impact of the global slowdown and maintaining external confidence in an increasingly fragile environment. While vulnerabilities have in most cases been reduced following the 1997–98 crises, including through the widespread adoption of flexible exchange rate regimes, significant risks remain. On the macroeconomic side, there is in some cases room for countercyclical policies, but in many countries the scope is constrained, especially where external financing requirements or fiscal imbalances are large. Slowing growth is also likely to add to pressures on corporate sectors and financial systems, and it will be essential to press ahead with structural reforms in these areas, especially in those countries that have been lagging in the process. The international community will also need to stand ready to support these efforts and to help address contagion pressures if they intensify, including through support for strengthened policy packages and through the use of the IMF's Contingent Credit Line Facility.

With past experience suggesting that slowing growth is likely to have a disproportionate impact on the poor, the global effort to reduce poverty becomes of even higher priority. The central re-

Table 1.5. Major Advanced Economies: General Government Fiscal Balances and Debt[1]
(Percent of GDP)

	1985–94	1995	1996	1997	1998	1999	2000	2001	2002	2006
Major advanced economies										
Actual balance	−3.8	−4.1	−3.4	−2.0	−1.3	−1.0	—	−0.8	−0.7	0.6
Output gap[2]	−0.5	−2.2	−2.0	−1.4	−1.2	−0.8	—	−1.4	−2.1	−0.1
Structural balance	−3.4	−3.2	−2.6	−1.3	−0.8	−0.7	−0.5	−0.4	0.1	0.7
United States										
Actual balance	−4.7	−3.3	−2.4	−1.3	—	0.7	1.9	1.2	1.2	1.3
Output gap[2]	−1.3	−3.2	−2.8	−1.6	−0.5	0.4	1.3	−0.5	−1.4	—
Structural balance	−4.2	−2.3	−1.5	−0.7	0.2	0.6	1.5	1.3	1.6	1.5
Net debt	51.4	59.6	59.2	57.0	53.4	48.9	43.6	40.9	38.0	25.8
Gross debt	65.7	72.9	72.8	70.3	66.7	63.4	57.3	54.1	50.7	35.9
Japan										
Actual balance	0.6	−3.5	−4.2	−3.2	−4.5	−7.0	−8.2	−7.4	−6.5	−1.3
Excluding social security	−2.5	−6.3	−6.7	−5.8	−6.5	−8.8	−9.5	−8.2	−7.0	−2.3
Output gap[2]	1.1	−1.2	0.4	0.4	−2.5	−3.1	−3.1	−4.8	−5.7	−0.2
Structural balance	0.3	−3.2	−4.3	−3.4	−3.6	−6.0	−7.3	−5.9	−4.7	−1.3
Excluding social security	−2.9	−6.0	−6.9	−5.9	−6.0	−8.2	−9.0	−7.4	−6.1	−2.4
Net debt	13.5	12.7	16.0	17.5	29.5	36.0	43.5	51.0	57.2	59.6
Gross debt	70.6	87.1	92.5	96.8	110.2	120.4	130.7	142.1	150.9	150.3
Euro area										
Actual balance	−4.9	−5.3	−4.4	−2.7	−2.2	−1.3	0.2	−1.0	−1.0	0.3
Output gap[2]	−0.3	−1.3	−2.0	−1.9	−1.3	−1.1	−0.1	−0.8	−1.2	—
Structural balance	...	−4.3	−3.1	−1.5	−1.3	−0.7	−0.7	−0.7	−0.4	0.2
Net debt	46.1	65.2	65.8	65.6	64.0	63.0	60.7	59.6	58.4	50.4
Gross debt	60.8	76.7	77.7	76.9	75.0	73.9	71.4	69.7	68.4	58.6
Germany[3]										
Actual balance[4]	−1.9	−3.3	−3.4	−2.7	−2.2	−1.6	1.2	−2.2	−1.8	—
Output gap[2]	−0.2	0.2	−0.9	−1.4	−1.3	−1.4	−0.3	−1.5	−1.7	—
Structural balance	−1.4	−3.3	−2.7	−1.6	−1.2	−0.7	−1.1	−1.4	−0.8	—
Net debt	24.9	49.4	51.1	52.2	52.0	52.4	51.6	50.9	50.9	44.9
Gross debt	43.8	58.3	59.8	60.9	60.7	61.1	60.3	59.6	59.6	53.6
France										
Actual balance[4]	−3.3	−5.5	−4.1	−3.5	−2.6	−1.6	−1.4	−0.8	−1.6	0.6
Output gap[2]	−0.3	−2.7	−3.3	−3.1	−1.8	−1.2	−0.3	−0.8	−1.2	—
Structural balance	−2.9	−3.7	−1.9	−1.5	−1.4	−0.9	−1.1	−1.0	−1.0	0.6
Net debt	28.3	45.8	48.1	49.6	49.8	48.9	48.0	48.8	47.4	41.5
Gross debt	36.9	54.6	57.1	59.3	59.5	58.5	57.5	57.8	57.8	51.8
Italy										
Actual balance[4]	−10.5	−7.6	−7.1	−2.7	−2.8	−1.8	−0.3	−1.3	−0.9	−0.3
Output gap[2]	−0.1	−1.1	−2.0	−2.3	−2.4	−2.7	−1.8	−2.0	−2.0	—
Structural balance	−10.4	−7.0	−6.2	−1.7	−1.8	−0.6	−0.7	−0.5	−0.1	−0.2
Net debt	93.2	116.6	116.0	113.7	110.1	108.4	104.4	101.9	99.9	84.8
Gross debt	99.5	123.2	122.6	120.1	116.2	114.5	110.2	107.6	105.6	89.8
United Kingdom										
Actual balance[4]	−3.2	−5.4	−4.1	−1.5	0.3	1.5	4.0	0.7	0.2	—
Output gap[2]	0.4	−1.1	−0.9	−0.4	—	−0.1	0.3	−0.3	−0.6	−0.2
Structural balance	−2.5	−4.4	−3.4	−1.0	0.5	1.5	1.6	0.7	0.5	0.2
Net debt	26.6	37.0	46.5	45.0	42.3	39.5	35.1	31.5	29.4	26.1
Gross debt	43.5	52.0	52.2	49.9	47.0	44.4	41.3	38.6	36.3	31.6
Canada										
Actual balance	−6.9	−5.3	−2.8	0.2	0.5	1.6	3.2	2.8	2.9	2.3
Output gap[2]	−2.0	−4.4	−5.3	−3.6	−3.3	−1.6	0.2	−0.6	−1.3	−0.7
Structural balance	−5.6	−2.8	0.1	2.1	2.1	2.5	3.1	3.2	3.6	2.6
Net debt	66.3	88.6	87.8	84.1	81.2	74.9	66.3	60.0	54.7	36.3
Gross debt	98.0	120.4	120.3	117.6	115.7	112.3	102.6	95.3	88.5	64.3

Note: The methodology and specific assumptions for each country are discussed in Box A1.
[1]Debt data refer to end of year; for the United Kingdom they refer to end of March.
[2]Percent of potential.
[3]Data before 1990 refer to west Germany. For net debt, the first column refers to 1988–94. Beginning in 1995, the debt and debt-service obligations of the Treuhandanstalt (and of various other agencies) were taken over by general government. This debt is equivalent to 8 percent of GDP, and the associated debt service to ½ to 1 percent of GDP.
[4]Includes one-off receipts from the sale of mobile telephone licenses equivalent to 2.5 percent of GDP in 2000 for Germany, 0.5 percent of GDP in 2001 for France, 1.2 percent of GDP in 2000 for Italy, and 2.4 percent of GDP in 2000 for the United Kingdom.

sponsibility for addressing poverty must of course lie with national governments of the countries concerned, and in this regard the New African Initiative announced by the Organization of African Unity—and supported by the G-8 at the Genoa summit—is a welcome step forward. Such efforts should be accompanied by increased support from the industrial countries, including further trade liberalization; debt relief under the enhanced HIPC initiative; a fully-funded strategy to fight the AIDS pandemic and other diseases; and increased efforts to achieve the U.N. target for official aid flows, which, as a percentage of donor country GDP, have declined steadily over the past decade (Figure 1.5).

In this connection, an increase in aid flows by 0.1 percentage points from today's average level of 0.24 percent of GNP would substantially exceed the $10 billion the United Nations has identified as needed to begin a comprehensive program of HIV/AIDS prevention and treatment.[6] Moreover, with only one-fifth of total overseas development aid flows now going to the least developed countries, there should be scope to direct more of the increased aid to the poorest nations.

Finally, the successful launch of new multilateral trade negotiations, possibly at the upcoming WTO Ministerial meeting in Doha, would boost global growth prospects and help strengthen the trading system. As discussed in Chapter II, the potential gains for both advanced and developing countries from further trade liberalization are substantial (for developing countries, the benefit is estimated at twice the present level of official aid flows). A failure to make progress toward a new round could reduce confidence in the multilateral trading system, a development that would likely hurt the poorest countries most of all. Moreover, in an environment of slowing global growth, protectionist pressures—which are never far below the surface, and signs of which have already begun

[6]"A Global Partnership for African Economic Development," address by IMF Managing Director Horst Köhler to the United Nations Economic and Social Council, Geneva, July 16, 2001. The text can be found at http://www.imf.org/external/np/speeches/2001/071601.htm.

Figure 1.5. Net Overseas Aid Disbursement by Major Development Assistance Committee (DAC) Countries[1]
(Percent of GNP)

Aid flows have steadily declined as a percentage of GNP in recent years, and—apart from Denmark, Netherlands, and Sweden—most countries are well below the United Nations target.

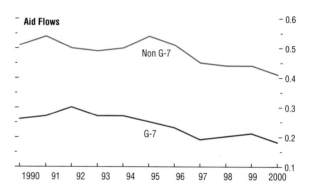

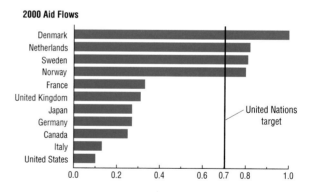

[1]Based on total amounts provided by donors, excludes debt forgiveness of non-ODA claims. 2000 data are provisional.

Figure 1.6. United States: A Sharp Slowdown in the Business Sector

(Percent change from four quarters earlier unless otherwise indicated)

The current slowdown has been marked by a sharp fall in business investment, especially in equipment and software. Core inflation remains subdued.

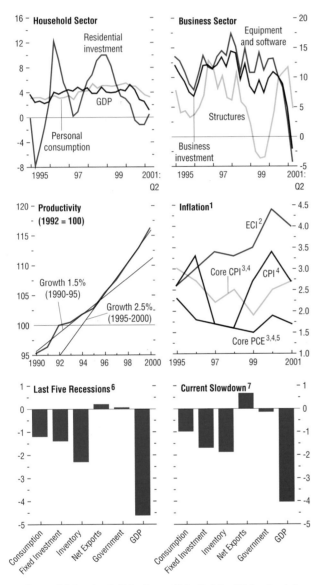

Sources: U.S. Department of Labor, Bureau of Labor Statistics; U.S. Department of Commerce, Bureau of Economic Analysis; and IMF staff estimates.

[1]Data for 2001 CPI, Core CPI, and core personal consumption expenditure (PCE) refer to percent change from July 2001 over July 2000; employment cost index (ECI) refers to change from 2001:Q2 over 2000:Q2.

[2]Employment cost index, fourth quarter over fourth quarter.

[3]Core inflation rates exclude changes in food and energy prices.

[4]Percentage change from December-over-December.

[5]Chain type price index for personal consumption expenditures.

[6]Difference in average percent contribution to growth, comparing the year before the last five cyclical peaks with the period between these peaks and subsequent troughs.

[7]Difference in percent contribution to growth between 1999:Q2 to 2000:Q2 and 2000:Q2 to 2001:Q2, annualized.

to emerge—would prove considerably more difficult to contain.

How Quickly Can Growth Pick Up in North America?

The sharp slowdown in U.S. economic activity that began in mid-2000 continued through the first eight months of 2001, and the September 11 terrorist attack has further increased downside risks, although at the time of writing it is too early to assess the economic consequences. The downturn through early September has been driven primarily by a significant weakening in business investment, marked by a sharp falloff in equipment and software purchases and a rapid depletion of inventories. Exports have also weakened substantially, although, with imports also falling sharply, the negative contribution of net trade to growth has diminished. In contrast, private consumption growth—while weakening—has remained relatively robust; and residential construction growth has also picked up, aided by the reduction in long-term interest rates since mid-2000. The decline in growth so far has been about the same as the average peak-to-trough decline in previous downturns, with broadly similar relative contributions of consumption, investment, and other demand components (Figure 1.6). Within investment, the contribution of business equipment and software to the slowdown has been substantially larger than in the past, reflecting the technology downturn, and that of construction (residential and nonresidential) has been somewhat smaller.[7]

The baseline projection, which was completed before the September 11 terrorist attack, envisages a modest recovery in the coming period, with GDP growth of 1.3 percent for the year as a

---

[7]In addition, recent revisions to historical national accounts data for 1998 to 2000 have led to a significant reduction in estimated GDP growth in 2000, from 5 percent to 4.1 percent, because of lower inventory and software investment. These same revisions also lifted the personal saving rate to 1 percent (from –0.1 percent) because of a reduction in corporate profits and increase in personal income.

Box 1.3. An Historical Analogy to the Terrorist Attack on the United States: The Kobe Earthquake

The 1995 earthquake in Kobe, Japan was the most costly natural disaster in modern history. Striking on January 17, it resulted in over 5,000 deaths, 35,000 casualties, and property damage of around $120 billion (or about 2½ percent of Japan's annual GDP). In addition to the direct impact on life and property, the regional economy (accounting for about 4 percent of Japan's total output) was severely affected by the disruption of transportation, including the closure of Kobe's important port facilities. In terms of the financial impact, Japanese stock prices fell by about 6 percent following the earthquake.

In the event, the direct impact on activity, as measured by indicators such as industrial production, was relatively small. The more important hit to overall output came through a contraction in consumer spending in the first quarter of 1995, leading to a decline in real GDP of 0.3 percent (quarterly rate). Activity recovered in subsequent quarters, however, and GDP for the year as a whole expanded by 1½ percent compared with slightly over ½ percent in 1994.

Comparing the Kobe earthquake with the recent terrorist attack in the United States, the direct impact of the earthquake was larger, both in absolute terms and relative to Japan's economy. The second-round effects on other industries are harder to assess. The earthquake caused immense dislocation in the surrounding area, but the terrorist attack may have a more far-reaching impact by disrupting U.S. financial activity and air transportation. Finally, since the terrorist attack was a deliberate action with long-term security implications, the effects on consumer psychology may well not be comparable.

whole, picking up to 2.2 percent in 2002. Such a scenario could—if accompanied by improved growth performance in other major countries and an orderly depreciation of the U.S. dollar—be consistent with a gradual reduction in the current account deficit to more sustainable levels, accompanied by a steady improvement in the household savings ratio. But, as emphasized earlier, there are also significant downside risks in the outlook, generally stemming from interrelated uncertainties about the extent of overinvestment in the economy, the medium-term outlook for productivity growth, and the robustness of household balance sheets, confidence, and consumer spending. The September 11 terrorist attack will have a short-term effect on activity, and has clearly exacerbated these risks, particularly with respect to confidence and consumer spending (Box 1.3 considers some possible parallels between the economic consequences of this attack and the Kobe earthquake in Japan).

Macroeconomic policies have been significantly eased. Since the beginning of the year, the U.S. Federal Reserve has reduced interest rates by 350 basis points, including a 50 basis points cut as part of a global monetary easing on September 17, accompanied by other measures to ensure adequate liquidity in financial markets for settlement of transactions. Fiscal policy has also been eased, initially by the implementation of a tax cut package in mid-year and by the recent approval of an emergency $40 billion spending package following the terrorist attack. This macroeconomic stimulus should support activity in the period ahead, allowing demand to recover modestly by the end of the year as assumed in the baseline. However, confidence has been further shaken by the terrorist attack, exacerbating risks that the pace of recovery may be slowed by the lagged effect on consumption of the decline in equity market valuations over the last year—possibly offset in part by rising house prices—as well as by the need to work off past overinvestment in the technology sector.

As in most other industrial countries, headline inflation has risen in the United States, mainly due to higher energy costs, and some measures of core inflation have edged up (though others, notably the personal consumption deflator, have remained relatively muted). At the same time, the combination of weakening productivity as activity slowed and a pickup in employment costs has led to a sharp rise in unit labor costs since mid-2000. With energy prices declining, product markets remaining highly competitive, and with activity slowing, the risks of sustained inflationary pressures appear relatively modest at the present juncture. Such pressures could become more of a concern, however, if underlying productivity growth—which has played a key role in absorbing wage increases in recent years—were to slow sharply, especially if accompanied by a sharp downward adjustment in the U.S. dollar.

With underlying inflation subdued, there is scope for further monetary easing to support the economy if weakness persists. On the fiscal side, policy is expected to be more expansionary, reflecting the approved $40 billion in extra spending and other measures that may be taken to meet assistance and reconstruction needs and the expenses of U.S. efforts to combat terrorism in the wake of the September 11 attack. The automatic stabilizers can also be allowed to work to cushion the impact of a weaker U.S. economy. However, at present, the need for and the potential effectiveness of other discretionary fiscal actions is not clear. Beyond the immediate aftermath of recent developments, both multi-year tax cuts and spending increases will have to be implemented flexibly over the medium term to ensure that sufficient resources are available to finance these measures and to meet fiscal obligations associated with the aging of the population.

Growth in *Canada* is expected to slow to 2 percent in 2001 and 2.2 percent in 2002, with the outlook largely reflecting Canada's close trade and financial linkages with the United States. Household spending has remained relatively robust, underpinned by tax cuts earlier in the year and generally firm labor market conditions, while business investment—especially in machinery and equipment—has declined sharply. Reflecting the latter trend, imports have also fallen, more than offsetting a decline in exports and propelling the

current account position to a record surplus. In the event of further slowing in activity, monetary easing would continue to be the preferred response—official interest rates having already been lowered by 175 basis points between January and August 2001 and a further 50 basis points on September 17. In addition, with Canada's fiscal surplus remaining proportionately the largest among the Group of Seven (G-7) countries, the automatic stabilizers should be allowed to work fully during the current slowdown. Over the medium term, continued emphasis needs to be given to reducing debt and preparing to meet rising public pension and health care costs associated with population aging.

Japan: A Somber Short-Term Outlook, But a New Opportunity for Reform

In Japan, the economic situation has continued to deteriorate, and it is now likely that the economy has, for the fourth time in the last 10 years, slipped back into recession. For 2000 as a whole, activity increased by 1.5 percent, close to the average during the 1990s. This expansion was underpinned by relatively strong investment and export growth, reflecting rising profits and buoyancy in the high tech sector. However, even though the pattern of growth is difficult to interpret given data problems,[8] the underlying pace of activity appears to have slowed from mid-2000 as external demand weakened and global electronics demand fell back. While real GDP rose marginally in the first quarter of 2001, reflecting a temporary boost to private consumption from increased purchases of household appliances in advance of environmental regulations introduced on April 1, 2001, output fell sharply in the second quarter, with significant falls in public and private investment offsetting a rise in private consumption. These deteriorating prospects, along with concerns about the pace of corporate restructuring, have been reflected in a sharp weakening in equity markets, exacerbated by the September 11

---

[8]See Box 1.2, October 2000 *World Economic Outlook*, for a discussion of measurement problems in the Japanese national accounts.

terrorist attack, while unemployment has reached an all time high of 5 percent. The yen has also depreciated significantly since late 2000, although this has been partly reversed since July.

The outlook for the remainder of the year remains very uncertain. On the positive side, the adoption of the new monetary framework in March—which has brought overnight interest rates back to zero—has been supportive, and the August and September increases in the target for reserves held at the central bank are further welcome steps, as are plans for a modest supplementary budget. However, private consumption remains extremely weak, reflecting declining incomes and concerns about rising unemployment and future corporate restructuring; business confidence continues to deteriorate; private credit is still declining; and moderate deflation persists. GDP is projected to decline by 0.5 percent in 2001—well below the 0.6 percent increase expected at the time of the May 2001 *World Economic Outlook*—followed by a modest recovery of growth to 0.2 percent in 2002. Moreover, significant downside risks remain, associated both with the possibility of a slower global recovery and with the future path of domestic policies—both fiscal and structural—which are discussed further below. These risks are of particular concern in a climate where growth in the other main currency areas is weakening, and will adversely affect the rest of the region (Box 1.4).

Japan's disappointing performance over the past decade has been aggravated by a series of macroeconomic shocks, but the roots of its problems can be found in the failure to address the excess stocks of capital and debt created in the bubble years and more broadly in a slow pace of adjustment to globalization and technological change. The financial situation of the banking system remains difficult: banks have substantial exposure to financial risks on holdings of equities and government paper, exacerbated by the further sharp decline in equity markets in recent weeks and the introduction of mark to market accounting at the end of September; credit risks remain on so-called "gray-zone" loans, for which limited provisioning has so far been made; and

core profitability is weak. In the corporate sector, there has been some shift toward more dynamic sectors—notably high tech, electrical machinery, and parts of transportation and communications—but little progress in addressing debt and capital overhangs and reducing labor costs, or in strengthening profitability (Figure 1.7).

Despite this somber outlook, a new and reformist government that enjoys strong popular support recently took office and there is now a renewed opportunity for change. In March, the authorities announced a package of banking and corporate reforms—including accelerated disposal of nonperforming loans by the major banks, measures to reduce banks' equity holdings, and guidelines to aid corporate restructuring and debt forgiveness—followed in June by a seven point plan of action focusing on fiscal consolidation and reform plus some regulatory improvements, and in September by the announcement of a concrete timetable for a number of structural measures. Although many details remain to be fleshed out, policymakers will need to resist pressures from vested interests, and to take full advantage of this opportunity to decisively address Japan's structural problems. On the banking and corporate side, the priorities are to extend debt writeoffs to regional banks; further strengthen implementation of classification and provisioning standards, especially for "gray-zone" loans; provide targeted public capital injections if and where necessary to avoid systemic concerns; and ensure that restructuring plans are sufficiently rigorous to force a turnaround in distressed corporates. These measures should be accompanied by reforms to boost flexibility and productivity, including strengthening competition policy and increasing labor mobility.

As the authorities have stressed, such a program is likely to have an adverse impact on growth and employment in the short run, although the impact would be reduced if rapid and thorough reforms boost confidence in longer-term prospects, and some reforms (for instance in the property sector) could enhance growth. Against this background, macroeco-

Figure 1.7. Japan: Banking and Corporate Sector

The financial position of the banking system remains very weak, especially given credit risks on classified loans, while limited progress has been made in corporate restructuring.

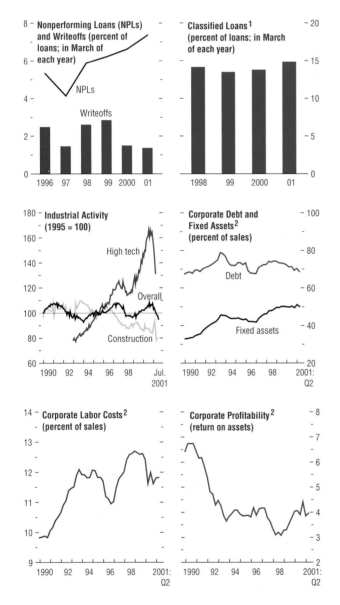

Sources: Ministry of Finance; Ministry of International Trade and Industry; Nikkei Telecomm; Nomura database; and IMF staff calculations.

[1]Defined as the sum of watch list loans (Class 2), doubtful loans (Class 3), and unrecoverable loans (Class 4), net of collateral, guarantees, and specific loan loss provisions.

[2]Seasonally adjusted data.

nomic policies should be supportive, although the room for maneuver is clearly limited, with short-term interest rates already close to zero and public debt very high. While the monetary easings in August and September should help to support activity, there remains scope for more aggressive use of the flexibility available under the new monetary framework with the aim of achieving a rapid end to deflation, even if this were to result in some moderate weakening of the yen. On the fiscal side, it will be important that the withdrawal of fiscal stimulus remains moderate until a recovery is clearly under way, and the authorities' intention to introduce a modest supplementary budget in the fall is therefore welcome. In this connection, it would be desirable to shift the composition of government outlays from public works toward expenditures that would be supportive of restructuring, including a strengthened social safety net, and the recently announced expenditure guidelines include an important step in that direction. This should be accompanied by the development and announcement of a clear and credible medium-term plan to put the government finances on a sounder footing, which could encompass a medium-term debt target, enunciation of the broad objectives and directions of tax, expenditure, and social security policy, and greater fiscal transparency.

How Serious Is the Slowdown in Western Europe?

In the euro area, the slowing in growth that began in the second half of 2000—most markedly in Germany—has continued and spread more widely in 2001. While interpretation of developments is complicated by recent data revisions, particularly in Germany, the slowdown appears to have been driven by weakening domestic demand growth, resulting in part from higher oil and food prices which have squeezed real incomes; downturns in equity markets and the technology sector (in particular telecommunications); and, in some countries, weakening employment growth (Figure 1.8). On the external side, export growth has slowed in response to weaker global demand—both in the United States and in Asia—and import growth has also turned down sharply. In addition to the direct impact of the global slowdown through trade channels, activity is also likely to have been affected by spillovers through corporate and financial linkages—including the expansion of U.S. operations by euro-area businesses and the rapid growth in European investors' holdings of U.S. equities (Chapter II). As the outlook deteriorated, the euro weakened further in the first half of 2001 and moved close to a record low against the U.S. dollar, before firming since July. The reasons for the euro's persistent weakness are still not well understood, but recent evidence suggests that differences in economic performance in the euro area and the United States, and portfolio adjustments as a result of the advent of the euro, have played an important role.

Underlying these overall trends have been some divergences in economic developments in individual euro-area economies (see Box 1.5). Among the three largest economies, gross fixed investment has weakened particularly sharply in Germany, where construction activity has fallen off significantly. More recently, destocking has contributed to stagnant overall activity in Germany—and possibly also in Italy, where a buildup of inventories led to relatively strong growth in the first quarter. The French economy initially appeared to be holding up relatively well against the global slowdown, supported by tax cuts and ongoing employment growth. With consumer and business confidence having fallen significantly, however, and unemployment recently moving up, the pace of activity has weakened and is expected to be similar to that of Germany and Italy during the second half of 2001 and in 2002. In the periphery, growth prospects remain generally stronger, notably in *Greece* and *Ireland*. Indeed, in Ireland the global slowdown has—somewhat fortuitously—helped to reduce the danger of overheating. Current account deficits are expected to remain relatively

Figure 1.8. Euro Area: Weakening Growth, Rising Inflation
(Percent change from four quarters earlier unless otherwise noted)

Business confidence and domestic demand have weakened sharply in the current slowdown and inflation has increased.

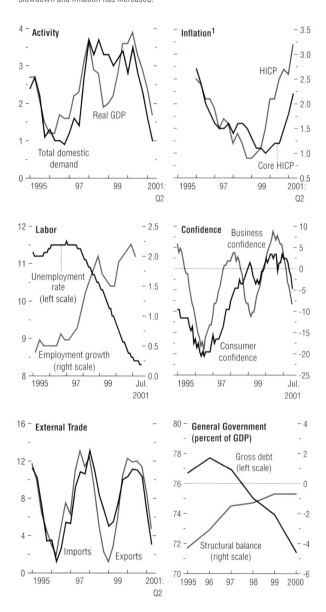

Sources: Eurostat; European Central Bank; European Commission; IMF, *International Financial Statistics;* and IMF staff estimates.
[1]Harmonized index of consumer price index.

Box 1.4. The Japanese Economic Slowdown and East Asia

The short-term outlook for Japan has worsened steadily since mid-2000 as the high-tech driven expansion succumbed to the slump in global electronics demand, while domestic demand remained weak. Real GDP is now expected to decline by 0.5 percent in 2001, followed by a modest rebound in 2002, fueled by a pickup in global growth. This represents a significant change from expectations a year ago, when the recovery seemed likely to continue in 2001, with the IMF forecasting growth of 1¾ percent. Given the size of the Japanese economy, this 2¼ percentage point markdown of the growth outlook has significant implications for the world economy, and East Asia in particular.

The transmission channels from Japan to the rest of the region include:

Trade. While the region has become relatively less reliant on trade with Japan in recent years, the linkages remain significant, with around 12 percent of East Asian exports being sold to Japan and 20 percent of imports coming from Japan (see the Table). A slowing Japanese economy would reduce trade turnover with regional partners, thus impacting their growth outlook. In the region, Indonesia has the most significant trade links with Japan (about one-half of this is petroleum), followed closely by China (which sells mostly lower-end goods to Japan). Hong Kong SAR and Singapore have the lowest reliance.

Stock market pullback. Given the relatively strong linkages between Japan and a number of East Asian markets, a further decline in the already depressed Japanese stock markets could push regional equity markets down, with investors scaling back their exposures to East Asian equity as an asset class. The linkage is particularly strong with Hong Kong SAR, but Korea, Singapore, and Thailand also have significant linkages. However, if investors see differing prospects between Japan and the rest of East Asia, then it is possible that funds may be pulled out of Japan and put into other Asian markets, thus boosting stock prices there.

Problems related to the banking sector. As the economy slows down, it is likely that the lending capacity of banks would be restricted by capital constraints as loan-loss charges are increased. Given that Japanese banks remain major lenders to the region, reports of further banking sector distress could be destabilizing, with Thailand having the highest exposure.

Continued stagnation or contraction in the corporate sector. While Japanese foreign direct investment (FDI) has declined and its banks have reduced lending to many East Asian countries since the Asian crisis, Japan nonetheless remains an important source of capital. Firm-level difficulties could impact Japan's FDI to the rest of East Asia.

Indicators of Linkages Between Japan and East Asia
(In percent, data as of 2000 unless otherwise stated)

	Share of Exports to Japan	Exports to Japan (percent of GDP)	External Debt/GDP	Share of Debt Denominated in Yen	Stock Market Correlation[1]	Share of Bank Lending from Japanese Banks	Share of FDI from Japan
Indonesia	22	8	97	21	0.03	25	13
Thailand	16	9	66	32	0.21	37	25
Korea	11	4	28	17[2]	0.32	18	16
Hong Kong SAR	6	7	...	...	0.40	32	...
Malaysia	13	13	48	30[2]	0.12	27	14
Philippines	14	7	76	27	0.09	18	7
Singapore	7	11	...	...	0.30	27	23
China	16	4	14	16[2]	0.00	18	7

Sources: CEIC Database; IFS; WEO; and IMF staff calculations.
[1]Daily correlation with the Nikkei 225 after controlling for the impact of the S&P 500, using data from January 1999 to June 2001.
[2]Refers to long-term debt in 1998.

The impact of the Japanese economy on East Asia can be analyzed through multicountry macroeconomic models, such as the Oxford Economic Model (OEM) and the G-cubed (Asia Pacific) model (Callen and McKibbin, forthcoming). Simulation results from the OEM, which highlight the trade linkages between countries, suggest that a 2 percentage point decline in Japan's growth outlook for 2001 (from the October 2000 baseline) would reduce growth rates of the East Asian economies, ranging from one-fifth of a percentage point in China, Korea, Malaysia, and the Philippines to about one-third of a percentage point in Indonesia, Hong Kong SAR, Singapore, and Thailand. Results from the G-cubed model, which incorporates intertemporal optimizing behavior of agents and explicit financial market linkages, highlight that the factors underlying the growth slowdown are crucial, as demand shocks like fiscal consolidation may have a negative short-term impact for the region, but would be ultimately beneficial by lowering interest rates and stimulating demand. If the slowdown results from a supply shock, such as a decline in productivity, however, the region's trade dynamics could be affected in a prolonged manner.

Weaker Japanese growth could also have implications for the exchange rate of the yen, although since the Asian crisis, reduced levels of external debt and more flexible exchange rate arrangements have reduced vulnerability to external shocks. It is possible that a depreciating yen would exert pressure on regional currencies, especially on countries competing with Japan in third markets or with major yen exposure. However, a more depreciated yen would have the beneficial effect of reducing the yen component of the East Asian countries' external debt.

Simulation results from the OEM suggest a modest initial negative impact on the region from a depreciation of the yen, and subsequent positive impact as Japan's growth and regional trade pick up. The impact could be somewhat different if the depreciation is induced by an increase in Japan's risk premium. Incorporating this channel into the G-cubed model shows a net positive impact on the region, with the negative impact on net exports (due to competitive pressure) more than offset by the reduced cost of capital and higher capital inflows (that mirror the capital outflows from Japan following the rise in its risk premium).

high in Greece and *Portugal* in 2001, coming down gradually in 2002.

Recent data suggest that activity and confidence are continuing to weaken in the major countries, and, in contrast to the United States, there is relatively little policy easing in place. Nevertheless, interest rates have been cut by 100 basis points since May. Moreover, although fiscal policy is broadly neutral in the area as a whole, tax cuts in some countries are providing a boost to consumption. Demand is also likely to be supported by the abatement of earlier oil and food price shocks, completion of inventory corrections, a still quite favorable exchange rate, and a modest strengthening of activity in the United States. Against this background, euro-area GDP growth is projected to average 1.8 percent in

2001—still the highest of the three major currency areas—and to rise to 2.2 percent in 2002. But the downside risks to this forecast have been increased by the September 11 terrorist attack, particularly if the global recovery is slower than expected or consumer confidence continues to weaken. The strong intraregional linkages would transmit these risks throughout the euro area. Furthermore, individual euro-area countries face particular risks: for example, *Finland* and Ireland are vulnerable to the high technology slowdown.

The oil and food price shocks that have dampened domestic demand have also led to a sharp rise in headline inflation, peaking at 3.4 percent in May. Core inflation has also risen, albeit more moderately, to just over 2 percent. Some of the

Box 1.5. Relative Euro-Area Growth Performances: Why Are Germany and Italy Lagging Behind France?

Since mid-2000, domestic demand growth has been weaker in Germany and Italy than in France (see the Figure).[1] These developments mirror a pattern of divergence among the three largest euro-area economies. Since the last area-wide recession in 1992–93, output growth has averaged about 2 percent for France, 1.7 percent for Italy, and 1.5 percent for Germany. The small, but cumulatively important, differences in growth over this horizon can largely be traced back to differences in potential growth—linked, among other factors, to the rate of growth in the labor force, which in France was twice as high as that in the other two countries, together with somewhat greater effectiveness in pursuing supply-side friendly structural reforms. Moreover, disappointing potential growth through most of the 1990s suggests that Germany has yet to fully shake off the lingering effects of unification.

Against this backdrop, developments can be analyzed by focusing on four subperiods:

- *From trough to Stage 3 of EMU:* Starting from the cyclical trough in 1993 to early 1997, France and Germany—linked through the de facto fixed exchange rate in the ERM—moved mostly in lockstep. By contrast, the depreciation of the lira upon Italy's exit from the Exchange Rate Mechanism (ERM) in September 1992 provided a boost to exports. Growth in all countries was dampened by macroeconomic policies geared toward promoting disinflation and convergence to Maastricht criteria. The negative fiscal impulse was about 2 percentage points of GDP in both Germany and France, and over 3 percent in Italy. Employment growth was weak in all three countries, but especially in Germany, reflecting the lack of labor market reforms, confidence effects, and less than exemplary output performance.

[1]Care should be taken in analyzing such short-term trends in growth rates. For example, the rapid upswing in German growth in early 2000 has to some extent created base effects that tend to exaggerate the degree of the current downturn.

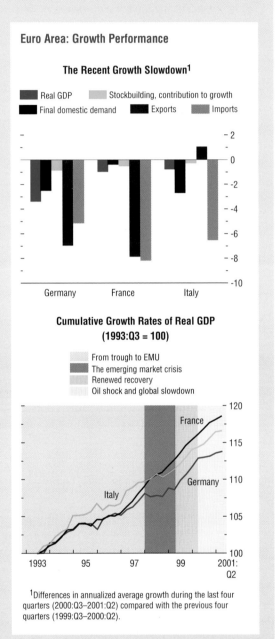

Euro Area: Growth Performance

The Recent Growth Slowdown[1]

[1]Differences in annualized average growth during the last four quarters (2000:Q3–2001:Q2) compared with the previous four quarters (1999:Q3–2000:Q2).

- *The emerging market crises:* After four years of fitful recovery, growth resumed by late 1997. France, in particular, benefited from strong domestic demand led by an investment boom—linked to improved profitability and increased capacity utilization—and employment-friendly tax relief that supported consumption. German growth continued to sputter as the lack of wage moderation and labor market reforms prolonged the labor shakeout begun in the early 1990s. Italy also did less well than France, as lagged effects of the earlier fiscal tightening, lack of progress in structural reforms, and initial uncertainties about membership in the monetary union all combined to weaken demand. Supported by strong U.S. demand and falling oil prices, the recovery started to pick up steam in all countries by mid-1998, but stalled in Germany and Italy as the spillovers from the emerging market crises hit Europe. These spillovers were particularly damaging for Germany and Italy because of their relatively larger manufacturing sectors and higher dependence on extra euro-area exports to emerging markets, and on cyclically sensitive capital and intermediate investment goods.

- *Renewed recovery:* As global activity rebounded following the Asian and Russian crises, the expansion took off again in mid-1999 and kept a sound footing for about one year, underpinned by lower energy prices and a depreciating euro. By this time, fiscal policy had turned roughly neutral in all three countries, while monetary conditions remained accommodative, as the tightening cycle initiated by the European Central Bank (ECB) had been offset by further declines in the euro. However, indicators of cost competitiveness—including ULC-based real effective exchange rates, export shares, and profitability indexes—suggest that conversion rates at the

euro's launch may have provided France with a relative competitive advantage vis-à-vis Germany and Italy.

- *The oil shock and global slowdown:* By mid-2000 the persistent jump in energy prices started to sap the recovery in all three economies. Final domestic demand faltered in the latter half of 2000, particularly in Germany and Italy, as oil and food price shocks eroded disposable income and gradually dragged down business confidence.[2] As the global economy slowed in the second half of 2000, exports fell back in both Germany and France, albeit from relatively high rates, but have held up surprisingly well in Italy where favorable movements in external competitiveness have sustained gains in market share. In most cases, previously legislated tax cuts turn out to have been fortuitously timed to provide some countercyclical support. At the same time, the continuation in the ECB's tightening cycle contributed to the slowdown felt throughout the euro area in the first half of 2001.

Looking ahead, as the effects of external shocks dissipate and European economic integration deepens, growth differences between Germany, France, and Italy should gradually narrow. At the same time, however, disparities in the pace of structural reforms, particularly in labor markets, will continue to create a potential for new divergences in economic performance, as fresh external shocks buffet the euro area.

[2]The term-of-trade loss in 2000 was equivalent to around 1.7 percent of GDP in both Germany and Italy but only 0.9 percent of GDP in France.

forces driving headline inflation—notably higher energy and food prices—now appear to be dissipating and, with demand pressures also easing, both headline and core inflation are expected to fall below 2 percent in 2002. Citing the improved outlook for prices, the ECB reduced interest rates by 25 basis points in August (following a similar cut in May), and rates were lowered by a further 50 basis points on September 17 in

conjunction with other major central banks. There would be scope for additional reductions if there is a further material weakening in demand and inflation developments remain favorable. The scope for monetary policy flexibility will also depend on prospects for continued wage moderation—especially in the key German wage rounds in early 2002—as well as developments in the exchange rate.

On the fiscal side, the structural balance in the euro area is expected to remain broadly constant, with fiscal stimulus in some countries (notably Germany) offset by tightening elsewhere (including in Austria, Spain, and Greece). Actual fiscal balances are projected to weaken, reflecting slowing growth and the assumed unhindered operation of the automatic stabilizers. Some countries—including France, Germany, and Italy—will have difficulty reaching the fiscal targets for 2001 set by their respective national stability programs. From a short-term cyclical perspective, a tightening of fiscal policy would generally be inappropriate at the present stage. At the same time, however, it is essential to maintain the credibility of the fiscal framework in the Stability and Growth Pact, especially given the substantial fiscal challenges from aging populations in coming years. One way to address this dilemma could be to allow revenues to fluctuate with the cycle, while emphasizing and maintaining expenditure targets in medium-term stability programs—implying greater focus of policy on structural rather than actual fiscal balances. Such an approach would avoid promoting procyclical fiscal impulses; had it been applied in the past, this policy would have encouraged a faster reduction in structural deficits in 1999 and 2000, when cyclical conditions were more favorable.

The relatively disappointing growth performance of the euro area, with the unemployment rate seemingly stabilizing well above the 8 percent mark, points to the need to boost productive potential through a reinvigoration of the structural reform effort. Although important progress has been made, there remains a substantial unfinished agenda, including in reforming labor markets, especially tax and benefit systems, and linking wages more closely to productivity; promoting effective integration of euro area capital markets, together with strengthening mechanisms for financial crisis management; reforming pension and healthcare arrangements; and ensuring effective competition and completing the internal market. Recent developments have been mixed. Important pension system reforms have been enacted in Germany. But other measures—including new labor market restrictions in Germany and France, and delays in product market reform in France—tend to convey the opposite signals regarding prospects for structural adjustment.

Domestic demand has remained surprisingly strong in the *United Kingdom*, partially offsetting the effects of a weak manufacturing sector and slowing exports. Robust demand growth and household confidence have been underpinned by record low unemployment and buoyant growth in earnings, while fiscal measures have added support to spending. Inflation, which had been declining, has risen back closer to the 2½ percent target; labor markets remain tight; and property prices have been increasing rapidly. Given the weakening of global demand and the persistent strength of sterling, however, the Bank of England lowered interest rates by 25 basis points in August and a further 25 basis points on September 18 in the aftermath of the terrorist attack, bringing this year's interest rate cuts to 1¼ percentage point. The monetary policy stance is finely balanced: if domestic demand weakens or the external outlook deteriorates further, there could be scope for additional monetary easing, but if domestic demand remains strong and labor market conditions tighten, an increase in interest rates may be warranted.

Growth in *Denmark, Norway,* and *Sweden* is expected to slow to under 2 percent in 2001, largely in response to weaker export market conditions. Inflation has also picked up, partly the result of increases in energy and food prices, and this has constrained real income growth. Although inflation concerns had militated against further easing, interest rates were cut by 50 basis points in Denmark and Sweden on September 17 in conjunction with other central banks. Sweden—which is particularly exposed to the global electronics slowdown (largely through the telecommunications sector)—has experienced sharp falls in stock prices and weakness in the krona. Concerned about increased inflation risks, the Riksbank has inter-

Table 1.6. Selected Western Hemisphere Countries: Real GDP, Consumer Prices, and Current Account Balance
(Annual percent change unless otherwise noted)

	Real GDP				Consumer Prices[1]				Current Account Balance[2]			
	1999	2000	2001	2002	1999	2000	2001	2002	1999	2000	2001	2002
Western Hemisphere	**0.2**	**4.2**	**1.7**	**3.6**	**8.8**	**8.1**	**6.2**	**4.9**	**−3.2**	**−2.5**	**−3.0**	**−3.0**
Mercosur[3]	**−0.3**	**3.1**	**1.4**	**3.2**	**3.4**	**5.0**	**4.5**	**3.9**	**−4.5**	**−3.8**	**−4.2**	**−3.8**
Argentina	−3.4	−0.5	−1.4	2.6	−1.2	−0.9	−0.6	0.6	−4.2	−3.2	−2.9	−2.8
Brazil	0.8	4.5	2.2	3.5	4.9	7.0	6.2	4.8	−4.8	−4.2	−5.0	−4.5
Uruguay	−2.8	−1.3	1.0	2.5	5.7	4.8	5.4	9.5	−2.4	−2.9	−2.7	−2.2
Andean region	**−3.3**	**3.5**	**2.7**	**3.5**	**13.0**	**12.8**	**8.9**	**6.8**	**0.8**	**3.2**	**0.3**	**−0.1**
Chile	−1.1	5.4	4.0	4.7	3.3	3.8	3.4	3.3	−0.1	−1.4	−2.2	−2.3
Colombia	−4.1	2.8	2.1	2.8	10.9	9.2	7.8	6.6	—	−0.2	−2.3	−2.7
Ecuador	−7.3	2.3	4.0	4.0	52.2	96.2	40.6	11.9	6.9	5.3	−1.3	−3.0
Peru	0.9	3.1	0.5	4.0	3.5	3.8	3.1	2.6	−3.8	−3.1	−2.9	−3.4
Venezuela	−6.1	3.2	3.3	2.8	23.6	16.2	12.8	12.9	3.6	10.8	4.9	4.6
Central America and Caribbean	**3.9**	**6.4**	**1.4**	**4.1**	**14.0**	**8.9**	**6.5**	**4.8**	**−3.4**	**−3.5**	**−3.1**	**−3.5**
Dominican Republic	8.0	7.8	3.0	5.6	6.5	7.7	9.7	4.7	−2.5	−5.4	−4.1	−4.4
Guatemala	3.5	3.3	2.0	3.7	5.3	6.0	6.2	4.0	−5.6	−4.5	−4.9	−4.3
Mexico	3.7	6.9	0.8	4.0	16.6	9.5	6.3	4.8	−2.9	−3.1	−2.8	−3.3

[1]In accordance with standard practice in the *World Economic Outlook*, movements in consumer prices are indicated as annual averages rather than as December/December changes during the year, as is the practice in some countries.
[2]Percent of GDP.
[3]Includes Argentina, Bolivia, Brazil, Paraguay, and Uruguay.

vened directly in the foreign exchange market several times since June 2001 and, in July, raised its official interest rate. However, substantial foreign ownership of equity in the high-technology sector in Sweden, as in Finland, should help to limit the downturn in domestic wealth and demand. In Norway, high oil prices are offsetting weakness in the non-oil economy, through, among other things, a resurgence of oil-related investment. Elsewhere in Europe, growth in *Switzerland* is expected to slow to below 2 percent in 2001 and 2002, largely due to weaker exports and investment activity. With inflation still subdued, the Swiss National Bank has been able to lower interest rates—including on September 17. Further cuts would be warranted should evidence of a marked slowing of activity persist. Ongoing public expenditure restraint will be needed to support planned tax cuts and rising costs associated with population aging, together with further structural reforms—including in the network industries—to raise the trend rate of growth. In *Iceland*, growth is projected to slow sharply, due mostly to a weakening of private consumption, and this should contribute to

some lowering of the still-high current account deficit. The authorities should continue to strengthen the financial system's ability to absorb shocks.

Latin America: How Will Argentina's Crisis Affect the Region?

In Latin America, following a strong recovery in 2000, GDP growth is projected to decline by 2.5 percentage points to 1.7 percent in 2001, 2 percentage points lower than projected at the time of the May 2001 *World Economic Outlook* (Table 1.6). Growth projections have been revised downwards for most countries, reflecting the increasing impact of the global economic slowdown, particularly for *Mexico* and *Chile*; the economic difficulties in *Argentina*, which have adversely affected a number of neighboring countries; and exogenous factors, including political uncertainties and the energy crisis in *Brazil*. Reflecting these developments, capital flows to the region weakened in the first half of the year, and—with the important exception of the Mexican peso—most regional currencies

Figure 1.9. Selected Western Hemisphere Countries: Overall Public Sector Deficit and Public Debt
(Percent of GDP)

Fiscal consolidation remains essential in many countries in Latin America, especially those where domestic debt remains high and vulnerable to exchange rate developments.

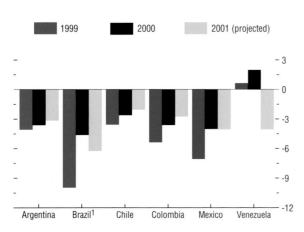

Overall Public Sector Deficit

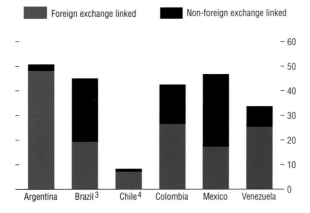

Foreign and Domestic Government Debt[2]
(end-2000)

Source: IMF staff estimates.

[1]About 4 percentage points of Brazil's deficit in 1999 were accounted for by the impact of the depreciation of the *real* on public sector debt.

[2]Unless noted otherwise, data refer to gross stocks of government debt, including that of public enterprises, but excluding central bank liabilities.

[3]Includes also central bank liabilities (monetary base) net of liquid foreign exchange assets.

[4]Adding debt owed by the central bank net of liquid foreign exchange assets would substantially raise the domestic debt component, while taking the (net) foreign exchange linked component into the negative range. Figures do not include recognition bonds related to pension system conversion.

were under downward pressure. As the crisis deepened in Argentina from early July, accompanied by signs of contagion within the region, these pressures have significantly increased. Sentiment remains very fragile, particularly following the September 11 terrorist attack on the United States and the associated possibility of increasing flight to quality in financial markets. As a result, there is substantial downside risk to the outlook.

In many countries, the central vulnerability remains a high external financing requirement, typically linked to a large public sector deficit and high public debt (Figure 1.9). With a substantial share of public debt denominated in foreign exchange, and in some cases a considerable proportion being short term, depreciating exchange rates and higher interest rates have—along with slowing growth—put additional pressures on fiscal positions across the region. Given the need to maintain external confidence, most countries have little scope to allow the automatic stabilizers to operate, and some will need to tighten the underlying stance of fiscal policy to avoid adverse debt dynamics. At the same time, with exchange rates weakening, the scope for monetary easing is in several cases also constrained. This will, unfortunately, add to pressures on activity and exacerbate the already high level of unemployment across much of the region.

Developments in the region have continued to be overshadowed by the situation in *Argentina*. Following the crisis in November 2000, economic conditions temporarily improved, but sentiment deteriorated sharply once again in March 2001, due to a further weakening of the fiscal position, political turmoil, and renewed concerns about Argentina's high external financing requirement, accompanied by a sharp rise in spreads, which also affected neighboring countries. The deteriorating situation in the region, and particularly the depreciation of the Brazilian *real*, in turn adversely affected Argentina. In response, the authorities further strengthened their program through revenue and expenditure measures designed to bring the fiscal position back on track, along with a series of initiatives to boost productivity and competitiveness; a $29.5 billion debt swap, which—while effectively locking in prevailing market rates—substantially reduced financing needs in 2001–05; and, in late June, a package of tax reforms, including trade measures that resulted in a modest effective depreciation of the peso for non-energy trade, and linked the value of the peso for non-energy trade to a basket of the U.S. dollar and the euro.

The authorities' program, along with the more general improvement in sentiment in international markets since April, resulted in a reduction in spreads through mid-June. In early July, however, confidence weakened seriously, prompted initially by concerns about the late June reforms, and then by increasing difficulties in raising domestic financing. As a result, interest rate spreads rose sharply, there was a substantial outflow of deposits from the banking system, and the stock market plummeted. In response, the authorities have committed to strengthening fiscal adjustment, and ensuring that it is sustainable over the medium term, through full implementation of the zero deficit law approved by the Argentine Congress on July 29; the introduction of legislation to reform the revenue sharing arrangement with the provinces; and measures to strengthen tax administration and the public banks. This has been supported by an augmentation of Argentina's program with the IMF, part of which will be available to support a voluntary and market-based operation to increase the viability of Argentina's debt profile. But, while private sector deposits have begun to recover, economic activity and confidence are still weak. The situation remains very difficult, and it will be critical now to focus on prompt and full implementation of the measures that have been announced.

Following a strong recovery from the 1998–99 recession, Brazil was buffeted by a series of adverse shocks in the first half of 2001, including contagion from Argentina, political uncertainties, and the emergence of a serious energy crisis requiring stringent electricity rationing. While

the impact of these shocks is difficult to gauge—the duration of electricity rationing, for example, will depend in part on the autumn rainfall—output fell in the second quarter and there are downside risks to activity in the period ahead. External confidence also weakened, reflected in widening yield spreads and slowing capital inflows, and the *real* depreciated steadily, putting upward pressure on inflation. In response, the authorities appropriately raised interest rates, and also undertook additional foreign borrowing to boost reserves and support the currency. As the situation in Argentina worsened in early July, these pressures markedly increased, with spreads rising above 1000 basis points, and the *real* plumbing new lows against the U.S. dollar. Against this background, the authorities have further tightened fiscal and monetary policies, including by increasing their target for the primary surplus from 3 percent to 3.35 percent for 2001 and 3.5 percent for 2002, and by accelerating structural reforms. These policies have been supported by a new $15 billion Stand-By Arrangement with the IMF, and the authorities have indicated that they do not intend to draw on IMF resources unless it is deemed necessary owing to changes in external economic and financial market conditions. In *Uruguay*, prospects have also weakened due to developments in Argentina and Brazil, as well as a serious outbreak of foot and mouth disease. To absorb external shocks and protect competitiveness, the authorities have increased the pace of depreciation of the exchange rate band, and widened the band. Additional fiscal tightening to control public debt dynamics, as well as an intensification of structural reforms, will also be needed.

Mexico's main vulnerability continues to be the possibility of a further weakening of activity in the United States. Through the first three quarters of 2000, with growth running at over 7 percent, the central policy concern was to avoid overheating; however, GDP and domestic demand growth have since weakened markedly as the growth of exports to the United States—which account for 25 percent of GDP—declined sharply. With GDP having fallen in the first two quarters of 2001 on a seasonally adjusted basis, output growth is projected to decline to under 1 percent for the year as a whole, recovering thereafter in tandem with activity in the United States. The current account deficit is now expected to decline to 2.8 percent of GDP in 2001, and capital inflows have remained strong—reflecting the continuing impact of North American Free Trade Agreement membership on direct investment, including the purchase of a major domestic bank by a foreign bank. Correspondingly, the peso appreciated significantly and inflation pressures declined, providing room for some monetary policy easing. Following the renewed crisis in Argentina, a portion of this appreciation has been reversed, and spreads have risen moderately. With lower growth resulting in a revenue shortfall, the authorities have taken offsetting measures to protect their fiscal targets; early passage of the tax reform remains critical to reduce medium-term fiscal vulnerabilities.

GDP growth in the Andean region is also expected to moderate as a result of the deteriorating external and regional environment, and some countries have experienced moderate contagion from Argentina. Growth in *Chile* has slowed and the outlook remains vulnerable to further slowing in the global economy (which would also depress export prices). Concerns about external financing are rather lower than elsewhere in the region, reflected in a continued relatively low yield spread. The authorities have lowered interest rates, and the new practice of targeting the structural fiscal balance will allow the automatic stabilizers to function. However, the recent depreciation of the peso may constrain monetary policy easing in the future (although so far it does not appear to have affected inflationary expectations). Among the smaller Andean countries, growth in *Ecuador* is expected to strengthen, aided by the construction of the new oil pipeline, and inflation has continued to decline as dollarization takes hold. But further action is needed to address banking sector weaknesses, which remain an important source of vulnerability, and the recent

Constitutional Court decision overturning the earlier increase in the VAT rate has added to fiscal uncertainties. In *Venezuela*, growth has also remained well sustained, but has been heavily dependent on rapid public expenditure growth, financed by buoyant oil revenues. With weak private investment and business confidence, and large capital outflows persisting, the economy remains vulnerable to lower oil prices. In contrast, growth is expected to weaken in *Colombia*, owing to lower coffee prices and weaker-than-expected investment. The stance of macroeconomic policies appears generally prudent, but much continues to depend on progress with the peace process, and maintaining the pace of structural reform in the run up to the coming elections. In *Peru*, growth has slowed sharply, mainly reflecting political uncertainties prior to the recent elections. The key challenge facing the new government is to restore confidence in a difficult external environment, through prudent macroeconomic policies and accelerated reforms, notably privatization.

Despite weakening tourism revenues, countries in the *Caribbean region* continued to experience solid growth and low inflation in 2000, underpinned by generally sound macroeconomic policies and buoyed by investment in natural gas and petrochemicals (*Trinidad and Tobago*), and tourism and infrastructure (*Grenada* and *St. Kitts and Nevis*). Prospects for the region in 2001 and the medium term may prove more difficult, due to the impact of the U.S. downturn on tourism; the erosion of preferential access for bananas and sugar into the European Union; and the decline in the offshore financial services industry in response to increased international scrutiny and a tightening of the regulatory framework. *Trinidad and Tobago* should continue to register strong growth, based on natural gas and services, and *Jamaica's* long period of economic stagnation could now be ending, based on a pickup in mining, tourism, and other services, as well as a steady decline in interest rates. Elsewhere, and particularly within the *Eastern Caribbean Currency Union*, countries should move quickly to strengthen their public finances, especially by containing the government wage bill, which is key to enhancing competitiveness, and pressing ahead with privatization and other structural reforms to offset the deteriorating external environment. Regulation and supervision of the offshore financial centers should also be strengthened.

Emerging Asia: Hard Hit by External Shocks

The outlook for the emerging markets of Asia has continued to deteriorate. From mid-2000, industrial production and exports slowed sharply, driven by the global slowdown, especially in the high technology sector, and more recently by weakening growth in Europe and Japan (Figure 1.10). Coming on top of a variety of earlier shocks, including higher oil prices, political uncertainties, and in some cases weakening confidence as a result of lagging structural reforms, growth prospects have declined further for most of the newly industrialized countries and members of the Association of South East Asian Nations (ASEAN) (Table 1.7). These shocks have been accompanied by a decline in stock markets, capital outflows, and periodic pressures on exchange rates. External trade accounts for a lower share of activity in the two largest economies of the region—China and India— but, while China's economic performance is expected to be relatively well-sustained, growth in India is projected to weaken in 2001 as a result of a range of domestic shocks together with falling exports.

Looking forward, growth in most Asian countries is expected to pick up in 2002, supported by an upturn in global activity and in the electronics cycle; and it is encouraging that foreign direct investment commitments continue to hold up quite well. However, there are important risks to the outlook, particularly given the increased global economic and financial market uncertainty following the September 11 terrorist attack on the United States. Specific concerns include the possibilities of a more prolonged downturn in the United States; a lagging recovery in the technology sector; and the weakening

Figure 1.10. Selected Asia-Pacific Countries: Weakening Export Growth[1]
(Percent change; U.S. dollars)

The newly industrialized economies and members of the Association of South East Asian Nations (ASEAN) are experiencing much weaker external demand, especially for technology.

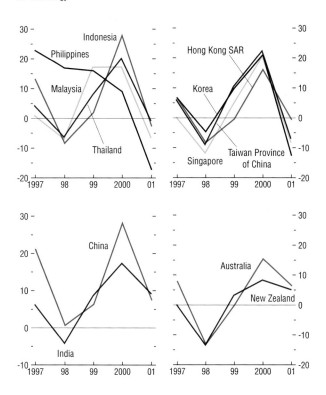

Source: IMF staff estimates.
[1]Export of goods.

Table 1.7. Selected Asian Countries: Real GDP, Consumer Prices, and Current Account Balance
(Annual percent change unless otherwise noted)

	Real GDP				Consumer Prices[1]				Current Account Balance[2]			
	1999	2000	2001	2002	1999	2000	2001	2002	1999	2000	2001	2002
Emerging Asia[3]	**6.4**	**7.0**	**5.1**	**5.9**	**2.1**	**1.8**	**2.7**	**3.1**	**3.8**	**3.0**	**2.1**	**1.6**
Newly industrialized Asian economies	**7.9**	**8.2**	**1.0**	**4.3**	**—**	**1.2**	**2.1**	**2.1**	**7.1**	**4.9**	**5.0**	**4.8**
Hong Kong SAR	3.0	10.5	0.6	4.0	−4.0	−3.7	−1.4	0.6	7.3	5.4	6.6	7.5
Korea	10.9	8.8	2.5	4.5	0.8	2.3	4.4	3.4	6.0	2.4	2.6	2.1
Singapore	5.9	9.9	−0.2	4.0	0.1	1.4	1.5	1.7	25.9	23.7	21.0	19.8
Taiwan Province of China	5.4	6.0	−1.0	4.0	0.2	1.3	0.1	0.8	2.9	2.9	2.5	2.6
ASEAN-4	**2.8**	**5.0**	**2.4**	**4.1**	**10.2**	**3.0**	**6.6**	**5.0**	**9.2**	**8.0**	**4.8**	**3.9**
Indonesia	0.8	4.8	3.0	4.3	20.7	3.8	10.8	7.0	4.1	5.2	3.2	2.0
Malaysia	6.1	8.3	1.0	4.8	2.7	1.5	1.5	2.0	15.9	9.4	6.6	5.7
Philippines	3.4	4.0	2.5	3.5	6.6	4.3	6.5	5.7	10.0	12.5	6.4	7.2
Thailand	4.2	4.4	2.0	4.0	0.3	1.5	2.5	2.7	10.2	7.5	4.4	3.2
South Asia[4]	**6.4**	**5.8**	**4.5**	**5.6**	**4.8**	**4.0**	**3.8**	**5.5**	**−1.1**	**−1.1**	**−1.0**	**−1.1**
Bangladesh	5.4	6.0	5.5	5.0	6.4	2.3	3.1	5.5	−1.4	−1.2	−1.7	−1.8
India	6.8	6.0	4.5	5.7	4.7	4.0	3.6	5.5	−0.7	−0.9	−0.8	−0.9
Pakistan	4.1	3.9	3.9	4.6	4.1	4.4	5.1	5.1	−2.8	−2.1	−2.0	−2.0
Formerly centrally planned economies[5]	**7.0**	**7.9**	**7.4**	**7.1**	**−1.1**	**0.4**	**1.0**	**1.6**	**1.6**	**1.8**	**0.9**	**0.1**
China	7.1	8.0	7.5	7.1	−1.4	0.4	1.0	1.5	1.6	1.9	1.0	0.2
Vietnam	4.2	5.5	4.5	6.0	4.1	−1.7	0.6	4.3	4.5	2.1	1.3	−2.7

[1]In accordance with standard practice in the *World Economic Outlook*, movements in consumer prices are indicated as annual averages rather than as December/December changes during the year, as is the practice in some countries.
[2]Percent of GDP.
[3]Includes developing Asia, newly industrialized Asian economies, and Mongolia.
[4]Includes Bangladesh, India, Maldives, Nepal, Pakistan, and Sri Lanka.
[5]Includes Cambodia, China, Lao People's Dem. Rep., Mongolia, and Vietnam.

outlook for Japan (Box 1.4). Further deterioration in external financial conditions could also create difficulties for some regional economies. Given the improvement in economic fundamentals since the Asian crisis—including large current account surpluses, higher reserves, reductions in short-term external debt, and widespread adoption of flexible exchange rates—most countries are in a better position to manage such risks. However, a further slowdown in growth would exacerbate pressures on already weak financial and corporate sectors, aggravate the fiscal deficit in India, and complicate reform efforts in China. While the room for policy maneuver varies, macroeconomic policies should remain supportive of activity to the extent possible, accompanied by accelerated progress in financial and corporate reforms, especially in countries where this has lagged.

The economic slowdown has continued to be steepest among the four newly industrialized

economies and *Malaysia*, which were furthest advanced in recovery from the 1997–98 crisis, are highly open, and—apart from *Hong Kong SAR*—are highly exposed to the technology sector (see Chapter III, Box 3.4). Export growth in all five has turned down sharply, accompanied by a rapid decline in industrial production, particularly in Malaysia, *Singapore,* and *Taiwan Province of China.* These developments have been exacerbated by slowing domestic demand growth, driven by declining consumer and business confidence—in some cases linked to banking and corporate sector weaknesses—and falling asset prices. In Taiwan Province of China, where GDP is now expected to decline in 2001, the sharp slowing in activity has increased concerns about the health of the financial system—including low banking sector profitability and the rising number of nonperforming loans. The external vulnerability of the economy is limited though by high foreign exchange reserves and low public debt. While business and household confidence have held up reasonably well in *Korea*, and unemployment remains low, downturns in industrial production and exports point to a further weakening in economic activity in 2001. The ASEAN countries (apart from Malaysia) are somewhat less open, and the main effect of global and domestic developments has been to further weaken an already faltering recovery. In the *Philippines* and *Thailand,* growth has been adversely affected by the electronics slowdown, banking system weaknesses, corporate vulnerabilities (Thailand), and a sizable budget deficit (Philippines). In Indonesia, market sentiment has improved following the recent peaceful resolution of the political crisis, reflected among other things in the strengthening of the rupiah by roughly 25 percent. The recent tightening of fiscal and monetary policy and the new government's intention to accelerate reforms are encouraging, but major challenges remain—particularly addressing concerns about fiscal sustainability and decentralization, containing inflation, and accelerating progress with bank and corporate restructuring.

Policy options for combating sustained weakness in domestic demand and output differ widely. Most countries have moved to reduce interest rates, and further scope for easing remains in many if necessary, consistent with maintaining low inflation rates. In Thailand, an increase in policy interest rates in early June created uncertainty over the course of monetary policy. However, since then the central bank has clarified its intention to maintain a supportive policy stance and has ruled out further rate increases in the near term. Inflation risks are more pressing in Indonesia, and the central bank has had to raise interest rates to address these concerns. In several cases, including Korea, Malaysia, Taiwan Province of China, and Thailand, sizable fiscal packages have been recently introduced to support growth; in others, notably Indonesia and the Philippines, room for maneuver is constrained by high levels of government deficits or debt.

China is expected to continue growing strongly in 2001, in part because total exports, and especially exports of high technology goods, comprise a much lower share of GDP than in most other emerging Asian economies. Indeed, although exports have slowed markedly in 2001—indicating that China is not immune to the global slowdown—overall activity remained strong in the first half of 2001, led by buoyant private consumption and strong public investment resulting from the September 2000 fiscal package. China's near-term vulnerability to external shocks is also limited both by its high level of foreign reserves and by strong inflows of foreign direct investment—running at around $40 billion a year since 1996 and showing a strong pickup in commitments over the past year. The key economic challenges, which have become more urgent with impending entry to the World Trade Organization, remain to strengthen the banking sector, which, despite recent loan transfers to asset management companies, remains burdened by high levels of nonperforming loans; move forward with enterprise restructuring; and, over the medium term, strengthen the fiscal position to cover the costs of bank and corporate reforms and meet outstanding pension liabilities. A gradual shift to more flexible exchange rate management would also be desirable at the appropriate time.

India is also relatively insulated from the global slowdown, given the nature of its IT sector (which is focused on services, where India remains highly cost competitive) and its relatively closed economy. Nonetheless, activity has slowed sharply, reflecting the effects of drought, energy price hikes, the waning effect of the substantial fiscal stimulus introduced during the late 1990s, and the devastating earthquake in Gujarat. As a result, growth in 2001 is projected to drop to around 4.5 percent (or 5 percent in FY 2001/02), well below levels considered necessary to make significant inroads into poverty (see Box 1.6). With signs of a favorable monsoon, the economy is expected to recover gradually in the latter half of 2001 and into 2002, and India's

Box 1.6. The Growth-Poverty Connection in India

Over the last three decades, India's poverty rate has declined significantly. Social development indicators, such as life expectancy, literacy, and infant mortality rates, have also improved. Despite this progress, around 260 million people (26 percent of the population) still live below the poverty line, which continues to present a major policy challenge.[1]

Between 1974–2000, the percentage of the population living below the poverty line fell from 55 percent to 26 percent (see the Figure). The decline was fairly uniform across rural and urban areas. Rural poverty, which constitutes roughly three-quarters of the national poor, declined from 56 percent in 1974 to 27 percent in 2000, while during the same period, urban poverty dropped from 49 percent to 24 percent. Interstate differentials in poverty also narrowed, but they still remain large—while 6 percent of the state of Punjab's population lives below the poverty line, in Bihar the incidence of poverty is now around 43 percent. The rate of reduction in poverty during this period has been generally steady, with the largest reduction having taken place between 1994–2000.

Analysis of poverty trends in India, however, has been complicated by statistical problems. Although the data on poverty in India are believed to be among the best among developing countries, there are a number of areas of concern, in particular related to the coverage and frequency of the National Sample Surveys (NSS), from which poverty estimates are constructed.[2] In addition, concerns have been

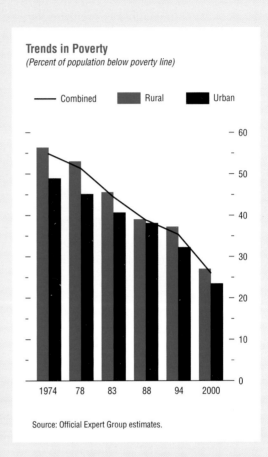

Trends in Poverty
(Percent of population below poverty line)

— Combined   ▇ Rural   ▇ Urban

Source: Official Expert Group estimates.

raised regarding the accuracy of the price deflators used in estimating real consumption expenditure, and the use of estimation procedures that do not reflect the increasing monetization and changing consumer preferences, particularly in the rural economy. More recently, questions have arisen regarding the poverty estimates from 2000. Some analysts have cautioned that confusion on the part of both respondents and enumerators due to changes in the survey questionnaires may have resulted in measurement errors and a possible downward bias to the poverty rate.

---

[1]India's official poverty line, based on a nutritional norm, is determined at 49 rupees per capita monthly expenditure at 1973–74 prices for rural areas, and 57 rupees per month for urban areas. This official poverty line is lower than the World Bank's dollar-a-day (at purchasing power parity) poverty line, according to which 47 percent of India's population lived in poverty in 1994, compared with the official estimate of 35 percent for the same year.

[2]The NSS carries out two types of consumer surveys—an annual survey with limited sample size and coverage, and a more comprehensive survey with a larger sample conducted roughly every five years. Although estimates from the smaller samples are made public,

they are not used to construct official poverty estimates. Nonetheless, most analyses on the time series properties of poverty have supplemented the estimates from the large-sample surveys with those from the small-sample surveys.

Despite these issues, several stylized facts have emerged from the extensive body of research on poverty in India. *First,* at the microeconomic level, poverty rates appear to be higher among women; those who are illiterate; landless laborers; and those who belong to the lower castes (see National Council of Applied Economic Research, 1996). *Second,* at the macroeconomic level, growth has been a major influence on poverty. Empirical studies show that both higher agricultural yields and increases in nonfarm output have significantly reduced poverty rates. In addition to growth, low inflation, education, public development spending, and land reforms—particularly tenancy reforms—have also played key roles in reducing poverty. *Lastly,* poverty alleviation programs (food subsidy, rural works, and self-employment schemes) have not been very cost effective, largely due to poor targeting, leakages, and abuse. However, some progress has recently been made in rationalizing and better targeting these programs (World Bank, 2000).

In the last few years, some analysts have raised concerns that the positive link between growth and poverty reduction, evidenced in the past, may have weakened in the 1990s. Critics contend that, although the reforms in the early 1990s raised economic growth markedly, the benefits in terms of poverty reduction were relatively muted. Supplementing poverty estimates from the five-yearly large sample surveys with the annual small-sample surveys for the period 1974–97, a recent analysis shows that although poverty increased in the initial years of the reforms (1991–92), the trend was sharply reversed in the later years as the benefits of the reforms began to filter through the economy.[3] However, other factors that were previously poverty reducing, such as low inflation and high public development spending, appear to have been less effective during this period.

The 2000 survey data—which showed a marked decline in the poverty rate after 1997 during a period of relatively robust growth—provides further evidence that growth has been pro-poor in India. In addition, the fact that per capita consumption—based on national account statistics—grew rapidly during the past decade, at a rate even faster than the growth implied by the NSS surveys, while income distribution worsened only marginally, appears to confirm this conclusion.

[3]See Aziz (forthcoming) who examines the experience with poverty at the state level during 1974–97, using estimates from both the five-yearly large sample and annual small-sample surveys.

external position is also projected to remain relatively comfortable. However, the recent slowdown—and associated fiscal revenue shortfalls—is expected to cause the public sector deficit to rise to more than 11 percent of GDP in FY 2001/02. It remains critical that steps are taken to assure fiscal sustainability and lay the foundations for strong and sustained growth—including by moving ahead with proposed fiscal responsibility legislation and by implementing the ambitious structural reform agenda recently laid out in the Prime Minister's Economic Advisory Council.

Agricultural conditions are contributing to a divergence in short-term economic prospects for *Pakistan* and *Bangladesh*. Severe drought in Pakistan has held down growth and weakened the trade balance, adding to the already-severe financial vulnerabilities—including low reserves, high public debt, and a large financing gap—while agricultural output and external trade in Bangladesh have picked up following a flood-affected slowdown in 2000. Partly reflecting these trends, tax revenues have been below expectations in Pakistan, but have grown strongly in Bangladesh. In both countries, further progress in needed to improve medium-term budgetary positions, including improvements in tax administration and spending discipline. Further privatization of public banks and enterprises, to-

Table 1.8. European Union Accession Candidates: Real GDP, Consumer Prices, and Current Account Balance
(Annual percent change unless otherwise noted)

	Real GDP				Consumer Prices[1]				Current Account Balance[2]			
	1999	2000	2001	2002	1999	2000	2001	2002	1999	2000	2001	2002
E.U. accession candidates	−0.1	4.9	1.1	4.7	25.3	24.3	20.5	14.7	−4.1	−5.1	−2.8	−3.6
Turkey	−5.0	7.5	−4.3	5.9	64.9	54.9	51.9	32.7	−0.7	−4.9	3.0	−0.4
Excluding Turkey	2.1	3.8	3.4	4.2	11.2	12.9	8.8	7.5	−5.7	−5.3	−5.3	−5.0
Baltics	−1.7	5.1	4.5	5.2	1.8	2.2	2.3	3.1	−9.3	−6.3	−6.7	−6.4
Estonia	−0.7	6.9	4.5	5.0	3.3	4.0	5.7	3.8	−4.7	−6.4	−7.2	−6.8
Latvia	1.1	6.6	6.0	6.0	2.4	2.6	2.3	3.0	−9.7	−6.8	−6.3	−5.8
Lithuania	−3.9	3.3	3.6	4.7	0.8	1.0	0.6	2.8	−11.2	−6.0	−6.7	−6.6
Central Europe	3.1	3.9	3.1	4.0	6.9	8.6	5.3	5.0	−5.7	−5.2	−5.1	−4.9
Czech Republic	−0.4	2.9	3.3	3.9	2.1	4.0	3.9	3.8	−2.9	−4.6	−5.0	−4.9
Hungary	4.5	5.2	4.5	4.5	10.0	9.8	9.4	6.4	−4.3	−3.6	−4.8	−4.8
Poland	4.1	4.1	2.5	3.7	7.3	10.1	5.7	5.7	−7.5	−6.3	−5.2	−5.0
Slovak Republic	1.9	2.2	3.0	4.4	10.7	12.0	7.2	6.0	−5.7	−3.7	−7.3	−6.4
Slovenia	5.2	4.9	4.5	4.0	6.2	8.9	7.0	5.0	−3.9	−3.2	−2.7	−2.4
Southern and South Eastern Europe	−0.7	2.8	4.2	4.6	30.9	32.9	24.1	18.2	−4.0	−5.1	−5.7	−5.2
Bulgaria	2.4	5.8	4.5	5.0	2.6	10.4	6.8	3.2	−5.3	−5.8	−6.0	−5.7
Cyprus	4.5	5.1	4.2	4.0	1.8	4.1	2.2	2.5	−2.4	−5.0	−3.6	−3.0
Malta	4.0	4.7	4.1	4.3	2.1	2.4	1.8	2.0	−3.4	−14.5	−5.9	−5.1
Romania	−2.3	1.6	4.1	4.5	45.8	45.7	33.8	26.0	−4.1	−3.9	−6.0	−5.5

[1]In accordance with standard practice in the *World Economic Outlook*, movements in consumer prices are indicated as annual averages rather than as December/December changes during the year as is the practice in some countries.
[2]Percent of GDP.

gether with liberalization of energy and other key sectors, would also support investment, diversification, and sustained growth.

Growth in *Australia* and *New Zealand* is expected to slow significantly in 2001—albeit by much less than other countries in the region—accompanied by declining inflation and smaller current account deficits. The export sectors of both countries have been performing well, supported by more depreciated real exchange rates, although the sustainability of recent export growth may be at risk if external markets continue to weaken. Domestic demand has been more patchy: investment—particularly residential construction—has been weak, but recent data point to a strong rebound in Australia, and consumer confidence and spending in both countries have held up relatively well. Interest rates in Australia have been cut substantially, supporting a bounce back in activity after the slowdown in the second half of 2000, which in part reflected an unwinding of the buildup of demand ahead of changes in the tax regime in

mid-2000. Faced with tighter labor markets and high capacity utilization, interest rate reductions in New Zealand have been more moderate. Nevertheless, provided inflation remains subdued, both countries have scope for further rate reductions—particularly if external and domestic demand weaken under the impact of the global slowdown.

The economic performance of individual *Pacific island countries* has varied quite widely over the years, reflecting differences in the strength of economic policy implementation, the political environment, and the timing and severity of particular external shocks. Thus, real GDP contracted sharply in *Fiji* and the *Solomon Islands* in 2000, where confidence was badly shaken by political disturbances and civil unrest, but picked up strongly in *Samoa*, which benefited from continued sound policies and a diversion of tourism from Fiji. The global economic slowdown is likely to dampen growth in 2001, particularly in countries where the tourism sector is relatively large.

Emerging Europe: A Difficult Balance Between Short- and Medium-Term Objectives

Following a strong pickup in 2000, regional GDP growth is expected to fall to 1.1 percent in 2001 (Table 1.8), due largely to a sharp decline in output in Turkey. GDP growth in most other countries in the region is expected to weaken moderately, as export growth—which has so far held up relatively well, buoyed by foreign direct investment and corporate restructuring—is increasingly affected by weakening demand in Europe, particularly Germany (Figure 1.11). Correspondingly, little progress is expected in reducing external current account deficits, which, although largely financed by foreign direct investment, remain a source of vulnerability. So far, contagion from the Turkish crisis has been limited, although some countries—including Poland and Hungary—experienced some pressures on exchange rates as conditions in Argentina deteriorated in early July. In most countries, unemployment—linked to labor market rigidities and high labor taxation—is also a serious concern.

For the regional aggregates, developments have been dominated by the crisis in *Turkey*, where a combination of weakening economic fundamentals, policy slippages, and increased political uncertainty culminated in a major speculative attack and the floating of the lira in late February. The extremely high interest rates experienced during the crisis period, combined with the large overnight borrowing of the state banks and official support for intervened private banks, resulted in a substantial increase in public debt and in a rapid shortening in its maturity. While interest rates eased in the immediate aftermath of the crisis, they have remained at high levels, putting fiscal sustainability and economic recovery at risk. Along with extreme uncertainty about exchange rates and inflation, high real interest rates hampered the real economy and increased pressures on the already fragile banking system. The key challenge facing the new economic team has been to restore confidence and to bring down interest rates rapidly and in a sus-

Figure 1.11. Emerging Europe: Export Growth[1]
(Percent change from four quarters earlier unless otherwise noted)

Exports in emerging Europe have been growing strongly over recent years, partly reflecting the impact of corporate restructuring and foreign direct investment. However, export growth has recently weakened under the impact of the global slowdown.

Export Growth

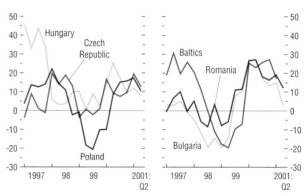

Exports as percent of GDP (2000)

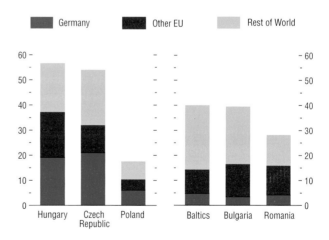

Sources: IMF, *Direction of Trade Statistics;* and various central bank websites.
[1] Export of goods only.

tainable fashion. To this end, the authorities' revised program focuses on addressing key structural weaknesses, particularly in the banks; reducing the public sector borrowing requirement and helping ensure debt sustainability, while centering monetary policy on inflation reduction; and strengthening the social dialogue to promote wage moderation and social protection. The program is supported by substantial additional external financing and resources from international financial institutions, including the IMF.

To date, performance has been mixed. As expected, output growth has declined rapidly, although there are signs that business confidence may be leveling off, and exports and tourism are expected to pick up sharply due to the depreciation of the lira. The authorities have made significant progress toward restructuring the banking system; the fiscal outturn has been stronger than expected; inflation has shown signs of moderating; and, following some earlier slippages, policy implementation has significantly improved. Even so, while domestic interest rates have declined somewhat, they remain well above programmed levels, reflecting continued market perceptions of high risk, as well as external factors (including contagion effects from the crisis in Argentina). Given the still very difficult economic situation and the need to further strengthen external confidence, flawless implementation of the program, together with full and undivided political support, remains essential.

In other countries in the region, macroeconomic and structural policies have continued to center on early accession to the European Union, including the adoption of the *acquis communautaire* (the detailed body of laws and regulations that underpins the European Union). With ongoing uncertainties over the timing of enlargement, and signs that popular support could be eroding in both accession and EU countries, the agreement by EU leaders at the Göteborg summit in June to seek to conclude negotiations with the most advanced countries by the end of 2002, with entry in 2004, is particularly welcome. But with discussions in the most difficult areas

still under way, much remains to be done—by both the EU and the accession countries—if this objective is to be achieved.

In Central Europe, key challenges are how best to set the fiscal-monetary policy mix in light both of cyclical conditions, and the need to make progress toward the medium-term goals of reducing fiscal and external deficits. In *Poland*, where activity has weakened sharply and inflation is declining, interest rates have been reduced, most recently in August, accompanied by a broadly cyclically neutral relaxation of the budget deficit target. With interest rates still remaining very high in real terms, there appears scope for further easing. Next year's budget needs to avoid any new spending commitments and tax exemptions to avoid the emergence of imbalances and resume progress toward medium-term fiscal consolidation. In contrast, in *Hungary* the expansion remains reasonably robust and inflation has returned to double digit levels. The recent widening of the exchange rate band is facilitating the necessary tightening of monetary conditions but needs to be supported by a tighter fiscal stance. In the *Czech Republic*, demand and activity remained strong in the first quarter but have since shown signs of slowing. The Central Bank raised its policy interest rate for the first time since March 1998, against a backdrop of rising headline inflation, as well as a projected expansion of the underlying budget deficit (excluding privatization reserves and expenditures related to bank restructuring). Over the medium term, all countries face serious fiscal challenges related to aging, high tax burdens on labor, and expenditures required for EU accession, underscoring the need to rationalize other current expenditures including through restructuring the civil service and improving the targeting of social spending (see Christou and Daseking, forthcoming).

Activity in the Baltics is projected to remain relatively robust, with a moderate slowdown in *Estonia*—in part reflecting its exposure to the electronics sector—offset to some extent by *Lithuania*'s continuing recovery from the 1999 recession. Given the openness of these economies, however, they remain vulnerable to weaker external demand, particularly in Europe. Budget deficits in all three Baltic countries have been sharply reduced in the past two years, contributing to the decline in external current account deficits across the region. While external deficits nonetheless remain high—partly because of higher oil prices—vulnerabilities are reduced by the high level of foreign direct investment and generally low external debt. Over the medium term, the key challenge is to consolidate this progress while meeting higher expenditure needs for EU accession, as well as pension reform; and, in Lithuania and *Latvia*, to support eventual repegging of their currencies to the euro (in Lithuania, planned for 2002).

In southeastern Europe, the expansion in *Bulgaria* has been underpinned by sound macroeconomic policies, although the slowdown in Europe and the crisis in Turkey have begun to affect export revenues. The key challenge for the new government is to maintain the momentum of structural reform necessary to establish a fully functioning and competitive market economy. In *Romania*, which has adopted a "stop-go" approach to reform and macroeconomic stability in recent years, GDP growth has become increasingly driven by domestic demand, accompanied by a significant widening of the current account deficit. To reduce these pressures, and support a further reduction in inflation, fiscal policy will need to be tightened, including through measures to strengthen the financial performance of public enterprises. It is also essential to reinvigorate the reform process, including through more rapid progress in privatization and improved governance.

In the *Federal Republic of Yugoslavia*, which faces an enormous task of economic reconstruction and a crushing burden of external debt, the new government has moved with impressive speed and commitment to formulate and begin to implement an ambitious program of stabilization and reform. Macroeconomic policies are focused on reducing inflation, which peaked at over 100 percent at the end of 2000, through strict restraint on credit expansion—especially quasi-fiscal lending to state enterprises—while

increasing reliance on noninflationary sources of finance such as foreign assistance and privatization revenues. This is being accompanied by wide-ranging structural reforms, including the almost complete liberalization of the trade and foreign exchange system, fiscal reforms, and the initiation of a bank resolution strategy. However, with much remaining to be done, it will be critical that the momentum of reform is sustained, supported by continued generous assistance from the international community including through debt restructuring.

Commonwealth of Independent States (CIS): Recovery Continues, But Reforms Lag

Following the recession induced by the Russian crisis in 1998, the CIS experienced a strong and widespread recovery in 1999–2000. In *Russia* and the energy exporting countries, the combination of higher oil prices and sharply depreciated exchange rates led to a surge in GDP growth to 8.6 percent in 2000 (Table 1.9), accompanied by the emergence of large fiscal and balance of payments surpluses. Despite the terms of trade shock from higher oil prices, GDP growth also appears to have picked up significantly in the energy importing countries, supported by strong import demand from Russia, exchange rate depreciation, and a variety of country-specific factors.

In 2001, regional GDP growth is projected at 4.4 percent, 3.5 percentage points lower than in 2000. The decline in 2001 largely reflects the partial reversal of the factors that had boosted growth earlier, including real exchange rate appreciation, particularly in countries where the strength of the balance of payments has contributed to rapid monetary growth and rising inflationary pressures; weaker-than-expected activity in Western Europe; and lower energy prices. Correspondingly, GDP growth in Russia and the energy exporting countries—which have been adversely affected by all these factors—is projected to halve to 4.3 percent, with a smaller decline in GDP growth in energy importing countries. To date, contagion from the crises in

Table 1.9. Commonwealth of Independent States: Real GDP, Consumer Prices, and Current Account Balance

(Annual percent change unless otherwise noted)

	Real GDP				Consumer Prices[1]				Current Account Balance[2]			
	1999	2000	2001	2002	1999	2000	2001	2002	1999	2000	2001	2002
Commonwealth of Independent States	**4.6**	**7.9**	**4.4**	**4.0**	**70.6**	**25.0**	**21.6**	**13.0**	**1.5**	**3.5**	**2.5**	**1.7**
Russia	5.4	8.3	4.0	4.0	85.7	20.8	22.1	12.9	11.7	18.0	11.5	7.9
Excluding Russia	2.8	6.9	5.4	4.1	42.1	34.8	20.6	13.1	−0.1	0.2	0.1	—
More advanced reformers	**1.4**	**6.7**	**6.1**	**4.7**	**16.9**	**19.7**	**11.5**	**9.4**	**−0.7**	**3.2**	**1.4**	**0.3**
Armenia	3.3	6.0	6.5	6.0	0.7	−0.8	4.5	3.0	−16.6	−14.6	−14.1	−12.1
Azerbaijan	7.4	11.1	8.5	8.5	−8.5	1.8	2.5	2.5	−13.2	−2.7	−6.1	−17.3
Georgia	3.0	1.8	3.5	3.8	19.1	4.0	5.9	5.2	−7.9	−6.0	−5.6	−4.9
Kazakhstan	2.8	9.5	6.0	5.0	8.4	13.3	9.4	7.5	1.0	8.0	5.0	4.3
Kyrgyz Republic	3.7	5.0	5.0	4.5	35.9	18.7	9.1	7.8	−22.9	−15.6	−8.5	−6.0
Moldova	−3.4	1.9	5.0	5.0	39.3	31.3	12.8	10.0	−2.6	−8.4	−6.9	−5.3
Ukraine	−0.2	5.8	6.2	4.0	22.7	28.2	14.9	12.3	2.6	4.7	2.9	2.6
Less advanced reformers	**5.7**	**7.4**	**4.1**	**3.0**	**111.9**	**71.2**	**41.5**	**20.9**	**−0.1**	**—**	**—**	**—**
Belarus	3.4	5.9	2.5	2.2	293.7	169.0	69.0	23.7	−1.6	−1.3	−1.3	−1.8
Tajikistan	3.7	8.3	5.0	5.0	27.5	32.9	39.9	10.7	—	—	—	—
Turkmenistan	16.0	17.6	10.0	6.0	23.5	8.0	15.0	15.0	−16.0	2.7	2.0	2.0
Uzbekistan	4.3	4.0	3.0	2.0	29.1	25.0	26.1	22.2	−1.0	1.4	1.4	2.1
Memorandum												
Net energy exporters[3]	5.5	8.6	4.3	4.2	75.3	19.6	20.7	12.4	9.9	16.7	10.7	7.2
Net energy importers[4]	1.6	5.2	4.7	3.5	56.1	44.9	25.0	14.9	—	0.1	—	—

[1]In accordance with standard practice in the *World Economic Outlook*, movements in consumer prices are indicated as annual averages rather than as December/December changes during the year as is the practice in some countries.
[2]Percent of GDP.
[3]Includes Azerbaijan, Kazakhstan, Russia, and Turkmenistan.
[4]Includes Armenia, Belarus, Georgia, Kyrgyz Republic, Moldova, Tajikistan, Ukraine, and Uzbekistan.

Turkey and Argentina has been relatively modest: spreads on both Russian and Kazakh eurobonds have fallen for the year as a whole, aided by high energy prices and limited financing needs (although some pressures emerged temporary at the end of June as the situation in Argentina deteriorated and oil prices declined). However, those countries where Turkey accounts for a significant share of exports (including *Georgia*) are likely to be adversely affected during the year.

On the macroeconomic side, the policy challenges vary widely. In Russia, despite some weakening in oil prices from their late 2000 peaks and continued high capital outflows, the external current account and overall balance of payments are expected to remain in strong surplus. The authorities face the difficult task of creating appropriately tight domestic liquidity conditions to restrain inflation while avoiding an overly rapid real appreciation of the ruble that could threaten economic growth. Despite stronger-

than-expected fiscal surpluses, inflation is running ahead of projections, suggesting that monetary policy may need to be tightened. Similar challenges are faced in *Kazakhstan*, which is experiencing rapid growth driven by buoyant oil exports, and has set up an oil stabilization fund to help manage the inflows. *Ukraine's* growth, inflation, and external position have performed significantly better than expected based on sound macroeconomic policies, substantial excess capacity, and competitive wage and exchange rates; the effects of earlier structural reforms, especially in agriculture, have been an important contributing factor in 2001.

Inflation has continued to decline across the region, but remains at high levels in a few countries, particularly *Belarus, Tajikistan* and *Uzbekistan*. In these cases, it will be essential to avoid further slippage in macroeconomic policy through maintaining strict fiscal discipline and reducing recourse to directed credit, which continues to undermine monetary policy in a number of cases. In *Armenia*, Georgia, *Kyrgyz Republic, Moldova* and Tajikistan, the dramatic increase in external debt over the past decade is a serious threat to external and fiscal sustainability (Figure 1.12) and is of particular concern given these countries' very low per capita income and high poverty levels. The rise appears to stem from sharp increases in energy prices and the loss of transfers from the central government of the former USSR early in the transition, resulting in large current account deficits. Regional and internal conflicts, policy failures and weak governance, and sharp currency devaluations following the 1998 Russia crisis also played an important role.[9] These factors were compounded by overestimation of implementation capacity and underestimation of the difficulties of transition by the governments, international financial institutions, and other creditors. Also, in some cases the financing received by these countries was not appropriately concessional, and related investments suffered from inadequate project planning. While policies to strengthen domestic adjustment and growth performance will help alleviate the situation, a number of these countries could face serious difficulties if the external environment deteriorates or if economic growth does not respond to reforms as expected. In this event, additional assistance from the international community will be needed to avoid an abrupt adjustment that could have a serious impact on the poor.

Looking to the longer term, the reinvigoration of the structural reform process—particularly in institution building and governance, enterprise restructuring, the financial sector, and transforming the role of the state—remains the key to sustainable growth in the CIS. Indicators of structural reform produced by the European Bank for Reconstruction and Development (EBRD) suggest that little progress was made between 1998

[9]For a detailed discussion, see "Armenia, Georgia, Kyrgyz Republic, Moldova, and Tajikistan: External Debt and Fiscal Sustainability," jointly prepared by the European II Department of the IMF and the Europe and Central Asia Region of the World Bank, available at http://www.imf.org/external/np/eu2/2001/edebt/eng/index.htm

Figure 1.12. Commonwealth of Independent States (CIS): Continuing Recovery But Disappointing Progress on Reform [1]
(Annual percent change unless otherwise noted)

GDP growth has picked up since the Russian crisis and inflation is declining, although it remains high in a number of countries. But progress in structural reform has been disappointing, while high external debt in some countries is a serious concern.

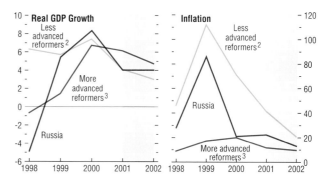

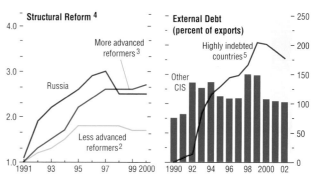

Source: European Bank for Reconstruction and Development, *Transition Report 2000.*
[1] Shaded areas indicate IMF staff projections
[2] Belarus, Tajikistan, Turkmenistan, and Uzbekistan.
[3] Armenia, Azerbaijan, Georgia, Kazakhstan, Kyrgyz Republic, Moldova, and Ukraine.
[4] Simple average of EBRD indicators for eight structural reform indicators. A score of 1 represents conditions before reform in a centrally planned economy; a score of 4 1/3 shows structural characteristics comparable to those in advanced economies.
[5] Armenia, Georgia, Kyrgyz Republic, Moldova, and Tajikistan.

Table 1.10. Selected African Countries: Real GDP, Consumer Prices, and Current Account Balance
(Annual percent change unless otherwise noted)

	Real GDP				Consumer Prices[1]				Current Account Balance[2]			
	1999	2000	2001	2002	1999	2000	2001	2002	1999	2000	2001	2002
Africa	**2.5**	**2.8**	**3.8**	**4.4**	**11.5**	**13.6**	**12.6**	**8.0**	**−3.6**	**0.5**	**−0.9**	**−1.4**
Maghreb	**2.5**	**2.4**	**5.0**	**5.0**	**2.0**	**1.3**	**3.1**	**4.8**	**−0.6**	**7.2**	**4.9**	**2.8**
Algeria	3.2	2.4	3.8	4.9	2.6	0.3	3.0	6.8	—	16.8	12.0	8.0
Morocco	−0.7	0.8	6.0	4.5	0.7	1.9	3.4	3.0	−0.5	−1.7	−2.1	−1.9
Tunisia	6.2	5.0	6.2	6.1	2.7	3.0	2.9	2.7	−2.1	−3.7	−3.1	−3.1
Sub-Sahara[3]	**2.8**	**2.9**	**3.8**	**4.5**	**19.1**	**23.5**	**20.2**	**11.0**	**−7.2**	**−2.4**	**−4.6**	**−5.3**
Cameroon	4.4	4.2	5.3	5.5	2.9	0.8	2.0	2.0	−4.1	−1.7	−2.0	−1.3
Côte d'Ivoire	1.6	−2.3	−1.0	3.5	0.7	2.5	4.0	3.6	−4.2	−5.4	−5.5	−4.3
Ghana	4.4	3.7	4.0	5.0	12.4	25.0	33.0	19.0	−11.5	−9.2	−6.9	−4.9
Kenya	1.3	−0.2	1.3	2.0	6.1	7.1	5.0	5.0	−2.3	−2.1	−5.6	−6.2
Nigeria	1.1	3.8	3.1	2.2	6.6	6.9	21.1	17.1	−9.5	4.9	−0.8	−4.6
Tanzania	4.8	5.1	5.9	6.2	6.3	6.2	5.2	4.4	−3.9	−0.7	−2.8	−3.6
Uganda	7.9	4.4	4.9	6.3	−0.2	6.3	4.3	5.0	−7.6	−8.8	−7.6	−10.4
South Africa	**1.9**	**3.1**	**2.8**	**3.4**	**5.2**	**5.4**	**6.1**	**4.5**	**−0.4**	**−0.3**	**0.1**	**1.4**
Memorandum												
Oil importers	2.6	2.8	3.9	4.4	11.0	13.5	11.8	6.7	−2.9	−2.7	−3.0	−2.7
Oil exporters	2.2	2.9	3.7	4.2	13.3	13.8	15.4	12.5	−5.8	9.7	4.8	2.1

[1]In accordance with standard practice in the *World Economic Outlook*, movements in consumer prices are indicated as annual averages ather than as December/December changes during the year, as is the practice in some countries.
[2]Percent of GDP.
[3]Excludes South Africa.

and 2000 (Figure 1.12), despite relatively favorable macroeconomic conditions (and in some cases reform actually moved backwards). Against that background, the 10-year reform program announced by the Russian government is encouraging, and the recently implemented tax reform is a major step forward (although the revenue implications will need to be monitored carefully, especially if oil prices decline further). New legislation in a broad range of areas is progressing through the Duma, including proposals on simplification of business regulations, money laundering, land code, and pension reform. The government has also approved strategies for reform of two key utilities—electricity and railways. Elsewhere, the experience remains mixed. While the momentum of reforms has picked up in some countries (including Armenia and Azerbaijan), in others—including many of the countries least advanced in transition—the reform process remains stalled. In a number of these, where further liberalization is being blocked by vested interests that benefit

from a situation of partial reform, a major domestic political initiative will be needed to achieve further progress.

Africa: Supporting Growth and Poverty Reduction

Growth in Africa is projected to reach close to 4 percent this year, driven by a substantial improvement in the Maghreb region—especially as *Morocco* recovers from drought—and a more modest increase in activity in sub-Saharan Africa (Table 1.10).[10] Inflation is expected to remain subdued in the Maghreb, as well as most countries of sub-Saharan Africa, although it remains a concern in some countries—notably in *Angola*, the *Democratic Republic of Congo*, and *Zimbabwe*, but also in *Ghana* and *Nigeria*. While the regional current account deficit remains small—reflecting large surpluses in oil and gas producers—many sub-Saharan African countries continue to experience large deficits, in part driven by weak non-

[10]However, IMF forecasts of African growth have in the past been too optimistic, reflecting a combination of adverse shocks, including conflicts, as well as shortfalls in policy implementation.

fuel commodity prices, high oil prices, and still high external debt servicing costs.

With exports accounting for more than one-third of African GDP, the global slowdown will weaken external trading conditions—particularly trade with the European Union, which absorbs around 40 percent of the region's exports. More significant though for external balances and economic activity in most African countries are market conditions for individual commodities—which are not well correlated in all cases with the global cycle (Figure 1.13; see also Appendix I). In the energy-producing countries, including *Algeria* and Nigeria, high oil and gas prices continue to support growth in domestic demand and improvements in fiscal and external balances. At the same time, these gains risk being cut short by looser macroeconomic policies—notably but not exclusively in Nigeria—particularly if the oil market were to weaken further.

Most nonfuel commodity prices remain weak (as noted in Appendix I, the main exceptions are some timber and meat prices). Among food and beverages, the most significant development has been the severe drop in coffee prices—down more than 60 percent since 1997—which has contributed to weak export growth and high external trade deficits in *Kenya* and *Uganda*. Agricultural commodity prices have also come down substantially since 1997, including cotton (a key export of *Benin*, *Chad*, and *Mali*) and tobacco (important for *Malawi* and Zimbabwe). Prices of aluminum and copper—of particular significance for *Mozambique* and *Zambia*, respectively—have declined since the beginning of 2001 and could fall further as global demand weakens, although recent increases in these countries' export volumes are helping to offset the lower prices. The prolonged decline in gold prices continues to weigh on export earnings of *South Africa*.

Global and commodity market developments notwithstanding, local influences still play the dominant role in the economic prospects of most African countries. In particular, the outlook for private investment, economic diversification, and longer-term growth is generally brighter in countries that have pursued sound macroeconomic

Figure 1.13. Selected African Countries: Sensitive to Commodity Markets[1]
(Percent change; countries grouped according to key sources of export earnings)

Commodity market developments have a major impact on overall economic activity in many African countries.

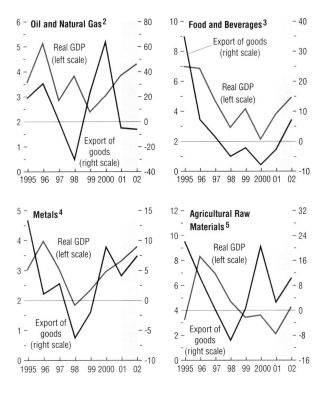

[1]Shaded area indicates IMF staff projections.
[2]Algeria, Angola, Cameroon, Republic of Congo, Equatorial Guinea, Gabon, and Nigeria.
[3]Burundi, Comoros, Côte d'Ivoire, Ethiopia, Guinea-Bissau, Kenya, Mauritania, Mauritius, Rwanda, São Tomé and Príncipe, and Uganda.
[4]Central African Republic, Ghana, Guinea, Mozambique, Namibia, Niger, Sierra Leone, South Africa, and Zambia.
[5]Benin, Chad, Malawi, Mali, Sudan, and Zimbabwe. This category includes cotton and tobacco.

Box 1.7. Economic Growth, Civil Conflict, and Poverty Reduction in Sub-Saharan Africa

Efforts to reduce poverty in sub-Saharan Africa have been disappointing over the past two decades, and its poverty gap with the rest of the world has widened significantly. While the share of sub-Saharan Africa's population earning less than $1 per day fell by 1½ percentage points over the 1990–98 period (see the Table), the proportion fell by 4 percentage points in south Asia and by 12½ percentage points in east Asia (Chen and Ravallion, 2000). In low- and middle-income countries, the decline in poverty during the 1990s closely tracked trends in per capita economic growth.

This relationship is confirmed in a number of recent empirical studies. Ravallion and Chen (1997), for example, find that the share of the population living on less than $1 per day falls by 3 percent for every 1 percent increase in mean per capita income, while Dollar and Kraay (2000) find a 1 percent increase in economic growth is associated with a 1 percent increase in income of the poor. Such studies, however, to a large extent have not focused specifically on Africa, owing to the paucity of quality data on income of the poor. Nonetheless, trends in broader "nonincome" poverty (or human development) indicators, which are more readily available for sub-Saharan Africa, also closely track changes in economic growth.

Infant mortality rates fell by 20 percent in sub-Saharan Africa from 1980 to 1998, a relatively modest improvement compared to the declines of around 30 to 50 percent achieved in other regions of the world. Similarly, life expectancy in-

creased by only 4 percent in sub-Saharan Africa during this period and remains well below average lifespans elsewhere. This poor progress in raising life expectancy in sub-Saharan Africa is partially explained by the high incidence of HIV/AIDS in a number of countries. Cross-country empirical analysis highlights the important role of growth in explaining broader "nonincome" poverty reduction in sub-Saharan Africa.[1] It has been estimated that a 10 percent increase in per capita GDP is associated with a 1 percent increase in life expectancy, a 3 percent to 4 percent decline in infant mortality rates, and a 3½ percent to 4 percent increase in the rate of primary school enrollment.[2] The analysis also finds that civil conflict, income distribution, and social service delivery are also significant factors affecting poverty in Africa. Implementing structural adjustment programs does not significantly affect life expectancy or infant mortality rates, though adjusters tend to have higher primary school enrolment rates—it is the economic growth resulting from adjustment programs that reduces poverty.

Considering in more detail the impact of escalating civil conflict, a study of six African countries that experienced extensive economic losses during sustained civil conflicts in the 1980s and

[1]See Moser and Ichida (2001) for a more detailed discussion.

[2]Based on the estimation of a reduced-form poverty equation, employing a panel of 46 sub-Saharan African countries covering the period 1972–97.

Poverty Indicators and Growth

	Life Expectancy at Birth (in years)		Infant Mortality Rate (per 1000)		Share of Population Living Below $1 Per Day		Real GDP Growth Rate Per Capita (Avg.)	
	1980	1998	1980	1998	1990	1998	1980–90	1990–99
Low- and middle-income countries	**58**	**65**	**87**	**59**			**1.3**	**1.4**
East Asia and Pacific	. . .	69	55	35	28	15	5.7	5.9
Europe and Central Asia	68	69	41	22	2	5	1.9	−3.3
Latin America and Caribbean	65	70	61	31	17	16	−1.3	0.9
Middle East and North Africa	59	68	95	45	2	2	−1.1	−0.1
South Asia	54	62	119	75	44	40	3.9	3.2
Sub-Saharan Africa	48	50	115	92	48	46	−1.0	−0.2

Source: World Bank, World Development Indicators, 2000; Chen and Ravallion (2000).

1990s finds that real per capita GDP at the end of the conflict period averaged only 55 percent of its prewar level.[3] Moreover, while there was an initial postwar rebound in agricultural output, the destruction of the capital base—both human and physical—limited the extent of medium-term gains. Consequently, five years after the end of the conflict, real per capita GDP had increased on average to only about 75 percent of prewar levels.

More generally, a comparison of poverty and income trends for conflict and nonconflict countries in sub-Saharan Africa over the 1972 to 1997 period reveals the following:[4]

- The infant mortality rate for nonconflict countries fell by 36½ percent, compared with a decline of 25½ percent for conflict countries. Excluding conflict-affected countries, the infant mortality rate in sub-Saharan Africa compares much more favorably (at 82 per 1000 in 1997) with that in south Asia.
- Life expectancy increased by 17½ percent for nonconflict countries compared with 9½ percent for conflict-affected countries, even though improvements in life expectancy generally stalled in the 1990s owing to the spread of HIV/AIDS.
- Gross primary school enrollment increased from 61 to 89 percent over 1972 to 1992 in nonconflict countries, compared with an increase from 46 to 66 percent in conflict countries.
- Economic performance, which experienced an initial surge in the 1970s, also differed substantially between the two groups of countries: real GDP per capita (in purchasing power parity terms) grew at an average annual rate of 5½ percent in nonconflict countries over the 1972–97 period, compared with 3 percent in conflict countries. Real per capita GDP (in U.S. dollar terms, converted at 1990 exchange rates) increased at an average rate of 1 percent annually for nonconflict countries compared with a decline of 1½ percent annually for conflict countries.

[3]Moser, Staines, and Engstrom (forthcoming).
[4]Conflict countries over the 1972–97 period comprised Angola, Burundi, Chad, Democratic Republic of the Congo, Ethiopia, Guinea-Bissau, Liberia, Mozambique, Nigeria, Rwanda, Sierra Leone, Sudan, and Uganda. These countries represented 55 percent of the population in sub-Saharan Africa in 1990.

and structural policies. Reflecting this, relatively strong growth—around 5 percent and above—is expected to continue in *Botswana, Cameroon,* Mozambique, *Tanzania,* and Uganda. In contrast, poor policy performance, often combined with political uncertainty and/or conflict, has markedly adverse effects on prospects for sustained growth and for reductions in poverty (see Box 1.7). In Zimbabwe, for example, the turbulent land reform program and inappropriate macroeconomic policies are expected to lead to the economy contracting by around 8½ percent in 2001, with inflation reaching more than 90 percent by the end of the year; in *Côte d'Ivoire,* the recent political uncertainty has hurt public finances and contributed to a weak investment climate and a fall in output. Local weather conditions can also have a major impact on year-to-year changes in output and prices, especially given the importance of agriculture in many African economies. The pickups projected for Kenya, Morocco, and Mozambique, for example, reflect in part the return of more normal weather following adverse conditions in 2000.

The central challenge remains how best to improve the environment for growth and investment, particularly through improving public service delivery—including education and poverty relief; promoting conflict resolution and prevention; strengthening infrastructure; liberalizing trade, to reverse Africa's declining share in world trade; and improving governance. The main responsibility for such progress must, of course, lie with African governments themselves: recent developments are encouraging in this regard, including the *New African Initiative,* which emphasizes the principles of African ownership, leadership, and accountability in eliminating home-grown obstacles to sustained growth. These efforts are being supported by the enhanced initiative for Heavily Indebted Poor Countries (or HIPC Initiative); through June 2001, 23 countries, mainly in Africa, had qualified for and begun to receive debt relief totaling some $34 billion—implying that on average their debt-to-GDP ratios will be halved.[11] Annual savings in debt service will represent about $1 billion on average in the initial years, which is substantially exceeded by the increase in social spending of more than $1½ billion—mainly on health and education, including programs to combat HIV/AIDS. For many sub-Saharan countries, the HIV/AIDS pandemic represents the largest threat to medium-term growth. In addition to the HIPC initiative, encouraging progress has been made in lowering the costs of antiretroviral drug therapies and in providing support through the International Partnership against AIDS in Africa, drawing together African governments, the United Nations, and public, private, and community sectors internationally. But, given the scale of the problem, an enormous effort lies ahead—including developing the health sector infrastructure to support advanced treatments, providing further financial support to countries affected, and stepping up HIV/AIDS awareness and prevention efforts.

Looking at the three largest economies of the region, South Africa's vulnerability to external shocks has been substantially reduced as a result of sound macroeconomic policies, with public spending effectively restrained, the budget deficit limited to around 2½ percent of GDP, and inflation expected to come back within the target range of 3 to 6 percent. These policies have helped sustain recent gains in external competitiveness and have enabled the Reserve Bank to lower its benchmark interest rates by 100 basis points in June. Furthermore, higher private capital inflows—including receipts from the sale of De Beers—have allowed the Reserve Bank to

lower its net open forward position to $5 billion as of mid-2001, down from $22.5 billion in 1998. Short-term prospects have been weakened by the global slowdown, however, given South Africa's relatively strong trade and financial linkages with the advanced economies. In addition, regional uncertainty has increased as a result of the ongoing economic and political difficulties in Zimbabwe. Major challenges lie ahead. As in many other African economies, extremely high unemployment (over 35 percent in South Africa) and minimal progress in raising per capita incomes underscore the need for wide-ranging structural reforms to improve the investment climate, boost employment, and raise growth to a rate that can make sizable inroads on poverty. In particular, further progress is needed with measures directed at improving education and training, increasing labor market efficiency, restructuring and privatizing state-owned enterprises, and liberalizing external trade.

In Nigeria, the spending of windfall gains from higher oil prices has led to a substantial boost to activity. But serious macroeconomic imbalances threaten these gains: sharply higher government spending, especially at state and local levels, has been accompanied by rapid monetary expansion, a surge in inflation, and disorder in the foreign exchange markets. Efforts to restore macroeconomic stability, particularly by restraining public spending at all levels and saving a larger portion of oil proceeds, remain an urgent priority. These measures need to be supported by wide-ranging institutional and structural reforms directed at improving the climate for private investment and economic diversification. Key steps include moving ahead with plans to privatize state-owned enterprises; building the public sector's capacity to formulate and implement reforms; and maintaining the drive to identify and weed out corruption.

Algeria's fiscal and external balances have also improved significantly as a result of strong growth in oil revenues. But, with a substantial share of oil revenues being set aside in a stabiliza-

---

[11]See Box 1.5, "The Enhanced HIPC Initiative in Africa," of the May 2001 *World Economic Outlook.*

Table 1.11. Selected Middle Eastern Countries: Real GDP, Consumer Prices, and Current Account Balance

(Annual percent change unless otherwise noted)

	Real GDP				Consumer Prices[1]				Current Account Balance[2]			
	1999	2000	2001	2002	1999	2000	2001	2002	1999	2000	2001	2002
Middle East[3]	**3.0**	**5.5**	**4.5**	**4.4**	**12.0**	**9.4**	**9.6**	**8.9**	**3.1**	**11.6**	**8.9**	**6.1**
Oil exporters[4]	**2.6**	**5.9**	**5.0**	**4.5**	**15.8**	**12.1**	**12.3**	**11.0**	**5.2**	**15.9**	**12.4**	**8.6**
Saudi Arabia	−0.8	4.5	2.2	2.7	−1.3	−0.6	−0.6	0.9	0.3	9.0	8.1	3.6
Iran, Islamic Rep. of	3.1	5.8	5.0	5.0	20.4	12.6	16.0	13.0	6.4	13.0	7.3	5.8
Kuwait	−0.6	3.6	0.8	3.0	3.0	1.7	2.5	2.5	17.0	39.3	35.3	30.8
Mashreq[5]	**4.1**	**4.1**	**3.2**	**4.2**	**2.0**	**2.2**	**2.3**	**3.2**	**−3.5**	**−2.9**	**−3.1**	**−2.3**
Egypt	6.0	5.1	3.3	4.8	3.8	2.8	2.4	3.0	−1.9	−1.2	−0.2	−0.7
Jordan	3.1	3.9	3.5	4.5	0.6	0.7	1.4	2.1	5.0	0.7	−2.7	−2.5

[1]In accordance with standard practice in the *World Economic Outlook*, movements in consumer prices are indicated as annual averages rather than as December/December changes during the year, as is the practice in some countries.
[2]Percent of GDP.
[3]Includes Bahrain, Egypt, Islamic Rep. of Iran, Iraq, Jordan, Kuwait, Lebanon, Libya, Oman, Qatar, Saudi Arabia, Syrian Arab Republic, United Arab Emirates, and Republic of Yemen.
[4]Includes Bahrain, Islamic Rep. of Iran, Iraq, Kuwait, Libya, Oman, Qatar, Saudi Arabia, and United Arab Emirates.
[5]Includes Egypt, Jordan, Lebanon, and Syrian Arab Republic.

tion fund—expected to total close to 20 percent of GDP by the end of 2001—and sustained monetary discipline and low inflation, Algeria should be able to avoid the same extent of boom-bust cycle that Nigeria may face. Some developments are of concern, however, including a surge of public wage and capital expenditure and a pickup in monetary growth that may add to inflation pressures. Maintaining prudent macroeconomic policies, together with increasing the pace of privatization, trade liberalization, and other structural reforms, would help promote private-sector led investment and growth—particularly needed in non-energy sectors of the economy.

The Middle East: Managing Oil Price Volatility

The economies of the Middle East face a range of external and domestic pressures. Most notable among these are oil market developments, including the increased uncertainties in the market following the September 11 terrorist attack in the United States; the stance of domestic policies—particularly fiscal policy; the regional security situation; and the global economic slowdown, especially—in the case of *Israel*—in the high-technology sector. While the region as a whole is expected to register relatively robust growth of 4.5

percent in 2001 and 4.4 percent in 2002, the short- to medium-term outlook varies quite widely from country to country (Table 1.11).

Although non-oil growth is likely to accelerate in 2001 owing in part to ongoing structural reforms, total growth in most regional oil producers is expected to moderate, mainly reflecting limits on oil production under quotas agreed to by the Organization of the Petroleum Exporting Countries (OPEC) as well as somewhat lower oil prices. In *Iran*, this impact is largely offset by strong growth in non-oil activities—driven in part by a recovery in agriculture from last year's drought and by a pickup in domestic demand. Given the need to sustain relatively high growth to generate employment for a rapidly growing labor force, policy emphasis needs to be placed on macroeconomic stabilization, as well as on pushing ahead with reform efforts directed at liberalizing and opening the economy. Expenditure restraint is being applied in most oil-producing countries, as they attempt to mute the boombust cycles experienced under earlier oil price fluctuations and, in *Saudi Arabia*, to reduce high domestic debt (Figure 1.14). In addition, official net foreign assets have continued to increase. With all the oil exporting countries recognizing the need for economic diversification, the maintenance of firm macroeconomic policies would

Figure 1.14. Selected Middle Eastern Oil Producing Countries: Fiscal Restraint Apparent[1]

Faced with higher export earnings, most oil producing countries are now showing greater fiscal restraint as they seek to avoid boom-bust cycles of the past.

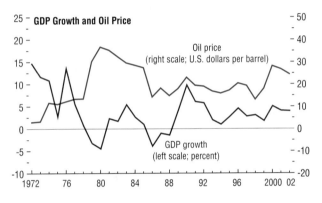

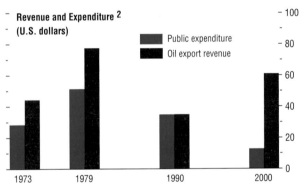

[1] Data for 2001 and 2002 are IMF staff projections. Oil producers include Bahrain, Islamic Rep. of Iran, Kuwait, Libya, Oman, Qatar, Saudi Arabia, and United Arab Emirates.
[2] Increase (in U.S. dollars) in the three years following each oil price shock compared with the three years before.

help to strengthen the climate for private investment, as would restructuring and privatization in the dominant state-owned enterprise sector.

For the countries of the Mashreq (see Table 1.11), economic growth is projected to be somewhat lower than in the Middle East as a whole, in part the result of the difficult security situation. Economic vulnerabilities are acute in *Lebanon,* where the government deficit and debt have reached very high levels; a comprehensive strategy to address these concerns needs to be implemented rapidly. In *Egypt,* real GDP growth is projected to ease to 3.3 percent in 2001, largely reflecting the recent slowing of credit expansion from earlier unsustainable rates. The fluctuation band for the pound was devalued by 6½ percent in early August, and widened to +/−3 percent (from +/−1½ percent). The 25 percent currency depreciation against the dollar since mid-2000 will, over time, help stimulate the traded goods sector, but continuing flexibility will be needed to avoid balance of payments constraints as economic growth recovers. Prospects for recovery over the year ahead will depend, in part, on the speed with which investor confidence strengthens and on developments within the region. In the Mashreq as a whole, reforms directed at further trade liberalization and developing a supportive business environment would improve the longer-term outlook for growth.

Economic activity in Israel weakened sharply in the final quarter of 2000, led by a falloff in investment and exports, and GDP growth is expected to decline from 6.2 percent in 2000 to 0.7 percent this year. This slowdown is mainly a result of the global high-technology slump and of the deterioration in regional security—the latter leading to lower numbers of foreign tourists, a poorer investment climate, and, through labor shortages, weakness in the construction and agricultural sectors. But, having pursued generally sound macroeconomic policies over the past decade and achieved substantial declines in inflation and public debt, Israel has some room for maneuver on the macroeconomic front. In addition, sound banking policies over the same period have helped to make this sector resilient to shocks. Inflation outturns and expectations have fallen, providing scope for a more aggressive easing of monetary policy without jeopardizing inflation targets. The automatic fiscal stabilizers should be allowed to work, but additional discretionary easing of the fiscal stance should be resisted as public expenditures and debt remain high (in relation to GDP) in comparison to most other advanced economies.

Appendix I: Primary Commodities and Semiconductor Markets

The slowdown in global growth is reducing demand for semiconductors and for a number of primary commodities, weakening already depressed prices: for example, metals prices have generally declined since the beginning of the year and, in mid-2001, prices of oil and oil products also turned down. While weaker global demand is likely to hold down commodity price pressures more generally, developments in many specific commodities—including most food and beverage items—are driven more by supply side shocks, including changes in production patterns (leading, for example, to a marked reduction in coffee prices) and animal diseases (driving up meat prices). Uncertainties about the global economic outlook, including prospects for oil and other commodity markets, have been heightened by the September 11 terrorist attack and its possible aftermath.

Oil

In 1998, in the wake of the Asian financial crisis, slowing demand growth for energy, and important production increases (above their target) by OPEC countries, oil prices fell to about $11 dollars per barrel, a price not experienced even in nominal terms since the mid-1980s. The rapid and steep decline in prices led to a revival of OPEC's efforts to control supplies entering the oil market. Initial efforts were not particularly effective as members found it difficult to reintroduce controls that they had

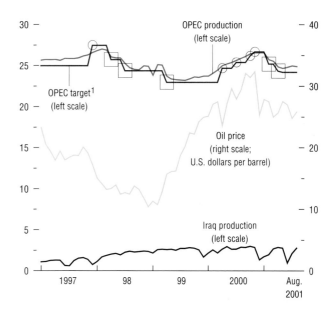

Figure 1.15. OPEC Target and Actual Production of Oil
(Millions barrels per day unless otherwise indicated)

Source: Bloomberg Financial Markets, LP.
[1]Circles denote increases in OPEC target production and squares denote decreases in OPEC target production.

Figure 1.16. Commercial Stocks and Prices

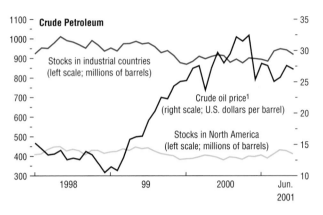

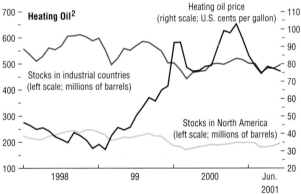

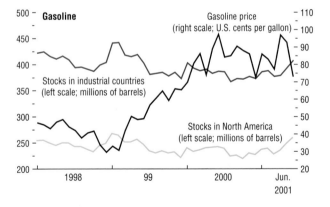

Sources: International Energy Agency, *Oil Market Report*.
[1] Crude oil price is the IMF's indicator price, an average of West Texas Intermediate, U.K. Brent, and Dubai.
[2] Products for which a large part is used as heating fuel, including diesel, other gas oil, and LPG.

largely abandoned in the previous decade. However, the further prices fell, the more efforts to reach a workable agreement were intensified. During the first half of 1999, rising demand for oil, reflecting the strength of world economic growth as well as the need to build up stocks, and firmer compliance to production targets by OPEC members, contributed to a significant rebound in oil prices: these reached $25 per barrel by December 1999 and, with demand increasing and compliance remaining high, averaged over $28 per barrel in 2000 (Figure 1.15).

From January to August 2001, prices remained within OPEC's target band of $22 to $28 per barrel, although fluctuating quite widely. Prices moved close to the upper end of this range early in 2001 and again in late May. But the increasingly sluggish pace of global economic activity, together with rising stocks of oil and oil products, led to a substantial weakening of prices in June and July (Figure 1.16). In the United States in particular, gasoline prices for current and near-term delivery fell sharply over this period as stocks built up to levels last seen in mid-1999—supported also by rising gasoline imports, higher crude stocks (6 percent above mid-2000 levels), and high capacity utilization in refineries. Immediately following the September 11 terrorist attack, crude spot prices initially increased, but then receded back to levels prevailing in the week before the attack—dampened by reassurances by OPEC members of production increases if they became necessary, and falling demand for crude and products, particularly for jet fuel, associated with air transport restrictions.

On the supply side, in an attempt to maintain oil prices within their targeted price band, OPEC has reduced oil production—lowering output by about 1½ million barrels a day on February 1 and a further 1 million barrels a day on April 1—and in late July announced another 1 million barrel reduction to take effect in September. Non-OPEC production, particularly in Russia, has increased modestly in 2001, and Iraq has resumed oil exports after suspending shipments briefly to protest United Nations economic sanctions.[12]

The outlook for oil prices also depends on global economic growth, especially in the major industrial countries, and on prospects for continuing cohesion within OPEC—where futures prices indicate that market participants generally expect OPEC's target price band to be maintained. Following the September 11 terrorist attack, futures prices increased slightly for the near term and decreased for long-term contracts. As of mid-September, crude prices were around $27 at the end of 2001, weakening to around $22 by the end of 2002. In addition to economic and political uncertainties surrounding the oil market, the vulnerability of markets for oil products to disruptions in production and distribution also needs to be emphasized. For example, with capacity utilization in U.S. refineries currently running at around 93 percent and little recent investment to enhance capacity, product markets have little room for maneuver in the event of unexpected breakdowns or other supply disruptions.

Agricultural Commodities

Production of most agricultural commodities failed to adjust to slower demand growth in 1997–98 and, with a succession of good harvests, it has been difficult to absorb inventories accumulated in those two years. As a result, prices generally remain well below their levels of the mid- to late 1990s (Figure 1.17). While the current slowing in global demand may exacerbate price weakness, low prices for most of these commodities tend to stem from supply rather than demand conditions. In particular, price declines over recent years have led to some strategic shifting among annual crops but have generally not led to a decrease in overall production. The situation has been most serious for tree and other

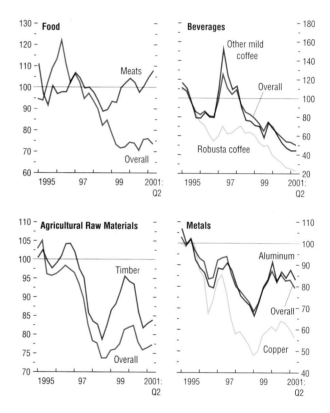

Figure 1.17. Indices of Commodity Prices
(1995 average = 100)

Sources: *Yellow sheets*, Urnerbarry Publications; *The National Business Review*; Bloomberg Financial Markets, LP; *Tropical Timbers Journal*; U.S. Forest Service, USDA; London Metals Exchange; World Bank and IMF staff calculations.

[12]Iraq's agreement with the United Nations to export oil in return for food and medicine expires on November 30, 2001, which adds to the uncertainty regarding supply in the near term.

perennial crops—notably coffee, but also cocoa, sugar, palm oil, coconut oil, cotton, and natural rubber. Noteworthy exceptions to the overall weakness in agricultural commodity markets are timber and meat prices. Timber prices have been supported by strong construction demand, particularly in the United States, and by institutional factors, including quotas and trade controls. Meat prices have been affected by livestock disease problems in Europe and South America and by measures taken to control these problems.

The most extreme case of low agricultural commodity prices is coffee. In the first seven months of 2001, prices of robusta and arabica coffee were about 30 percent and 50 percent, respectively, of their inflation-adjusted averages for the previous 30 years. During the past three years the price of coffee has progressively deteriorated: demand growth has been insufficient to absorb increasing supplies, particularly from Brazil and Vietnam, leading to accumulation of inventories. In the past, such situations have usually been alleviated by frosts in Brazil. This "solution," however, has now become less likely, as the coffee growing area in Brazil has been shifting and is now concentrated in areas less exposed to frost. Brazil has become the largest producer of robusta coffee—grown in frost free areas—in addition to maintaining its traditional position as the largest producer of arabica coffee. Vietnam has aggressively entered the market during the past two decades and now ranks as the world's second robusta producer. On the demand side, consumption growth has been sluggish. Attempts to promote coffee consumption in markets where per capita consumption is low have met with little success, and attempts by the Association of Coffee Producing Countries to set up an export retention scheme have not come to fruition.

Metals

Inventories and prices of metals have reacted quite promptly over recent years to signals of weakening or strengthening in global activity.

Table 1.12. Volatility Measures

	Standard deviation of monthly growth rates
Industrial production[1]	
G-7 countries	0.5
Newly industrialized economies of Asia[2]	7.0
ASEAN-4[3]	3.7
Non-oil commodity price index[4]	1.7
World sales of semiconductors[4]	14.7

[1]Calculated for de-meaned series, 1993M2-2001M3.
[2]Comprising Hong Kong SAR, Korea, Singapore, and Taiwan Province of China.
[3]Comprising Indonesia, Malaysia, Philippines, and Thailand.
[4]Calculated for de-meaned series, 1991M1-2001M4.

The large inventories of metals accumulated in the aftermath of the 1997–98 financial and economic crises were run down in 2000, but there is renewed accumulation in 2001 as industrial production weakens. For example, aluminum prices declined by 15 percent and copper prices by 18 percent between January and the end of August, 2001 (Figure 1.17). For these and most other metals, prices are expected to pick up in 2002 as recovery takes hold. Short-term risks are probably on the downside, however, and, even with some pickup in 2002, prices generally appear likely to remain well below their levels of the mid-1990s. Gold prices initially moved up sharply in response to the September 11 terrorist attack and then came down again—remaining though above their level of the first half of 2001.

Semiconductors

Microchips are an increasingly important item in international trade and, while not a primary commodity, exhibit many of the characteristics of primary commodities. The electronics industry has been hit hard by the global slowdown. Semiconductor prices have fallen sharply, with sales to all major markets weakening significantly since mid-2000, following rapid growth over the previous year (Figure 1.18). While orders for new equipment have been reduced or canceled, adjustment of supply has been slow—in part because of the difficulties in operating plants at less than optimal capacity—and inventories have become overinflated.

As discussed earlier, ASEAN members and the newly industrialized economies of Asia (NIEs), apart from Indonesia and Hong Kong SAR, have been heavily exposed to recent fluctuations in the electronics industry. With exports of electronic goods ranging from about one-third of total exports in Thailand up to around two-thirds in Malaysia and the Philippines, rising global demand for electronics contributed to the strong recovery of growth among the emerging Asian economies after the 1997–98 crises, and the collapse in demand since mid-2000 has led to a sharp weakening in regional activity. Indeed, industrial production among the NIEs and ASEAN economies has been substantially more volatile than in the large industrial economies over the past decade, reflecting both the fluctuations of world semiconductor sales and the increasing concentration of Asian production in electronics (Table 1.12).

Appendix II: Alternative Scenarios— How Might Medium-Term Productivity Growth Affect the Short-Term Outlook?

As sound macroeconomic policies have stabilized inflation expectations, private sector views on future growth are an increasingly important factor behind the business cycle. Accordingly, the underlying growth rate of productivity is a major concern for the global economy. In the United States, the uncertainty is centered on the size of the increase in productivity growth associated with information technology revolution (discussed in detail in Chapter III) and on the linked issue of whether the boom in the late 1990s generated significant overinvestment. Elsewhere, uncertainties about the rate of growth of potential output are associated with the speed of technology catch-up and, most notably in the euro area and Japan, the impact of future structural reforms.

Some of these issues have been explored in previous *World Economic Outlooks*. Chapter II of the October 2000 edition reported simulations

Figure 1.18. Semiconductor Sales and Prices
(Year on year percent changes in three-month averages unless otherwise indicated)

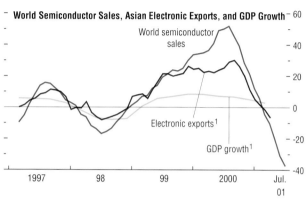

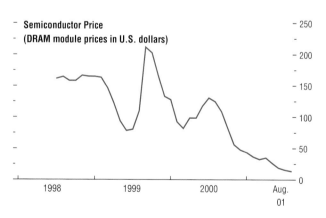

Sources: CEIC Data Company Limited; and Primark Datastream.
[1]Includes Hong Kong SAR, Indonesia, Korea, Malaysia, Philippines, Singapore, Taiwan Province of China, and Thailand.

Table 1.13. Potential Output Growth Rates in the Baseline

	1996–2001	2002–2006	Increase
United States	3.2	3.2	—
Euro area	2.4	2.6	0.2
Japan	1.6	1.6	—
Other industrial countries	2.8	2.8	—

Figure 1.19. Illustrative Country Scenario: Productivity Uncertainty

(Percent, deviations from baseline)

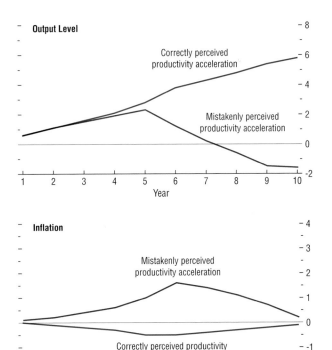

Source: October 2000 *World Economic Outlook*, page 54.

illustrating the impact of failing to realize that five years ago the growth of total factor productivity had accelerated or decelerated. These simulations, which combine a change in future productivity growth with a reassessment of the current cyclical position, illustrate how faulty assessments of past and future growth trends can create significant cyclical disturbances. Figure 1.19 illustrates the path of real output and inflation in a situation where people assume that productivity growth has risen by ½ percent either correctly or incorrectly (in the incorrect case it is assumed that they realize their mistake after five years). This simulation is intended to reflect the practical consequences of the difficulty in identifying long-term productivity trends, particularly in the presence of cycles, data revisions, and other effects. As can be seen, it is hard to distinguish the two paths over the initial five-year period, but in the scenario where the perception is incorrect there is a significant fall in activity once the error is realized as the excesses associated with earlier exuberance need to be corrected. The alternative scenarios reported below extend this type of analysis by looking at how alternative assumptions about past and future potential output growth could impact the global economy over the next few years.

Before describing these scenarios, however, it is useful to characterize the assumptions embodied in the current forecast discussed in the main body of this chapter. Table 1.13 reports the average rate of potential output growth assumed for the three major currency areas and for the other advanced economies. In the *United States*, the growth of potential output is assumed to stay steady at 3¼ percent over the next five years, toward the lower end of the generally accepted range of 3 percent to 4 percent.[13] In *Japan*, where potential output growth has been falling over the late 1990s, it is assumed to rise from its current value of 1¼ percent to 1¾ percent by 2006 as structural reforms are implemented. In the *euro area*, progress on structural reforms and uptake of IT also is assumed to fuel an increase in the growth of potential, which rises by about ¼ percent between 1996–2001 and 2002–06. A similar level and increase is assumed for the United Kingdom, the largest member of the other advanced countries group, although for the aggregate of the *other industrial countries* growth of potential output stays at around 2¾ percent.

How might changes in these rates of growth in potential affect the economic outlook in the next few years? This appendix explores two possibilities, both of which are assumed to occur at the beginning of 2002:

- *Future U.S. total factor productivity growth is ½ percent higher than in the baseline.* This moves potential output from the lower to the upper part of the current range of estimates, particularly once the additional capital accumulation associated with higher productivity is factored into the equation. As evidence of higher growth in the United States gradually accumulates over the next five years and is incorporated into expectations, the dollar and U.S. equity markets are assumed to gradually strengthen.
- *Potential output disappoints in the industrial countries.* In the "lower industrial countries productivity" scenario, it is assumed that underlying U.S. total factor productivity has been growing at ¼ percent lower than in the baseline since 1996. As a result, in addition to a slowing of future productivity, there is a significant current overhang of investment due to the reduction in underlying potential output, and thus a lower desired level of the capital stock. At the same time, productivity growth from 2002 on-

wards is assumed to be ½ percent lower than in the baseline in the rest of the advanced economies as the gains from structural reforms and IT catch-up disappoint. As a result, by 2006, total factor productivity is 2½ percent lower than in the baseline in all advanced economies. Two separate assumptions are made about financial market expectations. In the "immediate realization" scenario, markets realize the new realities immediately—including the need for an investment correction in the United States— leading to an abrupt fall in the U.S. dollar against the euro and the currencies of most other advanced economies as capital flows reverse (U.S. equity markets also fall abruptly). This does not occur against the yen, however, because of the lack of monetary policy options in the face of continuing difficulties in the Japanese economy. In the "gradual adjustment" scenario, the realization of the new environment occurs more slowly, leading to a more sluggish adjustment of exchange rates and equity markets.

In all scenarios, monetary policies are assumed to follow a forward looking Taylor rule, responding to changes in future core inflation and the current output gap, while the fiscal authorities allow automatic stabilizers to operate but do not initiate any discretionary policies.

The results of higher U.S. potential output growth are reported in Table 1.14 and Figure 1.20. As the evidence for strong productivity growth and continuing high real returns in the United States accumulates, this provides a steady upward boost to the U.S. dollar and stock market. Buoyant future expectations about profits and wages raises investment and, to a somewhat lesser extent, consumption, raising domestic demand and output by more than the rise in potential, only partly offset by tighter monetary policy as inflationary pressures emerge. The resulting surge in U.S. imports supports activity in the rest of the world, even

---

[13]These data incorporate recent revisions to the GDP accounts for 1998–2000, which significantly lowered output and productivity growth in 2000.

Table 1.14. Alternative Scenario: Faster U.S. Productivity Growth
(Percent deviation from baseline unless otherwise specified)

	2002	2003	2004	2005	2006
World real GDP	0.3	0.5	0.7	0.9	1.3
United States					
Real GDP	0.8	1.1	1.8	2.4	3.2
Potential output	0.6	1.2	1.8	2.5	3.3
Real domestic demand	0.9	1.3	2.0	2.8	3.8
Real investment	2.3	2.6	4.0	5.5	7.9
Real effective exchange rate	0.4	0.4	0.7	1.0	1.4
Current account ($billion)	−11.5	−22.5	−37.8	−59.1	−89.7
Net private Sector Saving (percentage points of GDP)	−0.2	−0.1	−0.2	−0.4	−0.6
CPI Inflation (percentage points)	—	0.1	0.1	0.1	0.2
Short-term interest rate (percentage points)	0.3	0.2	0.3	0.4	0.6
Euro area					
Real GDP	0.2	0.2	0.2	0.3	0.5
Potential output	—	—	—	—	−0.1
Real domestic demand	0.1	—	−0.1	−0.1	−0.2
Real investment	0.2	−0.2	−0.6	−1.1	−1.8
Real effective exchange rate	−0.2	−0.3	−0.5	−0.8	−1.3
Real U.S. dollar exchange rate	−0.5	−0.5	−1.0	−1.5	−2.4
Current account ($billion)	4.6	7.9	13.6	21.2	30.7
Net private sector saving (percentage points of GDP)	—	0.1	0.2	0.3	0.3
CPI inflation (percentage points)	—	0.1	0.2	0.3	0.4
Short-term interest rate (percentage points)	0.2	0.4	0.6	0.9	0.9
Japan					
Real GDP	0.2	0.2	0.2	0.3	0.4
Potential output	—	—	—	—	−0.1
Real domestic demand	0.1	0.1	—	—	−0.1
Real investment	0.3	−0.0	−0.4	−0.7	−1.3
Real effective exchange rate	−0.4	−0.5	−0.9	−1.4	−1.9
Real U.S. dollar exchange rate	−0.5	−0.7	−1.3	−2.0	−2.7
Current account ($billion)	2.2	5.8	8.9	13.7	20.3
Net private sector saving (percentage points of GDP)	—	0.1	0.2	0.2	0.3
CPI inflation (percentage points)	—	0.1	0.1	0.2	0.3
Short-term interest rate (percentage points)	0.1	0.3	0.4	0.7	1.1
Other industrial economies					
Real GDP	0.2	0.2	0.3	0.4	0.5
Real domestic demand	0.1	0.1	—	−0.1	−0.2
Current account ($billion)	4.8	8.5	14.8	23.3	36.4
Industrial countries					
Real GDP	0.4	0.6	0.8	1.1	1.5
Real domestic demand	0.4	0.5	0.8	1.0	1.4
Current account ($billion)	0.2	−0.2	−0.6	−0.9	−2.3
Developing countries					
Real GDP	0.1	0.2	0.3	0.4	0.6
Real domestic demand	0.2	0.3	0.4	0.7	0.9
Current account ($billion)	−0.2	0.2	0.6	0.9	2.3

though investment elsewhere falls in the medium-term as capital is diverted to the United States. With the United States acting as the locomotive of the world economy, existing imbalances expand. The U.S. current account deficit grows by $90 billion and net private saving steadily slips by more than ½ percentage point of GDP. In short, this scenario is a contin-uation of the U.S.-led expansion that character-ized the later part of the 1990s, and the imbal-ances and consequent financial uncertainties that were created.

Could such a situation be sustained over a prolonged period of time? Significant deficits of an order of magnitude not dissimilar to that currently being experienced by the United

States, as well as low saving rates, were sustained over the period 1880–1913 by several areas of new European settlement, including Australia and Canada (but not the United States). In this case, however, the areas of new European settlement were exploiting a resource (new land) that was not available in the European countries supplying the capital, and was complemented by large inflows of labor. By contrast, the United States is currently exploiting a technology whose components are highly traded (see Chapter III). Even if, as assumed in this scenario, the United States was able to further expand its existing productivity advantage over the other main industrial countries, this situation would be unlikely to last for an extended period of time, especially if structural reforms are introduced. As the gap between the output potential of the United States and the rest of the world widened, the opportunities for catch-up through copying U.S. organizational techniques would likewise increase. At some point, the greater expected real return to the United States, and associated capital flows and exchange rate strength, would reverse, ideally in a gradual fashion.

The second set of scenarios looks at the consequences of a slowing of productivity growth around the world, together with a realization that overly optimistic assumptions about recent rates of growth of potential output growth have led to significant investment and consumption overhangs within the United States.

When it is realized that current U.S. potential output is 1½ percent lower than initially assumed, investment falls in order to restore the desired capital output ratio. More generally, lower productivity growth in the United States and elsewhere also depresses wealth, and hence investment and consumption. The most dramatic version of this scenario, reported in Table 1.15, is when financial markets correctly reassess the situation immediately, which leads to a significant reduction in existing international imbalances at considerable short-term costs to global output and demand. In this case, the U.S. equity market falls by 20 percent as the

Figure 1.20. Impact of Changes in Productivity Growth
(Deviation in percent from baseline real GDP)

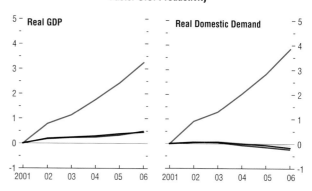

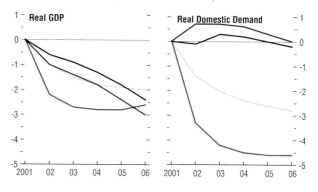

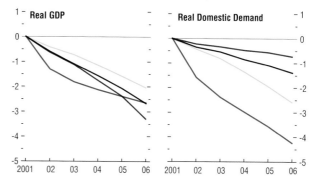

Source: IMF MULTIMOD simulations.

Table 1.15. Alternative Scenario: Immediate Realization of Slower Productivity Growth
(Percent deviation from baseline unless otherwise specified)

	2002	2003	2004	2005	2006
World real growth	−1.2	−1.6	−1.8	−2.1	−2.3
United States					
Real GDP	−2.2	−2.7	−2.8	−2.8	−2.6
Potential output	−1.6	−2.1	−2.6	−3.1	−3.5
Real domestic demand	−3.3	−4.2	−4.5	−4.6	−4.6
Real investment	−2.7	−7.0	−7.7	−8.2	−8.4
Real effective exchange rate	−7.1	−7.3	−7.4	−7.9	−8.7
Current account ($billion)	40.1	86.4	119.3	144.2	160.5
Private lending (percentage points of GDP)	0.4	0.7	0.8	0.8	0.8
CPI inflation (percentage points)	0.5	0.1	−0.1	−0.1	0.1
Short-term interest rate (percentage points)	−0.4	−0.7	−0.5	−0.1	0.1
Euro area					
Real GDP	−1.0	−1.4	−1.8	−2.4	−3.0
Potential output	−0.5	−0.9	−1.4	−1.8	−2.3
Real domestic demand	0.7	0.7	0.6	0.3	—
Real investment	1.2	2.6	2.6	2.7	2.8
Real effective exchange rate	10.4	10.1	9.9	9.8	9.6
Real U.S. dollar exchange rate	17.8	17.7	17.5	17.6	17.9
Current account ($billion)	−9.5	−35.3	−55.2	−72.6	−88.2
Private lending (percentage points of GDP)	−0.2	−0.9	−1.2	−1.4	−1.2
CPI inflation (percentage points)	−1.6	−0.8	−0.5	−0.4	−0.3
Short-term interest rate (percentage points)	−1.6	−1.9	−2.2	−2.3	−2.3
Japan					
Real GDP	−1.0	−1.5	−1.8	−1.9	−2.0
Potential output	−0.5	−1.0	−1.6	−2.1	−2.7
Real domestic demand	−1.4	−2.0	−2.4	−2.6	−2.8
Real investment	−0.9	−2.3	−2.7	−3.0	−3.1
Real effective exchange rate	−6.2	−6.2	−6.4	−6.6	−6.8
Real U.S. dollar exchange rate	0.2	0.2	−0.1	−0.2	−0.2
Current account ($billion)	−2.3	−2.3	−1.5	1.8	10.1
Private lending (percentage points of GDP)	−0.1	−0.2	−0.3	−0.7	−0.2
CPI inflation (percentage points)	0.4	0.0	−0.1	−0.1	−0.1
Short-term Interest Rates (percentage points)	−0.2	−0.2	−0.2	—	0.1
Other industrial economies					
Real GDP	−0.6	−0.9	−1.3	−1.8	−2.4
Real domestic demand	−0.2	0.3	0.2	—	−0.2
Current account ($billion)	−21.8	−49.3	−62.2	−73.5	−84.4
Industrial countries					
Real GDP	−1.4	−1.8	−2.1	−2.4	−2.5
Real domestic demand	−1.3	−1.7	−1.9	−2.2	−2.3
Current account ($billion)	6.4	−0.5	0.3	−0.1	−2.0
Developing countries					
Real GDP	−0.5	−0.7	−1.0	−1.2	−1.3
Real domestic demand	−0.5	−1.0	−1.3	−1.5	−1.8
Current account ($billion)	−6.4	0.5	−0.3	0.1	2.0

consequences of the investment overhang are realized, and the dollar falls by a similar amount against the euro and around 15 percent against other industrial country currencies, except the yen, as the consequences for capital flows are realized, boosting real exports and reducing real imports. Consistent with the depreciation of the real exchange rate, U.S. domestic demand falls by 4¼ percent compared to baseline by 2003 and stays broadly level thereafter. This reflects the resolution of the excesses of the previous boom based in overly optimistic potential output assumptions, which leads to a rapid reduction in investment (which in turn further reduces the rate of growth of potential output) and, to a lesser extent, private consumption.

Table 1.16. Alternative Scenario: Gradual Realization of Slower Productivity Growth

(Percent deviation from baseline unless otherwise specified)

	2002	2003	2004	2005	2006
United States					
Real GDP	−1.3	−1.8	−2.1	−2.4	−2.6
Potential output	−1.5	−1.9	−2.3	−2.8	−3.2
Real domestic demand	−1.6	−2.4	−3.0	−3.6	−4.2
Real investment	−1.4	−3.8	−4.8	−5.8	−6.9
Real effective exchange rate	−1.9	−3.6	−5.1	−6.7	−8.6
Current account ($billion)	13.0	28.8	45.5	66.1	87.8
Net private sector savings	0.1	0.2	0.3	0.4	0.6
CPI inflation (percentage points)	0.2	0.3	0.4	0.5	0.7
Short-term interest rate (percentage points)	0.0	0.1	0.2	0.5	0.9
Euro area					
Real GDP	−0.6	−1.1	−1.7	−2.4	−3.3
Potential output	−0.5	−1.0	−1.4	−1.8	−2.3
Real domestic demand	−0.2	−0.3	−0.5	−0.6	−0.7
Real investment	0.6	1.6	2.3	3.0	3.8
Real effective exchange rate	2.1	3.7	6.0	8.1	10.9
Real U.S. dollar exchange rate	3.5	6.8	10.2	13.8	18.4
Current account ($billion)	−4.1	−9.1	−15.7	−27.0	−39.5
Net private sector savings	—	−0.2	−0.3	−0.5	−0.6
CPI inflation (percentage points)	−0.3	−0.5	−0.6	−0.8	−1.0
Short-term interest rate (percentage points)	−0.3	−0.6	−1.0	−1.6	−1.9
Japan					
Real GDP	−0.4	−0.7	−1.1	−1.6	−2.0
Potential output	−0.5	−1.0	−1.5	−2.0	2.5
Real domestic demand	−0.4	−0.8	−1.3	−1.9	−2.6
Real investment	0.3	0.5	−0.1	−0.7	−1.5
Real effective exchange rate	−1.4	−2.7	−3.9	−5.1	−6.6
Real U.S. dollar exchange rate	—	—	—	—	—
Current account ($billion)	−3.5	−5.2	−4.8	−2.2	4.2
Net private sector savings	−0.1	−0.3	−0.3	−0.3	−0.2
CPI inflation (percentage points)	0.1	0.1	0.1	0.1	0.2
Short-term Interest Rates (percentage points)	−0.1	—	—	0.1	0.2
Other industrial economies					
Real GDP	−0.6	−1.1	−1.6	−2.1	−2.6
Real domestic demand	−0.3	−0.5	−0.8	−1.1	−1.3
Current account ($billion)	−7.2	−15.2	−23.1	−32.8	−45.3
Industrial countries					
Real GDP	−0.8	−1.3	−1.7	−2.2	−2.6
Real domestic demand	−0.8	1.2	−1.6	−2.0	−2.4
Current account ($billion)	−1.7	−0.7	1.5	3.2	5.5
Developing countries					
Real GDP	−0.3	−0.5	−0.7	−1.0	−1.2
Real domestic demand	−0.4	−0.6	−0.9	−1.2	−1.6
Current account ($billion)	1.7	0.7	−1.5	−3.2	−5.5

Monetary conditions are eased significantly, although the reduction in short-term interest rates is constrained by the inflationary impulse from the depreciation of the dollar. Real GDP shows a similar, if less dramatic, fall, being reduced by 2½ percent by 2003. With the retrenchment in real domestic demand over one-and-a-half times the fall in real output, the current account balance steadily improves, by

about $160 billion in 2006, when private sector borrowing has fallen by three-quarters of a percentage point of GDP. These effects would be even larger if future productivity growth was assumed to be more robust in the rest of the world. An alternative scenario reported in the October 2000 *World Economic Outlook* suggests that if future growth in the euro area and Japan is ½ percent a year higher than in the baseline, the U.S. current account would increase by around $50 billion after five years.

Turning to the rest of the world, despite the significant reduction in future productivity growth, real domestic demand rises *above* baseline in the euro area and remains close to baseline in the other industrial country group. In response to the exchange rate appreciation and resulting lower inflation, the authorities in these regions lower short-term interest rates, leading to somewhat looser monetary conditions. This boosts investment and consumption, which are also supported by the diminution in capital flows to the United States. The impact on real net exports of exchange rate appreciation and weak demand in the United States, however, is such that output remains mildly below the (weaker) path for potential output. In Japan, by contrast, the lack of room for monetary easing means that domestic demand cannot substitute for the loss of external demand. Domestic demand falls by 2 percent compared to baseline and real GDP by 1½ percent after two years, associated with a rapid reduction in real imports, and continues to deteriorate at a slower rate thereafter. In developing countries, domestic demand is trimmed by slightly more than real GDP, as lower demand from the advanced economies pushes output below baseline—an outcome that could be exacerbated by significant financial turbulence in emerging markets. The counterpart to the decrease in the U.S. current account deficit is deteriorating balances in the euro area and the other industrial country group.

In the case when financial markets realize the fall in productivity more slowly, the responses of domestic demand, real GDP, and the current account are correspondingly more gradual over time (Table 1.16). In the case when the dollar depreciates, by 2006 the longer-term real GDP outcomes are similar to the "immediate realization" case, although the divergences in real domestic demand and the current account are less dramatic. As a result, the U.S. current account balance improves by $90 billion by 2006, about two-thirds of the

value in the "immediate realization" case, although some of the relative price effects may still not have occurred. Finally, when this scenario is repeated with the U.S. dollar being kept at its approximate baseline values, changes in net exports are more subdued, keeping the path of real GDP and domestic demand more closely correlated in the United States and elsewhere. By 2006, real GDP and real domestic demand are significantly lower in the United States than elsewhere despite the fact that the fall in total factor productivity is identical across countries, largely reflecting the impact of weaker U.S. investment over the intervening five years. As a result, even in this case, the U.S. current account improves by around $75 billion by 2006.

References

Aziz, Jahangir, forthcoming, "India's Interstate Poverty Dynamics," IMF Working Paper (Washington: International Monetary Fund).

Callen, Tim, and Warwick McKibbin, forthcoming, "Japan and Asia: Policy and Prospects," in *Japan: Selected Issues* (Washington: International Monetary Fund).

Chen, Shaohua and Martin Ravallion, 2000, "How Did the World's Poorest Fare un the 1990s?" World Bank Policy Research Working Paper No. 2409 (Washington: World Bank).

Christou, Costas, and Christina Daseking, forthcoming, "Balancing Fiscal Priorities: Challenges for the Central European Countries on the Road to EU Accession," in *The Road to EU Accession, a Collection of Papers Covering the Czech Republic, Hungary, Poland, the Slovak Republic, and Slovenia,* by an IMF staff team led by Robert A. Feldman and C. Maxwell Watson (Washington: International Monetary Fund).

Dollar, David, and Aart Kraay, 2000, "Growth is Good for the Poor," World Development Research Group (Washington: World Bank).

Moser, Gary, and Toshihiro Ichida, 2001, "Economic Growth and Poverty Reduction in Sub-Saharan Africa," IMF Working Paper 01/112 (Washington: International Monetary Fund).

Moser, Gary, Nicholas Staines, and Lars Engstrom, forthcoming, " Economic Development in Post-Conflict

Countries in Sub-Saharan Africa," IMF Working Paper (Washington: International Monetary Fund).

National Council of Applied Economic Research, 1996, "Human Development Profile of India: Interstate and Inter Group Differentials" (New Delhi).

Ravallion, Martin, and Shaohua Chen, 1997, "What Can New Survey Data Tell Us About Recent Changes in Distribution and Poverty?" *World Bank Economic Review*, Vol. 11, No. 2, pp. 357–82.

World Bank, 2000, *India: Reducing Poverty, Accelerating Development* (Washington: World Bank).

CHAPTER II

INTERNATIONAL LINKAGES: THREE PERSPECTIVES

The three essays in this chapter focus on current policy issues involving interactions across national economies. Given that the global economy is in a synchronized slowdown in economic activity, the first two essays are devoted to an examination of the international business cycle linkages among the seven major advanced economies—hereafter called the Group of Seven (G-7) countries—and between the advanced and developing economies. The final essay looks at the issues involved in the proposed launching of a new multilateral trade round under the auspices of the World Trade Organization (WTO).

In examining the international business cycle linkages among the G-7 countries, the first essay notes the paradox that while economic and financial interdependence has increased with rapid globalization in recent years, there has been skepticism as to the importance of these linkages. The skepticism stems from the experience of the early 1990s when, in contrast with the 1970s and 1980s, the downturn in activity in the United States was not synchronized with those in continental Europe or Japan. The essay finds that there has indeed been a rapid increase in cross-border links, especially in the financial domain, over the past decade that is contributing to the broad nature of the current global slowdown, but that their importance was obscured in the early 1990s by two unusually large and idiosyncratic shocks—German reunification in continental Europe and the rise and fall of the asset bubble in Japan.

The second essay looks at the relatively underresearched area of cyclical connections between advanced and developing economies. At an aggregate level there is a clear correlation between the two cycles. By examining the main international transmission channels of shocks—trade and financial markets—the essay concludes that developing regions of the world such as Asia,

whose goods often compete with or complement those in the industrial core, are likely to be more dependent on cyclical conditions in the advanced economies than regions such as the Middle East and sub-Saharan Africa, whose cycles are much more dependent on conditions in commodity markets.

The final essay moves from cycles to longer term structural improvements to the global economy, and examines the state of play in launching a new multilateral trade round after the failure to do so in Seattle in 1999. It outlines the significant benefits that trade can provide for the global economy, including enhanced prospects for growth and development. It concludes that, while the situation has improved since the debacle in Seattle, there are still many issues that need to be resolved before a new round can begin.

Business Cycle Linkages Among Major Advanced Economies

Recent developments have refocused attention on the international business cycle linkages among advanced economies. The issue of whether, and how far, the current U.S. slowdown in growth will affect activity elsewhere, in particular in Europe, has been widely debated. The debate takes place against the background of two apparently contradictory features of the recent experience with business cycle linkages in the 1990s. On the one hand, the remarkable asymmetries in economic fluctuations in the major currency areas experienced during this decade have implied weak international business cycle linkages. On the other hand, some feel that increasing international economic interdependence, especially in financial markets, must have enhanced underlying international business cycle linkages. This essay documents the evolution of international business cycle linkages

Table 2.1. Cross-Correlations of Output Gaps in Group of Seven (G-7) Countries, 1974–2000 and 1991–2000[1]
(Shaded entries are correlation coefficients for the period 1991–2000)

	United States	Japan	Germany	France	Italy	United Kingdom	Canada
United States	. . .	0.28	0.47	0.35	0.46	0.66	0.78
Japan	−0.60	. . .	0.65	0.55	0.53	0.27	0.10
Germany	−0.57	0.53	. . .	0.61	0.74	0.23	0.26
France	−0.10	0.05	0.72	. . .	0.70	0.50	0.32
Italy	−0.28	0.38	0.75	0.74	. . .	0.45	0.50
United Kingdom	0.68	−0.36	−0.38	−0.14	0.15	. . .	0.60
Canada	0.79	−0.66	−0.38	0.15	0.08	0.82	. . .

Source: IMF staff calculations.

[1]Output gaps at business cycle frequencies (6–32 quarters) were computed with the approximate bandpass filter proposed by Baxter and King (1999). Correlation coefficients were calculated on the basis of an autocorrelation-heteroscedasticity consistent estimate of the variance-covariance matrix of the output gaps.

among the G-7 countries since 1974, when the generalized floating of the major currencies was introduced. It examines how international economic interdependence in goods and assets markets has changed, reflects on how it may have affected the international transmission of disturbances, and discusses the implications for the current cycle.

Recent Developments in Perspective

Common elements in business cycle fluctuations across countries have long been noted in the literature on business cycles (see, for example, Haberler, 1958). The timing of recessions or contractions in economic activity is often conspicuously similar, as the almost synchronous downturns in all G-7 countries during the 1974–75 and 1980 recessions illustrate. Recoveries and expansions in economic activity also frequently coincide, although the average duration of expansions varies widely among G-7 countries (McDermott and Scott, 2000). Moreover, and most relevant for this essay, the direction and magnitude of output fluctuations around potential output tend to be similar, as

evinced by the generally large positive bilateral correlations among output gaps in all G-7 countries at business cycle frequencies between 1974 and 2000 (Table 2.1).[1] From the 1980s, the mounting evidence on strong and systematic positive comovements led to the notion of a world business cycle or an international business cycle.[2]

Developments during the early 1990s, however, did not fit the notion of an international business cycle. Recessions occurred with noticeable differences in timing—in 1990–91 in the United States, the United Kingdom, and Canada, and in 1992–93 in Japan, Germany, France, and Italy. As a result, almost half of the correlation coefficients for the 1990s period became negative and the average correlation coefficient among output gaps in G-7 countries dropped from 0.60 during 1974–90 to 0.12 during the last decade (see shaded entries in Table 2.1).

Should the notion of the international business cycle be reconsidered in light of these developments? To put the experience of the 1990s in perspective, it is useful to compare the actual output gap in each G-7 country to a common

[1]To ensure consistency across countries, output gaps (actual output minus potential output as a fraction of potential output) for all G-7 countries were calculated by using potential output measures derived with the approximate bandpass filter proposed by Baxter and King (1999) rather than potential output estimates typically used in the *World Economic Outlook*. The business cycle component of a variable is defined as the sum of all components fluctuating at frequencies between $1\frac{1}{2}$ and 8 years (6–32 quarters).

[2]See, among others, Swoboda (1983), Camen (1987), Gerlach (1988), Canova and Dellas (1993), Gregory, Head, and Raynauld (1997), and Gregory and Head (1999).

component (Figure 2.1). The latter quantifies the international business cycle element in that country's output gap and was extracted with a so-called generalized dynamic factor model, which is a technique used to identify and estimate a small number of factors that explain a substantial fraction of output fluctuations across countries.[3] These estimated factors reflect global shocks affecting all countries and country-specific shocks with significant spillovers on all other G-7 countries. Although the set of underlying factors is the same for all seven countries and was estimated simultaneously, the common component for each country is different because the model allows for country-specific dynamic responses to the shocks captured by the factors. The difference between the output gap and the common component shows the idiosyncratic part in a country's output fluctuation—that is, the country-specific disturbances net of significant spillover effects on other countries.

Asymmetric shocks explain why the contribution of the international business cycle to output fluctuations in each country varies widely over time. Noticeable differences between output gaps and the common component emerged in Germany from the late 1980s through the early 1990s, reflecting the impulse from German reunification, which was transmitted to other European countries but not to the United States or Japan. There have also been significant differences in Japan since 1993, related to the bursting of the bubble in Japanese asset prices in the early 1990s and the subsequent protracted economic difficulties.[4] The disturbances were large enough to alter radically the correlation patterns among output gaps in G-7 countries during the 1990s, as shown by the rolling eight-year correlation windows in Figure 2.2. Most notably, the

[3]See Forni and others (2000) for details on the generalized dynamic factor model and Lumsdaine and Prasad (1999) and Clark and Shin (1998) on other approaches to identify and estimate common components.

[4]See Chapter IV of the October 1998 *World Economic Outlook* on Japan's financial problems since the early 1990s and their impact on the real economy.

Figure 2.1. Common Components in Group of Seven (G-7) Output Gaps[1]

(Actual output gaps and common components as fraction of potential GDP)

The international business cycle as captured by the common component is an important driving force behind business cycle fluctuations in G-7 countries.

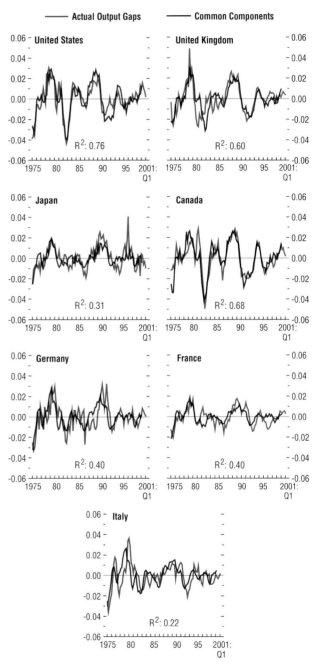

Source: IMF staff calculations.
[1]Common components are based on two factors, as estimated with the generalized dynamic factor model approach of Forni and others (2000). R^2 is the coefficient of determination for each country in the common components model and is a measure for the degree of variation in the output gap that is explained by the common component.

Figure 2.2. Group of Seven (G-7) Countries: Selected Bilateral Output Gap Correlations[1]
(Rolling eight-year correlation windows)

Asymmetric disturbances in the early 1990s led to radical changes in the correlation patterns among output gaps in the United States, Japan, and Germany, while other correlations remained much more stable.

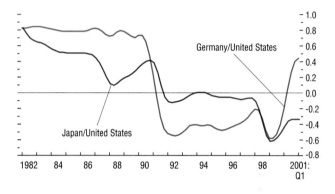

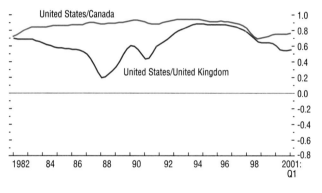

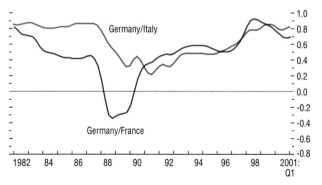

Source: IMF staff calculations.
[1] Labels indicate the correlation pair.

correlation between output gaps in the United States and Japan and the United States and the euro area countries turned negative.[5] This emphasizes the importance of the magnitudes, origin, and kind of disturbances for international business cycle linkages. It also highlights how sensitive the average correlations of output gaps are to the particular time period chosen for the analysis.

Global shocks and shocks with significant spillovers must have also been important, however, as the common components contributed prominently to changes in output gaps in all G-7 countries during 1974–2000, even though cross-country variations were significant. The common components seem dominant in the United States, Canada, and the United Kingdom. In the euro area countries (Germany, France, and Italy), they seem less important, as shown by the more frequent and sometimes sizable difference between output gaps and common components. In Japan, the common component is also less important than the idiosyncratic component in explaining output gap movements. These cross-country differences and the noticeable timing differences in peaks and troughs of output gaps and common components (especially in Japan and the euro area countries) make it difficult to say that there is a single world cycle across the major advanced economies.

Several observations hint at the role that structural factors and policy regimes play in determining the strength of international business cycle linkages. First, some linkages have been less affected by asymmetric shocks than others. Comovements among output gaps in the United States, Canada, and the United Kingdom remained positive during the entire 1990s. Similarly, business cycle linkages in the euro area countries remained strong or, perhaps not unexpectedly in view of the integration occurring in

[5]Eight-year correlation windows were chosen because this length approximates the duration of an average business cycle (see also Baxter and King, 1999). The finding of negative correlations is robust with regard to the window length.

the European Monetary System, grew stronger during the 1990s. The close affiliation of the business cycle in the United Kingdom with that in the United States, despite much more important trade links with the euro area countries, may have been the result of strong financial market linkages, as discussed below.[6] Second, the United States appears prominent in the international transmission of disturbances. The strong correlation between the common component and output gaps in the United States compared to Japan or Germany suggests that U.S. disturbances, such as the monetary policy shocks leading to the 1990–91 recession, generally affected all G-7 countries while the international transmission of disturbances originating in other major currency areas may have been weaker. This asymmetry is likely to reflect differences in country size and the depth of financial markets. Finally, the wide variations in common components in the G-7 countries at any point in time suggest that economies reacted differently to disturbances as a result of differences in economic structure and, sometimes, the conduct of stabilization policies.

At the current conjuncture, the strong common components in national business cycle fluctuations observed during the 1970s and 1980s appear to have resurfaced. The asymmetries in business cycle fluctuations in the Anglo-Saxon countries (the United States, Canada, and the United Kingdom) and the euro area countries disappeared in 1999 and 2000, as output gaps moved in the same direction. However, the asymmetries have persisted in the case of Japan.

Increased Economic Interdependence and the International Business Cycle

The strength of international business cycle linkages among the seven major advanced economies depends not only on the magnitude and origin of disturbances but also on the structure of international trade in goods, services, and financial assets. This structure of economic interdependence is a dynamic process, driven mostly by secular trends related to technological progress and regulatory changes. For example, as noted by Mussa (2000), the increasing merchandise trade interdependence since the 1950s has been the result of declining transaction costs following the substantial, progressive reduction in artificial barriers to international commerce in the context of multilateral and regional trade liberalization (see the third essay on global trade issues) and advances in transportation and communication technology. However, despite remarkable declines in cross-border transaction costs and corresponding increases in interdependence, national borders remain important barriers to trade in goods, services, and financial assets. Trade within countries continues to exceed cross-country trade by a surprisingly large margin, even when taking into account impediments, such as distance or different languages, that make cross-border transactions different from within-country transactions (see Obstfeld and Rogoff, 2000).

Trade Linkages

The strength of trade-related spillovers ensuing from disturbances in one or more countries depends on the depth of trade interdependence. Export and import shares in major advanced countries indicate that overall trade interdependence generally increased during 1974–2000 (Table 2.2). For merchandise trade, the level and direction of direct trade interdependence among G-7 countries during the 1990s remained very similar to the 1970s. Except for Canada, where trade was boosted following the introduction of the Canada-U.S. Free Trade Agreement (effective 1989) and the North American Free Trade Agreement (effective 1994), the average export and import shares to

---

[6]Artis and Zhang (1999) or Kontolemis and Samiei (2000) provide recent discussions of the business cycle in the United Kingdom.

Table 2.2. Trade Interdependence in Group of Seven (G-7) Countries, 1974–2000
(Period averages in percent of GDP)

	United States	Japan	Germany	France	Italy	United Kingdom	Canada
Merchandise imports from other G-7 Countries							
1974–1980	3.6	3.2	7.2	7.6	9.0	9.2	18.2
1991–2000	4.9	2.4	8.0	9.1	8.1	10.4	24.2
Merchandise exports to other G-7 Countries							
1974–1980	2.9	3.9	7.8	6.5	8.3	6.5	17.3
1991–2000	3.4	3.8	8.9	8.8	9.2	8.4	27.8
Merchandise imports							
1974–1980	7.8	11.3	19.9	17.7	20.3	24.4	23.2
1991–2000	10.2	6.8	20.4	19.3	17.4	22.4	30.7
Merchandise exports							
1974–1980	6.7	11.3	22.8	16.2	17.7	20.6	22.1
1991–2000	7.5	9.1	22.9	19.7	18.8	19.5	30.8
Imports of goods and services[1]							
1974–1980	9.0	12.5	24.2	20.4	22.5	28.1	24.5
1991–2000	12.1	8.5	26.0	22.1	21.7	27.3	34.5
Exports of goods and services[1]							
1974–1980	8.5	12.8	26.3	19.5	22.1	27.6	24.6
1991–2000	10.7	10.2	26.6	23.7	24.4	26.3	36.3

Sources: IMF, *Direction of Trade Statistics*; and OECD.
[1]Based on national accounts data.

and from other G-7 countries, measured in percent of GDP, rose by 2 percentage points or less.[7] National accounts data, which include exports and imports of services, also show small increases in trade interdependence.[8] Unfortunately, consistent direction of trade statistics are generally unavailable for services, but it seems plausible that interdependence in services trade among the G-7 countries has contributed at least proportionally to the overall increase, given that the services share in consumption tends to increase with per capita income.

The small increase in trade interdependence among G-7 countries between 1974 and 2000

suggests that, except for Canada, the nature and strength of dynamic trade-related output and terms of trade effects of a disturbance in any of the G-7 countries on output in the other G-7 countries are unlikely to have changed significantly during this period. This is not to say that the trade channel is unimportant; on the contrary, there is some evidence that bilateral output comovements tend to be stronger with closer merchandise trade links.[9] However, using standard income and price elasticities from estimated export and import equations for G-7 countries, small increases in trade shares do not generate substantial changes in output comove-

[7]The overall trade interdependence between G-7 countries could also have risen because of trade with third countries. However, magnitudes of the variation in overall merchandise trade shares of G-7 countries do not suggest significant changes in indirect trade interdependence.

[8]National accounts data suggest that, consistent with traded good prices rising less than nontraded good prices, trade volume growth was generally somewhat higher than growth in trade values. For the impact on business cycle linkages that changes in trade interdependence may have, however, trade values seem more relevant.

[9]See, among others, Canova and Dellas (1993) and Frankel and Rose (1998). The correlation between the bilateral output gap correlation coefficients during 1974–2000 reported in Table 2.1 and average bilateral import shares during this period is 0.45. However, the strong output comovements are not likely to reflect trade effects alone, since closer trade links are partly related to factors such as proximity and similar conduct of policies, which affect the strength of business cycle linkages themselves as well.

ments.[10] It also seems very unlikely that the actual change in trade interdependence among G-7 countries would have led to significantly higher correlations among country-specific disturbances that could have strengthened cross-country output correlations.[11] More generally, simulations of large multicountry models, such as the IMF's MULTIMOD, also suggest that trade linkages alone are unlikely to generate the output correlations found in actual data.

Financial Market Linkages

Financial markets are another important channel for transmitting disturbances internationally, with the mechanisms of transmission based on cross-border diversification of assets and liabilities on the one hand and cross-border asset price arbitrage on the other. Innovations related to advances in information technology and financial liberalization are rapidly integrating financial markets.

Cross-border diversification of assets and liabilities in the G-7 countries has greatly increased over the last two decades. Foreign assets and liabilities of residents in all major advanced economies more than doubled as a percentage of GDP between 1980 and 2000, with a remarkable acceleration in the 1990s (except in Japan), often reaching levels close to 100 percent of GDP by the end of the millennium (Figure 2.3). While some asymmetries between assets and liabilities are noticeable depending on whether the

---

[10]Using standard income elasticities for total exports and imports may lead to an underestimation of the impact that the recent changes in trade shares may have had on output comovements. As noted by Kose and Yi (2001), trade is increasingly characterized by vertical specialization, that is, by countries specializing in particular stages of the value-added chain of goods production rather than in producing entire goods. This process should in principle lead to time-varying income elasticities for total exports and imports, so that output correlations could increase even with unchanged shares of overall trade in GDP.

[11]As noted by Canova and Dellas (1993), among others, output comovements also depend on the correlation of disturbances. Frankel and Rose (1998) conjectured that increased trade integration could raise the covariance of productivity shocks because of the technology transfer involved in the international trade in capital goods and some inputs.

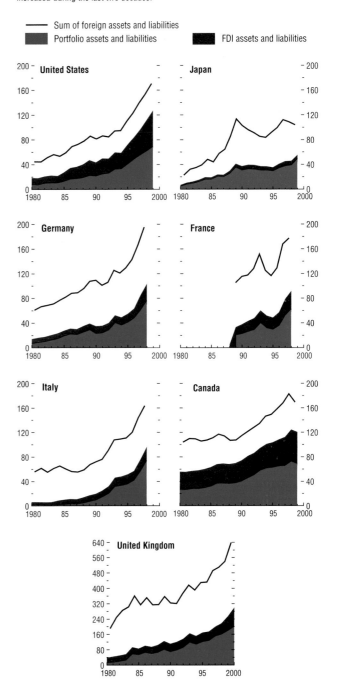

Figure 2.3. Group of Seven (G-7) Countries: Asset Market Interdependence
(Percent of GDP)

Cross-border diversification of assets and liabilities in the G-7 countries greatly increased during the last two decades.

— Sum of foreign assets and liabilities
■ Portfolio assets and liabilities ■ FDI assets and liabilities

Sources: IMF, *Balance of Payments Statistics* and *International Financial Statistics*.

Figure 2.4. Group of Seven (G-7) Countries: Net Foreign Assets
(Percent of GDP)

Changes in net foreign assets were only one factor behind the broad trend toward asset and liability diversification.

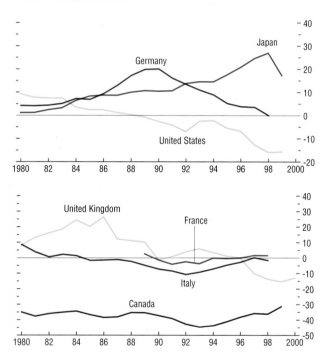

Sources: IMF, *Balance of Payments Statistics* and *International Financial Statistics*.

country is a net debtor or creditor, the broad trend toward two-way diversification—buying foreign assets while at the same time issuing liabilities to nonresidents—clearly accounts for the main part of the increases (Figure 2.4). Hence, the increase in cross-border diversification is only partly related to savings-investment imbalances, the persistence of which is in itself a reflection of more asset market integration.

Most of the increase in foreign assets and liabilities reflected rises in portfolio and foreign direct investment holdings, both of which involve a substantial equity element, except in the case of Japan, where banks led the increase in foreign exposure in the latter part of the 1980s. Again with the exception of Japan, foreign direct investment (FDI) and portfolio flows accelerated (Figure 2.5), especially during the last few years, although the sharply rising equity prices in all major advanced countries but Japan during the 1990s also played an important part in the increased stocks of foreign assets and liabilities.

Assessing the extent of cross-border diversification among G-7 countries would require data on bilateral asset holdings and capital flows. As in the case of trade in services, such data are generally not available.[12] Partial evidence based on data on bilateral cross-border asset holdings for the case of the United States shows that the general trend toward increased financial market interdependence noted above also holds for the G-7 countries (Figure 2.6). U.S. residents' holdings of foreign assets in G-7 countries and holdings of U.S. assets by residents of other G-7 countries as a percentage of GDP increased substantially between 1994 and 2000.[13] Distinguished by type of investment, FDI is the most important vehicle for investment, both for U.S. residents and nonresidents. Distinguished by destination or origin of investment, the relative importance of G-7 countries during 1994–2000 remained broadly unchanged for equity. For FDI, the share of G-7 countries de-

---

[12]See, however, IMF (2000) for a survey on the distribution of portfolio assets and liabilities at the end of 1997 by destination and instruments for 29 countries.

[13]The data exclude official holdings of foreign assets.

clined somewhat, suggesting that with globalization, U.S. firms were looking to establish themselves in new markets while firms from other countries sought to deepen their engagement in the United States. With regard to bonds, the share of U.S. residents' holdings in G-7 countries increased sharply, largely on account of holdings in the United Kingdom. However, this is likely to reflect that country's position as a financial center, so that the increase probably reflects holdings of bonds issued by residents in countries other than the United Kingdom as well.[14]

As a result of increased cross-border diversification, portfolio assets as a share of household financial wealth more than doubled between 1981–85 and 1996–99 in most G-7 countries (Table 2.3).[15] The international diversification of wealth is most prominent in the United Kingdom, where the share of foreign assets in total household financial assets was about 25 percent on average during 1996–99. However, this large share partly reflected that country's role as an international financial center and is correspondingly mirrored in foreign portfolio liabilities that are also large. Germany and France follow next in the ranking of cross-border wealth diversification, with shares in excess of 10 percent during 1996–99. In Japan, Canada, and the United States, the share of foreign assets in total household financial assets remained below 10 percent on average during 1996–99. Nevertheless, despite the remarkable increases in holdings of foreign assets in terms of GDP, cross-border diversification in terms of household wealth—the relevant denominations

[14]The data are based on the location of the financial intermediary conducting the transaction.

[15]Official household wealth data are not available for Italy. Also, unfortunately, portfolio assets and liabilities data classified by ownership are not readily available. The comparison does not imply that households account for all or even most of the increase in cross-border asset and liability diversification. On the contrary, there is evidence (e.g., flow of funds data for the United Kingdom) suggesting that financial intermediaries account for most of the rising cross-border diversification. However, as households own directly or indirectly a substantial share of liabilities of financial intermediaries (e.g., mutual fund shares), it is plausible that their financial decisions may have been at least partly affected by cross-border diversification.

Figure 2.5. Group of Seven (G-7) Countries: Gross Foreign Direct Investment and Portfolio Flows[1]
(Percent of GDP)

FDI and portfolio flows accelerated during the 1990s.

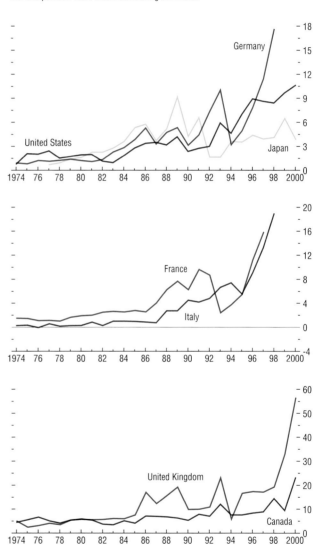

Sources: IMF, *Balance of Payments Statistics and International Financial Statistics.*
[1]Sum of credit and debit items.

Figure 2.6. U.S. Asset Markets and Group of Seven (G-7) Countries
(Percent of U.S. GDP)

Group of Seven countries account for a significant and rather stable share in both U.S. residents' holdings of foreign assets and nonresidents' holdings of U.S. assets.

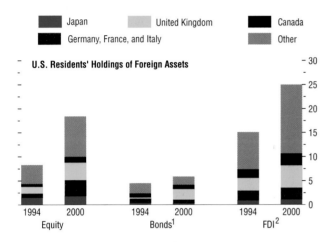

U.S. Residents' Holdings of Foreign Assets

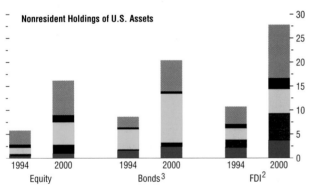

Nonresident Holdings of U.S. Assets

Source: U.S. Department of Commerce, *Survey of Current Business.*
[1]Excluding official holdings of foreign bonds.
[2]At market value. Bilateral holdings estimated using shares based on data on a historical cost basis.
[3]Excluding official holdings of U.S. bonds. Private holdings of U.S. treasury bonds estimated using shares based on private holdings of U.S. corporate and agency bonds.

for consumption and savings decisions—remained limited even at the end of 1999.[16]

Besides sources of financing, firms also diversified their operations internationally through the expansion of existing affiliates as well as through a wave of mergers and acquisitions, as reflected in the increased stocks and flows of foreign direct investment. Firm-level financial data indicate that for listed companies, sales revenue from operations of foreign affiliates generally account for an increasing share in total sales revenue in the major advanced countries (Table 2.4). Sales revenue from foreign affiliates are much more important for European and Canadian firms than for U.S. or Japanese companies, reflecting in part the much higher degree of openness of these economies and in part the high degree of interdependence within the European Union or NAFTA for Canada. The rapid increase in FDI flows compared to exports or imports may be an indication that, for multinational companies, mergers and acquisition and capital accumulation abroad have been a substitute for trade, so that trade data alone do not adequately reflect international economic interdependence at the firm level. Disturbances abroad that have little effect on trade flows may still affect the local economy through their impact on revenue and profits of foreign affiliates.

Financial innovations have also increased the scope for cross-border asset price arbitrage, implying that comparable risks should be priced similarly in all countries. As illustrated in Figure 2.7, equity market linkages as measured by the correlation between equity returns are generally strong and positive, as expected with significant asset market interdependence.[17] Although eq-

---

[16]Despite noticeable increases during the 1990s, the actual extent of cross-border portfolio diversification remains below the optimum implied by most models of optimal portfolio allocation, and the so-called home bias in portfolio allocation remains a puzzle in a world with seemingly highly integrated capital markets (see, for example, Tesar and Werner, 1995, or Lewis, 1999).
[17]De Santis and Gerard (1997) and Dumas, Harvey, and Ruiz (2000), among others, found evidence that is broadly consistent with identical pricing of equity market risk in advanced economies.

Table 2.3. Foreign Portfolio Assets and Household Wealth in Selected Group of Seven (G-7) Countries
(Period averages of end-year data)

	United States	Japan	Germany	France	United Kingdom	Canada
Foreign portfolio assets as percent of household financial assets						
1981–85	1.0	3.3	. . .	. . .	12.6	2.1
1986–90	1.8	7.2	. . .	. . .	17.3	2.9
1991–95	4.1	7.7	9.6	5.6	23.2	4.4
1996–99	6.6	8.9	15.0	10.9	25.6	6.6
Foreign portfolio equity assets as percent of household financial assets						
1981–85	0.3	0.0	. . .	. . .	7.5	1.7
1986–90	1.0	0.0	. . .	. . .	9.8	2.1
1991–95	2.7	1.2	3.8	2.0	10.5	3.4
1996–99	4.8	1.7	7.3	3.2	11.8	5.1
Memorandums items:						
Household financial assets as percent of household net worth						
1981–85	69.7	42.5	. . .	37.8	51.9	58.6
1986–90	71.7	41.5	. . .	49.6	52.7	63.9
1991–95	76.9	50.1	. . .	55.2	64.1	67.3
1996–99	82.2	58.2	. . .	58.8	68.8	70.2

Sources: IMF, Balance of Payments Statistics; and national household balance sheet data.

Table 2.4. International Revenue Diversification of Listed Joint Stock Companies in the Group of Seven (G-7) Countries[1]
(Revenue from sales of foreign affiliates as percent of domestic sales; period averages)

	United States	Japan	Germany	France	Italy	United Kingdom	Canada
1990–94	42.6	30.5	74.8	129.6	80.2	99.4	49.2
1995–2000	46.3	33.6	96.9	222.9	90.5	99.9	74.6

Source: Thompson Financial; Worldscope Database.
[1]The data are sales-weighted firm averages based on a balanced panel of firms. The number of firms and their share in total output vary across countries. Only firms that report international sales are included in the panel.

uity returns were already closely connected in the mid-1970s, the links have intensified, as shown by the rise in correlations between equity returns in each country and aggregate equity returns in G-7 countries between 1974 and 2000 in all countries but Japan and the United States.[18] Only Japan registered a significant fall in the correlation of local equity returns with the G-7 market portfolio, presumably reflecting protracted corporate balance sheet problems and the resulting decline in correlations with output

gaps in other G-7 countries. Interest rate linkages are, of course, well known and tend to be even stronger than equity market linkages. Evidence based on similar calculations shows that total returns in U.S. dollars on large bond portfolios in each G-7 country are highly correlated with the G-7 bond market portfolio and that the correlation coefficients often exceed those for excess equity returns.[19]

Since asset market interdependence, especially the cross-border diversification of wealth,

[18]This is consistent with Longin and Solnik (1995), who found an increase in the correlation of returns across seven major equity markets during 1959–1991, and Stulz (1999), who noted a small increase in the correlation between local equity returns and the return on the MSCI world market portfolio between October 1979 and March 1995.

[19]Based on Salomon Brothers total return indices on bond portfolios for the period 1985–2000.

Figure 2.7. G-7 Equity Return Linkages[1]
(Rolling correlation windows; returns are excess returns in U.S. dollars)

Correlation between equity returns in G-7 countries generally increased during the last two decades.

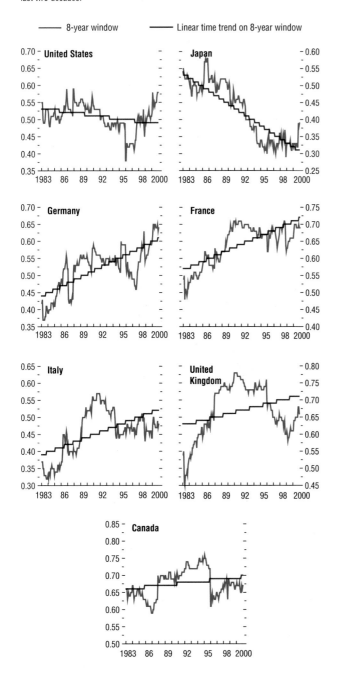

Sources: Primark Datastream; and IMF staff calculations.
[1]The correlation is between local excess equity returns and the return on a PPP-weighted equity portfolio for the other G-7 countries. Excess returns are calculated as the nominal monthly returns on the Morgan Stanley Capital International total return indices (in U.S. dollars) minus the one-month U.S. dollar interest rate in the Eurodollar market.

which only began to accelerate from the early to mid-1990s, broad-based empirical evidence on changes in the transmission of shocks through financial market linkages has yet to emerge. Nevertheless, the increased international interdependence in financial markets over the last two decades is likely to have raised the potential for stronger output comovements. As changes in the structure of financial market linkages occurred gradually, their rising impact on the magnitude of output comovements during the last two decades may have been overshadowed by the impact of disturbances.

The international transmission of disturbances will probably be amplified by the increased financial market interdependence, since many disturbances influence not only demand but also financial market prices. For example, the close affiliation of the business cycle in the United Kingdom with that of the United States rather than the euro area—its major trading partner—may reflect the dominance of financial factors over traditional trade linkages, although the United Kingdom's alignment with the euro area cycle has increased since 1999. The structure of the country's financial system, characterized by direct finance through securities and adjustable rate credit, resembles that of the United States, and has allowed asset prices to play an important and direct role in the transmission of business cycles, unlike the more bank-based financial systems in the euro area.

The speed with which disturbances are transmitted abroad is also likely to increase somewhat, as financial market prices and trading activities are more reactive to news and events than goods market prices or trade flows. Consequently, sentiments about the current state of the economy and prospects for the future as measured by confidence indices can be expected to affect sentiment elsewhere. This is consistent with the recently observed strong comovements in confidence indices across major advanced economies, and evidence of confidence spillovers (see Box 2.1). Moreover, there is evidence that asset price spillovers are especially high in times of heightened volatility in international financial markets

Box 2.1. Confidence Spillovers

In view of the spillover effects of the recent U.S. slowdown on global activity, an intriguing question is the extent to which measures of business confidence are becoming more synchronized across countries. Such cross-border confidence effects would, of course, partly reflect underlying business cycle linkages. But, in addition, there may be information "cascades," as firms quite rationally pay attention to cross-border measures of confidence.[1] There is also the possibility of "fads" or irrational "imitation" of business sentiment.[2] These factors raise the prospect that confidence linkages could, themselves, be becoming a potential channel through which economic shocks can be transmitted across countries.

To assess confidence linkages and the extent of spillover or contagion effects, a comparable set of measures for business confidence was obtained for the major industrial economies. The evidence suggests that business confidence measures do tend to move together, but that the degree and strength of synchronization differs significantly among countries and over time (see the Figure). Given the weight of the United States economy and its financial markets, consider first the linkages between the United States and other major countries. Not surprisingly, the strongest link is between the United States and Canadian business confidence (see the Table). Analyses based on vector autoregressions (VAR) suggest that the United States business confidence leads Canadian business confidence by a quarter or so (for detailed results, see Kumar and Kashiwase, forthcoming).

The confidence correlations change significantly in the case of Europe. In the United Kingdom, changes in the United States business confidence appear to have the largest impact relatively quickly, but in the most recent period, the linkage appears to be moderating somewhat.

[1]See, for instance, Avery and Zemsky (1998) and Bikhchandani, Hirshleifer, and Welch (1998).
[2]See Shiller (1998) on fads and other irrationalities in financial markets, and Kumar and Persaud (forthcoming) on spillover effects.

Business Confidence in G-7 Countries

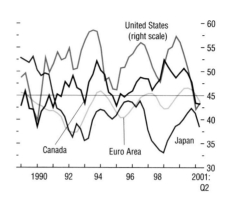

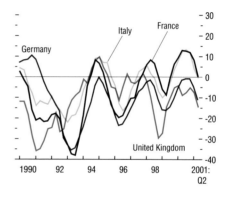

Sources: National Association of Purchasing Managers; Bank of Japan; Eurostat; and Statistics Canada.

For the euro area as a whole, spillover effects from the United States appear to occur mainly after a period of two quarters or so. The size of the correlations has been historically rather limited but there has been a substantial increase during the most recent period. There is also some evidence of a feedback effect, with changes in confidence overseas reverberating back on to confidence measure in the United States. In contrast, the correlation in business confidence between the United States and Japan is consistently negative for the past decade as a whole. The negative long-run correlation in the two measures likely reflects the idiosyncratic shock in Japan with the bursting of the asset

Box 2.1 *(concluded)*

Confidence Linkages Across G-7 Countries
(Correlation with contemporaneous and lagged U.S. business confidence)

	Contemporaneous	1 quarter lag	2 quarter lag	3 quarter lag
Canada				
1990–2001	0.57	0.60	0.44	0.29
1999–2001	0.77	0.85	0.80	0.31
United Kingdom				
1990–2001	0.45	0.58	0.51	0.55
1999–2001	. . .	0.31	0.47	0.28
Euro area				
1990–2001	. . .	0.11	0.31	0.39
1999–2001	. . .	0.11	0.56	0.80
Japan				
1990–2001	–0.38	–0.32	–0.38	–0.43
1999–2001	0.41	–0.25	0.06	0.53

Source: IMF staff calculations.

price bubble and the subsequent protracted economic difficulties.

Consider next confidence linkages *within* Europe, which may be expected to be increasing given the increasing integration among the European economies. The contemporaneous correlation among the three largest euro area economies, especially since the inception of the euro, is high. But, in addition, business confidence in Germany leads confidence in other countries. France and the United Kingdom also appear to have an appreciable influence on Italian business confidence. In the case of the United Kingdom, although there has been an increase in the contemporaneous correlation with France and Germany, the interlinkages are less pronounced.

The variation in the strength and dynamics of confidence linkages among G-7 countries appears consistent with the findings on business cycle linkages reported in the essay. However, two additional exercises examined the extent to which confidence linkages may reflect extrane-

ous factors including information cascades. The first analyzed changes in business confidence *relative to* changes in economic activity and found that the recent increase in synchronization of business confidence between the United States and the euro area, and within the euro area, was substantially greater than could be expected on the basis of comovement in economic activity alone. A second examined the cross-country correlation in residuals obtained from regressing business confidence on measures of activity or leading indicators and found that, except for Japan, the residuals were significantly correlated, with a marked increase in the correlation between the United States and the euro area, and within the euro area. These findings suggest that while a large part of the confidence linkages are due to business cycle linkages, an increasing part may be due to factors not immediately related to economic activity, thereby constituting an additional mechanism for the transmission of economic and financial disturbances.

or bear markets (see, for example, Stulz, 1999, or Dahlquist, Hördah, and Sellin, 2000).

Conclusions and Policy Implications

Over the last four quarters, the seven major advanced economies have for the first time since

the early 1980s experienced a broadly synchronized growth slowdown. The breadth of synchronization was surprising in light of the experience with international business cycle linkages during the 1990s, when recessions occurred with noticeable differences in timing. However, from a historical perspective, the synchronous slowdown is less surprising in view of the nature of recent shocks, all of which were either global (the repricing of information technology stocks and the increase in real crude oil prices) or positively correlated country-specific shocks (monetary tightening in the United States, the euro area, and, to a much lesser extent, in Japan). As shown in this essay, such combinations of shocks were generally associated with strong linkages in the past. More generally, a review of international business cycle linkages during 1974–2000 suggests that their strength varied over time, depending on the nature, magnitude, and origin of disturbances that affect each economy.

The analysis also suggests that the business cycle linkages during 1974–2000 were largely shaped by the characteristics of disturbances. Economic financial interdependence across countries also played a role, although integration across countries remains surprisingly small compared with integration within countries. Looking forward, the international business cycle will likely become a more important driving force behind fluctuations in economic activity in major advanced countries because of the large scope for increased trade and financial interdependence. In particular, if cross-border wealth diversification continues to expand at a rapid pace, foreign assets and liabilities will soon account for substantial shares of household wealth; and with the continued internationalization of firms' operations through foreign direct investment, disturbances in other economies will increasingly affect profits and investment decisions in the domestic economy.

The dependence of the international business cycle on the characteristics of disturbances, which are unpredictable, raises important lessons for policymakers. Prudent policymaking requires the monitoring and assessment of macroeconomic developments and policies abroad,

since the impact of shocks that are either global or highly correlated across countries on economic activity in other countries can often provide important information about their possible effects on the domestic economy. This monitoring and assessment of developments abroad also complements the insights from available multicountry macroeconometric models. The models tend to focus primarily on trade linkages, as many aspects of financial market linkages are not yet satisfactorily integrated. As a result, the historical effects of international business cycle linkages identified by these models (and most other analysis) often appear to be too small to explain the observed strong cross-country output correlations, leaving a high level of uncertainty as to the forces behind the international business cycle.

How Do Fluctuations in the G-7 Countries Affect Developing Countries?

The ongoing slowdown in the major industrial countries, which began in the United States last year, has had an increasingly important impact on developing countries. This essay looks at the key mechanisms through which business cycle fluctuations in the industrial countries affect developing ones—an area that to date has been relatively underresearched—and discusses how these effects have varied both by regions (focusing on Africa, Asia, the Middle East, and Western Hemisphere) and by analytic groups (particularly fuel and primary commodity producers). In common with the previous essay, output gaps for all countries are extracted using a bandpass filter, using annual data covering the period 1971–2000.[20] The industrial country cycle is proxied by the cycle in the G-7 economies, while the developing country aggregates are calculated from data on 66 countries (Table 2.5).[21]

---

[20]See Baxter and King (1999). The filter incorporates fluctuations with frequencies of between 2 and 8 years.

[21]Given the long sample period, the "developing country" group includes Korea, Israel, and Singapore, three countries currently classified as advanced economies due to their rapid development over the period. The composite data for regional or analytic groups has been calculated using the methodology described in the Statistical Appendix. (Similar results are obtained when the output aggregates are calculated using trade weights, as opposed to GDP valued at purchasing power parities weights).

Table 2.5. Countries Included in the Developing Country Aggregates

Africa		Asia		Middle East		Western Hemisphere	
Algeria	+	Afghanistan		Bahrain	+	Argentina	
Bostwana	*	Bangladesh		Egypt		Brazil	
Comoros		Bhutan	*	Iran	+	Chile	*
Djibouti		Cambodia	*	Iraq	+	Colombia	
Gabon	+	China		Israel		Costa Rica	
Gambia	*	India		Jordan		Dominican Republic	
Ghana	*	Indonesia		Kuwait	+	Ecuador	
Kenya		Korea		Libya	+	El Salvador	
Lesotho		Malaysia		Oman	+	Guatemala	
Mauritius		Myanmar	*	Qatar	+	Haiti	
Morocco		Nepal		Saudi Arabia	+	Jamaica	
Namibia	*	Pakistan		Syrian Arab Republic		Mexico	
Nigeria	+	Papua New Guinea	*	Turkey		Panama	
South Africa		Philippines		United Arab Emirates	+	Peru	*
Sudan	*	Singapore				Trinidad and Tobago	+
Swaziland	*	Sri Lanka				Uruguay	
Tunisia		Thailand				Venezuela	+
Zimbabwe	*						

Note: The symbols + and * indicate that the country is a fuel or primary product exporter, respectively.

Main Features of Output Fluctuations in Developing Countries

Output fluctuations in the G-7 and developing countries have been irregular in both intensity and duration, and have varied widely across regions (Figure 2.8). In contrast to the G-7 countries, where the amplitude of fluctuations has been declining over time, owing in part to the remarkable stability in North America during the 1990s, output fluctuations in the developing countries have increased slightly during the 1990s, largely as a result of a series of crises in emerging markets.[22] This was true in Asia, which—particularly when China and India are excluded—had experienced relatively moderate fluctuations during the previous two decades. There was also substantial output volatility in Western Hemisphere countries, reflecting the Mexican and Brazilian crises, although not to the extent experienced in the 1982 debt crisis. Elsewhere, the fuel and primary commodity exporters, and the associated developing country regions (the Middle East and sub-Saharan Africa) also experienced significant volatility.

As can be seen from Figure 2.8, output fluctuations in the developing countries as a group have been fairly synchronized and positively correlated with the output fluctuations in the G-7 countries for most of the 1971–2000 period (the most important exception being from the late 1980s through the mid-1990s). These linkages are quite important—simple regressions indicate that a 1 percent change in real GDP growth in the G-7 countries is associated with a 0.4 percent change in growth in developing countries, while a 1 percentage point decrease in the world real interest rate is associated with a 0.3 percent increase in developing country growth. The correlations between the cycles in the G-7 countries and in developing country regions or groups are significantly lower than among the cycles in the G-7 countries themselves, reflecting the developing countries' greater diversity in terms of structures of production and institutional arrangements and their greater vulnerability to external and domestic shocks. The magnitude of output fluctuations also tend to be larger in developing countries, thereby magnifying the impact of a given level of correlation.[23] For the period as a whole, output

---

[22]Agénor, McDermott, and Prasad (2000) document the main features of macroeconomic fluctuations for 12 middle-income developing countries.

[23]This is even more true at the individual developing country level. See Kose, Otrok, and Whiteman (2000).

Table 2.6. Output Correlation with the Group of Seven (G-7) Countries

	1971–2000	1971–80	1981–90	1991–2000
Africa	0.33	0.20	0.51	0.67
Asia	0.15	0.03	0.57	−0.04
Middle East	0.26	0.31	0.06	0.04
Western Hemisphere	0.32	0.42	0.16	0.18
Fuel exporters	0.32	0.41	−0.06	0.27
Primary goods exporters	0.07	0.07	0.08	0.21
Developing countries	0.45	0.52	0.62	0.10

Source: IMF staff estimates.

fluctuations in Africa, Western Hemisphere, and fuel exporters have been tied most closely with the advanced economies (Table 2.6), with a somewhat smaller correlation for Asian countries, and very little for primary commodity exporters.

The degree of correlation has, however, varied substantially over time, reflecting idiosyncratic shocks in both developing and the seven major advanced economies. Notably, rolling moving averages of these correlations indicate that the comovement between the G-7 countries and developing countries fell markedly in the 1990s (Figure 2.9). This decrease appears to stem from three main developments: the decoupling of the cycles in G-7 countries (caused by German reunification and underlying difficulties in Japan); the diversification of export markets away from the G-7 countries to other advanced and developing economies; and—as noted already—a series of emerging market crises, particularly in Asia and the Western Hemisphere. As the cycles in the G-7 countries became more synchronized in the late 1990s, however, output synchronization between these countries and developing countries has increased once again (Figure 2.9, top panel).

From the previous discussion, it follows that the relationship between the cycles of G-7 and developing countries is quite volatile and is affected strongly by idiosyncratic shocks in each group.[24]

[24]See Razin and Rose (1994) and Kraay and Ventura (2001) for a discussion of the causes of output volatility in developing countries; and Mendoza (1995) and Kose (forthcoming) for analyses of the sources of business cycle fluctuations in developing countries using dynamic stochastic models.

Figure 2.8. Output Fluctuations in the Group of Seven (G-7) and Developing Countries
(Percentage deviations from trend output)

Output fluctuations have been irregular and varied widely across regions and analytic groups.

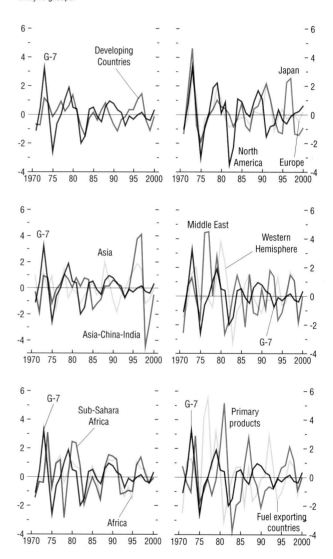

Sources: IMF, *International Financial Statistics*; and IMF staff calculations.

Figure 2.9. Output Comovements Between the Developing and the Group of Seven (G-7) Countries
(Rolling eight-year correlation windows)

Correlations indicate that output comovement between the G-7 countries and the developing countries and regions, with the exception of Africa, has weakened in the 1990s. However, correlations increased in the late 1990s.

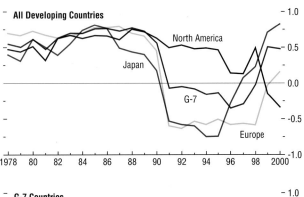

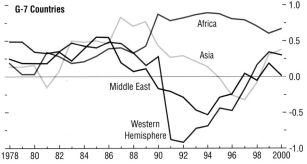

Sources: IMF, *International Financial Statistics*; and IMF staff calculations.

At the same time, however, there is also clear evidence that there is also an important degree of comovement, and the remainder of this essay investigates this issue in more detail.

What Accounts for Output Comovement?

The academic literature has focused on three key factors that might explain the extent of output comovement between advanced and developing economies. These are:

- *Increased trade and financial integration with the global economy,* as increased international trade and financial flows facilitate the transmission of demand and productivity shocks across countries (Frankel and Rose, 1998). On the trade side, this is particularly important for those countries and regions that trade most with the G-7 countries.

- *The size of the developing country,* with larger countries expected to have higher comovements with the advanced economies after controlling for other factors such as openness (Head, 1995). This presumably reflects their more diversified economic structure, making them less susceptible to country specific-shocks.[25] This relationship between country size and output comovements appears stronger for high-income developing countries, although some small countries, such as those that rely on tourism, are also closely integrated with the cycle in the G-7 countries.

- *The size and volatility of capital inflows.* While capital account openness would generally be expected to increase global linkages, high and volatile capital flows can lead to credit booms and busts that reduce correlations with the cycle in G-7 countries (Gourinchas, Valdés, and Landerretche, 2001).

To assess the relative importance of these factors, the staff of the *World Economic Outlook* esti-

---

[25]Moreover, shocks affecting their globally integrated industries, such as information technology, could contribute to the world cycle (Kraay and Ventura, 2001).

Table 2.7. Developing Countries: Determinants of Output Comovement

	Comovement with	
	G-7 Countries	North America
Trade openness[1]		
10 percentage points of GDP rise	0.019 +	0.018 +
Trade intensity with G-7 countries[2]		
10 percentage points of exports rise	0.035 +	0.017
Country size[3]		
10 percent increase in the size of the average country	0.003 +	0.003 +
Capital account openness[4]		
Movement from close to open	0.056	0.019
Net private capital flows[5]		
10 percentage point of GDP rise	−0.025	−0.104 +

Note: The symbol + indicates that the coefficient is significant. The dependent variables are the correlation coefficients between the cyclical component of real GDP of country i and the G-7 countries and North America, respectively. The regressors include a constant, a dummy for the Western Hemisphere region, exports of fuel (as percent of total exports), and the regressors reported above. While both the constant and the dummy were statistically significant, fuel exports was not.

[1]Country i's ratio of total exports plus imports over GDP.
[2]Country i's exports to the G-7 countries over its total exports.
[3]Country i's U.S. dollar GDP over global U.S. dollar GDP.
[4]Country i's restrictions on capital account transaction.
[5]Net private flows to country i.

mated a linear cross-section model, in which the correlation between the cycles of 58 individual developing countries and the G-7 economies was regressed against the degree of trade openness, the share of trade with the G-7 countries, the share of fuel exports, the size of the country, a measure of capital account openness, the level of net private capital flows, and a Western Hemisphere dummy.[26] The exercise was also undertaken using the correlation with North America alone. The results, shown in Table 2.7, confirm the importance of trade openness and trade intensity with the G-7 countries; and the size of the country is also found to be significant (although the impact is relatively small). The variables for capital account restrictiveness and

the level of net private capital flows are also correctly signed, although they were not statistically significant.

How Are External Shocks Transmitted to Developing Countries?

The previous discussion has highlighted several structural factors explaining the degree of output comovement over time. The remainder of this essay focuses in more detail on the trade and financial channels through which shocks can be transmitted to developing countries. The relative importance of these channels depends on the nature of the external shocks and the characteristics of the developing regions (see Box 2.2).

Trade Channel

There are two major ways for an external shock to be transmitted through international trade to developing countries: by affecting export volumes, and by changing the terms of trade. Typically, a slowdown in the advanced economies weakens the demand for developing countries' exports, as shown by the generally strong positive correlation between the volume of exports from individual developing countries and the business cycle in the G-7 countries (Figure 2.10, upper panel). Import volumes, by contrast, are not highly correlated with fluctuations in G-7 countries.

With the important exception of oil exporters, there is a strong positive correlation between the terms of trade and the business cycle in the G-7 countries (Figure 2.10, middle panel).[27] This positive correlation reflects conditions in both manufacturing and non-oil commodity prices. Many developing countries produce low value added manufactures for which competition is fierce, and prices tend to fluctuate in tandem with demand from industrial countries—the ma-

---

[26]All variables were averaged over the period 1971–2000. Other regional dummies were also included as regressors, but were dropped from the final specification because they were statistically insignificant. The Western Hemisphere dummy apparently is significant because, in contrast to other regions, dependence on the markets of the seven major advanced economies has increased over time.

[27]See also Mendoza (1995) and Kose (forthcoming).

Figure 2.10. Trade Developments in Developing Countries and the Cycle in the Group of Seven (G-7) Countries
(Histogram of Correlation Coefficients; axis indicate percent)

For a large number of countries in the sample, there is a procyclical association between their volume of exports, terms of trade, and trade balance and the G-7 cycle.

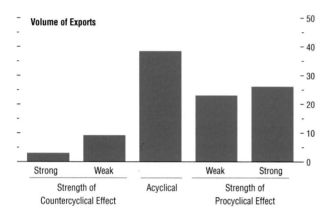

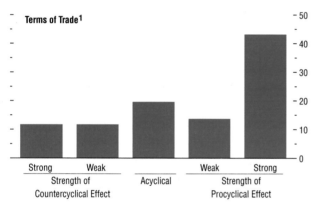

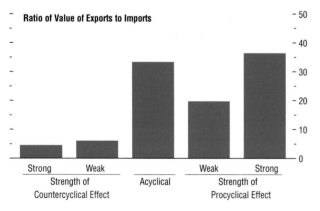

Sources: IMF, *International Financial Statistics*; and IMF staff calculations.
[1]Excludes fuel producing countries.

jor market.[28] During the recent slowdown, developments in the microprocessor market have clearly exemplified this phenomenon (see Appendix I of Chapter I). In addition, while individual commodity prices are often dominated by supply factors, aggregates of non-fuel commodity prices are affected by the cycle in the advanced economies. This relationship is especially relevant for metals whose prices are closely related to the cycle in industrial production.[29] Supply factors and the impact of changes in the oil price on activity in advanced economies explain the weak negative correlation between oil prices and the cycle of the G-7 countries.

In sum, a slowdown in the G-7 countries is normally associated with both a reduction in export volumes and a terms of trade deterioration in most developing countries, and, therefore, a weakening in their trade and current account balances. Taking these two factors together, there is a generally positive correlation between the ratio of the value of exports to imports in the developing countries and the business cycle in the G-7 countries (Figure 2.10, lower panel).

Financial Channel

External shocks can be transmitted to the developing countries through changes in the size and composition of capital flows, as well as in financing costs. Many small, poor countries rely on official flows for financing. A recent study reveals that, except for a number of African countries, these flows are volatile and are positively correlated with the cycle in donor countries, providing an additional procyclical impulse to countries relying on official financing.[30] More-

[28]Baxter and Kouparitsas (2000) find that a country's terms of trade volatility is, among other factors, related to its trade structure in terms of commodity composition and direction of trade.

[29]The importance of demand factors can also be induced from the persistence of commodity price movements and positive correlations of prices of individual commodities. See Deaton (1999).

[30]See Pallage and Robe (forthcoming). This study also reported that net official development assistance, over the 1969–95 period, averaged 12.5 percent of recipients' GDP for the African countries and 4 percent of recipients' GDP for the countries outside Africa.

Box 2.2. Channels of Business Cycle Transmission to Developing Countries

As developing countries become more integrated into the world economy, macroeconomic fluctuations in these countries have become increasingly affected by external influences, including business cycles in advanced economies. These influences can be transmitted through three basic channels: trade, finance, and direct sectoral linkages. This box provides a brief summary of these three channels, which are closely interrelated, and discusses how their relative importance has evolved in recent years.

The Trade Channel

- *Foreign demand shocks.* Business cycles in advanced economies have a significant effect on their demand for developing country commodities, intermediate goods, and finished products. As their trade relationships with industrial countries have expanded rapidly in recent decades, developing countries have become increasingly affected by aggregate demand conditions in industrial countries. This is true of many Asian and Latin American countries that have strong trade relationships with industrial countries. Countries in sub-Saharan Africa that largely rely on a narrow set of commodity exports and have limited trade with industrial countries, however, are much less directly influenced by business cycles in these countries.[1]
- *Aggregate productivity shocks.* For many developing countries, technology transfers occur mainly through imports from industrial countries. Technological spillovers and their effects on macroeconomic fluctuations therefore tend to be stronger for countries that have strong trade relationships with industrial countries, although this also depends on the nature of products traded. Industrial country productivity shocks have been estimated to account for 5 to 20 percent of the variation in developing country output (see Kouparitsas, 1996).

- *Terms of trade fluctuations.* Some authors have estimated that terms of trade shocks could account for as much as 50 percent of output fluctuations in developing economies.[2] These shocks include variations in commodity prices that are often influenced by cyclical conditions in advanced economies. The volatility of commodity prices tends to have large spillover effects within developing countries that rely on exports of commodities and other primary products for much of their export earnings (and, in some cases, for a significant fraction of their national incomes). In this vein, commodity price shocks have been shown to be important determinants of investment and output fluctuations among commodity-exporting African countries (Deaton and Miller, 1995; and Kose and Riezman, 2001).

The Financial Channel

- *Private capital flows.* Foreign direct investment and other forms of capital flows from industrial to developing countries have expanded considerably in recent decades. Many developing countries now rely heavily on external financing for their domestic investment and current account deficits (see Chapter IV). The magnitude and volatility of capital flows from industrial countries can therefore have a significant influence on developing country investment and output. The effects of capital inflows and their reversals on domestic activity in developing economies are well documented (see Mendoza, 2001). The phenomenon of financial contagion also implies that macroeconomic disturbances in one or a few developing countries could get transmitted rapidly via the financial channel to other developing countries. Rising correlations of stock market fluctuations, as evidenced by recent shocks to stock prices in the technology sector, are another aspect of this phenomenon. As developing countries strengthen their linkages to international financial markets,

---

[1]See Agénor, McDermott and Prasad (2000); Hoffmaister, Roldos, and Wickham (1998); and Ahmed and Loungani (forthcoming).

[2]Mendoza (1995); his sample includes 23 developing countries and covers the period 1961–90.

Box 2.2 *(concluded)*

the financial channel is likely to become an increasingly important channel of transmission of fluctuations to these countries.

- *Aid and other financial flows.* The volatility of aid flows can also affect macroeconomic fluctuations in some developing countries. Bulir and Hamann (forthcoming) document that, in many sub-Saharan African economies, which are generally heavily dependent on aid, aid flows are both volatile and positively related to their own cycle.
- *Global financial market conditions.* Changes in world interest rates and investors' appetite for risk, along with perceptions of riskiness of investments in developing countries, are likely to influence the quantity of capital flows to these countries. The ability of developing countries to conduct countercyclical macroeconomic policies could also be constrained by externally generated changes in interest rates and spreads. Existing evidence indicates that the effects of world real interest rate shocks on output volatility in most developing countries are rather small. However, one study finds that this effect tends to be much greater for countries with a high level of external indebtedness, while another finds that changes in U.S. interest rates significantly affect growth in some developing countries, with debtor countries again tending to experience a much larger impact (see Kose, forthcoming; and Arora and Cerisola, 2000).

Sectoral Interdependence

- *Similarities in economic structure.* These similarities imply that sector-specific shocks—

including productivity shocks and shocks to the composition of import demand from industrial countries—tend to have similar effects on aggregate fluctuations across national borders. Several studies find that the high degree of business cycle synchronization across the major East Asian economies compared to those in Latin America may in large part be attributable to similarities in the sectoral composition of output in these countries (Imbs, 1999; and Loayza, Lopez, and Ubide, 1999).

- *Shocks to the technology sector.* This sector is relatively important in many emerging market economies, particularly those in East Asia, and shocks to this sector emanating from advanced economies have had a significant impact on aggregate output fluctuations in those countries. Chapter I discussed the importance of the technology cycle for East Asian economies during the current downturn.

Developing countries are becoming more closely linked to industrial countries through trade and financial linkages as well as increasing similarities in industrial structure. These forces of global integration are likely to result in rising commonality of business cycle fluctuations across industrial and developing countries. Recent crises in emerging market economies show that, while the financial channel plays an increasingly important role in transmitting business cycles to these countries, the other channels associated with trade and sectoral interdependence also significantly affect macroeconomic fluctuations in developing economies.

---

over, the study finds only a few differences between the cyclical behavior of bilateral and multilateral assistance, although the latter is more volatile than the former.

For most other countries, the main source of finance is through private markets, and—as dis-

cussed in Chapter IV—these linkages have been increasing rapidly over time, suggesting that private capital flows are becoming more important.[31] At the same time—and crucially from the perspective of business cycle linkages—the composition of flows has also changed markedly. In

---

[31]Nevertheless, only a few middle-income developing countries have received a very large fraction of these inflows.

the 1970s, "other" net capital flows, largely comprising net bank loans, were the dominant form of finance; in the 1980s, capital flows in general were weak, although foreign direct investment remained relatively stable. The 1990s, in contrast, saw a sharp increase in foreign direct investment flows—often associated with "greenfield" projects, but increasingly also associated with merger and acquisition and privatization of existing businesses.[32] This was accompanied by a surge in portfolio flows, following the development of emerging bond markets in the late 1980s and of emerging equity markets shortly thereafter.

In terms of the cyclical behavior of capital flows, an important distinction can be made between interest-bearing instruments and equity finance. The former comprise bank loans and bonds while the latter includes corporate foreign direct investment and the equity portion of portfolio flows.[33] For interest-bearing debt, the cost of this capital depends on interest rates in advanced economies and the additional spread charged to developing countries. As seen in Figure 2.11, net private capital flows to developing countries since the 1980s have been negatively correlated with the world real interest rate. A simple linear regression relating these two variables suggests that a 1 percent decline in international real interest rates is associated with a rise in capital inflows to developing countries of 0.3 percent of GDP since the early 1980s. One recent study confirms this negative relationship for 15 large developing countries over the 1990s.[34]

This countercyclical behavior plausibly reflects the fact that lower interest rates both make such

[32]Albuquerque (2001) provides evidence that the foreign direct investment share of developing countries with poor access to capital markets is higher than that for other countries.

[33]Unfortunately, the split between portfolio bond and equity flows is difficult to obtain on a consistent basis.

[34]Montiel and Reinhart (2001) find evidence that capital flows also respond to short-run macroeconomic policies—such as sterilized intervention and, to lesser degree, capital controls—of the developing countries.

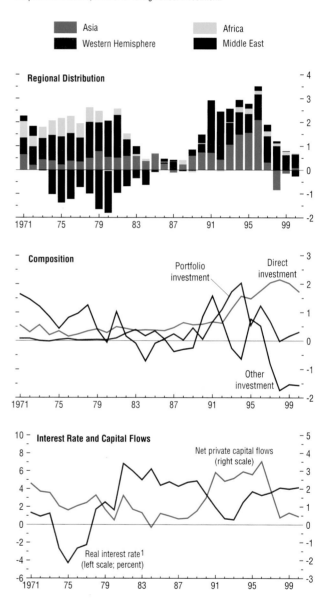

Figure 2.11. Developing Countries: Net Private Capital Flows
(Percent of GDP; unless otherwise noted)

Net external financing has increased over time and its composition has switched, in the past two decades, in favor of foreign direct investment.

Sources: IMF, *International Financial Statistics*; and IMF staff calculations.
[1]The world real interest rate is proxied by the difference between the Euro-dollar rate in London and the rate of inflation in the G-7 countries.

Figure 2.12. Stock Returns Comovement Between the Developing and the Group of Seven (G-7) Countries[1]
(Correlation between the G-7 and other markets; rolling 12-month windows)

Correlations between the technology stock returns in the G-7 countries and other developing markets have been high and increased further in the last few years. But correlations between the non-technology stocks returns have been weaker and more volatile.

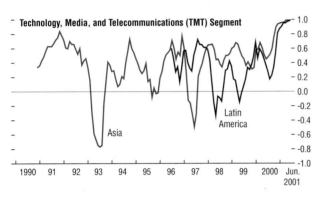

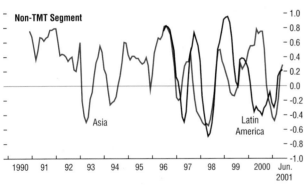

Sources: Primark Data Stream; and IMF staff estimates.
[1] Twelve-month returns.

financing more attractive and reduces market spreads, as the cost of servicing existing debt is reduced. It is difficult to obtain long time series, as spreads are not available for bank loans. Examining bond spreads over the 1990s, a recent study by the IMF finds that emerging market bond spreads are positively linked to the U.S. Federal Funds interest rate, 10-year U.S. treasury interest rates, the U.S. high yield interest rate spread, and the performance and volatility of U.S. stock market indices, although country-specific factors also play an important role in determining such spreads (IMF, 2001b). Given the short time period, however, there are questions about the strength of the positive relation between the Federal Fund interest rate and emerging market bond spreads, as this relation seems to be most evident when there are extreme events in emerging markets.

In contrast, equity-based flows are much less likely to be countercyclical. Foreign direct investment inflows, indeed, show relatively little cyclical variation (Figure 2.11), although related flows associated with operations such as exchange rate hedging can show up elsewhere in the financial accounts. Moreover, portfolio equity flows are likely to be positively related to the business cycle, since equity markets tend to be highly correlated and the correlation between advanced and emerging market equity prices has been rising over time.[35] Figure 2.12 highlights the close association between returns across markets, particularly for IT shares. In consequence, the cyclicality of capital flows is likely to depend increasingly on their composition; and for those regions that depend relatively more on portfolio equity flows—such as Asia—there is a greater chance that capital flows could be procyclical.

Implications for the Current Cycle

The discussion above has highlighted that developing countries' output comovement with the

[35]See IMF (2001b), and Froot, O'Connell, and Seasholes (2001).

advanced economies depends on trade integration, the composition of their trading partners and export products, and the size and composition of the net private capital flows. These linkages are quite strong—for the period since 1971 a linear regression suggests that a 1 percent reduction in output growth in the G-7 countries is associated with a 0.4 percent reduction in output growth in the developing countries while a 1 percentage point reduction in the world real interest rate is associated with a 0.3 percent increase in output growth of the developing countries. To the extent that output growth in the G-7 countries falls faster than the international real interest rates, as has been the case of a typical recession in these countries, output growth in the developing countries as a whole will be negatively affected. How do these considerations feed into the current outlook?

The emerging markets of Asia are probably most affected by the current slowdown in the industrial countries. On the trade side, both export volumes and prices (particularly in IT products) are sensitive to slower growth in the G-7 countries, while the region's relatively high dependence on equity finance provides a further channel for negative spillovers. Elsewhere, the impact of the business cycle in the G-7 countries on developing regions may be smaller. The main impact in Africa will probably come through declining terms of trade and, for a number of countries, lower official financing flows, while the impact in the Middle East and other fuel exporters largely depends on developments in oil prices.

In Mexico and the remainder of Central America, the impact of the current slowdown in G-7 countries will be negative, as the trade channel clearly dominates. Elsewhere in the Western Hemisphere, however, the combination of relatively limited trade links, high levels of interest bearing debt, and the need for significant bond financing could mean that the benefits of lower interest rates offset the negative effects through

activity. In practice, however, these benefits are being limited by several factors, including the high level of spreads reflecting problems in specific countries, and the strength of the U.S. dollar—the currency in which most debts are denominated—which is increasing debt burdens. Moreover, the recent slowdown in foreign net investment to these countries has further complicated the financing position of the region.

The World Trading System: From Seattle to Doha

The failure to start a new round of multilateral trade negotiations at the third ministerial conference of the World Trade Organization (WTO) in Seattle in 1999, owing to major divisions both between industrial and developing countries and among industrial countries, was a setback for the multilateral trading system. However, after a hiatus, momentum is gathering in the WTO for the start of a new round of negotiations, possibly to be launched at the ministerial conference in Doha, Qatar in November.[36] The negotiators will face significant challenges, including the desire by some countries to bring new and complicated policy issues under multilateral rules and the need to take into account the interests of a large and diverse membership of countries. But the benefits are even larger. At stake are enhanced global growth prospects from further trade liberalization (where, despite past successes, much remains to be done) and the reinforcement of free trade as an element of globalization that can continue to raise living standards in rich and poor countries alike. This essay takes stock of the current state of the world trading system and presents the issues that are likely to form the core of discussions for the next round.

Global Trade Growth

The extraordinary growth of the global economy since World War II has been driven, to

---

[36]See Chapter V of the October 1999 *World Economic Outlook* for a discussion of trends and issues in the global trading system during the 1990s.

Figure 2.13. World Trade and Developing Countries
(Percent of total)

Developing countries have become more important players in world trade and trade between them has increased significantly.

Share of Developing Countries' Exports Destined to Other Developing Countries

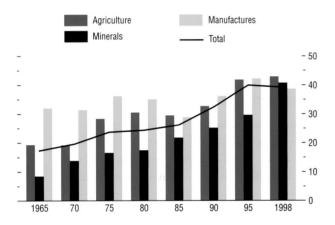

Product Composition of World Merchandise Exports

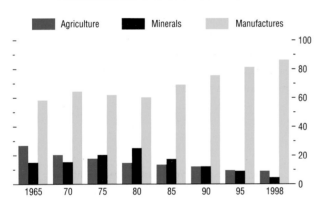

Manufactures' Share in Total Exports

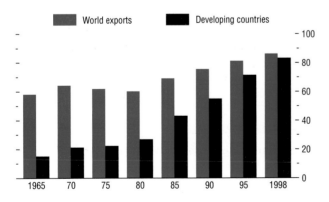

Source: Global Trade Analysis Project (GTAP) database, version 5.

some extent, by the liberalization of trade.[37] The cornerstone of this liberalization has been eight rounds of multilateral trade negotiations, of which the Uruguay Round, completed in 1994, is the most recent. Industrial countries have liberalized mainly within this multilateral framework, although regional arrangements, such as the European Union (EU) and North American Free Trade Agreement (NAFTA), have also been important. Historically, developing countries have relied less on multilateral trade rounds, pursuing unilateral liberalization as they shifted away from the import substitution policies of the 1960s and 1970s. More recently, many of these countries have complemented unilateral liberalization with regional trading arrangements and commitments undertaken in the Uruguay Round. By 1999, there were more than 140 regional trade agreements in force, most of them including developing or transition economies.

Partly as a result, during the past 20 years, the volume of world trade grew twice as fast as world real GDP (6 percent versus 3 percent), deepening economic integration. Developing countries as a group achieved the fastest expansion of trade and, as a result, have become more important players in world trade, including as markets for each other's products. They now account for one-third of world trade, up from about a quarter in the early 1970s, and 40 percent of their exports now go to other developing countries (Figure 2.13). Developing countries have also contributed to a shift in world trade toward manufactures and commercial services, particularly emerging market countries that have participated in the geographic dispersion of production processes and the rapid expansion of intra-

[37]See "Postwar Economic Achievement" in Chapter VI of the October 1994 *World Economic Outlook.* Also, the close connection between trade and growth has been well documented. See, for example, Bhagwati (1978) on individual country experiences; on cross-country growth analysis, see Sachs and Warner (1995), Edwards (1998), and Frankel and Romer (1999). Rodriguez and Rodrik (2000) dispute the cross-sectional statistical evidence on the relationship between openness and growth, and Rodrik (1999) concludes that "...openness is part of a development strategy; it does not substitute for it."

industry trade. However, a large number of developing countries did not participate in these trends. Poorer developing countries, especially in Africa, have seen their share of world trade decline, and many of them continue to be dependent on traditional commodity exports.[38] These countries, which generally maintain relatively restrictive trading regimes, comprise about 75 developing and transition economies that are eligible for concessional lending from the IMF and the World Bank, including virtually all the least-developed countries and the heavily indebted poor countries.

Trade Policies

Despite the failure to initiate a new trade round at the WTO Ministerial conference in Seattle, global trade has continued to expand, and there has been no major sign of backtracking on Uruguay Round commitments, which are being broadly implemented on schedule. This translates into more open markets as tariffs are reduced and nontariff barriers, such as voluntary export restraints and restrictive licensing, are eliminated. The (unweighted) average post-Uruguay Round bound tariff rate in industrial countries for manufacturing products is now quite low, at around 4 percent, whereas for developing countries the figure stands at 20 percent, although applied tariffs are lower.[39]

Countries are increasingly pursuing trade liberalization through regional trading arrangements. In the six years since the establishment of the WTO, 90 new regional trading arrangements have been reported to the WTO, compared to 124 during the first 46 years of the General Agreement on Tariffs and Trade (GATT) system (1948–1994), and many of the 124 were also reported only since the early 1990s. This process has continued since Seattle. In addition to the network of agreements with EU accession candidates and the Mediterranean countries, the EU

has recently concluded free trade agreements with Mexico and South Africa and launched negotiations with MERCOSUR. In the Americas, the United States and 33 other countries have established a timetable for negotiations to form a Free Trade Area of the Americas by 2005. In Asia, major traders such as Korea, Japan, Singapore, and Hong Kong SAR are moving for the first time toward bilateral free trade agreements. In Africa, efforts to promote regional trade integration have intensified. There has been substantial progress in implementing a customs union in the West African Economic and Monetary Union, particularly since January 2001 and, despite some difficulties, in the Central African Economic and Monetary Community, and a free trade area has been established in part of the Common Market for Eastern and Southern Africa.

Unilateral liberalization, a major avenue used by developing and transition economies to liberalize their trade regimes, has also continued in the past two years. Despite the 1997–98 crisis, trade liberalization actually accelerated in Asia, particularly for countries with IMF-supported programs (such as Korea and Indonesia). In Africa, South Asia, the Caribbean and, to a lesser extent, the Middle East, many countries continued to open their trade and investment regimes unilaterally. Central European countries have also generally reduced their tariff rates in preparation for accession to the EU and the adoption of the Common External Tariff.

But not all developments have been positive. There was a clear trend toward increased antidumping activity, both by industrial and developing countries (Figure 2.14), and growing concern about nontransparent barriers in the form of technical and health standards. Industrial countries have backloaded their WTO commitments in textiles and clothing made in the context of the Uruguay Round, so that the majority of quotas will only be dismantled in 2005. In

---

[38]The trade performance of sub-Saharan Africa was discussed in Chapter II of the May 2001 *World Economic Outlook*.
[39]Reflecting liberalization beyond WTO Commitments, applied tariffs in developing countries average 13 percent. The scope that this provides to raise tariffs to bound rates increases uncertainty regarding market access conditions.

agriculture, the tariffication of quantitative restrictions under the Uruguay Round has resulted in extremely high tariff rates, and minimum access levels negotiated during the Uruguay Round have yet to be reached; and while direct export subsidies have been reduced, total producer support to farming in OECD countries has changed little compared to the base period (1986–88) for the Uruguay Round (Figure 2.15). In addition, the spread of regional trading arrangements is seen by some as potentially detrimental to the world trading system, particularly in the context of the lack of progress on the multilateral front.[40]

Some regional initiatives have suffered delays or setbacks. Trade liberalization in the member countries of Asia-Pacific Economic Cooperation (APEC) seems to have lost momentum, particularly as members reached the stage of making market access concessions. Beset by a stalling economy and financial difficulties, Argentina has recently begun to levy tariffs on previously duty-free imports from other MERCOSUR members. In the Association of South East Asian Nations (ASEAN), resistance has emerged regarding the reduction of tariffs on politically "sensitive" products (automobiles, for example). In Africa, the number of overlapping and internally inconsistent initiatives, particularly in eastern and southern Africa, is a source of concern.

Global Trade Issues After the Uruguay Round

The Uruguay Round was one of the most impressive multilateral trade negotiations in terms

Figure 2.14. Number of Antidumping Investigations Initiated

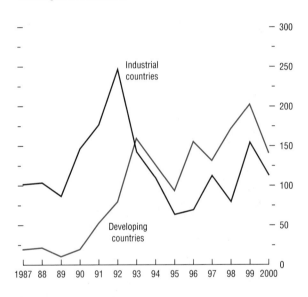

Source: World Trade Organization (WTO).

[40]Regional trading arrangements, appropriately designed, can provide net benefits from trade creation, offer an intermediate step toward a broader process of integration into the world economy, and lock-in reciprocal liberalization. At the same time, they discriminate against nonmembers and can lead to trade diversion and a loss of overall competitiveness. These risks are mitigated when regional arrangements are outward oriented and complemented by unilateral liberalization and periodic multilateral trade rounds. See Vamvakidis (1999) for an assessment of the relative merits of regional versus broad liberalization and World Bank (2000) for an in-depth analysis of the costs and benefits of regional trade agreements.

of scope and outcomes. Capping the achievements of previous rounds, it will virtually eliminate nontariff barriers by 2005 and cut tariffs substantially. The gains from lowering trade barriers alone have been estimated at around $200 billion a year, of which between $50 and $90 billion will go to developing countries.[41] The Uruguay Round also created the WTO, brought international trade rules to areas previously excluded or subject to weak rules (agriculture, textiles and clothing, services, and trade-related investment measures and intellectual property rights), and strengthened the dispute settlement mechanism.[42] In addition, in contrast to previous negotiations, developing countries played a much more active role and accepted the same obligations as other WTO members as part of the "single undertaking" of the round. Finally, the Uruguay Round provided for a future work program—the so-called built-in agenda—including a relatively rapid resumption (by January 2000) of multilateral negotiations to carry forward liberalization in agriculture and services— the core elements of the agenda—and reviews of the agreements on intellectual property rights, trade-related investment measures, and the dispute settlement mechanism.

Despite these achievements, the multilateral trading system faces important challenges. First, even after full implementation, protection will remain concentrated in areas of interest to developing countries. While rules and disciplines were extended to agriculture and services, little liberalization was achieved in these sectors. In manufactures, high tariffs will apply to textiles and clothing after quotas are finally dismantled in 2005, and other labor-intensive products still face tariff peaks and tariff escalation that constrain developing countries in their efforts to ex-

Figure 2.15. Selected OECD Countries: Agricultural Producer Support, 1986-2000
(Billions of U.S. dollars)

Producer support to farming has remained high in most OECD countries.

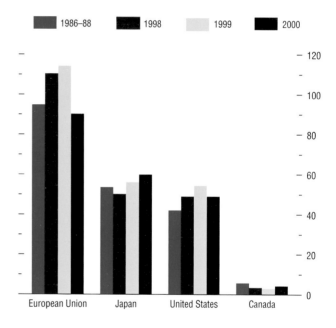

Source: OECD, *Agricultural Policies in OECD Countries* (Paris: OECD, 2001).

[41]Kirmani and others (1994) provide a detailed review of the Uruguay Round.

[42]The WTO incorporated a number of agreements, including three multilateral trade agreements—the General Agreement on Tariffs and Trade, The General Agreement on Trade in Services, and the Agreement on Trade-Related Aspects of Intellectual Property Rights—and procedures for dispute settlement.

pand and diversify their exports into higher value-added products. Moreover, developing countries themselves have high import tariffs; average applied tariffs on industrial goods are three times as high as those of industrial countries. These barriers impose costs on all countries and provide an opportunity for substantial gains from reciprocal trade liberalization (Box 2.3).

Second, the changing realities of international commerce have revealed the need to update and adapt the architecture of the trading system. With the deepening of economic integration through international trade and investment flows and the declining importance of restrictions at the border, attention has shifted to so-called new issues such as behind-the-border measures that limit the contestability of markets. Thus, there have been calls—variously by industrial and developing countries—for new or strengthened rules under the WTO dealing with competition policy, investment, government procurement, antidumping and other safeguard measures, health and product standards, and e-commerce. Also, as trade and the process of globalization have become a more visible part of industrial country economies, civil society has sought the incorporation of so-called non-trade concerns such as labor and environmental standards into the international trading system (Box 2.4).

A third challenge relates to implementation and institutional issues of concern to developing countries. Many developing countries feel that they are bearing the costs of implementing difficult and complex agreements in areas such as trade-related intellectual property rights and customs valuation without seeing the benefits of improved market access in areas of interest to them. Poorer developing countries have had trouble implementing these and other commitments because of a lack of institutional capacity and financial resources. They note that nonbinding pledges by industrial countries to provide significant technical assistance have yet to materialize. In addition, the governance and negotiating procedures (including a lengthy and com-

plex accession process) of the WTO make it difficult for many poor countries to pursue their legitimate interests.

These challenges, each in their own way, contributed to the impasse in Seattle. The diverse interests of the membership proved difficult to consolidate into a single negotiating agenda. The European Union and Japan promoted their concept of a comprehensive round embracing many of the new issues but downplaying agricultural liberalization, while the United States and some other countries proposed a more limited approach centered on the built-in agenda with greater emphasis on agricultural liberalization and some selective additions, such as labor standards. Some developing countries preferred to focus on the implementation of existing Uruguay Round Agreements, while others felt that a comprehensive round should include negotiations on antidumping. The discussion rapidly stalled on a wide range of issues related to agriculture, the implementation of certain Uruguay Round Agreements, new or non-trade issues (investment, competition policy, the environment, and labor standards), and antidumping. Inadequate preparation for the launching of the round, a lack of transparency and inclusiveness in the pre-negotiations, and the absence of a spirit of engagement and compromise contributed to the impasse. As a result, many developing countries felt excluded from the process and believed that their concerns and institutional and capacity constraints were not fully recognized.

Since Seattle, the WTO has sought to restore confidence in the multilateral trading system, with a particular focus on developing countries. An Implementation Review Mechanism has been put in place to examine, on a case-by-case basis, requests for the extension of time periods for implementation of Uruguay Round commitments, and there have been renewed efforts to improve the effectiveness and coordination of technical assistance to poorer countries. Ongoing discussions have been initiated to improve the WTO's negotiating procedures so that developing countries are not excluded from the process, and more time has been available for

Box 2.3. Potential Welfare Gains from a New Trade Round

Even after eight rounds of multilateral trade negotiations and the full implementation of commitments under the Uruguay Round, significant protection will still exist in industrial and developing countries.[1] As further reductions in trade barriers would be the quintessential element of a new trade round, the question of the potential welfare gains from reductions in the remaining barriers to trade and their distribution across countries naturally arises.

Quantifying the welfare gains and losses from trade liberalization is a difficult task. The results depend critically on the underlying model, the specification and quantification of trade barriers (which is notoriously difficult, especially for services), and the scope and extent of liberalization. Accordingly, available estimates of welfare gains of various trade policy options differ widely. In addition, many economists believe that these estimates significantly underestimate the true welfare gains because they do not adequately capture important dynamic effects, such as the availability of new goods (see Romer, 1994; and Feenstra, 1995). With these caveats in mind, this box summarizes some representative estimates of the welfare gains from full trade liberalization after the implementation of all commitments under the Uruguay Round.

The welfare gains reported below are based on simulations of two widely used computable general equilibrium models, which represent conservative and liberal estimates of the gains from trade liberalization. The Global Trade Analysis Project (GTAP) model is a static model with perfect competition, in which the welfare gains are limited to the reallocation of existing resources—capital and labor—according to each country's comparative advantage.[2] The Michigan Model, in contrast, incorporates imperfect competition in the manufacturing and services sectors.[3] This tends to generate larger welfare gains in these sectors since trade liberalization also reduces prices through greater competition and increasing returns to scale.

The potential global welfare gains from eliminating remaining trade barriers after the Uruguay Round are substantial (see the Table). The calculations suggest that full merchandise trade liberalization in 2005 would yield annual welfare gains between $146 and $489 billion (½ to ¾ percent of GDP) for industrial countries and between $108 billion and $188 billion (1¼ to 3 percent of GDP) for developing countries. As a percent of GDP, the gains for developing countries are larger compared to industrial countries because their trade barriers and associated distortions are, on average, significantly higher.

The simulation results are also consistent with one of the basic results from international trade theory: countries gain from trade under almost any conditions and the largest welfare gains from trade liberalization accrue to the countries that actually liberalize rather than to their trading partners. For example, according to GTAP model-based simulations, if only developing countries were to liberalize fully their merchandise trade regime in 2005 (post-Uruguay Round), they would reap annual welfare gains of $65 billion compared to $108 billion with worldwide full liberalization, that is, about 60 percent of the gains.[4]

Turning to the gains from worldwide trade liberalization by sector, free trade in agricultural products would yield important welfare benefits for developing countries according to both

---

[3]See Brown and others (2001) for the simulations and look for the model on the Internet at www.ford-school.umich.edu/rsie/model.

[4]Two recent papers by Zarazaga (1999, 2000) that survey the quantitative welfare benefits from unilateral trade liberalization in individual countries confirm that welfare gains are typically substantial when compared to those from multilateral or regional trade liberalization.

---

[1]IMF (2001a) summarizes the current state of trade restrictions in the world economy.

[2]See Anderson and others (2000) for the simulations and Hertel (1997) on the model.

Box 2.3 *(concluded)*

Welfare Gains from Post-Uruguay Round Trade Liberalization[1]
(In billions of U.S. dollars at 1995 exchange rates and prices)

| | Types of Products Liberalized | | | | |
	Agricultural	Manufacturing	All merchandise	Services	All
GTAP Model					
Industrial countries	122	24	146	. . .	. . .
Developing countries[2]	46	63	108	. . .	. . .
World	168	87	254	. . .	. . .
Michigan Model					
Industrial countries	7	482	489	998	1,487
Developing countries[2]	26	162	188	182	370
World	33	644	677	1,181	1,857

Sources: Anderson and others (2000); and Brown and others (2001).
[1]Figures may not add up because of rounding.
[2]Including newly industrialized countries in Asia, which are classified as advanced countries in the *World Economic Outlook*.

models, especially for the low-income developing countries, which would gain most from progress in this domain (see IMF, 2001a). Similarly, both models imply that, for developing countries as a whole, the welfare gains from worldwide liberalization of trade in manufactures would exceed those from agricultural products, reflecting the increasing importance of manufacturing exports in larger and more advanced developing countries.

For industrial countries, the results of the models differ. Simulations based on the GTAP model suggest that the most important welfare gains from merchandise trade liberalization would result from eliminating restrictions on trade in agricultural products, because trade barriers and subsidies remain high. The welfare gains from eliminating the already low import tariffs on manufactures (except for textiles and apparel) would be small. The Michigan Model, in contrast, suggests that the removal of import tariffs for manufactures could generate important welfare gains in advanced economies because of increased competitive pressures and scale effects. At the same time, the model predicts much smaller welfare gains from liberalizing trade in agricultural goods because of welfare losses experienced by net agricultural exporters, as the redirection of resources to agriculture lowers competition and raises prices in manufacturing and services. However,

the simulations likely underestimate the gains from liberalizing trade in agriculture because the simulated policy change does not include the elimination of subsidies to agriculture and because of some specific modeling assumptions.

Removing barriers to trade in services in the new round would increase the global welfare gain considerably in view of the dominant role of the services sectors in most economies and the typically still large trade barriers in these sectors. The results from the Michigan Model simulations, which include services, suggest that these gains would be about twice as large as those from merchandise trade liberalization in the case of industrial countries and would be about equal for developing countries.

Overall, the simulation results suggest important welfare gains for all countries from further post-Uruguay Round multilateral trade liberalization, even though the dynamic gains from trade are not taken into account. The gains differ across countries depending on the type of products included in the liberalization package. Given these differences, the inclusion of a wide range of sectors in the new trade round will be important for its success, because it will allow for the concessions among trade negotiators that will be needed to overcome resistance against further liberalization from vested interests.

Box 2.4. Critics of a New Trade Round

Critics of a new trade round raise two main concerns. The first is that globalization—and particularly trade liberalization—has widened the gap between rich and poor, so that the benefits are not fairly shared. The second is that, with the decline in protection at the border, the focus of trade negotiations has shifted to the realm of domestic policy, limiting the scope for governments to address social problems that arise.

Has Globalization Widened the Gap Between Rich and Poor?

There is a perception that open trade and the process of globalization are widening the gap between the rich and the poor, both within and across countries. Within industrial countries, globalization has been viewed with concern because it is thought to reduce relative wages and employment opportunities of unskilled workers. The substantial body of research on this issue generally finds that import competition *per se* has had a relatively small effect on the relative wages of unskilled workers in industrial countries. Instead, such workers have been mainly affected by technological change and migration (for a review of the evidence, see Burtless and others, 1998). That said, the adverse effects of labor market developments on unskilled workers, from whatever source, underlines the need for continued attention to social safety nets and education.

Turning to the international dimension, the balance of evidence strongly suggests that openness to trade stimulates growth.[1] While for many developing countries the income gap has widened relative to industrial countries, a group of successful integrators is catching up with the rich countries by combining openness with stable macroeconomic conditions, limited govern-

ment interference, and institutional and infrastructure investment.[2] A recent study by Dollar and Kraay (2001) of post-1980 integrators confirms these findings and provides evidence on within-country equity. The study examines a group of countries that have increased trade as a share of GDP substantially over the past 20 years, including China, Hungary, India, Malaysia, Mexico, the Philippines, and Thailand, and that account for over half of the population of the developing world. These countries introduced reforms in many areas as they opened up to trade, including protection of property rights and universal education, and have seen their economic performance improve substantially, narrowing the gap with rich countries, reducing poverty rates, and, as a group, avoiding any systematic increase in within-country inequality.

These and other studies provide significant evidence that increased openness to trade can assist countries in the context of an overall development strategy to improve economic performance and thus raise living standards. In contrast to the successful integrators, the poor economic performance of many of the countries that have fallen behind reflects a combination of poor policies, high indebtedness, weak institutions, and protection at home and abroad, often exacerbated by civil strife and poor initial circumstances. Helping these countries take advantage of trade for growth and development is a major challenge facing the international community. An essential ingredient of strategies to assist them is the removal of trade barriers, particularly in the areas most important for their development: agriculture, textiles and clothing, labor-intensive manufactures, and labor-based services. A new trade round would provide the opportunity for industrial and developing countries to jointly make progress in these areas. To

[1]See for example, Frankel and Romer (1999); Coe, Helpman, and Hoffmaister (1997); and Bhagwati and Srinivasan (1999). Rodriguez and Rodrik (2000) dispute the empirical evidence on the causal link from trade policies to growth, instead emphasizing institutional development.

[2]See *World Economic Outlook*, Chapter IV, May 1997, which also finds that openness without complementary reforms does not raise growth; and World Bank (1996).

Box 2.4 *(concluded)*

benefit from improved market access, these countries will also need to strengthen their own policies. In addition, much greater assistance (aid for trade) from their development partners will be needed to help them build the capacity to trade and to participate effectively in the WTO.

Are Trade-Rules Encroaching on Domestic Policy Space?

The essence of the WTO (and the earlier General Agreement on Tariffs and Trade) is that it incorporates a rules-based trading system with a dispute settlement mechanism and sanctions for transgressors alongside a mechanism for the negotiation of progressive liberalization of trade. As barriers to trade "at the border" have come down, other obstacles to trade that increasingly touch on domestic policy have become relevant, such as industrial subsidies and intellectual property rights (incorporated in past negotiations) and, more recently, investment and competition policies. While many find this trend necessary for trade rules to remain relevant, others find it contentious, particularly as it touches on wider social issues and impinges on areas traditionally left to domestic decision-making processes.

In this context, some industrial-country-based interest groups argue that there is a need for greater international coordination or convergence of rules, to temper the pressure toward unfettered free trade and avoid a destructive "race to the bottom." In their view, without such protection, companies looking for a competitive advantage will lower costs by moving to low-income countries with limited legal protection for workers and looser environmental standards. As indicated earlier, existing evidence does not support the thesis that opening up to trade generally degrades domestic institutions (see also Bhagwati and Hudec, 1996). In addition, there is an issue of whether trade rules are the ideal vehicle for accomplishing strengthened environmental and labor standards, which are not directly trade issues. A better-targeted approach, avoiding the threat of trade sanctions that would adversely affect workers in the relevant industries, would center on cooperative efforts through specialized means and institutions. Finally, and most important, using the trade system to enforce uniform standards in these areas can impose costs on developing countries that undermine their competitiveness and comparative advantage, reducing aggregate welfare and acting as a form of trade protection.

Indeed, and in contrast, many nongovernmental organizations (NGOs) and developing countries argue that in a number of areas existing trade rules are already too stringent and should be modified to provide greater flexibility to individual countries, consistent with their capabilities and stage of development. They suggest that the rich countries dominate trade negotiations and set the rules in their own interest and point to the costs of raising regulatory and other standards to industrial country norms, as well as the impact of rules on intellectual property rights on such issues as local production of cheap medicines to fight devastating diseases, such as AIDS. While there is merit in many of these specific suggestions for more flexibility, at a fundamental level it should be recognized that a rules-based system tends to protect the weak against the powerful—developing countries that have taken cases to the WTO's dispute settlement process have generally been successful—and that, for example, protection of intellectual property rights spurs innovation.

Given the contentious nature of the debate on trade policies and rules, and the complex web of costs and benefits that arises from them, the most legitimate way of resolving such differences is through a new trade round. Direct negotiations between governments representing their citizens' interests is the best way to revise and develop a trading system that strikes an appropriate balance between the advantages of a rules-based trading system—one that meets the needs of a continuously integrating world economy—and the legitimate desire for freedom to pursue economic policies and social goals and make decisions at the national level.

consultations to prepare for the upcoming ministerial meeting, something that was crucially lacking in the run-up to Seattle. Finally, concrete steps have been taken by some industrial countries to grant duty- and quota-free access to their markets (European Union, New Zealand and Norway), or to grant enhanced concessions under their Generalized System of Preferences.

In addition, progress is being made under the mandated built-in agenda, and discussions in services and agriculture have now been brought to a point where the "true bargaining" (i.e., the exchange of concessions) can take place. However, progress on negotiations in these areas is unlikely until a broader new negotiating agenda is agreed and set in motion.

The Run-Up to the Doha Ministerial Conference

Prospects for a new trade round have improved in view of recent progress although substantial challenges remain to bringing all parties to the table. Advocates of a "comprehensive" round (the European Union and Japan) seem to be ready to show greater flexibility in their approach. In a revised version of its proposed agenda, the EU Commission recognizes that its initial agenda (presented before Seattle) was too ambitious in the new areas, and not ambitious enough on market access and the implementation of existing agreements.[43] The Commission now proposes that agreements on the new issues could be plurilateral, and shows a more positive attitude toward market access, both in agriculture and non-agricultural products.[44] The Commission also stands ready to tackle other issues of concern to developing countries, such as the rules on antidumping, and to lower its expectations in areas such as the environment.

Developing countries, led by the so-called like-minded group, which includes India, Pakistan, Malaysia, and Egypt, have been reluctant to come to the table until they see progress on implementation issues and "tangible" improvements in market access from commitments in the previous round, particularly in areas such as agriculture and textiles and clothing, where they have a comparative advantage. They are most likely to support an agenda oriented toward further liberalization in those sectors, and one that takes into account tariff peaks and tariff escalation in all sectors, as well as subsidies on agricultural products. A key question for most developing countries is how far beyond core market access issues they will be ready to go, in particular regarding the new issues such as investment, competition policies, and the environment.

Another unknown factor is the position of the United States with respect to the negotiations. The government has made frequent statements in support of the launch of a new round in Doha, and has signaled its willingness to consider the extension of talks beyond the mandated built-in agenda. However, it is unclear how broad an agenda the United States would support. The prospects for obtaining trade promotion authority from the U.S. Congress, and the conditions that could be attached, are also uncertain.

Finally, there is a growing consensus that the agenda has to address the needs and concerns of the developing countries and encourage their full participation. This includes not only market access opportunities, but also complementary assistance for capacity building. In this regard, the United States and the European Union have stated in a joint communiqué that they are committed to the launch of a new round that will "equally address the needs and priorities of developing countries, demonstrate that the trading system can respond to the concerns of civil society, and promote sustainable development."[45] They are ready to reinforce and improve the

---

[43]European Commission, "State of Play and Strategy for the New Round," January 2001, available on the Internet at http://www.europa.eu.int.

[44]Plurilateral agreements, a feature of the GATT system, provide for limited and flexible participation in contrast to the "single undertaking" of the Uruguay Round.

[45]Joint statement issued in Göteborg, June 14, 2001.

provision of technical assistance to build capacity in the poorer countries to implement agreements and to support negotiations, and they will make efforts to secure the early accession of candidate countries to the WTO, especially the poorer countries. They have also pledged to work to improve the dispute settlement system for all countries in the WTO.

Conclusion

A successful, ambitious round of multilateral trade negotiations would result in major benefits for the world economy. A round would contribute to the restoration of market confidence and create new export opportunities; strengthen the multilateral trading system, which was debilitated after Seattle; and stimulate economic reforms by encouraging countries to extend regional liberalization to all WTO members. A new round could thus contribute substantially to global economic growth over the longer term. The potential welfare gains from eliminating remaining trade barriers on merchandise trade are considerable—ranging from $250 billion to $680 billion a year, excluding dynamic effects. About one-third of these gains would accrue to developing countries, more than twice the annual flow of aid to these countries. The gains from the liberalization of services are likely to be even larger given the size of this sector, its importance in overall competitiveness, and still high protection.

A new round should be sufficiently broad in scope to allow for trade-offs across sectors and issues. The goals for market access should be ambitious, aiming for substantial reduction or elimination of trade barriers where remaining protection is highest—agriculture, labor-intensive manufactures, and services. Both industrial and developing countries stand to gain substantially from liberalization in these areas. To facilitate free and nondiscriminatory trade, multilat-

eral trade rules need to be clarified and strengthened, particularly in areas susceptible to capture by protectionist interests (e.g., antidumping and other safeguard measures, health, safety, and environmental standards) and the dispute settlement mechanism further developed. The full participation of all WTO members in the development of the rules-based trading system is essential, and trade agreements should provide for flexibility in implementing commitments, recognizing the capacity constraints and development needs of the poorer countries.

The failure to make tangible progress toward a new round of trade negotiations would reduce confidence in the multilateral trading system and the commitment to further trade liberalization.[46] Lacking a broader context that would allow for concessions, negotiations in agriculture and services under the built-in agenda could languish. While there was no resort to protectionism after the financial crises of the late 1990s and the failure of the Seattle Ministerial Conference, protectionist pressures will be much more difficult to contain if the world economy slows down for a sustained period of time and there is little prospect of advancing on the multilateral trade front. Failure to continue to develop the rules and the dispute settlement procedures, and to thereby give confidence to trading partners and their major constituencies that the multilateral system remains relevant and responsive, could erode support for it. In this environment, increased resort to regional trading arrangements could ultimately have adverse consequences for the world economy. The GATT/WTO was created precisely to prevent the emergence of hostile trading blocks. In the absence of a new round, the primacy of multilateralism over regionalism may be threatened, a development that would be particularly detrimental to the poorest countries, which could be further marginalized.

---

[46]The first 50 years of the multilateral trading system saw almost continuous multilateral negotiations. The Tokyo Round was completed in 1979 and the Uruguay Round launched in 1986, after a series of Ministerial Conferences in 1982–86 that gradually developed the design for it. The Uruguay Round negotiations were completed in late 1993, almost eight years ago.

References

Agénor, Pierre-Richard, John McDermott, and Eswar Prasad, 2000, "Macroeconomic Fluctuations in Developing Countries: Some Stylized Facts," *The World Bank Economic Review*, Vol. 14 (May), pp. 251–85.

Ahmed, Shaghil, and Prakash N. Loungani, forthcoming, "Business Cycles in Asia," IMF Working Paper (Washington: International Monetary Fund).

Albuquerque, Rui, 2001, "The Composition of International Capital Flows: Risk Sharing Through Foreign Direct Investment" (unpublished; Rochester, New York: University of Rochester).

Anderson, Kym, Joe Francois, Thomas W. Hertel, Bernard Hoekman, and Will Martin, 2000, "Potential Gains from Trade Reform in the New Millennium," paper presented at the Third Annual Conference on Global Economic Analysis, Monash University, Mt. Eliza, Australia, June.

Arora, Vivek, and Martin Cerisola, 2000, "How Does U.S. Monetary Policy Influence Economic Conditions in Emerging Markets?" IMF Working Paper No. 00/148 (Washington: International Monetary Fund).

Artis, Michael J., and Wenda Zhang, 1999, "Further Evidence on the International Business Cycle and the ERM: Is There a European Business Cycle?" *Oxford Economic Papers*, Vol. 51 (January), pp. 120–32.

Avery, Christopher, and Peter Zemsky, 1998, "Multidimensional Uncertainty and Herd Behavior in Financial Markets," *American Economic Review*, Vol. 88 (September), pp. 724–48.

Baxter, Marianne, and Robert G. King, 1999, "Measuring Business Cycles: Approximate Band-Pass Filters for Economic Time Series," *Review of Economics and Statistics*, Vol. 81 (November), pp. 575–93.

Baxter, Marianne, and Michael Kouparitsas, 2000, "What Causes Fluctuations in the Terms of Trade?" NBER Working Paper No. 7462 (Cambridge, Massachusetts: National Bureau of Economic Research).

Bhagwati, Jagdish, 1978, *Foreign Trade Regimes and Economic Development: Anatomy and Consequences of Exchange Control Regimes* (Cambridge, Mass.: Ballinger).

Bhagwati, Jagdish, and Robert Hudec, 1996, *Fair Trade and Harmonization: Prerequisites for Free Trade?* (Cambridge, Mass.: MIT Press).

Bhagwati, Jagdish, and T.N. Srinivasan, 1999, "Outward-Orientation and Development: Are Revisionists Right?" Discussion Paper No. 806 (New Haven: Yale University, Economic Growth Center).

Bikhchandani, Sushil, David Hirshleifer, and Ivo Welch, 1998, "Learning from the Behavior of Others: Conformity, Fads and Informational Cascades," *Journal of Economic Perspectives*, Vol.12 (summer), pp. 151–70.

Brown, Drusilla K., Alan V. Deardorff, and Robert M. Stern, 2001, "CGE Modeling and Analysis of Multilateral and Regional Negotiating Options," Discussion Paper No. 468 (Ann Arbor: University of Michigan, Research Seminar in International Economics).

Bulir, Ales, and Javier Hamann, forthcoming, "How Volatile and Predictable Are Aid Flows, and What Are the Policy Implications?" IMF Working Paper (Washington: International Monetary Fund).

Burtless, Gary, Robert Z. Lawrence, Robert E. Litan, Robert J. Shapiro, 1998, *Globaphobia*, (Washington, D.C.: The Brookings Institution).

Camen, Ulrich, 1987, "Concepts and Measurement of World Business Cycles," (unpublished; Geneva, Switzerland: The Graduate Institute of International Studies).

Canova, Fabio, and Harris Dellas, 1993, "Trade Interdependence and the International Business Cycle," *Journal of International Economics*, Vol. 34 (February), pp. 23–47.

Canova, Fabio, and Jane Marrinan, 1998, "Sources and Propagation of International Output Cycles: Common Shocks or Transmission?" *Journal of International Economics*, Vol. 46 (October), pp. 133–66.

Clark, Todd E., and Kwanho Shin, 1998, "The Sources of Fluctuations Within and Across Countries," Research Working Paper No. 98–04 (Kansas City, Missouri: Federal Reserve Bank of Kansas City).

Coe, David T., Elhanan Helpman, and Alexander W. Hoffmaister, 1997, "North-South R&D Spillovers," *Economic Journal*, Vol. 107 (January), pp. 134–49.

Dahlquist, Magnus, Peter Hördahl, and Peter Sellin, 2000, "Measuring International Volatility Spillovers," in *International Financial Markets and the Implications for Monetary and Financial Stability*, BIS Conference Papers Vol. 8 (Basel: Bank for International Settlements).

Deaton, Angus, 1999, "Commodity Prices and Growth in Africa," *Journal of Economic Perspectives*, Vol. 13 (summer), pp. 23–40.

———, and Robert Miller, 1995, "International Commodity Prices, Macroeconomic Performance, and Politics in Sub-Saharan Africa," *Studies in International Finance*, No. 79 (Princeton: Princeton University, Department of Economics).

De Santis, Giorgio, and Bruno Gerard, 1997, "International Asset Pricing and Portfolio Diversification with Time-Varying Risk," *Journal of Finance*, Vol. 52 (December), pp. 1881–1912.

Dollar, David, and Aart Kraay, 2001, "Trade, Growth, and Poverty," Policy Research Paper No. 2587 (Washington: World Bank).

Dumas, Bernard, Campbell R. Harvey, and Pierre Ruiz, 2000, "Are Common Swings in International Stock Returns Justified by Subsequent Changes in National Outputs?" INSEAD Working Paper No. 2000/02 FIN (Fontainebleau, France: INSEAD).

Edwards, Sebastian, 1998, "Openness, Productivity and Growth: What Do we Really Know?" *Economic Journal*, Vol. 108 (March), pp. 383–98.

Feenstra, Robert C., 1995, "Estimating the Effects of Trade Policy," in *Handbooks in International Economics*, Vol. 3, ed. by Gene M. Grossman, and Kenneth Rogoff, (Amsterdam: Elsevier, North-Holland).

Forni, Mario, Marc Hallin, Marco Lippi, and Lucrezia Reichlin, 2000, "The Generalized Dynamic Factor Model: Identification and Estimation," *The Review of Economics and Statistics*, Vol. 82 (November), pp. 540–54.

Frankel, Jeffrey A., and David Romer, 1999, "Does Trade Cause Growth?" *American Economic Review*, Vol. 89 (June), pp. 379–99.

Frankel, Jeffrey A., and Andrew K. Rose, 1998, "The Endogeneity of the Optimum Currency Area Criteria," *Economic Journal*, Vol. 108 (July), pp. 1009–25.

Froot, Kenneth, Paul O'Connell, and Mark Seasholes, 2001, "The Portfolio Flows of International Investors," *Journal of Financial Economics*, Vol. 59 (February), pp. 151–93.

Gerlach, H. M. Stefan, 1988, "World Business Cycles under Fixed and Flexible Exchange Rates," *Journal of Money, Credit, and Banking*, Vol. 20 (November), pp. 621–32.

Gourinchas, Pierre-Olivier, Rodrigo Valdés, and Oscar Landerretche, 2001, "Lending Booms: Latin America and the World," NBER Working Paper No. 8249 (Cambridge, Mass.: National Bureau of Economic Research).

Gregory, Allan W., and Allen C. Head, 1999, "Common and Country-Specific Fluctuations in Productivity, Investment, and the Current Account," *Journal of Monetary Economics*, Vol. 44 (December), pp. 423–51.

———, and Jacques Raynauld, 1997, "Measuring World Business Cycles," *International Economic Review*, Vol. 38 (August), pp. 677–701.

Haberler, Gottfried, 1958, *Prosperity and Depression, A Theoretical Analysis of Cyclical Movements* (Cambridge, Mass.: Harvard University Press, 4th ed.).

Head, Allen, 1995, "Country Size, Aggregate Fluctuations, and International Risk Sharing," *Canadian Journal of Economics*, Vol. 28 (November), pp. 1096–1119.

Hertel, Thomas W., ed., 1997, *Global Trade Analysis: Modeling and Applications*, (Cambridge, U.K. and New York: Cambridge University Press).

Hoffmaister, Alexander, Jorge Roldós, and Peter Wickham, 1998, "Macroeconomic Fluctuations in Sub-Saharan Africa," *IMF Staff Papers*, International Monetary Fund, Vol. 45 (March), pp. 132–60.

Imbs, Jean, 1999, "Co-Fluctuations," CEPR Discussion Paper No. 2267 (London: Centre for Economic Policy Research).

IMF, 2000, *Results of the 1997 Coordinated Portfolio Investment Survey* (Washington: International Monetary Fund Committee on Balance of Payments Statistics).

———, 2001a, "Market Access for Developing Countries' Exports," (Washington: International Monetary Fund). Available on the Internet at http://www.imf.org/external/np/madc/eng/042701.htm.

———, 2001b, *International Capital Markets: Developments, Prospects, and Key Policy Issues*, World Economic and Financial Surveys (Washington: International Monetary Fund).

———, 2001c, *World Economic Outlook*, May 2001, *Fiscal Policy and Macroeconomic Stability*, World Economic and Financial Surveys (Washington: International Monetary Fund).

Kirmani, Naheed, Nur Calika, Richard Harmsen, Michael Leidy, Arvind Subramannin, and Peter Uimonen, 1994, *"International Trade Policies: The Uruguay Round and Beyond,"* Vol. 2, World Economic and Financial Surveys (Washington: International Monetary Fund).

Kontolemis, Zenon G., and Hossein Samiei, 2000, "The U.K. Business Cycle, Monetary Policy and EMU Entry," IMF Working Paper No. 00/210 (Washington: International Monetary Fund).

Kose, Ayhan, forthcoming, "Explaining Business Cycles in Small Open Economies: How Much Do World Prices Matter?" *Journal of International Economics.*

———, and Raymond Riezman, 2001, "Trade Shocks and Macroeconomic Fluctuations in Africa," *Journal of Development Economics,* Vol. 65 (June), pp. 55–88.

Kose, Ayhan, and Kei-Mu Yi, 2001, "International Trade and Business Cycles: Is Vertical Specialization the Missing Link?" *American Economic Review,* Vol. 91 (May), pp. 371–75.

Kose, Ayhan, Christopher Otrok, and Charles Whiteman, 2000, "International Business Cycles: World, Region, and Country-Specific Factors," (unpublished; Iowa City: University of Iowa, Department of Economics).

Kouparitsas, Michael, 1996, "North-South Business Cycle," Working Paper 96–9 (Chicago: Federal Reserve Bank of Chicago).

Kumar, Manmohan S., and Avinash Persaud, forthcoming, "Investor Risk Appetite and Contagion Effects," IMF Working Paper (Washington: International Monetary Fund).

Kumar, Manmohan S., and Ken Kashiwase, forthcoming, "Spillovers in Business Confidence in Major Industrial Economies," IMF Working Paper (Washington: International Monetary Fund).

Kraay, Aart, and Jaume Ventura, 2001, "Comparative Advantage and the Cross-Section of Business Cycles," NBER Working Paper No. 8104 (Cambridge, Mass.: National Bureau of Economic Research).

Lewis, Karen K., 1999, "Trying to Explain Home Bias in Equities and Consumption," *Journal of Economic Literature,* Vol. 37 (June), pp. 571–608.

Loayza, Norman, Humberto Lopez, and Angel Ubide, 1999, "Sectorial Macroeconomic Interdependencies—Evidence for Latin America, East Asia and Europe," IMF Working Paper No. 99/11 (Washington: International Monetary Fund).

Longin, François, and Bruno Solnik, 1995, "Is the Correlation in International Equity Returns Constant: 1960–1990?" *Journal of International Money and Finance,* Vol. 14 (February), pp. 3–26.

Lumsdaine, Robin L., and Eswar S. Prasad, 1999, "Identifying the Common Component in International Economic Fluctuations: A New Approach," IMF Working Paper No. 99/154 (Washington: International Monetary Fund).

McDermott, C. John, and Alasdair Scott, 2000, "Concordance in Business Cycles," IMF Working Paper No. 00/37 (Washington: International Monetary Fund).

Mendoza, Enrique, 1995, "The Terms of Trade, the Real Exchange Rate, and Economic Fluctuations," *International Economic Review,* Vol. 36 (February), pp. 101–137.

———, 2001, "Credit, Prices, and Crashes: Business Cycles with a Sudden Stop," NBER Working Paper No. 8338 (Cambridge, Mass.: National Bureau of Economic Research).

Montiel, Peter, and Carmen Reinhart, 2001, "The Dynamics of Capital Movements to Emerging Economies During the 1990s," in *Short-Term Capital Flows and Economic Crises,* ed. by Stephany Griffith-Jones, Manuel Montes, and Anwar Nasution (New York: Oxford University Press).

Mussa, Michael, 2000, "Factors Driving Global Economic Integration," paper presented at a symposium sponsored by The Federal Reserve Bank of Kansas City on "Global Opportunities and Challenges," Jackson Hole, Wyoming, August 25, 2000.

Obstfeld, Maurice, and Kenneth Rogoff, 2000, "The Six Major Puzzles in International Macroeconomics: Is There a Common Cause?" NBER Working Paper No. 7777 (Cambridge, Mass.: National Bureau of Economic Research).

Pallage, Stéphane, and Michael Robe, forthcoming, "Foreign Aid and the Business Cycle," *Review of International Economics.*

Poterba, James M., 2000, "Stock Market Wealth and Consumption," *Journal of Economic Perspectives,* Vol. 14 (spring), pp. 99–118.

Razin, Assaf, and Andrew Rose, 1994, "Business-Cycle Volatility and Openness: An Exploratory Cross-Sectional Analysis," in *Capital Mobility: The Impact on Consumption, Investment and Growth,* ed. by Leonardo Leiderman and Assaf Razin (New York: Cambridge University Press).

Rodriguez, Francisco, and Dani Rodrik, 2000, "Trade Policy and Economic Growth: A Skeptic's Guide to Cross-National Evidence," in *NBER Macroeconomics Annual 2000,* ed. by Ben Bernanke and Kenneth Rogoff (Cambridge, Mass.: MIT Press).

Rodrik, Dani, 1999, *The New Global Economy and Developing Countries: Making Openness Work,* (Washington: Overseas Development Council).

Romer, Paul, 1994, "New Goods, Old Theory, and the Welfare Costs of Trade Restrictions," *Journal of Development Economics,* Vol. 43, pp. 5–38

Sachs, Jeffrey, and Andrew Warner, 1995, "Economic Reform and the Process of Global Integration," *Brookings Papers on Economic Activity: 1*, pp. 1–118.

Shiller, Robert J., 1998, "Human Behavior and the Efficiency of the Financial System," NBER Working No. Paper 6375 (Cambridge, Mass.: National Bureau of Economic Research).

Stulz, Rene, 1995, "International Portfolio Choice and Asset Pricing," in *Finance*, ed. by Robert A. Jarrow, Vojislav Maksimovic, and William T. Ziemba (Amsterdam: North Holland).

———, 1999, "International Portfolio Flows and Securities Markets," in *International Capital Flows*, ed. by Martin Feldstein (Chicago: University of Chicago Press).

Swoboda, Alexander K., 1983, "Exchange Rate Regimes and European-U.S. Policy Interdependence," *Staff Papers*, International Monetary Fund, Vol. 30 (March), pp. 75–112.

Tesar, Linda L., and Ingrid M. Werner, 1995, "Home Bias and High Turnover," *Journal of International Money and Finance*, Vol. 14 (August), pp. 467–92.

Vamvakidis, Athanasios, 1999, "Regional Trade Agreements or Broad Liberalization: Which Path Leads to Faster Growth?" *IMF Staff Papers*, Vol. 46 (March), pp. 42–68.

World Bank, 1996, *Global Economic Prospects and the Developing Countries* (Washington: World Bank).

———, 2000, *Trade Blocs* (Washington: World Bank).

Zarazaga, Carlos E. J. M., 1999, "Measuring the Benefits of Unilateral Trade Liberalization Part 1: Static Models," Economic and Financial Review, Third Quarter (Dallas: Federal Reserve Bank of Dallas).

———, 2000, "Measuring the Benefits of Unilateral Trade Liberalization Part 2: Dynamic Models," Economic and Financial Review, First Quarter (Dallas: Federal Reserve Bank of Dallas).

THE INFORMATION TECHNOLOGY REVOLUTION

The world is in the midst of an all-purpose technological revolution based on information technology (IT), defined here as computers, computer software, and telecommunications equipment. The macroeconomic benefits of the IT revolution are already apparent in some economies, especially the United States. Historical experience has shown that such revolutions have often been accompanied by financial booms and busts, and the IT revolution has been no exception. But, while spending on IT goods is likely to remain weak in the immediate future, as past overinvestment unwinds, the longer-term benefits for the global economy are likely to continue, or even accelerate, in the years to come.

While technological change is an ongoing process, there are periods during which technological progress is especially rapid, resulting in new products and falling prices of existing products that have widespread uses in the rest of the economy. Such periods are generally identified with all-purpose technological revolutions. Earlier examples include textiles production and steam power in the industrial revolution, railroads in the nineteenth century, and electricity in the early twentieth century (the automobile could also be included, but its development was relatively gradual). The effects of such revolutions have generally occurred in three (often overlapping) main stages. First, technological change raises productivity growth in the innovating sector; second, falling prices encourage capital deepening; and, finally, there can be significant reorganization of production around the capital goods that embody the new technology.

At the core of the current IT revolution are advances in materials science, leading to increases in the power of semiconductors, in turn resulting in rapidly declining semiconductor prices (Figure 3.1). Over the past four decades, the capacity of semiconductor chips has doubled

Figure 3.1. United States: Relative Prices of Information Technology Goods[1]
(1999:Q1 = 100; logarithmic scale)

Steep declines in the prices of computer components, such as microprocessors, have led to persistent declines in computer prices.

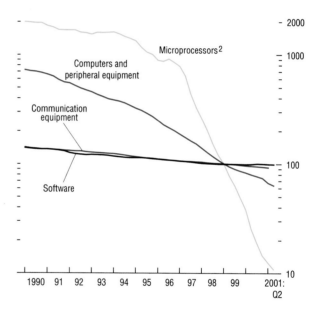

Sources: U.S. Commerce Department, Bureau of Economic Analysis for investment price deflators of computers and peripheral equipment, communication equipment, and software. U.S. Department of Labor, Bureau of Labor Statistics, for producer price index of microprocessors.
[1]Relative to the GDP deflator.
[2]Microprocessor (semiconductor) price indices do not hold quality constant prior to 1997, failing to capture the rapid decline in quality adjusted prices.

Figure 3.2. Information Technology Investment in the United States[1]
(Four-quarter percent change)

Investment in computers, software, and communication equipment grew at extraordinary rates during the 1990s.

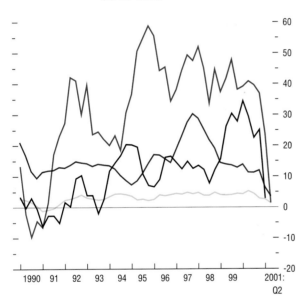

Source: U.S. Department of Commerce, Bureau of Economic Analysis.
[1]Real gross fixed investment.

roughly every 18–24 months—a phenomenon known as "Moore's Law," after a prediction made in 1965 by Gordon Moore, then Research Director at Fairchild Semiconductor. Cheaper semiconductors have allowed rapid advances in the production of computers, computer software, and telecommunications equipment, leading to steep price declines in these industries as well. The rapidly falling prices of goods that embody IT have stimulated extraordinary investment in these goods, resulting in significant capital deepening (Figure 3.2). This capital deepening has led, in some countries, to an acceleration in overall productivity growth and may be encouraging changes in the organization of production, which could lead to further improvements in productivity growth.

This chapter focuses on the macroeconomic consequences of the IT revolution, including lessons from past all-purpose technological revolutions, the impact on productivity growth, the distribution of the benefits between producers and users, the consequences for the business cycle and financial markets, and implications for macroeconomic policies.[1] In assessing these consequences, the chapter concentrates on the countries most involved in the IT revolution: the advanced economies and those emerging economies in Asia that are major producers of IT equipment (Figure 3.3).[2]

Past All-Purpose Technological Revolutions

The main all-purpose technological revolutions in the past have been textiles production, steam power, railroads, and electricity.[3] Past revo-

---

[1]The chapter examines the role of IT goods in investment, as personal consumption of IT goods is just a small fraction of private gross fixed capital spending on IT goods (about 7 percent in the United States in 2000).

[2]For more cross-country comparisons of IT production and use, see OECD (2000).

[3]This section draws extensively on Crafts (2001), which was commissioned for the *World Economic Outlook.* These points are consistent with the work of other economic historians, including David (1990 and 2000), DeLong (2001), and White (1990).

lutions have clearly yielded large benefits, though measurement difficulties associated with new or improved goods abound, and economic historians have had to adjust retrospectively for quality changes (Table 3.1). For example, railroads offered clear benefits in the form of faster and more comfortable travel. Yet the price of rail travel was often higher than the alternative, so it is important to account for the quality of a new service, such as speed and comfort, in calculating the gains from the invention of railroads.

Information technology has a number of striking similarities with past revolutions, but also some notable differences. Of the similarities, four stand out:

- The gains from the new technology initially came through the capital deepening caused by the fall in relative prices, but—when the efficiency gains from the reorganization of production were large—these benefits dominated in the long run. Table 3.1 shows that, in the case of the adoption of electricity in the United States, the contribution to growth was dominated by capital deepening over the initial period (1899–1919) but by gains from reorganization in usage at the end of the period (1919–1929).

- The initial gains were focused on industrial countries.[4] For example, Table 3.2 shows how railroads were initially adopted in the advanced economies of the day. Almost a century passed between the opening of the Liverpool and Manchester Railway in 1830 and the global adoption of railroads by 1920. However, as discussed below, there appears to be a difference in the rate of diffusion of IT to developing countries. In the very long run, the benefits depend on particular circumstances. For example, Table 3.3 shows that for freight transportation the eventual social savings were largest in Mexico, which largely lacked water transport.

[4]However, early users can also end up with significant costs if the technology gets superceded. For example, extensive canal systems were built in the United Kingdom and the United States, only to be made obsolete by the invention of railroads.

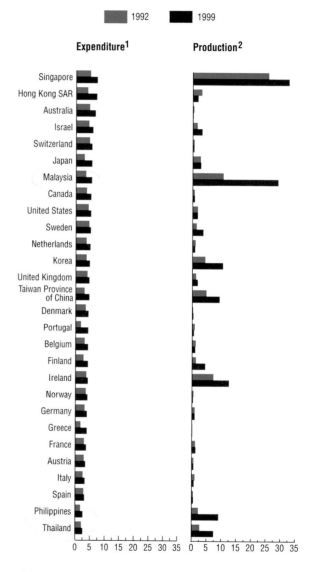

Figure 3.3. Information Technology (IT) Expenditure and Production
(Percent of GDP)

Spending on IT (as a share of GDP) is spread relatively evenly across countries, while IT production sectors are large in only a few economies.

Sources: WITSA (2001) for expenditure data; Reed Electronics Research (2001) for production; and IMF staff estimates.
[1]Information technology expenditure comprises hardware, software and telecommunications equipment.
[2]IT production comprises gross output of active components, electronic data processing equipment (adjusted for inputs of active components), and telecommunications equipment (adjusted for inputs of active components).

Table 3.1. Contribution of New Technology to Economic Growth
(Percent per year)

	Time Period	Capital Deepening	Technological Progress in Production	Technological Progress in Usage	Total
Steam—United Kingdom	1780–1860	0.19	. . .	0.32	0.51
Railroads—United Kingdom	1840–1870	0.13	0.10	. . .	0.23
	1870–1890	0.14	0.09	. . .	0.23
Railroads—United States	1839–1870	0.12	0.09	. . .	0.21
	1870–1890	0.32	0.24	. . .	0.56
Electricity—United States	1899–1919	0.34	0.07	—	0.41
	1919–1929	0.23	0.05	0.70	0.98
Information Technology—United States	1974–1990	0.52	0.17	. . .	0.69
	1991–1995	0.55	0.24	. . .	0.79
	1996–2000	1.36	0.50	. . .	1.86

Source: Crafts (2001). The estimates for information technology do not reflect the recent revisions to the U.S. national income and products accounts for 1998–2000.

Table 3.2. Railroad Mileage, 1840–1920
(Percent of world total)

	1840	1880	1920
North America	51.5	45.5	43.3
Europe	46.3	37.9	23.7
Rest of the world	2.2	16.6	33.0
World	100.0	100.0	100.0
Memorandum			
World (Thousands of miles)	5.49	220.76	674.89

Source: Woodruff (1966).

- The gains went largely to users, not producers. The benefits were mostly transferred to users through the fall in the relative price of goods embodying the new technology, while profits and wages in producing industries were rarely exceptional by comparison. The classic case is textiles production in the industrial revolution in Britain, where about half of the benefits from falling prices were exported via worsening terms of trade. Also, the new technology led to a reorganization of production, which marked the beginning of the factory system during the early phase of the industrial revolution. As these technological spillovers were localized, they helped maintain Britain's export competitiveness for many years.

- Technological revolutions have generally led to financial market excesses. The best documented cases are railroads and electricity. Figure 3.4 compares the paths of the stock prices of innovating firms, investment in goods embodying new technology, and real GDP in the "railway mania" in Britain in the 1840s and in the "IT mania" in the United States in recent years. As in other cases, while the collapse of the railroad bubble in the 1840s did not lead to an economy-wide recession, it did lead to significant consolidation in the industry.

There are also two important differences:

- The fall in the relative price of IT goods has been exceptionally sharp—there appears to be no historical equivalent to the sustained, rapid fall in semiconductor prices associated with Moore's Law.[5] As a result, while recognizing the difficulties of comparing data across historical episodes, the benefits of IT seem to be coming faster than those of previous all-purpose technological revolutions.

- Compared to past episodes, the production of goods embodying the new technology is much more globalized. This reflects the high price-to-weight ratio of IT goods, which makes them readily tradable. The

[5]For example, the real price of electricity in the United States fell by 7 percent per year between 1900–1920 (Brookes and Wahhaj, 2000), while the real (quality-adjusted) price of computers fell by 20 percent per year between 1990–2000.

Table 3.3. Social Savings from Railways[1]
(Percent of GNP)

	Year	Passenger	Freight
Brazil	1887	. . .	4.5
	1913	1.6	22.0
England and Wales	1865	. . .	4.1
	1890	. . .	10.2
India	1900	. . .	9.0
Mexico	1895	. . .	14.6
	1910	0.6	31.5
Russia	1907	1.0	4.6
Spain	1878	. . .	6.5
	1912	. . .	18.5
United States	1859	. . .	3.7
	1890	2.6	4.7–10.0

Source: Crafts (2001).
[1]Social savings measure benefits in terms of willingness to pay, that is, the area under the demand curve.

closest historical parallel is cotton textiles in the industrial revolution in Britain, where about half of production was exported.

Labor Productivity Growth

The rapidly growing literature on IT and labor productivity growth addresses two main issues: measurement problems and the contribution of IT to labor productivity growth.[6] New goods and rapidly falling relative prices complicate the measurement of output, and different countries use different statistical methodologies to address these issues. In some countries, hedonic methods are used to adjust prices for quality changes, while chain weighting is used to address the substitution bias in fixed-weight aggregation methods (Box 3.1). In addition, the coverage of the IT sector in official statistics is often inadequate: in most countries, national accounts simply do not distinguish IT production, investment, or consumption. Reflecting these problems, cross-country comparisons often use hedonic prices from the U.S. Bureau of Economic Analysis (adjusted for exchange rate changes)

[6]The idea that IT could contribute to labor productivity growth precedes the recently observed acceleration in productivity. See, for example, Kelkar (1982).

Figure 3.4. Initial Phase of Technological Revolutions
(Investment in percent of GDP and real GDP in annual percent change)

Both the railroad and information technology (IT) revolutions led to initial booms in stock prices and investment.

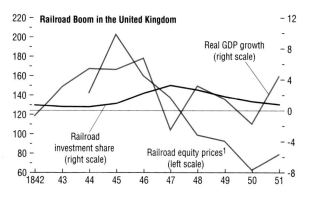

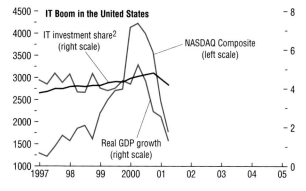

Sources: Hawke (1970) for railroad investment and Mitchell (1988) for GDP data.
[1]Railroad equity price is the average of the closing price in pounds sterling at the end end of July for four British railroad companies: London & North Western, Great Western Railway, London & Lancashire Railway, and the Midland Railway.
[2]Defined as private investment in information processing equipment and software.

Box 3.1. Measurement Issues

There are three important methodological issues in measuring the contribution of information technology (IT) to economic growth.[1] The first issue is how to adjust price indices for new goods and for improvements in the quality of existing goods. In the U.S. national accounts (and increasingly in other countries as well), the price deflators for many IT goods are based on hedonic price indices, which attempt to capture quality changes (see the Table). Hedonic price indices rely on the assumption that the value of a good is an aggregate of individual characteristics. Hence, the price of a new good can be based on the characteristics that it offers. Hedonic price equations for computers, for example, usually contain elements like the clock rate, RAM, and hard disk memory.

While hedonic methods are not a perfect way of adjusting prices for quality changes, they are more systematic than the available alternatives. For example, in Germany, the monetary value of quality changes is estimated on a case-by-case basis according to a set of rules, which may be difficult to apply in cases of extremely large quality changes and thus likely to understate the magnitude of the quality-adjusted price fall.[2] Given the highly tradable nature of IT goods, exchange-rate-adjusted hedonic prices in different countries often track each other closely, and at least two countries have opted to use the U.S. hedonic price index for computers, adjusted for exchange rate movements.

The impact of using hedonic methods on macroeconomic aggregates (in countries that do not already use them) will depend on the structure of production and demand. In IT-producing countries, measured real output of IT goods will tend to increase, boosting measured real GDP

Selected Economies: Features of National Accounts

	Hedonic Price Index for Computers	Chain Weights
Australia	Yes[1]	Yes
Belgium	No	No
Canada	Yes	Yes
China	No	No
Denmark	Yes[1]	No
Finland	No	No
France	Yes[2]	Yes
Germany	No	No
Hong Kong SAR	No	No
India	No	No
Indonesia	No	No
Ireland	No	No
Italy	No	No
Japan	Yes	No
Korea	No	No
Malaysia	No	No
Netherlands	No	Yes
Norway	No	Yes
Philippines	No	No
Singapore	No	No
Spain	No	No
Sweden	Yes	No
Taiwan Province of China	No	No
Thailand	No	No
United Kingdom	No	Yes
United States	Yes	Yes

Source: Gust and Marquez (2000) and national authorities.
[1]Uses U.S. hedonic index, adjusted for exchange rate movements
[2]Hedonic prices used for microcomputers only.

and real exports. As a result, the measured contribution of IT to growth (through TFP growth in the IT sector) will tend to rise. In IT-using countries, real investment in and real imports of IT goods will tend to increase, boosting the contribution of IT to growth through capital deepening and lowering the contribution of TFP growth.[3]

The second issue is how to aggregate the output of goods with large relative price changes. Goods with rapidly declining relative prices tend to be used in new ways with lower marginal product, so any fixed-weight aggregation method—such as the traditional Laspeyres index—will place inappropriately large weights on these rapidly-growing goods (substitution bias) and thus

---

[1]A fourth issue is that, given the high depreciation rates of many IT capital goods, it would be better to use net output to measure productivity. In the United States, real net domestic product (NDP) grew ¼ percent more slowly than real GDP between 1995–2000. See Landefeld and Fraumeni (2001).

[2]The deflator for IT equipment declined by about four-fifths between 1991–1999 in the United States, but only by about one-fifth in Germany. See Deutsche Bundesbank (2000).

[3]Schreyer (2001) finds that the impact of using hedonic prices (in advanced economies that do not already use them) on real GDP growth is small.

tend to overstate the growth of the aggregate. The further back the base year, the larger is the weight on these fast-growing goods and therefore the greater is the overstatement. This problem is well illustrated by the 1998 growth rate of fixed-weight real GDP in the United States: using 1995 base prices, it was 4.5 percent; using 1990 base prices, it was 6.5 percent; using 1980 base prices, it was 18.8 percent; and using 1970 base prices, it was 37.4 percent (Whelan, 2000).

To address the substitution bias in fixed-weight measures, an increasing number of countries calculate real aggregates using chain weights, based on prices that are updated every year. For example, the United States now aggregates across sectors using the so-called "ideal chain index" popularized by Irving Fisher.[4] The principal benefit of chain weights is that measured real GDP growth does not depend on some arbitrary price structure and is therefore independent of the choice of base year. The main drawback is that, except in the base year, the level of real GDP is not necessarily equal to the sum of its real components, because the weighting scheme takes account of shifting relative prices, and cannot be interpreted as the quantity of output had all prices remained fixed at their base period levels.

The final issue is how to allocate IT spending, especially software spending, between final and intermediate expenditure.[5] In general, business

spending on intermediate goods, which are fully incorporated into output, is subtracted from gross output to yield value added (to avoid double counting). Information technology spending is considered investment if, and only if, the corresponding products can be physically isolated, so that IT products embodied in equipment (such as microprocessors) are considered intermediate goods. In practice, the ratio of IT investment to IT intermediate consumption differs substantially across countries, reflecting different statistical practices in different countries (see Colecchia, 2001). For example, France asks buyers to classify their spending, while the United States relies on production data provided by sellers together with input-output tables. In countries that classify a larger proportion of business spending on IT goods as investment, measured GDP growth will be higher when such spending is rising rapidly.

Studies that compare the statistical methodologies used in France, Germany, and the United Kingdom to those used in the United States suggest that differences in the allocation of software spending between intermediate and final expenditure have the largest impact on measured output growth.[6] Differences in the allocation of software spending account for an annual growth differential of about 0.3 percentage points between France and the United States, which both use hedonic prices and chain weighting, while the combined effect of differences in quality adjustment, aggregation, and allocation of software spending accounts for an annual growth differential between both Germany and the United Kingdom, and the United States of about 0.4 percentage points.

---

[4]The real growth rate is calculated as the geometric average of the growth rates of a Paasche index (which uses current period prices as weights) and a Laspeyres index (which uses previous period prices as weights). See Landefeld and Parker (1998) and Vavares, Prakken, and Guirl (1998) for a description of the methodology and a discussion of related issues.

[5]The 1993 System of National Accounts (SNA93) stipulates that software purchases by firms should be considered investment expenditure.

[6]See Deutsche Bundesbank (2001), Lequiller (2001), and Wadhwani (2000).

and data on IT production and use from private sources, an approach also taken in this chapter.[7]

Information technology can contribute to labor productivity growth through both capital

---

[7]Expenditure data are from the World Information Technology Services Alliance (2001); production data are from Reed Electronics Research (2001). While the data from private sources cover a broad set of countries, they are not compiled in the same comprehensive manner as national accounts data.

Table 3.4. Contribution of Information Technology (IT) to the Acceleration in Productivity in the United States

	Gordon (2000)	Jorgenson and Stiroh (2000)	Oliner and Sichel (2000)	U.S. Council of Economic Advisers (2001)
Period under study	1995–1999	1995–1998	1995–1999	1995–2000
Acceleration in labor productivity	1.33	0.95	1.16	1.63
Capital deepening	0.33	0.29	0.33	0.38
IT-related	. . .	0.34	0.50	0.62
Other	. . .	−0.05	−0.17	−0.23
Total factor productivity growth	0.31	0.65	0.80	1.19
IT production	0.29	0.24	0.31	0.18
Rest of economy	0.02	0.41	0.49	1.00
Other factors	0.69	0.01	0.04	0.04
Cyclical effect	0.50	. . .	. . .	0.04
Price measurement	0.14	. . .	. . .	. . .
Labor quality	0.05	0.01	0.04	0.00

Source: Stiroh (2001) and U.S. Council of Economic Advisers (2001). See studies for data and methodological differences. The estimates do not reflect the recent revisions to the U.S. national income and products accounts, which were substantial for 2000.

deepening and total factor productivity (TFP) growth.[8] Capital deepening refers to the change in labor productivity attributable to higher levels of capital per worker. TFP growth refers to improvements in the efficiency with which capital and labor are combined to produce output. The existing literature has established that IT is contributing to labor productivity growth through both increases in the levels of IT capital per worker ("IT-related capital deepening") and TFP growth in IT production, though the precise magnitudes of these contributions remain a subject of debate. The main outstanding issue is whether IT has contributed to TFP growth more generally by increasing the efficiency of production, either through usage or knowledge spillovers from the production of IT goods. The literature consists of country-specific and cross-country studies.

Country-specific work broadly follows the pioneering studies on the United States, which generally agree that IT-related capital deepening and TFP growth in IT production made important contributions to the acceleration in labor productivity in the late 1990s.[9] Labor productivity growth in the nonfarm business sector increased from about 1½ percent in 1973–95 to about 2½ percent in 1996–2000. About ¼ to ½ percentage point of the acceleration in labor productivity was attributed to capital deepening, more than accounted for by investment in IT, and about another ¼ percentage point to TFP growth in IT production (Table 3.4).[10] However, there is no consensus on the effect of IT on generalized TFP growth. The debate focuses on whether the remainder of the acceleration reflects cyclical factors or an increase in underlying TFP growth, and—even if it is the latter—the

[8]Under standard assumptions, labor productivity growth (the change in output per unit of labor input) can be expressed as:

$$\left(\frac{\hat{Y}}{L}\right) = \alpha\left(\frac{\hat{K}}{L}\right) + \hat{A}$$

where Y is output, L is labor, K is capital, α is the share of capital in national income, A is the level of total factor productivity, and $\wedge$ denotes a percentage change.

[9]See Gordon (2000), Jorgenson and Stiroh (2000), Oliner and Sichel (2000), and U.S. Council of Economic Advisors (2001).

[10]The recent annual revisions to the U.S. national accounts reduced average annual labor productivity growth in the nonfarm business sector during 1996–2000 from 2.8 percent to 2.5 percent, mostly reflecting weaker labor productivity in 2000, and slightly reduced the contribution of IT-related capital deepening to growth, mainly through lower software investment.

extent to which this acceleration in generalized TFP reflects IT. One study attributes the additional ½ percentage point acceleration in labor productivity to cyclical factors, while other studies view this acceleration as structural. More recent studies suggest that little of the acceleration in labor productivity is due to changes in factor utilization, factor accumulation, or returns to scale, and that virtually all of the acceleration is accounted for by IT-using and IT-producing industries (see Box 3.2). Together, these results—if they are borne out by further empirical work—suggest that we may soon see an impact of IT on generalized TFP growth.

Another economy that has seen an acceleration in labor productivity in the 1990s is Australia. Using data released by the Australian Bureau of Statistics, work done by the IMF suggests that IT-related capital deepening and generalized TFP growth played important roles in the acceleration in labor productivity (see Cardarelli, 2001). In particular, IT-related capital deepening increased rapidly during the 1990s, accounting in recent years for about two-thirds of the growth contribution of capital deepening. While the national accounts do not separately identify IT producing sectors, employment and trade data suggest that IT production in Australia is very small, implying that TFP growth in IT production was not important in the acceleration in labor productivity. Conversely, IMF staff does find some evidence across Australian industries of a positive relationship between IT-related capital deepening and TFP growth. This evidence is consistent with the idea that increased IT use has been associated with a reorganization of economic activities, supported by structural reforms.

In most other advanced economies, labor productivity has not accelerated in recent years, implying that any positive contribution of IT must have been offset elsewhere:

- In Japan, labor productivity growth did not increase during the 1990s, despite relatively high levels of overall and IT-related capital deepening. An official study finds that the contribution of IT-related capital deepening to growth increased by about ½ to ¾ percentage points between the early and late 1990s (Japan, Economic Planning Agency, 2000). However, the contribution of non-IT-related capital deepening declined by a corresponding amount. There are no Japan-specific studies on the contribution of IT production or use to TFP growth.

- In France, labor productivity growth fell in the second half of the 1990s. Work by IMF staff attributes this fall to a decline in overall capital deepening, reflecting reduced investment in labor-saving equipment as wage growth remained moderate.[11] Although overall capital deepening fell, the contribution of IT-related capital deepening to growth increased from zero to ¼ percent. While TFP growth rebounded in the second half of the 1990s, this was likely related to the overall economic recovery (and procyclical TFP) and not to IT production, which is relatively small in France. The extent to which this rebound may, or may not, have been related to IT use remains to be established.

- In the United Kingdom, labor productivity has not accelerated, despite a rate of investment in IT capital that is almost as high as in the United States. Work by IMF staff suggests that both IT-related capital deepening and TFP growth in IT production made important contributions to labor productivity growth in the late 1990s (see Kodres, forthcoming, and Oulton, 2001). However, these contributions were offset by decreases in TFP growth outside of the IT sector.

- In most economies in emerging Asia, labor productivity growth fell in the late 1990s, partly reflecting the crisis-related slowdown in output growth. Preliminary work by IMF staff finds that the contributions of IT-re-

[11]See Estevão and Levy (2000). Mairesse, Cette, and Kocoglu (2000) also use aggregate data to assess the impact of IT on labor productivity growth and get similar results. Using micro data, Crépon and Heckel (2000) find a somewhat larger impact of IT on labor productivity growth.

Box 3.2. Has U.S. Total Factor Productivity Growth Accelerated Outside of the Information Technology Sector?

The literature on the contribution of information technology (IT) to labor productivity growth in the United States in the late 1990s has established that it has had benefits through capital deepening in the economy at large and technological progress in the IT sector, though the precise magnitudes of these contributions remain under debate.[1] About ¼ to ½ percent of the acceleration in labor productivity was due to capital deepening, with an IT contribution of ⅓ to ⅔ percent slightly offset by a decline in deepening elsewhere. However, part of the increase in capital deepening may have been temporary, reflecting the investment boom of the late 1990s (see Table 3.4).[2] Finally, about another ¼ percent was due to total factor productivity (TFP) growth in IT production.

Looking forward, an important issue is whether IT has already contributed to underlying TFP growth outside of the IT sector ("generalized" TFP growth). This could occur either through knowledge spillovers from the production of IT goods or business reorganization stemming from the usage of IT goods ("IT spillovers"). These types of benefits provide an incentive for additional investment in IT and have been responsible for a significant portion of the long-term increase in output in most other all-purpose technological revolutions. This box examines what the recent U.S. literature has to say on this issue, a discussion that has generally been subsumed within a more general debate about the sources of the acceleration in labor productivity since 1996.

Those who have been more skeptical of the importance of IT in the observed acceleration of TFP in the late 1990s have argued that it largely reflects cyclical factors associated with the boom over that period, which induced temporary increases in TFP.[3] Indeed, the slowdown in activity and labor productivity since mid-2000 provides some credence to the view that cyclical factors may have played some role, as do recent revisions to the national income accounts that have reduced labor productivity growth in 2000 by 1¼ percent, and for the full 1996–2000 period by over ¼ percent a year.

In addition, these skeptics also used initial evidence that increases in labor productivity growth were concentrated in the computer and semiconductor sectors to question whether the rest of the economy was benefiting from the new technology. Subsequent industry-level analysis, however, indicates that a significant acceleration in labor productivity has also occurred outside of the IT-producing sector, and has been concentrated in IT-using sectors (these results are not adjusted for recent data revisions). In particular, studies have found that the industries outside the IT sector that invested most aggressively in IT in the early 1990s subsequently showed the largest gains in labor productivity growth (and, together with IT-producing industries, accounted for virtually all of the acceleration in labor productivity); that strong labor productivity growth in three IT-intensive sectors (finance, retail trade, and wholesale trade) reflected improvements in the way that businesses were organized and how they used technology; and that, using the income rather than the output side of the national accounts, about half of the acceleration in labor productivity occurred outside of the IT sector.[4] While consistent with the view that part of the increase in U.S. labor productivity growth is structural, the industry-level results do not eliminate the possibility that much of the observed acceleration in TFP could be cyclical. The observed acceleration in labor productivity could reflect capital deepening as well as strong cyclical

---

[1]See Gordon (2000), Jorgenson and Stiroh (2000), and Oliner and Sichel (2000). For a review of this literature, see De Masi (2000).

[2]Most of these initial studies ended their analysis in 1999, and are hence not significantly affected by recent data revisions that lowered estimated labor productivity growth marginally in 1998 and 1999 but quite substantially in 2000.

[3]These arguments were raised most notably in Gordon (2000).

[4]Stiroh (2001), Baily and Lawrence (2001), and Nordhaus (2001).

effects, as the IT-using sectors expanded particularly rapidly during the late 1990s boom.

Finally, some recent studies have directly addressed the issue of cyclicality in the acceleration in productivity (using the unrevised data). Using proxies for factor utilization, capital accumulation, and returns to scale, one study found that cyclical and other temporary reasons affected year-by-year estimates of TFP growth but did not account for the general acceleration in labor productivity in the second half of the 1990s (Basu, Fernald, and Shapiro, 2001). Another study found that most of the acceleration in labor productivity reflected a structural increase, with the cyclical component contributing almost nothing (U.S. Council of Economic Advisers, 2001). While these results are suggestive of a structural acceleration in TFP, it is noto-

riously difficult to accurately identify unobservable cyclical components, especially before an entire cycle has been observed.

In summary, while evidence suggests that there has been some increase in underlying labor productivity growth in the United States over the last five years due to IT, there remains considerably more uncertainty about the magnitude and duration of any acceleration in underlying TFP. Evidence of rapid technological innovation in the IT sector is incontrovertible. Evidence of accelerated capital deepening is strong (although investment in IT goods might slow—possibly quite sharply—in the short term). Finally, there is insufficient evidence to come to a firm conclusion on whether there has been a rise in underlying TFP growth outside of the IT sector associated with reorganization of production.

lated capital deepening and TFP growth in the IT sector to labor productivity growth increased during the course of the 1990s, but were more than offset by declining contributions from other sectors (Box 3.3). The increase in IT-related capital deepening reflected the maintenance of high levels of IT investment despite the growth slowdown associated with the Asian crisis.

Cross-country studies also find that IT-related capital deepening and TFP growth in IT production contributed to labor productivity growth in the second half of the 1990s. The cross-country evidence comes in two forms: one set of studies estimates the contribution of IT-related capital deepening using the conventional growth accounting framework, while the others focus on the role played by IT-using (and IT-producing) sectors.[12] Studies following the first approach find that IT-related capital deepening has indeed made an important contribution to growth across a range of countries (Table 3.5). Given

the rapid fall in the relative price of IT capital equipment, its contribution to the growth of the capital stock exceeds its nominal share in investment. For example, one study finds that falling prices of capital goods accounted for about one-third of the real growth of the capital stock in the United States between 1995–99 (Colecchia, 2001).

Another way to measure the impact of information technology is to estimate the contributions of the IT-producing sector and of IT-intensive sectors to economic growth through capital deepening. In other words, the contribution of IT is measured as overall capital deepening by IT-related sectors, rather than as the IT-related capital deepening of all sectors. The findings of one such study (Van Ark, 2001) are reported in Table 3.6. This study suggests that industries producing IT equipment or industries using IT equipment intensively contributed between 0.5 and 0.9 percentage points, or between 28 and 57 percent, to economic growth. For most G-7

---

[12]Studies following the first approach are Colecchia (2001), Daveri (2001), Roeger (2001), and Schreyer (2000). For the second approach, see Lee and Pilat (2001) and Van Ark (2001).

Table 3.5. Contribution of Information Technology Capital Deepening to GDP Growth in the G-7 Economies
(Percentage points)

	Colecchia (2001) 1995–99	Daveri (2001) 1991–1999	Roeger (2001) 1995–1999
Canada[1]	0.4	. . .	. . .
France	0.4	0.4	0.3
Germany[2]	0.3	0.5	0.3
Italy	0.3	0.3	0.3
Japan	0.3	. . .	. . .
United Kingdom	. . .	0.8	0.4
United States	0.9	0.9	0.7

Note: Colecchia (2001) and Daveri (2001) refer to business sector growth, while Roeger (2001) uses GDP growth. In addition to computers and telecommunications equipment, Colecchia (2001) and Daveri (2001) include software, while Roeger (2001) includes semiconductors.
[1]The Colecchia (2001) estimate excludes software.
[2]The Daveri (2001) estimate covers the period 1992–1999.

Table 3.6. Contribution of Information Technology (IT) Activities to GDP Growth, 1990–98
(Percent per year)

	Real GDP Growth	Contribution of IT-Related Industries		
		Total	IT-Using	IT-Producing
Canada	2.1	0.8	0.6	0.2
Denmark	1.8	0.5	0.3	0.2
Finland	1.6	0.7	0.0	0.7
France	1.3	0.5	0.2	0.3
Germany	1.1	0.5	0.4	0.1
Italy	1.4	0.7	0.5	0.2
Japan	1.4	0.8	0.5	0.3
Netherlands	2.5	1.0	0.7	0.3
United Kingdom	2.1	1.0	0.6	0.4
United States	3.2	1.4	0.9	0.5

Source: Van Ark (2001). For Germany, the numbers refer to 1991–97.

economies, the contribution of IT-using sectors is much stronger than the contribution of the IT-producing sector.

The contribution of technological progress in IT production to labor productivity growth is also fairly uncontroversial. Substantial TFP growth in the IT sector, which is the counterpart of the rapid declines in quality-adjusted IT prices, made significant contributions to labor productivity growth in countries with relatively large IT-producing sectors.

The impact of IT on generalized TFP growth can be assessed by examining the cross-country relationship between TFP growth and IT production and use. As in studies of the United States, the cross-country evidence on IT spillovers is ambiguous. There is some evidence of a positive effect of IT spending on the acceleration in TFP growth across 14 advanced economies (see Gramlich, 2001). Work by IMF staff extends this approach to a broader sample of countries and applies a richer specification. It finds that the effect of IT expenditure on TFP growth is ambiguous, with the estimated coefficients and standard errors being sensitive to the specification, time period, and set of countries

included in the regression (see Haacker and Morsink, 2001).

In summary, the weight of the evidence suggests that IT is already making an important contribution to labor productivity growth through technological progress in IT production and IT-related capital deepening. Convincing evidence of the impact of IT on the general efficiency of production is not yet available.

Who Benefits—Producers or Users?

While most of the existing literature on the macroeconomic consequences of IT has focused on labor productivity, the allocation of the potential welfare benefits has received less attention. In principle, the benefits of a technological revolution could accrue to owners (in the form of higher profits), labor (through higher wages), or users (through lower prices). In the IT revolution, profits and wages have risen somewhat, but these changes are small relative to the sharp fall in the relative prices of IT goods. This suggests that IT-using countries tend to benefit somewhat more than IT-producing countries, because producing countries lose some of the gains through deteriorating terms of trade.[13] As noted earlier, historical experience suggests that

[13]In some developing countries producing IT goods, the IT industry may also pay wages considerably above those prevailing elsewhere.

Box 3.3. Information Technology and Growth in Emerging Asia

While most of the literature on information technology (IT) and growth covers the advanced economies of North America, Europe, and Japan, many emerging market economies in Asia are important producers and users of IT goods. The IMF has begun a cross-country study of the impact of IT-related capital deepening on labor productivity growth in China, Hong Kong SAR, Indonesia, Korea, Malaysia, Philippines, Singapore, Taiwan Province of China, and Thailand (Lee and Khatri, 2001). As the statistical authorities in these economies do not use hedonic methods to adjust price indices for quality changes or use chain weighting to calculate real growth rates (see Box 3.1), and the national accounts do not distinguish IT production, IT consumption, and IT investment, the IMF study uses consistent cross-country data on IT spending from the World Information Technology Services Alliance (WITSA) and price data from the U.S. Bureau of Economic Analysis, adjusted for exchange rate changes.

Estimates of IT capital stocks (relative to GDP) for emerging Asian economies and the United States are shown in the Figure.[1] IT capital stocks as a ratio of GDP are largest in the United States and the newly industrialized economies (NIEs), followed by the ASEAN-4 countries, and then China, reflecting differences in income per capita. In all economic areas, the stock of telecommunications capital is largest, followed by IT hardware and then IT software. In addition, the proportions differ significantly, with hardware being a much larger part of the IT capital stock in the United States and the Asian NIEs than elsewhere. This is important for calculations of capital deepening, as the relative price declines that drive the additional benefits to IT, as opposed to other capital investment, are much larger in the hardware sector than elsewhere.

Results based on the standard growth accounting decomposition show that the contribu-

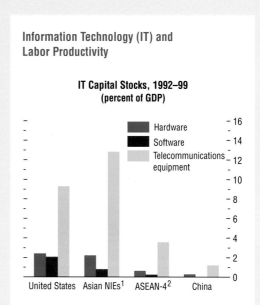

Information Technology (IT) and Labor Productivity

IT Capital Stocks, 1992–99
(percent of GDP)

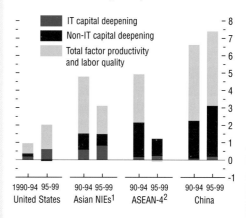

Contributions to Labor Productivity Growth, 1990–99
(percent)

Source: IMF staff estimates.

[1] Simple average of the Asian newly industrialized economies (NIEs): Hong Kong SAR, Korea, Singapore, and Taiwan Province of China.

[2] Simple average of the four members of the ASEAN-4: Indonesia, Malaysia, Philippines, and Thailand.

tion of IT-related capital deepening to labor productivity growth in emerging Asia increased during the 1990s (see the Figure). This contribution was already important in the first half of 1990s in the newly industrialized economies of Asia, and increased even further in the second

[1] These calculations use a perpetual inventory method.

Box 3.3 *(concluded)*

half of the 1990s. In the ASEAN-4 and China, the contribution of IT-related capital deepening started from a low base and roughly doubled to around ¼ percent in the ASEAN countries and in China.

This capital deepening, however, has occurred against a background in which labor productivity growth in the emerging market economies of Asia dropped from 5 percent in the first half of the 1990s to 2½ percent in the second half of the 1990s. The sharp decline in labor productivity growth in Asia's emerging markets between

the early and late 1990s mainly reflected the crisis-related growth slowdown. In particular, the abrupt deceleration in total factor productivity (TFP) and the slowdown in non-IT-related capital deepening in the Asian NIEs and the ASEAN-4 were related to the 1997–98 crisis, as suggested by the contrast with China. It is remarkable, therefore, that the contribution of IT capital to growth increased in all countries, reflecting continued strong IT investment. Indeed, in some crisis-affected countries, strong IT investment helped growth to recover.

the main beneficiaries of technological revolutions have in practice been the users. This is well illustrated by the experience with textiles production in the industrial revolution in the United Kingdom, where about half of the welfare gains were exported through terms of trade losses.

One way of demonstrating the impact of falling technological prices on the international distribution of IT benefits is through an illustrative exercise to calculate the impact of introducing hedonic prices for IT goods and chain-weighting on real GDP and real domestic demand. Intuitively, the results illustrate how rapidly falling relative prices of IT goods increase output, and how trade between countries transfers some of these benefits from countries that produce IT goods to countries that consume them. As shown in the (upper-bound) estimates in Table 3.7, on the production side, the technological improvements incorporated in the fall in relative prices of IT goods raise the annualized growth in output, most notably in Singapore and

Malaysia.[14] However, because most of these goods are exported to the rest of the world, and hence exchanged for non-IT goods, which are rapidly becoming relatively more expensive, the benefits to real domestic demand are significantly smaller. Conversely, countries that import IT goods from abroad gain from the continuing improvement in their terms of trade.

Another more theoretically attractive way of looking at the welfare gains from falling IT prices is to calculate the change in consumer surplus, broadly defined. The increase in consumer surplus is represented by the area between the initial price, P_0, and the final price, P_1, under the demand curve for IT products (see Figure 3.5).[15] The entire demand curve is used because, assuming a perfectly competitive environment, all the benefits end up with consumers, even if this includes intermediate or investment goods.[16] Following the methodology used in earlier studies on U.S. data, IMF staff estimated demand curves for IT hardware, software, and telecommunications equipment, using

[14]Specifically, it is assumed that a country switches from deflating the output of the IT sector (for output) or purchases of IT goods (for real domestic demand) by the GDP deflator to using U.S. hedonic prices (adjusted for exchange rate movements) and chain-weighting to take account of substitution effects (see Box 3.1). This is an upper bound calculation because it is extremely unlikely that any country priced IT goods as equal to the GDP deflator, which implies that no relative price benefits from the IT revolution are included in the calculations that do not use hedonic prices.

[15]This concept is known as "social savings" in the economic history literature (see Crafts, 2001).

[16]The highly competitive environment in which most IT companies operate suggests that this assumption may be reasonable, although there are obvious exceptions. Brookes and Wahhaj (2000) suggest that overall profit rates in the IT sector are not exceptional.

Table 3.7. Illustrative Estimates of the Impact of Falling Prices of Information Technology (IT) Goods on GDP, Terms of Trade, and Domestic Demand[1]

(Percent per year, in order of magnitude of impact on domestic demand)

Country	GDP	Terms of Trade (Contribution to GDP Growth)	Domestic Demand (Contribution to GDP Growth)
United States	0.38	0.28	0.67
Sweden	−0.09	0.50	0.41
Canada	0.11	0.26	0.37
Australia	0.03	0.30	0.33
United Kingdom	0.30	0.02	0.32
Korea	0.85	−0.59	0.27
Singapore	6.71	−6.46	0.25
Denmark	−0.01	0.26	0.25
Israel	0.27	−0.04	0.23
Taiwan Province of China	0.58	−0.37	0.21
Norway	0.03	0.18	0.20
Hong Kong SAR	0.20	−0.01	0.20
Finland	−0.09	0.28	0.19
Netherlands	0.13	0.05	0.18
Malaysia	3.31	−3.13	0.18
Ireland	2.10	−1.93	0.18
Switzerland	0.03	0.15	0.17
Japan	0.37	−0.19	0.17
Belgium	0.10	0.03	0.12
Germany	0.04	0.08	0.12
France	0.10	0.02	0.12
Portugal	0.07	0.05	0.12
Austria	0.03	0.09	0.12
Italy	0.09	0.01	0.11
Brazil	0.17	−0.07	0.10
Philippines	1.13	−1.03	0.10
Spain	0.03	0.06	0.09
Thailand	0.96	−0.87	0.09
Greece	0.01	0.04	0.06

Source: Bayoumi and Haacker (2001).
[1]The impact of falling IT prices on real GDP, real domestic demand, and real net exports is calculated by deflating IT final expenditure by exchange-rate-adjusted U.S. hedonic prices (rather than the GDP deflator) and then chain weighting.

Figure 3.5. Demand for Information Technology (IT) Goods and Consumer Surplus[1]

As the price of IT goods falls, consumer surplus increases.

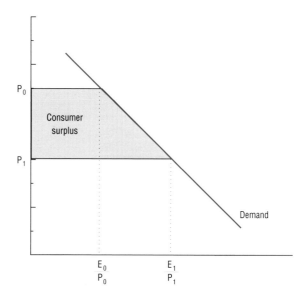

[1]P_0 is the initial price; P_1 is the final price. E_0 is the initial nominal expenditure; E_1 is the final nominal expenditure.

panel data on IT-related sales for 41 countries over the years 1992–99 and exchange rate adjusted prices from the U.S. National Income and Products Accounts.[17] Based on the estimated demand curves, the consumer surplus for the year 1999 was then calculated as the gain from the fall in prices between 1992 and 1999.

[17]The IMF staff study is Bayoumi and Haacker (2001). The earlier study of the United States is Brynjolfsson (1996).

Figure 3.6. Increase in Consumer Surplus, 1992–99
(Percent of GDP)

The increase in consumer surplus due to the fall in relative prices of information technology goods ranged from 1¼–4 percent of GDP in advanced and emerging Asian economies.

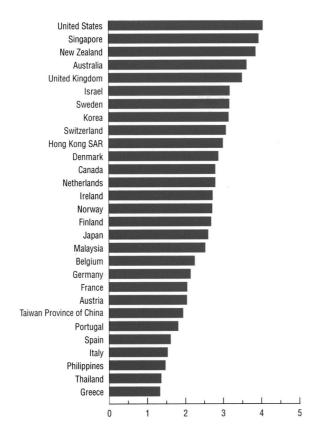

Source: Bayoumi and Haacker (2001).

While the results should be interpreted with caution, given the strong underlying assumptions, the estimated increases in consumer surplus are quite large, already amounting to several percentage points of GDP (Figure 3.6). The gain in consumer surplus depends not only on the total amount of IT spending (as a ratio to GDP), but also on the composition of IT spending. Countries with relatively high levels of spending on electronic data processing equipment, the prices of which declined more quickly than for telecommunications equipment and for software, experienced higher increases in the surplus. Cross-country comparisons indicate some interesting variations in consumer surplus gains. The countries with the largest gains in consumer surplus (greater than 3½ percent of GDP) are the United States, Singapore, New Zealand, Australia, and the United Kingdom. Other countries with large gains (2½ to 3½ percent of GDP) are in northern Europe (Sweden, Switzerland, Denmark, Netherlands, Ireland, Norway, and Finland), in Asia (Korea, Hong Kong SAR, Japan, and Malaysia), or have close links to the United States (Israel and Canada). The smallest benefits accrue to most continental European countries, particularly in southern Europe, as well as some important producers of IT goods (the Philippines, Taiwan Province of China, and Thailand). For these Asian countries, however, the consumer surplus gains remain large relative to other countries outside of the sample with similar income per capita, indicating that the IT-producing sector is creating valuable technological spillover.

The IT revolution also affects the distribution of labor income within countries. The development of IT increases the demand for highly skilled workers who can push the technological frontier forward and make the new technology accessible to the rest of the workforce. Even the initial adoption of IT increases the relative demand for skilled labor, as the introduction of computer systems often involves the routinization of simple, repetitive tasks (in service firms) or the automation of production processes (in manufacturing), although the IT-producing sector—which is important in some countries—itself produces many unskilled jobs. Outside of IT, computers can substitute more readily for human labor and judgment in clerical and production jobs, than in managerial and professional jobs.[18] Information technology also increases the returns to the use of marketing and problem solving skills to improve the match between customer-specific needs and existing products and to develop new products. However, over the longer term, as IT becomes more user-friendly and IT equipment becomes more readily available, IT will facilitate the creation of value by less-skilled workers.[19]

In summary, as in past technological revolutions, many of the benefits of the IT revolution accrue to users rather than the producers of IT-related goods. While some countries experienced large increases in real GDP, much of these gains were offset by a deterioration in their terms of trade, although there were also beneficial spillovers through greater IT use. The gains from technological progress, whether measured by an increase in domestic demand or in the consumer surplus, are mainly linked to a country's spending on IT-related goods. Within countries, the IT revolution is raising the wages of more-skilled workers relative to less-skilled workers, though the skill bias may wane in the long run.

Business Cycle Implications

The rapid growth of IT production and use around the world have important implications for the sources and propagation of the business cycle. As IT production becomes a larger share of total output, IT-related shocks are playing a greater role in driving macroeconomic fluctuations, while the increasing use of IT may be speeding up the pace of macroeconomic adjustment. At the same time, the IT revolution has strengthened real and financial linkages across countries, with the result that exports, foreign direct investment, and stock markets in IT-producing countries are vulnerable to shifts in the global demand for IT goods. Also, the heavy reliance of IT firms on equity financing opens up the possibility that swings in investor sentiment (as distinct from changes in fundamentals) may play an independent driving force in global IT cycles.

Domestic Business Cycle

Information technology-related shocks are playing a greater role in driving macroeconomic fluctuations, as IT production becomes a larger share of total output. Some observers have noted the parallels between the current combination of rapid technological progress, more integrated capital markets, and greater macroeconomic discipline, and the economic environment in the late nineteenth and early twentieth centuries (see Bank for International Settlements, 2001). During that period, technology shocks and their impact on investment and on aggregate spending have been acknowledged as a main driving force of business cycles.[20] This contrasts with much of the post-World War II period, during which fiscal and monetary policies played more pivotal roles in stimulating or slowing economic activity.

The diffusion of IT may improve inventory management by reducing time lags in the collection, transmission, and processing of information. Consistent with this idea, inventories-to-sales ratios in Australia, Canada, and the United States declined from the 1980s to the 1990s. Information technology can also help firms ensure that, for a given shock, their inventory

---

[18]Empirical evidence for advanced economies mostly confirms that IT has thus far increased the demand for and relative wages of more-skilled labor. See Autor, Katz, and Krueger (1998); Autor, Levy, and Murnane (2001); Berman, Bound, and Machin (1998); and Bresnahan, Brynjolfsson, and Hitt (1999). However, Di Nardo and Pischke (1997) suggest that the wage differential may simply reflect the fact that higher-wage workers use computers on their jobs.

[19]Already today, a retail sales clerk not only facilitates sales in the conventional manner, but also automatically engenders a book of accounts, inventory control, and supplier re-orders. See Greenspan (2001b).

[20]See Hicks (1982) for a concise review of early business cycle models and the relative importance of real versus monetary factors in this connection.

Figure 3.7. Exports of Information Technology (IT) Goods[1]
(Percent of global exports)

IT goods have become increasingly important components of world trade.

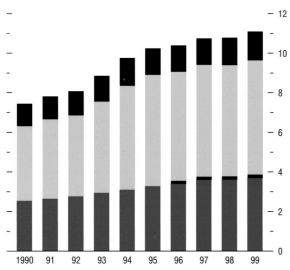

Source: United Nations Trade Statistics.
[1]IT exports of selected goods for 32 countries. Selected IT goods are electronic data equipment, software, electronic components, and telecommunications equipment. Sample of countries includes Australia, Austria, Belgium-Luxembourg, Brazil, Canada, Denmark, Finland, France, Germany, Greece, Hong Kong SAR, India, Indonesia, Ireland, Israel, Italy, Japan, Korea, Malaysia, Netherlands, Norway, Philippines, Portugal, Singapore, South Africa, Spain, Sweden, Switzerland, Taiwan Province of China, Thailand, United Kingdom, and the United States.
[2]Software data begins in 1996.

buildup is smaller than it would otherwise have been—though IT by itself cannot mitigate the size or the frequency of the underlying shocks. The international evidence on recent trends in the volatility of inventories and its contribution to the volatility of output is consistent with this view (Box 3.4).

Anecdotal evidence that IT may speed up the pace of macroeconomic adjustment comes from the abruptness of the recent global slowdown, especially in the United States. After the growth of spending on consumer durables slowed in the middle of 2000 in the United States, more advanced supply-chain management allowed firms to quickly identify the initial backup in inventories, and more flexible manufacturing processes enabled firms to adjust production levels rapidly. As a result, a round of inventory rebalancing—especially in the auto sector—quickly took hold and the economic slowdown intensified, leading to a sharper-than-expected slowdown. One implication of faster economic adjustment is that monetary policy may need to adjust more quickly than before (Greenspan, 2001a).

International Business Cycle

The IT revolution has strengthened real and financial linkages across countries. One important dimension of these linkages is the rapidly growing share of IT goods in world trade, which has risen from some 7½ percent in 1990 to 11 percent in 1999 (Figure 3.7), reflecting both the growing demand for new technology and the high price to weight ratio of IT goods, which contributes to their greater tradability. The growth of IT-related trade has been particularly impressive among Asian emerging markets, notably Korea, Malaysia, Philippines, Singapore, and Thailand (Figure 3.8). Adding other electronic components, which are mostly associated with the production of IT goods, the total share of electronic goods now exceeds 50 percent of overall exports in a number of East Asian countries. A similar, though weaker, upward trend in the export share of IT goods was also observed for the United States and Europe.

One important implication of these developments is to render those countries' export earnings more vulnerable to shifts in the global demand for IT equipment and components. As noted in the Chapter I Appendix on commodity prices, the prices of IT goods have undergone large swings in recent years. In particular, semiconductor prices have displayed marked cycles with about a four-year periodicity, which partly reflects the typical two-year lead time in building chip factories, as well as the fact that the bulk of such investment is usually made in the later stages of the cyclical upswing when firms are better placed to finance their expansion out of retained earnings. In addition to this cobweb-type mechanism, the sector experienced a succession of favorable shocks in the late 1990s, including the deregulation of local telecommunications in the United States, Y2K concerns, and the commercialization of the Internet. The resulting increase in production capacity is aggravating the oversupply situation in the current retrenchment. The link between the domestic business cycle and the international electronics cycle is particularly noteworthy in several small, open Asian economies, which, as noted earlier, have become highly specialized in the production and exports of semiconductors and IT-related equipment (Box 3.5).

Besides trade linkages, much of the globalization of the IT sector and its increasing role in global business cycle transmission has taken place via foreign direct investment. The rapid overseas expansion of large IT companies such as Intel, Cisco, Compaq, IBM, Motorola, Sony, Ericsson, and Nokia, provides anecdotal evidence in this regard. A more systematic indicator of this trend can be derived from firm-level data on the ratio of sales of foreign subsidiaries to total global sales. This ratio would approach one for companies with extended multinational operations, and zero for companies that operate in only one country.[21] Using firm-level data from a sample of publicly

[21]This definition of international sales is net of exports, so it does not overlap with export data.

Figure 3.8. Trade in Information Technology (IT) Goods[1]
(Percent of total exports for country or group)

The share of IT goods in total exports has risen markedly in Asia.

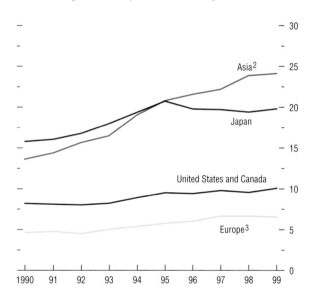

Sources: United Nations Trade Database; and IMF staff estimates.
[1] Exports of electronic data processing equipment and active components.
[2] Includes Australia, Hong Kong SAR, Korea, Malaysia, Philippines, Singapore, Taiwan Province of China, and Thailand.
[3] Includes Austria, Belgium-Luxembourg, Denmark, France, Germany, Italy, Netherlands, Norway, Finland, Greece, Ireland, Portugal Spain, Sweden, and Switzerland.

Box 3.4. Has the Information Technology Revolution Reduced Output Volatility?

Over the past 20 years output volatility has fallen significantly in most G-7 countries. The standard deviation of quarterly real output growth has almost halved from the 1980s to the 1990s in Canada, Germany, the United Kingdom, and the United States, remained broadly stable in France and Italy, and risen in Japan. This volatility decline partly reflects longer-term structural changes, such as the shift toward services, financial deepening, and improved monetary and fiscal policies. More recently, however, attention has focused on whether information technology (IT) has contributed to the volatility decline.

This box explores whether the adoption of IT by firms has contributed to the volatility decline from the 1980s to the 1990s through improved inventory management. Information technology can affect inventory behavior through at least two channels:

• By increasing the quality of information used by businesses and the speed with which they receive it (for example, through bar coding and real-time transmission of sales information from retailers to distributors).

• Computer aided design (CAD) has made capital equipment easier and faster to produce, reducing set-up times and the incentive to produce in large quantities because of high fixed costs.

Both channels may allow companies to operate with lower inventories and use unsold stocks more efficiently as a buffer against changes in sales. Consistent with this view, inventory-to-sales ratios have declined in recent years, particularly in industries and countries that have adopted IT more quickly. Based on company-level data for G-7 countries, the Figure shows inventories as a share of annual sales from 1988–2000 for three industry classifications: durable consumer goods (electronics, automobiles, and household goods), nondurable consumer goods (beverages, food products, and personal care products) and IT (computer hardware and software).[1] Relative

to annual sales, inventories of durable consumer goods have fallen by about one-fifth since 1988 and from a higher level than inventories of nondurable consumer goods, mainly driven by companies in Japan, the United Kingdom, and the United States, rather than Canada or continental Europe. There is a larger and more generalized decline in the inventory-to-sales ratio in the IT sector, which has almost halved since 1988. This suggests that at least some of the decline in inventory levels since the late 1980s is due to IT-related effects, as the adoption of IT is likely most advanced in the IT sector.[2] In 2000, the aggregate inventory-to-sales ratio was lowest in the United States, followed by the United Kingdom, Canada, and Japan, and higher in France, Germany, and Italy.

How has this change in inventories affected output volatility? From the standard breakdown of real output into final sales and inventory investment, it is possible to decompose the change in the volatility of real output growth into that coming from changes in sales growth, changes in the growth of inventory investment, and the change in correlation between these variables.[3] Hence, any decline in output volatility that is not attributable to a reduction in the variance of sales growth is linked either to greater predictability of inventory growth or better use of inventories to smooth irregularities in the path of final sales.

Turning to individual countries, the variance of quarterly real GDP growth in the United

[1]These industry-level ratios represent weighted averages of inventories to annual sales, where company sales as a share of the industry total are used as weights. Fiscal year-end data on inventories and sales are downloaded from Worldscope for up to 2,743 firms (in 1999).

[2]The marked decline in inventory levels in the IT sector, relative to other sectors, may also reflect cyclical factors.

[3]From this decomposition, the variance of real output growth can be written as

$$\text{var}(\Delta y_t) = \text{var}(\Delta s_t) + \text{var}(\Delta I_t) + 2\,\text{cov}(\Delta s_t, \Delta I_t)$$

where Δy_t is real output growth, Δy_t is the growth contribution of final sales, and ΔI_t is the growth contribution of changes in inventory investment. Sales and inventory changes have been broadly stable as components of GDP from the 1980s to the 1990s across G-7 countries, so that changes in their growth contributions derive mainly from changes in the volatility of the growth rates of sales and inventory investment.

States fell by 68 percent between the 1980s to the 1990s, while the variance of sales growth declined by 50 percent (see the Figure). Hence, inventories provided a significant additional reduction in the volatility of output growth, reflecting both a large fall in the volatility of inventories and better "timing" of inventory changes. Inventories also played a significant role in the reduction of output volatility in Canada and the United Kingdom. By contrast, in the continental European countries, there was little sign of a significant contribution from inventories to the decline in output volatility, consistent with lower usage of IT in these countries.

Japan is the one G-7 country where output volatility has increased substantially.[4] As can be seen from the Figure, inventories contributed modestly to this rise in volatility, despite significant usage of IT in the economy. While the variability of changes in inventories has fallen, as expected given the decline in the inventory-to-sales ratio, inventory investment did not offset movements in sales as much as in the past. This suggests that much of the ability of producers to better offset changes in sales in the United States and elsewhere may be in part a cyclical phenomenon that comes with lower output volatility, rather than improved inventory management.

In conclusion, the results are consistent with the idea that IT is helping to reduce output variability through better inventory control. Though some of the decline in output volatility in the G-7 countries probably reflects cyclical factors, it is striking that the volatility of inventory changes has fallen substantially in both Japan (where sales volatility has risen) and the United States. It is more difficult to determine whether inventories are also being used more efficiently, in terms of acting as a better buffer against changes in sales. While anecdotal evidence suggests that this may be occurring, hard

[4]See Box 1.2 in the October 2000 *World Economic Outlook* for a discussion of the reasons for this different evolution of output volatility.

Inventories and Output Volatility

Global Inventories-to-Sales Ratios
(inventories in percent of annual sales)

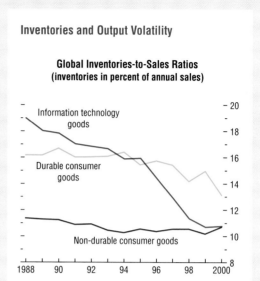

Change in Volatility of Output and Sales Growth
Among the Group of Seven Countries[1]
(percent)

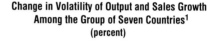

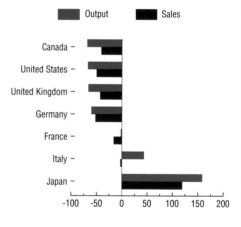

Sources: Thomson Financial, Worldscope database; and IMF staff estimates.
[1]Change in the variance of quarterly real GDP growth, between 1981:Q1–1990:Q4 and 1991:Q1–2000:Q4. The change in variance is then decomposed into inventory and sales components. See text for explanation of calculations.

evidence at the macroeconomic level is more difficult to identify. Going forward, the current slowdown will be instructive in assessing to what extent the IT revolution has improved inventory management.

Box 3.5. The Information Technology Slump and Short-Term Growth Prospects in East Asia

The sensitivity of East Asia's economic performance to cyclical developments in global information technology (IT) markets has increased significantly over the past two decades, with the rapid growth of the IT sector's share of regional production, investment, and exports. By 2000, IT sector exports accounted for 30 percent of total exports of goods from East Asia, equivalent to nearly 10 percent of GDP.[1] This increased sensitivity is clearly reflected in the region's recent growth performance: the slump in global IT markets since mid-2000 is one of the principal factors dampening exports and GDP growth in East Asia in 2001, just as the boom in the IT sector boosted the regional economic recovery in 1999–2000. The increasingly commodity-like characteristics of many IT products—for example, the strong cycles in prices—means that East Asian economies are now experiencing to varying degrees the sort of export and output variability traditionally associated with commodity exporters.

The slump in the IT sector began in the first half of 2000 with a significant reversal of the earlier speculative run-up in IT sector stock prices worldwide, and was followed by a sharp weakening of global sales volumes and prices for IT components and products in late 2000 and into 2001. In the first four months of 2001, global sales of semiconductors were down around 10 percent from the same period in 2000. The impact on Asia of the downturn in the electronics sector is being felt both through trade channels, including weaker trade volumes and prices, and through financial market channels, including the impact of lower regional stock market prices on investment and consumer spending, and weaker foreign direct investment and portfolio investment inflows to the region.

This box examines the impact of the IT sector slump on East Asian growth through the trade channel. More specifically, a simple model is

used to estimate the impact on regional economies of a 10 percent decline in the growth of the volume of IT sector exports. The analysis highlights the importance of three factors influencing the effects of the export shock across the region: (1) the magnitude of exports of electronics, *net* of imported intermediate inputs, relative to GDP; (2) the responsiveness of other GDP expenditure components to weaker export earnings; and (3) indirect trade spillovers from weaker growth elsewhere in the region.

Electronics exports are equivalent to nearly 10 percent of GDP for the Asian region as a whole, and to 20 percent of GDP in the smaller regional economies (see the Figure). For most countries in the region, however, electronics production and exports include a high proportion—between 50 and 75 percent—of imported intermediate inputs, mainly sourced within the region. As a result, a fall in electronics exports leads automatically to a decline in such imports, significantly dampening the spillover into domestic expenditure. The size of IT sector net exports relative to GDP varies substantially across the region—from as much as 25 percent of GDP for Malaysia, to less than 1 percent of GDP for Hong Kong SAR (excluding re-exports)—so the estimated initial impact on the region's economies also varies widely.

An additional consequence of the high import content of electronics exports in most countries in the region is that the fall in electronics prices affects both import and export prices within the region, having an ambiguous effect on terms of trade. The most commodity-like electronics components, such as memory chips, have experienced much larger price falls than many other electronics components. As a result, countries importing such components and exporting other electronics products could even experience terms of trade improvements.

The estimates and assumptions employed in this analysis regarding the responsiveness of different expenditures to lower export growth suggest that, in Malaysia and Singapore in particular, lower multipliers (reflecting higher marginal savings rates) will tend to cushion the

[1]In this analysis, East Asia includes China, Hong Kong SAR, Indonesia, Japan, Korea, Malaysia, Philippines, Singapore, Taiwan Province of China, and Thailand.

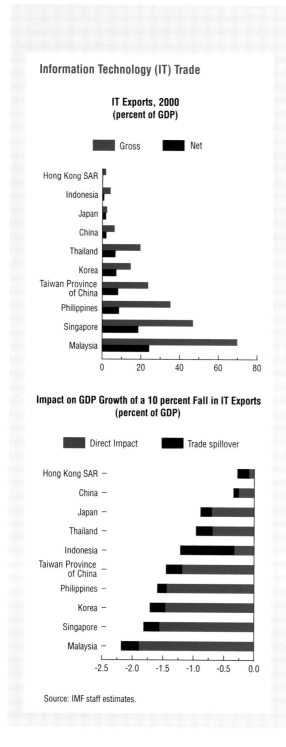

Information Technology (IT) Trade

IT Exports, 2000
(percent of GDP)

Gross　Net

Hong Kong SAR
Indonesia
Japan
China
Thailand
Korea
Taiwan Province of China
Philippines
Singapore
Malaysia

0　20　40　60　80

Impact on GDP Growth of a 10 percent Fall in IT Exports
(percent of GDP)

Direct Impact　Trade spillover

Hong Kong SAR
China
Japan
Thailand
Indonesia
Taiwan Province of China
Philippines
Korea
Singapore
Malaysia

-2.5　-2.0　-1.5　-1.0　-0.5　0.0

Source: IMF staff estimates.

impact of the IT shock.[2] Conversely, in Indonesia and Japan, higher multipliers (reflecting lower marginal savings rates) tend to accentuate the impact of the external shock. In the Philippines, the effect of a low savings rate is substantially off-set by the high responsiveness of nonelectronics imports to weaker domestic demand.

Overall, the direct impact of a 10 percent fall in regional electronics exports is estimated to cut GDP growth in the region by about ½ per-centage point. The adverse impact on growth in Malaysia, Singapore, Korea, the Philippines, and Taiwan Province of China is substantially greater (see the Figure), largely reflecting the impor-tance of IT net exports to their economies. In addition to the direct impact of the IT shock to growth in the region, weaker growth will also re-duce nonelectronics imports by countries in the region, leading to a further, second-round con-traction of other countries' nonelectronics ex-ports and GDP. Analysis using bilateral trade shares to estimate the contraction in nonelec-tronics trade within the region suggests that these second-round effects would cut growth in the region by an additional ¼ percentage point, bringing the total growth reduction to ¾ of a percentage point, and nearly double that for East Asia excluding China and Japan. Indonesia is likely to be the country most strongly affected by the second-round trade spillover effects, re-flecting the unusually high proportion of its ex-ports going to other countries in the region, as well as relative sensitivity of Indonesian con-sumption to changes in export income.

[2]Private consumption elasticities are based on a re-cent analysis by J.P. Morgan Chase & Co. (2001), while private investment is assumed to be 2½ times as re-sponsive as private consumption. Public sector expen-diture is assumed to be unchanged. The responses of nonelectronics imports are based on elasticities esti-mated in Senhadji (1998).

traded and mostly very large companies in ad-vanced economies, Figure 3.9 shows that the ratio of international sales (net of exports) to total sales in the IT sector has trended up

markedly since the early 1990s relative to the non-IT sector. Much of this increase has been due to the globalization of hardware and soft-ware production.

Figure 3.9. Globalization of Information Technology (IT) Firms[1]
(Percent)

The ratio of international sales to total sales is higher for IT firms than for non-IT firms and has risen sharply in the past two years.

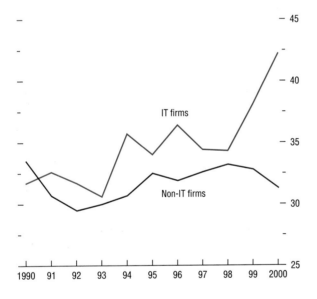

Sources: Thomson Financial, Worldscope database; and IMF staff estimates.
[1]Ratio of international sales to total sales, weighted by each firm's total sales.

The strengthening of real linkages—through both merchandise trade and the expansion of overseas subsidiaries of IT firms—has had an important counterpart in financial market linkages. The cross-border correlations of stock prices since the mid-1990s have been higher for the IT sector than for non-IT sectors, reflecting the greater exposure of IT firms to common expectational shocks (regarding the future profitability of IT) and the greater internationalization of IT firms—a shock to the earnings of an IT firm in one country can have a substantial impact on other countries, through its effect on the company's worldwide consolidated balance sheet (Figure 3.10). More rigorous statistical analysis, which decomposes a firm's stock returns into a global business cycle factor, a country-affiliation factor, and an industry-affiliation factor, shows that IT firms have experienced by far the most significant increase in the contribution of the industry affiliation factor to the determination of firms' stock returns (see Brooks and Catão, 2000).

At the same time, the strength of cross-border financial linkages among IT firms opens up the possibility that swings in investor sentiment (as opposed to investors' rational response to changes in fundamentals) may play an independent driving force in global IT cycles. While it is difficult to establish the extent to which the 1995–2000 rise in IT stock prices constituted a bubble, or the extent to which prices now reflect fundamentals, it is clear that those financial market developments can have important business cycle implications. This is because, as discussed in the following paragraphs, the availability of external funds appears to have been a key determinant of investment by IT firms, implying that the higher cost and more limited availability of external funds—relating to the current weakness in stock prices—may be expected to restrain investment in the sector on a global scale, at least in the near term.

Financing Information Technology

As in past technological revolutions, the initial phase of the IT revolution appears to have been characterized by excessive optimism about the potential earnings of innovating firms. This over-optimism led for several years to soaring stock prices of IT firms, which made equity finance cheaper and more readily available, which in turn boosted investment by IT firms. The association between stock prices and the relative cost of capital for IT producers can be seen in the upper left panel of Figure 3.11, which plots the ratio of the market value of equity to the book value of equity—a widely used measure of the relative cost of investment often known as Tobin's q.[22] Partly reflecting soaring optimism about the prospective benefits of IT, the Tobin's q of the IT sector rose much more rapidly than that of the rest of the economy in the 1990s and remained higher even in 2000.[23] During the same period, the investment expenditure (scaled by total assets) in the IT sector also rose markedly relative to the rest of the economy (upper right panel of Figure 3.11), similar to the "railway mania" in Britain in the 1840s that was discussed earlier.

These developments echo the findings of a large literature in empirical finance that postulates that capital structure and external financing conditions play a key role in firms' investment decisions.[24] In a world where information is costly and not fully available to investors, a firm's internal funds (retained earnings) tend to be significantly cheaper than external funds (like new debt or equity), as internal funds dispense with costly monitoring of the firm's management decisions. Likewise, the choice between

[22]The definition of the non-IT sector excludes banks and financial institutions since, by the nature of their operations, they tend to display very high leverage ratios and large maturity mismatches between assets and liabilities, which would distort the comparison with other sectors. The empirical analysis presented in this section is based on company level information covering 19 advanced economies, obtained from the Worldscope database.

[23]Hall (2001) argues that the higher Tobin's q in the IT sector reflects higher human capital, which is not captured by balance-sheet measures of capital. However, this argument implies that the recent sharp swings in IT stock prices primarily reflect rapid changes in human capital.

[24]Fazzari, Hubbard, and Petersen (1988), Gertler and Gilchrist (1994), and Hubbard (1998).

Figure 3.10. Stock Prices[1]
(1995 average = 100; monthly averages)

The stock prices of information technology (IT) firms have been highly correlated across countries.

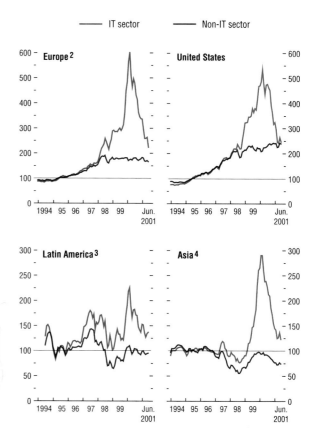

Source: Thomson Financial Datastream.
[1]Weighted by market value.
[2]Includes Austria, Belgium, Denmark, Finland, France, Germany, Greece, Ireland, Italy, Luxembourg, Netherlands, Norway, Portugal, Spain, Sweden Switzerland, and the United Kingdom.
[3]Includes Argentina, Brazil, Chile, Colombia, Mexico, and Peru.
[4]Includes China, Hong Kong SAR, India, Indonesia, Japan, Korea, Malaysia, Philippines, Singapore, Taiwan Province of China, and Thailand.

Figure 3.11. Information Technology (IT) Financing in Advanced Economies[1]
(Percent)

There are significant differences in financial structure between IT and non-IT firms.

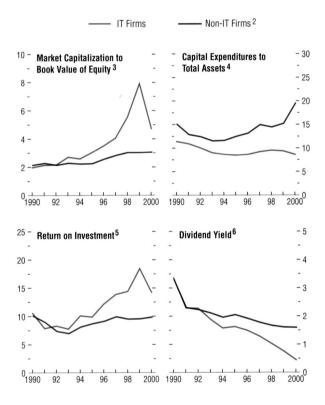

different instruments of external funds—namely between equity and debt finance as well as between short-term debt and long-term debt—also appears to have an important bearing on the firm's ability to finance new investment projects and hence on how the firm's stocks are valued. In particular, some have argued that firms with high debt to asset ratios, and with high ratios of short-term debt to total debt, are more likely to pass up good investment opportunities for fear of bankruptcy and hence have diminished growth prospects (see Myers, 1977; and Myers and Majluf, 1984).

Looking at the financial performance of IT firms and their capacity to finance new investment with retained earnings, a distinguishing feature of the sector has been its high rates of return on investment and higher earnings relative to the non-IT sector (Figure 3.11). Yet, despite higher earnings, IT firms have remained highly dependent on external finance. Retained earnings (as a share of total earnings) have been increasingly used to finance investment needs, but this has been insufficient to fill the financing gap. This is apparent from the ratios of the dividend yield and retained earnings to investment, both of which trended down during the 1990s, pointing to decreases in liquidity and the sector's capacity for self-financing.[25]

When resorting to external funds, IT firms have been considerably less reliant on debt than the average non-IT firm. Moreover, the ratio of debt to assets of IT firms declined in the second half of the 1990s, during the bull market for IT stocks.[26] At the same time, the share of short-term debt in total debt is higher for IT firms than for non-IT firms. This trend was reinforced in the past two years by heavy short-term borrow-

[25]Within IT, this trend has been more marked for hardware and software producing firms relative to telecoms. Because telecom firms tend to be larger, and financially more established, ratios of net cash flows to assets and retained earnings to investment tend to be higher than in the software and hardware subsectors.

[26]Again, this is particularly the case among hardware and software producers than among telecom companies.

ing by telecommunications firms in Europe (Figure 3.12).

The greater reliance of the IT sector on equity relative to debt and on short-term relative to long-term debt is explained by several factors. First, firms specializing in the development of new technology tend to be younger, have a less established credit reputation, and are riskier from a bondholder's perspective. Under these circumstances, equity financing tends to be cheaper, especially during periods of euphoria about the economic prospects for the adoption of new technologies. Second, one of the main distinguishing characteristics of the IT revolution compared to past technological revolutions is that the optimal firm size is much smaller.[27] This implies that IT firms have a limited stock of fixed assets to pledge as a collateral against loans, which tends to increase borrowing costs. Third, to the extent that new IT ventures tend to be riskier, subject to greater earnings volatility, but also have projects with higher expected returns, theory suggests that equity tends to be superior to debt financing (see Myers, 1977). Greater reliance on short-term debt relative to long-term debt also reflects a combination of demand and supply factors. On supply side, greater long-term risks imply that the yield curve faced by younger and smaller IT firms will tend to be steeper. On the demand side, higher depreciation rates in IT imply that tangible assets will tend to have a relatively short life span, so that maturity matching considerations will point toward a more intensive use of short-term debt.

These capital structure characteristics of the IT sector have significant economywide implications. Higher intensity in the use of external funds tends to foster the development of domestic financial systems. In particular, greater reliance on the use of equity financing tends to favor the development of domestic stock markets—a desirable feature, especially for developing countries. Interestingly, these characteristics of IT firms have

[27]Digital technology and the Internet tend to reduce the optimal firm size to the extent that they increase opportunities for outsourcing and lower fixed costs.

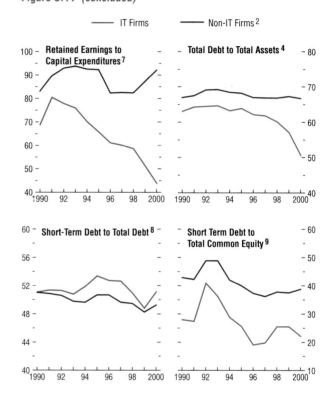

Figure 3.11 *(concluded)*

Source: Thomson Financial, Worldscope database.
[1] Advanced economies include Australia, Austria, Belgium, Canada, Denmark, Finland, France, Germany, Ireland, Italy, Japan, Luxembourg, Netherlands, New Zealand, Norway, Spain, Sweden, Switzerland, United Kingdom, and the United States.
[2] Excludes financial firms.
[3] Ratio for each firm weighted by its book value of equity.
[4] Ratio for each firm weighted by its total total assets.
[5] Ratio for each firm weighted by its total sales.
[6] Ratio for each firm weighted by its market capitalization.
[7] Ratio for each firm weighted by its capital expenditures.
[8] Ratio for each firm weighted by its total liabilities.
[9] Ratio for each firm weighted by its total common equity.

Figure 3.12. Short-Term Debt to Book Value of Equity[1]
(Percent)

The reliance of telecommunications firms in Europe on short-term debt increases sharply in 2000.

—— Information technology (IT) hardware firms
—— Software firms
—— Telecommunication services firms
—— Non-IT firms, excluding financial firms

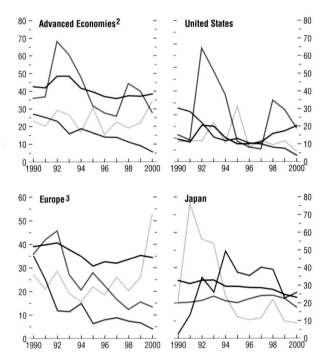

Source: Thomson Financial, Worldscope database.
[1]Weighted by the firm's book value of equity.
[2]Countries include Australia, Austria, Belgium, Canada, Denmark, Finland, France, Germany, Ireland, Italy, Japan, Luxembourg, Netherlands, New Zealand, Norway, Spain, Sweden, Switzerland, United Kingdom, and the United States.
[3]Countries include Austria, Belgium, Denmark, France, Germany, Italy, Luxembourg, Netherlands, Norway, Finland, Ireland, Spain, Sweden, and Switzerland.

been observed across a variety of economies, including both those where bank loans have been the main source of business financing (as in Germany and Japan) and those where the stock market has played a more central role (as in Canada, the United Kingdom, and the United States). At the same time, however, greater reliance on external finance, the stock market, and on short-term debt also makes the IT sector more vulnerable to changes in macroeconomic conditions and shifts in investor confidence. As in previous technological revolutions, this could pave the way for substantial industry consolidation and for a relatively protracted period of lower investment and slowdown in the diffusion of the new technology.

Prospects for the Information Technology Revolution

While global demand for IT goods is falling sharply at present, reflecting in part a retreat from the unsustainably high level of a year ago, IT adoption will likely continue to expand in the medium term. As users bring their IT spending back into line with their medium-term needs, short-term prospects for IT-producing countries and for the contribution of IT-related capital deepening to labor productivity growth may be limited. However, in the medium term, the diffusion of IT is likely to make substantial contributions to productivity growth, as the increasing use of computers and telecommunications equipment streamlines business processes and organization, boosting the efficiency with which other factors of production are used.

Advanced Economies

Further innovation in the production of IT equipment, leading to TFP growth in the IT sector, and additional purchases of IT equipment, resulting in IT-related capital deepening, are highly likely in the medium term. As Moore's Law is likely to continue to hold for some time, advances in semiconductor technology will continue to drive declines in computer prices

(Jorgenson, 2001). Imminent innovations in semiconductors include larger chips, which will reduce costs by 30 percent, and thinner circuit lines, which will allow manufacturers to etch more transistors on a single chip. As a result, the relative price of computer power is likely to continue to fall sharply at least for several years.

In conjunction with the continued fall in computer prices, two characteristics of IT equipment suggest that in the medium term IT investment and adoption will likely remain strong. Given that computers depreciate rapidly, firms will probably invest in computers at a faster rate than they do in other forms of capital in order to maintain a given level of the capital stock. The rapid replacement of IT equipment means that new technology becomes "embodied" in the capital stock at a faster rate than is the case for longer-lived assets (Ferguson, 2001). Second, empirical research has shown that the demand for computers—unlike that for other classes of capital—is quite sensitive to movements in the cost of capital (Tevlin and Whelan, 2000). The combination of this higher price elasticity and rapid decline in relative computer prices is likely to sustain investment in IT equipment, though investment may slow from the frenetic pace of the late 1990s, implying slower capital deepening and therefore slower labor productivity growth. This is consistent with the idea that firms and individuals are still finding new uses for IT, implying a price elasticity of demand for IT goods and services greater than unity, so that technological progress (and hence falling prices) results in a growing sector over time.[28]

Beyond TFP growth in IT production and IT-related capital deepening, the reorganization of production around IT may have a positive impact on productivity growth over the medium term. There is already microeconomic evidence of productivity gains associated with the invention of new processes, procedures, and organizational structures that leverage IT (see Brynjolfsson and Hitt, 2000, and Litan and Rivlin, 2000). Specifically, IT can sharply reduce transaction costs in the production and distribution of goods and services, especially in data-intensive industries, such as medical care and financial services, and reduce communication costs, enabling firms to improve supply chain management, assess customers' needs more effectively, and enhance internal efficiency. Microeconomic evidence suggests that IT is already having a disproportionately large impact on business performance by enabling complementary organizational innovations (new processes and structures). Together, IT and reorganization are leading to cost reductions and product-quality improvements.

Information technology is likely to affect not only the organization of workplaces but also firms' sourcing and location decisions. By reducing information and communication costs, which are important barriers to cross-border transactions, IT has the potential to raise international trade, reduce home-market bias, boost cross-border financial flows, and facilitate technology transfer. Recent work suggests that standard measures of distance in empirical models of international trade may partly capture information costs—adding measures of information flows to these models sharply diminishes the role of distance (Portes and Rey, 1999).

The overall impact of IT on the location of production in central versus peripheral areas is less clear. On the one hand, lower transaction and communication costs, combined with goods production that is increasingly characterized by flexible specialization rather than economies of scale, will tend to favor the dispersion of economic activity. Indeed, cities based on large-scale concentrated manufacturing are already past history in some countries (Glaeser, 1998). On the other hand, the combination of increasingly up-to-date information about shifting consumer preferences, the rising importance of intermediates in production, and easier outsourcing, will tend to favor locating production near to markets. If

---

[28]By contrast, the price elasticity of demand for agricultural goods is considerably less than unity, so that technological progress (and falling prices) results in a shrinking sector over time.

Table 3.8. Selected Economies: Indicators of Information Technology (IT) Use

Country	IT/GDP (In percent) Change 1992–99	IT/GDP (In percent) 1999	IT per Capita (Nominal U.S. dollars) Growth 1992–99 (percent)	IT per Capita (Nominal U.S. dollars) 1999	Personal Computers (per 100 people) Change 1990–2000	Personal Computers (per 100 people) 2000	Telephone Lines (per 100 people) Change 1990–2000	Telephone Lines (per 100 people) 2000
Developing								
Argentina	1.0	3.4	78.0	294.3	4.4	5.1	12.0	21.3
Brazil	2.3	5.8	199.4	267.4	4.1	4.4	8.4	14.9
Chile	1.1	5.7	121.8	321.0	7.5	8.6	15.5	22.1
China	3.0	4.9	465.7	37.9	1.6	1.6	8.0	8.6
India	1.8	3.5	220.8	15.4	0.5	0.5	2.6	3.2
Indonesia	–0.3	1.4	7.0	13.7	0.9	1.0	2.5	3.1
Korea	–0.5	4.4	53.8	521.5	15.3	19.0	15.4	46.4
Malaysia	2.1	5.5	61.8	168.4	9.7	10.5	12.2	21.1
Mexico	5.2	1.0	30.6	231.8	4.3	5.1	6.0	12.5
Philippines	0.9	2.7	82.6	33.6	1.6	1.9	2.9	3.9
South Africa	1.8	7.2	49.5	240.6	5.5	6.2	3.2	12.5
Advanced								
Canada	1.6	5.3	31.6	1,808.7	28.3	39.0	11.1	67.6
Denmark	1.0	4.5	45.3	2,540.3	31.6	43.1	13.8	70.5
France	0.8	3.8	27.5	1,706.6	23.4	30.5	8.5	58.0
Germany	0.9	4.1	29.4	1,699.9	23.4	33.6	16.0	60.1
United Kingdom	0.7	4.7	52.0	1,979.5	23.0	33.8	12.6	56.7
United States	0.9	5.2	57.9	2,792.1	36.8	58.5	12.8	67.3

Sources: ITU Statistical Yearbook, 1999; World Information Technology Services Alliances, *Digital Planet*, 2001.

outsourcing involves the proliferation of new intermediaries supplying various services (such as accounting, marketing, purchasing), which still rely in part on people providing the services in person, then close proximity is also valuable because it economizes on the cost of time.

Developing Countries

Looking ahead, it appears likely that usage of information technology products will continue to expand rapidly in developing countries, but productivity benefits will accrue only slowly. As in advanced economies, expanded usage is driven by the rapid decline in prices of information technology products. Enhanced productivity through that use, however, is a development task that may require complementary human capital, efficient (de)regulation of the telecommunications infrastructure and of information flows, and, more generally, overcoming organizational rigidities that limit the benefits from new ideas and technologies. As such, even though information technology will contribute to raising the absolute levels of productivity in developing coun-

tries, it may increase the productivity gap between advanced economies and developing countries.

The rate of diffusion of IT to developing countries has been rapid compared to earlier all purpose technologies. Just 10 years after the "start" of the IT revolution, developing countries (with about 85 percent of the world's population) already had about a 10 percent share of Internet subscribers in 2000. By contrast, it took more than 80 years from the opening of the first rail line in 1830 for developing countries to account for 30 percent of the world's rail track in 1913. Though from a low base, IT expenditure rose throughout the 1990s for most developing countries and for many of them at a rate significantly greater than in advanced economies (Table 3.8). Investment spending slowed when economic conditions were unfavorable, as in Indonesia in the late-1990s, but the expenditures typically grew substantially, with the result that much larger numbers of personal computers and telephone lines per capita were in use at the end of the 1990s than at the start, which, in turn, enabled a more widespread use of the

Internet. This trend toward more widespread use is likely to continue.

What explains the patterns of diffusion of these new technologies? A recent analysis points to several important factors (Dasgupta, Lall, and Wheeler, 2001). Countries with relatively high growth rates, greater urbanization, and a superior economic policy environment have expanded their use of cell phones and Internet connections at a faster pace than others. Once these factors are controlled for, those with low usage have caught up. Other studies, such as those by Caselli and Coleman (2001) and Lee (2000), reinforce these findings. High levels of human capital are strongly correlated with the rate of adoption of information technology. Since the new technology is typically embodied in new equipment, high investment rates speed up adoption (Chile, for example, has one of the highest investment rates in Latin America and Malaysia and Korea achieved historically high investment rates in the 1990s). Finally, a policy regime that is open to imports and foreign direct investment creates a window to the world and hence raises the likelihood of adopting new technologies in general, and computers in particular.

The implications are, therefore, mixed. Strong growth and good policies raise the rate of IT adoption, which, in turn, has long-term beneficial growth effects; this implies the likelihood of a "virtuous" circle—with growth, policies, urbanization, education, and information technology reinforcing each other. However, those with the least developed infrastructures are also closing the IT usage gap. An important finding is that in some of the poorest countries, the ratio of Internet users to telephones is no lower, and often higher, than in advanced economies. The suggestion, therefore, is the latent demand for access to IT (and to the international knowledge networks) is strong even in poor countries. The critical question in the case of such countries is whether the new technolo-

gies could be productively used to accelerate the pace of development.

Information technology presents the attractive possibility of bypassing older technologies ("leapfrogging"). For example, countries with old-fashioned mechanical telephone systems can skip the analog electronic era and go straight to advanced digital technologies, and that certainly is happening. Leapfrogging is also made possible in a more radical developmental sense. Education can potentially be delivered at much lower expense to a much wider group of people. People on the margins of domestic and international markets can be brought into the mainstream through the provision of better information and the reduction of transactions costs. Again, some are realizing this potential. Bangladesh's Grameen Bank, a pioneer in the area of microfinance, has launched an effort to build cell phone and Internet access in rural areas. The range of IT applications and their creative deployment for raising productivity is large and includes factories, banks, ports, and, more recently, the business of governments themselves. Continued innovation and the relentless decline in costs is likely to further bolster these trends.

Despite the many specific examples of IT benefits in developing countries, the aggregate impact has thus far been limited.[29] This reflects in part some fundamental constraints, including the lack of complementary human capital, telecommunications sectors that are not yet sufficiently responsive, and organizational rigidities. With regard to human capital, IT may in some instances reduce the demand for human capital by embodying "intelligence" in information products and services, thus facilitating development. For example, electronic course content may sometimes substitute partially for trained teachers. Such substitutability between human capital in the old-fashioned sense and IT is likely to increase with the maturation of the technologies and the delivery systems. By contrast, the

---

[29]In a cross-country analysis, Pohjola (2000) shows that IT helps raise growth in advanced economies but not in developing countries.

complementary human capital requirements of IT are often significant, especially in business and government applications. For example, factory floor microelectronics-based technologies were expected to improve efficiency even in low wage environments by reducing waste and increasing throughput. However, as a series of engineering-economic studies showed, the achievement of those efficiencies required strong quality control ability, which was more a function of industrial literacy than sophisticated machinery (Mody, Suri, and Sanders, 1992).

Telecommunications infrastructure is paramount. The ratio of Internet users to telephone lines varies across countries in a much smaller range than does the number of telephone lines per capita. Thus, the latent demand for connections to the web—despite the high costs of doing so in most developing countries—is being constrained by the availability of telephone line connections. Privatization has brought significant gains but the process of awarding privatization contracts and the extent of subsequent market competition have remained controversial. In particular, regulatory oversight has proved complex and demanding, with considerable scope for regulatory overreach. New challenges lie ahead in setting standards and regulations, taxing and regulating electronic transactions, undertaking antitrust actions, and protecting privacy.

Finally, the widespread adoption and effective use of new technologies requires organizational flexibility and the willingness to take risks.[30] For example, though the potential exists for considerable efficiency improvements in the running of governments, rigid bureaucratic structures have often prevented a more aggressive adoption. While this concept is linked to the quality of human capital, it refers further to the organizational capacity to engineer change.

In summary, the unprecedented decline in IT prices has implied a faster rate of diffusion than in previous technological revolutions. The present constraints on more productive uses of the

technology are real, but a continued vigorous effort to harness the potential of IT is likely to pay dividends, as these become available over the next two or three decades.

Policy Implications

The IT revolution raises at least three important questions for policymakers. First, how can countries promote the use of IT and maximize its impact on growth? Second, how should macroeconomic policies take into account the uncertainty over any acceleration in productivity? And, finally, what are the implications of IT for fiscal, monetary, and financial policies in the long run?

Structural Policies

Differences in recent and prospective productivity performance across advanced economies reinforces the case for aggressive structural reform. Among the G-7 countries, the United States has seen large IT investment translate into an increase in underlying labor productivity growth, while in Japan and Europe it is more difficult to discern any positive impact on growth. This difference likely reflects, at least in part, less flexible labor markets and less efficient services sectors—especially telecommunications, finance, and distribution—in Japan and Europe. Such rigidities limit firms' abilities to exploit new opportunities, including those afforded by information technology. For example, employment practices—as reflected in official regulations, union rules, or simply employee culture—can restrict firms from offering appropriate incentive compensation, changing the tasks of existing employees, or dismissing workers. Indeed, theoretical work has emphasized the importance of workers (and managers) continually taking on new tasks to on-the-job learning in human capital accumulation (Lucas, 1993). Equally, an inefficient distribution sector not only raises the price of IT goods,

---

[30]Abramowitz and David (1996) discuss the limitations that arise from weak "social capability."

thus stifling adoption, but also may prevent its effective use—for example, by sharply increasing delivery times (Mann, Eckert, and Knight, 2000).

The implications of the IT revolution for structural policies may run even deeper, to the very foundations underpinning market-based economic systems. The use of IT, and the related reorganization of economic activity, almost inevitably creates new challenges for educational systems as well as legal and institutional arrangements, as illustrated by past technological revolutions. In the United States in the nineteenth century, innovative activity was stimulated by the development of the patent system, especially the growth of intermediaries (agents and lawyers) who specialized in trading patent rights, well before the rise of large-scale businesses and their founding of in-house research and development laboratories (Lamoreaux and Sokoloff, 1999). Similarly, the advent of mass production, the large corporation, and the continent-wide market in the United States in the late nineteenth and early twentieth centuries required not only improvements in production technology, but also legal and institutional changes, including limited liability, investment banking, a common market, and antitrust policy (DeLong, 2001).

Macroeconomic Policies Under Productivity Uncertainty

The considerable uncertainty about the precise magnitude and likely duration of the acceleration in underlying productivity has important implications for macroeconomic policies. Specifically, uncertainty about the acceleration complicates the assessment of the sustainability of the external current account position and potential output. With regard to the external current account, economic theory tells us that a country-specific positive productivity shock tends to increase the external current account deficit, by causing investment to rise (reflecting the increased marginal product of capital) and saving to fall (as households anticipate greater future

income). While recent empirical work finds some support for this effect in the United States in the late 1990s, the results for other major advanced economies are mixed (Marquez, 2001; see also Glick and Rogoff, 1995). More generally, uncertainty about the current and prospective impact of IT on productivity growth across countries makes it difficult to assess the extent to which global current account imbalances reflect structural or cyclical factors.

The difficulty of correctly assessing potential output at a time of changing productivity growth is well illustrated by the experience of the 1970s. In the United States, real-time official estimates of potential output, which were used by the U.S. Federal Reserve, failed to capture the slowdown in productivity growth that occurred in the early 1970s (see Figure 3.13 and Orphanides, 2000). Partly as a result, monetary policy may have tried to "stabilize" output at too high a level, contributing to rising inflation. More generally, in a situation where productivity growth is uncertain, the costs of maintaining an inappropriate policy stance rise rapidly over time, as discussed in Chapter II of the October 2000 *World Economic Outlook* and also mentioned in Appendix II of Chapter I.

How should macroeconomic policies be formulated with a "broken speedometer?" If the structure of the economy is changing, policymakers should place more weight on recent observations, which reflect these changes, and less weight on the distant past, which does not. Equally, policymakers should focus on observable variables, such as current inflation, rather than on unobservable concepts, such as the output gap, which depend on historical data (see Orphanides, 1998; and Swanson, 2000). In other words, policymakers should "attenuate" their response to less reliable indicators. There is evidence that the U.S. Federal Reserve in the ate 1990s placed less weight on the output gap and the unemployment rate, and more weight on inflation and a wide array of early warning indicators of emerging inflation, including credit conditions, wages, salaries, and other employment costs, profit

Figure 3.13. United States: Evolving Official Estimates of the Output Gap[1]
(Percent of potential GDP)

In the 1970s, policymakers severely underestimated the output gap, resulting in a monetary policy stance that was—in retrospect—too expansionary.

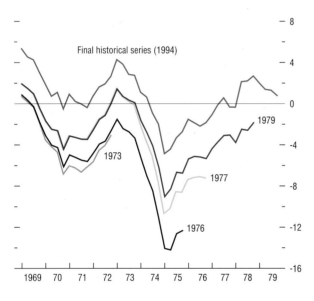

Source: Orphanides (2000).
[1]Except for the final historical series, each line shows the historical series for the output gap based on data available in the first quarter of the year shown. The final historical series is estimated with data available at the end of 1994.

margins, the stock market, and the monetary aggregates.[31]

As with monetary policy, the implication of increased uncertainty about productivity growth for countercyclical fiscal policy is to place more weight on recent observed indicators rather than on historical patterns. With regard to medium-term fiscal objectives, increased uncertainty about productivity growth calls for greater prudence in budget projections, because the political economy of the budget process means that it is easier to spend unexpected windfalls than to make up for unexpected deficits.

Long-Term Effects on Macroeconomic Policies

In the long run, IT may affect fiscal, monetary, and financial policies in fundamental ways. First, IT has the potential to transform the way that governments do their work. Governments can use IT to improve the procurement of goods and services; the quality and delivery of the government services; especially information; and the efficiency with which applications are filed and taxes are paid. However, IT may undermine a government's ability to collect certain taxes, such as sales taxes in the United States, though the associated revenue loss is estimated to be small.[32] In addition, IT may make it more difficult to define a "permanent establishment" for taxing the sale of digital products, like music, photographs, medical and financial advice, and educational services (Tanzi, 2000).

Information technology also has the potential to reduce the demand for bank reserves held at the central bank, which would affect the central

[31]See Meyer (2000) and the minutes of the June 2000 and August 2000 Federal Open Market Committee meetings.
[32]Sales taxes are collected by states. The U.S. Supreme Court has ruled that a state has no jurisdiction to require an out-of-state merchant with no employees or other physical presence in a state to collect the tax. For a more detailed discussion of the law, see U.S. General Accounting Office (2000). Goolsbee (2001) puts the revenue loss at about $612 million (less than 0.01 percent of GDP) in 1999, rising to $6.88 billion (0.06 percent of GDP) in 2004.

bank's ability to conduct monetary policy. At present, central banks have enormous leverage, even though the size of their balance sheet is small in relation to that of the private sector, because base money—especially bank reserves at the central bank—is the medium of final settlement. IT could allow final settlements to be carried out by the private sector without the need for clearing through the central bank. For example, private parties could settle a transaction by transferring wealth from one electronic account to another, with pre-agreed algorithms determining which financial assets were sold by the purchaser and bought by the seller (King, 1999). The key to any such development is the ability of information and communication systems to allow instantaneous verification of creditworthiness, thereby enabling private sector real time gross settlement to occur with finality. While there would be a new need to ensure the integrity of the systems used for settlement purposes, base money would no longer have a unique role and central banks would lose their ability to implement monetary policy. However, the demand for bank reserves at the central bank is likely to remain strong for many years, given their current key role in final settlement (Cecchetti, 2001).

Finally, as the financial services industry adopts IT, the regulation and supervision of financial systems will need to respond. The IT revolution is transforming financial services by changing the speed, scope, and nature of information, computation, and communication. Financial institutions are offering new products, developing new processes, and facing stiffer competition from nonfinancial institutions. Banks' risk management will have to adapt to greater risks in operations (the use of increasingly complex technology by employees who do not fully understand it), counterparty location (the physical or legal location of a financial institution will become more difficult to identify), and systemic risk (from accidents to or sabotage of common software or the Internet) (Turner, forthcoming). In identifying and addressing new challenges, prudential oversight will need to be flexible, stress guidance rather than detailed rules, rely more on improved disclosure requirements, and extend to new providers of financial services.

Conclusion

To date, the IT revolution has largely followed the pattern of past technological revolutions, including an initial phase characterized by a boom and bust in the stock prices of innovating firms, as well as in spending on goods embodying the new technology. The IT revolution is different from past technological revolutions in the globalization of production, which has strengthened real and financial linkages across countries. The rapid growth in the production of IT goods implies that changes in global demand conditions, driven mainly by IT-using advanced economies, have a significant impact on the exports of IT-producing countries. While positive demand shocks helped to boost IT production in 1999 and 2000, the current slump in global IT spending is a heavy drag on these IT-producing countries.

Notwithstanding the adverse impact of the current IT slump on some countries, the economic benefits of the IT revolution are already significant and will likely continue. Thus far, the benefits arise mainly from the fall in the relative prices of semiconductors and computers, and accrue primarily to the users of these products. There is evidence that TFP growth in IT production and IT-related capital deepening have boosted labor productivity growth in some countries, and it is likely that—in the coming years—economic activities in a variety of countries will be increasingly reorganized to take advantage of IT, yielding further benefits. The fall in relative prices of IT goods has also led to significant increases in consumer surplus in IT-using countries. Over the near term, despite the relatively rapid diffusion of the technology around the globe, the IT revolution is likely to benefit advanced economies more than developing countries. In the long run, however, the distribution of the benefits will depend on specific country characteristics rather than relative incomes.

The IT revolution has important policy implications. Structural policies should encourage the widespread adoption and effective use of IT, including by promoting flexible labor markets and efficient service sectors. Uncertainty about the precise magnitude and likely duration of the acceleration in productivity imply that policymakers should place less weight on variables about which uncertainty has increased, such as the output gap, and more weight on observable variables, like actual inflation and a wide array of indicators of future inflation.

References

Abramovitz, Moses, and Paul A. David, 1996, "Convergence and Deferred Catch-up: Productivity Leadership and the Waning of American Exceptionalism," in *The Mosaic of Economic Growth,* ed. by Ralph Landau, Timothy Taylor, and Gavin Wright (Stanford: Stanford University Press).

Autor, David H., Lawrence F. Katz, and Alan B. Krueger, 1998, "Computing Inequality: Have Computers Changed the Labor Market?" *Quarterly Journal of Economics*, Vol. 113 (November), pp. 1169–1213.

Autor, David H., Frank Levy, and Richard J. Murnane, 2001, "The Skill Content of Recent Technological Change: An Empirical Investigation," NBER Working Paper No. 8337 (Cambridge, Mass.: National Bureau of Economic Research).

Baily, Martin, and Robert Lawrence, 2001, "Do We Have a New E-Conomy," NBER Working Paper No. 8243 (Cambridge, Mass.: National Bureau of Economic Research).

Bank for International Settlements, 2001, *71st Annual Report* (Basel: BIS).

Basu, Susanto, John G. Fernald, and Matthew D. Shapiro, 2001, "Productivity Growth in the 1990s: Technology, Utilization, or Adjustment?" NBER Working Paper No. 8359 (Cambridge, Mass.: National Bureau of Economic Research).

Bayoumi, Tamim, and Markus Haacker, 2001, "It's Not What You Make, It's How You Use IT," (unpublished; Washington: International Monetary Fund, Research Department).

Berman, Eli, John Bound, and Stephen Machin, 1998, "Implications of Skill-Biased Technological Change: International Evidence," *Quarterly Journal of Economics*, Vol. 113 (November), pp. 1245–79.

Bresnehan, Timothy F., Erik Brynjolfsson, and Lorin M. Hitt, 1999, "Information Technology, Workplace Organization, and the Demand for Skilled Labor: Firm-Level Evidence," NBER Working Paper No. 7136 (Cambridge, Mass.: National Bureau of Economic Research).

Brookes, Martin, and Zaki Wahhaj, 2000, "Is the Internet Better Than Electricity?" Global Economics Papers No. 49, Goldman Sachs (New York: Goldman Sachs).

Brooks, Robin, and Luis Catão, 2000, "The New Economy and Global Stock Returns," IMF Working Paper No. 00/216 (Washington: International Monetary Fund).

Brynjolfsson, Erik, 1996, "The Contribution of Information Technology to Consumer Welfare," *Information Systems Research*, Vol. 7 (September), pp. 281.

———, and Lorin M. Hitt, 2000, "Beyond Computation: Information Technology, Organizational Transformation, and Business Performance," *Journal of Economic Perspectives*, Vol. 14 (Fall), pp. 23–48.

Cardarelli, Roberto, 2001, "Is Australia a 'New Economy'?" in *Australia: Selected Issues and Statistical Appendix*, IMF Country Report No. 01/55 (Washington: International Monetary Fund).

Caselli, Francesco, and Wilbur John Coleman II, 2001, "Cross-Country Technology Diffusion: The Case of Computers," NBER Working Paper No. 8130 (Cambridge: Mass.: National Bureau of Economic Research).

Cecchetti, Stephen G., 2001, "The New Economy and the Challenges for Monetary Policy," paper for a conference on "New Technologies: Consequences and Challenges for Central Banks," Banque de France, February 1–9. Available on the Internet at *http://www.econ.ohio-state.edu/cecchetti/ pub_pol_papers.shtml.*

Colecchia, Alessandra, 2001, "The Impact of Information and Communications Technologies on Output Growth: Issues and Preliminary Findings," OECD Directorate for Science, Technology, and Industry Working Paper No. 11 (Paris: Organization for Economic Cooperation and Development).

Crafts, Nicholas, 2000, "The Solow Productivity Paradox in Historical Perspective," paper presented to the conference on "Long-Term Trends in the World Economy," University of Copenhagen, December.

———, 2001, "Historical Perspectives on the Information Technology Revolution," (unpublished; Washington: International Monetary Fund, Research Department).

Crépon, Bruno, and Thomas Heckel, 2000, "La Contribution de l'Information à la Croissance Française: Une Mesure à partir des Donnés d'Entreprises," *Economie et Statistique*, No. 339/340 pp. 93–116.

Dasgupta, Susmita, Somik Lall, and David Wheeler, 2001, "Policy Reform, Economic Growth and the Digital Divide: An Econometric Analysis," Development Research Group Working Paper No. 2567 (Washington: World Bank).

Daveri, Francesco, 2001, "Information Technology and Growth in Europe," (unpublished: Parma: University of Parma).

David, Paul A., 1990, "The Dynamo and the Computer: An Historical Perspective on the Modern Productivity Paradox," *American Economic Review, Papers and Proceedings*, Vol. 80 (May), pp. 355–61.

———, 2000, "Understanding Digital Technology's Evolution and the Path of Measured Productivity Growth: Present and Future in the Mirror of the Past," in *Understanding the Digital Economy,* ed. by Erik Brynjolfsson and Brian Kahin (Cambridge, Mass.: MIT Press).

DeLong, Bradford, forthcoming, "Do We Have a 'New' Macroeconomy?" in *Innovation Policy and the Economy, Volume 2*, ed. by Adam Jaffee, Joshua Lerner, and Scott Stern (Cambridge, Mass.: MIT Press).

———, 2001, "A Historical Perspective on the New Economy," remarks prepared for the Montreal New Economy Conference. June. Available on the Internet at *www.econ161.berkeley.edu.*

De Masi, Paula, 2000, "Does the Pickup in Productivity Growth Mean That There is a New Economy?" in *United States: Selected Issues,* IMF Staff Country Report No. 00/112 (Washington: International Monetary Fund).

DiNardo, John E., and Jorn-Steffen Pischke, 1997, "The Returns to Computers Revisited: Have Pencils Changed the Wage Structure Too?" *Quarterly Journal of Economics*, Vol. 112 (February), pp. 291–303.

Deutsche Bundesbank, 2000, "Problems of International Comparisons of Growth Caused by Dissimilar Methods of Deflation, With IT Equipment in Germany and the United States as a Case in Point," in *Monthly Report*, August.

———, 2001, "Problems of International Comparisons of Growth—A Supplementary Analysis," Appendix in *Monthly Report*, May.

Estevão, Marcello, and Joaquim Levy, 2000, "The New Economy in France: Development and Prospects," in *France: Selected Issues*, IMF Staff Country Report No. 00/148 (Washington: International Monetary Fund).

Fazzari, Steven, Glenn Hubbard, and Bruce Petersen, 1988, "Financing Constraints and Corporate Investment," *Brooking Paper on Economic Activity: 1,* Brookings Institution, pp. 141–206.

Ferguson, Roger W., 2001, "The Productivity Experience of the United States: Past, Present, and Future," speech given at the U.S. Embassy, The Hague, Netherlands, June. Available on the Internet at *www.federalreserve.gov/boarddocs/speeches/2001.*

Gertler, Mark, and Simon Gilchrist, 1994, "Monetary Policy, Business Cycles, and the Behavior of Small Manufacturing Firms," *Quarterly Journal of Economics,* Vol. 109, pp. 309–40.

Glaeser, Edward L., 1998, "Are Cities Dying?" *Journal of Economic Perspectives*, Vol. 12 (Spring), pp. 139–60.

Glick, Reuven, and Kenneth Rogoff, 1995, "Global versus Country-Specific Productivity Shocks and the Current Account," *Journal of Monetary Economics,* Vol. 35 (February), pp.159–92.

Goolsbee, Austan, 2001, "The Implications of Electronic Commerce for Fiscal Policy (and Vice Versa)," *Journal of Economic Perspectives*, Vol. 15 (Winter), pp. 13–23.

Gordon, Robert J., 2000, "Does the 'New Economy' Measure up to the Great Inventions of the Past?" *Journal of Economic Perspectives*, Vol. 14 (Fall), pp. 49–74.

Gramlich, Edward M., 2001, "The Productivity Growth Spurt in the United States," speech before the International Bond Congress, London, February 20. Available on the Internet at *www.federalreserve.gov/boarddocs/speeches/2001.*

Greenspan, Alan, 2001a, "Economic Developments," speech before the Economic Club of New York, May 24. Available on the Internet at *www.federalreserve.gov/boarddocs/speeches/2001.*

———, 2001b, "The Growing Need for Skills in the 21st Century," speech before the U.S. Department of Labor, June 20. Available on the Internet at *www.federalreserve.gov/boarddocs/speeches/2001.*

Gust, Christopher, and Jaime Marquez, 2000, "Productivity Developments Abroad," *Federal Reserve Bulletin,* The Federal Reserve Board (October).

Haacker, Markus, and James Morsink, 2001, "You Say You Want A Revolution: Information Technology and Growth," (unpublished, Washington: International Monetary Fund, Research Department).

Hall, Robert E., 2001, "Struggling to Understand the Stock Market," *American Economic Review, Papers and Proceedings*, Vol. 91 (May), pp. 1–11.

Hawke, Gary R., 1970, *Railways and Economic Growth in England and Wales, 1840–1870*, (Oxford: Clarendon Press).

Hicks, John, 1982, "Are there Economic Cycles?" in *Money, Interest, and Wages: Collected Essays on Economic Theory*, Vol. 2, ed. by John Hicks (Oxford: Basil Blackwell).

Hubbard, R. Glenn, 1998, "Capital-Market Imperfections and Investment," *Journal of Economic Literature*, Vol. 36 (March), pp. 193–225.

International Telecommunications Union, 1999, *Statistical Yearbook* (Geneva: International Telecommunications Union).

Japan, Economic Planning Agency, 2000, *Keizai Hakusho* (Economic Survey of Japan), in Japanese and English (Tokyo: Economic Planning Agency).

Jorgenson, Dale W., 2001, "Information Technology and the U.S. Economy," *American Economic Review*, Vol. 91 (March), pp. 1–32.

———, and Kevin J. Stiroh, 2000, "Raising the Speed Limit: U.S. Economic Growth in the Information Age," *Brookings Papers on Economic Activity: 1*, Brookings Institution, pp. 161–67.

J.P. Morgan Chase & Co., 2001, "The Asian Growth Hit From the U.S. Tech. Slowdown," in *Asia Economic Viewpoint* (February).

Kelkar, Vijay Laxman, 1982, "Long-Term Growth Possibilities in the OECD Economies: An Alternative View," in *Trade and Development Report* (Geneva: United Nations Conference on Trade and Development).

King, Mervyn, 1999, "Challenges for Monetary Policy: New and Old," in *New Challenges for Monetary Policy*, by the Federal Reserve Bank of Kansas City (Kansas City, MO: Federal Reserve Bank of Kansas City).

Kodres, Laura, forthcoming, "The New Economy in the United Kingdom," in an IMF Country Report.

Lamoreaux, Naomi R., and Kenneth L. Sokoloff, 1999, "Inventive Activity and the Market for Technology in the United States, 1840–1920," NBER Working Paper No. 7107 (Cambridge, Mass.: National Bureau of Economic Research).

Landefeld, J. Steven, and Barbara M. Fraumeni, 2001, "Measuring the New Economy," *Survey of Current Business* (March), pp. 23–40.

Landefeld, J. Steven, and Robert Parker, 1998, "BEA's Chain Indexes, Time Series, and Measures of Long-Term Economic Growth," *Survey of Current Business* (May), pp. 58–68.

Lee, Frank C., and Dirk Pilat, 2001, "Productivity Growth in ICT-Producing and ICT-Using Industries—A Source of Growth Differentials in the OECD?" OECD Directorate for Science, Technology, and Industry Working Paper No. 3 (Paris: Organization for Economic Cooperation and Development).

Lee, Il-Houng, and Yougesh Khatri, 2001, "The Role of the New Economy in East Asia," (unpublished; Washington: International Monetary Fund, Asia and Pacific Department).

Lee, Jong-Wha, 2000, "Education for Technology Readiness: Prospects for Developing Countries," background Paper for the *Human Development Report 2001*, United Nations Development Programme (New York: UNDP).

Lequiller, Francois, 2001, "La Nouvelle Economie et la Mesure de la Croissance du PIB," Serie des documents de travail de la Direction des Etudes et Syntheses Economiques, INSEE (Paris, February).

Litan, Robert E., and Alice M. Rivlin, 2000, "The Economy and the Internet: What Lies Ahead?" Brookings Conference Report No. 4, Brookings Institution.

Lucas, Robert E., Jr., 1993, "Making a Miracle," *Econometrica*, Vol. 61 (March), pp. 251–72.

Mairesse, Jacques, Gilbert Cette, and Yussuf Kocoglu, 2000, "Les Technologies de l'Information et de la Communication en France: Diffusion et Contribution à la Croissance," *Economie et Statistique*, No. 339/340, pp. 117–46.

Mann, Catherine L., Sue E. Eckert, and Sarah Cleeland Knight, 2000, *Global Electronic Commerce: A Policy Primer* (Washington: Institute for International Economics).

Marquez, Jaime, 2001, "Reassessing Explanations of the Inverse Relation Between Private Investment and the Current Account," (unpublished; Washington: Federal Reserve Board).

Meyer, Laurence H., 2000, "Structural Change and Monetary Policy," remarks prepared for the Joint Conference of the Federal Reserve Bank of San Francisco and the Stanford Institute for Economic Policy Research, San Francisco, March. Available on the Internet at *www.federalreserve.gov/boarddocs/ speeches/2001.*

Mitchell, Brian R., 1988, *British Historical Statistics* (Cambridge: Cambridge University Press).

Mody, Ashoka, Rajan Suri, and Jerry Sanders, 1992, "Keeping Pace with Change: Organizational and Technological Imperatives," *World Development*, Vol. 20 (December), pp. 1797–816.

Myers, Stewart, 1977, "Determinants of Corporate Borrowing," *Journal of Financial Economics*, Vol. 5 (November), pp. 147–75.

———, and Nicolas Majluf, 1984, "Corporate Financing and Investment Decisions When Firms Have Information that Investors do not Have," *Journal of Financial Economics*, Vol. 13 (June), pp. 187–221.

Nordhaus, William, 2001, "Productivity Growth and the New Economy," NBER Working Paper No. 8096 (Cambridge, Mass.: National Bureau of Economic Research).

Oliner, Stephen D., and Daniel E. Sichel, 2000, "The Resurgence of Growth in the Late 1990s: Is Information Technology the Story," *Journal of Economic Perspectives*, Vol. 14 (Fall), pp. 3–22.

OECD, 2000, *OECD Information Technology Outlook: ICTs, E-Commerce, and the Information Economy* (Paris: Organization for Economic Cooperation and Development).

Orphanides, Athanasios, 1998, "Monetary Policy Evaluation with Noisy Information," Finance and Economics Discussion Paper No. 1998–50 (Washington: Board of Governors of the Federal Reserve System).

———, 2000, "The Quest for Prosperity Without Inflation," European Central Bank Working Paper No. 15 (Frankfurt: European Central Bank).

Oulton, Nicholas, 2001, "ICT and Productivity Growth in the United Kingdom," Bank of England Working Paper No. 140, (London: Bank of England, July).

Pohjola, Matti, 2000, "Information Technology and Economic Growth: A Cross-Country Analysis," World Institute for Development Economics Research Working Paper No. 173 (Helsinki: United Nations University).

Portes, Richard, and Helene Rey, 1999, "The Determinants of Cross-Border Equity Flows," NBER Working Paper No. 7336 (Cambridge, Mass.: National Bureau of Economic Research).

Reed Electronics Research, 2001, *Yearbook of World Electronics Data* (Reed Business Information Ltd.).

Roeger, Werner, 2001, "The Contribution of Information and Communication Technologies to Growth in Europe and the United States: A Macroeconomic Analysis," *Economic Papers*, No. 147, European Commission (January).

Schreyer, Paul, 2000, "The Contribution of Information and Communication Technology to Output Growth: A Study of the G7 Countries," OECD Directorate for Science, Technology, and Innovation Working Paper No. 2000/2, (Paris: Organization for Economic Cooperation and Development).

———, 2001, "Computer Price Indices and International Growth and Productivity Comparisons," OECD Statistics Directorate (unpublished; Paris: Organization for Economic Cooperation and Development).

Senhadji, Abdelhak, 1998, "Time Series Estimation of Structural Import Demand Equations: A Cross-Country Analysis," *IMF Staff Papers*, International Monetary Fund, Vol. 45 (June), pp. 236–68.

Stiroh, Kevin J., 2001, "Information Technology and the U.S. Productivity Revival: What Do the Industry Data Say?" Staff Report No. 115 (New York: Federal Reserve Bank of New York).

Swanson, Eric T., 2001, "On Signal Extraction and Non-Certainty-Equivalence in Optimal Monetary Policy Rules," Finance and Economics Discussion Paper No. 2000–32 (Washington: Board of Governors of the Federal Reserve System).

Tanzi, Vito, 2000, "Globalization, Technological Developments, and the Work of Fiscal Termites," IMF Working Paper No. 00/181 (Washington: International Monetary Fund).

Tevlin, Stacey, and Karl Whelan, 2000, "Explaining the Investment Boom of the 1990s," Finance and Economics Discussion Series No. 2000–11 (Washington: Board of Governors of the Federal Reserve System).

Turner, Philip, forthcoming, "Policy, Regulatory, and Legal Issues Associated with E-Finance in Emerging Markets," in *Open Doors: Foreign Participation in Financial Systems in Developing Countries* (Washington: Brookings Institution).

U.S. Council of Economic Advisers, 2001, *Economic Report of the President* (Washington: U.S. Government Printing Office).

U.S. Department of Commerce, Bureau of Economic Analysis (for hedonic price indices). Available on the Internet at *http://www.bea.doc.gov/bea/dn/ nipaweb/*

U.S. General Accounting Office, 2000, "Sales Taxes: Electronic Commerce Growth Presents Challenges,

Revenue Losses are Uncertain," Report to Congressional Requesters, GAO/GGD/OCE-00-165 (Washington).

Van Ark, Bart, 2001, "The Renewal of the Old Economy: Europe in an Internationally Comparative Perspective," (unpublished; Groningen: University of Groningen).

Vavares, Chris, Joel Prakken, and Lisa Guirl, 1998, "Macro Modeling with Chain-Type GDP," *Journal of Economic and Social Measurement*, Vol. 24, No. 2, pp. 123–42.

Wadhwani, Sushil, 2000, "Monetary Challenges in a New Economy," speech to the Hong Kong and Shanghai Banking Corporation Global Investment Seminar, October. Available on the Internet at *www.bankofengland.co.uk/speeches/speech103.pdf.*

Whelan, Karl, 2000, "A Guide to the Use of Chain Aggregated NIPA Data," Finance and Economics Discussion Paper No. 2000–35 (Washington: Board of Governors of the Federal Reserve System).

White, Eugene N., 1990, "The Stock Market Boom and Crash of 1929 Revisited," *Journal of Economic Perspectives*, Vol. 4 (spring), pp. 67–83.

Woodruff, William, 1966, *The Impact of Western Man* (London: Macmillan).

World Information Technology Services Alliance (WITSA), 2001, *Digital Planet.*

CHAPTER IV

INTERNATIONAL FINANCIAL INTEGRATION AND DEVELOPING COUNTRIES

Globalization of the world economy has been driven by a variety of forces: rising trade in goods, increasing international capital flows, greater technological spillovers, and growing labor mobility. This chapter examines the increase in capital movement and, in particular, the impact of international financial integration on developing countries. Views on this issue have changed since the early 1990s, when international financial deregulation, and the associated capital flows from industrial to developing countries, appeared to be fueling faster growth and catch-up. A series of financial crises, starting with industrial countries in the European Exchange Rate Mechanism (ERM) in 1992 and 1993 but then moving on in a significantly more virulent form to developing countries with the 1995 Tequila crisis in Mexico, the Asian crisis of 1997–98, and the Russian and Latin American crises in 1998–2000, have made clear that international capital flows have risks as well as benefits.

Opening the financial market to the rest of the world is a complex and often long-drawn out process that involves lifting restrictions on foreign direct investment (FDI) flows and long- and short-term financial instruments. The bulk of this chapter assesses the net benefits to output of international financial market integration, focusing on the channels through which capital flows from industrial to developing countries might affect economic activity in the recipient countries. The remaining part of the chapter describes the lessons learned from sequencing. On the positive side, less restrictive capital controls and higher international capital flows can increase investment possibilities, create technology spillovers, and deepen domestic capital markets. However, they can also create instability by leaving countries open to sudden reversals in capital flows. This risk can increase if domestic macroeconomic and financial policies are weak or in-

consistent, or if financial systems are not sufficiently developed to cope with large capital flows.

The chapter first documents the increase in financial integration over the last three decades, using two complementary measures of capital account liberalization, one of which has not been widely applied in previous analysis. These measures indicate that the industrial countries liberalized their capital accounts early on whereas in the developing countries the shift toward capital account liberalization in general was slow, but quickened in the early 1990s. These indicators are then used to examine whether countries with more open capital accounts have had a better economic performance than countries with more restrictive capital accounts. The analysis reveals a weak relationship between growth and capital account liberalization and, like other studies, has difficulty finding evidence of a significant relationship. That said, work using the new measure of openness suggests that it is possible to identify a significant impact from capital account liberalization on investment and financial development (as well as positive spillover from FDI to growth in countries with adequate human capital). The effect of a "typical" liberalization through these two channels is estimated to increase growth by ½ percent a year or more. But, opening up the capital account can also entail costs if it is not sequenced and implemented appropriately, particularly when the institutional framework is weak. This helps to explain the weaker direct relationship between liberalization and growth.

Prior to analyzing these issues in more detail, some definitions of key concepts are needed. First, in this chapter, international financial liberalization—or opening the capital account—will be simply referred to as liberalization, while the level of such integration will be referred to as openness. Both concepts refer to the degree to which restrictions on financial transactions based upon citizenship or residency, or related to cross-border transactions, have been eliminated.[1] Second, domestic financial liberalization, which relates to the reduction of distortions in the domestic financial system, will be referred to as domestic liberalization. While both forms of liberalization are important and often go hand in hand, the focus of this chapter is on the effects of international financial liberalization.

Trends in Capital Account Liberalization and Capital Flows

Generally speaking, the increasing financial links across countries, and especially between industrial and developing countries, have been associated with the liberalization of both international and domestic financial markets. This section describes the trends in capital account liberalization and the associated rapid growth of international capital flows.[2]

Before reviewing the experience over the last 30 years, two lessons from history are worth noting. First, at a general level, openness to trade and, to a somewhat lesser extent, open financial markets have been associated with higher growth and greater convergence across regions. The collapse of international trade and capital flows in the interwar period involved slow growth and little convergence. By contrast, the period since 1950, which has seen rapid opening of trade and financial markets, has had high rates of growth and some convergence, although progress was most rapid in the early part of the period, when trade links were growing fastest.[3] Second, the liberalized capital markets that were a feature of

the pre-1914 classical gold standard supported relatively larger capital flows than today, but had international financial crises that were, if anything, somewhat less frequent and less disruptive of output than those since 1973 (Bordo and others, 2001). The relatively greater stability before World War I appears to reflect the large degree of credibility of domestic policies associated with the gold standard, greater ties in terms of heritage between Britain (the major lender) and many of the important borrowers, and the fact that much of the money was used to finance railroads and other infrastructure, which was easily monitored and directly used in producing exports and hence earning foreign currency.

Since 1970, the experience of developing countries with capital account liberalization has differed dramatically from that of the industrial countries. Nevertheless, researchers face a common problem in both industrial and developing countries when attempting to measure financial openness (see Box 4.1). Liberalization involves a complex process of reducing controls across a wide array of assets. There are large differences in the nature, the intensity, and the effectiveness of the various impediments governments have put into place to limit the movement of cross-border capital flows. Consequently, there are often large gaps between the ideal set of indicators and the measures that are available in practice (see Eichengreen, 2001).

This chapter uses two indicators derived from different methodologies to measure capital account liberalization. Most formal empirical work analyzing the impact of capital account liberalization has used a *restriction* measure based on the restrictions on capital flows as reported to

[1]It should be noted that the use of the words "capital account" is inconsistent with the terminology in the 1993 System of National Accounts, which switched the name from capital account to financial account. To avoid confusion, this chapter uses the older and more generally understood term.

[2]Most of the analysis in this chapter is based on a sample of 55 developing countries listed in Table 4.2 (as well as, in some cases, 20 industrial countries). Because of data limitations, the reported regression analysis reports results for 38 developing countries. Given the long period over which the analysis is conducted, several countries currently defined as industrial (Cyprus, Israel, Korea, and Singapore) are included with developing country group. The following countries were excluded: countries with a population below 500,000 people, Heavily Indebted Poor Countries (which mostly receive official flows), and transition economies (partly due to lack of data). For recent studies of the HIPCs and of the transition economies, see the *World Economic Outlook* May 2000 and *World Economic Outlook* October 2000, respectively.

[3]See *World Economic Outlook*, May 2000; and O'Rourke (2001).

Box 4.1. Measuring Capital Account Liberalization

Assessing international capital account liberalization is complex, largely reflecting the difficulty in quantifying the extent and the effectiveness of capital controls. No fully satisfactory measure is available, which puts a premium on examining the results from alternative indicators. This chapter uses two measures derived from different methodologies to measure the effectiveness of capital controls. The first, used in most previous analysis of liberalization, is a *restriction* measure, constructed as an on/off indicator of the existence of rules/restrictions that inhibit cross-border capital flows or discriminate on the basis of citizenship or residence of transacting agents. The second and complementary indicator of capital account integration used in this chapter (and only recently available) is a measure of *openness* that is based on the estimated stocks of gross foreign assets and liabilities as a ratio to GDP.

The measure of restrictions comes from the International Monetary Fund's *Annual Report on Exchange Arrangements and Exchange Restrictions* (AREAER).[1] This publication provides a written description of current controls and, since 1967, on/off indicators of the presence or absence of restrictions on the current and capital account. Most studies focus on the indicator measuring restrictions on payments for capital transactions, the only measure that focuses on the capital account.[2] In 1996, however, the presentation was changed to a new system, which contains more detail on capital account restrictions, but is not backwardly compatible with the earlier indicator.

The main difficulty with the restriction measure is that it does not take into account the intensity of the controls, or differentiate across types of restrictions. Recent work has addressed this issue by assessing the intensity of enforce-

ment of the controls using the narrative information contained in the IMF's AREAER. However, due to the labor-intensive nature of this work, such measures for developing countries are currently only available for a few years in the 1970s and 1980s.[3] Other studies have proposed restrictiveness measures for a limited number of countries that focus on controls of international sales and purchases of equities over recent years.[4] Yet others have used interest rate differentials and forward premium/discount to assess the degree of capital mobility and capital account liberalization (see Frankel and MacArthur, 1988). The relatively small coverage of countries and time periods limits these extended measures of restrictions for broad cross-sectional studies of the impact of capital controls, such as the background study used for this chapter.

The second indicator of capital account liberalization uses gross holdings of international assets and liabilities to measure openness to capital transactions.[5] This measure looks directly at one of the consequences of liberalization, namely larger ownership of foreign assets in the country and liabilities elsewhere. It applies the same logic as similar variables used to measure domestic financial depth, such as the stock of credit to the private sector as a ratio of GDP, and trade openness, defined as the sum of exports and imports as a ratio to GDP. Stocks of financial assets are a better measure of capital account

---

[1]The first work to employ this dataset was Grilli and Milesi-Ferretti (1995).

[2]Some researchers supplement this information with the additional external restriction measures available in the AREAER; such as whether there is a separate exchange rate for current account and capital account transactions, whether there are restrictions on payments for current account transactions, whether there is the requirement of surrender or repatriation of export proceeds.

[3]See Quinn (1997). The data on developing countries are limited to three years: 1973, 1982, and 1988.

[4]Henry (2000) and Bekaert and Harvey (2000) compile from a variety of sources dates that countries liberalized their equity markets, while Edison and Warnock (2001) propose a measure that is based on restrictions of foreign ownership of domestic equities, using the ratio of the market capitalization of the country's Global index to the Investable index that is compiled by the International Finance Corporation (IFC) in their Emerging Market Database that is now maintained by Standard and Poor's.

[5]These *openness* measures have not been widely used in the literature. O'Donnell (2001) and Chanda (2000) employ a similar openness measure to the one described in the background study. Kraay (1998) defines openness using the sum of capital inflows and outflows as a ratio of GDP.

Box 4.1 *(concluded)*

openness than underlying flows, as they are less subject to temporary disturbances, although by their nature they tend to be a lagging indicator of policy changes. In addition, various sub-components, related to different types of financial transactions, can be analyzed.

The overall openness measure is computed by using the stock measures of both assets and liabilities of FDI and portfolio transactions (the latter encompassing equities and debt transactions).[6] When interpreting this measure, it is

important to recognize that cross-border capital movements are influenced by a wide range of policy outcomes and do not reflect barriers alone. For example, these measures are also affected by a range of policies and circumstances such as the stance of monetary and fiscal policy, the size of the domestic economy, and conditions in the rest of the world.

The background study for this chapter uses both measures. In general, the results using the restriction measure are not particularly encouraging. By contrast, as reported in the text, the openness measure and its subcomponents appear to provide more intuitively plausible results both in the raw data and the econometric analysis.

[6]The underlying stocks are calculated by accumulating the corresponding flows with appropriate valuation adjustments, and were constructed by Lane and Milesi-Ferretti (forthcoming).

the IMF by national authorities. This indicator directly measures capital controls, and countries are either classified as open or closed. By its nature, however, this measure does not capture differences in the degree of liberalization: for example, a country might liberalize some, but not all, categories of their capital account, and, in accordance with the restriction measure, it could still be labeled as closed. In addition, it is only available until 1995, when a new and more refined measure—not backward compatible—was introduced.

A second and complementary indicator of capital account integration is an *openness* measure (described in Box 4.1), based on the estimated gross stocks of foreign assets and liabilities as a ratio to GDP.[4] It is inspired by the use of similar variables to measure domestic financial depth, such as the stock of credit to the private sector as a ratio to GDP. The openness measure is created by calculating the gross level of FDI and portfolio assets and liabilities via the accumulation of the corresponding inflows and outflows.[5] If this gross stock measure is high, it im-

plies that a country is open, in the sense that it is or has been experiencing significant private sector flows to and from the rest of the world.

For both developing and industrial countries, international gross private capital flows have grown markedly, but with considerable variation over time (Figure 4.1). The openness measure has also increased over time, but in a more gradual and backward-looking fashion, as it measures the stock of assets (Figure 4.2). Clearly, however, the openness measure does not just capture the restrictiveness of capital controls, but also the impact of all other factors influencing the level of capital flows, such as the nature of domestic financial markets. In this respect, the openness measure of liberalization is analogous to measuring the trade regime through calculating the ratio of exports and imports to GDP, while the restriction measure of liberalization is similar to measures of trade restrictions in terms of tariff and nontariff barriers.

What do the restriction measure and the openness measure tell us about liberalization over time? In industrial countries the behavior

[4]These underlying stock data were developed and described by Lane and Milesi-Ferretti (forthcoming). A similar measure using the same underlying stock data has been considered by Chanda (2000) and O'Donnell (2001).
[5]Individual country data on stocks of bank loans are too fragmented to be included in the measure.

of the two measures is similar, and confirms that industrial countries have become considerably more open over time. A particularly rapid decline in controls occurred during the 1980s, when the members of the European Community, now the European Union, liberalized capital controls. Following this, there was a dramatic rise in cross-border capital flows. Based on the openness measure, the top four most open industrial countries have been: Canada, Netherlands, Switzerland, and the United Kingdom.

In developing countries, the story is more complex. In general, both measures suggest a less dramatic shift toward liberalization and openness than in industrial countries. The following points are worth noting:

- For the developing countries as a whole, the restriction measure suggests that, after a period of liberalization in the 1970s, the trend toward openness reversed in the 1980s. Liberalization resumed in the early 1990s, but the pace has been relatively slow; the measure indicates that the current level of the indicator on average is only at the same level as it was in the late 1970s.

- The openness measure shows a modest decline in openness to capital flows during the early 1970s, followed by a moderate increase in the 1980s, which accelerated sharply in the early 1990s. While the most recent acceleration may reflect a more rapid liberalization than the relatively crude restrictiveness measure suggests, it also reflects the increasing openness of industrial countries, as well as the more general trend toward globalization.

Within developing countries, there have been important differences across regions:

- For *Asia*, there has been an upward trend in the openness measure since the late 1970s, while the restriction measure has changed very little.[6] While it is probable that the re-

[6]Indonesia and Malaysia are defined as open using the restrictiveness measure from the early 1970s on, while Korea is classified as closed through the end of the sample in 1995.

Figure 4.1. Gross Capital Flows
(Percent of GDP)

Gross capital flows have risen over time, but are also volatile.

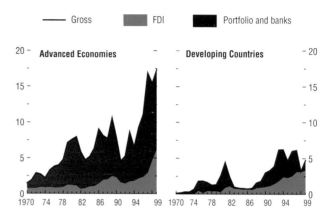

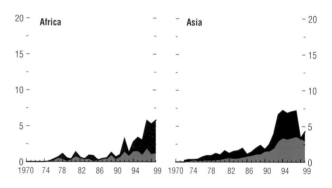

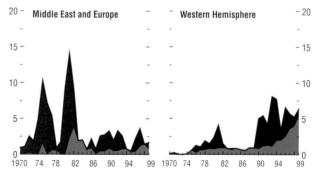

Sources: IMF, *International Financial Statistics*; and IMF staff estimates.
[1]For country coverage, see Table 4.2.

Figure 4.2. Summary of Measures of Capital Account Openness[1]

The two measures of liberalization show similar overall patterns, but the openness measure points to greater progress in the 1990s.

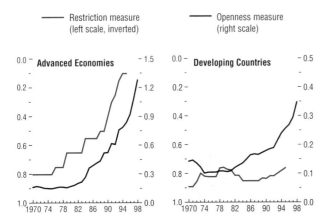

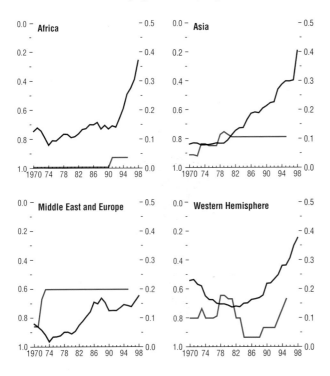

Sources: IMF, *Annual Report on Exchange Arrangements and Exchange Restrictions*, various issues; *International Financial Statistics*; and IMF staff calculations.

[1] The restriction measure is calculated as the "average" value of the on/off measure for the country group. The openness measure is calculated as the average stock of accumulated capital flows (as percent of GDP) in a country group.

[2] For country coverage, see Table 4.2.

strictiveness measure underestimates the degree of liberalization, the rapid rise in openness probably also reflects other factors, including the opening up of the Chinese economy, and the rapid development and growth—and associated capital requirements of—the newly industrialized economies and members of the Association of South East Asian Nations (ASEAN). While a substantial proportion of inflows take the form of foreign direct investment, there was a very large increase in portfolio and bank flows in the early 1990s, which ultimately proved unsustainable.

- For *Africa*, both the restriction measure and the openness measure show little change until the early 1990s. The substantial increase in openness in the 1990s is mainly due to events in a limited number of countries. In particular, this has involved large portfolio flows to South Africa, which has the most developed financial markets in the region, as well as large FDI flows to Lesotho and Nigeria, which reflected investments in resource production.

- In the *Middle East and Europe* the restriction index shows some liberalization in the early 1970s, as oil producers such as Oman, Qatar, Saudi Arabia, and the United Arab Emirates lowered restrictions. The openness measure shows a more gradual increase in liberalization. By contrast, gross capital flows spiked with the two oil price hikes, but have stagnated since then.

- For the *Western Hemisphere*, both measures show that, on average, the region was relatively open in the 1970s, with Argentina, Chile, and Mexico having liberalized. The openness of the region led to large bank-based inflows of oil surpluses in the mid- to late 1970s, but many countries then imposed controls in response to outflows during the 1980s debt crisis, sparked by the Mexican crisis in 1982. These capital controls were relatively ineffective, and capital flight continued through most of the "lost decade" until longer-term institutional reforms allowed the region to reenter international capital markets at the end of the 1980s. Hence, one of the lessons from the 1980s debt crisis is that imposing capital controls on markets that have been closely linked to the rest of the world may be of limited value in stemming outflows.

- After the setback of much of the 1980s, Latin American liberalization has continued through the late 1980s and early 1990s. As in Asia, the openness measure shows a much larger increase, fueled by portfolio flows and FDI. The U-shaped pattern observed in the indicators for the Western Hemisphere illustrate the endogeneity inherent in these measures; if the economic performance deteriorates, then a country might impose controls.

Finally, some countries have played a more important role than others in global capital markets over the last three decades. Among the industrial countries, since 1970 the United States and the United Kingdom were both dominant suppliers and users of capital. More generally, the Group of Five (France, Germany, Japan, United Kingdom, and United States) countries were the largest suppliers and users of capital, accounting for about two-thirds of all private capital inflows and outflows. For the developing countries, the bulk of capital flows have been directed toward Asia and Latin America (Figure 4.3). Asia (primarily China) received a higher portion of FDI than other regions, while countries in Latin America received a higher portion of portfolio flows than other regions. These regional differences mirror partly the general history of larger fiscal deficits in Latin America compared with Asia, leading to more floating of government bonds, as well as the earlier development of some capital markets in Latin America. For example, most investments in China are FDI flows, partly because local capital markets are less open and developed. More generally, the figures reflect that countries with relatively liberalized capital accounts receive higher capital flows whereas countries that are more closed receive moderate amounts of capi-

Figure 4.3. Concentration of Capital Flows: Largest Developing Country Users
(Average of 1970–2000)

The largest users of foreign direct investment (FDI) flows are generally in Asia, while portfolio flows are more concentrated in Latin America.

Largest Users of FDI

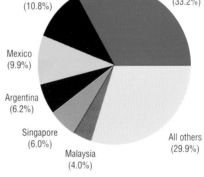

Largest Users of Portfolio Flows

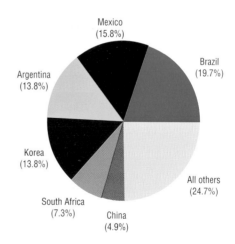

Sources: IMF, *International Financial Statistics*; and IMF staff estimates.

tal flows, mainly in the form of foreign direct investment.[7]

Overall, according to both the restriction and openness measures, most regions of the world today have been opening their capital accounts during the 1980s and 1990s.

The Impact of International Capital Account Liberalization on Growth

The impact of liberalization on growth depends crucially on the initial conditions and policies in the country. From a theoretical perspective, models of perfect markets and full information suggest that liberalization, by allowing a better allocation of resources across countries, benefits both lenders and borrowers and raises growth. In practice, however, this result depends critically on a variety of preconditions, including a supportive and consistent macroeconomic and institutional framework. One example is when liberalization is associated with a government pledge to maintain a pegged exchange rate that is unsustainable in the medium term. As a result of the unsustainable and inconsistent macroeconomic policy, consumers and producers borrow excessively in the short term from the rest of the world to bring forward purchases of (temporarily cheap) foreign goods, creating a domestic boom. When the exchange rate peg eventually collapses, however, domestic demand will collapse and international capital flows will reverse, often accompanied by serious banking system pressures.[8] A similar story could clearly be told for inadequate financial supervision. This, in a nutshell, is the tension between the benefits and costs of open liberalization. While an open capital account can provide great benefits if the appropriate institutional requirements are in place—notably adequate financial supervision

and consistent macroeconomic policies—it can be destabilizing if they are not.

Financial instability may also affect poverty levels and other social conditions. On the one hand, recent evidence shows that growth is one of the main factors contributing to the reduction of poverty and the improvement of social conditions, so that liberalization can help reduce poverty to the extent it increases the long-run impact on growth. On the other hand, liberalization can be associated with an increase in macroeconomic volatility and the occurrence of crises, which may entail social costs such as worsening income distribution, poverty levels, and health and education conditions. This is because the poor and less educated have very limited access to financial markets to hedge or diversify risk, and are thus hurt disproportionately more by economic contraction and by the frequently associated reduction in public health and education spending.[9] This points to the value of comprehensive social safety nets to help mitigate the impact of structural changes—including that associated with liberalization—on the population in general and the poor in particular.

Reflecting these considerations, experience with liberalization is quite varied. Hence, identifying "the impact" of capital market opening on growth has been difficult. In many respects, a more fruitful approach is to examine the main channels through which liberalization affects the economy. On the positive side, liberalization will tend to raise investment by supplementing domestic savings, as well as by allowing better risk diversification and greater consumption smoothing. In addition, foreign direct investment flows in particular can provide technology spillovers via the transfer of ideas. The impact on domestic financial intermediation, however, is mixed. Liberalization can improve the domestic finan-

[7]See Johnston and Ryan (1994); and Mody and Murshid (2001). The impact of liberalization on capital flows depends also on timing. When liberalization occurs in tranquil times, capital flows tend to increase, but when liberalization occurs during a crisis, capital flows tend either to not react or to decline—see Edison and Warnock (forthcoming).

[8]On these issues, see Eichengreen and others (1998); and Calvo and Végh (1999).

[9]On these issues, see, for example, Chapter IV in the May 2000 *World Economic Outlook*; Dollar and Kraay (2001); and Asian Development Bank (2001).

cial system over time by strengthening competition, providing access to best practices elsewhere (particularly if foreign financial institutions enter the market), and reducing resources spent on circumventing capital controls. However, excessive inflows facilitated by lax financial supervision, macroeconomic policy inconsistencies, or excessive zeal by foreign investors can overwhelm the ability of the domestic financial system to allocate funds efficiently, leading to future financial and social problems.

The opening part of this section provides a broad assessment of the relationship between capital market openness and growth, examining the raw data, the existing literature, and the results of a background study carried out by IMF staff and a consultant. The analysis finds a weak positive link between capital account liberalization and economic growth. A similar approach focusing on the channels suggests that capital market openness is linked over time with higher domestic private investment in developing countries, some positive spillovers from FDI, and a boost to domestic financial depth. However, excessive capital inflows can lead to financial instability, so that the net benefits will obviously depend, as already noted, on the strength of the domestic macroeconomic policies and financial structures.

Has Liberalization Led to Higher Growth?

Empirical work finds a weak positive relationship between international capital account liberalization and growth. For example, when countries are classified using the openness measures into open and closed, it appears that countries that are more open to international capital flows tend to grow faster than those countries classified as less open in the 1980s and 1990s (Figure 4.4). In this calculation open developing countries are defined as those whose openness measure exceeds the average value for the entire sample period for both industrial and developing countries, and the remainder are defined as closed. Although such a correlation ignores the numerous other factors that explain growth, and

Figure 4.4. Per Capita Growth by Liberalization in Developing Countries[1]
(Percent)

More liberalized countries tended to grow faster in the 1980s and 1990s, according to the openness measure.

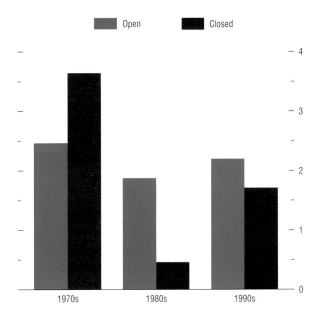

Sources: IMF, *International Financial Statistics*; and IMF staff calculations.
[1]A country is defined as open when its openness measure exceeds the average value for the entire sample period for both industrial and developing countries. The remaining countries are defined as closed. See Table 4.2 for country classification.

Table 4.1. Summary Studies on Capital Account Liberalization and Growth

Study	Number of Countries	Years Covered	Effect on Growth
Alesina, Grilli, and Milesi-Ferretti (1994)	20	1950–89	No effect
Grilli and Milesi-Ferretti (1995)	61	1966–89	No effect
Quinn (1997)	64	1975–89	Positive
Kraay (1998)	117	1985–97	No effect
Rodrik (1998)	95	1975–89	No effect
Klein and Olivei (2000)	92	1986–95	Positive
Chanda (2000)	116	1976–95	Positive
Arteta, Eichengreen, and Wyplosz (2001)	59	1973–92	Mixed
Bekaert, Harvey, and Lundblad (2001)	30	1981–97	Positive
Edwards (2001)	62	1980s	Positive

assumes that liberalized markets affect growth immediately, approaches using more sophisticated statistical models come to similar conclusions.

A growing number of academic studies have examined the relationship between capital account liberalization and growth by adding a measure of such liberalization to the conventional growth model (see Box 4.2). The results from these exercises have been mixed, with about half identifying a significant positive impact and the other half failing to find such a relationship (Table 4.1).[10] Overall, this suggests that liberalization is mildly beneficial for growth.

The wide divergence in results reflects a number of differences across studies. First, the country coverage is different, with some authors analyzing industrial countries, others developing countries, and others a mixture. Second, there are differences in the sample period, which may be particularly important for developing countries given the recent nature of many capital account liberalizations. Third, the applied methodology (cross-sectional, time series, or panel) and the estimation technique (ordinary least squares, instrumental variables, or generalized method of moments) differ across studies. In addition, there are some general drawbacks with the literature that analyzes the relationship between liberalization and growth. The restrictiveness measure of financial controls used in the bulk of these studies is relatively crude. Finally, capital controls are often treated as exogenous to the growth process, but in practice countries with particular macroeconomic and financial characteristics are especially prone to adopt controls, implying the potential for reverse causality.[11]

To delve into these issues more deeply, IMF staff and a consultant undertook a new study focusing on 38 developing countries over the period 1980 to 1999, using both the restriction measure of liberalization generally included in existing studies and the new openness measure of liberalization discussed earlier (Table 4.2). Particular attention was paid to exploring the results for developing countries using the openness measure, including how openness to portfolio flows and FDI affect the results, and how liberalization interacts with the channels discussed above—domestic investment and spillover, financial depth, and institutional arrangements. Details of the approach are contained in Box 4.2.[12]

On the central issue of the impact of liberalization on growth, the results are supportive of a mildly beneficial impact. The results, reported in Table 4.3, and other regressions using alternative sample periods, can be summarized as follows:

[10]For a comprehensive survey see Edison, Klein, Ricci, and Sløk (forthcoming).

[11]For example, a country with weak economic performance might choose to adopt capital controls and there is a danger in such a case to interpret incorrectly that the country's low growth depends on those controls.

[12]A comprehensive discussion of the results is contained in Edison, Levine, Ricci, and Sløk (forthcoming).

Table 4.2. Openness of the Capital Account

(According to the openness measure)

Algeria	**India**	**Papua New Guinea**[80,90]
Argentina	**Indonesia**	**Peru**
Bangladesh	**Israel**	**Philippines**
Botswana[80]	Jamaica[70,80,90]	Saudi Arabia
Brazil	**Jordan**	**Singapore**[70,80,90]
Chile[90]	**Kenya**	South Africa
China	**Korea**	**Sri Lanka**
Costa Rica[90]	**Lesotho**[90]	**Syrian Arab Republic**
Colombia	**Malaysia**[80,90]	**Thailand**
Dominican Republic	**Mauritius**	**Tunisia**[90]
Ecuador	**Mexico**[90]	Trinidad and Tobago[70,80,90]
Egypt[80]	**Morocco**	**Turkey**
El Salvador	Namibia[90]	United Arab Emirates
Gabon[70,80]	**Nepal**	**Uruguay**
Gambia	Nigeria[80,90]	Venezuela[90]
Guatemala	Oman	**Zimbabwe**
Haiti	**Pakistan**	

Note: The table lists the countries identified in the sample and indicates those that are classified as open (according to the openness measure defined in the text) in the 1970s, 1980s, and 1990s. A superscript 70 denotes that the country was open in the 1970s, superscript 80 that it was open in the 1980s, and superscript 90 that it was open in the 1990s. Developing countries in bold (plus Swaziland) were included in the regression sample. Tables and Figures in the text encompass four additional developing countries (Bhutan, Comoros, Cyprus, and Qatar) and 20 industrial countries (Australia, Austria, Canada, Denmark, Finland, France, Germany, Greece, Ireland, Italy, Japan, Netherlands, New Zealand, Norway, Portugal, Spain, Sweden, Switzerland, the United Kingdom, and the United States).

- *Increased international financial integration is generally associated with an economically meaningful rise in growth in developing countries, although these effects are generally not statistically significant.* When a developing country liberalizes, moving from a closed to open status, its per capita growth is estimated to rise on average by slightly over ¼ percent per year.[13] The lack of significance of most of the coefficients presumably reflects the wide diversity of developing country experiences with growth, including the financial instability associated with liberalization in many cases.
- *The growth effects on developing countries come through both FDI and portfolio liberalization.* On further examination, there are some intu-

Table 4.3. Liberalization and Economic Growth for Developing Countries

(Percent change in per capita growth per year)

	Restriction moves from closed to open	Openness moves from closed to open[1]
Overall liberalization	0.3	0.3
FDI liberalization	. . .	0.2
Portfolio liberalization	. . .	*0.3*

Note: Bold indicates significance at the 5 percent confidence level (using a one-tailed test), and italic indicates significance in regressions that account for endogeneity. Control variables are level of income in 1980; level of secondary schooling in 1980; inflation; and government balance. For the details of the analysis see Edison, Levine, Ricci, and Sløk (forthcoming).
[1]Overall, FDI, and portfolio openness are assumed to increase by 40, 30, and 10 percent of GDP, respectively. Each change is equivalent to the difference between the average of the corresponding stock for open and closed developing countries (defined as those above and below the average for all countries in the sample).

itive differences in results between the 1980s and 1990s that imply these relationships may have altered over time. While the benefits of FDI liberalization appear to have been higher in the 1990s than in the 1980s, that of portfolio liberalization appears to have been lower, consistent with the financial crises that affected many developing countries with access to portfolio flows during the 1990s.

Channels Linking Capital Account Liberalization with Growth

The debate over the impact of capital account liberalization on growth often reflects differences in the assumed potency of the various channels through which capital account liberalization may occur, including the impact on investment, the existence of technological spillovers, and the ability of the financial system to cope with large inflows. Higher investment, technological spillovers, and deeper financial markets are all associated with higher growth

---

[13]Liberalization is proxied by a move from one to zero when using the restriction indicator, or by the increase in the average level of the openness measure as a country moves from closed to open. The calculation implies that the overall FDI and portfolio openness measures are assumed to increase by 40, 30, and 10 percent of GDP, respectively, in the move from closed to open. Table 4.2 contains details on the countries defined as open and closed using the openness measure for the 1970s, 1980s, and 1990s.

Box 4.2. The Impact of Capital Account Liberalization on Economic Performance

The background study whose results are reported in this chapter, as with earlier studies, uses a standard growth model (Eichengreen, 2001). This model, which has been widely used to test numerous hypotheses about which factors affect economic growth, relates real per capita GDP growth to initial per capita GDP (to capture the convergence effect), and various other conditioning variables.[1] In the background study, a relatively standard set of such variables were included: the initial level of education attainment (proxying the level of human capital), a measure of the government surplus as a share of GDP, and a measure of average inflation (both controlling for macroeconomic stability).[2] Some studies also include real investment as an explanatory variable of growth, but since investment is a key channel through which capital account liberalization might affect growth, it was not included.

In the background study by IMF staff and a consultant, the basic growth model was estimated using cross-sectional data, averaged over the period 1980–99 (as well as the 1980s and 1990s separately) for a data set consisting of 57 industrial and developing countries.[3] All models were estimated with ordinary least squares (OLS) and, to examine causality, instrumental variables (IV).[4]

---

[1]As an illustration of its wide use, Sala-i-Martin (1997) in the paper entitled "I just ran two million regressions" attempts to map which of the numerous variables used in studies variables are most important in determining growth. Other survey studies include Levine and Renelt (1992) and Barro and Sala-i-Martin (1995).

[2]In some cases the model is augmented for additional factors such as political stability, government corruption, black market exchange rate premium, and trade with the rest of the world.

[3]The country coverage is given in Table 4.2. Note that, because of the long period covered by the study, three countries currently included in the advanced country group—Israel, Korea, and Singapore—were included in the developing country group.

[4]The instruments are those commonly adopted in the literature: the composition of religious beliefs (share of population embracing catholic, muslim, or other religion), the origin of the legal system (French, German, or English), the latitude, and an index of ethnic diversity developed by Easterly and Levine (1997).

Basic Growth Regression

	Ordinary Level Squares	Instrumental Variables
Level of GDP in 1980	−0.0102 (0.0045)	−0.0058 (0.0037)
Level of schooling in 1980	0.0155 (0.0067)	0.0099 (0.0064)
Government balance (percent of GDP)	0.1220 (0.0660)	0.0829 (0.1220)
Inflation	−0.0154 (0.0094)	−0.0309 (0.0145)
R^2	0.2861	0.1617

Note: The coefficient is reported, with standard errors in parenthesis.

The Table shows that in the basic growth model the control variables are generally statistically significant.

Building upon this model, five aspects of the relationship between capital account liberalization and economic performance were examined using a variety of dependent and independent variables. The results presented in the text tables are derived as follows:[5]

- *The overall impact of capital account liberalization on growth.* The basic growth model was extended by including either the IMF restriction measure or the openness measure (see Box 4.1). The end of the period was used for openness, given that the stock of foreign assets as a ratio to GDP is a somewhat backward-looking measure of liberalization (average values give very similar results). The two components of the last measure—FDI openness and portfolio openness—were also tested separately. For all countries and for all measures the results were positive, but generally not significant.

- *The impact of capital account liberalization on private investment.* In these regressions, private investment as a ratio to GDP was introduced as the dependent variable instead of real per capita growth. The control variables were kept

---

[5]For the details of the statistical analysis, see Edison, Levine, Ricci, and Sløk (forthcoming).

the same, as the key source of growth in the Solow growth model that underlies the empirical specification is investment. Overall, the results show that there are relatively strong positive links between liberalization and private investment.

- *The impact of capital account liberalization on technology transfers to developing countries.* To test the impact of FDI spillovers, three additional variables were added to the basic growth model—private investment (to eliminate the benefits of FDI through this channel), FDI openness (measured both as stocks and as flows), and the interaction of FDI with human capital. The interaction term can be used to measure the impact of human capital on FDI spillovers that are not connected with private investment. The results suggest that higher levels of human capital raise the benefits from opening up to FDI.

- *The impact of capital account liberalization on financial development.* In these regressions, measures of financial development were substi-

tuted for growth in the specification. In one regression, private sector credit and a ratio to GDP was used and, in another, stock market turnover as a ratio to GDP. The regressions generally support a significant link from liberalization to financial development.

- *The role of institutions when opening the capital account.* This was examined by successively adding into the basic growth regression various variables capturing the quality of the institutional and policy environment, as well as interaction terms between such variables and capital flows into the basic growth model. The institutional and policy variables are: a measure of law and order, the two measures of financial development discussed earlier, and fiscal balance as a ratio to GDP. The impact of the institutional environment on the benefits of liberalization can then be measured through the interaction terms. As in the case of the overall impact of liberalization on growth, the coefficients are generally correctly signed but not statistically significant.

(King and Levine, 1993). Financial crises are associated with generally temporary, but often large, losses in output (Barro, 2001).

Does Capital Account Liberalization Promote Domestic Investment?

Greater access to foreign saving associated with opening the capital account generally leads to greater capital inflows and—if these flows are managed appropriately—more investment and higher growth. This is particularly true for poorer countries and for "greenfield" FDI, in which a company is starting a new enterprise from scratch. By contrast, the impact on investment in industrial countries is likely to be much more muted, as they have continuous access to capital markets and most FDI flows involve the purchase of an existing enterprise.

Simple comparisons of investment rates across developing countries indicate that openness is indeed generally associated with higher domestic

investment and hence somewhat higher growth. More liberalized economies have investment ratios that are higher than closed economies (Figure 4.5) and this behavior is associated with higher FDI inflows (including many relatively poor economies with open capital accounts, which typically rely primarily on FDI inflows— Box 4.3). Of course, some of this correlation may reflect other characteristics—open countries also tend to be richer and often have more stable macroeconomic environments.

Recent academic studies that control for such factors confirm a positive association between *capital inflows* and investment, although some authors have found that this effect has declined during the 1990s. Some of these studies focus specifically on FDI inflows, while others examine the strength of this relationship for various categories of inflows (see Bosworth and Collins, 1999). The evidence across a wide range of developing country groups indicates that all forms

Table 4.4. Liberalization and Private Investment for Developing Countries

(Investment as a ratio to GDP)

	Restriction moves from closed to open	Openness moves from closed to open[1]
Overall liberalization	1.2	*1.9*
FDI liberalization	. . .	**1.9**
Portfolio liberalization	. . .	*1.0*

Note: Bold indicates significance at the 5 percent confidence level (using a one-tailed test), and italic indicates significance in regressions that account for endogeneity. Control variables are level of income in 1980; level of secondary schooling in 1980; inflation; and government balance. For the details of the analysis, see Edison, Levine, Ricci, and Sløk (forthcoming).

[1]Overall, FDI, and portfolio openness are assumed to increase by 40, 30, and 10 percent of GDP, respectively. Each change is equivalent to the difference between the average of the corresponding stock for open and closed developing countries (defined as those above and below the average for all countries in the sample).

Figure 4.5. Private Investment and Foreign Direct Investment (FDI) Inflows by Liberalization in Developing Countries[1]

(Percent of GDP)

Open economies tended to invest more, and attracted more FDI flows, according to the openness measure.

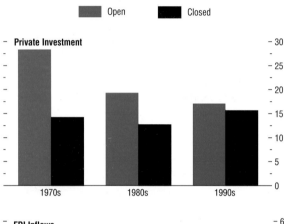

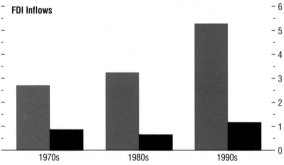

Sources: IMF, *International Financial Statistics*; and IMF staff calculations.
[1]A country is defined as open when its openness measure exceeds the average value for the entire sample period for both industrial and developing countries. The remaining countries are defined as closed. See Table 4.2 for country classification.

of capital inflows can increase investment, but that this is particularly true of FDI flows (for a recent survey of this literature, see the World Bank, 2001).

The impact of capital account *liberalization* on domestic investment has received less attention in the academic literature (see Henry, 2000). The results from the background study indicate that liberalization is associated with higher domestic investment in developing countries, particularly when the openness measure for FDI is used (Table 4.4).[14] Increasing the openness measure by the average gap between countries defined as closed and open is associated with a rise in the private investment ratio of about 2 percentage points of GDP, somewhat larger than the effect implied by the restrictions measure.[15] These openness coefficients are in general significant and, with the exception of the FDI measure, the estimates using instrumental variables indicate that the relationship appears to be causal, implying that liberalization increases investment ratios. Using a standard coefficient be-

[14]The background study examined this issue using a similar approach to that taken to examine the impact on growth, but with the ratio of private investment to GDP replacing economic growth as the dependent variable.

[15]Results using total investment indicate a somewhat larger impact, with similar results in terms of significance and causality.

Box 4.3. Foreign Direct Investment and the Poorer Countries

Foreign direct investment (FDI) flows provide one mechanism for helping to integrate poorer countries into the global economy. Such flows have become increasingly important over the past decade and offer considerable promise for boosting economic performance.

As shown in the Table, FDI flows to all developing countries increased by more than six-fold between 1986–90 and 1996–99. FDI flows to the 49 countries classified by the United Nations as least developed countries, rose by a similar factor—from an annual average of just $0.6 billion to $3.6 billion over the same period. In contrast, official development assistance, traditionally the major source of capital financing for the least developed countries, has declined over the past decade. While FDI continues to flow mainly between advanced economies, the share to poorer countries rose modestly in the 1990s.[1] More important, FDI inflows are often large relative to the size of economies of the least developed countries. During 1997–99, these inflows averaged 8 percent of gross fixed capital formation for all least developed countries, and for six of these countries, exceeded 30 percent of fixed capital formation.

Though still concentrated, FDI flows to poorer countries, have become increasingly dispersed. During 1996–99, 10 countries received 74 percent of the total flows to the 49 least developed countries, compared with 84 percent during 1991–95 and 92 percent during 1986–1990.[2] Countries such as Cambodia, Mozambique, and Uganda were able to join the group of top recipients, following substantial changes in their economic and/or political environments. Moreover, while a significant share of FDI remains in natural resources, investments in other sectors have also become more important.

FDI and ODA Flows
(Billions of U.S. dollars, annual averages)

	1986–90	1991–95	1996–99
Foreign direct investment			
World	160.9	229.1	641.8
Developed	133.0	149.8	459.7
All developing	27.9	79.3	182.2
Least developed	0.6	1.8	3.6
Official development assistance			
Least developed	13.9	16.6	12.7

Source: UNCTAD, FDI in Least Developed Countries at a Glance (April 2001), Figure 2, pp..2 and Table 3, pp. 8.

For example, most of the inward FDI stock in Cambodia and Uganda is in manufacturing, while most of the stock in Cape Verde and Nepal is in services.

Growing FDI inflows promise a variety of potential benefits to poor country recipients. FDI flows could provide a relatively stable and growing source of finance for poorer countries, and they have tended to be considerably less volatile than other types of capital inflows for middle- and high-income countries. Notably, FDI flows stagnated, but did not collapse during the recent financial crises.[3]

How do FDI flows affect recipient countries?

- FDI inflows tend to raise domestic investment, including in low-income and sub-Saharan African countries. While the link between capital inflows and investment may have weakened during the 1990s, this is probably due to shifts within FDI, toward mergers and acquisitions instead of "greenfield" investments (i.e., a firm started from scratch), and thus is less relevant for poorer countries where mergers and acquisitions account for less than 10 percent of direct investments.[4]
- Multinational corporations tend to pay higher wages than domestic enterprises and can offer valuable training opportunities to workers.

[1]This share rose from just 0.4 percent in the late 1980s to 0.8 percent in the early 1990s. It declined somewhat to 0.6 percent during 1996–99 as flows to advanced economies surged.

[2]The least developed countries with the largest FDI inflows during 1996–99 were Angola, Cambodia, Ethiopia, Lesotho, Mozambique, Myanmar, Sudan, Tanzania, Uganda, and Zambia.

[3]See for example, Mody and Murshid (2001); and Wei (2001).

[4]See for example, Bosworth and Collins (1999); Mody and Murshid (2001); and United Nations Conference on Trade and Development, or UNCTAD (2000).

Box 4.3 *(concluded)*

- Multinational corporations can also promote the transfer of technology, with possible spillovers to domestic firms. However, empirical evidence on such transfers or spillovers is mixed (for a recent review, see Hanson, 2001).
- Evidence on economic growth is also mixed. Some studies find a positive relationship only for countries above a minimum "threshold" of absorptive capacity—measured by education of the workforce, capital infrastructure or other development indicators.[5] By promoting investment in poorer countries, FDI can help move them closer to this threshold.

Recent analyses find that those developing countries with stronger policy environments attract a larger share of the total FDI flow to developing countries, while higher levels of corruption act as a deterrent. These factors are likely to be particularly important for countries hoping to attract flows outside of the natural resource sector, given the greater range of alternative locations. Many countries compete to attract FDI flows using a range of financial incentives. However, such incentives can significantly reduce the benefits from FDI flows accruing to the domestic economy—for example, through foregone tax revenues and increased distortions. Their role in attracting multinational corporations is unclear.[6]

Some examples of poorer countries that have recently attracted increased FDI inflows, based on improved structural and macroeconomic performance are:

[5]For example, see Borensztein, De Gregorio, and Lee (1998); and Eichengreen (2001).
[6]See Hanson (2001); Wei (2001); and UNCTAD (1996).

- *Uganda,* where FDI inflows began to grow in 1993, averaging $182 million per year during 1997–99, or nearly 20 percent of gross fixed capital formation. The sectoral distribution of FDI has been quite diverse, with 52 percent of the 1998 stock allocated to manufacturing, 35 percent to services (including transport and telecommunications) and 13 percent to the primary sector. Uganda was one of the first countries to benefit from the Initiative for the Heavily Indebted Poor Countries (or HIPC Initiative) reflecting its commitment to sound macroeconomic policy since 1987, including private-sector led development and poverty reduction.
- *Bolivia,* which was also an early HIPC participant, saw its FDI flows rise after a successful program to eliminate a hyperinflation in 1985, followed by ongoing structural reform. From minimal levels in the late 1980s, FDI flows grew to an average of $818 million a year during 1996–99. At the same time domestic gross fixed capital formation increased considerably. FDI inflows remained high in 1999 despite short-term macroeconomic difficulties.
- *Bangladesh,* where FDI inflows surged from minimal levels before 1995 to an annual average of $170 million during 1996–99 (about 4 percent of domestic investment). This growth followed a program of macroeconomic policy reforms undertaken since the early 1990s, and moves more recently to encourage (domestic and foreign) private investment. The FDI flows have been allocated to the energy sector (especially gas and power), to manufacturing (textiles, garments and electronics), and to transportation and telecommunications services.

tween investment and growth would indicate that this increase in the investment ratio would raise growth by 0.3 percent a year.

Does Capital Account Liberalization Promote Technology Spillovers?

A second channel through which capital account liberalization can have a positive impact is through technology spillovers. These spillovers are most clear in the case of foreign direct investment, especially through foreign firms incorporating new technologies in their subsidiaries. As new technologies are generally developed and adapted by firms in industrial countries, foreign direct investment may be the most efficient way for developing economies to gain access to them. In addition, this knowledge may become more widely available in the country over time, as employees with experience in the techniques used in foreign companies switch to other firms. Finally, foreign investment could increase competition in the host-country industry, and hence force local firms to become more productive by adopting more efficient methods or by investing in human and/or physical capital.

Recent analyses using macroeconomic data suggest that FDI can have a positive impact on growth, particularly when the receiving country has a highly educated workforce, allowing it to exploit FDI spillovers (Borensztein, De Gregorio, and Lee, 1998). In a similar vein, other studies have found that FDI spillovers are greatest in richer countries, while in poor countries the technologies being used are often less attuned to the needs of the economy, limiting the benefits from technological spillovers (the mining industry is often a good example of this type of effect; see Blomström, Lipsey, and Zejan, 1994). The evidence on spillovers between foreign-owned and domestic-owned firms is less clear-cut. While studies find that sectors with a higher degree of foreign ownership exhibit faster productivity growth, firm-level data provide little evidence of spillovers (Aitken and Harrison, 1999; and Blomström, 1986).

The background study confirmed existing results that FDI spillovers appear to depend on human capital. The results in Table 4.5 indicate that higher levels of human capital raise the benefits from FDI liberalization and flows. For a country with a high level of human capital, such as Korea, increasing the openness measure by the average gap between closed and open economies can raise growth by as much as a quarter of a percent a year. Further, in both cases this relationship appears to be causal, which is important given the highly endogenous nature of FDI openness and human capital. Slightly more than two-thirds of the countries in the sample have sufficient human capital to gain (to varying degrees) from such spillovers.

Table 4.5. Liberalization and FDI Spillovers for Developing Countries
(Percent change in per capita growth per year)

	FDI openness rises by 30 percent of GDP	Gross FDI flows rise by 3 percent of GDP
FDI term	*−1.87*	*−1.88*
Interaction between FDI and human capital	*0.50*	*0.48*
Percentage of countries benefiting from FDI spillover	71	68

Note: Bold indicates significance at the 5 percent confidence level (using a one-tailed test), and italic indicates significance in regressions that account for endogeneity. Control variables are level of income in 1980; level of secondary schooling in 1980; inflation; and government balance. Three additional variables were added to the basic growth specification—the private investment ratio, FDI openness (or actual FDI flows), and the interaction of FDI with human capital. Adding private investment (which is highly significant) eliminates the direct impact of FDI through capital formation, so that the coefficients of FDI and its interaction with human capital measure the spillover effects of FDI on growth. For details of the analysis see Edison, Levine, Ricci, and Sløk (forthcoming).

Capital Account Liberalization and Domestic Financial Development

The interaction between capital account liberalization and financial development is a double-edged sword, holding out the promise of medium-term benefits to growth through deeper domestic capital markets, but also carrying the risk of severe financial difficulties if the appropriate institutional framework is not in place. On the positive side, liberalization associated with steady inflows of capital can gradually deepen domestic financial systems, particularly when control on foreign ownership of banks is relaxed (see Chapter 5 in IMF, 2000). For example, in Latin America, foreign involvement in banking systems increased dramatically in the 1990s, particularly in Argentina and Mexico, which resulted in higher levels of financial development. In addition, greater foreign ownership of the banking sector may actually help reduce a country's vulnerability to financial contagion. International banks with their large capital base and geographically diversified operations may be less susceptible to a domestic bank run or financial panic and may serve as a safe haven for local depositors. There is also ample evidence at the firm, sector, and macroeconomic level that a deeper and more efficient financial system can, in turn, raise growth through more efficiently allocating resources among competing projects.[16]

Does Liberalization Benefit Domestic Financial Depth in the Medium Term?

There does appear to be a positive long-term correlation between financial depth and capital account openness, presumably reflecting, at least in part, the fact that domestic and international financial market deregulation are often carried out in tandem (Williamson and Mahar, 1998). Figure 4.6 illustrates the relationship between openness and two measures of financial development that have been linked to higher growth in past analysis—the value of credit to the private sector as a ratio of GDP and stock market turnover (as the ratio of total stock market turnover to GDP). For both measures there is a strong positive correlation, partly reflecting joint characteristics, such as richer countries tend to have more open international financial markets and deeper domestic financial markets.

The existing academic literature, which takes account of other factors, such as income per capita, confirms that capital account liberalization is associated with financial development in the longer term. For example, one recent study found that countries with open capital accounts enjoy a significantly greater increase in financial depth than countries that maintain capital account restrictions, although this link appears to be closest for industrial countries (see Klein and Olivei, 2000; and Bailliu, 2000). Other work, focusing on large emerging market economies, finds that stock markets become larger and more liquid after the capital account is opened (see Levine and Zervos, 1998; and Henry, 2000).

Further evidence of a positive link was found in the background study. The results suggest

Figure 4.6. Financial Development by Liberalization in Developing Countries[1]
(Percent of GDP)

Open economies generally have greater domestic financial development, according to the openness measure.

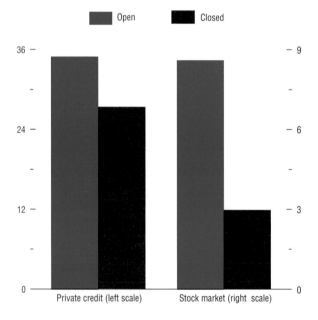

Sources: IMF, *International Financial Statistics*; and IMF staff calculations.
[1]A country is defined as open when its openness measure exceeds the average value for the entire sample period for both industrial and developing countries. The remaining countries are defined as closed. See Table 4.2 for country classification.

[16]For firm level evidence, see Demirgüç-Kunt and Maksimovic (1998); for industry-level evidence, Rajan and Zingales (1998); for cross-country evidence, Beck, Levine, and Loayza (2000).

Table 4.6. Liberalization and Domestic Financial Development for Developing Countries
(Percentage increase)

	Restriction moves from closed to open	Openness moves from closed to open[1]
Private credit[2]		
Overall liberalization	35.8	**19**
FDI liberalization	. . .	15
Portfolio liberalization	. . .	**12**
Stock market turnover[2]		
Overall liberalization	54.7	***90***
FDI liberalization	. . .	86
Portfolio liberalization	. . .	***40***

Note: Bold indicates significance at the 5 percent confidence level (using a one-tailed test), and italic indicates significance in regressions that account for endogeneity. Control variables are level of income in 1980; level of secondary schooling in 1980; inflation; and government balance. For the details of the analysis see Edison, Levine, Ricci, and Sløk (forthcoming).

[1]Overall, FDI, and portfolio openness are assumed to increase by 40, 30, and 10 percent of GDP, respectively. Each change is equivalent to the difference between the average of the corresponding stock for open and closed developing countries (defined as those above and below the average for all countries in the sample).

[2]As a ratio to GDP.

that liberalization has large and (in the case of the openness measure) significant effects on both measures of domestic financial depth. For example, increasing the openness measure by the average gap between a closed and open economy raises private credit as a ratio to GDP by 20 percent and almost doubles stock market turnover (Table 4.6). Based on standard estimates of the link between financial deepening and growth, this could raise growth by a quarter of a percent. Turning to the results for portfolio and FDI openness, as expected, the impact on financial deepening of liberalization of portfolio flows appears to be both significant, and, in the case of stock market turnover, causal. Liberalization of foreign direct investment also appears to have a positive impact, although it is not significant. In short, there is suggestive evidence that over longer periods successful liberalization, particularly on the portfolio side, is linked to deeper domestic financial markets.

Financial Instability: The Cost of Liberalization

These potential long-term benefits, however, need to be set against the danger that open international financial markets can also create financial problems, including financial crises, with large output costs. The problems are generally associated both with excessive inflows and outflows and, more generally, the volatility of net capital flows. Figure 4.7 shows that volatility of net capital inflows has increased substantially over time, particularly for countries that experienced more extensive capital account liberalization. The increase in volatility has been more pronounced for portfolio flows than FDI flows, reflecting the more long-term relationship implicit in FDI. Volatility has been particularly high in the 1990s, when many developing countries had recently liberalized. In this decade, higher volatility of capital flows has also been associated with somewhat lower growth (Figure 4.8).

As noted above, the 1990s have been characterized by numerous exchange rate and financial crises, often associated with a drastic contraction of economic activity.[17] In most cases, the crises are associated with large inflows of capital—especially portfolio inflows—which are not efficiently channeled to the most productive investment opportunities, leading to a progressive deterioration in the balance sheets of the domestic financial sector.[18] This reflects the limited depth of financial markets in many developing countries, as well as the reduced incentive of lending agencies to screen for good projects when more credit is easily available, and the maturity mismatch in trying to finance long-term projects with short-term money. Asymmetric information between foreign investors and domestic borrowers may allow inflows to continue even as balance sheets deteriorate (see Eichengreen and others, 1998). When international investors decide that repayment difficulties and default risks may arise, however, large net inflows are quickly replaced by outflows, which can degenerate into exchange rate and financial crises. These effects

---

[17]For a discussion of financial crises, see *World Economic Outlook,* May 1998 and May 1999.

[18]See Calvo and Reinhart (2000) and the discussion in Chapter IV of the May 2001 *World Economic Outlook.*

Figure 4.7. Volatility of Net Capital Flows and Liberalization [1]
(Billions of U.S. dollars)

According to the openness measure, portfolio and bank flows have been very volatile, particularly in the 1990s. Foreign direct investment (FDI) flows have instead been steadier.

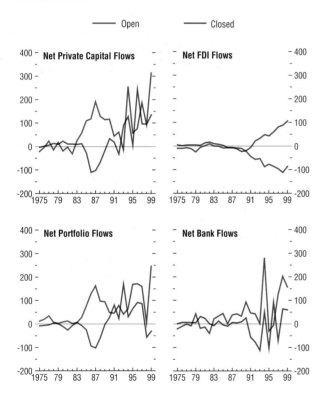

Sources: IMF, *International Financial Statistics*; and IMF staff calculations.
[1]A country is defined as open when its openness measure exceeds the average value for the entire sample period for both industrial and developing countries. The remaining countries are defined as closed. See Table 4.2 for country classification.

can rapidly spread through global financial markets, particularly at the regional level, affecting financing in other countries with open capital markets.

In addition to sudden reversals of capital flows, there are other possible costs. As with any policy change that provides access to greater resources, liberalization can exacerbate existing distortions within an economy. For example, if high levels of protection are supporting an inefficient industry, providing access to foreign saving may allow more capital to flow to this sector, thereby accentuating the underlying problem. This reflects the general issue of the law of the second best, namely that in the presence of other distortions, removing one particular distortion does not necessarily improve the overall outcome. That said, the major costs of liberalization appear to have been focused on excessive capital inflows followed by sudden reversals.

Policy responses to a reversal of inflows can attempt to deal with the short-term problem of outflows directly through reimposing capital controls and/or deal with the longer term issue of improving financial supervision and strengthening macroeconomic policies. In response to crises in the 1990s, most countries have focused on supervision and policy, tightening monetary policies during the crisis to regain investor confidence, moving away from exchange rate pegs, and instituting financial and (where necessary) corporate structural reforms. The most notable countries to have reimposed capital controls after a crisis are Malaysia and Russia. In both cases, controls appear to have provided some breathing space in which to implement more fundamental policy reforms, but at the cost of weakening the confidence of international investors, thereby increasing the cost of funding from abroad, weakening FDI flows somewhat, and producing large administrative costs. In Malaysia, the effectiveness of capital controls was enhanced by macroeconomic and structural adjustments. The authorities' strong enforcement capacity and favorable exchange rate developments also played an important role.[19] In Russia, in the absence of rapid structural reforms, controls have done little to stem underlying capital flight—a similar experience to that of the 1980s debt crisis. There is also Chile, which imposed capital controls on inflows in the face of an increase in such capital. The aim was to discourage short-term inflows but not long-term ones and to increase the potency of monetary policy. In Chile's case, the breathing space provided was used to implement significant structural reforms.

Empirical evidence on the connection between institutional arrangements and performance is difficult to come by, largely reflecting the difficulties of measuring institutional quality. Earlier work has found that, while higher levels of gross capital flows increased growth over the 1990s, the volatility of capital flows lowered growth, which is suggestive of a significant role for institutional factors (Mody and Murshid, 2001). The background study also finds some evidence that stronger institutions increase the benefits from capital inflows. Data limitations for developing countries restricted the proxy variables to measures of financial depth and fiscal policies, as appropriate data on such important issues as financial supervision or corporate governance were not available. The results suggest that three indicators of domestic financial market efficiency (private credit as a ratio to GDP, stock market turnover as a ratio to GDP, and a measure of the underlying degree of law and order) tend to boost the growth benefits of capital flows, although the coefficients are generally small and statistically insignificant (Table 4.7).[20] On the macroeconomic side, a stronger fiscal position also appears to enhance the growth benefits from international capital flows.

These results suggest that domestic institutional failures, such as weak financial supervision and regulation, can lead to crises and output

---

[19]Malaysia has subsequently reversed all controls on portfolio capital flows that were imposed in September 1998.

[20]Arteta, Eichengreen, and Wyplosz (2001) also investigate the relationship with law and order.

Figure 4.8. Growth by Volatility of Gross Portfolio Flows in Countries with Open Capital Markets[1]
(Percent)

In the 1990s, higher volatility has been associated with somewhat lower growth.

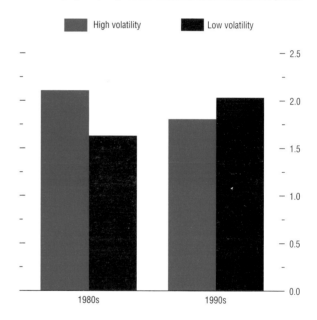

Sources: IMF, *International Financial Statistics*; and IMF staff calculations.
[1]Volatility is measured by the standard deviation of gross portfolio flows over 1970–99. Countries are classified as high volatility if their standard deviation is above the average.

Table 4.7. The Benefits of Capital Flows from Stronger Institutions in the 1990s
(Increase in per capita growth per year)

Private credit doubles	0.15
Stock market turnover doubles	0.07
Law and order improves from worst to best	0.43
Fiscal balance rises by 10 percent of GDP	0.13

Note: Bold indicates significance at the 5 percent confidence level (using a one-tailed test), and italic indicates significance in regressions that account for endogeneity. The estimates are derived from the coefficient of the interaction (product) term of gross capital flows and the respective measure of institution; they are evaluated at the average level of gross capital flows over the sample. Control variables are level of income in 1990; level of secondary schooling in 1990; inflation; government balance; gross capital flows; and the respective measure of institution. For the details of the analysis see Edison, Levine, Ricci, and Sløk (forthcoming).

losses. Therefore, adequate financial supervision and regulation is also essential to ensure that the domestic lending agencies do not undertake excessive risk due to the presence of limited liability (see Bhattacharya and Thakor, 1993). This is particularly true in the presence of explicit or implicit government guarantees of loans, which reduce the incentives of both domestic financial intermediaries and international lenders to control risk. More generally, weak corporate governance, poor accounting practices, and the absence of timely diffusion of accurate information on the macroeconomic situation and the financial sector raise the general level of uncertainty among international investors, worsening the aforementioned problems of asymmetric information between domestic and international investors.

Strong domestic fundamentals or institutions, however, do not rule out the possibility of crises, as shifts in portfolio preferences by external investors can also be a source of sudden changes in net capital flows. When the Hong Kong dollar came under pressure in October 1997, despite its solid fundamentals, investor sentiment toward Asia shifted sharply, and countries that had been awash with foreign money suddenly found it difficult or impossible to obtain new financing, or even experienced large net capital outflows.

These shifts in sentiment may reflect opportunities in other markets, as saving and investment opportunities fluctuate in the industrial countries—partly due to changes in interest rates (this is discussed further in Chapter II). However, the rapidity of the apparent shift in investor sentiment has also led to discussion of financial contagion and models of "self-fulfilling crisis," in which the vagaries of international investors determine whether a crisis occurs or not.[21] There is a growing empirical literature on contagion, focusing largely on the crises that occurred in the second half of the 1990s, that suggests that problems in one country did cause lenders to reduce their exposures to other countries in the region.

The international financial community can help countries that undertake capital account liberalization to reduce the associated costs. Promoting standards for improved transparency and wider dissemination of information—including the IMF's initiatives on data dissemination and financial and fiscal transparency—can reduce the asymmetry of information between domestic borrowers and international investors. Initiatives aimed at increasing private sector involvement in resolving financial crises are also aimed at inducing international investors to take full account of available information on borrowers' default risks. Nonetheless, the major effort to reduce the costs of capital account liberalization need to be undertaken by the countries themselves, by implementing appropriate policies and creating favorable domestic conditions. Sound macroeconomic policies, efficient supervision and regulation of the financial system, reduced government guarantees (e.g., though limited deposit insurance schemes), effective accounting and legal systems, and enhanced transparency improve the effectiveness of the financial system in channeling foreign resources to domestic productive activities, limit the systemic risks of this intermediation process, and help reduce the moral hazard of both domestic and international agents.

[21]For surveys on self-fulfilling crises, see Obstfeld (1998) and Jeanne (2000). For evidence on financial contagion, see Caramazza, Ricci, Salgado (2000) and Van Rijckeghem and Weder (2000).

It is often not possible—and not always desirable—to implement such a wide range of reforms at the same time. Some of the risks arising from capital account liberalization can be reduced by appropriately sequencing the stages of liberalization and coordinating them with complementary policies (including sound macroeconomic policy and reform). The next section explores how reforms related to liberalization can be sequenced.

Sequencing Capital Account Liberalization

Successful international capital account liberalization often requires careful sequencing of policies, requiring a detailed assessment of country-specific circumstances. In particular, it is important that reforms take place in an institutional environment that can support the opening of the capital account and avoid exchange rate or financial crises. In particular, focus is needed on the ordering of liberalization of types of flows, such as FDI, and long- and short-term financial instruments, as well as the speed at which the often numerous restrictions on such flows are lifted.

Two basic approaches have been put forward as being the best method to achieve financial integration:

- The *conventional* view emphasizes the preconditions for liberalization. In particular, this approach suggests that liberalization should come after macroeconomic stability has been achieved; financial reform has been implemented, and trade liberalization undertaken.[22] Based on this view, liberalization should occur gradually and late in the process of economic reform.

- The *political economy* view stresses the constraints imposed by political factors on reforms and the limited capacity of countries to reform themselves in the absence of external pressures. This view recognizes that

the approach to reform is often dictated as much by political feasibility as technical requirements and hence suggests that liberalization should come early in the process as a "big bang," serving as a catalyst for further economic reforms and helping to overcome opposition to reform.

The experiences of countries that have engaged in international financial market liberalization indicate that both views have merit (Box 4.4). However, the pace and timing of reforms are often not as important as the consistency of the reforms and policies that are followed at each particular point in time. For capital account liberalization, the coordination of specific reforms and policies in the domestic and external sectors, especially domestic financial sector reforms and the implementation of a consistent monetary and exchange rate policy mix, are considered the most important (Johnston, Darbar, and Echeverria, 1999). In Asia, for example, problems have generally occurred in situations where financial supervision was not sufficiently rigorous, while in Latin America problems have more often come through the macroeconomic policy mix.

In practice, liberalization in industrial countries has tended to follow the gradual and phased approach to economic reforms.[23] Developing countries, on the other hand, have followed both "big bang" and gradual approaches to liberalization of their capital accounts. The differences in experiences reflected existing conditions as much as the speed of reform and other factors.

While country experiences illustrate there is no simple rule for the sequencing and coordination of capital account liberalization with other policies, the following general three principles can help guide liberalization in any particular case (see Ishii and others, 2001):

- *Sound and sustainable macroeconomic policies are an important pre-condition for liberalization.* Macroeconomic instability can exacerbate

[22]See for example McKinnon (1973), Shaw (1973), and Hanson (1995).
[23]In those countries, capital account liberalization followed trade reforms and domestic financial reforms.

Box 4.4. Country Experiences with Sequencing Capital Account Liberalization

Country experiences illustrate that there is no unique correct approach to sequencing and coordinating capital account liberalization with other policies.[1] This box examines the experiences of eight advanced and emerging market economies that exemplify many of the issues that countries have encountered in the course of capital account liberalization. Four of the countries (Austria, Hungary, South Africa, and the United Kingdom) were able to fully or very substantially liberalize the capital account without suffering a systemic financial crisis, and no or only mild balance of payments problems. The four other countries (Korea, Mexico, Sweden, and Turkey) suffered severe financial system and external

crises, even though at least one (Korea) still maintained a broad range of capital controls.

The country experiences are summarized in the Table. Four important conclusions emerge from the analysis of these experiences:

- The pace of capital account liberalization had no systematic effect on the likelihood of a crisis. Of the four countries that experienced major financial sector disruptions following capital account liberalization, Korea, Mexico, and Sweden took a gradual approach to liberalization. Conversely, the United Kingdom and Hungary avoided crises even though they rapidly liberalized capital flows.

- Sequencing capital account liberalization in a particular way is not by itself sufficient to protect a country from crisis. Most of the coun-

[1]For a detailed discussion see Ishii and others (2001).

Summary of Country Experiences with Sequencing

	Pace and Sequencing of Liberalization	Financial Sector Policies	Macroeconomic Policies
1. Countries that avoided a crisis			
Austria	Gradual. Long-term flows liberalized before short-term flows.	Sound and well-supervised financial sector.	Stable macroeconomic environment.
Hungary	Rapid. FDI and other long-term flows liberalized before short-term flows.	Rapid financial sector reforms. Foreign bank participation encouraged early.	Macroeconomic stabilization following 1995 crisis.
South Africa	Gradual. Restrictions on non-residents' capital flows liberalized first.	Well-capitalized banks. Steps to strengthen prudential regulation and supervision.	Sound macroeconomic policies.
United Kingdom	Rapid.	Strong market discipline and prudential policies.	Generally sound policies, despite 1992 ERM exchange rate crisis.
2. Countries that experienced a crisis			
Korea	Gradual and partial. Financial institutions not subject to significant restrictions on short-term external borrowing, but limits on long-term external borrowing.	Weaknesses in the financial sector. Poor corporate governance and high leverage.	Sound macroeconomic policies, with low inflation and stable public finances.
Mexico	Gradual. FDI liberalized first. Capital account substantially liberalized on the eve of the 1994 crisis.	Poorly supervised and managed financial sector that relied heavily on short-term foreign borrowing.	Growing macroeconomic imbalances inconsistent with the tightly managed exchange rate regime.
Sweden	Gradual, but accelerated in late 1980s. Long-term flows generally liberalized before short-term flows.	Extensive domestic financial liberalization, but with inadequate supervision.	Expansionary macroeconomic policies leading to an unsustainable credit and asset price boom.
Turkey	Rapid. Most capital controls removed between 1988 and 1991. Direct investment liberalized slightly earlier than portfolio investment.	Weak banks, poor supervision, government ownership.	Growing macroeconomic imbalances and uncertain policy setting marked by high and variable inflation and interest rates.

tries studied here liberalized FDI and other long-term flows before short-term flows. Even so, some of them (for example Mexico and Sweden) experienced serious crises. This does not mean that the order in which flows are liberalized is irrelevant. Korea liberalized short-term flows before long-term flows, which encouraged excessive short-term foreign borrowing and left the economy vulnerable to external shocks.

- Financial sector stability is of paramount importance. All of the countries that avoided a crisis following capital account liberalization paid careful attention to the soundness of the financial sector and put in place strong prudential policies. The financial system in the United Kingdom, for example, was able to withstand recession and withdrawal from the ERM owing, among other things, to effective supervision and strong market discipline. By contrast, there were major weaknesses in the financial sector in all of the countries that experienced a crisis.

- Stable macroeconomic policies are important to an orderly capital account liberalization. All of the countries that avoided crises had sound macroeconomic policies in place. For example, Austria consistently geared its macroeconomic policies to maintaining the peg with the deutsche mark. By contrast, in Mexico, Sweden, and Turkey, a fixed or tightly managed exchange rate was maintained for too long in the face of expansionary policy settings. A counter-example is provided by Korea, where sound macroeconomic policies offered no protection from vulnerabilities stemming from deep-seated structural problems in the financial and corporate sectors.

financial sector weaknesses; and financial and capital account liberalization in such circumstances can accentuate such instability. Sound macroeconomic policies are essential to defusing this two-way linkage.

- *A series of financial sector reforms should be implemented during liberalization, if they do not already exist.* In particular, market-based monetary arrangements and associated central banking reforms should be implemented early to foster domestic financial liberalization. Prudential regulation and supervision and financial restructuring policies should be phased in to complement other reforms aimed at enhancing competitive efficiency and market development to help manage risks in liberalization and to foster financial sector stability.

- *The pace, timing, and sequencing of liberalization need to take account of social and regional considerations.* In particular, account needs to be taken of the authorities' commitment to and ownership of a reform strategy, as well as other considerations, such as membership in regional groups. Also, the operational and institutional arrangements for policy transparency and data disclosure—including monetary and financial policy transparency—need to be adapted to support capital account opening.

These principles are consistent with various speeds of capital account liberalization; and they do not imply that liberalization should be unduly delayed. Countries should therefore feel able to proceed with both capital account liberalization and financial sector development and reform in accord with these principles, and, as quickly as they can, develop the ability to effectively manage the risks associated with international capital flows.

Policy Considerations

The remarkable growth of cross-border capital flows has been in part associated with the reduction in impediments to capital movements and in part associated with the general trends in globalization. Recent experience has made it clear that international financial market liberalization can have both favorable and adverse effects. On the positive side, over time liberalization can significantly raise domestic investment, create spillovers to the rest of the economy from technological transfer (particularly for FDI flows) and deepen domestic financial markets (particularly for portfolio flows). Estimates reported in this chapter provide evidence that, for a "typical" liberalization, these benefits are associated with an increase in growth of a half of a percent a year or more (a quarter percent from higher investment, a quarter percent from greater domestic financial development, and up to a quarter percent from FDI spillovers). As experience has shown, however, liberalization entails significant risks. In particular, weak financial supervision and inconsistent macroeconomic policies can be associated with excessive capital inflows that are allocated inefficiently and lead to rapid capital outflows. As a result, strong overall growth benefits from liberalization are difficult to identify.

The challenge for emerging market countries, therefore, is to maximize net benefits from liberalization. For those countries that already have significant involvement in international capital markets, the key requirement is to create institutions that strengthen the positive aspects of financial integration. In this respect, the lessons of the financial crises of the 1990s underscore the importance of strong macroeconomic policies and sound financial systems, which enable countries to protect themselves against adverse swings in investor sentiment. The experience of the debt crisis in the 1980s and of the Asian and Russian crises more recently also suggests that imposing capital controls during crises on financial systems that have been liberalized internationally has only a limited impact on outflows and may distract governments from their prime task of strengthening the financial and macroeconomic environment.

For those countries that are not involved—or only partially involved—in global capital markets, capital account liberalization should remain the ultimate goal, but the pace at which it can be achieved will vary significantly. Country experiences suggest that successful capital account liberalization requires careful sequencing of policies that may help to reduce the likelihood of external or financial sector instabilities. These experiences illustrate that there is no simple rule for sequencing either the speed or the order of liberalization of capital flows. Rather, reforms and policies need to be implemented consistently at each point. Two of the most important areas of reform relate to the support and reinforcement of sound macroeconomic policy and financial sector reform. If these two factors are not in place it may be best for a country to adopt a slow and gradual approach to opening the capital account.

Finally, turning to the poorest developing countries, on the positive side, FDI flows can play an important role. However, a top priority should be to implement policies that make their country more attractive for domestic savings and investment so as to encourage foreign capital. Improvements in financial development, especially if associated with stronger financial and policy institutions, can also help cushion the negative impact of liberalization on social conditions by reducing the poor's exposure to macroeconomic volatility and financial crises. It would be a mistake for these countries to think that involvement with global capital markets offers a magic, near-term fix for their problems. Creating the conditions and institutions that make savings and investment attractive will, however, over time offer poorer countries opportunities for higher living standards, through, among other sources, capital inflows from abroad.

References

Aitken, Brian, and Ann Harrison, 1999, "Do Domestic Firms Benefit from Direct Foreign Investment?" *American Economic Review*, Vol. 89 (June), pp. 605–18.

Alesina, Alberto, Vittorio Grilli, and Gian Maria Milesi-Ferretti, 1994, "The Political Economy of Capital Controls," in *Capital Mobility: The Impact on Consumption, Investment, and Growth*, ed. by Leonardo Leiderman and Assaf Razin (Cambridge: Cambridge University Press for CEPR).

Arteta, Carlos, Barry Eichengreen, and Charles Wyplosz, 2001, "On the Growth Effects of Capital Account Liberalization" (unpublished; Berkeley: University of California).

Asian Development Bank, 2001, *Asian Development Outlook* (Oxford: Oxford University Press).

Bailliu, Jeannine, 2000, "Private Capital Flows, Financial Development, and Economic Growth in Developing Countries," Bank of Canada Working Paper No. 2000–15 (Ontario, Canada: Bank of Canada).

Barro, Robert J., 2001, "Economic Growth in East Asia Before and After the Financial Crisis," NBER Working Paper No. 8330 (Cambridge, Mass.: National Bureau of Economic Research).

———— and Xavier Sala-i Martin, 1995, *Economic Growth* (Cambridge, Mass.: MIT Press).

Bekaert, Geert, and Campbell Harvey, 2000, "Foreign Speculators and Emerging Equity Markets," *The Journal of Finance*, Vol. 55 (April), pp. 565–613.

Bekaert, Geert, Campbell R. Harvey, and Christian Lundblad, 2001, "Does Financial Liberalization Spur Growth?" NBER Working Paper No. 8245 (Cambridge, Mass.: National Bureau of Economic Research).

Beck, Thorsten, Ross Levine, and Norman Loayza, 2000, "Finance and the Sources of Growth," *Journal of Financial Economics*, Vol. 58 (Oct.–Nov.), pp. 261–300.

Bhattacharya, Sudipto, and Anjan V. Thakor, 1993, "Contemporary Banking Theory," *Journal of Financial Intermediation*, Vol. 3 (October), pp. 2–50.

Blomström, Magnus, 1986, "Foreign Investment and Productive Efficiency," *Journal of Industrial Economics*, Vol. 35 (September), pp. 97–110.

————, Robert Lipsey, and Mario Zejan, 1994, "What Explains Developing Country Growth?" NBER Working Paper No. 4132 (Cambridge: National Bureau of Economic Research).

Bordo, Michael, Barry Eichengreen, Daniela Klingebiel, and María Soledad Martínez-Peria, 2001, "Is the Crisis Problem Growing More Severe?," *Economic Policy*, Vol. 16 (April), pp. 51–82.

Borensztein, Eduardo, José De Gregorio, and Jong-Wha Lee, 1998, "How Does Foreign Direct Investment Affect Growth?" *Journal of International Economics*, Vol. 45 (June), pp. 115–35.

Bosworth, Barry, and Susan Collins, 1999, "Capital Flows to Developing Economies: Implications for Saving and Investment," *Brookings Papers on Economic Activity:1* (Washington: Brookings Institution).

Calvo, Guillermo, and Carlos Végh, 1999, "Inflation Stabilization and BOP Crises in Developing Countries," in *Handbook of Macroeconomics*, ed. by John Taylor and Michael Woodford (New York: North-Holland), pp. 1531–1614.

Calvo, Guillermo, and Carmen Reinhart, 2000, "When Capital Inflows Come to a Sudden Stop: Consequences and Policy Options," in *Reforming the International Monetary and Financial Systems*, ed. by Peter Kenen and Alexander Swoboda (Washington: International Monetary Fund), pp. 175–201.

Caramazza, Francesco, Luca Ricci, and Ranil Salgado, 2000, "Trade and Financial Contagion in Currency Crises," IMF Working Paper 00/55 (Washington: International Monetary Fund).

Chanda, Areendam, 2000, "The Influence of Capital Controls on Long Run Growth: Where and How Much?" (unpublished; Providence, Rhode Island: Brown University, Department of Economics).

Demirgüç-Kunt, Asli, and Vojislav Maksimovic, 1999, "Institutions, Financial Markets, and Firm Debt Maturity," *Journal of Financial Economics*, Vol. 54 (December), pp. 295–336.

Diaz-Alejandro, Carlos, 1985, "Good-Bye Financial Repression, Hello Financial Crash, *Journal of Development Economics*, Vol. 19 (Sept.–Oct.), pp. 1–24.

Dollar, David, and Aart Kraay, 2001, "Growth is Good for the Poor," World Bank Policy Research Working Paper No. 2587 (Washington: World Bank).

Easterly, William, and Ross Levine, 1997, "Africa Growth Tragedy: Policies and Ethnic Divisions," *Quarterly Journal of Economics*, Vol. 112 (November), pp. 1203–50.

Edison, Hali, and Frank Warnock, 2001, "A Simple Measure of the Intensity of Capital Controls," International Finance Discussion Paper No. 705 (Washington: Board of Governors of the Federal Reserve, August).

————, forthcoming, "Cross-Border Listings, Capital Controls, and Equity Flows to Emerging Markets," (Washington: Board of Governors of the Federal Reserve).

Edison, Hali, Michael Klein, Luca Ricci, and Torsten Sløk, forthcoming, "Capital Account Liberalization and Economic Performance: A Review of the Literature," IMF Working Paper (Washington: International Monetary Fund).

Edison, Hali, Ross Levine, Luca Ricci, and Torsten Sløk, forthcoming, "The Relationship Between Capital Account Liberalization and Growth

Revisited," IMF Working Paper (Washington: International Monetary Fund).

Edwards, Sebastian, 2001, "Capital Mobility and Economic Performance: Are Emerging Economies Different?" NBER Working Paper No. 8076 (Cambridge, Mass.: National Bureau of Economic Research).

Eichengreen, Barry, 2001, "Capital Account Liberalization: What do Cross-Country Studies Tell Us?" (unpublished; Berkeley: University of California).

———, Michael Mussa, Giovanni Dell'Ariccia, Enrica Detragiache, Gian Maria Milesi-Ferretti, and Andrew Tweedie, 1998, Occasional Paper No. 172 (Washington: International Monetary Fund).

Frankel, Jeffrey, and Alan MacArthur, 1988, "Political vs. Currency Premia in International Real Interest Differentials: A Study of Forward Rates for 24 Countries," NBER Working Paper No. 2309 (Cambridge, Mass.: National Bureau of Economic Research).

Grilli, Vittorio, and Gian Maria Milesi-Ferreti, 1995, "Economic Effects and Structural Determinants of Capital Controls," *Staff Papers*, International Monetary Fund, Vol. 42 (September), pp. 517–51.

Hanson, Gordon, 2001, "Should Countries Promote Foreign Direct Investment?" G-24 Discussion Paper No. 9 (February).

Hanson, James, 1995, "Opening the Capital Account: Costs, Benefits and Sequencing," in *Capital Controls, Exchange Rates, and Monetary Policy in the World Economy*," ed. by Sebastian Edwards (Cambridge: Cambridge University Press).

Henry, Peter, 2000, "Stock Market Liberalization, Economic Reform, and Emerging Market Equity Prices," *Journal of Finance*, Vol. 55 (April), pp. 529–64.

International Monetary Fund, 1998, *World Economic Outlook, May 1998* (Washington: IMF).

———, 1999, *World Economic Outlook, May 1999* (Washington: IMF)..

———, 2000, *World Economic Outlook, May 2000* (Washington: IMF).

———, 2000, *World Economic Outlook, October 2000* (Washington: IMF).

———, 2001, *World Economic Outlook, May 2001* (Washington: IMF).

Ishii, Shogo, Karl Habermeier, Bernard Laurens, John Leimone, Judit Vadasz, and Jorge Ivan Canales-Kriljenko, 2001, "Capital Account Liberalization and Financial Sector Stability," (unpublished; Washington, D.C.: International Monetary Fund).

Jeanne, Olivier, 2000, "Currency Crises: A Perspective on Recent Theoretical Developments," *Special Papers in International Economics No. 20* (Princeton: Princeton University, Economics Department, International Economies Section).

Johnston, R. Barry, and Chris Ryan, 1994, "The Impact of Controls on Capital Movements on the Private Capital Account of Countries Balance of Payments," IMF Working Paper No. 94/78, (Washington: International Monetary Fund).

Johnston, R. Barry, Salid Darbar, and Claudia Echevarria, 1999, "Sequencing Capital Account Liberalization: Lessons from the Experiences in Chile, Indonesia, Korea, and Thailand," in *Sequencing Financial Sector Reforms: Country Experiences and Issues*, ed. by R. Barry Johnston and V. Sundararajan (Washington: International Monetary Fund).

King, Robert, and Ross Levine, 1993, "Finance and Growth: Schumpeter Might Be Right," *Quarterly Journal of Economics*, Vol. 108 (August), pp. 717–37.

Klein, Michael, and Giovanni Olivei, 2000, "Capital Account Liberalization, Financial Depth, and Economic Growth" (unpublished; Medford, Mass.: Tufts University).

Kraay, Aart, 1998, "In Search of the Macroeconomic Effects of Capital Account Liberalization," (unpublished; Washington: World Bank).

Lane, Philip, and Gian Maria Milesi-Ferretti, forthcoming, "The External Wealth of Nations," *Journal of International Economics*.

Levine, Ross, and Sara Zervos, 1998, "Stock Markets, Banks, and Economic Growth," *American Economic Review*, Vol. 88 (June), pp. 537–58.

Levine, Ross, and David Renelt, 1992, "A Sensitivity Analysis of Cross-Country Growth Regressions," *American Economic Review*, Vol. 82 (September), pp. 942–63.

McKinnon, Ronald, 1973, *Money and Capital in Economic Development* (New York: Oxford University Press).

Mody, Ashoka, and Antu Panini Murshid, 2001, "Growing Up With Capital Flows" (unpublished; Washington: International Monetary Fund).

Obstfeld, Maurice, 1998, "The Global Capital Market: Benefactor or Menace?" *Journal of Economic Perspectives*, Vol. 12 (Fall), pp. 9–30.

O'Donnell, Barry, 2001, "Financial Openness and Economic Performance" (unpublished; Dublin: Trinity College).

O'Rourke, Kevin, 2001, "Globalization and Inequality: Historical Trends," CEPR Discussion Paper No.

2865 (London: Centre for Economic Policy Research).

Quinn, Dennis, 1997, "The Correlates of Change in International Financial Regulation," *American Political Science Review*, Vol. 91 (September), pp. 531–51.

Rajan, Raghuram, and Luigi Zingales, 1998, "Financial Dependence and Growth," *American Economic Review*, Vol. 88 (June), pp. 559–86.

Rodrik, Dani, 1998, "Who Needs Capital-Account Convertibility" (unpublished; Cambridge, Mass.: Harvard University).

Sala-i-Martin, Xavier, 1997, "I Just Ran Two Million Regressions," *American Economic Review*, Vol. 87, pp. 178–83.

Shaw, Edward, 1973, *Financial Deepening in Economic Development* (New York: Oxford University Press).

UNCTAD, 1996, *Incentives and Foreign Direct Investment* (New York).

———, 2000, *World Investment Report 2000*.

Van Rijckeghem, Caroline, and Beatrice Weder, 2000, "Spillover Through Banking Centers—A Panel Data Analysis," IMF Working Paper No. 00/88 (Washington: International Monetary Fund).

Wei, Shang-Jin, 2001, "Domestic Crony Capitalism and International Fickle Capital: Is There a Connection?" (unpublished; Washington: Brookings Institution).

Williamson, John, and Molly Mahar, 1998, "A Survey of Financial Liberalization," *Essays in International Finance*, No. 211 (Princeton, New Jersey, Princeton University Press).

World Bank, 2001, *Global Development Finance* (Washington).

SUMMING UP BY THE ACTING CHAIR

The following remarks by the Acting Chair were made at the conclusion of the Executive Board's discussion of the World Economic Outlook. *They were made on September 7, 2001, prior to the terrorist attack in the United States.*

Executive Directors agreed that prospects for global growth have weakened further since the May 2001 *World Economic Outlook.* They noted in particular the substantial decline in growth in the United States over the past year; the serious deterioration in economic prospects for Japan; the weaker conditions and outlook in Europe; and the reduction in growth projections for most developing country regions. Directors observed that the slower GDP growth in almost all regions of the globe is accompanied by a sharp decline in trade growth. Financing conditions for emerging markets have also deteriorated, partly owing to renewed financial difficulties in some major countries, although Directors were encouraged that contagion effects have so far been more moderate than in preceding episodes.

Directors considered that a range of interrelated factors have contributed to the slowdown, including a reassessment of corporate profitability and associated adjustment in equity prices; higher energy and food prices; and earlier monetary policy tightening to contain demand pressures in the United States and in Europe. They noted in particular the role played by the boom and bust in stock prices of information technology (IT) firms, and the associated sharp fall in IT investment and output. More broadly, Directors considered that the faster-than-expected slowdown also reflects the strong cross-country trade and financial linkages that are now increasingly evident across countries.

With policymakers having generally moved promptly to ease macroeconomic policies, and the impact of earlier shocks now beginning to abate, Directors believed that there is a reasonable prospect that global growth will begin to pick up in the second half of 2001, although at a slower pace than earlier envisaged. They cautioned, however, that substantial downside risks remain, stemming largely from the increasingly synchronized nature of the slowdown, the financial difficulties faced by some major emerging market economies, and the prospect that slower growth could put pressure on weak financial and corporate sectors, particularly in Japan. Many Directors also stressed the need for appropriate policies ensuring that the imbalances built up in the major currency areas during the recent expansion—including the large U.S. current account deficit matched by current account surpluses elsewhere; the apparent overvaluation of the U.S. dollar; low U.S. household savings rates; and equity markets that are still richly valued by historical standards—are adjusted in an orderly way, while sustaining prospects for global growth. In this respect, a number of Directors noted that, to the extent that the U.S. external position reflects the strength of U.S. investment opportunities relative to those in the rest of the world, stronger growth-oriented policies in other countries could contribute to addressing the global imbalances. Several Directors also noted that the continued strength of the U.S. dollar against the euro—although easing somewhat in recent weeks—could inhibit recovery in the United States while reducing scope for monetary easing in the euro area; and that the recent strengthening of the yen, if continued, could further weaken economic prospects in Japan.

Given these uncertainties and risks, Directors agreed that renewed vigilance and a firm determination to act on the policy front are needed in all parts of the world. Macroeconomic policies in the advanced economies need to remain supportive of activity, and in Europe and Japan the determined pursuit of structural reforms will be essential to boost long-term growth. In emerging markets, the outlook remains heavily dependent on developments in the major industrial countries. While the situation varies markedly across countries, Directors underscored the need to maintain prudent macroeconomic policies and to accelerate structural as well as institutional reforms. The international community, including the Fund, needs to continue to stand ready to support these efforts and to help address contagion pressures if they intensify.

Directors underscored the substantial benefits that new multilateral trade negotiations would yield in terms of supporting growth and strengthening the rules-based trading system. They emphasized that prospects for increased trade and market opening under a new round will help to restore confidence, boost global growth prospects, and contain pressures for protection at a time of increasing economic sluggishness. Directors expressed a range of views on the possible scope of a new round. While many Directors supported a broad, balanced negotiation including both market access and trade rules, several other Directors preferred to focus mainly on the built-in agenda and implementation issues related to existing agreements. Directors considered that the goals for market access should be ambitious, with many Directors favoring liberalization across all sectors, and others emphasizing the large gains for both developed and developing countries that would accrue from liberalization in agriculture, textiles, and clothing, where trade barriers and subsidies remain high. These Directors stressed that a new round should address the particular concerns of developing countries, especially the poorest countries, which have participated less fully in the growth of world trade.

With past experience suggesting that slowing growth is likely to have a disproportionate impact on the poor, Directors stressed that the global effort to reduce poverty takes on even

more importance. The central responsibility for addressing poverty lies with the national governments of the countries concerned. In this connection, they welcomed the New African Initiative announced by the Organization of African Unity, emphasizing the role of African ownership, leadership, and accountability for planning and implementing reforms. Most Directors considered that such efforts should be accompanied by increased support from the advanced economies. Pending the launch and completion of a new round of trade negotiations, they called for greater efforts to increase market access for the exports of the poorest countries as part of a coherent approach to poverty alleviation, including debt relief under the enhanced HIPC Initiative, and higher official aid flows. Funding of the strategy to fight HIV/AIDS and other diseases is also imperative.

Major Currency Areas

Directors noted that output growth in the major currency areas has continued to weaken through the first half of 2001. While recent indicators are mixed, most Directors considered that there is a reasonable prospect of a gradual recovery in the United States in the second half of 2001. Nonetheless, Directors acknowledged that substantial uncertainties remain, including the outlook for productivity growth; the robustness of household balance sheets and spending—especially given losses in stock market wealth and rising unemployment; and the extent of over-investment in the economy. In this context, they agreed that monetary policy would need to remain flexible, providing further support if activity continues to weaken, and containing possible inflationary pressures if the recovery takes place more quickly than expected. Directors viewed the recent tax package as an appropriate and timely response to the present slowdown, while stressing that spending and tax provisions will need to be implemented flexibly to ensure that medium-term fiscal targets are reached.

Directors expressed serious concern about the deterioration in economic conditions in Japan, where prospects for near-term recovery remain highly uncertain—especially given the persistently low level of domestic confidence, weakening external demand, and very limited room for maneuver on the macroeconomic policy front. They were encouraged by the new government's stated determination to address underlying weaknesses in the banking and corporate sectors and to push forward reforms more generally, and urged that corrective measures be implemented vigorously. While these measures could lead to slower growth in the short-term, Directors also highlighted the improved confidence in Japan's future economic prospects that would result from the steadfast implementation of a wide-ranging reform package. It would, nevertheless, be important that macroeconomic policies support activity to the extent possible. In this regard, they recommended full use of the flexibility available under the new monetary policy framework, and a cautious approach to the withdrawal of fiscal stimulus until recovery is clearly underway. Directors welcomed the announcement of a modest supplementary budget in the fall, as well as the recent shift in expenditure priorities from public works toward outlays facilitating economic restructuring, including a strengthened social safety net, and urged that this be continued.

Directors observed that the economic slowdown in the euro area since mid-2000 has been driven by weaker growth of real incomes and exports, together with broader spillover effects from the global slowdown—reflecting increasing international linkages of corporate and financial sectors. While the still highly competitive exchange rate, the dissipation of recent price shocks, and tax cuts in some countries should support prospects for a recovery, they agreed that the outlook remains subject to uncertainty, especially if global recovery is delayed or consumer confidence falters further. Against this backdrop, Directors welcomed the recent interest rate cuts by the European Central Bank, and encouraged the authorities to continue to strike a careful balance between the need to preserve the credibility of their commitment to price sta-

bility and the use of any scope for further easing if warranted. On the fiscal side, Directors agreed that fiscal revenues should be allowed to fluctuate with the cycle, while maintaining expenditure targets under medium-term Stability Programs, although some Directors believed that there is room for full operation of automatic stabilizers only in countries with a sufficiently strong budgetary position. Overall, Directors underscored the central importance of accelerating structural reforms, including in labor markets and public pension arrangements, in order to raise potential output growth, lower unemployment, and reduce future fiscal pressures.

Emerging Markets

Directors noted that growth in Latin America has weakened sharply, reflecting the global slowdown, slowing capital inflows, and a variety of country-specific factors, including the difficult situation facing Argentina. Given generally high external financing requirements, many countries in the region have relatively little scope for anticyclical monetary and fiscal support, and indeed some countries have tightened policies further to maintain external confidence and avoid adverse debt dynamics. Against this backdrop, Directors welcomed the new adjustment program announced in Argentina, underscoring the need for full implementation of the zero deficit law and early reform of fiscal arrangements with the provinces. They also welcomed the strengthened economic program in Brazil and the recent tightening of fiscal policies in Mexico. Directors emphasized that the situation nevertheless remains fragile, and that the authorities in the region will need to continue to monitor developments closely and be ready to take additional measures if necessary.

Directors observed that growth in most countries of emerging Asia, with the notable exception of China, has slowed sharply since mid-2000, and that countries exposed to the global slowdown in the high technology sector have been especially affected. They considered that prospects for stronger growth in 2002 depend largely on a recovery of the global economy and the electronics cycle, as well as on developments in the Japanese economy. Directors agreed that macroeconomic policies should continue to support activity to the extent possible, although high levels of government deficit or debt constrain the room for maneuver in some cases. They also emphasized the need for more rapid progress in tackling financial sector, corporate, and other structural weaknesses. Welcoming the ongoing buoyancy of the Chinese economy, Directors encouraged the authorities to press ahead with reforms to strengthen the banking sector and restructure state-owned enterprises.

Directors observed that GDP growth in most countries in emerging Europe is generally expected to ease moderately, owing largely to the slowdown in western Europe. While the appropriate short term policy mix varies across countries in light of cyclical conditions, Directors agreed that medium-term policies should remain firmly oriented toward the objective of EU accession and fiscal consolidation, especially given the need to reduce high external current account deficits and address pressures associated with population aging. They noted that the wide-ranging reform and stabilization measures being implemented by Turkey have yet to result in a lowering of domestic real interest rates to levels that would support growth and help to ensure debt sustainability. Directors stressed that continued full implementation of the program remains critical to boost domestic and external confidence.

Directors observed that growth in Russia and other countries of the CIS remains relatively robust, following the decline from the exceptionally high levels of 2000. Policymakers in Russia and other energy-exporting countries should strike a delicate balance between creating sufficiently tight domestic liquidity conditions to hold down inflation and avoiding excessive and rapid appreciation of the real exchange rate. Directors stressed that the high level of external debt in a number of the poorest CIS countries is a serious concern, requiring close monitoring. Acceleration of structural reforms—particularly strengthening institutions and governance, re-

structuring enterprises and the financial sector, and transforming the role of the state—remains critical in most countries in the region.

Directors noted that growth in Africa is expected to be reasonably well sustained in 2001, although the outlook will depend on external developments and on the security situation in individual countries. While higher oil and gas prices have supported a pickup in growth among energy exporting countries, persistent weaknesses in most nonfuel commodity prices continue to constrain activity elsewhere. They noted that sound macroeconomic and structural policies are underpinning growth in an increasing number of countries, but that prospects for growth and poverty alleviation in some continue to be impaired by economic and political uncertainties, including ongoing conflict. Directors concurred with the need for wide-ranging policy efforts to improve the climate for investment, diversification, and growth: key measures would include strengthening the delivery of education, health care, and other public services; resolving and preventing conflict; improving governance; and liberalizing trade.

Directors noted that, in the Middle East, growth is expected to moderate in 2001 owing to lower oil production quotas and prices, the weakening global outlook, and the deteriorating regional security situation. They welcomed the firm fiscal restraint being applied in the oil-producing countries as they seek to avoid the boom-bust patterns experienced under previous oil price fluctuations. Directors highlighted the importance of maintaining firm macroeconomic policies, continuing trade liberalization, and improving the business climate in order to help promote diversification and growth.

Directors had a broad-ranging discussion of the macroeconomic impact of the IT revolution. They noted that to date, the IT revolution has largely followed the pattern of past technological revolutions, with an initial phase characterized by a boom and bust in the stock prices of innovating firms, as well as in spending on goods embodying the new technology. Directors noted that rapid technological progress in IT production has already led—through falling relative prices—to significant economic benefits, including through increased capital deepening and consumer surplus. Notwithstanding the current IT slump, they believed that the IT revolution will continue to have a positive impact on the global economy over the longer term as activity is reorganized to take advantage of IT. Directors highlighted the importance for many countries to strengthen structural policies further, including labor market policies and the improvement of human capital formation, in order to facilitate the reorganization of production and allow the full benefits of IT use to be captured.

Directors welcomed the analysis of the impact of international financial integration on developing countries. Noting the weak positive relationship that empirical work finds between international capital account liberalization and economic growth, Directors considered that these findings have to be assessed taking into account a variety of factors, including the partial nature of the analyses thus far, the degree to which sample countries meet the macroeconomic and institutional preconditions for successful capital account liberalization, and the varying impact of different types of capital flows

on enhancing growth prospects. They highlighted the significant long-term benefits that capital account liberalization can bring through raising domestic investment and deepening domestic financial markets, and noted in particular the beneficial role of foreign direct investment and the spillovers to the rest of the economy from technological transfer. At the same time, Directors agreed that opening up financial markets to the rest of the world is a complex and challenging process, which can involve significant risks by exposing countries to financial volatility and sudden reversals in capital flows. The challenge for developing countries is therefore to maximize the net benefits from liberalization over time. Directors agreed that this requires implementation of carefully designed policies in a wide range of areas that take into account each country's specific circumstances and stage of development. Directors concluded from the available country experience that, while there is no simple rule for sequencing either the speed or the order of capital account liberalization, as a rule such reforms need the support of both consistent macroeconomic policies and a sufficiently strong institutional framework, particularly in the financial sector.

STATISTICAL APPENDIX

The statistical appendix presents historical data, as well as projections. It comprises four sections: Assumptions, Data and Conventions, Classification of Countries, and Statistical Tables.

The assumptions underlying the estimates and projections for 2001–2002 and the medium-term scenario for 2003–2006 are summarized in the first section. The second section provides a general description of the data and of the conventions used for calculating country group composites. The classification of countries in the various groups presented in the *World Economic Outlook* is summarized in the third section. Note that the group of advanced economies now includes Cyprus.

The last, and main, section comprises the statistical tables. Data in these tables have been compiled on the basis of information available through the end of August 2001. The figures for 2001 and beyond are shown with the same degree of precision as the historical figures solely for convenience; since they are projections, the same degree of accuracy is not to be inferred.

Assumptions

Real effective *exchange rates* for the advanced economies are assumed to remain constant at their average levels during the period July 23–August 17, 2001. For 2001 and 2002, these assumptions imply average U.S. dollar/SDR conversion rates of 1.271 and 1.274, respectively.

Established *policies* of national authorities are assumed to be maintained. The more specific policy assumptions underlying the projections for selected advanced economies are described in Box A1.

It is assumed that the *price of oil* will average $26.80 a barrel in 2001 and $24.50 a barrel in 2002.

With regard to *interest rates*, it is assumed that the London interbank offered rate (LIBOR) on six-month U.S. dollar deposits will average 4.1 percent in 2001 and 3.7 percent in 2002; that the three-month certificate of deposit rate in Japan will average 0.2 percent in 2001 and 0.1 in 2002; and that the three-month interbank deposit rate for the euro will average 4.3 percent in 2001 and 4.0 percent in 2002.

With respect to *introduction of the euro*, on December 31, 1998 the Council of the European Union decided that, effective January 1, 1999, the irrevocably fixed conversion rates between the euro and currencies of the member states adopting the euro are:

1 euro	= 13.7603	Austrian schillings
	= 40.3399	Belgian francs
	= 1.95583	Deutsche mark
	= 5.94573	Finnish markkaa
	= 6.55957	French francs
	= 340.750	Greek drachma[1]
	= 0.787564	Irish pound
	= 1,936.27	Italian lire
	= 40.3399	Luxembourg francs
	= 2.20371	Netherlands guilders
	= 200.482	Portuguese escudos
	= 166.386	Spanish pesetas

See Box 5.4 in the October 1998 *World Economic Outlook* for details on how the conversion rates were established.

Data and Conventions

Data and projections for 182 countries form the statistical basis for the *World Economic*

---

[1]The conversion rate for Greece was established prior to inclusion in the euro area on January 1, 2001.

Box A1. Economic Policy Assumptions Underlying the Projections for Selected Advanced Economies

The short-term *fiscal policy assumptions* used in the *World Economic Outlook* are based on officially announced budgets, adjusted for differences between the national authorities and the IMF staff regarding macroeconomic assumptions and projected fiscal outturns. The medium-term fiscal projections incorporate policy measures that are judged likely to be implemented. In cases where the IMF staff has insufficient information to assess the authorities' budget intentions and prospects for policy implementation, an unchanged structural primary balance is assumed, unless otherwise indicated. Specific assumptions used in some of the advanced economies follow (see also Tables 14–16 in the Statistical Appendix for data on fiscal and structural balances).[1]

United States. The U.S. fiscal projections are based on the Administration's August Mid-Session Review, adjusted for the IMF staff's macroeconomic assumptions. This covers legislation enacted as of August, notably the Economic Growth and Tax Reconciliation Act of 2001. In addition, the fiscal projections assume that tax reduction measures scheduled to expire during the forecast period will be extended. These include provisions providing relief from the alternative minimum tax and other "temporary" tax credits such as the research and experimentation credit that have been consistently renewed in the past. The Administration's stated medium-term fiscal objective implies unified federal budget surpluses equivalent to prospective surpluses in the Social Security trust fund.

Japan. The projections take account of the FY2000 supplementary budget and the FY2001 budget. The ¥11 trillion stimulus package announced in October 2000 includes additional public investment of ¥5 trillion (headline figure), most of which would take place in the first half of CY2001. Local governments are projected to largely offset their share in the stimulus package with cuts in own-account expenditures elsewhere. For FY2002 projections, the impact of a ¥30 trillion cap on new JGB issues on public investment is factored into the calculations, which also assume a supplementary budget with an effective demand component of about ¥1 trillion (to take place toward the end of 2001).

Germany. Fiscal projections are generally based on the national authorities' medium-term expenditure plans from June 2001, which are consistent with the targets of Germany's Stability Program 2000. The expenditure plans include the costs associated with the pension reform of May 2001, which will be phased in beginning 2002. Projections for revenue and cyclical expenditure are based on the IMF staff's macroeconomic framework and take into account the effects of the tax reform package of July 2000, to be implemented in stages during 2001–05.

France. The projections are based on the authorities' announced policies. For 2001 and 2002, the projection incorporates the estimates presented in the May 2001 *Debat d'Orientation Budgetaire* and the guidelines announced in the *lettres de cadrage* for the 2002 budget, adjusted for the IMF staff's weaker macroeconomic scenario. For the outer years, the projections are broadly consistent with the authorities' stability program, adjusted for the differences between the IMF staff's and the authorities' macroeconomic assumptions. The multiyear tax cut plan announced in 2000 is assumed to be implemented fully and to have an impact as estimated by the authorities.

---

[1]The output gap is actual less potential output, as a percent of potential output. Structural balances are expressed as a percent of potential output. The structural budget balance is the budgetary position that would be observed if the level of actual output coincided with potential output. Changes in the structural budget balance consequently include effects of temporary fiscal measures, the impact of fluctuations in interest rates and debt-service costs, and other noncyclical fluctuations in the budget balance. The computations of structural budget balances are based on IMF staff estimates of potential GDP and revenue and expenditure elasticities (see the October 1993 *World Economic Outlook*, Annex I). Net debt is defined as gross debt less financial assets of the general government, which include assets held by the social security insurance system. Estimates of the output gap and of the structural balance are subject to significant margins of uncertainty.

Italy. The fiscal projections for 2002–06 build on the authorities' program targets, as published in the medium-term program released in July 2001 (DPEF 2002–06), adjusted for differences in macroeconomic assumptions.

United Kingdom. The fiscal projections are based on the March 2001 budget. Additionally, the projections incorporate more recent statistical releases from the Office for National Statistics, including provisional budgetary outturns through March 2001. The main difference with respect to the official budgetary projections is that the staff projections are based on potential growth of 2¾ percent rather than the 2¼ percent underlying official projections. They also include an adjustment for the proceeds of the recent UMTS license auction (about 2.4 percent of GDP) received in fiscal year 2000/01 to conform to the Eurostat accounting guidelines. These proceeds are not included in the computation of the structural balance.

Canada. The fiscal outlook assumes tax and expenditure policies in line with those outlined in *Economic Update* of the Department of Finance Canada from May 17, 2001, adjusted for the staff's economic projections. In line with the recent announcement in the *Economic Update,* the staff expects a federal government budget surplus of CAN$15 billion for the fiscal year 2000/01, reflecting an upward revision from previous CAN$10 billion announced by Government in October 2000. Over the medium-term, the staff assumes that the federal government budget will be in surplus by CAN$3 billion a year, an amount equivalent to the contingency reserve. The consolidated fiscal position for the provinces is assumed to evolve in line with their stated medium-term targets.

Australia. The fiscal projections through the fiscal year 2004/05 are based on the 2001/02 budget, which was published by the Australian Treasury in May 2001. For the remainder of the projection period, the IMF staff assumes unchanged policies.

Belgium. Fiscal projections are based on existing policies and on the government's medium-term tax and expenditure plans announced in the 2001 budget. The projections incorporate the IMF staff's assumptions for economic growth and interest rates and assume that a large part of the savings on interest expenditures—resulting from ongoing large primary surpluses—are devoted to further fiscal consolidation. Revenues from UMTS licenses amounting to 0.2 percent of GDP are included in the deficit figures for 2001.

Greece. The fiscal projections are based on the authorities' policies presented in the 2001 budget, adjusted for different macroeconomic assumptions. For the 2002–06 period, primary current expenditures are assumed to maintain their share of GDP, while the current revenue share is projected to decline slightly (by ¼ percent of GDP), as social insurance contributions—which are tied to wages—are expected to grow less rapidly than output. Thus, the overall surplus is projected to grow largely in line with a reduction in interest expenditures, which is the result of euro area membership.

Korea. The fiscal projections for 2001 are based on the government's budget, adjusted for the IMF staff's macroeconomic assumptions. The projections do not include the supplementary budget submitted to the National Assembly in June 2001, which was approved in September 2001. For the medium term, the projections are based on the IMF staff's assumptions for economic growth and interest rates.

Netherlands. The 2000 budget balance includes revenues from the sale of mobile phone licenses of NLG 5.9 billion (0.7 percent of GDP). The fiscal projections through 2002 reflect the government's rules-based approach to fiscal policy, which comprises medium-term real expenditure ceilings, and a baseline path for revenues adjusted for the staff's growth projections. As permitted under the rules, spending is projected to be increased up to the ceiling. The revenue baseline path includes the effects of the tax cuts as part of the tax reform package implemented in 2001. The tax revenue projection for 2002 incorporates a small additional tax cut of 0.2 percent of GDP. For the period after 2002, real spending is assumed to grow by an annual aver-

Box A1 *(concluded)*

age of 1.6 percent. The revenue ratio is projected to fall by, on average, 0.3 percent of GDP per year, reflecting the notion that part of current revenue windfalls are non-permanent.

Portugal. The fiscal projections for 2001 are based in the IMF staff's estimate of the effects of the 2001 budget and changes in fiscal policy since the announcement of the budget, as well as the staff's macroeconomic framework. For 2002–05 a constant structural primary balance is assumed.

Spain. Fiscal projections through 2004 are based on the policies outlined in the national authorities' updated stability program of January 2001. Projections for subsequent years assume no significant changes in those policies.

Sweden. Projections for 2001 are based on the central government budget outturn for the first half of 2001, the policies and projections (for general government) underlying the Spring Budget Bill published in April 2001. The projections also take account of the authorities' medium-term fiscal objective of a general government surplus of 2 percent of GDP over the economic cycle, the Ministry of Finance's medium-term fiscal projections for 2002–04, and the nominal ceilings on central government expenditures for the same period. The surpluses projected by staff include tax reductions amounting to 2 percent of GDP by 2003. These reductions, while somewhat greater than those assumed in the authorities' announced medium-term projections, are consistent with their medium-term fiscal objective.

Switzerland. The projections for 2001–2004 are based on official budget plans that include measures to balance the Confederation's budget by 2001 and strengthen the finances of social security. Beyond 2004, the general government's structural balance is assumed to remain unchanged.

Monetary policy assumptions are based on the established policy framework in each country. In most cases, this implies a nonaccommodative stance over the business cycle: official interest rates will therefore increase when economic indicators suggest that prospective inflation will rise above its acceptable rate or range; and they will decrease when indicators suggest that prospective inflation will not exceed the acceptable rate or range, that prospective output growth is below its potential rate, and that the margin of slack in the economy is significant. On this basis, the London interbank offered rate (LIBOR) on six-month U.S. dollar deposits is assumed to average 4.1 percent in 2001 and 3.7 percent in 2002. The projected path for U.S. dollar short-term interest rates reflects the assumption that the U.S. Federal Reserve will lower the target Federal Funds rate by another 25 basis points in the third quarter of 2001, and then hold rates constant until a 25 basis point increase in the final quarter of 2002. The interest rate on six-month Japanese yen deposits is assumed to average 0.2 percent in 2001 and 0.1 percent in 2002, with the current monetary policy framework being maintained. The rate on six-month euro deposits is assumed to average 4.3 percent in 2001, reflecting the assumption of moderate easing in the remainder of the year, and 3.9 in 2002. Changes in interest rate assumptions compared with the May 2001 *World Economic Outlook* are summarized in Table 1.1.

Outlook (the World Economic Outlook database). The data are maintained jointly by the IMF's Research Department and area departments, with the latter regularly updating country projections based on consistent global assumptions.

Although national statistical agencies are the ultimate providers of historical data and definitions, international organizations are also involved in statistical issues, with the objective of harmonizing methodologies for the national compilation of statistics, including the analytical frameworks, concepts, definitions, classifications, and valuation procedures used in the production of economic statistics. The World Economic Outlook database reflects information from both national source agencies and international organizations.

The completion in 1993 of the comprehensive revision of the standardized *System of National Accounts 1993* (*SNA*) and the IMF's *Balance of Payments Manual* (*BPM*) represented important improvements in the standards of economic statistics and analysis.[2] The IMF was actively involved in both projects, particularly the new *Balance of Payments Manual*, which reflects the IMF's special interest in countries' external positions. Key changes introduced with the new *Manual* were summarized in Box 13 of the May 1994 *World Economic Outlook*. The process of adapting country balance of payments data to the definitions of the new *BPM* began with the May 1995 *World Economic Outlook*. However, full concordance with the *BPM* is ultimately dependent on the provision by national statistical compilers of revised country data, and hence the *World Economic Outlook* estimates are still only partially adapted to the *BPM*.

The members of the European Union have recently adopted a harmonized system for the compilation of the national accounts, referred to as ESA 1995. All national accounts data from 1995 onward are now presented on the basis of the new system. Revision by national authorities of data prior to 1995 to conform to the new system has progressed, but has in some cases not been completed. In such cases, historical *World Economic Outlook* data have been carefully adjusted to avoid breaks in the series. Users of EU national accounts data prior to 1995 should nevertheless exercise caution until such time as the revision of historical data by national statistical agencies has been fully completed. See Box 1.2, *Revisions in National Accounts Methodologies*, in the May 2000 *World Economic Outlook*.

Composite data for country groups in the *World Economic Outlook* are either sums or weighted averages of data for individual countries. Arithmetically weighted averages are used for all data except inflation and money growth for the developing and transition country groups, for which geometric averages are used. The following conventions apply.

- Country group composites for exchange rates, interest rates, and the growth rates of monetary aggregates are weighted by GDP converted to U.S. dollars at market exchange rates (averaged over the preceding three years) as a share of world or group GDP.
- Composites for other data relating to the domestic economy, whether growth rates or ratios, are weighted by GDP valued at purchasing power parities (PPPs) as a share of total world or group GDP.[3]
- Composite unemployment rates and employment growth are weighted by labor force as a share of group labor force.
- Composites relating to the external economy are sums of individual country data after conversion to U.S. dollars at the average market exchange rates in the years indicated for balance of payments data and at end-of-year market exchange rates for debt denominated in currencies other than U.S. dollars. Composites of changes in foreign trade volumes and prices, however, are arithmetic averages of percentage changes for individual countries weighted by the U.S. dollar value of exports or imports as a share of total world or group exports or imports (in the preceding year).

For central and eastern European countries, external transactions in nonconvertible curren-

---

[2]Commission of the European Communities, International Monetary Fund, Organization for Economic Cooperation and Development, United Nations, and World Bank, *System of National Accounts 1993* (Brussels/Luxembourg, New York, Paris, and Washington, 1993); and International Monetary Fund, *Balance of Payments Manual, Fifth Edition* (Washington: IMF, 1993).

[3]See Box A1 of the May 2000 *World Economic Outlook* for a summary of the revised PPP-based weights and Annex IV of the May 1993 *World Economic Outlook*. See also Anne Marie Gulde and Marianne Schulze-Ghattas, "Purchasing Power Parity Based Weights for the *World Economic Outlook*," in *Staff Studies for the World Economic Outlook* (International Monetary Fund, December 1993), pp. 106–23.

cies (through 1990) are converted to U.S. dollars at the implicit U.S. dollar/ruble conversion rates obtained from each country's national currency exchange rate for the U.S. dollar and for the ruble.

Unless otherwise indicated, multiyear averages of growth rates are expressed as compound annual rates of change.

Classification of Countries

Summary of the Country Classification

The country classification in the *World Economic Outlook* divides the world into three major groups: advanced economies, developing countries, and countries in transition.[4] Rather than being based on strict criteria, economic or otherwise, this classification has evolved over time with the objective of facilitating analysis by providing a reasonably meaningful organization of data. A few countries are presently not included in these groups, either because they are not IMF members, and their economies are not monitored by the IMF, or because databases have not yet been compiled. Cuba and the Democratic People's Republic of Korea are examples of countries that are not IMF members, whereas San Marino, among the advanced economies, is an example of an economy for which a database has not been completed. It should also be noted that, owing to a lack of data, only three of the former republics of the dissolved Socialist Federal Republic of Yugoslavia (Croatia, the former Yugoslav Republic of Macedonia, and Slovenia) are included in the group composites for countries in transition.

Each of the three main country groups is further divided into a number of subgroups. Among the advanced economies, the seven largest in terms of GDP, collectively referred to as the major advanced countries, are distin-

guished as a subgroup, and so are the 15 current members of the European Union, the 12 members of the euro area,[5] and the four newly industrialized Asian economies. The developing countries are classified by region, as well as into a number of analytical and other groups. A regional breakdown is also used for the classification of the countries in transition. Table A provides an overview of these standard groups in the *World Economic Outlook*, showing the number of countries in each group and the average 2000 shares of groups in aggregate PPP-valued GDP, total exports of goods and services, and population.

General Features and Compositions of Groups in the *World Economic Outlook* Classification

Advanced Economies

The 29 advanced economies are listed in Table B. The seven largest in terms of GDP—the United States, Japan, Germany, France, Italy, the United Kingdom, and Canada—constitute the subgroup of *major advanced economies,* often referred to as the Group of Seven (G-7) countries. The current members of the *European Union* (15 countries), the euro area (12 countries), and the *newly industrialized Asian economies* are also distinguished as subgroups. Composite data shown in the tables for the European Union and the euro area cover the current members for all years, even though the membership has increased over time.

In 1991 and subsequent years, data for *Germany* refer to west Germany *and* the eastern Länder (i.e., the former German Democratic Republic). Before 1991, economic data are not available on a unified basis or in a consistent manner. Hence, in tables featuring data expressed as annual percent change, these apply to

---

[4]As used here, the term "country" does not in all cases refer to a territorial entity that is a state as understood by international law and practice. It also covers some territorial entities that are not states, but for which statistical data are maintained on a separate and independent basis.

[5]Data shown are aggregates of country data and do not reflect official statistics at this time.

Table A. Classification by *World Economic Outlook* Groups and Their Shares in Aggregate GDP, Exports of Goods and Services, and Population, 2000[1]

(Percent of total for group or world)

	Number of Countries	GDP		Exports of Goods and Services		Population	
		← Share of total for →					
		Advanced economies	World	Advanced economies	World	Advanced economies	World
Advanced economies	**29**	**100.0**	**57.1**	**100.0**	**75.7**	**100.0**	**15.4**
Major advanced economies	7	79.5	45.4	62.9	47.7	74.3	11.5
United States		38.5	22.0	18.8	14.2	29.7	4.6
Japan		12.8	7.3	9.2	7.0	13.6	2.1
Germany		8.1	4.6	11.0	8.4	8.9	1.4
France		5.6	3.2	6.6	5.0	6.3	1.0
Italy		5.4	3.1	5.1	3.9	6.1	0.9
United Kingdom		5.5	3.1	6.7	5.1	6.3	1.0
Canada		3.5	2.0	5.5	4.2	3.3	0.5
Other advanced economies	22	20.5	11.7	37.1	28.1	25.7	4.0
Memorandum							
European Union	15	35.0	20.0	47.6	36.0	40.2	6.2
Euro area	12	28.0	16.0	37.9	28.7	32.3	5.0
Newly industrialized Asian economies	4	6.0	3.4	13.1	9.9	8.6	1.3
		Developing countries	World	Developing countries	World	Developing countries	World
Developing countries	**125**	**100.0**	**37.0**	**100.0**	**20.0**	**100.0**	**77.9**
Regional groups							
Africa	51	8.6	3.2	10.3	2.1	15.7	12.2
Sub-Sahara	48	6.6	2.4	7.6	1.5	14.2	11.1
Excluding Nigeria and South Africa	46	3.8	1.4	3.8	0.8	10.5	8.2
Developing Asia	25	58.3	21.6	46.2	9.2	66.8	52.0
China		31.2	11.6	18.4	3.7	27.0	21.1
India		12.6	4.6	3.9	0.8	21.4	16.6
Other developing Asia	23	14.5	5.4	23.7	4.7	18.4	14.3
Middle East, Malta, and Turkey	16	10.5	3.9	20.9	4.2	6.6	5.1
Western Hemisphere	33	22.6	8.4	22.7	4.5	10.9	8.5
Analytical groups							
By source of export earnings							
Fuel	18	9.0	3.3	21.5	4.3	7.0	5.4
Nonfuel	109	91.0	33.7	78.5	15.7	93.0	72.4
of which, primary products	42	6.5	2.4	5.9	1.2	10.9	8.5
By external financing source							
Net debtor countries	113	97.3	36.0	87.8	17.6	99.3	77.3
of which, official financing	43	5.6	2.1	5.1	1.0	13.8	10.8
Net debtor countries by debt-servicing Experience							
Countries with arrears and/or rescheduling during 1994–98	55	24.6	9.1	24.0	4.8	29.0	22.6
Other groups							
Heavily indebted poor countries	40	5.1	1.9	4.3	0.9	13.6	10.6
Middle East and north Africa	21	10.3	3.8	20.3	4.1	7.5	5.9
		Countries in transition	World	Countries in transition	World	Countries in transition	World
Countries in transition	**28**	**100.0**	**5.9**	**100.0**	**4.3**	**100.0**	**6.7**
Central and eastern Europe	16	39.2	2.3	51.4	2.2	29.7	2.0
CIS and Mongolia	12	61.1	3.6	48.8	2.1	71.4	4.8
Russia		42.0	2.5	34.3	1.5	36.8	2.5
Excluding Russia	11	19.1	1.1	14.5	0.6	34.6	2.3

[1]The GDP shares are based on the purchasing-power-parity (PPP) valuation of country GDPs.

Table B. Advanced Economies by Subgroup

	European Union		Euro Area	Newly Industrialized Asian Economies	Other Countries
Major advanced economies	France Germany Italy United Kingdom		France Germany Italy		Canada Japan United States
Other advanced economies	Austria Belgium Denmark Finland Greece Ireland	Luxembourg Netherlands Portugal Spain Sweden	Austria Belgium Finland Greece Ireland Luxembourg Netherlands Portugal Spain	Hong Kong SAR[1] Korea Singapore Taiwan Province of China	Australia Cyprus Iceland Israel New Zealand Norway Switzerland

[1]On July 1, 1997, Hong Kong was returned to the People's Republic of China and became a Special Administrative Region of China

west Germany in years up to and including 1991, but to unified Germany from 1992 onward. In general, data on national accounts and domestic economic and financial activity through 1990 cover west Germany only, whereas data for the central government and balance of payments apply to west Germany through June 1990 and to unified Germany thereafter.

Developing Countries

The group of developing countries (125 countries) includes all countries that are not classified as advanced economies or as countries in transition, together with a few dependent territories for which adequate statistics are available.

The *regional breakdowns* of developing countries in the *World Economic Outlook* conform to the IMF's *International Financial Statistics (IFS)* classification—*Africa, Asia, Europe, Middle East,* and *Western Hemisphere*—with one important exception. Because all of the non-advanced countries in Europe except Malta and Turkey are included in the group of countries in transition, the *World Economic Outlook* classification places these two countries in a combined *Middle East, Malta, and Turkey* region. In both classifications, Egypt and the Libyan Arab Jamahiriya are included in this region, not in Africa. Three additional regional groupings—two of them

constituting part of Africa and one a subgroup of Asia—are included in the *World Economic Outlook* because of their analytical significance. These are *sub-Sahara, sub-Sahara excluding Nigeria and South Africa,* and *Asia excluding China and India.*

The developing countries are also classified according to *analytical criteria* and into *other groups.* The analytical criteria reflect countries' composition of export earnings and other income from abroad, a distinction between net creditor and net debtor countries, and, for the net debtor countries, financial criteria based on external financing source and experience with external debt servicing. Included as "other groups" are currently the heavily indebted poor countries (HIPCs), and Middle East and north Africa (MENA). The detailed composition of developing countries in the regional, analytical, and other groups is shown in Tables C through E.

The first analytical criterion, by *source of export earnings,* distinguishes between categories: *fuel* (Standard International Trade Classification—SITC 3) and nonfuel and then focuses on *nonfuel primary products* (SITC 0,1,2,4, and 68).

The financial criteria focus on *net creditor* and *net debtor countries* which are differentiated on the basis of two additional financial criteria: by

Table C. Developing Countries by Region and Main Source of Export Earnings

	Fuel	Nonfuel, Of Which Primary Products
Africa		
Sub-Sahara	Angola Congo, Rep. of Equatorial Guinea Gabon Nigeria	Benin Botswana Burkina Faso Burundi Central African Rep. Chad Congo, Democratic Rep. of Côte d'Ivoire Gambia, The Ghana Guinea Guinea-Bissau Liberia Madagascar Malawi Mali Mauritania Namibia Niger Somalia Sudan Swaziland Tanzania Togo Zambia Zimbabwe
North Africa	Algeria	
Developing Asia	Brunei Darussalam	Bhutan Cambodia Myanmar Papua New Guinea Solomon Islands Vanuatu Vietnam
Middle East, Malta and Turkey	Bahrain Iran, Islamic Rep. of Iraq Kuwait Libya Oman Qatar Saudi Arabia United Arab Emirates	
Western Hemisphere	Trinidad and Tobago Venezuela	Belize Bolivia Chile Guyana Honduras Nicaragua Paraguay Peru Suriname

official external financing and by *experience with debt servicing*.[6]

The *other groups* of developing countries (see Table E) constitute the HIPCs and MENA countries. The first group comprises 40 of the countries (all except Nigeria) considered by the IMF and the World Bank for their debt initiative, known as the HIPC Initiative.[7] Middle East and north Africa, also referred to as the MENA countries, is a *World Economic Outlook* group, whose composition straddles the Africa and Middle East and Europe regions. It is defined as the Arab League countries plus the Islamic Republic of Iran.

Countries in Transition

The group of countries in transition (28 countries) is divided into two regional subgroups: *central and eastern Europe, and the Commonwealth of Independent States and Mongolia.* The detailed country composition is shown in Table F.

One common characteristic of these countries is the transitional state of their economies from a centrally administered system to one based on market principles. Another is that this transition involves the transformation of sizable industrial sectors whose capital stocks have proven largely obsolete. Although several other countries are also "in transition" from partially command-based economic systems toward market-based systems (including China, Cambodia, the Lao People's Democratic Republic, Vietnam, and a number of African countries), most of these are largely rural, low-income economies for whom the principal challenge is one of economic development. These countries are therefore classified in the developing country group rather than in the group of countries in transition.

[6]During the 1994–98 period, 55 countries incurred external payments arrears or entered into official or commercial bank debt-rescheduling agreements. This group of countries is referred to as *countries with arrears and/or rescheduling during 1994–98.*

[7]See David Andrews, Anthony R. Boote, Syed S. Rizavi, and Sukwinder Singh, *Debt Relief for Low-Income Countries: The Enhanced HIPC Initiative,* Pamphlet Series, No. 51 (Washington: International Monetary Fund, November 1999)

Table D. Developing Countries by Region and Main External Financing Source

Countries	Net Debtor Countries		Countries	Net Debtor Countries	
	By main external financing source			By main external financing source	
	Net debtor countries	Of which official financing		Net debtor countries	Of which official financing
Africa			**Developing Asia**		
Sub-Sahara			Afghanistan, Islamic State of	•	
Angola	•		Bangladesh	•	•
Benin	•	•	Bhutan	•	•
Burkina Faso	•	•	Cambodia	•	•
Burundi	•	•	China	•	
Cameroon	•	•	Fiji	•	
Cape Verde	•	•	India	•	
Central African Rep.	•	•	Indonesia	•	
Chad	•	•	Kiribati	•	
Comoros	•	•	Lao People's Democratic Rep.	•	•
Congo, Democratic Rep. of	•	•	Malaysia	•	
Congo, Rep. of	•	•	Maldives	•	
Côte d'Ivoire	•		Myanmar	•	
Djibouti	•		Nepal	•	•
Equatorial Guinea	•		Pakistan	•	
Eritrea	•		Papua New Guinea	•	
Ethiopia	•	•	Philippines	•	
Gabon	•	•	Samoa	•	•
Gambia, The	•	•	Solomon Islands	•	
Ghana	•		Sri Lanka	•	•
Guinea	•	•	Thailand	•	
Guinea-Bissau	•	•	Tonga	•	•
Kenya	•		Vanuatu	•	
Lesotho	•		Vietnam	•	
Liberia	•	•	**Middle East, Malta, and Turkey**		
Madagascar	•	•	Bahrain	•	
Malawi	•	•	Egypt	•	
Mali	•	•	Iran, Islamic Rep. Of	•	
Mauritania	•	•	Iraq	•	
Mauritius	•		Jordan	•	
Mozambique, Rep. of	•	•	Lebanon	•	•
Namibia	•		Malta	•	
Niger	•	•	Oman	•	•
Nigeria	•		Syrian Arab Rep.	•	
Rwanda	•	•	Turkey	•	•
São Tomé and Príncipe	•	•	Yemen, Rep. of	•	
Senegal	•	•	**Western Hemisphere**		
Seychelles	•		Antigua and Barbuda	•	•
Sierra Leone	•		Argentina	•	•
Somalia	•		Bahamas, The	•	•
South Africa	•		Barbados	•	
Sudan	•		Belize	•	•
Tanzania	•	•	Bolivia	•	
Togo	•	•	Brazil	•	•
Uganda	•	•	Chile	•	•
Zambia	•	•	Colombia	•	•
Zimbabwe	•		Costa Rica	•	
North Africa			Dominica	•	
Algeria	•	•	Dominican Rep.	•	•
Morocco	•		Ecuador	•	•
Tunisia	•		El Salvador	•	
			Grenada	•	

Table D (concluded)

| Countries | Net Debtor Countries | | Countries | Net Debtor Countries | |
| | By main external financing source | | | By main external financing source | |
	Net debtor countries	Of which official financing		Net debtor countries	Of which official financing
Guatemala	•	•	Paraguay	•	
Guyana	•	•	Peru	•	
Haiti	•	•	St. Kitts and Nevis	•	
Honduras	•	•	St. Lucia	•	
Jamaica	•		St. Vincent and the Grenadines	•	
Mexico	•	•	Suriname	•	
Netherlands Antilles	•	•	Trinidad and Tobago	•	
Nicaragua	•	•	Uruguay	•	
Panama	•		Venezuela	•	

Table E. Other Developing Country Groups

Countries	Heavily Indebted Poor Countries	Middle East and North Africa	Countries	Heavily Indebted Poor Countries	Middle East and North Africa
Africa			Tanzania	•	
Sub-Sahara			Togo	•	
Angola	•		Uganda	•	
Benin	•		Zambia	•	
Burkina Faso	•		**North Africa**		
Burundi	•		Algeria		•
Cameroon	•		Morocco		•
Central African Rep.	•		Tunisia		•
Chad	•		**Developing Asia**		
Congo, Democratic Rep. of	•		Lao People's Democratic Rep.	•	
Congo, Rep. of	•		Myanmar	•	
Côte d'Ivoire	•		Vietnam	•	
Djibouti		•	**Middle East, Malta,**		
Ethiopia	•		**and Turkey**		
Gambia, The	•		Bahrain		•
Ghana	•		Egypt		•
Guinea	•		Iran, Islamic Rep. Of		•
Guinea-Bissau	•		Iraq		•
Kenya	•		Jordan		•
Liberia	•		Kuwait		•
Madagascar	•		Lebanon		•
Malawi	•		Liberia	•	
Mali	•		Libya		•
Mauritania	•	•	Oman		•
Mozambique, Rep. of	•		Qatar		•
Niger	•		Saudi Arabia		•
Rwanda	•		Syrian Arab Rep.		•
São Tomé and Príncipe	•		United Arab Emirates		•
Senegal	•		Yemen, Rep. of	•	•
Sierra Leone	•		**Western Hemisphere**		
Somalia	•	•	Bolivia	•	
Sudan	•	•	Guyana	•	
			Honduras	•	
			Nicaragua	•	

Table F. Countries in Transition by Region

Central and Eastern Europe		Commonwealth of Independent States and Mongolia
Albania	Lithuania	Armenia
Belarus	Macedonia, former Yugoslav Republic of	Azerbaijan
Bosnia and Herzegovina	Poland	Belarus
Bulgaria	Romania	Georgia
Croatia	Slovak Republic	Kazakhstan
Czech Republic	Slovenia	Kyrgyz Republic
Estonia	Yugoslavia, Federal Republic of (Serbia/Montenegro)	Moldova
Hungary		Mongolia
Latvia		Russia
		Tajikistan
		Turkmenistan
		Ukraine
		Uzbekistan

List of Tables

Table 1. Summary of World Output[1]

(Annual percent change)

| | Ten-Year Averages | | 1993 | 1994 | 1995 | 1996 | 1997 | 1998 | 1999 | 2000 | 2001 | 2002 |
	1983–92	1993–2002										
World	**3.4**	**3.5**	**2.2**	**3.7**	**3.7**	**4.0**	**4.2**	**2.8**	**3.6**	**4.7**	**2.6**	**3.5**
Advanced economies	**3.3**	**2.7**	**1.4**	**3.4**	**2.7**	**2.9**	**3.5**	**2.7**	**3.4**	**3.8**	**1.3**	**2.1**
United States	3.4	3.3	2.7	4.0	2.7	3.6	4.4	4.3	4.1	4.1	1.3	2.2
European Union	2.6	2.2	−0.4	2.8	2.4	1.7	2.6	2.9	2.7	3.4	1.8	2.2
Japan	3.9	0.9	0.5	1.0	1.6	3.3	1.9	−1.1	0.8	1.5	−0.5	0.2
Other advanced economies	4.6	4.2	4.2	5.8	5.1	4.1	4.6	1.2	5.7	5.9	1.5	3.5
Developing countries	**4.7**	**5.4**	**6.3**	**6.7**	**6.2**	**6.6**	**5.8**	**3.5**	**3.9**	**5.8**	**4.3**	**5.3**
Regional groups												
Africa	2.0	3.1	0.5	2.3	2.9	5.6	3.1	3.3	2.5	2.8	3.8	4.4
Developing Asia	7.3	7.2	9.4	9.7	9.0	8.3	6.5	4.0	6.1	6.8	5.8	6.2
Middle East, Malta, and Turkey	3.5	3.6	3.2	0.3	4.7	5.1	5.1	4.1	1.0	6.0	2.3	4.8
Western Hemisphere	2.3	3.2	4.0	5.0	1.7	3.6	5.3	2.3	0.2	4.2	1.7	3.6
Analytical groups												
By source of export earnings												
Fuel	2.6	3.0	0.5	0.1	3.0	3.8	4.1	3.3	1.3	4.9	4.5	4.2
Nonfuel	5.0	5.7	7.1	7.4	6.5	6.8	5.9	3.6	4.2	5.9	4.3	5.4
of which, primary products	2.6	4.4	3.9	5.3	6.5	5.7	5.7	3.2	2.2	3.8	3.3	4.8
By external financing source												
Net debtor countries	4.8	5.5	6.5	6.9	6.3	6.6	5.9	3.6	4.0	5.8	4.4	5.4
of which, official financing	2.8	4.0	1.6	2.5	5.3	5.3	4.2	3.9	3.7	4.0	4.6	5.4
Net debtor countries by debt-servicing experience												
Countries with arrears and/or rescheduling during 1994–98	2.7	3.7	3.5	4.6	5.2	5.0	4.4	−0.4	2.1	4.5	3.4	4.4
Countries in transition	**0.1**	**−0.2**	**−8.9**	**−8.6**	**−1.5**	**−0.5**	**1.6**	**−0.8**	**3.6**	**6.3**	**4.0**	**4.1**
Central and eastern Europe	...	3.0	−0.3	3.0	5.6	3.9	2.5	2.3	2.0	3.8	3.5	4.2
Commonwealth of Independent States and Mongolia	...	−2.0	−12.6	−14.6	−5.5	−3.3	1.0	−2.8	4.6	7.8	4.4	4.0
Russia	...	−1.9	−13.0	−13.5	−4.2	−3.4	0.9	−4.9	5.4	8.3	4.0	4.0
Excluding Russia	...	−2.2	−11.8	−17.0	−8.6	−3.0	1.4	1.6	2.8	6.8	5.4	4.1
Memorandum												
Median growth rate												
Advanced economies	3.2	3.0	0.7	4.1	2.9	3.0	3.8	3.3	3.7	3.8	1.7	2.5
Developing countries	3.4	4.0	3.3	3.8	4.4	4.6	4.5	3.7	3.4	3.9	3.8	4.5
Countries in transition	−0.1	1.8	−8.1	−3.0	2.1	3.0	3.7	3.8	3.1	5.1	4.5	4.5
Output per capita												
Advanced economies	2.9	2.0	0.8	2.7	2.1	2.3	2.8	2.0	2.8	2.4	0.7	1.6
Developing countries	2.5	3.8	4.4	5.0	4.5	4.8	4.2	2.0	2.3	4.3	2.9	3.9
Countries in transition	−0.5	—	−9.0	−8.6	−1.4	−0.3	2.0	−0.6	4.1	6.5	4.4	4.5
World growth based on market exchange rates	**3.0**	**2.7**	**1.0**	**2.9**	**2.8**	**3.2**	**3.5**	**2.2**	**3.0**	**3.9**	**1.6**	**2.5**
Value of world output in billions of U.S. dollars												
At market exchange rates	18,121	30,394	25,090	27,050	29,609	30,847	30,788	30,793	31,627	32,326	32,178	33,633
At purchasing power parities	22,806	39,476	30,467	32,170	33,996	36,032	38,227	39,652	41,585	44,549	47,473	50,612

[1]Real GDP.

Table 2. Advanced Economies: Real GDP and Total Domestic Demand
(Annual percent change)

	Ten-Year Averages		1993	1994	1995	1996	1997	1998	1999	2000	2001	2002	Fourth Quarter[1]		
	1983–92	1993–2002											2000	2001	2002
Real GDP															
Advanced economies	**3.3**	**2.7**	**1.4**	**3.4**	**2.7**	**2.9**	**3.5**	**2.7**	**3.4**	**3.8**	**1.3**	**2.1**	...	...	...
Major advanced economies	3.2	2.5	1.3	3.1	2.3	2.7	3.2	2.8	3.0	3.4	1.1	1.8	2.8	0.7	2.6
United States	3.4	3.3	2.7	4.0	2.7	3.6	4.4	4.3	4.1	4.1	1.3	2.2	2.8	0.8	3.1
Japan	3.9	0.9	0.5	1.0	1.6	3.3	1.9	−1.1	0.8	1.5	−0.5	0.2	2.5	−0.9	1.0
Germany	3.1	1.4	−1.1	2.3	1.7	0.8	1.4	2.0	1.8	3.0	0.8	1.8	2.5	0.8	2.4
France	2.2	2.0	−0.9	1.8	1.9	1.1	1.9	3.5	3.0	3.4	2.0	2.1	3.1	1.3	2.6
Italy	2.3	1.7	−0.9	2.2	2.9	1.1	2.0	1.8	1.6	2.9	1.8	2.0	2.6	1.1	3.2
United Kingdom	2.5	2.8	2.3	4.4	2.8	2.6	3.5	2.6	2.3	3.1	2.0	2.4	2.6	1.7	2.9
Canada	2.6	3.3	2.4	4.7	2.8	1.6	4.3	3.9	5.1	4.4	2.0	2.2	3.5	1.7	2.4
Other advanced economies	3.9	3.6	1.9	4.6	4.3	3.8	4.2	2.2	4.9	5.3	1.9	3.3	...	...	...
Spain	3.2	2.8	−1.0	2.4	2.8	2.4	3.9	4.3	4.0	4.1	2.7	2.8	3.8	2.5	3.6
Netherlands	2.8	2.8	0.8	3.2	2.3	3.0	3.8	4.3	3.7	3.5	1.4	2.2	3.0	1.2	2.3
Belgium	2.3	2.1	−1.5	3.0	2.6	1.2	3.4	2.4	2.7	4.0	1.7	2.0	...	...	...
Sweden	1.7	2.4	−2.2	4.1	3.7	1.1	2.1	3.6	4.1	3.6	1.7	2.5	2.3	1.8	2.6
Austria	2.6	2.1	0.5	2.4	1.5	2.0	1.3	3.3	2.8	3.3	1.6	2.6	...	...	...
Denmark	1.9	2.5	—	5.5	2.8	2.5	3.0	2.8	2.1	3.2	1.4	2.0	2.8	2.0	0.7
Finland	1.6	3.6	−1.1	4.0	3.8	4.0	6.3	5.3	4.0	5.7	2.0	2.6	5.5	1.3	2.7
Greece[2]	2.1	2.7	−1.6	2.0	2.1	2.4	3.5	3.1	3.4	4.3	4.3	3.8	...	...	...
Portugal	3.0	2.6	−1.4	2.4	2.9	3.7	3.8	4.7	3.4	3.4	1.6	1.7	3.4	1.0	1.8
Ireland	3.7	7.9	2.7	5.8	10.0	7.8	10.8	8.6	10.9	11.5	6.3	4.9	...	...	...
Luxembourg	5.5	5.5	8.5	4.1	3.5	2.9	7.3	5.0	7.3	8.5	4.2	4.3	...	...	...
Switzerland	1.9	1.3	−0.5	0.5	0.5	0.3	1.7	2.3	1.5	3.5	1.6	1.7	2.8	1.0	2.6
Norway	2.9	3.1	2.7	5.5	3.8	4.9	4.7	2.4	1.1	2.3	1.9	2.2	...	...	...
Israel	4.5	4.3	3.6	6.9	6.8	4.5	3.3	2.7	2.6	6.2	0.7	5.4	...	...	...
Iceland	1.8	3.0	0.6	4.5	0.1	5.2	4.7	4.5	4.1	3.6	1.7	0.7	...	...	...
Cyprus	6.3	4.0	0.7	5.9	6.1	1.9	2.5	5.0	4.5	5.1	4.2	4.0	...	...	...
Korea	8.7	5.3	5.5	8.3	8.9	6.8	5.0	−6.7	10.9	8.8	2.5	4.5	4.6	2.8	4.8
Australia	3.1	4.1	3.8	5.0	4.4	3.7	3.8	5.6	4.7	3.8	2.3	3.8	2.0	3.9	3.9
Taiwan Province of China	8.5	5.2	7.0	7.1	6.4	6.1	6.7	4.6	5.4	6.0	−1.0	4.0	3.8	—	3.7
Hong Kong SAR	6.4	3.7	6.1	5.4	3.9	4.5	5.0	−5.3	3.0	10.5	0.6	4.0	6.6	0.7	4.7
Singapore	7.0	6.7	12.7	11.4	8.0	7.7	8.5	0.1	5.9	9.9	−0.2	4.0	11.0	−2.1	3.0
New Zealand	1.8	3.3	5.2	5.8	4.3	3.6	2.2	−0.1	3.8	3.7	1.8	2.9	1.8	2.3	2.7
Memorandum															
European Union	2.6	2.2	−0.4	2.8	2.4	1.7	2.6	2.9	2.7	3.4	1.8	2.2	...	...	...
Euro area	2.7	2.1	−0.8	2.3	2.3	1.5	2.4	2.9	2.7	3.5	1.8	2.2	...	...	...
Newly industrialized Asian economies	8.2	5.2	6.5	7.7	7.5	6.3	5.8	−2.4	7.9	8.2	1.0	4.3	5.4	1.6	4.7
Real total domestic demand															
Advanced economies	**3.4**	**2.8**	**1.1**	**3.4**	**2.7**	**3.0**	**3.3**	**3.0**	**3.9**	**3.7**	**1.3**	**2.2**	...	...	...
Major advanced economies	3.3	2.6	1.1	3.1	2.2	2.8	3.2	3.5	3.7	3.6	1.2	2.0	2.9	0.8	2.6
United States	3.4	3.8	3.3	4.4	2.5	3.7	4.7	5.4	5.0	4.8	1.4	2.6	3.5	0.8	3.6
Japan	3.9	0.9	0.4	1.3	2.1	3.8	1.0	−1.4	0.9	1.1	0.2	−0.1	2.5	−0.6	0.5
Germany	3.0	1.2	−1.1	2.3	1.7	0.3	0.6	2.4	2.6	2.0	—	1.9	2.1	−0.2	2.4
France	2.2	1.8	−1.6	1.9	1.8	0.7	0.7	4.2	3.0	3.6	1.8	2.1	3.1	1.2	2.4
Italy	2.7	1.3	−5.1	1.7	2.0	0.9	2.7	3.1	3.0	2.3	1.0	1.9	1.2	1.6	2.6
United Kingdom	2.7	3.2	2.2	3.4	1.8	3.1	3.7	4.6	3.8	3.7	2.8	2.8	2.9	2.6	2.8
Canada	3.0	3.0	1.6	3.2	1.8	1.2	6.1	2.3	4.0	4.5	2.5	2.8	2.7	4.7	0.4
Other advanced economies	4.0	3.3	1.0	4.8	4.5	3.8	3.6	1.1	4.9	4.4	1.4	3.0	...	...	...
Memorandum															
European Union	2.8	2.1	−1.6	2.4	2.1	1.4	2.3	3.9	3.3	3.1	1.5	2.2	...	...	...
Euro area	2.8	1.8	−2.2	2.1	2.1	1.1	2.0	3.8	3.3	3.0	1.2	2.1	...	...	...
Newly industrialized Asian economies	8.4	4.1	6.1	8.5	7.8	6.8	4.0	−9.2	7.5	6.7	−0.1	3.9	...	...	...

[1]From fourth quarter of preceding year.
[2]Based on revised national accounts for 1988 onward.

Table 3. Advanced Economies: Components of Real GDP
(Annual percent change)

	Ten-Year Averages		1993	1994	1995	1996	1997	1998	1999	2000	2001	2002
	1983–92	1993–2002										
Private consumer expenditure												
Advanced economies	**3.3**	**2.8**	**1.9**	**3.0**	**2.6**	**2.7**	**2.8**	**3.0**	**4.0**	**3.6**	**2.2**	**2.3**
Major advanced economies	3.2	2.7	1.9	2.8	2.3	2.4	2.6	3.4	3.8	3.4	2.3	2.2
United States	3.4	3.7	3.4	3.8	3.0	3.2	3.6	4.8	5.0	4.8	2.8	2.6
Japan	3.6	1.2	2.0	2.5	1.5	1.9	1.1	0.2	1.2	0.5	0.7	0.5
Germany	3.1	1.5	0.1	1.0	2.0	1.0	0.6	1.8	3.1	1.5	1.8	2.3
France	1.8	1.7	–0.1	0.7	1.5	1.3	0.1	3.6	3.2	2.7	2.4	1.9
Italy	2.9	1.5	–3.7	1.5	1.7	1.2	3.2	3.1	2.3	2.9	1.3	1.9
United Kingdom	3.0	3.3	2.9	2.9	1.7	3.6	3.9	4.0	4.4	3.7	3.0	2.9
Canada	2.8	3.0	1.8	3.0	2.1	2.6	4.6	3.0	3.4	3.6	3.7	2.6
Other advanced economies	3.8	3.3	1.8	4.1	3.8	3.9	3.6	1.8	4.9	4.4	2.0	2.9
Memorandum												
European Union	2.7	2.1	–0.4	1.7	1.8	2.0	2.1	3.4	3.4	2.8	2.1	2.3
Euro area	2.7	1.9	–0.9	1.3	1.9	1.6	1.8	3.2	3.3	2.7	1.9	2.2
Newly industrialized Asian economies	8.2	4.8	7.1	8.0	7.0	6.6	5.1	–4.5	7.4	6.6	1.4	3.9
Public consumption												
Advanced economies	**2.6**	**1.7**	**0.9**	**1.0**	**1.1**	**1.7**	**1.4**	**1.6**	**2.4**	**2.5**	**2.3**	**2.2**
Major advanced economies	2.4	1.6	0.7	0.9	0.8	1.2	1.1	1.3	2.5	2.6	2.4	2.2
United States	2.4	1.4	–0.4	0.2	—	0.5	1.8	1.4	2.2	2.8	2.8	2.5
Japan	3.1	2.9	3.2	2.8	4.3	2.8	1.3	1.9	4.0	3.6	2.2	2.4
Germany	1.7	1.1	0.1	2.4	1.5	1.8	0.4	1.2	1.6	1.2	1.0	–0.3
France	2.5	1.8	4.3	0.5	—	2.2	2.1	–0.1	2.0	2.3	1.9	2.4
Italy	2.5	0.5	–0.2	–0.8	–2.1	1.1	0.3	0.4	1.6	1.7	1.3	1.5
United Kingdom	1.2	1.7	–0.8	1.4	1.6	1.7	–1.4	1.1	4.0	2.3	3.8	3.8
Canada	2.4	0.7	—	–1.3	–0.6	–1.4	–0.8	1.8	2.6	2.2	3.0	1.6
Other advanced economies	3.7	2.2	2.0	1.3	2.1	3.6	2.4	2.7	2.0	2.3	2.0	2.1
Memorandum												
European Union	2.2	1.5	1.0	1.0	0.8	1.6	0.8	1.4	2.4	1.9	1.9	1.6
Euro area	2.4	1.4	1.3	1.0	0.7	1.6	1.3	1.4	2.1	1.8	1.5	1.2
Newly industrialized Asian economies	6.4	2.6	3.7	0.8	2.6	8.0	3.3	1.8	–0.7	2.5	1.5	2.4
Gross fixed capital formation												
Advanced economies	**4.0**	**3.8**	**—**	**4.6**	**4.0**	**5.7**	**5.7**	**5.4**	**5.2**	**5.1**	**0.4**	**2.2**
Major advanced economies	3.9	3.8	0.2	4.2	3.1	5.9	5.6	6.1	5.5	4.9	0.4	1.8
United States	3.9	6.5	5.7	7.3	5.4	8.4	8.8	10.2	7.8	6.7	1.1	3.7
Japan	5.1	–0.6	–3.1	–1.2	0.1	7.3	0.7	–4.2	–0.8	0.6	–2.3	–3.0
Germany	3.7	0.3	–4.5	4.0	–0.7	–0.8	0.6	3.0	4.2	2.3	–3.2	–1.2
France	2.5	2.1	–6.6	1.5	2.1	—	–0.1	7.2	6.2	6.2	3.4	1.8
Italy	2.3	2.0	–10.9	0.1	6.0	3.6	2.1	4.3	4.6	6.1	1.7	3.5
United Kingdom	3.6	4.0	0.8	3.6	2.9	4.9	7.5	10.1	5.4	2.8	0.9	1.4
Canada	2.6	4.5	–2.0	7.5	–2.2	4.4	15.2	2.4	7.4	6.8	2.8	4.2
Other advanced economies	4.8	4.1	–0.8	6.4	7.4	5.3	6.1	2.6	4.1	6.0	0.4	3.5
Memorandum												
European Union	3.3	2.5	–5.6	2.6	3.6	2.4	3.5	6.4	5.6	4.5	1.0	1.8
Euro area	3.3	2.1	–6.6	2.2	3.3	1.8	2.7	5.6	5.6	4.7	0.8	1.7
Newly industrialized Asian economies	9.9	3.9	7.9	10.3	10.4	7.2	4.4	–9.0	—	9.5	–2.5	2.9

Table 3 *(concluded)*

| | Ten-Year Averages | | 1993 | 1994 | 1995 | 1996 | 1997 | 1998 | 1999 | 2000 | 2001 | 2002 |
	1983–92	1993–2002										
Final domestic demand												
Advanced economies	**3.7**	**2.8**	**1.2**	**2.9**	**2.6**	**3.2**	**3.1**	**3.1**	**3.9**	**3.8**	**1.8**	**2.2**
Major advanced economies	3.6	2.7	1.2	2.6	2.1	3.0	2.9	3.5	3.9	3.6	1.9	2.1
United States	3.3	3.9	3.1	3.8	2.9	3.7	4.3	5.3	5.2	5.0	2.4	2.8
Japan	3.9	0.9	0.6	1.5	1.5	3.6	1.0	–0.8	1.1	1.0	0.1	–0.1
Germany	5.9	1.2	–1.0	2.0	1.3	0.7	0.5	1.9	3.0	1.6	0.5	1.0
France	2.1	1.8	–0.4	0.8	1.2	1.3	0.6	3.4	3.5	3.3	2.5	2.0
Italy	2.7	1.4	–4.5	0.8	1.7	1.7	2.4	2.8	2.6	3.3	1.4	2.2
United Kingdom	2.7	3.1	1.8	2.7	1.9	3.4	3.5	4.5	4.5	3.3	2.8	2.8
Canada	2.7	2.8	0.7	2.8	0.7	2.0	5.5	2.6	4.1	4.0	3.3	2.8
Other advanced economies	4.0	3.3	1.3	4.2	4.3	4.2	3.9	1.8	4.1	4.5	1.6	2.9
Memorandum												
European Union	3.5	2.1	–1.2	1.7	1.9	2.0	2.1	3.6	3.7	3.0	1.8	2.1
Euro area	3.7	1.9	–1.7	1.4	1.9	1.6	1.9	3.3	3.6	3.0	1.6	1.9
Newly industrialized Asian economies	8.4	4.2	6.7	7.8	7.6	7.1	4.5	–5.6	4.0	7.0	0.3	3.5
Stock building[1]												
Advanced economies	**0.1**	**—**	**–0.1**	**0.5**	**0.1**	**–0.2**	**0.2**	**—**	**—**	**—**	**–0.6**	**—**
Major advanced economies	0.1	—	–0.1	0.5	—	–0.2	0.3	0.1	–0.2	—	–0.7	—
United States	0.1	–0.1	—	0.7	–0.5	—	0.4	0.2	–0.2	–0.1	–1.1	–0.2
Japan	—	—	–0.2	–0.2	0.6	0.3	—	–0.6	–0.2	0.1	—	—
Germany	0.1	0.1	–0.1	0.3	0.3	–0.5	—	0.5	–0.4	0.4	–0.5	0.8
France	0.1	—	–1.2	1.0	0.5	–0.6	0.1	0.8	–0.4	0.3	–0.7	0.1
Italy	—	–0.1	–0.7	0.8	0.2	–0.7	0.3	0.3	0.4	–1.0	–0.4	–0.3
United Kingdom	—	0.1	0.4	0.7	—	–0.4	0.3	0.1	–0.7	0.4	—	—
Canada	0.2	0.2	0.9	0.4	1.1	–0.7	0.7	–0.3	–0.1	0.5	–0.8	—
Other advanced economies	0.1	—	–0.3	0.6	0.2	–0.3	–0.2	–0.6	0.6	–0.1	–0.1	0.1
Memorandum												
European Union	—	—	–0.4	0.7	0.2	–0.5	0.1	0.4	–0.3	0.1	–0.3	0.2
Euro area	0.1	—	–0.6	0.6	0.3	–0.5	0.1	0.4	–0.2	—	–0.3	0.2
Newly industrialized Asian economies	0.1	–0.2	–0.6	0.7	0.3	–0.3	–0.6	–3.3	2.7	–0.3	–0.3	0.4
Foreign balance[1]												
Advanced economies	**–0.1**	**—**	**0.3**	**–0.1**	**0.1**	**—**	**0.2**	**–0.4**	**–0.5**	**—**	**0.1**	**–0.1**
Major advanced economies	–0.1	–0.2	0.2	—	0.2	–0.1	0.1	–0.8	–0.8	–0.3	—	–0.2
United States	–0.1	–0.5	–0.6	–0.4	0.1	–0.1	–0.3	–1.3	–1.1	–0.9	—	–0.3
Japan	0.1	—	0.1	–0.2	–0.5	–0.4	1.0	0.3	–0.1	0.4	–0.6	0.3
Germany	–0.3	0.2	—	0.1	0.1	0.5	0.9	–0.4	–0.7	1.1	0.8	–0.1
France	0.1	0.2	0.7	—	0.1	0.4	1.2	–0.6	—	–0.1	0.3	0.1
Italy	–0.3	0.5	4.3	0.6	1.0	0.2	–0.6	–1.2	–1.3	0.6	0.8	0.1
United Kingdom	–0.4	–0.5	0.1	0.9	1.0	–0.5	–0.3	–2.0	–1.5	–0.8	–0.8	–0.6
Canada	–0.3	0.4	1.0	1.6	1.1	0.4	–1.7	1.7	1.3	0.2	–0.5	–0.5
Other advanced economies	–0.1	0.5	1.0	–0.1	–0.1	0.1	0.7	1.0	0.3	1.2	0.4	0.3
Memorandum												
European Union	–0.2	0.2	1.2	0.4	0.4	0.2	0.4	–1.0	–0.6	0.4	0.3	—
Euro area	–0.2	0.3	1.4	0.3	0.2	0.4	0.5	–0.8	–0.6	0.6	0.5	0.1
Newly industrialized Asian economies	0.2	1.4	0.6	–0.8	0.1	–0.3	1.9	6.5	1.8	2.8	0.9	0.7

[1]Changes expressed as percent of GDP in the preceding period.

Table 4. Advanced Economies: Unemployment, Employment, and Real Per Capita GDP
(Percent)

	Ten-Year Averages[1]		1993	1994	1995	1996	1997	1998	1999	2000	2001	2002
	1983–92	1993–2002										
Unemployment rate												
Advanced economies	**7.0**	**6.7**	**7.5**	**7.4**	**7.1**	**7.1**	**6.9**	**6.8**	**6.4**	**5.8**	**6.0**	**6.2**
Major advanced economies	6.9	6.5	7.2	7.0	6.7	6.8	6.6	6.3	6.1	5.7	5.9	6.3
United States[2]	6.8	5.2	6.9	6.1	5.6	5.4	5.0	4.5	4.2	4.0	4.7	5.3
Japan	2.5	3.9	2.5	2.9	3.1	3.3	3.4	4.1	4.7	4.7	5.0	5.6
Germany	7.3	8.2	7.6	8.1	7.9	8.6	9.5	8.9	8.2	7.5	7.5	7.9
France	9.8	11.0	11.7	12.3	11.7	12.3	12.3	11.8	11.2	9.5	8.7	8.5
Italy[3]	10.7	10.9	10.1	11.1	11.6	11.6	11.7	11.8	11.4	10.6	9.5	9.1
United Kingdom	9.0	7.3	10.4	9.7	8.7	8.2	7.1	6.3	6.0	5.6	5.2	5.3
Canada	9.7	8.7	11.4	10.4	9.4	9.6	9.1	8.3	7.6	6.8	7.4	7.3
Other advanced economies	7.2	7.5	8.6	8.7	8.2	8.1	7.8	8.1	7.3	6.2	6.3	6.1
Spain	18.9	18.6	22.7	24.2	22.9	22.2	20.8	18.8	15.9	14.1	13.0	12.6
Netherlands	7.9	5.1	6.5	7.6	7.1	6.6	5.5	4.1	3.2	2.8	3.6	3.9
Belgium	9.0	8.7	8.8	10.0	9.9	9.7	9.4	9.5	8.8	7.0	7.1	7.3
Sweden	2.7	6.5	8.2	8.0	7.7	8.1	8.0	6.5	5.6	4.7	4.1	4.1
Austria	3.5	4.0	4.0	3.8	3.9	4.3	4.4	4.5	3.9	3.7	3.7	3.6
Denmark	9.3	7.8	12.0	11.9	10.1	8.6	7.8	6.5	5.6	5.2	5.2	5.4
Finland	5.5	12.7	16.4	16.6	15.4	14.6	12.6	11.4	10.3	9.8	9.9	10.4
Greece	7.7	10.5	9.7	9.6	10.0	10.3	9.6	10.8	12.0	11.3	10.9	10.7
Portugal	6.7	5.5	5.5	6.8	7.2	7.3	6.7	5.0	4.4	4.0	3.9	4.1
Ireland	15.5	8.7	15.5	14.1	12.1	11.5	9.8	7.4	5.6	4.3	3.7	4.0
Luxembourg	1.5	2.9	2.1	2.7	3.0	3.3	3.3	3.3	2.9	2.6	2.7	2.6
Switzerland	0.9	3.5	4.5	4.7	4.2	4.7	5.2	3.9	2.7	1.9	1.8	1.9
Norway	3.8	4.2	6.1	5.5	5.0	4.9	4.1	3.2	3.2	3.4	3.3	3.3
Israel	7.7	8.3	10.0	7.8	6.9	6.7	7.7	8.5	8.9	8.8	9.0	8.6
Iceland	1.3	3.2	4.4	4.8	5.0	4.3	3.9	2.7	1.9	1.4	1.4	2.0
Cyprus	2.9	3.2	2.7	2.7	2.6	3.1	3.4	3.4	3.6	3.5	3.6	3.8
Korea	3.1	3.6	2.8	2.4	2.0	2.0	2.6	6.8	6.3	4.1	4.0	3.5
Australia	8.3	7.9	10.6	9.4	8.2	8.2	8.2	7.7	7.0	6.3	6.8	6.7
Taiwan Province of China	2.1	2.8	1.5	1.6	1.8	2.6	2.7	2.7	2.9	3.0	4.6	4.8
Hong Kong SAR	2.3	3.9	2.0	1.9	3.2	2.8	2.2	4.7	6.3	5.0	5.6	5.3
Singapore	3.3	2.8	2.7	2.6	2.7	2.0	1.8	3.2	3.5	3.1	3.2	3.1
New Zealand	6.6	6.8	9.5	8.2	6.3	6.1	6.7	7.5	6.8	6.0	5.5	5.7
Memorandum												
European Union	9.4	9.6	10.6	11.1	10.7	10.8	10.5	9.8	9.1	8.1	7.7	7.7
Euro area	9.7	10.2	10.7	11.5	11.2	11.4	11.4	10.8	9.9	8.8	8.4	8.4
Newly industrialized Asian economies	2.8	3.4	2.4	2.2	2.1	2.2	2.5	5.4	5.3	3.8	4.3	4.0
Growth in employment												
Advanced economies	**1.3**	**0.9**	**−0.1**	**1.1**	**1.2**	**1.0**	**1.5**	**1.0**	**1.3**	**1.4**	**0.5**	**0.5**
Major advanced economies	1.2	0.8	—	1.0	0.9	0.8	1.4	1.0	1.1	1.2	0.3	0.3
United States	1.8	1.4	1.5	2.3	1.5	1.5	2.3	1.5	1.5	1.3	0.2	0.6
Japan	1.3	−0.1	0.2	0.1	0.1	0.5	1.1	−0.7	−0.8	−0.2	−0.6	−0.7
Germany	0.9	0.2	−1.4	−0.2	0.1	−0.3	−0.2	1.1	1.2	1.6	0.1	—
France	0.2	0.8	−1.2	0.1	0.8	0.1	0.5	1.4	1.4	2.4	1.6	0.4
Italy	0.4	0.1	−4.1	−1.6	−0.6	0.5	0.4	1.1	1.3	1.9	1.5	0.6
United Kingdom	0.5	0.9	−0.9	1.0	1.4	1.1	2.0	1.1	1.3	1.0	0.6	0.5
Canada	1.5	1.9	0.8	2.0	1.9	0.8	2.3	2.7	2.8	2.6	1.8	1.8
Other advanced economies	1.4	1.4	−0.4	1.3	2.2	1.7	1.6	1.0	2.1	2.1	1.2	1.2
Memorandum												
European Union	0.6	0.7	−1.9	−0.2	0.8	0.7	1.0	1.8	1.7	2.0	0.9	0.5
Euro area	0.6	0.7	−2.0	−0.4	0.6	0.6	0.8	2.0	1.8	2.2	1.0	0.6
Newly industrialized Asian economies	2.5	1.3	1.5	2.8	2.5	2.1	1.7	−2.7	1.5	1.3	1.3	1.5

Table 4 *(concluded)*

	Ten-Year Averages[1]		1993	1994	1995	1996	1997	1998	1999	2000	2001	2002
	1983–92	1993–2002										
Growth in real per capita GDP												
Advanced economies	**2.9**	**2.0**	**0.8**	**2.7**	**2.1**	**2.3**	**2.8**	**2.0**	**2.8**	**2.4**	**0.7**	**1.6**
Major advanced economies	2.8	1.8	0.7	2.4	1.7	2.1	2.6	2.2	2.5	1.8	0.6	1.3
United States	2.4	2.1	1.5	3.0	1.7	2.6	3.4	3.3	3.3	0.9	0.4	1.3
Japan	3.4	0.7	0.2	0.7	1.3	3.1	1.7	–1.3	0.6	1.4	–0.7	0.1
Germany	5.1	1.3	–1.8	2.1	1.4	0.5	1.2	2.0	1.8	3.1	0.8	1.8
France	1.8	1.6	–1.3	1.4	1.4	0.7	1.5	3.1	2.6	3.8	1.7	1.7
Italy	2.3	1.8	0.5	1.9	2.7	1.0	1.8	1.8	1.6	2.9	1.8	2.1
United Kingdom	2.2	2.5	2.1	4.0	2.4	2.2	3.1	2.2	1.8	3.1	1.8	2.2
Canada	1.4	2.3	1.2	3.5	1.7	0.5	3.2	3.0	4.2	3.5	1.1	1.4
Other advanced economies	3.2	2.9	1.2	3.8	3.5	2.9	3.6	1.5	4.2	4.9	1.3	2.7
Memorandum												
European Union	3.0	2.0	–0.5	2.4	2.1	1.4	2.3	2.7	2.4	3.5	1.7	2.1
Euro area	3.2	1.9	–1.0	2.0	2.0	1.2	2.2	2.8	2.5	3.6	1.6	2.1
Newly industrialized Asian economies	7.0	4.0	5.5	6.3	6.0	4.7	4.5	–3.6	6.8	7.1	—	3.3

[1]Compound annual rate of change for employment and per capita GDP; arithmetic average for unemployment rate.
[2]The projections for unemployment have been adjusted to reflect the new survey techniques adopted by the U.S. Bureau of Labor Statistics in January 1994.
[3]New series starting in 1993, reflecting revisions in the labor force surveys and the definition of unemployment to bring data in line with those of other advanced economies.

Table 5. Developing Countries: Real GDP
(Annual percent change)

| | Ten-Year Averages | | 1993 | 1994 | 1995 | 1996 | 1997 | 1998 | 1999 | 2000 | 2001 | 2002 |
	1983–92	1993–2002										
Developing countries	**4.7**	**5.4**	**6.3**	**6.7**	**6.2**	**6.6**	**5.8**	**3.5**	**3.9**	**5.8**	**4.3**	**5.3**
Regional groups												
Africa	2.0	3.1	0.5	2.3	2.9	5.6	3.1	3.3	2.5	2.8	3.8	4.4
Sub-Sahara	1.7	3.1	0.9	1.9	3.7	5.1	3.7	2.6	2.5	3.0	3.5	4.2
Excluding Nigeria and South Africa	1.9	3.5	0.4	1.6	4.2	5.4	4.6	3.8	3.1	2.8	3.9	5.0
Developing Asia	7.3	7.2	9.4	9.7	9.0	8.3	6.5	4.0	6.1	6.8	5.8	6.2
China	10.2	9.2	13.5	12.6	10.5	9.6	8.8	7.8	7.1	8.0	7.5	7.1
India	5.4	6.1	5.0	6.9	7.7	7.3	4.9	5.8	6.8	6.0	4.5	5.7
Other developing Asia	5.3	4.2	6.3	6.9	7.7	6.7	3.8	−5.2	3.6	5.0	3.1	4.5
Middle East, Malta, and Turkey	3.5	3.6	3.2	0.3	4.7	5.1	5.1	4.1	1.0	6.0	2.3	4.8
Western Hemisphere	2.3	3.2	4.0	5.0	1.7	3.6	5.3	2.3	0.2	4.2	1.7	3.6
Analytical groups												
By source of export earnings												
Fuel	2.6	3.0	0.5	0.1	3.0	3.8	4.1	3.3	1.3	4.9	4.5	4.2
Nonfuel	5.0	5.7	7.1	7.4	6.5	6.8	5.9	3.6	4.2	5.9	4.3	5.4
of which, primary products	2.6	4.4	3.9	5.3	6.5	5.7	5.7	3.2	2.2	3.8	3.3	4.8
By external financing source												
Net debtor countries	4.8	5.5	6.5	6.9	6.3	6.6	5.9	3.6	4.0	5.8	4.4	5.4
of which, official financing	2.8	4.0	1.6	2.5	5.3	5.3	4.2	3.9	3.7	4.0	4.6	5.4
Net debtor countries by debt-servicing experience												
Countries with arrears and/or rescheduling during 1994–98	2.7	3.7	3.5	4.6	5.2	5.0	4.4	−0.4	2.1	4.5	3.4	4.4
Other groups												
Heavily indebted poor countries	2.1	4.4	1.9	2.8	6.2	6.1	5.2	3.9	3.8	3.8	4.4	5.5
Middle East and north Africa	3.0	3.7	1.4	2.3	2.9	5.2	3.7	4.7	3.0	5.0	4.7	4.6
Memorandum												
Real per capita GDP												
Developing countries	2.5	3.8	4.4	5.0	4.5	4.8	4.2	2.0	2.3	4.3	2.9	3.9
Regional groups												
Africa	−0.8	0.7	−2.1	−0.2	0.9	3.1	0.7	0.9	−0.1	0.3	1.4	1.9
Developing Asia	5.4	5.8	7.6	8.1	7.5	6.8	5.2	2.6	4.9	5.6	4.6	5.0
Middle East, Malta, and Turkey	0.3	1.5	0.9	−1.4	2.2	2.6	2.8	2.4	−0.9	3.2	0.3	2.8
Western Hemisphere	0.2	1.6	2.2	3.3	0.3	1.8	3.7	0.7	−1.7	3.2	0.2	2.1

Table 6. Developing Countries—by Country: Real GDP[1]

(Annual percent change)

	Average 1983–92	1993	1994	1995	1996	1997	1998	1999	2000
Africa	**2.0**	**0.5**	**2.3**	**2.9**	**5.6**	**3.1**	**3.3**	**2.5**	**2.8**
Algeria	1.9	−2.1	−0.9	3.8	3.8	1.1	5.1	3.2	2.4
Angola	2.1	−24.0	1.3	7.1	7.9	6.2	3.1	3.4	2.1
Benin	1.6	3.5	4.4	4.6	5.5	5.7	4.5	5.0	5.3
Botswana	9.7	2.1	3.5	4.5	5.7	6.7	5.9	6.1	7.7
Burkina Faso	3.6	−0.8	1.2	4.0	6.0	4.8	6.2	6.2	2.2
Burundi	4.0	−5.9	−3.7	−7.3	−8.4	0.4	4.5	−0.8	—
Cameroon	0.3	−3.2	−2.5	3.3	5.0	5.1	5.0	4.4	4.2
Cape Verde	1.3	12.7	11.5	3.8	3.8	4.7	7.6	7.9	6.7
Central African Republic	0.5	3.1	2.6	7.6	−4.9	3.9	5.5	3.5	2.6
Chad	6.3	−2.1	5.7	1.3	2.4	4.5	6.7	0.5	0.6
Comoros	1.7	3.0	−5.3	3.6	−1.3	4.2	1.2	1.9	−1.1
Congo, Dem. Rep. of	−1.4	−13.5	−3.9	0.7	−1.3	−5.6	−1.6	−10.4	−4.3
Congo, Rep. of	5.8	−1.0	−5.5	4.0	4.3	−0.6	3.7	−3.0	4.5
Côte d'Ivoire	0.6	−0.2	2.0	7.1	6.9	6.2	5.8	1.6	−2.3
Djibouti	0.1	−6.7	−0.9	−3.5	−4.1	−0.7	0.1	2.2	0.7
Equatorial Guinea	2.4	6.3	5.1	14.3	29.1	71.2	22.0	50.1	16.9
Eritrea	...	−2.5	9.8	2.9	6.8	7.9	3.9	0.8	−8.2
Ethiopia	−0.2	12.0	1.6	6.2	10.6	5.2	−1.2	6.3	5.3
Gabon	1.9	3.9	3.7	5.0	3.6	5.7	3.5	−9.6	−1.0
Gambia, The	3.2	6.1	3.8	−3.4	6.1	4.9	3.5	6.4	5.6
Ghana	4.1	5.0	3.3	4.0	4.6	4.2	4.7	4.4	3.7
Guinea	3.8	5.5	4.3	5.1	4.2	4.8	4.9	3.9	1.8
Guinea-Bissau	2.6	2.1	3.2	4.4	4.6	5.5	−28.1	7.8	9.3
Kenya	3.4	0.4	2.7	4.4	4.2	2.1	1.6	1.3	−0.2
Lesotho	5.3	3.7	3.7	5.9	9.5	4.8	−3.0	2.4	3.3
Liberia	...	...	...	...	...	...	...	...	...
Madagascar	1.2	2.1	—	1.7	2.1	3.7	3.9	4.7	4.8
Malawi	2.6	9.7	−10.3	16.7	7.3	3.8	3.3	4.0	1.7
Mali	4.1	−4.7	2.6	7.0	4.3	6.7	4.9	6.6	4.3
Mauritania	4.8	5.5	4.6	4.6	5.5	3.2	3.7	4.1	5.1
Mauritius	6.2	6.7	4.5	3.8	5.2	5.8	6.0	5.9	3.6
Morocco	3.5	−1.0	10.4	−6.6	12.2	−2.2	6.8	−0.7	0.8
Mozambique, Rep. of	—	8.7	7.5	4.3	7.1	11.0	12.6	7.5	2.1
Namibia	2.5	16.9	7.7	0.7	2.8	9.7	5.4	5.3	−0.4
Niger	−0.7	1.4	4.0	2.6	3.4	2.8	10.4	−0.6	3.0
Nigeria	3.8	2.2	−0.6	2.6	6.4	3.1	1.9	1.1	3.8
Rwanda	2.5	−8.1	−50.2	34.4	15.8	12.8	9.5	5.9	5.6
São Tomé and Príncipe	−0.5	1.1	2.2	2.0	1.5	1.0	2.5	2.5	3.0
Senegal	1.6	−2.2	2.9	5.2	5.1	5.0	5.7	5.1	5.6
Seychelles	5.2	6.5	−0.8	−0.6	4.7	4.3	2.3	−3.0	1.2
Sierra Leone	−1.4	0.1	3.5	−10.0	−24.8	−17.6	−0.8	−8.1	3.8
Somalia	...	...	...	...	...	...	...	...	...
South Africa	0.7	1.2	3.2	3.1	4.2	2.5	0.7	1.9	3.1
Sudan	1.7	6.2	2.0	3.0	10.5	10.2	6.1	5.1	8.3
Swaziland	6.6	3.3	3.5	3.5	4.2	3.8	3.5	3.5	2.5
Tanzania	3.4	1.2	1.6	3.6	4.5	3.5	3.3	4.8	5.1
Togo	1.4	−16.9	17.5	6.9	9.7	4.3	−2.1	2.7	−0.5
Tunisia	4.2	2.2	3.2	2.4	7.1	5.4	4.8	6.2	5.0
Uganda	3.4	8.6	6.4	11.9	8.6	5.1	4.6	7.9	4.4
Zambia	0.7	−0.1	−13.3	−2.5	6.5	3.4	−1.9	2.4	3.6
Zimbabwe	2.5	1.1	7.1	−0.6	8.7	3.7	2.5	−0.2	−5.1

Table 6 *(continued)*

	Average 1983–92	1993	1994	1995	1996	1997	1998	1999	2000
Developing Asia	**7.3**	**9.4**	**9.7**	**9.0**	**8.3**	**6.5**	**4.0**	**6.1**	**6.8**
Afghanistan, Islamic State of	...	...	...	...	...	...	...	...	...
Bangladesh	4.6	4.3	4.5	4.8	5.0	5.3	5.0	5.4	6.0
Bhutan	6.6	6.1	6.4	7.4	6.1	7.3	5.5	5.9	6.1
Brunei Darussalam	...	0.5	1.8	3.1	1.0	3.6	−4.0	2.5	3.0
Cambodia	...	4.0	3.9	6.7	5.5	3.7	1.8	5.0	4.0
China	10.2	13.5	12.6	10.5	9.6	8.8	7.8	7.1	8.0
Fiji	2.5	4.1	5.4	2.5	2.7	−0.9	1.4	8.0	4.9
India	5.4	5.0	6.9	7.7	7.3	4.9	5.8	6.8	6.0
Indonesia	6.3	7.3	7.5	8.2	8.0	4.5	−13.1	0.8	4.8
Kiribati	0.2	0.8	7.2	6.5	4.1	1.6	6.6	2.1	−1.7
Lao P.D. Republic	4.7	5.9	8.1	7.1	6.9	6.5	4.0	5.0	5.7
Malaysia	6.6	9.9	9.2	9.8	10.0	7.3	−7.4	6.1	8.3
Maldives	10.0	6.2	6.6	7.2	8.8	11.2	7.9	8.5	5.6
Myanmar	1.0	5.9	6.8	7.2	6.4	5.7	5.8	10.9	5.5
Nepal	4.6	3.8	8.2	3.5	5.3	5.0	3.0	4.4	6.5
Pakistan	5.8	2.7	4.4	4.9	2.9	1.8	3.1	4.1	3.9
Papua New Guinea	3.5	18.2	5.9	−3.3	7.7	−3.9	−3.8	3.1	0.3
Philippines	1.0	2.1	4.4	4.7	5.8	5.2	−0.6	3.4	4.0
Samoa	14.3	1.7	−0.1	6.2	7.3	0.8	2.5	3.5	6.8
Solomon Islands	2.8	2.0	5.4	10.5	3.5	−2.3	0.5	−0.5	−1.0
Sri Lanka	4.1	6.9	5.6	5.5	3.8	6.4	4.7	4.3	6.0
Thailand	8.4	8.4	9.0	9.3	5.9	−1.4	−10.8	4.2	4.4
Tonga	1.8	3.7	5.0	4.8	−1.4	−4.4	−1.5	—	1.5
Vanuatu	2.8	4.5	1.3	2.3	0.4	0.6	6.0	−2.5	4.0
Vietnam	5.9	8.1	8.8	9.5	9.3	8.2	3.5	4.2	5.5
Middle East, Malta, and Turkey	**3.5**	**3.2**	**0.3**	**4.7**	**5.1**	**5.1**	**4.1**	**1.0**	**6.0**
Bahrain	3.5	12.9	−0.2	3.9	4.1	3.1	4.8	4.0	3.9
Egypt	4.5	2.5	3.9	4.7	5.0	5.3	5.7	6.0	5.1
Iran, Islamic Republic of	2.6	2.1	0.9	2.9	5.9	2.7	3.7	3.1	5.8
Iraq	...	...	...	...	...	...	...	...	...
Jordan	9.0	5.6	5.0	6.4	2.1	3.1	2.9	3.1	3.9
Kuwait	−1.7	46.0	1.7	9.7	8.6	−2.5	1.7	−0.6	3.6
Lebanon	2.2	7.0	8.0	6.5	4.0	4.0	3.5	1.0	−0.7
Libya	0.6	−10.6	−2.7	0.9	5.2	−1.2	2.9	2.5	3.0
Malta	4.7	4.5	5.7	6.2	4.0	4.9	3.4	4.0	4.7
Oman	7.2	6.1	3.8	4.8	2.9	6.2	2.7	−1.0	4.9
Qatar	0.2	−0.6	2.3	2.9	4.8	25.4	6.2	2.4	10.5
Saudi Arabia	2.6	−0.6	0.5	0.5	1.4	2.0	1.7	−0.8	4.5
Syrian Arab Republic	2.8	5.0	7.7	5.8	4.4	1.8	7.6	−1.8	2.5
Turkey	5.0	7.7	−4.7	8.1	6.9	7.6	3.1	−5.0	7.5
United Arab Emirates	2.1	2.2	8.5	7.9	6.2	6.7	4.3	3.9	5.0
Yemen, Republic of	...	0.4	−3.6	34.7	5.9	8.1	4.9	0.6	5.2

Table 6 *(concluded)*

	Average 1983–92	1993	1994	1995	1996	1997	1998	1999	2000
Western Hemisphere	**2.3**	**4.0**	**5.0**	**1.7**	**3.6**	**5.3**	**2.3**	**0.2**	**4.2**
Antigua and Barbuda	6.8	5.1	6.2	−5.0	6.1	5.6	3.9	3.2	2.5
Argentina	1.7	6.3	5.8	−2.8	5.5	8.1	3.8	−3.4	−0.5
Bahamas, The	2.0	1.7	0.9	0.3	4.2	3.3	3.0	5.9	5.0
Barbados	0.6	0.8	4.0	3.1	1.7	6.4	4.1	1.3	3.2
Belize	6.1	3.3	1.8	3.3	2.0	3.6	3.4	5.6	10.3
Bolivia	1.2	4.3	4.7	4.7	4.4	5.0	5.2	0.4	2.4
Brazil	2.0	4.9	5.9	4.2	2.7	3.3	0.2	0.8	4.5
Chile	5.9	7.0	5.7	10.6	7.4	7.4	3.9	−1.1	5.4
Colombia	3.7	5.4	5.8	5.2	2.1	3.4	0.6	−4.1	2.8
Costa Rica	4.4	6.3	4.9	4.0	0.3	5.8	8.0	8.0	4.5
Dominica	4.3	1.9	2.1	1.6	3.1	2.0	2.4	0.9	0.5
Dominican Republic	2.7	2.9	4.3	4.7	7.2	8.3	7.3	8.0	7.8
Ecuador	2.4	2.0	4.4	2.3	2.0	3.4	0.4	−7.3	2.3
El Salvador	2.7	7.4	6.0	6.4	1.8	4.3	3.2	2.0	3.0
Grenada	4.2	−1.2	3.3	3.1	3.1	4.0	7.3	7.5	6.4
Guatemala	2.0	3.9	4.0	4.9	3.0	4.1	5.1	3.5	3.3
Guyana	−0.1	8.2	8.5	5.0	7.9	6.2	−1.7	3.0	2.5
Haiti	−0.7	−2.4	−8.3	4.4	2.7	1.1	3.1	2.1	1.2
Honduras	3.2	6.2	−1.3	4.1	3.6	5.1	2.9	−1.9	6.2
Jamaica	2.6	1.5	1.0	0.2	−1.5	−1.7	−0.5	—	1.5
Mexico	1.8	2.0	4.4	−6.2	5.2	6.8	5.0	3.7	6.9
Netherlands Antilles	0.7	5.3	5.9	0.6	2.3	1.4	−2.1	−1.9	−2.3
Nicaragua	−1.8	−0.2	3.3	4.2	5.0	4.9	4.2	6.7	5.9
Panama	1.7	5.5	2.9	1.8	2.4	4.4	4.0	4.1	4.5
Paraguay	2.8	4.1	3.1	4.7	1.3	2.6	−0.4	0.5	−0.4
Peru	−1.0	4.8	12.8	8.6	2.5	6.7	−0.5	0.9	3.1
St. Kitts and Nevis	5.0	6.7	5.1	3.7	6.5	6.8	1.1	2.8	2.6
St. Lucia	7.1	2.0	2.1	4.1	1.4	0.6	2.9	3.0	2.0
St. Vincent and the Grenadines	6.1	2.3	−2.0	8.3	1.2	3.1	5.7	4.0	3.5
Suriname	0.2	−9.5	−5.4	7.1	6.7	5.6	1.9	5.0	2.9
Trinidad and Tobago	−3.1	−1.4	3.6	4.0	3.8	3.1	4.8	6.8	5.6
Uruguay	2.5	2.7	7.3	−1.4	5.6	5.0	4.5	−2.8	−1.3
Venezuela	2.4	0.3	−2.3	4.0	−0.2	6.4	0.2	−6.1	3.2

[1]For many countries, figures for recent years are IMF staff estimates. Data for some countries are for fiscal years.

Table 7. Countries in Transition: Real GDP[1]

(Annual percent change)

	Average 1983–92	1993	1994	1995	1996	1997	1998	1999	2000
Central and eastern Europe	...	**−0.3**	**3.0**	**5.6**	**3.9**	**2.5**	**2.3**	**2.0**	**3.8**
Albania	−3.6	9.6	9.4	8.9	9.1	−7.0	8.0	7.3	7.8
Bosnia and Herzegovina	...	...	...	32.4	85.8	39.9	10.0	10.0	4.6
Bulgaria	9.5	−12.1	−7.8	4.3	−10.9	−7.0	3.5	2.4	5.8
Croatia	...	−8.0	5.9	5.9	6.0	6.6	2.5	−0.4	3.7
Czech Republic	...	0.1	2.2	5.9	4.3	−0.8	−1.2	−0.4	2.9
Estonia	...	−8.2	−1.8	4.6	4.0	10.4	5.0	−0.7	6.9
Hungary	−1.0	−0.6	2.9	1.5	1.3	4.6	4.9	4.5	5.2
Latvia	...	−14.9	0.6	−0.8	3.3	8.6	3.9	1.1	6.6
Lithuania	...	−16.2	−9.8	3.3	4.7	7.3	5.1	−3.9	3.3
Macedonia, former Yugoslav Rep. of	...	−7.5	−1.8	−1.1	1.2	1.4	2.9	2.7	5.0
Poland	0.9	4.3	5.2	6.8	6.0	6.8	4.8	4.1	4.1
Romania	...	1.5	3.9	7.3	3.9	−6.1	−4.8	−2.3	1.6
Slovak Republic	...	−3.7	4.9	6.7	6.2	6.2	4.1	1.9	2.2
Slovenia	...	2.8	5.3	4.1	3.5	4.6	3.8	5.2	4.9
Commonwealth of Independent States and Mongolia	...	**−12.6**	**−14.6**	**−5.5**	**−3.3**	**1.0**	**−2.8**	**4.6**	**7.8**
Russia	...	−13.0	−13.5	−4.2	−3.4	0.9	−4.9	5.4	8.3
Excluding Russia	...	−11.8	−17.0	−8.6	−3.0	1.4	1.6	2.8	6.8
Armenia	...	−14.1	5.4	6.9	5.9	3.3	7.3	3.3	6.0
Azerbaijan	...	−23.1	−19.7	−11.8	1.3	5.8	10.0	7.4	11.1
Belarus	...	−7.0	−12.6	−10.4	2.8	11.4	8.3	3.4	5.9
Georgia	...	−29.3	−10.4	2.6	10.5	10.6	2.9	3.0	1.8
Kazakhstan	...	−9.2	−12.6	−8.3	0.5	1.6	−1.9	2.8	9.5
Kyrgyz Republic	...	−15.5	−19.8	−5.8	7.1	10.0	2.1	3.7	5.0
Moldova	...	−1.1	−31.1	−1.4	−5.9	1.6	−6.5	−3.4	1.9
Mongolia	1.6	−2.9	2.3	6.3	2.4	4.0	3.5	3.2	1.1
Tajikistan	...	−11.1	−21.4	−12.5	−4.4	1.7	5.3	3.7	8.3
Turkmenistan	...	−10.0	−17.3	−7.2	−6.7	−11.3	5.0	16.0	17.6
Ukraine	...	−14.2	−22.9	−12.2	−9.8	−3.3	−1.9	−0.2	5.8
Uzbekistan	...	−2.3	−4.2	−0.9	1.6	2.5	4.3	4.3	4.0
Memorandum									
EU accession candidates	...	2.3	0.7	6.4	4.7	4.1	2.6	−0.1	4.9

[1]Data for some countries refer to real net material product (NMP) or are estimates based on NMP. For many countries, figures for recent years are IMF staff estimates. The figures should be interpreted only as indicative of broad orders of magnitude because reliable, comparable data are not generally available. In particular, the growth of output of new private enterprises of the informal economy is not fully reflected in the recent figures.

Table 8. Summary of Inflation
(Percent)

	Ten-Year Averages		1993	1994	1995	1996	1997	1998	1999	2000	2001	2002
	1983–92	1993–2002										
GDP deflators												
Advanced economies	**4.5**	**1.8**	**2.7**	**2.2**	**2.3**	**1.9**	**1.7**	**1.4**	**0.8**	**1.4**	**1.7**	**1.6**
United States	3.3	2.0	2.4	2.1	2.2	1.9	1.9	1.2	1.4	2.3	2.3	2.1
European Union	5.5	2.3	3.5	2.7	3.1	2.6	1.9	2.0	1.4	1.5	2.2	2.0
Japan	1.8	−0.6	0.5	0.1	−0.4	−0.6	0.3	−0.1	−1.4	−1.7	−1.5	−1.1
Other advanced economies	7.8	2.2	3.8	3.3	3.4	3.0	2.2	1.5	—	1.4	1.7	1.8
Consumer prices												
Advanced economies	**4.6**	**2.2**	**3.1**	**2.6**	**2.6**	**2.4**	**2.1**	**1.5**	**1.4**	**2.3**	**2.4**	**1.7**
United States	4.0	2.6	3.0	2.6	2.8	2.9	2.3	1.5	2.2	3.4	3.2	2.2
European Union	5.1	2.4	3.8	3.0	2.9	2.5	1.8	1.5	1.4	2.3	2.6	1.8
Japan	1.8	0.2	1.2	0.7	−0.1	0.1	1.7	0.6	−0.3	−0.6	−0.7	−0.7
Other advanced economies	7.9	2.7	3.4	3.3	3.8	3.2	2.4	2.6	1.0	2.2	2.7	2.1
Developing countries	**46.4**	**17.6**	**49.2**	**55.3**	**23.2**	**15.4**	**9.9**	**10.5**	**6.8**	**6.0**	**5.9**	**5.1**
Regional groups												
Africa	22.4	22.1	39.0	54.7	35.3	30.2	14.2	10.8	11.5	13.6	12.6	8.0
Developing Asia	9.9	7.0	10.8	16.0	13.2	8.3	4.8	7.7	2.5	1.9	2.8	3.3
Middle East, Malta, and Turkey	22.9	26.4	29.4	37.3	39.1	29.6	27.7	27.6	23.2	19.2	18.9	14.5
Western Hemisphere	170.2	37.2	194.6	200.3	36.0	21.2	12.9	9.9	8.8	8.1	6.2	4.9
Analytical groups												
By source of export earnings												
Fuel	15.3	22.9	29.2	36.2	42.6	35.1	19.4	17.2	16.2	12.9	13.0	11.5
Nonfuel	51.6	17.1	51.8	57.7	21.3	13.5	8.9	9.9	5.8	5.3	5.3	4.5
of which, primary products	75.2	23.0	46.7	62.9	29.7	27.0	15.9	14.1	12.2	13.3	12.0	7.3
By external financing source												
Net debtor countries	48.4	18.1	51.1	57.5	23.8	15.8	10.2	10.8	6.9	6.1	6.1	5.2
of which, official financing	37.3	20.0	37.5	64.3	30.0	22.6	11.2	10.6	10.7	10.4	8.8	5.5
Net debtor countries by debt-servicing experience												
Countries with arrears and/or rescheduling during 1994–98	109.7	41.7	200.5	221.6	40.1	21.1	11.9	18.4	13.3	11.0	11.1	7.6
Countries in transition	**42.4**	**77.8**	**635.8**	**274.2**	**133.8**	**42.5**	**27.3**	**21.8**	**43.9**	**20.0**	**16.4**	**10.7**
Central and eastern Europe	. . .	25.6	79.9	45.6	24.7	23.3	41.8	17.1	10.9	12.6	8.7	7.4
Commonwealth of Independent States and Mongolia	. . .	112.3	1,246.1	508.1	235.6	55.9	19.1	25.0	70.4	25.0	21.6	12.9
Russia	. . .	95.0	878.8	307.5	198.0	47.9	14.7	27.8	85.7	20.8	22.1	12.9
Excluding Russia	. . .	154.2	2,440.9	1,334.5	338.8	75.5	29.6	19.3	41.8	34.6	20.5	13.0
Memorandum												
Median inflation rate												
Advanced economies	4.7	2.2	3.0	2.4	2.5	2.1	1.8	1.7	1.5	2.7	2.5	2.2
Developing countries	9.4	6.6	9.7	10.6	10.0	7.3	6.2	5.8	3.9	4.2	4.1	4.4
Countries in transition	95.8	72.3	472.3	132.1	40.1	24.1	14.8	10.0	8.0	9.5	6.9	5.5

Table 9. Advanced Economies: GDP Deflators and Consumer Prices
(Annual percent change)

| | Ten-Year Averages | | 1993 | 1994 | 1995 | 1996 | 1997 | 1998 | 1999 | 2000 | 2001 | 2002 | Fourth Quarter[1] | | |
	1983–92	1993–2002											2000	2001	2002
GDP deflators															
Advanced economies	**4.5**	**1.8**	**2.7**	**2.2**	**2.3**	**1.9**	**1.7**	**1.4**	**0.8**	**1.4**	**1.7**	**1.6**	...	...	...
Major advanced economies	3.7	1.5	2.3	1.8	1.9	1.7	1.5	1.1	0.8	1.3	1.5	1.5	1.3	1.6	1.7
United States	3.3	2.0	2.4	2.1	2.2	1.9	1.9	1.2	1.4	2.3	2.3	2.1	2.4	2.3	2.1
Japan	1.8	−0.6	0.5	0.1	−0.4	−0.6	0.3	−0.1	−1.4	−1.7	−1.5	−1.1	−1.9	−1.4	−0.4
Germany	2.8	1.4	3.7	2.5	2.0	1.0	0.7	1.1	0.5	−0.4	1.4	1.2	−0.3	1.8	1.3
France	4.4	1.3	2.4	1.8	1.7	1.4	1.2	0.9	0.3	0.8	1.5	1.4	1.1	1.6	1.3
Italy	8.3	3.1	3.9	3.5	5.0	5.3	2.4	2.7	1.6	2.2	2.4	2.0	2.2	2.8	2.0
United Kingdom	5.6	2.5	2.7	1.5	2.5	3.3	2.9	3.0	2.3	1.8	1.9	3.0	1.3	1.8	3.4
Canada	3.6	1.7	1.4	1.2	2.3	1.7	1.1	−0.4	1.4	3.7	2.9	2.0	3.4	2.8	2.0
Other advanced economies	7.9	2.7	4.4	3.8	3.9	3.0	2.5	2.3	0.8	1.7	2.2	2.0	...	...	...
Spain	8.2	3.4	4.5	3.9	4.9	3.5	2.2	2.3	2.9	3.5	3.5	2.6	...	...	...
Netherlands	1.4	2.4	1.9	2.3	1.8	1.2	2.0	1.7	1.7	3.7	4.8	2.7	...	...	...
Belgium	3.1	1.6	3.7	1.9	1.8	1.2	1.3	1.6	1.0	1.2	1.5	0.9	...	...	...
Sweden	6.8	1.8	2.6	2.4	3.5	1.4	1.7	0.9	0.5	0.8	1.9	1.8	...	...	...
Austria	3.2	1.6	2.8	2.8	2.3	1.3	1.2	0.7	0.9	1.2	1.7	1.5	...	...	...
Denmark	4.5	2.2	1.4	1.7	1.8	2.5	2.2	1.9	3.0	3.7	2.1	2.1	...	...	...
Finland	5.3	2.0	2.3	2.0	4.1	−0.2	2.1	3.0	−0.1	3.4	2.3	1.7	...	...	...
Greece	17.3	6.8	14.5	11.2	11.2	7.3	6.8	5.1	2.8	3.3	3.1	3.0	...	...	...
Portugal	16.1	4.5	7.0	6.1	7.4	3.8	3.1	4.3	3.4	2.6	4.2	3.1	...	...	...
Ireland	4.3	3.8	5.2	1.7	3.0	2.2	4.1	5.9	4.2	4.3	4.2	3.7	...	...	...
Luxembourg	3.4	2.2	0.8	4.9	4.3	1.7	3.3	1.5	1.1	1.4	1.5	1.5	...	...	...
Switzerland	3.3	1.1	2.7	1.6	1.1	0.4	−0.2	0.2	0.6	1.3	1.4	1.6	...	...	...
Norway	4.1	3.8	2.1	−0.2	3.1	4.3	3.0	−0.7	6.3	16.3	3.0	1.4	...	...	...
Israel	68.2	7.5	11.3	13.4	9.4	11.5	8.5	8.0	6.3	1.5	1.2	4.6	...	...	...
Iceland	23.8	3.7	2.3	1.9	2.8	1.9	3.5	5.3	3.8	3.6	6.4	5.6	...	...	...
Cyprus	5.1	3.1	4.9	5.1	3.6	1.9	2.5	2.3	2.1	4.1	2.2	2.5	...	...	...
Korea	6.9	3.3	7.1	7.7	7.1	3.9	3.1	5.1	−2.0	−1.6	1.6	1.9	...	...	...
Australia	5.8	1.5	1.6	0.8	1.5	2.2	1.6	0.1	1.0	3.3	2.1	1.4	...	...	...
Taiwan Province of China	2.2	1.3	3.6	2.0	2.0	3.1	1.7	2.6	−1.4	−1.6	−0.3	1.3	...	...	...
Hong Kong SAR	8.0	1.9	8.5	6.9	2.6	5.9	5.8	0.4	−5.4	−6.6	0.1	1.8	...	...	...
Singapore	2.2	1.1	3.3	2.9	2.6	0.7	0.8	−2.0	−2.3	1.8	1.5	1.7	...	...	...
New Zealand	7.3	1.7	2.3	1.4	2.1	2.0	0.8	0.8	−0.6	1.9	3.3	2.6	...	...	...
Memorandum															
European Union	5.5	2.3	3.5	2.7	3.1	2.6	1.9	2.0	1.4	1.5	2.2	2.0	...	...	...
Euro area	5.5	2.2	3.8	2.9	3.2	2.5	1.7	1.8	1.2	1.4	2.2	1.8	...	...	...
Newly industrialized Asian economies	5.4	2.4	6.0	5.5	4.7	3.7	2.9	3.2	−2.3	−1.9	0.8	1.7	...	...	...
Consumer prices															
Advanced economies	**4.6**	**2.2**	**3.1**	**2.6**	**2.6**	**2.4**	**2.1**	**1.5**	**1.4**	**2.3**	**2.4**	**1.7**	...	...	...
Major advanced economies	3.9	2.0	2.8	2.2	2.3	2.2	2.0	1.3	1.4	2.3	2.3	1.6	2.4	1.9	1.7
United States	4.0	2.6	3.0	2.6	2.8	2.9	2.3	1.5	2.2	3.4	3.2	2.2	3.4	2.9	2.3
Japan	1.8	0.2	1.2	0.7	−0.1	0.1	1.7	0.6	−0.3	−0.6	−0.7	−0.7	−0.6	−1.3	0.2
Germany[2]	2.3	1.9	4.5	2.7	1.7	1.2	1.5	0.6	0.7	2.1	2.5	1.3	2.4	2.1	1.3
France	4.4	1.5	2.1	1.7	1.8	2.1	1.3	0.7	0.6	1.8	1.8	1.1	2.0	1.6	1.0
Italy	7.4	3.0	4.6	4.1	5.2	4.0	1.9	2.0	1.7	2.6	2.6	1.6	2.8	2.2	1.7
United Kingdom[3]	5.3	2.6	3.0	2.4	2.8	3.0	2.8	2.7	2.3	2.1	2.2	2.4	2.1	2.4	2.5
Canada	4.4	1.8	1.8	0.2	1.9	1.6	1.6	1.0	1.7	2.7	3.1	2.3	3.1	2.9	2.0
Other advanced economies	7.7	2.9	4.2	4.1	3.8	3.2	2.3	2.4	1.3	2.4	3.0	2.2	...	...	...
Memorandum															
European Union	5.1	2.4	3.8	3.0	2.9	2.5	1.8	1.5	1.4	2.3	2.6	1.8	...	...	...
Euro area	5.0	2.4	4.0	3.2	3.0	2.5	1.7	1.3	1.2	2.4	2.7	1.7	...	...	...
Newly industrialized Asian economies	4.3	3.2	4.6	5.7	4.6	4.3	3.4	4.4	—	1.2	2.1	2.1	...	...	...

[1]From fourth quarter of preceding year.
[2]Based on the revised consumer price index for united Germany introduced in September 1995.
[3]Retail price index excluding mortgage interest.

Table 10. Advanced Economies: Hourly Earnings, Productivity, and Unit Labor Costs in Manufacturing
(Annual percent change)

| | Ten-Year Averages | | 1993 | 1994 | 1995 | 1996 | 1997 | 1998 | 1999 | 2000 | 2001 | 2002 |
	1983–92	1993–2002										
Hourly earnings												
Advanced economies	**6.1**	**3.5**	**4.2**	**3.4**	**3.2**	**3.0**	**2.8**	**3.3**	**3.3**	**4.4**	**4.5**	**2.9**
Major advanced economies	5.2	3.2	3.8	2.8	2.7	2.4	2.4	3.4	3.0	4.3	4.8	2.6
United States	4.1	3.7	2.8	2.8	2.1	1.3	1.9	5.4	4.0	6.5	6.9	3.6
Japan	3.9	1.2	2.7	2.3	2.4	1.7	3.1	0.9	–0.7	–0.1	1.2	–1.8
Germany	5.2	3.3	6.9	2.4	4.1	4.7	1.5	2.1	2.8	2.7	2.8	3.0
France	7.2	3.2	6.6	2.2	1.4	3.0	1.7	2.6	5.0	3.4	2.8	3.2
Italy	9.9	3.3	5.4	3.1	4.7	5.8	4.2	–1.4	2.9	2.7	3.0	2.7
United Kingdom	8.4	4.5	4.7	5.0	4.4	4.3	4.2	4.5	4.1	4.6	4.8	4.1
Canada	5.0	2.4	2.0	1.6	2.2	1.0	2.2	2.1	1.3	3.5	4.5	3.6
Other advanced economies	10.2	4.6	5.9	5.9	5.2	5.7	4.3	3.0	4.7	4.5	3.2	3.8
Memorandum												
European Union	7.5	3.7	5.9	3.5	3.9	4.4	3.1	2.4	3.5	3.4	3.6	3.4
Euro area	7.4	3.5	6.2	3.1	3.8	4.4	2.8	1.9	3.4	3.2	3.3	3.2
Newly industrialized Asian economies	13.4	6.5	9.2	11.4	7.9	10.2	5.6	0.9	9.3	7.0	0.7	4.0
Productivity												
Advanced economies	**3.3**	**3.4**	**2.1**	**4.8**	**3.9**	**3.1**	**4.4**	**2.5**	**4.1**	**5.9**	**1.5**	**1.7**
Major advanced economies	3.3	3.3	1.7	4.4	3.8	3.1	4.3	2.7	3.8	6.1	1.5	1.4
United States	3.0	3.7	1.9	3.0	3.9	3.5	4.2	5.4	4.6	6.7	1.6	2.0
Japan	2.9	1.8	–1.0	3.3	4.7	3.8	4.8	–4.2	3.6	6.8	–1.4	–2.1
Germany	3.9	5.1	3.0	9.0	4.5	6.0	7.3	4.8	3.1	6.6	3.5	3.2
France	3.4	3.7	0.7	6.8	6.0	1.0	5.6	5.5	2.9	5.4	1.5	1.8
Italy	3.3	2.5	0.6	6.0	3.6	3.7	2.3	–1.5	2.0	4.5	2.3	1.7
United Kingdom	4.8	2.3	4.9	4.5	–0.4	–1.0	0.9	0.6	3.8	5.4	2.6	1.7
Canada	2.6	2.2	4.9	4.5	1.5	–1.1	2.8	—	1.6	1.2	3.4	3.1
Other advanced economies	3.3	3.8	4.0	6.7	4.0	2.8	4.5	1.6	5.5	4.8	1.7	2.5
Memorandum												
European Union	3.6	3.6	3.0	7.3	3.6	2.5	4.3	2.7	2.8	5.0	2.4	2.2
Euro area	3.4	3.8	2.4	7.6	4.4	3.4	4.9	3.1	2.7	4.9	2.4	2.3
Newly industrialized Asian economies	7.9	6.1	4.7	7.1	7.9	6.3	7.1	–1.6	14.8	10.6	0.8	3.9
Unit labor costs												
Advanced economies	**2.8**	**0.1**	**2.0**	**–1.4**	**–0.7**	**—**	**–1.5**	**0.9**	**–0.7**	**–1.4**	**2.9**	**1.2**
Major advanced economies	1.9	—	2.1	–1.5	–1.1	–0.7	–1.8	0.8	–0.7	–1.7	3.3	1.2
United States	1.0	0.1	0.8	–0.2	–1.7	–2.1	–2.2	—	–0.5	–0.2	5.3	1.6
Japan	1.0	–0.6	3.7	–1.0	–2.2	–2.0	–1.6	5.3	–4.1	–6.4	2.7	0.3
Germany	1.2	–1.7	3.8	–6.1	–0.4	–1.2	–5.5	–2.6	–0.3	–3.6	–0.7	–0.2
France	3.6	–0.5	5.9	–4.4	–4.3	1.9	–3.7	–2.8	2.1	–1.9	1.3	1.4
Italy	6.4	0.8	4.8	–2.7	1.0	2.0	1.9	0.2	0.9	–1.7	0.7	1.0
United Kingdom	3.4	2.2	–0.2	0.5	4.8	5.3	3.3	3.9	0.3	–0.8	2.1	2.4
Canada	2.3	0.2	–2.8	–2.8	0.7	2.1	–0.6	2.2	–0.3	2.2	1.1	0.5
Other advanced economies	6.8	0.8	1.7	–0.8	0.9	2.6	–0.3	1.5	–0.4	–0.3	1.5	1.3
Memorandum												
European Union	3.9	0.2	2.9	–3.5	0.4	1.9	–1.1	–0.2	0.7	–1.4	1.1	1.2
Euro area	3.9	–0.2	3.8	–4.1	–0.5	1.0	–1.9	–1.1	0.7	–1.6	0.9	0.9
Newly industrialized Asian economies	4.3	0.2	3.5	2.6	–1.0	2.6	–1.5	2.7	–4.1	–3.2	—	0.2

Table 11. Developing Countries: Consumer Prices
(Annual percent change)

| | Ten-Year Averages | | 1993 | 1994 | 1995 | 1996 | 1997 | 1998 | 1999 | 2000 | 2001 | 2002 |
	1983–92	1993–2002										
Developing countries	**46.4**	**17.6**	**49.2**	**55.3**	**23.2**	**15.4**	**9.9**	**10.5**	**6.8**	**6.0**	**5.9**	**5.1**
Regional groups												
Africa	22.4	22.1	39.0	54.7	35.3	30.2	14.2	10.8	11.5	13.6	12.6	8.0
Sub-Sahara	26.3	26.8	47.9	68.5	40.9	36.5	17.4	12.9	14.5	17.5	15.6	9.0
Excluding Nigeria and South Africa	34.6	39.8	73.7	121.6	57.4	58.7	24.7	16.9	21.7	27.0	20.0	9.9
Developing Asia	9.9	7.0	10.8	16.0	13.2	8.3	4.8	7.7	2.5	1.9	2.8	3.3
China	7.6	6.4	14.7	24.1	17.1	8.3	2.8	-0.8	-1.4	0.4	1.0	1.5
India	9.3	7.4	6.4	10.2	10.2	9.0	7.2	13.2	4.7	4.0	3.6	5.5
Other developing Asia	13.0	8.5	8.3	8.1	9.1	7.7	6.8	22.1	9.1	3.3	6.2	5.4
Middle East, Malta, and Turkey	22.9	26.4	29.4	37.3	39.1	29.6	27.7	27.6	23.2	19.2	18.9	14.5
Western Hemisphere	170.2	37.2	194.6	200.3	36.0	21.2	12.9	9.9	8.8	8.1	6.2	4.9
Analytical groups												
By source of export earnings												
Fuel	15.3	22.9	29.2	36.2	42.6	35.1	19.4	17.2	16.2	12.9	13.0	11.5
Nonfuel	51.6	17.1	51.8	57.7	21.3	13.5	8.9	9.9	5.8	5.3	5.3	4.5
of which, primary products	75.2	23.0	46.7	62.9	29.7	27.0	15.9	14.1	12.2	13.3	12.0	7.3
By external financing source												
Net debtor countries	48.4	18.1	51.1	57.5	23.8	15.8	10.2	10.8	6.9	6.1	6.1	5.2
of which, official financing	37.3	20.0	37.5	64.3	30.0	22.6	11.2	10.6	10.7	10.4	8.8	5.5
Net debtor countries by debt-servicing experience												
Countries with arrears and/or rescheduling during 1994–98	109.7	41.7	200.5	221.6	40.1	21.1	11.9	18.4	13.3	11.0	11.1	7.6
Other groups												
Heavily indebted poor countries	51.4	32.3	60.3	92.0	49.6	46.5	21.1	17.5	16.9	18.9	14.5	7.7
Middle East and north Africa	15.5	13.7	19.5	21.8	24.2	16.7	11.2	10.5	10.1	7.8	8.3	8.0
Memorandum												
Median												
Developing countries	9.4	6.6	9.7	10.6	10.0	7.3	6.2	5.8	3.9	4.2	4.1	4.4
Regional groups												
Africa	9.5	8.6	9.8	24.7	11.8	7.7	7.8	5.8	4.2	5.3	4.7	4.5
Developing Asia	8.1	6.4	7.6	8.4	7.9	7.6	6.4	8.4	4.4	3.6	4.3	5.1
Middle East, Malta, and Turkey	6.6	3.9	6.4	4.9	6.4	6.8	3.1	3.0	2.2	1.5	2.5	2.8
Western Hemisphere	14.5	6.6	10.7	8.3	10.2	7.4	7.0	5.1	3.5	4.7	5.1	3.9

Table 12. Developing Countries—by Country: Consumer Prices[1]

(Annual percent change)

	Average 1983–92	1993	1994	1995	1996	1997	1998	1999	2000
Africa	**22.4**	**39.0**	**54.7**	**35.3**	**30.2**	**14.2**	**10.8**	**11.5**	**13.6**
Algeria	12.3	20.5	29.0	29.8	18.7	5.7	5.0	2.6	0.3
Angola	23.9	1,379.5	949.8	2,672.2	4,146.0	221.5	107.4	248.2	325.0
Benin	1.6	0.4	38.5	14.5	4.9	3.8	5.8	0.3	4.2
Botswana	12.4	14.3	10.5	10.5	10.1	8.8	6.5	7.2	8.5
Burkina Faso	0.4	0.6	24.7	7.8	6.1	2.3	5.0	−1.1	−0.2
Burundi	7.1	9.7	14.7	19.4	26.4	31.1	12.5	3.6	31.9
Cameroon	4.8	−3.7	12.7	25.8	6.6	5.1	—	2.9	0.8
Cape Verde	10.0	5.8	3.3	8.4	6.0	8.6	4.4	4.4	−2.5
Central African Republic	1.4	−2.9	24.5	19.2	3.7	1.6	−1.9	−1.5	3.1
Chad	2.4	31.4	41.3	9.1	11.8	5.9	4.4	−8.0	3.1
Comoros	1.1	2.0	25.3	7.1	2.0	3.0	3.5	3.5	4.5
Congo, Dem. Rep. of	200.5	1,893.1	23,760.5	541.8	616.8	198.5	106.9	269.6	553.7
Congo, Rep. of	−1.2	5.0	42.9	8.6	10.2	13.2	1.8	3.1	3.0
Côte d'Ivoire	3.8	2.1	26.0	14.3	2.7	4.2	4.5	0.7	2.5
Djibouti	5.3	4.4	6.5	4.9	3.5	2.5	2.2	2.0	2.4
Equatorial Guinea	13.0	1.6	38.9	11.4	6.0	3.0	3.0	6.5	6.0
Eritrea	...	4.6	11.6	10.7	9.3	1.3	16.6	8.3	9.4
Ethiopia	7.3	10.0	1.2	13.4	0.9	−6.4	3.6	3.9	4.2
Gabon	2.2	0.6	36.1	10.0	4.5	4.1	2.3	−0.7	1.0
Gambia, The	17.7	5.9	4.0	4.0	4.8	3.1	1.1	2.5	2.5
Ghana	33.2	24.9	24.9	59.5	46.6	27.9	19.3	12.4	25.0
Guinea	28.2	7.2	4.2	5.6	3.0	1.9	5.1	4.6	6.8
Guinea-Bissau	61.9	48.2	15.2	45.4	50.7	49.1	8.0	−2.1	9.1
Kenya	13.0	45.9	27.9	4.0	9.0	9.2	9.3	6.1	7.1
Lesotho	14.3	13.8	7.2	9.9	9.1	8.5	7.8	8.7	6.1
Liberia	...	...	...	...	...	...	...	...	...
Madagascar	14.0	9.3	39.0	49.0	19.8	4.5	6.2	9.9	11.9
Malawi	17.1	22.8	34.7	83.1	37.7	9.1	29.8	44.8	29.6
Mali	0.8	−0.6	24.8	12.4	6.5	−0.7	4.1	−1.2	−0.7
Mauritania	8.2	9.3	4.1	6.5	4.7	4.5	8.0	4.1	3.3
Mauritius	6.9	8.9	9.4	6.0	5.9	7.9	5.4	7.9	5.3
Morocco	6.4	5.2	5.1	6.1	3.0	1.0	2.7	0.7	1.9
Mozambique, Rep. of	48.1	42.3	63.1	54.4	44.6	6.4	0.6	2.9	12.7
Namibia	12.8	8.5	10.8	10.0	8.0	8.8	6.2	8.6	4.5
Niger	−0.8	−0.6	24.8	11.2	5.3	2.9	4.5	2.9	2.9
Nigeria	22.3	57.2	57.0	72.8	29.3	8.5	10.0	6.6	6.9
Rwanda	5.3	12.5	64.0	22.0	8.9	11.7	6.8	−2.4	3.9
Sâo Tomé and Príncipe	24.6	25.5	51.2	36.8	42.0	69.0	42.1	16.3	11.0
Senegal	3.4	−0.6	32.0	8.1	2.8	1.7	1.1	0.8	0.7
Seychelles	2.6	1.3	1.8	−0.3	−1.1	0.6	2.7	6.3	6.7
Sierra Leone	81.2	22.2	24.2	26.0	23.1	14.9	35.5	34.1	−0.9
Somalia	...	...	...	...	...	...	...	...	...
South Africa	14.6	9.9	8.8	8.7	7.3	8.6	6.9	5.2	5.4
Sudan	60.2	101.3	115.5	68.4	132.8	46.7	17.1	16.0	8.0
Swaziland	13.0	12.0	13.8	12.3	6.4	7.9	7.5	5.9	9.9
Tanzania	29.9	23.6	37.1	26.5	21.0	16.1	12.6	6.3	6.2
Togo	1.7	2.4	48.5	6.4	2.5	5.5	−1.4	2.0	−2.5
Tunisia	7.4	4.0	4.5	6.3	3.8	3.7	3.1	2.7	3.0
Uganda	92.3	30.0	6.5	6.1	7.5	7.8	5.8	−0.2	6.3
Zambia	67.5	183.3	54.6	34.9	43.1	24.4	24.5	26.8	26.1
Zimbabwe	17.8	27.6	22.2	22.6	21.4	18.8	32.3	58.2	55.7

Table 12 *(continued)*

	Average 1983–92	1993	1994	1995	1996	1997	1998	1999	2000
Developing Asia	**9.9**	**10.8**	**16.0**	**13.2**	**8.3**	**4.8**	**7.7**	**2.5**	**1.9**
Afghanistan, Islamic State of	...	...	...	...	...	...	...	...	...
Bangladesh	9.2	3.0	6.1	7.7	3.9	5.1	8.5	6.4	2.3
Bhutan	9.9	11.2	7.0	9.5	8.8	6.5	10.6	6.8	4.8
Brunei Darussalam	...	4.3	2.4	6.0	2.0	1.7	−0.4	−0.1	1.5
Cambodia	...	114.3	9.4	1.3	7.2	8.0	14.8	4.0	1.0
China	7.6	14.7	24.1	17.1	8.3	2.8	−0.8	−1.4	0.4
Fiji	6.1	5.2	0.6	0.3	4.9	3.4	5.9	2.0	2.4
India	9.3	6.4	10.2	10.2	9.0	7.2	13.2	4.7	4.0
Indonesia	8.1	9.7	8.5	9.4	7.9	6.2	58.0	20.7	3.8
Kiribati	2.7	6.1	5.3	4.1	−1.5	2.2	4.7	0.4	1.0
Lao P.D. Republic	34.7	6.3	6.8	19.4	13.0	19.3	87.4	134.0	27.1
Malaysia	2.6	3.6	4.1	3.5	3.5	2.7	5.3	2.7	1.5
Maldives	6.7	20.1	3.4	5.5	6.2	7.6	−1.4	3.0	−1.1
Myanmar	16.8	33.6	22.4	28.9	20.0	33.9	49.1	11.4	10.3
Nepal	8.6	8.9	8.9	7.7	7.2	8.1	8.3	11.4	3.4
Pakistan	7.3	10.0	12.4	12.3	10.4	11.4	6.2	4.1	4.4
Papua New Guinea	5.6	5.0	2.9	17.3	11.6	3.9	13.6	14.9	15.6
Philippines	13.5	6.9	8.4	8.0	9.0	5.9	9.7	6.6	4.3
Samoa	3.4	1.7	12.1	−2.9	5.4	6.9	2.2	0.3	1.0
Solomon Islands	11.2	9.2	13.3	9.6	11.8	8.1	12.4	8.3	6.0
Sri Lanka	11.7	11.7	8.4	7.7	15.9	9.6	9.4	4.7	6.2
Thailand	3.7	3.4	5.1	5.8	5.9	5.6	8.1	0.3	1.5
Tonga	10.0	3.1	2.4	0.5	2.6	2.0	3.1	3.9	5.3
Vanuatu	6.3	3.6	2.3	2.2	0.9	2.9	3.2	2.0	2.0
Vietnam	124.6	8.4	9.5	17.4	5.7	3.2	7.3	4.1	−1.7
Middle East, Malta, and Turkey	**22.9**	**29.4**	**37.3**	**39.1**	**29.6**	**27.7**	**27.6**	**23.2**	**19.2**
Bahrain	−0.2	2.6	0.4	3.1	−0.1	1.5	−0.3	−1.6	−0.4
Egypt	18.6	11.0	9.0	9.4	7.1	6.2	4.7	3.8	2.8
Iran, Islamic Republic of	18.6	22.9	35.2	49.4	23.2	17.3	20.0	20.4	12.6
Iraq	...	...	...	...	...	...	...	...	...
Jordan	5.0	3.3	3.6	2.3	6.5	3.0	3.1	0.6	0.7
Kuwait	8.1	0.4	2.5	2.7	3.6	0.7	0.1	3.0	1.7
Lebanon	89.9	24.7	8.0	10.6	8.9	7.7	4.5	−2.7	−0.4
Libya	7.7	7.5	10.7	8.3	4.0	3.6	3.7	2.6	−3.0
Malta	1.0	4.0	4.1	4.0	2.0	3.1	2.4	2.1	2.4
Oman	1.4	1.1	−0.7	−1.1	0.3	−0.2	−0.5	0.5	−1.0
Qatar	3.0	−0.9	1.4	3.0	7.1	2.7	2.9	2.2	2.4
Saudi Arabia	−0.4	0.8	0.6	5.0	0.9	−0.4	−0.2	−1.3	−0.6
Syrian Arab Republic	20.6	23.6	3.9	7.7	8.9	1.9	−0.4	−2.1	1.1
Turkey	52.4	66.1	106.3	93.7	82.3	85.7	84.6	64.9	54.9
United Arab Emirates	3.6	5.2	5.7	4.4	3.0	2.9	2.0	2.1	1.4
Yemen, Republic of	...	62.4	71.3	62.5	40.0	4.6	11.5	9.2	8.0

Table 12 *(concluded)*

	Average 1983–92	1993	1994	1995	1996	1997	1998	1999	2000
Western Hemisphere	**170.2**	**194.6**	**200.3**	**36.0**	**21.2**	**12.9**	**9.9**	**8.8**	**8.1**
Antigua and Barbuda	3.6	3.1	6.5	2.7	3.0	0.3	3.3	1.6	2.0
Argentina	346.3	10.7	4.2	3.4	0.2	0.5	0.9	−1.2	−0.9
Bahamas, The	5.1	2.7	1.3	2.1	1.4	0.5	1.3	1.3	1.6
Barbados	4.5	1.2	−0.1	1.9	2.4	7.7	−1.3	1.6	2.6
Belize	2.9	1.4	2.5	2.9	6.3	1.1	−0.9	−1.1	0.7
Bolivia	198.7	8.5	7.9	10.2	12.4	4.7	7.7	2.2	4.6
Brazil	475.8	1,927.4	2,075.8	66.0	15.8	6.9	3.2	4.9	7.0
Chile	21.1	12.7	11.4	8.2	7.4	6.1	5.1	3.3	3.8
Colombia	24.2	22.4	22.8	20.9	20.8	18.5	18.7	10.9	9.2
Costa Rica	19.3	9.8	13.5	23.2	17.6	13.3	11.7	10.1	11.5
Dominica	4.0	1.6	—	1.3	1.7	2.4	0.9	1.6	1.9
Dominican Republic	27.1	5.3	8.3	12.5	5.4	8.3	4.8	6.5	7.7
Ecuador	43.7	45.0	27.3	22.9	24.4	30.6	36.1	52.2	96.2
El Salvador	19.0	18.5	10.6	10.1	9.8	4.5	2.5	0.6	2.5
Grenada	3.2	2.8	2.6	2.2	2.8	1.3	1.4	0.5	2.2
Guatemala	15.5	13.4	12.5	8.4	11.0	9.2	6.6	5.3	6.0
Guyana	38.4	12.0	12.4	12.2	7.1	3.6	4.6	7.5	6.6
Haiti	10.1	18.8	37.4	30.2	21.9	16.2	12.7	8.1	11.5
Honduras	10.2	10.7	18.2	29.5	23.8	20.2	13.7	11.6	10.5
Jamaica	27.6	24.3	33.2	21.7	21.5	9.1	8.1	6.3	7.7
Mexico	59.3	9.8	7.0	35.0	34.4	20.6	15.9	16.6	9.5
Netherlands Antilles	2.5	1.9	1.9	2.8	3.4	3.1	1.2	0.8	4.7
Nicaragua	910.3	20.4	7.7	11.2	11.6	9.2	13.0	11.2	9.7
Panama	1.0	0.5	1.3	0.9	1.3	1.3	0.6	1.3	1.4
Paraguay	23.7	18.3	20.6	13.4	9.8	7.0	11.6	6.8	9.0
Peru	383.7	48.6	23.7	11.1	11.5	8.5	7.3	3.5	3.8
St. Kitts and Nevis	2.5	1.8	1.4	3.0	2.0	8.7	3.7	3.5	—
St. Lucia	3.1	0.8	2.7	5.9	0.9	0.1	2.8	3.5	4.0
St. Vincent and the Grenadines	3.4	4.3	1.0	1.7	4.4	0.4	2.1	1.0	0.8
Suriname	17.9	143.4	368.5	235.5	−0.8	7.3	19.0	98.8	59.1
Trinidad and Tobago	9.6	13.1	3.7	5.3	3.3	3.6	5.6	3.4	3.5
Uruguay	73.3	54.3	45.0	42.6	28.6	20.0	10.9	5.7	4.8
Venezuela	27.4	38.1	60.8	59.9	99.9	50.0	35.8	23.6	16.2

[1]For many countries, figures for recent years are IMF staff estimates. Data for some countries are for fiscal years.

Table 13. Countries in Transition: Consumer Prices[1]

(Annual percent change)

	Average 1983–92	1993	1994	1995	1996	1997	1998	1999	2000
Central and eastern Europe	...	**79.9**	**45.6**	**24.7**	**23.3**	**41.8**	**17.1**	**10.9**	**12.6**
Albania	16.0	85.0	22.6	7.8	12.7	32.1	20.9	0.4	0.0
Bosnia and Herzegovina	...	...	...	0.2	–13.7	9.5	0.6	3.4	5.0
Bulgaria	28.4	72.8	96.0	62.1	123.0	1,061.2	18.8	2.6	10.4
Croatia	...	1,516.6	97.5	2.0	3.5	3.6	5.7	4.1	6.2
Czech Republic	...	20.8	10.0	9.1	8.8	8.5	10.7	2.1	4.0
Estonia	...	89.8	49.3	29.0	23.1	11.2	8.1	3.3	4.0
Hungary	15.1	22.4	18.8	28.3	23.5	18.3	14.3	10.0	9.8
Latvia	...	109.2	35.9	25.0	17.6	8.4	4.7	2.4	2.6
Lithuania	...	410.4	72.1	39.5	24.7	8.8	5.1	0.8	1.0
Macedonia, former Yugoslav Rep. of	...	338.7	127.5	15.7	2.3	2.6	–0.1	–0.7	5.8
Poland	71.8	35.3	32.2	27.9	19.9	14.9	11.8	7.3	10.1
Romania	...	256.1	136.7	32.3	38.8	154.8	59.1	45.8	45.7
Slovak Republic	...	23.0	13.4	9.9	5.8	6.1	6.7	10.7	12.0
Slovenia	...	31.9	21.5	13.5	9.9	8.4	7.9	6.2	8.9
Commonwealth of Independent States and Mongolia	...	**1,246.1**	**508.1**	**235.6**	**55.9**	**19.1**	**25.0**	**70.4**	**25.0**
Russia	...	878.8	307.5	198.0	47.9	14.7	27.8	85.7	20.8
Excluding Russia	...	2,440.9	1,334.5	338.8	75.5	29.6	19.3	41.8	34.6
Armenia	...	3,731.8	5,273.4	176.7	18.7	14.0	8.7	0.7	–0.8
Azerbaijan	...	1,129.7	1,664.0	411.8	19.8	3.7	–0.8	–8.5	1.8
Belarus	...	1,190.2	2,434.1	709.3	52.7	63.8	73.0	293.7	169.0
Georgia	...	3,125.4	15,606.5	162.7	39.3	7.0	3.6	19.1	4.0
Kazakhstan	...	1,662.3	1,879.9	176.3	39.1	17.4	7.3	8.4	13.3
Kyrgyz Republic	...	772.4	190.1	40.7	31.3	22.6	12.0	35.9	18.7
Moldova	...	788.5	329.6	30.2	23.5	11.8	7.7	39.3	31.3
Mongolia	13.7	268.4	87.6	56.8	46.8	36.6	9.4	7.6	11.6
Tajikistan	...	2,194.9	350.4	610.0	418.2	88.0	43.2	27.5	32.9
Turkmenistan	...	3,102.4	1,748.3	1,005.2	992.4	83.7	16.8	23.5	8.0
Ukraine	...	4,734.9	891.2	376.4	80.2	15.9	10.6	22.7	28.2
Uzbekistan	...	534.2	1,568.3	304.6	54.0	70.9	29.0	29.1	25.0
Memorandum									
EU accession candidates	...	64.9	59.1	42.8	39.4	55.4	35.6	25.3	24.3

[1]For many countries, inflation for the earlier years is measured on the basis of a retail price index. Consumer price indices with a broader and more up-to-date coverage are typically used for more recent years.

Table 14. Summary Financial Indicators
(Percent)

	1993	1994	1995	1996	1997	1998	1999	2000	2001	2002
Advanced economies										
Central government fiscal balance[1]										
Advanced economies	−4.3	−3.7	−3.3	−2.7	−1.5	−1.6	−0.9	0.4	−0.3	−0.2
United States	−4.2	−3.0	−2.6	−1.8	−0.6	0.6	1.3	2.5	1.8	1.7
European Union	−5.9	−5.3	−4.6	−4.1	−2.4	−1.8	−1.0	0.4	−0.9	−0.9
Euro area	−5.3	−4.8	−4.3	−4.1	−2.7	−2.4	−1.7	−0.4	−1.3	−1.3
Japan	−2.6	−3.4	−3.9	−4.2	−3.9	−8.9	−7.9	−7.5	−6.2	−5.1
Other advanced economies	−2.1	−1.4	−1.0	−0.2	0.6	−0.1	0.1	1.6	0.8	1.0
General government fiscal balance[1]										
Advanced economies	−4.7	−4.0	−3.8	−3.1	−1.7	−1.2	−0.9	0.3	−0.5	−0.4
United States	−5.1	−3.8	−3.3	−2.4	−1.3	—	0.7	1.9	1.2	1.2
European Union	−6.3	−5.6	−5.3	−4.3	−2.5	−1.6	−0.7	0.9	−0.5	−0.7
Euro area	−5.9	−5.3	−5.3	−4.4	−2.7	−2.2	−1.3	0.2	−1.0	−1.0
Japan	−1.6	−2.2	−3.5	−4.2	−3.2	−4.5	−7.0	−8.2	−7.4	−6.5
Other advanced economies	−2.7	−1.9	−1.1	−0.2	0.6	−0.4	0.2	2.2	1.4	1.7
General government structural balance[2]										
Advanced economies	−3.9	−3.4	−3.2	−2.5	−1.3	−0.8	−0.6	−0.3	−0.3	0.1
Growth of broad money										
Advanced economies	3.8	2.6	4.4	4.9	5.0	6.5	. . .	. . .	. . .	. . .
United States	1.3	0.6	3.9	4.5	5.6	8.5	6.3	6.2	. . .	. . .
Euro area	6.3	2.3	5.7	4.0	4.6	4.7	6.9	4.9	. . .	. . .
Japan	1.4	2.9	3.2	2.9	3.8	4.4	2.6	2.2	. . .	. . .
Other advanced economies	8.0	9.5	8.8	8.7	6.3	10.4	. . .	. . .	. . .	. . .
Short-term interest rates[3]										
United States	3.5	3.1	4.4	5.7	5.1	4.9	4.8	6.0	3.7	3.2
Japan	2.4	1.9	0.8	0.3	0.3	0.2	—	0.2	—	—
Euro area	8.7	6.5	6.2	4.7	4.2	4.0	3.1	4.6	4.4	4.0
LIBOR	3.4	5.1	6.1	5.6	5.9	5.6	5.5	6.6	4.1	3.7
Developing countries										
Central government fiscal balance[1]										
Weighted average	−3.4	−2.8	−2.6	−2.2	−2.5	−3.9	−4.1	−3.0	−3.4	−3.0
Median	−4.2	−3.8	−3.3	−2.5	−2.4	−2.8	−3.2	−2.9	−2.6	−2.4
General government fiscal balance[1]										
Weighted average	−3.6	−3.8	−3.3	−3.3	−3.4	−4.9	−5.2	−3.8	−4.2	−3.8
Median	−4.1	−3.7	−3.2	−2.9	−2.4	−3.3	−3.2	−2.9	−2.5	−2.1
Growth of broad money										
Weighted average	90.4	67.7	24.3	23.1	22.1	17.4	15.1	11.2	13.3	13.0
Median	16.5	19.1	16.3	14.4	15.6	10.5	12.5	10.9	10.3	9.6
Countries in transition										
Central government fiscal balance[1]	−6.1	−7.4	−4.7	−4.6	−4.7	−3.6	−2.5	−0.6	−0.6	−0.9
General government fiscal balance[1]	−6.8	−7.5	−4.7	−5.8	−5.4	−4.9	−2.2	—	−1.0	−1.3
Growth of broad money	424.5	194.3	75.3	32.3	33.1	20.5	39.5	37.7	17.4	15.8

[1]Percent of GDP.
[2]Percent of potential GDP.
[3]For the United States, three-month treasury bills; for Japan, three-month certificates of deposit; for LIBOR, London interbank offered rate on six-month U.S. dollar deposits.

Table 15. Advanced Economies: General and Central Government Fiscal Balances and Balances Excluding Social Security Transactions[1]

(Percent of GDP)

	1993	1994	1995	1996	1997	1998	1999	2000	2001	2002
General government fiscal balance										
Advanced economies	**−4.7**	**−4.0**	**−3.8**	**−3.1**	**−1.7**	**−1.2**	**−0.9**	**0.3**	**−0.5**	**−0.4**
Major advanced economies	−5.0	−4.2	−4.1	−3.4	−2.0	−1.3	−1.0	—	−0.8	−0.7
United States	−5.1	−3.8	−3.3	−2.4	−1.3	—	0.7	1.9	1.2	1.2
Japan	−1.6	−2.2	−3.5	−4.2	−3.2	−4.5	−7.0	−8.2	−7.4	−6.5
Germany[2]	−3.1	−2.4	−3.3	−3.4	−2.7	−2.2	−1.6	1.2	−2.2	−1.8
France[2,3]	−6.0	−5.5	−5.5	−4.1	−3.5	−2.6	−1.6	−1.4	−0.8	−1.6
Italy[2]	−9.4	−9.1	−7.6	−7.1	−2.7	−2.8	−1.8	−0.3	−1.3	−0.9
United Kingdom[2,4]	−7.8	−6.9	−5.4	−4.1	−1.5	0.3	1.5	4.0	0.7	0.2
Canada	−8.7	−6.7	−5.3	−2.8	0.2	0.5	1.6	3.2	2.8	2.9
Other advanced economies	−3.7	−3.0	−2.7	−1.5	−0.7	−0.9	−0.2	1.4	0.8	0.9
Spain	−6.7	−6.1	−7.0	−4.9	−3.2	−2.6	−1.2	−0.3	−0.3	−0.3
Netherlands[2]	−3.1	−3.6	−4.2	−1.8	−1.1	−0.8	0.4	2.2	0.8	0.4
Belgium[2]	−7.3	−5.0	−4.3	−3.8	−1.9	−0.9	−0.7	0.1	0.1	—
Sweden	−11.9	−10.8	−7.9	−3.4	−2.0	1.8	1.9	3.1	3.3	2.4
Austria	−4.2	−4.8	−5.1	−3.8	−1.7	−2.3	−2.1	−1.1	−0.7	—
Denmark	−2.8	−2.4	−2.3	−1.0	0.5	1.1	3.1	2.5	1.9	2.0
Finland	−7.3	−5.7	−3.7	−3.2	−1.5	1.3	1.9	6.9	3.8	2.4
Greece	−13.8	−10.0	−10.2	−7.4	−4.0	−2.5	−1.8	−1.0	0.3	1.0
Portugal	−6.1	−6.0	−4.6	−4.0	−2.6	−1.9	−2.0	−1.5	−2.0	−2.0
Ireland	−2.3	−1.7	−2.2	−0.2	0.7	2.1	3.9	4.5	2.9	1.6
Luxembourg	5.2	4.2	2.2	2.7	3.6	3.3	2.3	4.1	4.2	4.6
Switzerland	−3.8	−2.8	−1.9	−2.0	−2.4	−0.4	−0.4	1.8	—	0.2
Norway	−1.4	0.4	3.5	6.6	7.9	3.4	5.8	14.7	16.1	14.6
Israel	−4.6	−3.5	−4.8	−5.5	−4.1	−3.6	−4.8	−2.9	−3.9	−3.7
Iceland	−4.5	−4.7	−3.0	−1.6	—	0.4	2.2	2.8	1.9	1.4
Cyprus	−2.4	−1.4	−1.0	−3.4	−5.3	−5.5	−4.0	−2.7	−2.7	−2.4
Korea[5]	1.3	1.0	1.3	1.0	−0.9	−3.8	−2.7	2.5	1.1	1.6
Australia[6]	−4.4	−3.5	−2.1	−0.9	−0.1	0.3	0.8	0.9	0.5	0.5
Taiwan Province of China	0.6	0.2	0.4	0.2	0.1	1.4	0.1	−0.5	−2.0	−0.7
Hong Kong SAR	2.1	1.1	−0.3	2.2	6.6	−1.9	0.8	−0.9	−0.2	−0.3
Singapore	14.4	13.9	12.2	9.3	9.2	3.6	4.5	7.9	6.1	7.3
New Zealand[7]	−0.7	2.2	3.6	2.7	1.6	1.0	0.4	0.6	0.7	0.9
Memorandum										
European Union	−6.3	−5.6	−5.3	−4.3	−2.5	−1.6	−0.7	0.9	−0.5	−0.7
Euro area	−5.9	−5.3	−5.3	−4.4	−2.7	−2.2	−1.3	0.2	−1.0	−1.0
Newly industrialized Asian economies	2.1	1.7	1.6	1.5	1.1	−1.4	−0.9	1.6	0.3	1.1
Fiscal balance excluding social security transactions										
United States	−5.3	−4.2	−3.7	−2.7	−1.7	−0.7	−0.3	0.3	−0.2	−0.2
Japan	−4.7	−5.0	−6.3	−6.7	−5.8	−6.5	−8.8	−9.5	−8.2	−7.0
Germany	−3.3	−2.5	−2.9	−3.1	−2.8	−2.3	−1.8	1.2	−2.1	−1.8
France	−5.1	−5.0	−4.8	−3.6	−3.1	−2.5	−1.8	−1.5	−1.2	−2.2
Italy	−5.4	−4.5	−5.6	−5.3	−0.7	1.3	2.6	3.6	2.6	2.9
Canada	−5.9	−3.9	−2.7	—	3.0	3.0	3.9	5.1	4.4	4.0

Table 15 *(concluded)*

	1993	1994	1995	1996	1997	1998	1999	2000	2001	2002
Central government fiscal balance										
Advanced economies	**-4.3**	**-3.7**	**-3.3**	**-2.7**	**-1.5**	**-1.6**	**-0.9**	**0.4**	**-0.3**	**-0.2**
Major advanced economies	-4.5	-3.8	-3.4	-3.0	-1.7	-1.8	-1.0	0.3	-0.4	-0.3
United States[8]	-4.2	-3.0	-2.6	-1.8	-0.6	0.6	1.3	2.5	1.8	1.7
Japan[9]	-2.6	-3.4	-3.9	-4.2	-3.9	-8.9	-7.9	-7.5	-6.2	-5.1
Germany[10]	-2.1	-1.5	-1.4	-2.2	-1.7	-1.5	-1.3	1.3	-1.3	-1.1
France[10]	-4.6	-4.6	-4.2	-4.6	-3.6	-3.7	-3.0	-2.4	-1.8	-2.2
Italy	-9.9	-9.1	-7.1	-6.8	-2.9	-2.8	-1.4	-1.0	-2.5	-2.3
United Kingdom	-8.2	-6.9	-5.5	-4.2	-1.5	0.3	1.4	4.0	0.7	0.2
Canada	-5.4	-4.5	-3.9	-2.0	0.7	1.0	0.9	1.8	1.2	1.1
Other advanced economies	-3.9	-3.2	-2.8	-1.7	-1.0	-1.0	-0.5	0.8	0.3	0.5
Memorandum										
European Union	-5.9	-5.3	-4.6	-4.1	-2.4	-1.8	-1.0	0.4	-0.9	-0.9
Euro area	-5.3	-4.8	-4.3	-4.1	-2.7	-2.4	-1.7	-0.4	-1.3	-1.3
Newly industrialized Asian economies	0.8	1.0	1.0	1.0	0.8	-1.3	-1.2	0.8	-0.3	0.4

[1]On a national income accounts basis except as indicated in footnotes. See Box A1 for a summary of the policy assumptions underlying the projections.

[2]Includes one-off receipts from the sale of mobile telephone licenses equivalent to 2.5 percent of GDP in 2000 for Germany, 0.5 percent of GDP in 2001 for France, 1.2 percent of GDP in 2000 for Italy, 2.4 percent of GDP in 2000 for the United Kingdom, 0.2 percent of GDP in 2001 for Belgium,and 0.7 percent of GDP in 2000 for the Netherlands.

[3]Adjusted for valuation changes of the foreign exchange stabilization fund.

[4]Excludes asset sales.

[5]Data include social security transactions (that is, the operations of the public pension plan).

[6]Data exclude net advances (primarily privatization receipts and net policy-related lending).

[7]Data from 1992 onward are on an accrual basis and are not strictly comparable with previous cash-based data.

[8]Data are on a budget basis.

[9]Data are on a national income basis and exclude social security transactions.

[10]Data are on an administrative basis and exclude social security transactions.

Table 16. Advanced Economies: General Government Structural Balances[1]

(Percent of potential GDP)

	1993	1994	1995	1996	1997	1998	1999	2000	2001	2002
Structural balance[2]										
Advanced economies	**−3.9**	**−3.4**	**−3.2**	**−2.5**	**−1.3**	**−0.8**	**−0.6**	**−0.3**	**−0.3**	**0.1**
Major advanced economies	−3.8	−3.3	−3.2	−2.6	−1.3	−0.8	−0.7	−0.5	−0.4	0.1
United States	−3.8	−2.8	−2.3	−1.5	−0.7	0.2	0.6	1.5	1.3	1.6
Japan	−1.5	−1.9	−3.2	−4.3	−3.4	−3.6	−6.0	−7.3	−5.9	−4.7
Germany[3,4]	−3.0	−2.4	−3.3	−2.7	−1.6	−1.2	−0.7	−1.1	−1.4	−0.8
France[4]	−3.5	−3.5	−3.7	−1.9	−1.5	−1.4	−0.9	−1.1	−1.0	−1.0
Italy[4]	−8.2	−7.8	−7.0	−6.2	−1.7	−1.8	−0.6	−0.7	−0.5	−0.1
United Kingdom[4]	−6.6	−5.5	−4.4	−3.4	−1.0	0.5	1.5	1.6	0.7	0.5
Canada	−4.4	−3.8	−2.8	0.1	2.1	2.1	2.5	3.1	3.2	3.6
Other advanced economies	−4.3	−4.0	−3.4	−2.0	−1.1	−0.7	−0.2	0.3	0.3	0.4
Spain	−5.0	−5.2	−5.1	−3.1	−1.8	−1.9	−1.1	−0.8	−0.4	—
Netherlands	−1.9	−2.7	−3.1	−0.9	−0.8	−1.4	−0.7	0.2	—	−0.1
Belgium	−5.2	−3.1	−2.7	−1.6	−0.5	0.4	0.4	−0.1	0.1	0.2
Sweden	−13.1	−11.8	−8.8	−4.9	−3.7	0.6	1.5	4.3	3.1	2.3
Austria	−3.7	−4.6	−4.8	−3.6	−1.2	−1.7	−1.7	−1.5	−0.3	0.4
Denmark	−1.1	−1.2	−1.7	−0.7	0.5	0.6	2.3	1.2	1.0	1.4
Finland	−0.9	−0.7	0.3	0.3	0.1	2.0	2.5	6.9	4.7	3.6
Greece	−5.9	−3.9	−3.5	−2.4	−1.2	−0.7	−0.5	−0.4	−0.1	0.1
Portugal	−5.4	−5.0	−3.5	−3.2	−2.3	−2.3	−2.6	−2.6	−2.1	−1.6
Ireland	−0.5	0.1	−1.9	0.1	0.1	1.5	2.9	2.9	1.6	1.0
Norway[5]	−7.9	−6.7	−4.5	−3.4	−2.6	−3.6	−3.5	−3.3	−2.8	−2.9
Australia[6]	−2.8	−2.3	−1.6	−0.7	0.1	0.2	0.5	0.7	0.6	0.7
New Zealand[7]	0.4	0.9	1.7	1.4	1.6	1.7	0.8	0.9	1.1	1.5
Memorandum										
European Union[8]	−5.0	−4.5	−4.4	−3.1	−1.4	−1.0	−0.2	−0.2	−0.3	−0.2
Euro area[8]	−4.5	−4.2	−4.3	−3.1	−1.5	−1.3	−0.7	−0.7	−0.7	−0.4

[1]On a national income accounts basis.

[2]The structural budget position is defined as the actual budget deficit (or surplus) less the effects of cyclical deviations of output from potential output. Because of the margin of uncertainty that attaches to estimates of cyclical gaps and to tax and expenditure elasticities with respect to national income, indicators of structural budget positions should be interpreted as broad orders of magnitude. Moreover, it is important to note that changes in structural budget balances are not necessarily attributable to policy changes but may reflect the built-in momentum of existing expenditure programs. In the period beyond that for which specific consolidation programs exist, it is assumed that the structural deficit remains unchanged.

[3]The estimate of the fiscal impulse for 1995 is affected by the assumption by the federal government of the debt of the Treuhandanstalt and various other agencies, which were formerly held outside the general government sector. At the public sector level, there would be an estimated withdrawal of fiscal impulse amounting to just over 1 percent of GDP.

[4]Excludes mobile telephone license receipts.

[5]Excludes oil.

[6]Excludes commonwealth government privatization receipts.

[7]Excludes privatization proceeds.

[8]Excludes Luxembourg.

Table 17. Advanced Economies: Monetary Aggregates
(Annual percent change)[1]

	1993	1994	1995	1996	1997	1998	1999	2000
Narrow money[2]								
Advanced economies	**8.1**	**4.4**	**5.3**	**4.4**	**4.2**	**5.3**	...	...
Major advanced economies	7.6	4.0	4.7	3.6	3.8	5.1	...	...
United States	10.6	2.5	−1.6	−4.5	−1.3	2.1	1.8	−1.7
Japan	3.4	4.9	12.8	10.0	8.9	6.1	11.8	4.1
Euro area	6.0	4.4	6.4	7.5	7.1	9.5	10.3	5.7
Germany	8.5	5.2	6.8	12.4	2.3	11.1	...	...
France	1.4	2.8	7.7	0.8	6.5	3.1	...	...
Italy	7.6	3.4	1.4	3.9	7.7	9.0	...	...
United Kingdom	6.0	6.8	5.6	6.7	6.4	5.3	11.7	4.6
Canada	14.4	8.7	7.6	17.8	10.6	8.7	8.5	14.2
Other advanced economies	10.8	6.6	8.3	8.3	6.2	6.4	...	...
Memorandum								
Newly industrialized Asian economies	18.0	9.3	10.5	5.8	−3.8	0.9	19.7	4.5
Broad money[3]								
Advanced economies	**3.8**	**2.6**	**4.4**	**4.9**	**5.0**	**6.5**	...	...
Major advanced economies	2.6	1.7	3.7	4.2	4.6	6.5	...	...
United States	1.3	0.6	3.9	4.5	5.6	8.5	6.3	6.2
Japan	1.4	2.9	3.2	2.9	3.8	4.4	2.6	2.2
Euro area	6.3	2.3	5.7	4.0	4.6	4.7	6.9	4.9
Germany	10.9	1.6	3.6	8.7	3.6	7.3	...	...
France	−2.9	1.8	4.6	−3.3	2.0	2.7	...	...
Italy	3.8	1.0	−1.9	3.8	9.0	5.6	...	...
United Kingdom	4.9	4.2	9.9	9.6	5.6	8.4	3.9	8.4
Canada	2.7	2.8	4.1	2.1	−1.3	1.4	5.1	5.5
Other advanced economies	9.3	6.6	7.6	8.8	7.0	6.7	...	...
Memorandum								
Newly industrialized Asian economies	15.6	16.5	13.0	11.4	11.3	19.8	16.9	14.2

[1]Based on end-of-period data except for Japan which is based on monthly averages.

[2]M1 except for the United Kingdom, where M0 is used here as a measure of narrow money; it comprises notes in circulation plus bankers' operational deposits. M1 is generally currency in circulation plus private demand deposits. In addition, the United States includes traveler's checks of nonbank issues and other checkable deposits and excludes private sector float and demand deposits of banks. Japan includes government demand deposits and excludes float. Germany includes demand deposits at fixed interest rates. Canada excludes private sector float.

[3]M2, defined as M1 plus quasi-money, except for Japan, Germany, and the United Kingdom, for which the data are based on M2 plus certificates of deposit (CDs), M3, and M4, respectively. Quasi-money is essentially private term deposits and other notice deposits. The United States also includes money market mutual fund balances, money market deposit accounts, overnight repurchase agreements, and overnight Eurodollars issued to U.S. residents by foreign branches of U.S. banks. For Japan, M2 plus CDs is currency in circulation plus total private and public sector deposits and installments of Sogo Bank plus CDs. For Germany, M3 is M1 plus private time deposits with maturities of less than four years plus savings deposits at statutory notice. For Italy, M2 comprises M1 plus term deposits, passbooks from the Postal Office, and CDs with maturities of less than 18 months. For the United Kingdom, M4 is composed of non-interest-bearing M1, private sector interest-bearing sterling sight bank deposits, private sector sterling time banks deposits, private sector holdings of sterling bank CDs, private sector holdings of building society shares and deposits, and sterling CDs less building society holdings of banks deposits and bank CDs and notes and coins.

Table 18. Advanced Economies: Interest Rates

(Percent a year)

	1993	1994	1995	1996	1997	1998	1999	2000	August 2001
Policy-related interest rate[1]									
Major advanced economies	**4.7**	**4.5**	**5.4**	**4.4**	**4.2**	**4.3**	...	...	...
United States	3.0	4.2	5.9	5.3	5.5	5.4	5.0	6.3	3.7
Japan	2.3	1.8	1.0	0.5	0.5	0.5	0.5	0.5	0.3
Euro area	...	...	...	...	...	3.3	2.7	4.0	4.5
Germany	7.4	5.3	4.4	3.2	3.1	3.3	...	...	...
France	8.6	5.6	6.3	3.7	3.3	3.4	...	...	...
Italy	10.5	8.8	10.7	8.6	6.6	4.9	...	...	...
United Kingdom	5.9	5.5	6.7	6.0	6.6	7.2	5.3	6.0	5.0
Canada	4.6	5.1	7.0	4.3	3.4	5.0	4.8	5.5	4.0
Short-term interest rate[2]									
Advanced economies	**5.5**	**4.5**	**4.7**	**4.3**	**4.0**	**4.0**	**3.5**	**4.5**	...
Major advanced economies	4.8	3.9	4.1	3.9	3.6	3.6	3.3	4.4	...
United States	3.5	3.1	4.4	5.7	5.1	4.9	4.8	6.0	3.5
Japan	2.4	1.9	0.8	0.3	0.3	0.2	—	0.2	0.0
Euro area	8.7	6.5	6.2	4.7	4.2	4.0	3.1	4.6	4.4
Germany	7.2	5.3	4.5	3.3	3.3	3.5	...	...	...
France	7.2	5.3	4.5	3.3	3.3	3.7	...	...	...
Italy	10.5	8.8	10.7	8.6	6.6	4.9	...	...	...
United Kingdom	6.0	5.6	6.8	6.1	6.9	7.4	5.5	6.1	5.0
Canada	4.9	5.4	7.0	4.3	3.2	4.7	4.7	5.5	4.1
Other advanced economies	8.7	7.4	7.3	6.1	5.7	5.7	4.2	5.1	...
Memorandum									
Newly industrialized Asian economies	8.5	9.0	9.2	8.7	9.4	9.8	5.5	5.6	4.5
Long-term interest rate[3]									
Advanced economies	**6.6**	**7.2**	**6.8**	**6.1**	**5.5**	**4.5**	**4.6**	**5.0**	...
Major advanced economies	6.2	6.8	6.4	5.8	5.2	4.2	4.5	4.9	...
United States	5.9	7.1	6.6	6.4	6.4	5.3	5.6	6.0	5.0
Japan	4.0	4.2	3.3	3.0	2.1	1.3	1.7	1.7	1.3
Euro area	8.3	8.4	8.6	7.2	5.9	4.8	4.6	5.4	...
Germany	6.4	7.1	6.9	6.2	5.6	4.6	...	...	...
France	6.9	7.4	7.6	6.4	5.6	4.8	...	...	...
Italy	11.3	10.6	12.2	9.4	6.9	4.9	...	...	...
United Kingdom	7.6	8.4	8.4	8.1	7.4	5.4	5.4	5.4	5.0
Canada	7.2	8.4	8.1	7.2	6.1	5.3	5.6	5.9	5.5
Other advanced economies	8.5	9.1	8.9	7.7	6.8	5.9	5.4	5.5	...
Memorandum									
Newly industrialized Asian economies	9.2	9.4	9.4	8.5	9.2	9.4	7.1	5.9	7.1

[1]For the United States, federal funds rate; for Japan, official discount rate; for Germany, repurchase rate; for France, day-to-day money rate; for Italy, three-month treasury bill gross rate; for the United Kingdom, base lending rate; for Canada, overnight money market financing rate; for the euro area, repurchase rate.

[2]For the United States, three-month certificates of deposit (CDs) in secondary markets; for Japan three-month CDs; for Germany, France and the United Kingdom, three-month interbank deposits; for Italy, three-month treasury bills gross rate; and for Canada, three-month prime corporate paper.

[3]For the United States, yield on ten-year treasury bonds; for Japan, over-the-counter sales yield on ten-year government bonds with longest residual maturity; for Germany, yield on government bonds with maturities of nine to ten years; for France, long-term (seven- to ten-year) government bond yield (Emprunt d'Etat à long terme TME); for Italy, secondary market yield on fixed-coupon (BTP) government bonds with two to four years' residual maturity; for the United Kingdom, yield on medium-dated (ten-year) government stock; and for Canada, average yield on government bonds with residual maturities of over ten years.

Table 19. Advanced Economies: Exchange Rates

	1993	1994	1995	1996	1997	1998	1999	2000	Exchange Rate Assumption[1] 2001
				National currency units per U.S. dollar					
U.S. dollar nominal exchange rates									
Japanese yen	111.2	102.2	94.1	108.8	121.0	130.9	113.9	107.8	122.7
Euro[2]	. . .	. . .	. . .	. . .	. . .	. . .	1.07	0.92	0.89
Deutsche mark	1.65	1.62	1.43	1.50	1.73	1.76	1.84	2.12	2.19
French franc	5.66	5.55	4.99	5.12	5.84	5.90	6.16	7.12	7.35
Italian lira	1,574	1,612	1,629	1,543	1,703	1,736	1,817	2,102	2,171
Pound sterling[2]	1.50	1.53	1.58	1.56	1.64	1.66	1.62	1.51	1.43
Canadian dollar	1.29	1.37	1.37	1.36	1.38	1.48	1.49	1.49	1.54
Spanish peseta	127.3	134.0	124.7	126.7	146.4	149.4	156.2	180.6	186.5
Netherlands guilder	1.86	1.82	1.61	1.69	1.95	1.98	2.07	2.39	2.47
Belgian franc	34.6	33.5	29.5	31.0	35.8	36.3	37.9	43.8	45.2
Swedish krona	7.78	7.72	7.13	6.71	7.63	7.95	8.26	9.16	10.35
Austrian schilling	11.6	11.4	10.1	10.6	12.2	12.4	12.9	14.9	15.4
Danish krone	6.48	6.36	5.60	5.80	6.60	6.70	6.98	8.10	8.36
Finnish markka	5.71	5.22	4.37	4.59	5.19	5.34	5.58	6.45	6.67
Greek drachma	229.2	242.6	231.7	240.7	273.1	295.5	305.6	361.0	382.0
Portuguese escudo	160.8	166.0	151.1	154.2	175.3	180.1	188.2	217.6	224.8
Irish pound	0.68	0.67	0.62	0.63	0.66	0.70	0.74	0.85	0.88
Swiss franc	1.48	1.37	1.18	1.24	1.45	1.45	1.50	1.69	1.70
Norwegian krone	7.09	7.06	6.34	6.45	7.07	7.55	7.80	8.80	9.02
Israeli new sheqel	2.83	3.01	3.01	3.19	3.45	3.80	4.14	4.08	4.24
Icelandic krona	67.60	69.94	64.69	66.50	70.90	70.96	72.34	78.62	98.67
Cyprus pound	0.50	0.49	0.45	0.47	0.51	0.52	0.54	0.62	0.64
Korean won	802.7	803.4	770.8	804.5	951.2	1,401.8	1,188.8	1,131.0	1,286.0
Australian dollar	1.47	1.37	1.35	1.28	1.35	1.59	1.55	1.72	1.93
New Taiwan dollar	26.39	26.46	26.49	27.46	28.70	33.46	32.27	31.07	34.58
Hong Kong dollar	7.74	7.73	7.74	7.73	7.74	7.75	7.76	7.79	7.80
Singapore dollar	1.62	1.53	1.42	1.41	1.48	1.67	1.69	1.72	1.74
									Percent change from previous assumption[3]
				Index, 1990 = 100					
Real effective exchange rates[4]									
United States	95.9	93.7	86.4	89.5	94.6	100.8	99.3	106.4	−0.4
Japan	131.0	138.8	145.9	124.2	118.0	109.4	123.3	131.3	−1.3
Euro[5]	99.2	97.2	101.6	102.2	92.1	89.1	84.9	76.0	0.9
Germany	110.5	113.8	122.3	120.9	114.0	111.3	108.3	102.4	0.4
France	97.4	96.4	97.3	94.3	90.4	90.0	89.3	85.8	0.3
United Kingdom	94.0	96.1	92.7	96.2	114.8	122.3	124.7	132.0	−0.6
Italy	84.8	80.0	73.6	84.3	86.2	84.6	84.4	81.7	0.3
Canada	94.5	88.7	88.1	89.0	91.6	86.1	85.6	86.4	—
Spain	101.1	94.8	93.9	96.3	93.9	95.7	95.9	94.7	0.3
Netherlands	101.4	102.4	104.8	101.7	97.1	98.3	97.7	95.5	0.4
Belgium	101.7	100.8	103.7	99.3	95.8	95.2	91.5	88.5	0.3
Sweden	80.7	80.0	80.5	90.8	88.5	87.1	84.4	83.9	−0.3
Austria	97.7	95.4	91.9	87.3	82.8	81.3	79.3	77.3	0.2
Denmark	100.3	99.4	102.4	100.5	97.9	99.3	98.9	95.5	0.5
Finland	64.2	67.4	74.3	68.7	64.7	63.8	61.4	58.5	0.5
Greece	98.5	100.4	106.5	109.3	113.3	109.6	110.3	106.8	0.3
Portugal	118.2	115.0	119.7	120.1	119.4	120.6	121.0	119.8	0.3
Ireland	80.1	75.1	70.3	66.8	62.6	56.7	53.0	48.0	0.6
Switzerland	96.8	104.9	111.5	111.6	108.1	114.0	113.3	112.5	0.9
Norway	97.6	97.4	103.0	105.4	110.2	111.6	117.3	119.9	0.1
Australia	89.0	93.5	92.7	108.8	113.6	102.2	104.4	99.0	−0.4
New Zealand	90.6	96.5	102.5	114.7	119.2	103.5	101.3	90.0	—

[1]Average exchange rates for the period July 23-August 17, 2001. See "Assumptions" in the Introduction to the Statistical Appendix.
[2]Expressed in U.S. dollars per currency unit.
[3]In nominal effective terms. Average July 23-August 17, 2001 rates compared with May 15-June 11, 2001 rates.
[4]Defined as the ratio, in common currency, of the normalized unit labor costs in the manufacturing sector to the weighted average of those of its industrial country trading partners, using 1989–91 trade weights.
[5]An effective euro is used prior to January 1, 1999. See Box 5.5 in the *World Economic Outlook*, October 1998.

Table 20. Developing Countries: Central Government Fiscal Balances
(Percent of GDP)

	1993	1994	1995	1996	1997	1998	1999	2000	2001	2002
Developing countries	**−3.4**	**−2.8**	**−2.6**	**−2.2**	**−2.5**	**−3.9**	**−4.1**	**−3.0**	**−3.4**	**−3.0**
Regional groups										
Africa	−7.7	−5.5	−3.9	−2.6	−3.0	−3.9	−3.3	−1.7	−2.0	−2.0
Sub-Sahara	−8.2	−5.9	−4.1	−3.3	−3.6	−3.9	−3.9	−2.8	−2.7	−2.3
Excluding Nigeria and South Africa	−8.1	−6.6	−5.0	−3.8	−4.0	−3.7	−4.0	−4.0	−3.1	−2.8
Developing Asia	−3.1	−2.6	−2.5	−2.0	−2.4	−3.5	−4.2	−3.9	−4.0	−3.7
China	−1.9	−1.6	−2.1	−1.6	−1.8	−3.1	−4.1	−3.6	−3.2	−2.9
India	−6.1	−5.5	−4.6	−4.2	−4.7	−5.3	−5.5	−5.4	−5.9	−5.8
Other developing Asia	−2.7	−2.1	−1.4	−1.0	−1.8	−2.9	−3.1	−3.2	−4.2	−3.4
Middle East, Malta, and Turkey	−7.5	−5.5	−3.8	−3.4	−3.5	−6.2	−3.8	0.3	−2.0	−2.6
Western Hemisphere	−0.3	−0.9	−1.9	−2.0	−1.9	−3.5	−4.4	−2.8	−3.1	−2.0
Analytical groups										
By source of export earnings										
Fuel	−7.6	−6.5	−3.4	−0.3	−0.8	−6.3	−1.2	6.1	4.7	1.9
Nonfuel	−2.8	−2.4	−2.5	−2.4	−2.6	−3.6	−4.4	−3.9	−4.3	−3.5
of which, primary products	−5.2	−3.6	−1.7	−1.0	−1.5	−1.4	−2.5	−2.8	−2.6	−2.1
By external financing source										
Net debtor countries	−3.1	−2.7	−2.6	−2.3	−2.5	−3.8	−4.2	−3.3	−3.8	−3.3
of which, official financing	−7.0	−5.3	−3.4	−2.0	−2.4	−3.4	−3.0	−1.7	−2.1	−2.8
Net debtor countries by debt-servicing experience										
Countries with arrears and/or rescheduling during 1994–98	−3.3	−2.3	−1.8	−1.1	−1.8	−4.0	−3.5	−0.5	−1.9	−2.1
Other groups										
Heavily indebted poor countries	−8.0	−6.1	−3.4	−2.4	−2.9	−2.2	−2.6	−2.6	−2.3	−2.1
Middle East and north Africa	−7.4	−5.6	−3.6	−1.4	−1.7	−5.1	−1.1	3.5	2.7	0.3
Memorandum										
Median										
Developing countries	−4.2	−3.8	−3.3	−2.5	−2.4	−2.8	−3.2	−2.9	−2.6	−2.4
Regional groups										
Africa	−6.2	−5.2	−3.9	−4.1	−3.0	−3.2	−3.3	−3.1	−2.8	−2.7
Developing Asia	−4.2	−3.4	−3.4	−2.4	−2.3	−2.5	−2.4	−3.6	−3.7	−3.4
Middle East, Malta, and Turkey	−7.5	−4.7	−4.7	−3.3	−2.6	−6.4	−2.3	4.1	2.4	−0.3
Western Hemisphere	−1.3	−1.0	−1.7	−2.0	−1.6	−2.3	−2.8	−2.8	−2.4	−2.1

Table 21. Developing Countries: Broad Money Aggregates
(Annual percent change)

	1993	1994	1995	1996	1997	1998	1999	2000	2001	2002
Developing countries	**90.4**	**67.7**	**24.3**	**23.1**	**22.1**	**17.4**	**15.1**	**11.2**	**13.3**	**13.0**
Regional groups										
Africa	30.8	41.3	22.8	21.9	18.3	17.0	20.1	19.2	12.3	11.7
Sub-Sahara	35.7	50.3	27.5	25.4	19.6	18.6	22.1	21.7	12.9	11.5
Developing Asia	27.3	25.0	22.7	20.6	18.1	18.3	14.0	12.1	13.5	13.2
China	43.0	34.9	29.5	25.3	19.6	14.8	14.7	12.3	14.0	13.5
India	16.5	20.1	14.6	16.2	17.1	20.4	17.0	15.9	16.1	15.6
Other developing Asia	20.7	18.5	20.6	18.3	17.0	21.1	11.3	9.4	10.9	11.0
Middle East, Malta, and Turkey	26.0	41.3	32.6	34.4	25.3	28.0	29.6	18.9	22.1	14.3
Western Hemisphere	288.9	155.4	23.1	21.8	26.2	12.9	10.3	6.0	10.1	12.4
Analytical groups										
By source of export earnings										
Fuel	21.2	25.8	17.1	21.2	16.1	13.0	16.6	17.3	13.7	11.3
Nonfuel	105.6	75.5	25.4	23.3	22.9	18.0	14.9	10.5	13.3	13.2
of which, primary products	51.0	57.1	30.4	30.4	21.3	13.8	23.2	18.6	13.4	12.9
By external financing source										
Net debtor countries	98.8	73.0	25.7	24.3	23.1	18.3	15.5	11.5	13.6	13.4
of which, official financing	31.1	41.0	20.8	19.3	16.6	16.6	23.2	24.0	15.4	14.3
Net debtor countries by debt-servicing experience										
Countries with arrears and/or rescheduling during 1994–98	394.1	226.6	27.4	18.4	22.9	18.7	14.7	11.3	11.9	16.8
Other groups										
Heavily indebted poor countries	58.4	84.9	37.2	39.6	23.0	20.5	34.3	30.7	17.3	13.8
Middle East and north Africa	16.7	14.4	12.7	12.3	10.0	10.1	11.7	12.3	11.2	9.8
Memorandum										
Median										
Developing countries	16.5	19.1	16.3	14.4	15.6	10.5	12.5	10.9	10.3	9.6
Regional groups										
Africa	13.6	32.4	16.2	14.4	15.4	8.8	13.5	13.0	10.5	9.6
Developing Asia	20.4	19.4	16.7	15.7	17.0	12.4	14.9	11.1	12.6	11.0
Middle East, Malta, and Turkey	9.3	11.4	9.9	8.3	9.7	8.5	11.5	10.0	9.2	7.5
Western Hemisphere	21.1	18.3	20.0	16.7	16.4	11.5	12.1	8.4	9.6	8.9

Table 22. Summary of World Trade Volumes and Prices
(Annual percent change)

	Ten-Year Averages		1993	1994	1995	1996	1997	1998	1999	2000	2001	2002
	1983–92	1993–2002										
Trade in goods and services												
World trade[1]												
Volume	5.3	6.9	3.5	8.9	10.1	6.7	10.3	4.1	5.3	12.4	2.7	5.2
Price deflator												
In U.S. dollars	2.2	−0.9	−3.9	2.7	8.9	−1.1	−5.9	−5.2	−1.5	−0.8	−2.3	0.6
In SDRs	−0.2	0.1	−3.1	0.2	2.7	3.3	−0.7	−3.8	−2.3	2.8	1.4	0.4
Volume of trade												
Exports												
Advanced economies	5.8	6.3	2.9	8.6	8.8	5.9	10.5	3.8	5.1	11.5	1.7	4.5
Developing countries	5.7	9.0	9.3	11.3	11.0	9.0	13.1	5.1	4.6	15.1	5.0	6.6
Imports												
Advanced economies	6.5	6.6	1.3	9.5	9.1	6.3	9.3	5.8	7.6	11.5	1.7	4.7
Developing countries	3.2	8.6	10.5	6.9	19.6	9.1	10.1	−1.6	2.1	16.6	6.4	8.0
Terms of trade												
Advanced economies	1.1	—	0.8	0.1	0.2	−0.3	−0.6	1.4	−0.2	−2.4	−0.3	0.9
Developing countries	−2.6	0.3	−1.5	1.2	2.9	1.7	−1.6	−7.7	4.4	6.8	−1.0	−1.7
Trade in goods												
World trade[1]												
Volume	5.6	7.2	4.2	10.0	11.0	6.4	10.5	4.6	5.6	12.8	2.2	5.3
Price deflator												
In U.S. dollars	2.0	−1.0	−4.6	2.7	9.2	−1.2	−6.2	−6.1	−1.5	0.2	−2.2	0.6
In SDRs	−0.4	—	−3.8	0.2	3.0	3.3	−1.0	−4.7	−2.3	3.9	1.5	0.4
World trade prices in U.S. dollars[2]												
Manufactures	4.7	−1.7	−5.7	3.1	10.3	−3.1	−8.0	−1.9	−1.8	−5.1	−3.1	−0.6
Oil	−5.2	2.6	−11.8	−5.0	7.9	18.4	−5.4	−32.1	37.5	56.9	−5.0	−8.6
Nonfuel primary commodities	0.8	−0.1	1.8	13.4	8.4	−1.2	−3.2	−14.7	−7.0	2.6	−2.6	4.5
World trade prices in SDRs[2]												
Manufactures	2.1	−0.7	−4.9	0.6	4.1	1.2	−2.9	−0.4	−2.6	−1.6	0.5	−0.8
Oil	−7.5	3.6	−11.1	−7.3	1.8	23.7	−0.2	−31.2	36.5	62.6	−1.4	−8.8
Nonfuel primary commodities	−1.6	0.9	2.7	10.6	2.3	3.3	2.2	−13.5	−7.7	6.4	1.0	4.2
World trade prices in euros[2]												
Manufactures	1.7	1.7	4.8	2.1	0.2	−0.6	4.9	−0.3	2.5	8.0	−2.0	−1.7
Oil	−7.9	6.2	−2.0	−6.0	−2.0	21.6	7.9	−31.0	43.6	78.4	−3.9	−9.6
Nonfuel primary commodities	−2.1	3.4	13.1	12.2	−1.6	1.5	10.5	−13.3	−2.9	16.6	−1.5	3.3

Table 22 *(concluded)*

	Ten-Year Averages		1993	1994	1995	1996	1997	1998	1999	2000	2001	2002
	1983–92	1993–2002										
Trade in goods												
Volume of trade												
Exports												
Advanced economies	6.1	6.6	3.2	9.6	9.6	5.7	10.8	4.3	5.1	11.8	1.3	4.7
Developing countries	6.0	9.0	9.1	11.6	12.3	9.1	12.3	4.8	4.8	16.1	4.0	6.3
Fuel exporters	4.7	4.9	4.7	2.7	17.0	7.4	4.1	1.8	0.7	7.4	2.4	2.2
Nonfuel exporters	6.9	10.2	10.9	14.8	10.9	9.6	14.8	5.7	5.7	18.3	4.5	7.6
Imports												
Advanced economies	6.8	7.0	2.2	11.1	9.9	5.8	9.9	5.9	8.5	11.7	1.1	4.7
Developing countries	3.3	9.1	11.8	7.9	20.1	9.4	9.9	0.2	1.3	16.6	6.5	8.4
Fuel exporters	−2.1	9.0	−2.5	−13.3	70.9	7.2	12.6	2.7	1.6	12.7	9.9	4.8
Nonfuel exporters	5.7	9.1	15.8	12.8	10.9	9.8	9.5	−0.2	1.2	17.3	5.9	9.0
Price deflators in SDRs												
Exports												
Advanced economies	0.5	−0.4	−3.8	0.3	3.3	1.8	−2.2	−3.4	−3.3	1.0	1.1	1.0
Developing countries	−3.5	1.5	−3.5	1.3	2.8	7.6	1.6	−10.7	4.9	13.1	1.0	−1.4
Fuel exporters	−8.1	2.9	−9.0	−1.7	−2.0	18.5	1.8	−26.6	27.3	46.3	−1.2	−6.9
Nonfuel exporters	−0.7	1.1	−1.3	2.3	4.3	4.6	1.5	−6.3	0.2	4.4	1.7	0.2
Imports												
Advanced economies	−0.6	−0.5	−5.5	−0.2	2.9	2.6	−1.6	−4.9	−3.3	3.8	1.4	0.2
Developing countries	−0.1	1.1	−0.5	−0.4	0.6	5.0	2.5	−4.1	−0.1	6.6	1.7	0.3
Fuel exporters	−0.7	—	−1.8	0.7	−7.6	1.6	2.4	0.5	−4.1	3.1	4.7	1.2
Nonfuel exporters	—	1.3	−0.1	−0.7	2.1	5.6	2.5	−4.8	0.6	7.2	1.2	0.1
Terms of trade												
Advanced economies	1.1	0.1	1.7	0.5	0.4	−0.8	−0.6	1.6	—	−2.7	−0.2	0.8
Developing countries	−3.4	0.4	−3.0	1.7	2.2	2.5	−0.8	−6.9	5.0	6.1	−0.7	−1.7
Fuel exporters	−7.5	2.9	−7.3	−2.4	6.1	16.6	−0.6	−26.9	32.7	41.9	−5.7	−8.0
Nonfuel exporters	−0.7	−0.2	−1.1	3.0	2.1	−0.9	−0.9	−1.6	−0.4	−2.5	0.5	0.1
Memorandum												
World exports in billions of U.S. dollars												
Goods and services	3,308	6,694	4,702	5,263	6,257	6,580	6,841	6,727	6,953	7,720	7,722	8,169
Goods	2,645	5,363	3,706	4,188	5,037	5,275	5,475	5,356	5,547	6,247	6,222	6,578

[1]Average of annual percent change for world exports and imports. The estimates of world trade comprise, in addition to trade of advanced economies and developing countries (which is summarized in the table), trade of countries in transition.

[2]As represented, respectively, by the export unit value index for the manufactures of the advanced economies; the average of U.K. Brent, Dubai, and West Texas Intermediate crude oil spot prices; and the average of world market prices for nonfuel primary commodities weighted by their 1987–89 shares in world commodity exports.

Table 23. Nonfuel Commodity Prices[1]
(Annual percent change; U.S. dollar terms)

| | Ten-Year Averages | | | | | | | | | | | |
	1983–92	1993–2002	1993	1994	1995	1996	1997	1998	1999	2000	2001	2002
Nonfuel primary commodities	**0.8**	**−0.1**	**1.8**	**13.4**	**8.4**	**−1.2**	**−3.2**	**−14.7**	**−7.0**	**2.6**	**−2.6**	**4.5**
Food	−0.1	−1.1	−1.3	5.2	8.1	12.2	−10.6	−12.6	−15.6	−0.5	2.6	5.3
Beverages	−6.0	−0.1	6.3	74.9	0.9	−17.4	32.6	−15.2	−21.3	−16.6	−16.8	4.5
Agricultural raw materials	3.3	0.8	16.2	9.5	4.3	−2.7	−6.8	−16.4	2.4	4.1	−1.0	2.0
Metals	1.8	0.1	−14.2	16.6	19.5	−11.9	3.7	−16.2	−1.5	12.1	−7.3	7.5
Fertilizers	−0.7	0.4	−15.4	8.0	10.6	13.7	1.1	2.8	−4.0	−5.3	−5.9	2.1
Advanced economies	**0.8**	**−0.4**	**−2.5**	**13.3**	**11.1**	**−2.3**	**−3.9**	**−15.7**	**−6.8**	**4.5**	**−3.7**	**5.5**
Developing countries	**0.4**	**−0.5**	**−0.4**	**15.8**	**9.5**	**−2.6**	**−1.4**	**−16.2**	**−9.2**	**2.2**	**−4.9**	**5.4**
Regional groups												
Africa	0.3	−0.3	3.5	16.6	8.0	−5.2	−1.1	−14.6	−8.3	1.2	−4.8	5.0
Sub-Sahara	0.3	−0.3	3.8	16.9	8.0	−5.8	−0.8	−14.7	−8.2	1.2	−5.1	5.1
Developing Asia	0.6	−0.5	2.0	13.5	8.2	−1.3	−3.5	−14.3	−8.0	0.9	−4.5	5.0
Excluding China and India	0.4	−0.8	3.1	13.9	7.4	−1.4	−4.0	−13.7	−9.2	−0.9	−5.0	5.2
Middle East, Malta, and Turkey	0.6	−0.3	−4.0	15.2	12.4	−3.4	−2.6	−15.4	−7.8	4.6	−3.9	5.7
Western Hemisphere	0.1	−0.7	−3.4	17.8	10.9	−2.8	0.4	−18.3	−10.6	3.5	−5.5	5.8
Analytical groups												
By source of export earnings												
Fuel	1.5	−0.2	−1.1	10.6	11.6	−7.2	—	−16.9	−3.5	7.5	−6.2	6.7
Nonfuel	0.3	−0.6	−0.5	16.0	9.5	−2.4	−1.5	−16.1	−9.3	2.0	−4.9	5.4
of which, primary products	0.8	−1.1	−5.3	18.8	14.0	−8.7	−1.0	−16.2	−11.4	3.3	−6.4	7.0
By external financing source												
Net debtor countries	0.3	−0.6	−0.4	15.8	9.5	−2.5	−1.5	−16.1	−9.2	2.2	−5.0	5.4
of which, official financing	−0.2	−0.9	4.9	21.1	9.2	−8.1	−0.3	−13.9	−12.0	−2.1	−7.9	5.6
Net debtor countries by debt-servicing experience												
Countries with arrears and/or rescheduling during 1994–98	−0.2	−0.7	−0.7	18.6	9.2	−4.2	0.5	−15.9	−10.6	1.5	−5.9	5.3
Other groups												
Heavily indebted poor countries	−1.2	−0.9	1.9	24.9	7.8	−6.9	2.0	−12.0	−14.6	−4.3	−7.1	5.2
Middle East and north Africa	0.4	−0.3	−2.4	15.3	11.4	−2.7	−2.8	−15.0	−8.5	3.6	−3.8	5.3
Memorandum												
Average oil spot price[2]	−14.3	17.5	−11.8	−5.0	7.9	18.4	−5.4	−32.1	37.5	56.9	−5.0	−8.6
In U.S. dollars a barrel	21.20	20.00	16.79	15.95	17.20	20.37	19.27	13.07	17.98	28.21	26.80	24.50
Export unit value of manufactures[3]	4.7	−1.7	−5.7	3.1	10.3	−3.1	−8.0	−1.9	−1.8	−5.1	−3.1	−0.6

[1]Averages of world market prices for individual commodities weighted by 1987–89 exports as a share of world commodity exports and total commodity exports for the indicated country group, respectively.
[2]Average of U.K. Brent, Dubai, and West Texas Intermediate crude oil spot prices.
[3]For the manufactures exported by the advanced economies.

Table 24. Advanced Economies: Export Volumes, Import Volumes, and Terms of Trade in Goods and Services
(Annual percent change)

| | Ten-Year Averages | | 1993 | 1994 | 1995 | 1996 | 1997 | 1998 | 1999 | 2000 | 2001 | 2002 |
	1983–92	1993–2002										
Export volume												
Advanced economies	**5.8**	**6.3**	**2.9**	**8.6**	**8.8**	**5.9**	**10.5**	**3.8**	**5.1**	**11.5**	**1.7**	**4.5**
Major advanced economies	5.6	5.7	1.7	8.0	8.1	5.8	10.6	3.7	3.8	10.8	1.2	3.8
United States	7.5	5.9	3.3	8.9	10.3	8.2	12.3	2.1	3.2	9.5	−1.2	3.2
Japan	4.8	3.4	−0.1	3.4	4.1	6.4	11.3	−2.3	1.3	12.1	−5.5	4.1
Germany	5.2	5.8	−5.5	7.6	5.7	5.1	11.2	6.8	5.6	13.2	4.9	3.9
France	5.1	6.1	—	7.7	7.7	3.5	11.8	8.2	3.9	13.4	2.7	2.7
Italy	4.7	6.3	9.0	9.8	12.6	0.6	6.4	3.6	—	10.2	6.9	4.9
United Kingdom	3.9	6.3	3.9	9.2	9.5	7.5	8.6	2.6	4.0	8.4	4.2	5.3
Canada	6.0	7.8	10.9	12.8	8.5	5.7	8.3	8.8	10.0	7.6	2.6	3.2
Other advanced economies	6.2	7.4	5.2	9.8	10.0	6.2	10.3	4.1	7.2	12.8	2.6	5.8
Memorandum												
European Union	4.9	6.5	1.2	8.9	8.9	4.8	10.2	6.1	5.0	11.6	4.6	4.6
Euro area	5.2	6.6	0.7	8.7	8.8	4.4	10.5	6.8	5.1	12.2	4.7	4.4
Newly industrialized Asian economies	9.3	8.3	10.0	11.3	12.8	7.6	10.7	0.6	8.3	16.3	−0.6	6.8
Import volume												
Advanced economies	**6.5**	**6.6**	**1.3**	**9.5**	**9.1**	**6.3**	**9.3**	**5.8**	**7.6**	**11.5**	**1.7**	**4.7**
Major advanced economies	6.2	6.5	0.5	8.8	7.9	6.5	9.4	7.7	7.7	11.4	1.5	4.2
United States	7.4	9.0	9.1	12.0	8.2	8.6	13.7	11.8	10.5	13.4	−1.0	4.4
Japan	5.7	3.9	−1.4	7.7	12.8	13.2	1.2	−6.8	2.9	9.9	0.2	1.5
Germany	5.5	5.3	−5.4	7.3	5.6	3.1	8.3	8.9	8.5	10.0	2.7	4.5
France	4.5	5.5	−3.7	8.2	8.0	1.6	6.9	11.9	4.2	15.2	1.8	2.6
Italy	6.7	4.7	−10.9	8.1	9.7	−0.3	10.1	9.0	5.1	8.3	4.5	4.9
United Kingdom	5.5	7.1	3.2	5.4	5.5	9.1	9.2	8.8	8.1	9.6	5.8	6.1
Canada	7.6	7.0	7.4	8.1	5.8	5.1	14.3	4.9	7.3	8.1	4.2	4.7
Other advanced economies	7.1	6.8	2.8	10.7	11.0	5.9	9.0	2.5	7.5	11.6	1.9	5.7
Memorandum												
European Union	5.6	6.1	−3.3	7.9	7.9	4.0	9.2	9.6	7.1	10.8	3.8	4.7
Euro area	5.8	5.9	−4.4	8.1	8.4	3.2	9.1	9.7	7.1	11.0	3.4	4.4
Newly industrialized Asian economies	12.8	7.1	10.7	13.1	14.5	7.7	8.1	−8.9	8.3	15.2	−2.0	7.1
Terms of trade												
Advanced economies	**1.1**	**—**	**0.8**	**0.1**	**0.2**	**−0.3**	**−0.6**	**1.4**	**−0.2**	**−2.4**	**−0.3**	**0.9**
Major advanced economies	0.9	—	0.6	—	−0.1	−0.3	−0.5	2.1	−0.2	−2.9	—	1.5
United States	0.1	0.7	1.0	—	−0.5	0.6	1.6	3.5	−0.9	−2.5	1.5	2.5
Japan	2.9	−0.6	2.0	1.5	−0.1	−5.4	−3.7	3.2	−0.7	−4.0	−0.8	1.9
Germany	−0.6	−0.1	2.5	0.1	0.8	−0.7	−1.9	2.0	0.6	−4.6	−0.9	1.3
France	0.6	−0.3	−1.7	0.2	0.1	−1.2	—	1.1	−0.3	−2.8	1.3	0.3
Italy	2.5	−1.0	−4.4	−0.9	−2.3	4.3	−1.5	2.0	−0.5	−6.0	−0.9	0.3
United Kingdom	0.3	0.4	0.3	−2.0	−2.5	1.0	2.7	2.2	1.1	0.5	−0.3	1.0
Canada	−0.2	—	−1.8	−0.6	2.9	1.7	−0.7	−4.1	1.1	4.2	−0.6	−1.3
Other advanced economies	1.4	−0.1	1.1	0.1	0.5	−0.1	−0.7	0.3	−0.2	−1.5	−0.8	−0.2
Memorandum												
European Union	0.7	−0.2	0.1	−0.5	−0.3	0.2	−0.5	1.5	—	−2.7	−0.3	0.5
Euro area	0.7	−0.3	0.2	−0.2	−0.1	0.1	−0.9	1.6	−0.2	−3.3	−0.2	0.4
Newly industrialized Asian economies	3.7	−0.7	2.3	—	0.1	−0.7	−1.2	0.3	−1.1	−4.6	−1.8	—
Memorandum												
Trade in goods												
Advanced economies												
Export volume	6.1	6.6	3.2	9.6	9.6	5.7	10.8	4.3	5.1	11.8	1.3	4.7
Import volume	6.8	7.0	2.2	11.1	9.9	5.8	9.9	5.9	8.5	11.7	1.1	4.7
Terms of trade	1.1	0.1	1.7	0.5	0.4	−0.8	−0.6	1.6	—	−2.7	−0.2	0.8

Table 25. Developing Countries—by Region: Total Trade in Goods
(Annual percent change)

	Ten-Year Averages		1993	1994	1995	1996	1997	1998	1999	2000	2001	2002
	1983–92	1993–2002										
Developing countries												
Value in U.S. dollars												
Exports	3.6	9.0	4.3	15.5	20.5	11.8	7.9	−7.8	9.7	25.4	1.2	5.0
Imports	4.6	8.1	9.9	9.8	19.0	9.5	6.6	−5.1	0.7	19.5	4.2	8.9
Volume												
Exports	6.0	9.0	9.1	11.6	12.3	9.1	12.3	4.8	4.8	16.1	4.0	6.3
Imports	3.3	9.1	11.8	7.9	20.1	9.4	9.9	0.2	1.3	16.6	6.5	8.4
Unit value in U.S. dollars												
Exports	−1.1	0.5	−4.3	3.8	9.0	3.0	−3.7	−12.0	5.8	9.0	−2.7	−1.2
Imports	2.3	0.1	−1.3	2.1	6.6	0.5	−2.9	−5.5	0.7	2.8	−2.0	0.5
Terms of trade	−3.4	0.4	−3.0	1.7	2.2	2.5	−0.8	−6.9	5.0	6.1	−0.7	−1.7
Memorandum												
Real GDP growth in developing country trading partners	4.1	3.3	3.2	4.3	3.6	3.9	4.1	1.7	3.4	4.7	1.8	2.9
Market prices of nonfuel commodities exported by developing countries	0.4	−0.5	−0.4	15.8	9.5	−2.6	−1.4	−16.2	−9.2	2.2	−4.9	5.4
Regional groups												
Africa												
Value in U.S. dollars												
Exports	1.8	4.5	−5.4	3.7	18.5	11.5	1.7	−13.6	7.1	25.8	−0.2	1.7
Imports	1.3	4.3	−4.0	5.4	20.4	1.7	4.2	−0.8	—	5.8	6.7	4.9
Volume												
Exports	2.8	3.8	1.7	—	8.7	8.2	4.5	0.7	3.4	6.1	1.5	3.5
Imports	1.2	5.4	0.9	4.7	12.0	5.3	8.2	5.4	2.3	5.6	6.8	3.3
Unit value in U.S. dollars												
Exports	−0.3	1.1	−6.8	6.3	9.2	3.2	−2.5	−14.4	4.1	19.0	−1.6	−1.3
Imports	1.7	−0.6	−4.5	2.3	7.6	−2.8	−3.2	−5.5	−1.8	0.8	0.5	1.7
Terms of trade	−1.9	1.7	−2.4	3.9	1.5	6.1	0.7	−9.4	6.0	18.1	−2.1	−2.9
Sub-Sahara												
Value in U.S. dollars												
Exports	2.0	4.3	−4.8	4.9	18.5	11.0	1.3	−13.9	5.7	22.5	−0.4	3.1
Imports	0.7	4.3	−3.4	3.2	21.8	4.4	6.8	−2.8	−1.2	6.2	6.0	4.6
Volume												
Exports	3.1	3.6	1.6	−0.7	9.7	9.9	3.8	−0.1	1.9	5.7	1.4	3.5
Imports	1.6	5.6	1.8	2.8	13.9	10.3	9.5	3.5	1.5	5.2	5.5	2.5
Unit value in U.S. dollars												
Exports	−0.3	1.2	−6.1	9.1	8.1	1.1	−2.3	−14.0	4.5	16.8	−1.7	0.2
Imports	1.0	−0.6	−4.9	2.2	7.1	−5.0	−1.8	−5.7	−2.1	1.7	1.2	2.2
Terms of trade	−1.2	1.8	−1.2	6.7	1.0	6.3	−0.5	−8.8	6.7	14.9	−2.9	−2.0

Table 25 *(concluded)*

	Ten-Year Averages		1993	1994	1995	1996	1997	1998	1999	2000	2001	2002
	1983–92	1993–2002										
Developing Asia												
Value in U.S. dollars												
Exports	10.6	11.6	11.6	23.9	23.2	10.0	12.2	−2.2	8.4	22.2	1.7	8.3
Imports	9.5	10.5	19.1	17.8	23.7	10.4	1.2	−13.5	8.9	27.2	5.4	10.4
Volume												
Exports	9.0	11.6	12.2	20.7	11.6	9.0	18.0	6.0	5.6	23.6	3.6	7.9
Imports	7.2	10.4	20.0	16.1	13.0	9.7	5.8	−6.6	6.7	22.6	8.7	10.7
Unit value in U.S. dollars												
Exports	1.9	0.3	−0.4	2.7	10.4	1.3	−4.8	−7.6	4.6	−0.9	−1.9	0.3
Imports	2.4	0.5	−0.4	1.6	9.5	1.1	−4.3	−7.8	5.2	4.4	−3.0	−0.3
Terms of trade	−0.5	−0.2	—	1.2	0.8	0.2	−0.4	0.2	−0.6	−5.1	1.2	0.6
Excluding China and India												
Value in U.S. dollars												
Exports	10.2	9.1	12.5	18.8	22.4	5.7	7.4	−3.9	10.1	18.7	−3.8	6.1
Imports	9.1	7.1	13.7	20.3	26.9	5.7	−0.7	−22.9	6.0	22.8	0.7	8.0
Volume												
Exports	10.3	8.2	10.3	16.5	10.3	2.0	11.0	8.5	3.6	16.9	−1.7	6.0
Imports	8.3	6.3	11.4	19.7	16.4	3.7	1.7	−14.1	0.1	15.7	4.3	8.1
Unit value in U.S. dollars												
Exports	0.3	1.2	2.1	2.1	10.9	3.9	−3.2	−11.3	9.8	1.5	−2.2	0.1
Imports	1.1	1.4	1.9	0.6	9.1	2.3	−2.4	−10.6	11.5	6.4	−3.3	−0.1
Terms of trade	−0.8	−0.2	0.1	1.5	1.6	1.5	−0.8	−0.8	−1.5	−4.6	1.1	0.2
Middle East, Malta, and Turkey												
Value in U.S. dollars												
Exports	−1.4	6.1	−3.8	7.9	14.3	17.1	0.8	−21.6	22.4	39.1	0.6	−3.8
Imports	0.7	4.1	3.0	−10.6	17.5	10.8	6.6	−1.2	−5.3	15.6	−0.3	8.1
Volume												
Exports	5.1	6.1	6.3	5.9	17.7	8.3	5.4	2.1	1.1	8.7	4.4	2.4
Imports	−0.3	9.4	7.7	−13.4	64.3	13.4	11.3	3.1	−1.2	14.8	1.6	6.6
Unit value in U.S. dollars												
Exports	−5.6	1.0	−9.1	1.9	4.0	9.8	−4.3	−22.9	21.1	29.0	−3.5	−6.1
Imports	2.0	−1.2	−3.6	2.9	−0.1	−1.6	−3.7	−3.6	−3.5	0.8	−1.2	1.4
Terms of trade	−7.4	2.3	−5.7	−1.0	4.1	11.5	−0.6	−20.0	25.4	27.9	−2.3	−7.4
Western Hemisphere												
Value in U.S. dollars												
Exports	4.0	9.3	7.8	15.4	22.3	10.6	9.8	−3.9	4.3	20.4	1.3	7.9
Imports	5.3	9.0	9.8	17.3	11.0	10.5	18.2	4.7	−6.6	15.0	4.0	8.2
Volume												
Exports	6.5	9.2	12.2	8.6	10.6	10.3	12.1	6.8	6.4	11.5	5.6	7.9
Imports	4.1	8.1	8.8	14.7	5.0	8.0	17.6	7.6	−4.9	12.5	5.8	7.4
Unit value in U.S. dollars												
Exports	0.3	0.3	−3.9	6.3	10.7	0.3	−1.8	−10.0	−1.7	8.5	−4.1	0.1
Imports	2.8	0.9	1.2	2.3	5.8	2.5	0.7	−2.7	−1.9	2.2	−1.6	0.9
Terms of trade	−2.5	−0.6	−5.0	4.0	4.6	−2.2	−2.5	−7.5	0.2	6.2	−2.5	−0.7

Table 26. Developing Countries—by Source of Export Earnings: Total Trade in Goods
(Annual percent change)

| | Ten-Year Averages | | 1993 | 1994 | 1995 | 1996 | 1997 | 1998 | 1999 | 2000 | 2001 | 2002 |
	1983–92	1993–2002										
Fuel												
Value in U.S. dollars												
Exports	−2.0	5.8	−5.7	2.5	13.8	20.7	0.5	−26.7	29.1	50.6	−2.9	−4.8
Imports	−1.1	3.3	−5.6	−10.8	13.1	3.2	8.8	0.8	−2.5	11.9	10.9	6.1
Volume												
Exports	4.7	4.9	4.7	2.7	17.0	7.4	4.1	1.8	0.7	7.4	2.4	2.2
Imports	−2.1	9.0	−2.5	−13.3	70.9	7.2	12.6	2.7	1.6	12.7	9.9	4.8
Unit value in U.S. dollars												
Exports	−5.9	1.9	−9.8	0.7	3.8	13.4	−3.5	−27.6	28.3	41.2	−4.8	−6.7
Imports	1.8	−1.0	−2.6	3.3	−2.1	−2.8	−2.9	−0.9	−3.3	−0.5	0.9	1.4
Terms of trade	−7.5	2.9	−7.3	−2.4	6.1	16.6	−0.6	−26.9	32.7	41.9	−5.7	−8.0
Nonfuel												
Value in U.S. dollars												
Exports	7.3	10.0	8.4	20.1	22.5	9.3	10.2	−2.5	5.5	18.9	2.5	8.0
Imports	7.1	9.1	14.3	14.6	20.0	10.6	6.2	−6.0	1.2	20.8	3.1	9.4
Volume												
Exports	6.9	10.2	10.9	14.8	10.9	9.6	14.8	5.7	5.7	18.3	4.5	7.6
Imports	5.7	9.1	15.8	12.8	10.9	9.8	9.5	−0.2	1.2	17.3	5.9	9.0
Unit value in U.S. dollars												
Exports	1.8	0.1	−2.1	4.9	10.5	0.1	−3.8	−7.6	1.0	0.7	−2.0	0.5
Imports	2.5	0.3	−1.0	1.8	8.2	1.1	−2.9	−6.2	1.4	3.3	−2.5	0.3
Terms of trade	−0.7	−0.2	−1.1	3.0	2.1	−0.9	−0.9	−1.6	−0.4	−2.5	0.5	0.1
Primary products												
Value in U.S. dollars												
Exports	4.9	7.7	2.1	18.0	25.3	4.4	5.9	−5.9	3.8	13.1	3.4	9.5
Imports	3.9	7.1	5.7	11.6	25.5	10.0	7.5	−2.0	−7.8	10.0	5.2	8.5
Volume												
Exports	3.0	7.5	9.0	7.9	8.5	10.4	7.3	7.6	7.6	6.7	4.9	5.6
Imports	1.8	7.3	9.2	9.8	18.0	9.7	10.5	6.2	−5.7	4.1	5.4	7.1
Unit value in U.S. dollars												
Exports	2.6	0.5	−6.1	11.9	15.9	−5.2	−0.8	−12.7	−3.4	5.6	−1.2	4.6
Imports	4.0	0.2	−4.0	3.3	6.5	0.9	−2.6	−8.0	−1.9	6.1	0.3	1.7
Terms of trade	−1.3	0.4	−2.3	8.3	8.8	−6.0	1.8	−5.1	−1.6	−0.5	−1.5	2.9

Table 27. Summary of Payments Balances on Current Account
(Billions of U.S. dollars)

	1993	1994	1995	1996	1997	1998	1999	2000	2001	2002
Advanced economies	**68.3**	**33.9**	**58.1**	**44.5**	**91.7**	**35.8**	**−121.1**	**−248.4**	**−223.1**	**−200.5**
United States	−82.5	−118.2	−109.9	−120.9	−139.8	−217.5	−324.4	−444.7	−407.1	−404.9
European Union	10.8	19.7	56.6	90.8	122.0	70.9	23.9	−22.5	0.3	5.2
Euro area[1]	24.7	16.9	53.4	81.5	102.0	63.8	28.7	−6.5	15.5	26.2
Japan	132.0	130.6	111.4	65.8	94.1	121.0	106.8	116.9	88.8	108.9
Other advanced economies	8.0	1.9	—	8.9	15.4	61.3	72.7	101.9	94.9	90.4
Memorandum										
Newly industrialized Asian economies	20.8	16.1	5.9	−0.9	10.7	68.0	66.1	50.6	47.5	48.9
Developing countries	**−119.1**	**−85.7**	**−96.2**	**−74.2**	**−59.1**	**−86.8**	**−10.5**	**60.2**	**22.4**	**−23.1**
Regional groups										
Africa	−11.3	−11.8	−16.6	−6.0	−7.8	−20.6	−15.5	2.1	−3.9	−6.4
Developing Asia	−33.0	−18.9	−42.5	−38.8	8.8	47.1	46.3	45.8	22.0	8.7
Excluding China and India	−19.4	−24.9	−38.5	−40.0	−25.1	22.5	33.8	29.4	14.5	10.9
Middle East, Malta, and Turkey	−28.8	−2.8	—	10.5	6.7	−23.0	15.0	60.9	62.2	37.0
Western Hemisphere	−45.9	−52.0	−37.1	−39.8	−66.8	−90.4	−56.3	−48.6	−57.9	−62.4
Analytical groups										
By source of export earnings										
Fuel	−23.6	−3.2	2.8	31.0	20.3	−29.6	19.0	97.9	73.3	49.6
Nonfuel	−95.5	−82.5	−98.9	−105.2	−79.4	−57.2	−29.5	−37.7	−50.9	−72.6
of which, primary products	−12.9	−11.6	−14.7	−17.1	−18.9	−19.1	−9.4	−9.8	−11.4	−12.5
By external financing source										
Net debtor countries	−103.9	−78.3	−98.3	−87.3	−70.3	−71.5	−24.4	2.5	−27.8	−56.4
of which, official financing	−8.1	−9.9	−11.8	−8.7	−5.0	−10.7	−6.3	2.6	−2.0	−6.8
Net debtor countries by debt-servicing experience										
Countries with arrears and/or rescheduling during 1994–98	−28.2	−18.6	−45.6	−42.0	−49.7	−58.9	−23.4	7.6	−15.7	−23.8
Countries in transition	**−7.9**	**2.3**	**−1.7**	**−16.7**	**−24.0**	**−28.5**	**−1.9**	**27.5**	**13.9**	**4.8**
Central and eastern Europe	−8.1	−3.2	−3.0	−14.9	−17.0	−20.2	−23.1	−19.8	−22.4	−22.2
Commonwealth of Independent States and Mongolia	0.2	5.5	1.3	−1.8	−7.1	−8.3	21.2	47.3	36.3	27.0
Russia	2.6	8.2	4.9	3.8	−0.4	−1.6	22.6	45.3	35.3	26.8
Excluding Russia	−2.4	−2.7	−3.6	−5.6	−6.6	−6.7	−1.4	2.0	0.9	0.2
Total[1]	**−58.6**	**−49.5**	**−39.8**	**−46.4**	**8.6**	**−79.6**	**−133.5**	**−160.7**	**−186.9**	**−218.7**
In percent of total world current account transactions	−0.6	−0.5	−0.3	−0.4	0.1	−0.6	−1.0	−1.0	−1.2	−1.3
In percent of world GDP	−0.2	−0.2	−0.1	−0.2	—	−0.3	−0.4	−0.5	−0.6	−0.7
Memorandum										
Emerging market countries, excluding Asian countries in surplus[2]	−102.8	−74.6	−75.7	−75.4	−106.6	−172.2	−60.8	40.2	9.3	−36.1

[1]Reflects errors, omissions, and asymmetries in balance of payments statistics on current account, as well as the exclusion of data for international organizations and a limited number of countries. See "Classification of Countries" in the introduction to this Statistical Appendix.

[2]All developing and transition countries excluding China, Hong Kong SAR, Korea, Malaysia, the Philippines, Singapore, Taiwan Province of China, and Thailand.

Table 28. Advanced Economies: Balance of Payments on Current Account

	1993	1994	1995	1996	1997	1998	1999	2000	2001	2002
					Billions of U.S. dollars					
Advanced economies	**68.3**	**33.9**	**58.1**	**44.5**	**91.7**	**35.8**	**−121.1**	**−248.4**	**−223.1**	**−200.5**
Major advanced economies	18.9	−6.2	6.4	−0.1	26.0	−54.0	−206.9	−335.5	−311.3	−292.0
United States	−82.5	−118.2	−109.9	−120.9	−139.8	−217.5	−324.4	−444.7	−407.1	−404.9
Japan	132.0	130.6	111.4	65.8	94.1	121.0	106.8	116.9	88.8	108.9
Germany	−9.8	−23.9	−20.7	−7.9	−2.7	−6.7	−17.9	−19.4	−14.4	−9.3
France	9.2	7.4	10.9	20.5	39.4	37.6	37.2	23.8	32.0	35.0
Italy	7.8	13.2	25.1	40.0	32.4	20.0	6.3	−5.7	−0.9	1.1
United Kingdom	−15.9	−2.2	−5.9	−0.9	10.8	−0.1	−16.0	−24.5	−23.3	−29.5
Canada	−21.8	−13.0	−4.4	3.4	−8.2	−8.3	1.1	18.1	13.7	6.8
Other advanced economies	49.4	40.1	51.7	44.7	65.7	89.8	85.9	87.1	88.2	91.5
Spain	−5.8	−6.6	0.2	0.4	2.5	−2.9	−12.8	−17.8	−13.5	−12.9
Netherlands	13.3	17.3	25.8	22.0	25.2	12.7	16.5	16.2	18.3	18.6
Belgium-Luxembourg	11.2	12.6	14.2	13.8	13.9	12.1	13.4	11.8	11.4	12.3
Sweden	−2.6	2.4	7.1	7.2	8.0	7.1	8.5	5.9	4.7	4.6
Austria	−1.4	−3.3	−6.1	−5.4	−6.5	−5.2	−6.6	−5.4	−5.5	−5.1
Denmark	4.7	2.7	1.9	3.1	1.1	0.3	2.6	2.7	3.5	4.0
Finland	−1.1	1.1	5.3	5.1	6.8	7.3	7.8	9.0	7.2	6.9
Greece	−0.7	−0.1	−2.9	−4.6	−4.8	−3.6	−5.1	−7.7	−7.5	−8.0
Portugal	0.2	−2.2	−0.1	−4.4	−6.2	−8.2	−10.2	−10.7	−10.3	−10.1
Ireland	1.8	1.5	1.7	2.0	1.9	0.8	0.4	−0.6	−1.2	−2.5
Switzerland	19.5	17.5	21.5	22.0	25.5	25.9	30.0	31.0	26.4	27.6
Norway	3.5	3.7	4.9	10.2	8.7	−1.3	6.1	23.1	24.2	23.3
Israel	−2.6	−3.4	−5.2	−5.4	−3.7	−1.4	−3.0	−1.4	−3.4	−3.1
Iceland	—	0.1	0.1	−0.1	−0.1	−0.6	−0.6	−0.9	−0.7	−0.5
Cyprus	0.1	0.1	−0.2	−0.5	−0.3	−0.6	−0.2	−0.4	−0.3	−0.3
Korea	1.0	−3.9	−8.5	−23.0	−8.2	40.4	24.5	11.0	10.9	9.6
Australia	−9.8	−17.2	−19.5	−15.8	−12.7	−18.2	−23.0	−15.4	−10.6	−10.4
Taiwan Province of China	7.0	6.5	5.5	10.9	7.1	3.4	8.4	8.9	7.1	7.8
Hong Kong SAR	8.6	2.1	−5.5	−1.6	−6.1	3.9	11.5	8.8	10.7	13.0
Singapore	4.2	11.4	14.4	12.8	17.9	20.3	21.8	21.8	18.8	18.4
New Zealand	−1.7	−2.1	−3.1	−3.9	−4.4	−2.2	−3.7	−2.8	−1.9	−1.9
Memorandum										
European Union	10.8	19.7	56.6	90.8	122.0	70.9	23.9	−22.5	0.3	5.2
Euro area[1]	24.7	16.9	53.4	81.5	102.0	63.8	28.7	−6.5	15.5	26.2
Newly industrialized Asian economies	20.8	16.1	5.9	−0.9	10.7	68.0	66.1	50.6	47.5	48.9
					Percent of GDP					
United States	−1.2	−1.7	−1.5	−1.5	−1.7	−2.5	−3.5	−4.5	−4.0	−3.8
Japan	3.0	2.7	2.1	1.4	2.2	3.1	2.4	2.5	2.2	2.6
Germany	−0.5	−1.1	−0.8	−0.3	−0.1	−0.3	−0.9	−1.0	−0.8	−0.5
France	0.7	0.5	0.7	1.3	2.8	2.6	2.6	1.8	2.5	2.6
Italy	0.8	1.3	2.3	3.2	2.8	1.7	0.5	−0.5	−0.1	0.1
United Kingdom	−1.7	−0.2	−0.5	−0.1	0.8	—	−1.1	−1.7	−1.7	−2.0
Canada	−3.9	−2.3	−0.8	0.5	−1.3	−1.3	0.2	2.5	1.9	0.9
Spain	−1.2	−1.3	—	0.1	0.5	−0.5	−2.1	−3.2	−2.3	−2.1
Netherlands	4.1	4.9	6.2	5.3	6.7	3.2	4.1	4.4	4.8	4.6
Belgium-Luxembourg	4.9	5.1	4.8	4.8	5.3	4.5	5.0	4.8	4.6	4.8
Sweden	−1.3	1.2	3.0	2.7	3.4	2.9	3.5	2.6	2.2	2.1
Austria	−0.8	−1.6	−2.6	−2.3	−3.2	−2.5	−3.2	−2.9	−2.9	−2.6
Denmark	3.4	1.8	1.1	1.7	0.7	0.1	1.5	1.7	2.2	2.5
Finland	−1.3	1.1	4.1	4.0	5.6	5.6	6.0	7.4	5.9	5.3
Greece	−0.8	−0.1	−2.4	−3.7	−4.0	−3.0	−4.1	−6.8	−6.5	−6.4
Portugal	0.3	−2.5	−0.1	−3.9	−5.8	−7.3	−8.8	−10.1	−9.4	−8.7
Ireland	3.6	2.7	2.5	2.8	2.4	0.9	0.4	−0.7	−1.2	−2.2
Switzerland	8.2	6.7	7.0	7.4	10.0	9.8	11.6	12.9	10.7	10.9
Norway	3.0	3.0	3.3	6.5	5.6	−0.9	4.0	14.3	15.0	14.4
Israel	−3.9	−4.5	−5.9	−5.6	−3.7	−1.4	−3.0	−1.3	−3.1	−2.7
Iceland	0.8	1.9	0.8	−1.8	−1.5	−6.9	−7.0	−10.3	−9.6	−6.5
Cyprus	1.5	1.2	−1.8	−5.2	−4.0	−6.7	−2.4	−5.0	−3.6	−3.0
Korea	0.3	−1.0	−1.7	−4.4	−1.7	12.6	6.0	2.4	2.6	2.1
Australia	−3.3	−5.1	−5.4	−3.9	−3.1	−5.0	−5.8	−4.0	−3.0	−2.8
Taiwan Province of China	3.1	2.7	2.1	3.9	2.4	1.3	2.9	2.9	2.5	2.6
Hong Kong SAR	7.4	1.6	−3.9	−1.0	−3.6	2.4	7.3	5.4	6.6	7.5
Singapore	7.3	16.3	17.3	14.1	19.0	24.8	25.9	23.7	21.0	19.8
New Zealand	−4.0	−4.1	−5.1	−6.0	−6.6	−4.1	−6.7	−5.6	−4.0	−3.8

[1]Calculated as the sum of the balances of individual euro area countries.

Table 29. Advanced Economies: Current Account Transactions
(Billions of U.S. dollars)

	1993	1994	1995	1996	1997	1998	1999	2000	2001	2002
Exports	2,933.7	3,303.7	3,959.3	4,078.6	4,191.0	4,163.4	4,266.7	4,643.3	4,586.9	4,863.0
Imports	2,843.4	3,229.8	3,868.3	4,018.9	4,120.1	4,100.4	4,339.7	4,857.9	4,801.4	5,049.5
Trade balance	90.3	73.9	91.0	59.7	70.9	62.9	−73.0	−214.6	−214.5	−186.5
Services, credits	835.4	892.1	1,006.3	1,062.6	1,096.3	1,111.6	1,154.9	1,195.7	1,204.0	1,273.5
Services, debits	775.1	826.3	938.1	985.3	1,002.4	1,039.0	1,082.8	1,125.7	1,144.7	1,206.2
Balance on services	60.3	65.8	68.2	77.3	93.9	72.5	72.1	70.0	59.3	67.3
Balance on goods and services	150.6	139.7	159.2	137.0	164.9	135.5	−0.9	−144.6	−155.2	−119.2
Income, net	−5.9	−15.8	−18.2	2.3	15.2	−3.9	−12.4	6.3	26.6	15.9
Current transfers, net	−76.4	−90.0	−82.9	−94.8	−88.3	−95.8	−107.7	−110.1	−94.6	−97.2
Current account balance	**68.3**	**33.9**	**58.1**	**44.5**	**91.7**	**35.8**	**−121.1**	**−248.4**	**−223.1**	**−200.5**
Balance on goods and services										
Advanced economies	**150.6**	**139.7**	**159.2**	**137.0**	**164.9**	**135.5**	**−0.9**	**−144.6**	**−155.2**	**−119.2**
Major advanced economies	81.3	71.0	84.5	55.9	74.9	16.8	−114.5	−257.2	−264.5	−235.2
United States	−68.8	−96.7	−96.4	−101.8	−107.8	−166.8	−261.8	−375.7	−353.5	−348.2
Japan	96.5	96.4	74.7	21.2	47.3	73.2	69.1	69.0	32.1	53.9
Germany	7.4	10.0	18.0	25.2	29.1	30.8	18.3	6.8	15.0	21.1
France	24.5	25.0	28.9	31.2	45.7	42.0	39.3	23.1	31.0	33.6
Italy	32.2	37.0	45.3	62.2	47.6	39.8	23.2	11.3	15.6	17.9
United Kingdom	−10.1	−7.0	−4.4	−6.5	0.8	−13.2	−24.1	−27.1	−34.8	−35.8
Canada	−0.4	6.3	18.4	24.4	12.1	10.9	21.5	35.4	30.0	22.4
Other advanced economies	69.3	68.7	74.7	81.1	89.9	118.7	113.6	112.5	109.3	116.0
Memorandum										
European Union	92.0	110.6	148.0	176.3	187.4	152.2	104.0	52.3	66.2	79.6
Euro area	84.7	99.5	128.0	156.0	162.3	147.5	105.7	58.7	83.6	97.5
Newly industrialized Asian economies	16.9	11.9	4.3	−0.9	6.5	63.7	60.4	44.4	37.9	38.7
Income, net										
Advanced economies	**−5.9**	**−15.8**	**−18.2**	**2.3**	**15.2**	**−3.9**	**−12.4**	**6.3**	**26.6**	15.9
Major advanced economies	21.2	15.1	5.3	34.8	35.4	22.2	7.1	21.3	39.5	31.4
United States	23.9	16.7	20.5	21.0	8.8	−6.2	−13.6	−14.8	−10.7	−14.7
Japan	40.6	40.3	44.4	53.6	55.6	56.6	49.7	57.7	64.7	65.1
Germany	16.6	3.0	0.1	0.9	−1.4	−7.2	−8.8	−1.1	−6.6	−7.5
France	−9.1	−6.8	−9.0	−2.7	2.6	8.6	11.0	13.4	13.8	14.8
Italy	−17.2	−16.7	−15.6	−15.0	−11.2	−12.3	−11.5	−12.4	−11.9	−11.9
United Kingdom	−12.8	−2.4	−12.4	−1.5	1.7	2.5	1.4	−3.2	7.9	2.3
Canada	−20.8	−19.0	−22.7	−21.6	−20.9	−19.7	−21.1	−18.3	−17.6	−16.7
Other advanced economies	−27.1	−30.9	−23.6	−32.5	−20.2	−26.1	−19.5	−14.9	−12.9	−15.5
Memorandum										
European Union	−46.8	−46.1	−54.5	−41.7	−29.2	−38.2	−34.9	−30.5	−24.1	−31.7
Euro area	−20.6	−33.0	−30.8	−28.1	−20.3	−35.1	−31.5	−21.8	−27.6	−29.9
Newly industrialized Asian economies	4.1	5.1	5.2	3.6	8.5	5.2	8.8	11.2	15.0	15.4

Table 30. Developing Countries: Payments Balances on Current Account

	1993	1994	1995	1996	1997	1998	1999	2000	2001	2002
					Billions of U.S. dollars					
Developing countries	**−119.1**	**−85.7**	**−96.2**	**−74.2**	**−59.1**	**−86.8**	**−10.5**	**60.2**	**22.4**	**−23.1**
Regional groups										
Africa	−11.3	−11.8	−16.6	−6.0	−7.8	−20.6	−15.5	2.1	−3.9	−6.4
Sub-Sahara	−10.3	−8.6	−12.4	−6.8	−10.6	−18.9	−14.9	−5.5	−9.4	−9.8
Excluding Nigeria and South Africa	−9.7	−7.1	−8.9	−7.8	−10.6	−13.7	−11.0	−7.1	−9.2	−9.5
Developing Asia	−33.0	−18.9	−42.5	−38.8	8.8	47.1	46.3	45.8	22.0	8.7
China	−11.9	7.7	1.6	7.2	37.0	31.5	15.7	20.5	11.2	2.7
India	−1.6	−1.7	−5.6	−6.0	−3.0	−6.9	−3.2	−4.2	−3.8	−4.9
Other developing Asia	−19.4	−24.9	−38.5	−40.0	−25.1	22.5	33.8	29.4	14.5	10.9
Middle East, Malta, and Turkey	−28.8	−2.8	—	10.5	6.7	−23.0	15.0	60.9	62.2	37.0
Western Hemisphere	−45.9	−52.0	−37.1	−39.8	−66.8	−90.4	−56.3	−48.6	−57.9	−62.4
Analytical groups										
By source of export earnings										
Fuel	−23.6	−3.2	2.8	31.0	20.3	−29.6	19.0	97.9	73.3	49.6
Nonfuel	−95.5	−82.5	−98.9	−105.2	−79.4	−57.2	−29.5	−37.7	−50.9	−72.6
of which, primary products	−12.9	−11.6	−14.7	−17.1	−18.9	−19.1	−9.4	−9.8	−11.4	−12.5
By external financing source										
Net debtor countries	−103.9	−78.3	−98.3	−87.3	−70.3	−71.5	−24.4	2.5	−27.8	−56.4
of which, official financing	−8.1	−9.9	−11.8	−8.7	−5.0	−10.7	−6.3	2.6	−2.0	−6.8
Net debtor countries by debt-servicing experience										
Countries with arrears and/or rescheduling during 1994–98	−28.2	−18.6	−45.6	−42.0	−49.7	−58.9	−23.4	7.6	−15.7	−23.8
Other groups										
Heavily indebted poor countries	−13.8	−10.2	−12.4	−12.8	−14.8	−16.3	−12.9	−9.1	−12.1	−14.3
Middle East and north Africa	−25.0	−11.4	−4.7	12.4	10.5	−28.6	14.2	77.2	61.2	39.6

Table 30 (concluded)

| | Ten-Year Averages | | 1993 | 1994 | 1995 | 1996 | 1997 | 1998 | 1999 | 2000 | 2001 | 2002 |
	1983–92	1993–2002										
	Percent of exports of goods and services											
Developing countries	**−11.1**	**−1.4**	**−15.8**	**−9.9**	**−9.3**	**−6.4**	**−4.7**	**−7.4**	**−0.8**	**3.9**	**1.4**	**−1.4**
Regional groups												
Africa	−10.1	−4.0	−11.5	−11.6	−13.8	−4.5	−5.7	−17.1	−12.1	1.4	−2.5	−4.0
Sub-Sahara	−12.7	−8.3	−13.9	−11.1	−13.4	−6.7	−10.2	−20.7	−15.5	−4.8	−8.3	−8.3
Excluding Nigeria and South Africa	−27.9	−15.8	−26.6	−18.8	−19.7	−15.8	−21.1	−29.9	−22.4	−12.7	−16.3	−15.8
Developing Asia	−5.0	1.1	−11.1	−5.1	−9.3	−7.7	1.6	8.7	8.0	6.5	3.1	1.1
China	8.1	0.8	−38.1	−15.9	−28.9	−22.6	4.3	22.7	21.2	16.4	7.3	2.6
India	−14.4	−6.8	−123.9	−59.9	−111.5	−94.2	19.7	103.0	90.1	74.4	33.0	12.1
Other developing Asia	−9.9	3.0	−10.6	−11.3	−14.3	−13.7	−8.0	7.9	10.9	8.2	4.2	3.0
Middle East, Malta, and Turkey	−12.5	11.2	−16.5	−1.5	—	4.2	2.6	−10.6	6.0	18.3	18.5	11.2
Western Hemisphere	−19.7	−15.7	−25.2	−25.1	−15.0	−14.6	−22.3	−31.0	−18.7	−13.6	−15.8	−15.7
Analytical groups												
By source of export earnings												
Fuel	−14.3	15.3	−13.7	−1.8	1.4	12.8	8.3	−16.0	8.1	28.4	21.8	15.3
Nonfuel	−10.1	−5.4	−10.1	−5.9	−6.3	−6.0	−2.3	—	0.2	−0.9	−1.4	−2.7
of which, primary products	−23.2	−12.1	−25.3	−19.5	−19.7	−21.7	−22.6	−23.9	−11.5	−10.8	−12.0	−12.1
By external financing source												
Net debtor countries	−10.9	−3.8	−16.0	−10.3	−10.8	−8.6	−6.3	−6.7	−2.2	0.2	−2.0	−3.8
of which, official financing	−13.9	−7.7	−19.2	−22.5	−22.0	−14.2	−7.6	−17.7	−9.5	3.1	−2.3	−7.7
Net debtor countries by debt-servicing experience												
Countries with arrears and/or rescheduling during 1994–98	−10.8	−6.0	−14.2	−8.5	−18.1	−14.8	−16.0	−20.9	−7.7	2.0	−4.2	−6.0
Other groups												
Heavily indebted poor countries	−34.7	−19.1	−40.7	−26.7	−26.6	−24.2	−26.8	−30.6	−22.2	−13.4	−17.2	−19.1
Middle East and north Africa	−13.2	12.7	−14.5	−6.4	−2.3	5.3	4.4	−14.9	6.1	23.8	19.0	12.7
Memorandum												
Median												
Developing countries	−18.0	−10.1	−19.2	−14.0	−13.1	−14.6	−11.7	−17.1	−11.5	−12.0	−11.8	−10.1

Table 31. Developing Countries—by Region: Current Account Transactions
(Billions of U.S. dollars)

	1993	1994	1995	1996	1997	1998	1999	2000	2001	2002
Developing countries										
Exports	620.7	716.7	863.7	965.8	1,042.3	960.7	1,053.5	1,321.1	1,336.5	1,403.2
Imports	663.2	728.3	866.5	948.9	1,011.1	959.6	965.9	1,154.3	1,202.5	1,309.9
Trade balance	−42.4	−11.5	−2.7	17.0	31.3	1.2	87.7	166.9	134.1	93.3
Services, net	−47.3	−39.3	−48.0	−55.4	−61.0	−49.7	−56.4	−61.4	−60.4	−65.0
Balance on goods and services	−89.7	−50.8	−50.7	−38.4	−29.7	−48.5	31.2	105.6	73.7	28.4
Income, net	−57.6	−63.1	−79.0	−74.0	−75.4	−79.6	−86.5	−92.3	−104.0	−101.3
Current transfers, net	28.2	28.2	33.2	37.7	45.6	40.8	44.2	46.6	52.2	49.4
Current account balance	**−119.1**	**−85.7**	**−96.2**	**−74.2**	**−59.1**	**−86.8**	**−10.5**	**60.2**	**22.4**	**−23.1**
Memorandum										
Exports of goods and services	752.0	864.9	1,032.6	1,158.8	1,257.9	1,167.5	1,257.7	1,547.7	1,578.4	1,663.5
Interest payments	82.2	87.7	102.8	106.7	108.4	115.8	118.3	117.2	116.0	114.5
Oil trade balance	114.9	112.7	127.2	159.7	150.6	98.9	143.5	231.8	215.6	194.2
Regional groups										
Africa										
Exports	82.0	85.1	100.8	112.4	114.4	98.8	105.8	133.1	132.8	135.1
Imports	78.2	82.5	99.3	101.0	105.2	104.4	104.4	110.4	117.8	123.6
Trade balance	3.8	2.6	1.5	11.4	9.2	−5.6	1.4	22.7	15.0	11.6
Services, net	−9.2	−9.5	−11.5	−10.4	−10.2	−10.3	−9.9	−11.6	−11.4	−13.1
Balance on goods and services	−5.5	−6.9	−10.0	1.0	−1.0	−15.9	−8.5	11.1	3.6	−1.6
Income, net	−16.2	−15.4	−17.2	−18.2	−18.5	−16.8	−19.0	−21.9	−20.6	−18.4
Current transfers, net	10.3	10.5	10.2	10.7	11.3	11.8	11.6	12.6	12.6	13.1
Current account balance	**−11.3**	**−11.8**	**−16.6**	**−6.0**	**−7.8**	**−20.6**	**−15.5**	**2.1**	**−3.9**	**−6.4**
Memorandum										
Exports of goods and services	98.3	102.1	120.0	133.4	136.1	120.4	128.1	155.4	155.8	159.4
Interest payments	13.6	13.9	16.5	16.2	16.0	15.8	15.3	16.2	15.7	14.8
Oil trade balance	20.2	18.5	21.6	30.7	29.4	19.3	25.5	47.3	45.0	41.7
Developing Asia										
Exports	247.9	307.1	378.4	416.3	467.0	456.6	494.8	604.6	614.9	666.0
Imports	277.9	327.4	404.9	447.2	452.4	391.2	426.0	542.0	571.3	630.9
Trade balance	−30.0	−20.2	−26.4	−30.7	14.8	65.4	68.9	62.7	43.7	35.2
Services, net	−4.7	−4.5	−11.6	−7.4	−12.1	−12.6	−19.3	−17.6	−21.0	−23.9
Balance on goods and services	−34.6	−24.7	−37.9	−38.2	2.7	52.8	49.7	45.1	22.7	11.4
Income, net	−14.0	−13.5	−24.5	−24.8	−23.6	−28.7	−29.3	−28.6	−30.9	−33.2
Current transfers, net	15.7	19.2	20.0	24.1	29.7	23.0	25.9	29.3	30.2	30.6
Current account balance	**−33.0**	**−18.9**	**−42.5**	**−38.8**	**8.8**	**47.1**	**46.3**	**45.8**	**22.0**	**8.7**
Memorandum										
Exports of goods and services	296.8	370.5	454.7	505.2	565.4	539.6	579.8	701.2	718.1	777.4
Interest payments	21.8	24.5	26.8	29.5	26.9	30.4	35.0	27.6	25.3	23.4
Oil trade balance	−11.2	−11.5	−13.6	−19.5	−22.2	−14.3	−23.0	−40.5	−42.1	−45.1

Table 31 *(concluded)*

	1993	1994	1995	1996	1997	1998	1999	2000	2001	2002
Middle East, Malta, and Turkey										
Exports	145.8	157.2	179.8	210.5	212.2	166.3	203.6	283.2	284.8	274.0
Imports	149.2	133.3	156.7	173.5	185.0	182.8	173.1	200.2	199.6	215.7
Trade balance	−3.4	23.9	23.1	37.0	27.1	−16.4	30.5	83.0	85.2	58.3
Services, net	−25.3	−16.7	−16.6	−26.9	−23.5	−12.4	−17.3	−20.1	−18.1	−19.1
Balance on goods and services	−28.7	7.3	6.5	10.1	3.6	−28.8	13.3	62.9	67.1	39.2
Income, net	9.4	5.1	6.7	12.7	14.4	17.5	14.7	13.6	7.2	13.4
Current transfers, net	−9.5	−15.2	−13.2	−12.3	−11.3	−11.6	−13.0	−15.6	−12.0	−15.5
Current account balance	**−28.8**	**−2.8**	**—**	**10.5**	**6.7**	**−23.0**	**15.0**	**60.9**	**62.2**	**37.0**
Memorandum										
Exports of goods and services	174.4	184.8	211.4	246.6	257.1	215.7	247.9	332.6	337.2	329.7
Interest payments	11.9	12.6	15.3	15.4	16.5	17.0	12.6	14.6	16.5	17.7
Oil trade balance	91.5	90.0	100.2	123.3	119.3	78.6	117.4	185.3	180.5	165.8
Western Hemisphere										
Exports	145.0	167.4	204.7	226.5	248.7	239.0	249.3	300.3	304.1	328.0
Imports	157.9	185.2	205.6	227.2	268.5	281.2	262.5	301.8	313.9	339.8
Trade balance	−12.9	−17.8	−0.9	−0.7	−19.7	−42.2	−13.2	−1.5	−9.8	−11.7
Services, net	−8.1	−8.6	−8.3	−10.7	−15.2	−14.4	−10.0	−12.0	−9.9	−8.9
Balance on goods and services	−21.0	−26.4	−9.2	−11.4	−35.0	−56.6	−23.2	−13.5	−19.7	−20.6
Income, net	−36.8	−39.3	−44.0	−43.7	−47.7	−51.5	−52.9	−55.4	−59.6	−63.1
Current transfers, net	11.8	13.6	16.1	15.2	15.9	17.7	19.8	20.3	21.4	21.3
Current account balance	**−45.9**	**−52.0**	**−37.1**	**−39.8**	**−66.8**	**−90.4**	**−56.3**	**−48.6**	**−57.9**	**−62.4**
Memorandum										
Exports of goods and services	182.5	207.6	246.5	273.6	299.4	291.8	301.8	358.4	367.3	397.0
Interest payments	35.0	36.7	44.2	45.6	48.9	52.6	55.5	58.9	58.5	58.5
Oil trade balance	14.4	15.7	19.0	25.3	24.0	15.3	23.6	39.7	32.2	31.7

Table 32. Developing Countries—by Analytical Criteria: Current Account Transactions
(Billions of U.S. dollars)

	1993	1994	1995	1996	1997	1998	1999	2000	2001	2002
By source of export earnings										
Fuel										
Exports	162.0	166.1	188.9	228.0	229.2	168.1	216.9	326.7	317.2	302.0
Imports	124.6	111.1	125.7	129.7	141.2	142.3	138.8	155.2	172.2	182.7
Trade balance	37.4	55.0	63.3	98.3	88.0	25.7	78.2	171.5	145.0	119.3
Services, net	−43.5	−35.1	−37.0	−50.3	−50.9	−40.7	−41.4	−50.3	−49.7	−51.1
Balance on goods and services	−6.1	19.9	26.2	48.0	37.1	−14.9	36.8	121.2	95.3	68.2
Income, net	3.8	0.2	−0.6	4.1	4.0	7.7	6.0	3.4	4.4	7.7
Current transfers, net	−21.3	−23.2	−22.8	−21.1	−20.8	−22.4	−23.8	−26.7	−26.4	−26.3
Current account balance	**−23.6**	**−3.2**	**2.8**	**31.0**	**20.3**	**−29.6**	**19.0**	**97.9**	**73.3**	**49.6**
Memorandum										
Exports of goods and services	172.2	176.7	200.4	241.2	245.3	184.7	233.4	344.1	336.4	323.2
Interest payments	14.7	15.3	18.1	17.4	19.4	19.6	13.8	14.9	14.5	13.9
Oil trade balance	127.0	123.6	141.0	179.3	175.2	118.0	166.7	269.2	257.0	238.7
Nonfuel exports										
Exports	458.6	550.7	674.8	737.8	813.1	792.6	836.5	994.5	1,019.4	1,101.2
Imports	538.6	617.2	740.8	819.1	869.9	817.3	827.2	999.1	1,030.4	1,127.2
Trade balance	−79.9	−66.5	−66.0	−81.3	−56.7	−24.6	9.5	−4.5	−10.8	−25.9
Services, net	−3.8	−4.2	−11.0	−5.1	−10.1	−9.1	−15.0	−11.1	−10.7	−13.8
Balance on goods and services	−83.6	−70.6	−76.9	−86.4	−66.8	−33.6	−5.5	−15.6	−21.6	−39.8
Income, net	−61.4	−63.2	−78.4	−78.1	−79.5	−87.3	−92.5	−95.7	−108.4	−109.0
Current transfers, net	49.5	51.4	56.0	58.8	66.4	63.2	68.0	73.2	78.6	75.7
Current account balance	**−95.5**	**−82.5**	**−98.9**	**−105.2**	**−79.4**	**−57.2**	**−29.5**	**−37.7**	**−50.9**	**−72.6**
Memorandum										
Exports of goods and services	579.7	688.3	832.2	917.6	1,012.6	982.8	1,024.3	1,203.6	1,242.0	1,340.3
Interest payments	67.6	72.4	84.8	89.3	89.0	96.2	104.6	102.3	101.5	100.6
Oil trade balance	−12.1	−10.9	−13.8	−19.6	−24.7	−19.2	−23.2	−37.3	−41.4	−44.5
Nonfuel primary products										
Exports	41.2	48.6	60.9	63.6	67.3	63.4	65.8	74.4	77.0	84.3
Imports	47.1	52.6	66.0	72.7	78.1	76.6	70.6	77.7	81.7	88.7
Trade balance	−6.0	−4.0	−5.2	−9.1	−10.8	−13.2	−4.8	−3.3	−4.8	−4.4
Services, net	−5.3	−5.2	−6.3	−6.5	−6.6	−5.6	−5.2	−6.3	−6.1	−7.3
Balance on goods and services	−11.3	−9.3	−11.4	−15.6	−17.4	−18.8	−10.0	−9.5	−10.8	−11.7
Income, net	−8.3	−9.0	−10.3	−9.9	−9.9	−9.4	−9.4	−10.5	−10.7	−11.5
Current transfers, net	6.7	6.7	6.7	8.0	8.1	8.7	9.6	9.8	9.8	10.2
Current account balance	**−12.9**	**−11.6**	**−14.7**	**−17.1**	**−18.9**	**−19.1**	**−9.4**	**−9.8**	**−11.4**	**−12.5**
Memorandum										
Exports of goods and services	51.2	59.6	74.6	78.7	83.4	80.0	82.0	90.7	94.4	103.1
Interest payments	7.8	8.0	9.6	9.1	8.9	9.4	8.8	9.7	10.1	10.2
Oil trade balance	−2.5	−2.5	−3.0	−3.9	−4.4	−3.8	−3.5	−4.2	−4.4	−7.3

Table 32 *(continued)*

	1993	1994	1995	1996	1997	1998	1999	2000	2001	2002
By external financing source										
Net debtor countries										
Exports	524.9	618.3	749.0	831.9	905.4	862.4	932.2	1,142.9	1,160.2	1,238.3
Imports	593.9	662.6	794.5	873.8	930.6	879.7	893.4	1,077.7	1,120.9	1,222.8
Trade balance	−68.9	−44.2	−45.4	−41.8	−25.1	−17.2	39.0	65.3	39.4	15.7
Services, net	−17.7	−16.7	−23.6	−18.8	−24.0	−22.2	−27.4	−25.2	−24.0	−27.6
Balance on goods and services	−86.6	−61.0	−69.0	−60.6	−49.1	−39.5	11.5	40.1	15.5	−11.9
Income, net	−69.6	−71.6	−87.3	−87.9	−90.5	−96.8	−103.7	−109.3	−121.3	−120.7
Current transfers, net	52.3	54.3	57.6	60.8	68.8	64.4	67.3	71.2	77.6	75.7
Current account balance	**−103.9**	**−78.3**	**−98.3**	**−87.3**	**−70.3**	**−71.5**	**−24.4**	**2.5**	**−27.8**	**−56.4**
Memorandum										
Exports of goods and services	650.8	761.0	912.3	1,018.4	1,112.2	1,059.9	1,126.4	1,358.7	1,390.6	1,486.3
Interest payments	80.3	85.3	100.1	103.7	104.6	111.9	115.5	114.0	112.5	111.0
Oil trade balance	39.2	38.9	43.9	58.1	50.8	34.6	55.6	90.0	77.0	69.2
Official financing										
Exports	32.0	32.8	40.5	47.1	51.1	45.9	51.1	66.9	68.9	70.4
Imports	38.6	42.9	51.5	55.2	55.2	56.5	58.0	64.9	71.6	78.0
Trade balance	−6.6	−10.0	−11.0	−8.1	−4.1	−10.5	−6.9	2.0	−2.7	−7.5
Services, net	−3.0	−3.1	−3.7	−3.5	−3.0	−4.2	−4.0	−3.8	−3.8	−5.3
Balance on goods and services	−9.6	−13.1	−14.7	−11.6	−7.1	−14.7	−10.9	−1.7	−6.5	−12.8
Income, net	−6.8	−6.0	−6.6	−6.6	−7.2	−6.0	−6.4	−7.8	−7.6	−6.4
Current transfers, net	8.2	9.1	9.5	9.6	9.3	10.0	11.0	12.2	12.0	12.4
Current account balance	**−8.1**	**−9.9**	**−11.8**	**−8.7**	**−5.0**	**−10.7**	**−6.3**	**2.6**	**−2.0**	**−6.8**
Memorandum										
Exports of goods and services	42.4	44.1	53.6	61.0	65.9	60.6	66.4	83.2	85.9	88.3
Interest payments	7.1	6.7	7.3	7.0	7.2	7.0	6.2	6.8	6.6	6.2
Oil trade balance	9.6	7.9	8.9	12.5	13.0	8.3	11.7	21.5	20.1	14.4
Net debtor countries by debt-servicing experience										
Countries with arrears and/or rescheduling during 1994–98										
Exports	166.0	183.2	208.1	233.5	252.6	232.4	259.4	328.9	324.1	339.6
Imports	162.4	176.4	221.3	241.4	260.1	242.0	233.4	267.1	284.6	307.1
Trade balance	3.6	6.9	−13.2	−7.8	−7.5	−9.6	26.0	61.7	39.5	32.6
Services, net	−17.0	−14.8	−19.0	−24.2	−30.7	−34.2	−31.9	−33.2	−33.6	−36.1
Balance on goods and services	−13.4	−7.9	−32.2	−32.1	−38.2	−43.8	−5.9	28.5	5.9	−3.6
Income, net	−30.1	−27.4	−31.0	−27.1	−29.7	−32.8	−34.7	−38.5	−40.0	−39.8
Current transfers, net	15.3	16.7	17.2	16.7	17.8	17.4	16.8	17.2	17.9	19.1
Current account balance	**−28.2**	**−18.6**	**−45.6**	**−42.0**	**−49.7**	**−58.9**	**−23.4**	**7.6**	**−15.7**	**−23.8**
Memorandum										
Exports of goods and services	198.5	220.1	251.5	284.7	311.1	282.1	305.6	379.8	377.0	396.7
Interest payments	30.8	29.7	36.2	37.8	39.4	43.4	45.0	47.1	47.3	46.5
Oil trade balance	35.0	35.0	38.7	50.0	48.1	36.5	55.6	88.3	83.7	78.2

Table 32 *(concluded)*

	1993	1994	1995	1996	1997	1998	1999	2000	2001	2002
Other groups										
Heavily indebted poor countries										
Exports	26.2	29.9	37.0	42.6	44.6	42.1	46.3	56.3	57.5	61.2
Imports	33.2	35.2	42.3	47.9	51.1	52.0	53.5	58.3	62.3	67.7
Trade balance	−7.0	−5.3	−5.3	−5.3	−6.5	−9.8	−7.2	−1.9	−4.7	−6.5
Services, net	−5.8	−5.2	−6.7	−7.3	−8.0	−7.8	−7.0	−8.2	−8.3	−10.0
Balance on goods and services	−12.9	−10.5	−12.1	−12.6	−14.5	−17.7	−14.2	−10.1	−13.1	−16.5
Income, net	−8.7	−7.7	−8.8	−9.5	−9.4	−8.7	−9.3	−10.6	−10.7	−9.6
Current transfers, net	7.7	8.0	8.0	8.8	8.7	9.7	10.3	11.2	11.3	11.4
Current account balance	**−13.8**	**−10.2**	**−12.4**	**−12.8**	**−14.8**	**−16.3**	**−12.9**	**−9.1**	**−12.1**	**−14.3**
Memorandum										
Exports of goods and services	33.9	38.1	46.7	53.2	55.3	53.3	57.8	68.2	70.1	74.7
Interest payments	6.6	6.6	7.3	7.3	7.0	7.4	6.5	6.6	6.7	6.1
Oil trade balance	2.9	3.5	4.4	6.1	6.3	3.5	6.9	12.3	11.1	7.9
Middle East and north Africa										
Exports	148.9	154.0	175.1	203.2	205.5	157.5	199.4	287.1	283.8	272.0
Imports	140.2	133.6	147.9	156.0	161.8	163.9	160.1	174.3	185.3	198.4
Trade balance	8.7	20.4	27.1	47.2	43.7	−6.4	39.3	112.8	98.5	73.6
Services, net	−30.6	−20.3	−21.4	−30.9	−31.3	−22.6	−23.0	−29.7	−30.0	−30.1
Balance on goods and services	−21.9	0.1	5.8	16.3	12.4	−29.0	16.3	83.0	68.5	43.5
Income, net	5.8	2.1	2.5	7.7	9.3	12.5	11.3	10.1	5.4	12.3
Current transfers, net	−8.9	−13.6	−13.0	−11.6	−11.1	−12.0	−13.3	−15.9	−12.7	−16.1
Current account balance	**−25.0**	**−11.4**	**−4.7**	**12.4**	**10.5**	**−28.6**	**14.2**	**77.2**	**61.2**	**39.6**
Memorandum										
Exports of goods and services	172.2	178.5	201.7	233.5	238.8	191.4	234.2	323.8	322.1	313.3
Interest payments	−12.9	−13.2	−16.2	−16.3	−16.9	−16.9	−11.7	−13.0	−12.8	−13.4
Oil trade balance	104.0	101.1	112.6	139.2	135.8	91.8	132.1	211.3	205.5	189.8

Table 33. Summary of Balance of Payments, Capital Flows, and External Financing
(Billions of U.S. dollars)

	1993	1994	1995	1996	1997	1998	1999	2000	2001	2002
Developing countries										
Balance of payments[1]										
Balance on current account	−119.1	−85.7	−96.2	−74.2	−59.1	−86.8	−10.5	60.2	22.4	−23.1
Balance on goods and services	−89.7	−50.8	−50.7	−38.4	−29.7	−48.5	31.2	105.6	73.7	28.4
Income, net	−57.6	−63.1	−79.0	−74.0	−75.4	−79.6	−86.5	−92.3	−104.0	−101.3
Current transfers, net	28.2	28.2	33.2	37.7	45.6	40.8	44.2	46.6	52.2	49.4
Balance on capital and financial account	138.3	113.3	118.3	112.3	117.7	114.6	33.2	−44.9	−6.0	36.9
Balance on capital account[2]	6.5	6.3	8.8	12.5	13.5	7.4	8.4	7.0	7.9	14.6
Balance on financial account	131.8	107.1	109.5	99.8	104.3	107.2	24.9	−51.9	−13.9	22.3
Direct investment, net	51.5	75.4	86.1	108.0	130.4	131.1	125.4	119.2	131.9	123.3
Portfolio investment, net	103.8	100.2	22.7	74.7	42.8	6.7	20.8	−6.9	−4.7	25.4
Other investment, net	16.3	−18.1	67.9	11.3	−12.6	−37.3	−90.1	−105.2	−89.2	−70.5
Reserve assets	−39.9	−50.4	−67.1	−94.2	−56.3	6.6	−31.3	−59.0	−52.0	−55.9
Errors and omissions, net	−19.2	−27.7	−22.2	−38.0	−58.6	−27.8	−22.6	−15.3	−16.3	−13.8
Capital flows										
Total capital flows, net[3]	171.7	157.4	176.6	194.0	160.5	100.5	56.2	7.1	38.0	78.2
Net official flows	49.0	23.8	32.4	4.1	22.8	33.7	26.6	13.1	31.5	3.9
Net private flows[4]	122.7	133.6	144.3	189.9	137.7	66.8	29.6	−5.9	6.5	74.3
Direct investment, net	51.5	75.4	86.1	108.0	130.4	131.1	125.4	119.2	131.9	123.3
Private portfolio investment, net	73.6	92.2	17.8	61.7	35.7	−2.0	11.8	−13.9	−0.9	23.3
Other private flows, net	−2.4	−34.0	40.5	20.1	−28.3	−62.3	−107.6	−111.3	−124.4	−72.3
External financing[5]										
Net external financing[6]	195.1	167.9	213.1	242.3	245.7	187.5	162.7	150.2	183.4	202.1
Nondebt-creating flows	97.2	101.2	115.3	153.6	169.1	145.5	141.0	148.6	153.8	160.7
Capital transfers[7]	6.5	6.3	8.8	12.5	13.5	7.4	8.4	7.0	7.9	14.6
Foreign direct investment and equity security liabilities[8]	90.7	94.9	106.5	141.1	155.7	138.1	132.6	141.6	145.9	146.0
Net external borrowing[9]	97.9	66.7	97.8	88.7	76.5	42.0	21.7	1.6	29.6	41.5
Borrowing from official creditors[10]	48.6	22.6	32.5	7.8	13.9	29.7	28.3	10.7	28.4	6.3
Of which,										
Credit and loans from IMF[11]	−0.1	−0.8	12.6	−2.9	0.8	8.5	1.3	−6.5	. . .	. . .
Borrowing from banks[12]	17.1	−27.7	21.2	22.5	28.6	27.1	−3.1	7.5	2.0	13.4
Borrowing from other private creditors	32.2	71.7	44.0	58.4	34.0	−14.9	−3.5	−16.5	−0.7	21.8
Memorandum										
Balance on goods and services in percent of GDP[13]	−2.4	−1.3	−1.1	−0.8	−0.6	−1.0	0.6	2.0	1.3	0.5
Scheduled amortization of external debt	122.5	126.3	154.1	197.6	220.8	225.7	256.3	252.1	226.5	213.0
Gross external financing[14]	317.6	294.2	367.2	439.9	466.4	413.2	419.0	402.3	409.9	415.1
Gross external borrowing[15]	220.4	193.0	251.9	286.3	297.3	267.7	278.0	253.7	256.1	254.5
Exceptional external financing, net	33.6	20.1	19.6	20.2	15.6	17.8	25.4	21.9	24.4	16.0
Of which,										
Arrears on debt service	4.8	−8.0	−2.4	−4.1	−7.6	0.2	13.4	−23.8	. . .	. . .
Debt forgiveness	1.8	1.3	1.9	8.8	14.3	1.5	1.6	1.8	. . .	. . .
Rescheduling of debt service	22.5	25.1	20.3	15.7	10.4	6.1	11.1	41.6	. . .	. . .
Countries in transition										
Balance of payments[1]										
Balance on current account	−7.9	2.3	−1.7	−16.7	−24.0	−28.5	−1.9	27.5	13.9	4.8
Balance on goods and services	−8.6	3.2	−4.5	−17.9	−19.1	−21.3	3.6	31.9	18.9	9.1
Income, net	−5.5	−5.1	−2.0	−4.7	−10.8	−14.3	−13.5	−12.5	−14.1	−13.3
Current transfers, net	6.2	4.3	4.8	5.8	5.9	7.1	8.0	8.1	9.1	9.1
Balance on capital and finalcial account	10.3	−1.6	5.6	24.0	27.1	36.3	7.0	−20.0	−15.5	−5.1
Balance on capital account[2]	2.5	10.3	−1.6	1.2	0.3	0.4	0.2	—	—	−0.1
Balance on financial account	7.8	−11.9	7.2	22.8	26.8	36.0	6.8	−20.0	−15.5	−5.0
Direct investment,net	6.0	5.3	13.1	12.4	15.6	21.6	23.6	22.7	26.9	31.3
Portfolio investment, net	8.7	17.1	14.6	13.4	24.4	12.2	1.8	6.2	7.7	7.4
Other investment, net	4.0	−29.0	17.3	−0.9	−3.9	4.1	−11.4	−27.3	−28.2	−29.1
Reserve assets	−10.9	−5.3	−37.8	−2.1	−9.4	−1.9	−7.2	−21.6	−21.9	−14.6
Errors and omissions, net	−2.4	−0.7	−3.9	−7.2	−3.1	−7.8	−5.1	−7.5	1.6	0.3

Table 33 (concluded)

	1993	1994	1995	1996	1997	1998	1999	2000	2001	2002
Capital flows										
Total capital flows, net[3]	18.7	−6.6	45.0	24.9	36.2	37.9	14.1	1.6	6.4	9.6
Net official flows	−1.1	−12.2	−7.1	2.6	32.9	17.2	0.5	−0.4	1.3	3.1
Net private flows[4]	19.7	5.7	52.1	22.3	3.2	20.7	13.6	2.0	5.1	6.4
Direct investment, net	6.0	5.3	13.1	12.4	15.6	21.6	23.6	22.7	26.9	31.3
Private portfolio investment, net	8.7	17.1	14.6	13.4	8.0	4.0	2.8	4.3	5.0	4.3
Other private flows, net	5.0	−16.8	24.5	−3.6	−20.3	−4.9	−12.8	−25.0	−26.7	−29.1
External financing[5]										
Net external financing[6]	19.0	13.4	31.8	35.3	74.9	56.6	42.4	24.4	34.2	39.6
Nondebt-creating flows	9.8	16.3	12.7	14.7	21.4	24.5	24.4	25.9	29.4	34.1
Capital transfers[7]	2.5	10.3	−1.6	1.2	0.3	0.4	0.2	—	—	−0.1
Foreign direct investment and equity security liabilities[8]	7.2	6.1	14.3	13.5	21.1	24.2	24.2	25.9	29.4	34.2
Net external borrowing[9]	9.2	−2.9	19.1	20.6	53.5	32.1	18.0	−1.5	4.8	5.5
Borrowing from official creditors[10]	2.0	−6.8	−3.8	2.9	32.9	17.2	0.4	−0.4	1.2	3.1
Of which,										
Credit and loans from IMF[11]	3.7	2.4	4.7	3.7	2.5	5.5	−3.6	−4.2	. . .	. . .
Borrowing from banks[12]	5.6	3.8	−2.2	4.6	4.5	5.4	−1.6	—	1.0	2.2
Borrowing from other private creditors	1.6	0.1	25.0	13.1	16.1	9.5	19.1	−1.0	2.5	0.2
Memorandum										
Balance on goods and services in percent of GDP[13]	−0.8	0.2	−0.3	−0.9	−0.9	−1.0	0.2	1.8	1.0	0.4
Scheduled amortization of external debt	25.3	23.9	26.6	25.6	19.3	23.1	27.4	30.6	29.7	31.0
Gross external financing[14]	44.3	37.3	58.4	60.9	94.2	79.7	69.8	55.1	63.9	70.6
Gross external borrowing[15]	34.5	21.0	45.7	46.2	72.8	55.2	45.4	29.2	34.5	36.5
Exceptional external financing, net	20.4	18.8	17.3	13.6	−20.9	7.8	7.6	5.2	0.4	0.3
Of which,										
Arrears on debt service	0.5	3.8	−0.5	1.1	−24.8	5.0	1.8	1.6	. . .	. . .
Debt forgiveness	2.1	—	0.9	0.9	—	—	—	—	. . .	. . .
Rescheduling of debt service	1.4	13.3	13.9	9.9	3.3	2.4	4.7	3.7	. . .	. . .

[1]Standard presentation in accordance with the 5th edition of the International Monetary Fund's *Balance of Payments Manual* (1993).

[2]Comprises capital transfers—including debt forgiveness—and acquisition/disposal of nonproduced, nonfinancial assets.

[3]Comprise net direct investment, net portfolio investment, and other long- and short-term net investment flows, including official and private borrowing. In the standard balance of payments presentation above, total net capital flows are equal to the balance on financial account minus the change in reserve assets.

[4]Because of limitations on the data coverage for net official flows, the residually derived data for net private flows may include some official flows.

[5]As defined in the *World Economic Outlook* (see footnote 6). It should be noted that there is no generally accepted standard definition of external financing.

[6]Defined as the sum of—with opposite sign—the goods and services balance, net income and current transfers, direct investment abroad, the change in reserve assets, the net acquisition of other assets (such as recorded private portfolio assets, export credit, and the collateral for debt-reduction operations), and the net errors and omissions. Thus, net external financing, according to the definition adopted in the *World Economic Outlook*, measures the total amount required to finance the current account, direct investment outflows, net reserve transactions (often at the discretion of the monetary authorities), the net acquisition of nonreserve external assets, and the net transactions underlying the errors and omissions (not infrequently reflecting capital flight).

[7]Including other transactions on capital account.

[8]Debt-creating foreign direct investment liabilities are not included.

[9]Net disbursement of long- and short-term credits, including exceptional financing, by both official and private creditors.

[10]Net disbursement by official creditors, based on directly reported flows and flows derived from information on external debt.

[11]Comprise use of International Monetary Fund resources under the General Resources Account, Trust Fund, and Poverty Reduction and Growth Facility (PRGF). For further detail, see Table 37.

[12]Net disbursement by commercial banks, based on directly reported flows and cross-border claims and liabilities reported in the International Banking section of the International Monetary Fund's *International Financial Statistics*.

[13]This is often referred to as the "resource balance" and, with opposite sign, the "net resource transfer."

[14]Net external financing plus amortization due on external debt.

[15]Net external borrowing plus amortization due on external debt.

Table 34. Developing Countries—by Region: Balance of Payments and External Financing[1]
(Billions of U.S. dollars)

	1993	1994	1995	1996	1997	1998	1999	2000	2001	2002
Africa										
Balance of payments										
Balance on current account	−11.3	−11.8	−16.6	−6.0	−7.8	−20.6	−15.5	2.1	−3.9	−6.4
Balance on capital account	3.2	2.5	2.9	7.0	8.3	3.4	4.2	3.0	4.3	9.9
Balance on financial account	10.1	10.9	14.4	1.2	0.3	15.3	9.0	−10.1	0.1	−4.4
Change in reserves (− = increase)	2.8	−5.7	−1.9	−9.1	−10.6	1.9	−3.6	−13.3	−10.5	−9.3
Other official flows, net	4.4	3.2	4.1	−2.5	2.1	3.6	1.8	−0.3	−0.1	−7.1
Private flows, net	2.9	13.4	12.2	12.7	8.8	9.8	10.8	3.5	10.8	12.0
External financing										
Net external financing	10.9	19.5	24.4	20.7	27.7	25.6	26.2	13.8	24.1	23.8
Nondebt-creating inflows	6.9	6.9	11.1	15.3	24.8	20.7	23.2	13.5	23.1	28.0
Net external borrowing	4.0	12.6	13.3	5.4	2.9	4.9	3.0	0.3	1.0	−4.2
From official creditors	4.5	3.2	4.5	−2.2	2.2	3.9	2.0	0.1	0.4	−6.7
Of which,										
Credit and loans from IMF	0.2	0.9	0.8	0.6	−0.5	−0.4	−0.2	−0.1	. . .	. . .
From banks	−0.2	2.4	1.1	0.4	0.4	3.5	0.7	—	−0.7	0.7
From other private creditors	−0.3	6.9	7.7	7.2	0.3	−2.5	0.3	0.2	1.2	1.7
Memorandum										
Exceptional financing	9.8	14.7	11.7	13.6	11.3	2.2	8.4	6.3	7.5	2.1
Sub-Sahara										
Balance of payments										
Balance on current account	−10.3	−8.6	−12.4	−6.8	−10.6	−18.9	−14.9	−5.5	−9.4	−9.8
Balance on capital account	3.2	2.5	3.0	6.9	8.3	3.3	3.9	3.0	4.3	9.9
Balance on financial account	8.9	7.7	10.4	2.1	2.9	13.7	7.8	−2.0	5.6	−1.1
Change in reserves (− = increase)	3.1	−3.7	−3.3	−6.3	−5.5	0.9	−4.0	−6.2	−3.3	−6.4
Other official flows, net	4.1	3.5	4.5	−2.2	3.1	4.0	2.3	0.6	0.5	−6.2
Private flows, net	1.7	7.9	9.2	10.6	5.4	8.9	9.4	3.6	8.4	11.5
External financing										
Net external financing	9.5	15.2	22.3	19.3	26.0	24.9	25.7	14.8	22.3	24.0
Nondebt-creating inflows	5.8	5.7	10.4	14.2	23.1	19.2	21.5	12.3	18.9	25.1
Net external borrowing	3.7	9.5	11.8	5.1	2.9	5.7	4.2	2.5	3.4	−1.2
From official creditors	4.2	3.5	4.9	−1.9	3.1	4.3	2.5	1.0	1.1	−5.7
Of which,										
Credit and loans from IMF	0.7	0.5	0.6	0.1	−0.5	−0.3	−0.1	—	. . .	. . .
From banks	−0.3	2.4	1.2	0.5	0.3	3.5	−0.1	−0.1	−0.7	0.7
From other private creditors	−0.1	3.6	5.8	6.5	−0.5	−2.1	1.8	1.6	3.0	3.8
Memorandum										
Exceptional financing	9.8	9.0	5.7	9.0	7.7	1.1	7.8	6.3	7.4	2.1
Developing Asia										
Balance of payments										
Balance on current account	−33.0	−18.9	−42.5	−38.8	8.8	47.1	46.3	45.8	22.0	8.7
Balance on capital account	1.3	2.4	3.3	3.7	3.6	2.4	1.4	0.7	2.0	3.3
Balance on financial account	41.8	28.2	60.3	64.0	27.5	−30.6	−36.0	−32.1	−16.9	−5.1
Change in reserves (− = increase)	−24.7	−44.0	−31.7	−37.5	−20.5	−16.5	−30.1	−18.2	−20.9	−21.7
Other official flows, net	11.4	12.2	8.0	−0.9	4.1	12.7	16.8	4.6	12.4	10.1
Private flows, net	55.0	60.0	84.0	102.5	43.9	−26.9	−22.6	−18.4	−8.4	6.5
External financing										
Net external financing	75.2	76.3	94.4	106.4	96.5	42.0	51.8	61.0	75.3	92.8
Nondebt-creating inflows	48.5	48.5	65.3	77.4	67.6	57.7	41.1	58.8	52.1	62.9
Net external borrowing	26.7	27.9	29.2	29.0	28.9	−15.7	10.7	2.2	23.1	29.9
From official creditors	10.9	11.6	6.8	−1.8	3.5	12.4	16.2	4.0	11.8	9.8
Of which,										
Credit and loans from IMF	0.6	−0.8	−1.5	−1.7	5.0	6.6	1.7	0.9	. . .	. . .
From banks	11.2	10.8	14.6	19.8	22.2	1.9	−11.0	−1.7	6.3	8.9
From other private creditors	4.6	5.5	7.7	11.1	3.1	−29.9	5.5	—	5.0	11.2
Memorandum										
Exceptional financing	1.7	1.2	0.4	0.7	0.5	14.0	14.8	15.9	16.0	13.6

Table 34 *(concluded)*

	1993	1994	1995	1996	1997	1998	1999	2000	2001	2002
Excluding China and India										
Balance of payments										
Balance on current account	−19.4	−24.9	−38.5	−40.0	−25.1	22.5	33.8	29.4	14.5	10.9
Balance on capital account	1.3	2.4	3.3	3.7	3.6	2.4	1.4	0.7	2.0	3.3
Balance on financial account	17.4	26.0	39.4	47.7	37.9	−23.5	−38.3	−27.0	−14.6	−12.3
Change in reserves (− = increase)	−18.4	−4.1	−11.3	−3.2	19.9	−7.4	−15.6	−1.6	1.7	−4.9
Other official flows, net	5.5	3.4	4.1	−3.2	2.6	7.1	9.7	2.8	7.7	2.6
Private flows, net	30.3	26.7	46.6	54.1	15.5	−23.2	−32.5	−28.2	−24.0	−9.9
External financing										
Net external financing	35.4	28.0	48.9	49.3	22.1	−3.3	−4.1	−0.5	7.0	16.8
Nondebt-creating inflows	19.1	9.3	25.5	30.7	14.8	12.9	−1.5	1.6	−1.1	11.0
Net external borrowing	16.3	18.7	23.4	18.6	7.3	−16.1	−2.6	−2.1	8.1	5.8
From official creditors	5.0	2.8	2.9	−4.1	2.0	6.8	9.2	2.2	7.1	2.2
Of which,										
Credit and loans from IMF	0.1	0.4	−0.3	−0.4	5.7	7.0	2.1	0.9	...	...
From banks	4.1	7.1	8.9	15.8	14.9	−1.0	−9.2	−4.8	0.8	0.6
From other private creditors	7.2	8.8	11.5	6.8	−9.5	−21.9	−2.6	0.6	0.2	3.0
Memorandum										
Exceptional financing	1.7	1.2	0.4	0.7	0.5	14.0	14.8	15.9	16.0	13.6
Middle East, Malta, and Turkey										
Balance of payments										
Balance on current account	−28.8	−2.8	—	10.5	6.7	−23.0	15.0	60.9	62.2	37.0
Balance on capital account	1.4	1.3	2.1	0.7	0.4	0.4	1.1	1.9	0.2	0.2
Balance on financial account	32.8	13.7	−1.3	−6.0	5.9	26.0	−7.4	−51.3	−53.3	−29.4
Change in reserves (− = increase)	2.6	−4.6	−10.3	−18.6	−11.4	12.5	−5.2	−24.5	−26.6	−22.1
Other official flows, net	2.7	0.6	2.5	1.8	0.6	2.4	0.9	0.7	8.1	−5.3
Private flows, net	27.4	17.7	6.5	10.9	16.8	11.2	−3.2	−27.6	−34.9	−2.0
External financing										
Net external financing	27.6	3.9	9.8	21.6	23.0	15.3	7.2	8.4	−10.7	4.9
Nondebt-creating inflows	5.8	6.2	6.9	7.5	4.7	4.5	4.8	8.2	3.8	10.4
Net external borrowing	21.7	−2.3	2.9	14.1	18.3	10.9	2.3	0.1	−14.5	−5.5
From official creditors	1.1	−1.2	−0.1	0.1	−0.8	−1.1	−1.8	3.3	11.0	−3.9
Of which,										
Credit and loans from IMF	—	0.4	0.4	0.1	0.2	−0.1	0.6	3.4	...	...
From banks	1.0	−8.8	−0.3	−3.0	1.0	6.5	5.0	2.8	−8.5	−1.6
From other private creditors	19.6	7.7	3.3	16.9	18.1	5.5	−0.9	−6.0	−17.0	—
Memorandum										
Exceptional financing	13.2	4.2	3.3	1.0	0.3	0.4	0.2	0.1	0.5	0.1
Western Hemisphere										
Balance of payments										
Balance on current account	−45.9	−52.0	−37.1	−39.8	−66.8	−90.4	−56.3	−48.6	−57.9	−62.4
Balance on capital account	0.6	—	0.5	1.2	1.3	1.2	1.8	1.4	1.4	1.2
Balance on financial account	47.1	54.3	36.1	40.6	70.5	96.5	59.2	41.6	56.2	61.1
Change in reserves (− = increase)	−20.7	4.0	−23.3	−29.0	−13.8	8.7	7.6	−3.1	6.0	−2.9
Other official flows, net	30.4	7.8	17.8	5.8	16.0	15.1	7.0	8.1	11.2	6.2
Private flows, net	37.4	42.4	41.6	63.8	68.3	72.7	44.6	36.7	39.0	57.8
External financing										
Net external financing	81.5	68.1	84.5	93.5	98.5	104.5	77.4	66.9	94.6	80.7
Nondebt-creating inflows	36.0	39.6	32.1	53.4	72.0	62.6	71.8	68.0	74.7	59.4
Net external borrowing	45.5	28.5	52.4	40.1	26.5	41.9	5.6	−1.0	20.0	21.2
From official creditors	32.0	9.0	21.3	11.6	9.0	14.5	11.8	3.3	5.2	7.0
Of which,										
Credit and loans from IMF	−0.9	−1.3	12.9	−2.0	−4.0	2.5	−0.9	−10.7	...	...
From banks	5.2	−32.1	5.8	5.3	5.0	15.2	2.1	6.3	4.8	5.4
From other private creditors	8.3	51.6	25.3	23.2	12.5	12.1	−8.4	−10.6	10.0	8.8
Memorandum										
Exceptional financing	8.9	0.1	4.1	4.9	3.5	1.2	2.0	−0.5	0.3	0.3

[1]For definitions, see footnotes to Table 33.

Table 35. Developing Countries—by Analytical Criteria: Balance of Payments and External Financing[1]
(Billions of U.S. dollars)

	1993	1994	1995	1996	1997	1998	1999	2000	2001	2002
By source of export earnings										
Fuel										
Balance of payments										
Balance on current account	−23.6	−3.2	2.8	31.0	20.3	−29.6	19.0	97.9	73.3	49.6
Balance on capital account	0.3	0.5	1.0	4.0	−0.2	0.1	0.8	1.9	−0.1	0.7
Balance on financial account	31.9	22.3	4.2	−27.7	−7.0	31.0	−6.9	−88.8	−63.4	−43.1
Change in reserves (− = increase)	10.4	1.0	0.7	−22.4	−13.7	19.2	5.4	−38.4	−31.6	−24.5
Other official flows, net	4.2	6.4	6.2	0.5	5.4	6.2	1.7	−1.6	−4.2	−3.9
Private flows, net	17.3	14.9	−2.7	−5.7	1.4	5.6	−14.0	−48.7	−27.6	−14.7
External financing										
Net external financing	16.0	13.1	3.6	9.9	13.8	15.4	—	−6.3	−6.9	−1.6
Nondebt-creating inflows	2.0	3.7	3.7	10.9	6.3	8.1	9.1	12.1	11.7	12.7
Net external borrowing	14.0	9.4	−0.1	−1.0	7.5	7.3	−9.1	−18.4	−18.6	−14.3
From official creditors	3.5	4.9	2.9	0.4	2.8	1.6	1.5	−0.4	−1.9	−2.4
Of which,										
Credit and loans from IMF	−0.8	0.4	−0.2	0.7	−0.3	−0.6	−0.5	−0.6	. . .	. . .
From banks	1.5	−1.2	−2.6	−6.9	−1.5	7.5	2.2	−0.8	−2.2	−1.4
From other private creditors	9.0	5.7	−0.4	5.5	6.2	−1.8	−12.8	−17.3	−14.5	−10.6
Memorandum										
Exceptional financing	16.4	12.8	11.9	9.8	7.4	5.2	4.0	2.6	2.2	—
Nonfuel										
Balance of payments										
Balance on current account	−95.5	−82.5	−98.9	−105.2	−79.4	−57.2	−29.5	−37.7	−50.9	−72.6
Balance on capital account	6.1	5.8	7.8	8.5	13.7	7.3	7.6	5.1	8.0	14.0
Balance on financial account	99.9	84.8	105.3	127.5	111.2	76.2	31.7	36.9	49.5	65.4
Change in reserves (− = increase)	−50.3	−51.3	−67.9	−71.8	−42.5	−12.5	−36.7	−20.6	−20.3	−31.5
Other official flows, net	44.8	17.4	26.2	3.7	17.4	27.6	24.8	14.7	35.7	7.8
Private flows, net	105.5	118.7	147.0	195.6	136.3	61.2	43.6	42.8	34.1	89.0
External financing										
Net external financing	179.1	154.8	209.5	232.3	231.8	172.0	162.7	156.5	190.3	203.7
Nondebt-creating inflows	95.2	97.5	111.7	142.7	162.8	137.4	131.9	136.4	142.0	147.9
Net external borrowing	83.9	57.3	97.8	89.6	69.0	34.7	30.8	20.0	48.3	55.8
From official creditors	45.1	17.6	29.6	7.4	11.2	28.1	26.7	11.0	30.3	8.6
Of which,										
Credit and loans from IMF	0.6	−1.2	12.8	−3.6	1.2	9.1	1.8	−6.0	. . .	. . .
From banks	15.6	−26.4	23.8	29.4	30.1	19.6	−5.3	8.2	4.2	14.8
From other private creditors	23.2	66.1	44.4	52.9	27.7	−13.1	9.4	0.8	13.8	32.4
Memorandum										
Exceptional financing	17.2	7.3	7.7	10.4	8.2	12.6	21.4	19.4	22.2	16.0
By external financing source										
Net debtor countries										
Balance of payments										
Balance on current account	−103.9	−78.3	−98.3	−87.3	−70.3	−71.5	−24.4	2.5	−27.8	−56.4
Balance on capital account	6.7	6.5	9.0	12.7	13.6	7.3	7.7	5.0	7.8	14.5
Balance on financial account	109.1	87.3	102.6	103.4	109.7	88.9	27.8	−0.1	29.3	48.9
Change in reserves (− = increase)	−48.1	−52.3	−67.5	−85.9	−47.8	−5.4	−35.3	−40.4	−33.0	−43.8
Other official flows, net	47.2	21.9	29.6	2.0	21.6	30.5	24.8	16.6	34.8	5.6
Private flows, net	110.0	117.7	140.5	187.3	135.9	63.8	38.4	23.8	27.4	87.1
External financing										
Net external financing	186.9	160.7	212.4	232.6	241.0	182.8	164.5	153.1	194.1	207.5
Nondebt-creating inflows	97.4	101.1	115.7	153.6	169.3	145.5	140.3	145.5	152.5	158.4
Net external borrowing	89.5	59.6	96.8	79.0	71.7	37.3	24.2	7.7	41.6	49.1
From official creditors	48.4	22.4	32.3	7.3	14.0	29.9	29.1	11.5	28.7	6.5
Of which,										
Credit and loans from IMF	−0.1	−0.8	12.6	−2.9	0.8	8.5	1.3	−6.5	. . .	. . .
From banks	14.2	−27.8	20.2	23.3	26.9	24.6	−5.4	7.2	2.8	14.6
From other private creditors	26.9	65.0	44.2	48.4	30.8	−17.1	0.5	−11.0	10.2	28.0
Memorandum										
Exceptional financing	33.6	20.1	19.6	20.2	15.6	17.8	25.4	21.9	24.4	16.0

Table 35 *(continued)*

	1993	1994	1995	1996	1997	1998	1999	2000	2001	2002
Official financing										
Balance of payments										
Balance on current account	−8.1	−9.9	−11.8	−8.7	−5.0	−10.7	−6.3	2.6	−2.0	−6.8
Balance on capital account	4.8	5.2	6.3	6.9	12.3	5.9	6.3	4.5	7.0	12.9
Balance on financial account	2.0	3.9	5.9	1.6	−7.2	5.4	0.5	−7.6	−4.7	−5.9
Change in reserves (− = increase)	−0.1	−3.4	−0.1	−3.1	−5.7	1.7	−0.7	−9.8	−8.7	−6.1
Other official flows, net	3.6	4.2	5.2	2.0	6.3	4.4	2.5	1.7	4.0	−1.5
Private flows, net	−1.5	3.1	0.9	2.6	−7.9	−0.7	−1.3	0.5	−0.1	1.7
External financing										
Net external financing	7.1	12.0	12.9	10.6	10.0	9.2	7.5	6.1	10.7	12.5
Nondebt-creating inflows	5.0	7.4	8.7	10.1	15.9	9.7	10.3	8.7	12.4	19.5
Net external borrowing	2.1	4.6	4.2	0.5	−5.9	−0.5	−2.8	−2.7	−1.7	−7.0
From official creditors	3.6	4.0	5.0	1.8	6.2	4.3	2.4	1.6	3.9	−1.7
Of which,										
Credit and loans from IMF	−0.5	1.1	1.1	0.9	0.2	—	—	−0.1	. . .	. . .
From banks	−0.8	—	0.5	1.1	1.2	0.1	—	0.1	0.4	1.0
From other private creditors	−0.6	0.6	−1.3	−2.5	−13.3	−4.9	−5.2	−4.4	−6.0	−6.3
Memorandum										
Exceptional financing	6.4	12.4	10.4	11.3	6.4	4.1	3.8	2.3	3.6	1.5
Net debtor countries by debt-servicing experience										
Countries with arrears and/or rescheduling during 1994–98										
Balance of payments										
Balance on current account	−28.2	−18.6	−45.6	−42.0	−49.7	−58.9	−23.4	7.6	−15.7	−23.8
Balance on capital account	4.3	4.6	7.0	10.2	11.3	5.1	4.9	2.8	5.4	12.0
Balance on financial account	25.8	25.3	38.8	39.0	55.5	59.6	22.1	−7.8	16.2	14.2
Change in reserves (− = increase)	−9.7	−16.3	−22.7	−22.0	−2.9	8.5	0.8	−24.6	−14.0	−13.1
Other official flows, net	3.2	2.2	2.8	−8.9	4.1	11.4	13.1	−1.9	4.6	−3.8
Private flows, net	32.4	39.5	58.8	69.9	54.4	39.7	8.2	18.7	25.5	31.0
External financing										
Net external financing	40.5	46.2	73.1	73.3	68.8	59.8	43.5	44.8	61.4	63.9
Nondebt-creating inflows	20.3	27.4	31.6	50.3	49.1	47.4	41.2	46.3	46.1	52.5
Net external borrowing	20.2	18.8	41.5	23.0	19.7	12.3	2.3	−1.5	15.2	11.4
From official creditors	3.1	2.0	2.5	−9.1	4.0	11.3	13.1	−1.8	4.8	−3.5
Of which,										
Credit and loans from IMF	−0.8	1.0	0.5	0.7	3.9	10.9	5.6	−5.3	. . .	. . .
From banks	−3.4	−37.0	4.7	8.3	14.3	11.6	−6.7	−1.0	2.4	3.5
From other private creditors	20.5	53.9	34.2	23.8	1.5	−10.6	−4.1	1.3	8.0	11.4
Memorandum										
Exceptional financing	31.5	19.1	19.1	19.8	15.0	16.0	21.8	18.1	19.6	12.6
Other groups										
Heavily indebted poor countries										
Balance of payments										
Balance on current account	−13.8	−10.2	−12.4	−12.8	−14.8	−16.3	−12.9	−9.1	−12.1	−14.3
Balance on capital account	3.4	4.2	5.6	10.2	11.3	4.8	4.9	3.0	6.0	12.5
Balance on financial account	8.9	5.9	6.0	1.8	2.7	11.6	6.8	5.4	6.3	1.9
Change in reserves (− = increase)	1.5	−2.7	−0.9	−3.2	−0.1	1.6	−2.7	−2.6	−3.1	−3.1
Other official flows, net	3.0	2.4	4.1	−2.2	4.3	4.9	3.3	2.7	3.0	−4.1
Private flows, net	4.4	6.2	2.9	7.2	−1.5	5.2	6.2	5.3	6.4	9.1
External financing										
Net external financing	11.0	12.3	14.8	15.7	15.0	16.1	16.3	12.0	17.3	19.1
Nondebt-creating inflows	5.7	7.2	9.5	14.8	17.2	11.0	12.1	8.8	12.5	20.4
Net external borrowing	5.3	5.1	5.3	0.9	−2.2	5.1	4.1	3.2	4.8	−1.3
From official creditors	3.2	2.7	4.8	−1.6	4.6	5.3	3.6	3.1	3.4	−3.8
Of which,										
Credit and loans from IMF	−0.2	0.5	0.6	0.3	—	0.2	0.2	0.1	. . .	. . .
From banks	−0.1	1.2	1.0	1.6	0.7	—	0.2	0.1	0.4	1.0
From other private creditors	2.3	1.2	−0.5	0.9	−7.5	−0.2	0.2	—	0.9	1.5
Memorandum										
Exceptional financing	9.3	8.7	5.9	10.7	5.1	−1.1	5.9	4.2	5.7	2.2

Table 35 *(concluded)*

	1993	1994	1995	1996	1997	1998	1999	2000	2001	2002
Middle East and north Africa										
Balance of payments										
Balance on current account	−25.0	−11.4	−4.7	12.4	10.5	−28.6	14.2	77.2	61.2	39.6
Balance on capital account	1.4	1.3	2.0	0.8	0.4	0.5	1.3	1.9	0.2	0.3
Balance on financial account	26.6	23.3	4.4	−10.0	−0.5	29.7	−4.2	−68.2	−52.5	−32.2
Change in reserves (− = increase)	2.8	−5.7	−4.3	−17.0	−13.0	13.9	1.3	−31.3	−32.9	−24.1
Other official flows, net	0.5	1.5	2.4	2.2	—	3.0	1.6	−4.3	−3.9	−2.7
Private flows, net	23.2	27.5	6.3	4.9	12.5	12.8	−7.1	−32.5	−15.7	−5.4
External financing										
Net external financing	16.9	16.7	7.5	14.8	14.4	12.9	−1.2	−4.6	−5.7	2.2
Nondebt-creating inflows	5.4	5.8	6.3	7.1	5.3	5.3	5.6	8.7	8.8	10.2
Net external borrowing	11.4	10.9	1.2	7.7	9.1	7.6	−6.8	−13.3	−14.5	−8.0
From official creditors	−1.1	−0.3	−0.2	0.5	−1.4	−0.4	−1.1	−1.7	−1.0	−1.3
Of which,										
Credit and loans from IMF	−0.5	0.5	0.2	0.6	0.3	−0.1	—	−0.1	. . .	. . .
From banks	−1.4	−1.7	−2.3	−6.1	−1.2	3.2	3.2	−0.8	−1.7	−1.7
From other private creditors	14.0	12.9	3.7	13.2	11.7	4.8	−8.9	−10.8	−11.8	−5.0
Memorandum										
Exceptional financing	13.4	10.0	9.5	6.9	5.4	2.9	2.4	1.7	2.1	1.5

[1]For definitions, see footnotes to Table 33.

Table 36. Developing Countries: Reserves[1]

	1993	1994	1995	1996	1997	1998	1999	2000	2001	2002
					Billions of U.S. dollars					
Developing countries	**324.8**	**380.2**	**448.2**	**541.1**	**591.3**	**604.2**	**641.3**	**684.8**	**736.8**	**792.5**
Regional groups										
Africa	19.7	24.7	26.6	31.2	41.9	39.6	39.7	50.4	61.0	70.1
Sub-Sahara	13.4	15.9	19.0	21.0	27.6	26.2	26.9	31.1	34.4	40.7
Developing Asia	125.5	174.3	200.8	246.5	264.9	289.8	322.9	330.8	351.6	373.3
Excluding China and India	91.8	100.4	106.2	118.0	96.3	112.1	131.3	123.5	121.8	126.6
Middle East, Malta, and Turkey	70.0	75.9	90.6	106.7	114.2	113.5	124.7	147.1	173.7	195.7
Western Hemisphere	109.6	105.4	130.3	156.8	170.2	161.3	154.1	156.5	150.5	153.4
Analytical groups										
By source of export earnings										
Fuel	51.5	53.4	55.8	74.4	86.4	80.0	84.0	120.8	152.5	176.8
Nonfuel	273.3	326.9	392.4	466.8	504.9	524.2	557.4	564.0	584.3	615.7
of which, primary products	39.8	48.9	53.8	58.3	62.1	59.0	59.7	59.4	63.5	68.1
By external financing source										
Net debtor countries	300.3	355.5	419.4	504.5	552.2	567.0	596.9	628.0	661.0	704.6
of which, official financing	27.6	30.7	30.8	33.2	37.2	35.1	34.7	43.4	52.0	58.1
Net debtor countries by debt-servicing experience										
Countries with arrears and/or rescheduling during 1994–98	93.2	110.6	128.7	155.2	152.6	148.3	146.2	165.2	179.2	192.1
Other groups										
Heavily indebted poor countries	22.2	24.2	26.7	28.3	28.9	27.9	29.9	31.3	34.5	37.5
Middle East and north Africa	68.6	75.7	84.2	99.0	108.6	106.0	112.7	142.9	175.8	199.9
					Ratio of reserves to imports of goods and services[2]					
Developing countries	**38.6**	**41.5**	**41.4**	**45.2**	**45.9**	**49.7**	**52.3**	**47.5**	**49.0**	**48.5**
Regional groups										
Africa	19.0	22.7	20.4	23.6	30.6	29.1	29.1	34.9	40.1	43.6
Sub-Sahara	17.0	19.5	19.4	20.6	25.7	24.9	25.9	28.0	29.7	33.2
Developing Asia	37.9	44.1	40.8	45.4	47.1	59.5	60.9	50.4	50.6	48.7
Excluding China and India	45.2	40.9	34.4	35.4	28.3	42.5	47.3	37.4	36.5	35.2
Middle East, Malta, and Turkey	34.5	42.7	44.2	45.1	45.1	46.4	53.1	54.5	64.3	67.4
Western Hemisphere	53.8	45.0	51.0	55.0	50.9	46.3	47.4	42.1	38.9	36.7
Analytical groups										
By source of export earnings										
Fuel	28.9	34.0	32.0	38.5	41.5	40.1	42.7	54.2	63.2	69.3
Nonfuel	41.2	43.1	43.2	46.5	46.8	51.6	54.1	46.3	46.2	44.6
of which, primary products	63.8	71.0	62.6	61.9	61.6	59.8	64.8	59.3	60.4	59.3
By external financing source										
Net debtor countries	40.7	43.3	42.7	46.8	47.5	51.6	53.5	47.6	48.1	47.0
of which, official financing	53.0	53.6	45.1	45.7	51.0	46.6	44.9	51.1	56.4	57.4
Net debtor countries by debt-servicing experience										
Countries with arrears and/or rescheduling during 1994–98	44.0	48.5	45.4	49.0	43.7	45.5	46.9	47.0	48.3	48.0
Other groups										
Heavily indebted poor countries	47.4	50.0	45.4	43.0	41.3	39.3	41.6	40.0	41.5	41.1
Middle East and north Africa	35.4	42.4	43.0	45.6	48.0	48.1	51.7	59.4	69.3	74.1

[1]In this table, official holdings of gold are valued at SDR 35 an ounce. This convention results in a marked underestimate of reserves for countries that have substantial gold holdings.
[2]Reserves at year-end in percent of imports of goods and services for the year indicated.

Table 37. Net Credit and Loans from IMF[1]

(Billions of U.S. dollars)

	1992	1993	1994	1995	1996	1997	1998	1999	2000
Advanced economies	**0.3**	—	—	**−0.1**	**−0.1**	**11.3**	**5.2**	**−10.3**	—
Newly industrialized Asian economies	—	—	—	—	—	11.3	5.2	−10.3	—
Developing countries	**−0.4**	**−0.1**	**−0.8**	**12.6**	**−2.9**	**0.8**	**8.5**	**1.3**	**−6.7**
Regional groups									
Africa	−0.2	0.2	0.9	0.8	0.6	−0.5	−0.4	−0.2	−0.1
Sub-Sahara	—	0.7	0.5	0.6	0.1	−0.5	−0.3	−0.1	—
Developing Asia	1.3	0.6	−0.8	−1.5	−1.7	5.0	6.6	1.7	0.9
Excluding China and India	0.1	0.1	0.4	−0.3	−0.4	5.7	7.0	2.1	0.9
Middle East, Malta, and Turkey	0.1	—	0.4	0.4	0.1	0.2	−0.1	0.6	3.3
Western Hemisphere	−1.6	−0.9	−1.3	12.9	−2.0	−4.0	2.5	−0.9	−10.7
Analytical groups									
By source of export earnings									
Fuel	−0.5	−0.8	0.4	−0.2	0.7	−0.3	−0.6	−0.5	−0.6
Nonfuel	—	0.6	−1.2	12.8	−3.6	1.2	9.1	1.8	−6.1
of which, primary products	—	−0.1	0.2	0.4	0.1	—	—	—	−0.2
By external financing source									
Net debtor countries	−0.4	−0.1	−0.8	12.6	−2.9	0.8	8.5	1.3	−6.7
of which, official financing	−0.1	−0.5	1.1	1.1	0.9	0.2	—	—	—
Net debtor countries by debt-servicing experience									
Countries with arrears and/or rescheduling during 1994–98	−1.0	−0.8	1.0	0.5	0.7	3.9	10.9	5.6	−5.5
Other groups									
Heavily indebted poor countries	−0.1	−0.2	0.5	0.6	0.3	—	0.2	0.2	—
Middle East and north Africa	−0.1	−0.5	0.5	0.2	0.6	0.3	−0.1	—	−0.3
Countries in transition	**1.6**	**3.7**	**2.4**	**4.7**	**3.7**	**2.5**	**5.5**	**−3.6**	**−4.2**
Central and eastern Europe	0.5	2.0	0.2	−2.7	−0.8	0.4	−0.4	—	−0.1
Commonwealth of Independent States and Mongolia	1.0	1.9	2.3	7.5	4.5	2.1	5.8	−3.6	−4.1
Russia	1.0	1.5	1.5	5.5	3.2	1.5	5.3	−3.6	−2.9
Excluding Russia	—	0.3	0.7	2.0	1.3	0.5	0.5	—	−1.2
Memorandum									
Total									
Net credit provided under:									
General Resources Account	0.644	3.374	0.594	15.633	0.291	14.355	18.811	−12.856	−10.741
Trust Fund	—	−0.060	−0.014	−0.015	—	−0.007	−0.001	−0.001	—
PRGF	0.733	0.253	0.998	1.619	0.325	0.179	0.374	0.194	−0.119
Disbursements at year-end under:[2]									
General Resources Account	31.217	34.503	37.276	53.275	51.824	62.703	84.961	69.913	55.756
Trust Fund	0.217	0.157	0.153	0.141	0.137	0.121	0.126	0.122	0.116
PRGF	5.041	5.285	6.634	8.342	8.392	8.049	8.788	8.761	8.199

[1]Includes net disbursements from programs under the General Resources Account, Trust Fund and Poverty Reduction and Growth Facility (formerly ESAF-Enhanced Structural Adjustment Facility). The data are on a transactions basis, with conversion to U.S. dollar values at annual average exchange rates.
[2]Converted to U.S. dollar values at end-of-period exchange rates.

Table 38. Summary of External Debt and Debt Service

	1993	1994	1995	1996	1997	1998	1999	2000	2001	2002
					Billions of U.S. dollars					
External debt										
Developing countries	**1,538.6**	**1,658.0**	**1,808.9**	**1,880.6**	**1,966.5**	**2,101.5**	**2,166.3**	**2,140.6**	**2,155.4**	**2,186.4**
Regional groups										
Africa	267.8	287.8	304.1	302.3	292.8	291.4	290.8	285.1	275.1	268.0
Developing Asia	466.7	519.2	579.1	615.1	660.5	681.9	715.8	693.5	697.0	711.1
Middle East, Malta, and Turkey	278.5	285.7	306.1	317.2	342.6	376.5	392.9	409.7	416.9	426.0
Western Hemisphere	525.6	565.4	619.6	646.0	670.7	751.7	766.9	752.2	766.3	781.3
Analytical groups										
By external financing source										
Net debtor countries	1,499.1	1,618.6	1,765.0	1,833.4	1,905.5	2,026.4	2,087.2	2,061.9	2,077.0	2,107.6
of which, official financing	161.6	175.6	182.4	181.2	171.9	173.2	171.6	163.2	161.3	155.8
Net debtor countries by debt-servicing experience										
Countries with arrears and/or rescheduling during 1994–98	683.6	727.4	767.0	797.8	826.5	882.0	914.4	898.5	900.8	907.1
Countries in transition	**236.3**	**260.1**	**276.1**	**299.1**	**308.6**	**360.4**	**358.4**	**358.9**	**367.0**	**374.7**
Central and eastern Europe	113.1	114.7	125.5	138.1	144.6	167.6	172.6	177.0	186.1	195.6
Commonwealth of Independent States and Mongolia	123.2	145.4	150.7	161.0	164.0	192.8	185.7	181.8	180.9	179.1
Russia	112.7	127.5	128.0	136.1	134.6	158.2	144.3	140.7	136.8	132.9
Excluding Russia	10.5	17.9	22.7	24.9	29.4	34.6	41.4	41.1	44.1	46.2
Debt-service payments[1]										
Developing countries	**174.6**	**194.8**	**237.5**	**277.6**	**305.4**	**313.8**	**353.4**	**337.8**	**330.4**	**315.2**
Regional groups										
Africa	28.7	29.3	33.1	30.8	29.2	28.1	27.5	28.0	29.4	26.9
Developing Asia	53.1	63.9	75.1	79.5	85.9	98.1	109.2	90.6	87.1	89.9
Middle East, Malta, and Turkey	21.4	26.0	32.1	42.7	37.6	39.1	39.8	41.4	47.4	44.3
Western Hemisphere	71.4	75.5	97.1	124.6	152.7	148.4	176.8	177.7	166.5	154.2
Analytical groups										
By external financing source										
Net debtor countries	171.0	186.9	229.4	264.8	296.8	305.6	346.4	330.7	321.3	306.3
of which, official financing	14.6	15.8	17.2	15.1	13.4	11.9	11.3	11.8	12.6	12.1
Net debtor countries by debt-servicing experience										
Countries with arrears and/or rescheduling during 1994–98	65.3	66.8	84.2	91.5	114.9	126.9	155.1	127.2	117.8	116.4
Countries in transition	**18.2**	**21.6**	**29.5**	**31.4**	**32.8**	**49.4**	**45.8**	**49.8**	**50.8**	**51.6**
Central and eastern Europe	11.5	14.8	19.7	21.4	23.2	28.6	27.7	32.2	31.4	31.8
Commonwealth of Independent States and Mongolia	6.7	6.8	9.8	10.0	9.6	20.8	18.2	17.6	19.4	19.9
Russia	6.2	4.3	6.4	6.9	5.9	16.3	12.9	11.3	14.3	14.7
Excluding Russia	0.5	2.5	3.5	3.1	3.7	4.5	5.3	6.4	5.2	5.2

Table 38 *(concluded)*

	1993	1994	1995	1996	1997	1998	1999	2000	2001	2002
					Percent of exports of goods and services					
External debt[2]										
Developing countries	**204.6**	**191.7**	**175.2**	**162.3**	**156.3**	**180.0**	**172.2**	**138.3**	**136.6**	**131.4**
Regional groups										
Africa	272.4	281.9	253.3	226.6	215.1	242.0	226.9	183.4	176.6	168.2
Developing Asia	157.3	140.1	127.4	121.7	116.8	126.4	123.5	98.9	97.1	91.5
Middle East, Malta, and Turkey	159.7	154.6	144.8	128.6	133.3	174.6	158.5	123.2	123.6	129.2
Western Hemisphere	288.0	272.4	251.4	236.1	224.0	257.6	254.1	209.9	208.7	196.8
Analytical groups										
By external financing source										
Net debtor countries	230.3	212.7	193.5	180.0	171.3	191.2	185.3	151.8	149.4	141.8
of which, official financing	381.2	398.0	340.2	296.9	260.7	285.6	258.5	196.2	187.9	176.4
Net debtor countries by debt-servicing experience										
Countries with arrears and/or rescheduling during 1994–98	344.3	330.4	305.0	280.3	265.6	312.7	299.2	236.6	238.9	228.7
Countries in transition	**130.6**	**128.7**	**106.9**	**106.6**	**104.2**	**126.7**	**130.7**	**107.7**	**104.1**	**101.4**
Central and eastern Europe	136.4	120.6	100.6	103.8	98.6	107.2	115.0	105.9	102.2	98.9
Commonwealth of Independent States and Mongolia	125.7	135.9	112.7	109.2	109.8	150.3	149.8	109.4	106.1	104.4
Russia	171.1	166.1	134.2	132.4	130.6	181.3	170.3	122.1	118.0	116.8
Excluding Russia	32.7	59.2	59.2	55.8	63.5	84.4	105.5	80.7	80.8	80.0
Debt-service payments										
Developing countries	**23.2**	**22.5**	**23.0**	**24.0**	**24.3**	**26.9**	**28.1**	**21.8**	**20.9**	**19.0**
Regional groups										
Africa	29.2	28.7	27.6	23.1	21.5	23.3	21.4	18.0	18.9	16.9
Developing Asia	17.9	17.3	16.5	15.7	15.2	18.2	18.8	12.9	12.1	11.6
Middle East, Malta, and Turkey	12.3	14.1	15.2	17.3	14.6	18.2	16.1	12.5	14.1	13.4
Western Hemisphere	39.1	36.4	39.4	45.5	51.0	50.9	58.6	49.6	45.3	38.8
Analytical groups										
By external financing source										
Net debtor countries	26.3	24.6	25.1	26.0	26.7	28.8	30.8	24.3	23.1	20.6
of which, official financing	34.3	35.8	32.0	24.7	20.3	19.6	17.0	14.2	14.6	13.7
Net debtor countries by debt-servicing experience										
Countries with arrears and/or rescheduling during 1994–98	32.9	30.3	33.5	32.1	36.9	45.0	50.7	33.5	31.2	29.4
Countries in transition	**10.1**	**10.7**	**11.4**	**11.2**	**11.1**	**17.3**	**16.7**	**14.9**	**14.4**	**14.0**
Central and eastern Europe	13.9	15.6	15.8	16.1	15.8	18.3	18.4	19.2	17.2	16.1
Commonwealth of Independent States and Mongolia	6.9	6.4	7.4	6.8	6.5	16.2	14.7	10.6	11.4	11.6
Russia	9.4	5.6	6.7	6.7	5.7	18.7	15.2	9.8	12.3	12.9
Excluding Russia	1.7	8.3	9.0	7.0	8.1	10.9	13.4	12.5	9.5	9.0

[1]Debt-service payments refer to actual payments of interest on total debt plus actual amortization payments on long-term debt. The projections incorporate the impact of exceptional financing items.
[2]Total debt at year-end in percent of exports of goods and services in year indicated.

Table 39. Developing Countries—by Region: External Debt, by Maturity and Type of Creditor

(Billions of U.S. dollars)

	1993	1994	1995	1996	1997	1998	1999	2000	2001	2002
Developing countries										
Total debt	**1,538.6**	**1,658.0**	**1,808.9**	**1,880.6**	**1,966.5**	**2,101.5**	**2,166.3**	**2,140.6**	**2,155.4**	**2,186.4**
By maturity										
Short-term	249.2	239.4	286.9	309.4	371.6	372.0	298.9	279.0	268.3	267.2
Long-term	1,289.4	1,418.7	1,522.0	1,571.3	1,594.9	1,729.6	1,867.4	1,861.5	1,887.1	1,919.2
By type of creditor										
Official	725.9	789.1	832.1	891.1	847.2	892.5	915.3	912.8	942.3	948.0
Banks	380.7	374.6	412.2	460.2	532.6	566.2	560.5	557.2	560.9	577.8
Other private	432.0	494.4	564.5	529.4	586.8	642.9	690.5	670.5	652.1	660.6
Regional groups										
Africa										
Total debt	**267.8**	**287.8**	**304.1**	**302.3**	**292.8**	**291.4**	**290.8**	**285.1**	**275.1**	**268.0**
By maturity										
Short-term	34.1	38.3	43.4	46.1	53.9	53.4	57.0	36.9	36.1	27.7
Long-term	233.7	249.5	260.7	256.3	238.8	238.0	233.7	248.2	239.0	240.3
By type of creditor										
Official	183.1	200.4	212.9	214.4	202.7	208.1	206.5	199.5	194.7	185.8
Banks	43.8	44.5	44.2	42.6	40.9	36.2	35.8	33.2	31.2	30.6
Other private	40.9	42.9	47.0	45.3	49.2	47.1	48.4	52.4	49.2	51.6
Sub-Sahara										
Total debt	**211.8**	**225.9**	**237.2**	**235.7**	**230.7**	**228.8**	**230.9**	**230.8**	**224.8**	**221.3**
By maturity										
Short-term	32.0	36.3	41.5	43.7	51.7	50.9	54.2	34.2	33.2	24.6
Long-term	179.9	189.6	195.7	192.0	179.0	177.9	176.7	196.6	191.6	196.7
By type of creditor										
Official	150.9	162.1	168.5	168.7	159.6	164.5	165.5	161.6	159.1	152.5
Banks	20.0	20.8	21.7	21.7	21.9	17.2	17.0	16.8	16.5	17.2
Other private	40.9	42.9	47.0	45.3	49.2	47.1	48.4	52.4	49.2	51.6
Developing Asia										
Total debt	**466.7**	**519.2**	**579.1**	**615.1**	**660.5**	**681.9**	**715.8**	**693.5**	**697.0**	**711.1**
By maturity										
Short-term	68.5	76.4	110.1	114.9	154.2	152.2	74.8	62.8	61.1	65.0
Long-term	398.2	442.8	469.0	500.2	506.3	529.7	641.0	630.7	635.9	646.1
By type of creditor										
Official	224.2	252.6	255.1	265.8	268.8	289.4	309.1	317.3	325.1	333.7
Banks	109.4	122.7	159.5	190.9	215.1	209.6	190.8	180.8	183.8	194.8
Other private	133.1	143.9	164.4	158.4	176.5	182.9	215.9	195.4	188.1	182.6
Middle East, Malta, and Turkey										
Total debt	**278.5**	**285.7**	**306.1**	**317.2**	**342.6**	**376.5**	**392.9**	**409.7**	**416.9**	**426.0**
By maturity										
Short-term	71.5	45.1	47.3	52.8	60.9	70.8	73.7	76.2	71.3	73.7
Long-term	207.0	240.6	258.8	264.4	281.6	305.6	319.2	333.6	345.6	352.3
By type of creditor										
Official	151.8	161.7	172.6	173.3	166.7	168.3	167.7	173.6	189.3	191.6
Banks	86.1	91.2	93.2	112.1	156.8	185.7	202.1	214.0	205.2	210.4
Other private	40.7	32.7	40.4	31.8	19.0	22.5	23.1	22.1	22.5	24.1
Western Hemisphere										
Total debt	**525.6**	**565.4**	**619.6**	**646.0**	**670.7**	**751.7**	**766.9**	**752.2**	**766.3**	**781.3**
By maturity										
Short-term	75.1	79.6	86.1	95.6	102.5	95.6	93.5	103.1	99.8	100.8
Long-term	450.5	485.8	533.5	550.5	568.2	656.2	673.5	649.1	666.6	680.5
By type of creditor										
Official	166.9	174.3	191.5	237.6	208.9	226.8	232.0	222.4	233.3	237.0
Banks	141.5	116.2	115.4	114.6	119.8	134.6	131.8	129.2	140.8	142.0
Other private	217.2	274.9	312.7	293.9	342.0	390.3	403.2	400.6	392.3	402.3

Table 40. Developing Countries—by Analytical Criteria: External Debt, by Maturity and Type of Creditor
(Billions of U.S. dollars)

	1993	1994	1995	1996	1997	1998	1999	2000	2001	2002
By source of export earnings										
Fuel										
Total debt	**277.1**	**291.7**	**303.1**	**301.4**	**314.4**	**337.6**	**345.8**	**341.7**	**341.0**	**342.3**
By maturity										
Short-term	53.4	41.3	40.4	43.4	52.3	60.9	63.4	40.6	40.9	41.3
Long-term	223.7	250.4	262.7	258.1	262.2	276.7	282.4	301.1	300.1	301.0
By type of creditor										
Official	136.6	149.0	164.0	162.2	161.1	166.0	166.0	163.6	163.4	162.9
Banks	87.4	88.4	84.5	100.0	110.9	123.7	129.0	129.3	129.1	129.9
Other private	53.0	54.3	54.5	39.3	41.5	47.9	50.7	48.8	48.5	49.5
Nonfuel										
Total debt	**1,261.5**	**1,366.3**	**1,505.8**	**1,579.2**	**1,652.1**	**1,763.9**	**1,820.6**	**1,798.9**	**1,814.4**	**1,844.1**
By maturity										
Short-term	195.8	198.1	246.5	266.0	319.3	311.1	235.5	238.4	227.5	225.9
Long-term	1,065.8	1,168.3	1,259.3	1,313.2	1,332.8	1,452.8	1,585.0	1,560.4	1,587.0	1,618.2
By type of creditor										
Official	589.3	640.1	668.1	728.9	685.1	726.5	749.3	749.3	778.9	785.1
Banks	293.3	286.2	327.7	360.2	421.7	442.5	431.4	427.9	431.9	447.9
Other private	378.9	440.1	510.0	490.1	545.3	595.0	639.9	621.7	603.6	611.1
Nonfuel primary products										
Total debt	**183.1**	**195.6**	**203.1**	**202.7**	**200.3**	**206.4**	**210.2**	**212.3**	**216.6**	**216.7**
By maturity										
Short-term	23.2	25.0	28.0	27.7	27.5	26.0	24.1	25.6	26.8	17.0
Long-term	159.9	170.6	175.1	175.1	172.8	180.4	186.1	186.8	189.8	199.6
By type of creditor										
Official	124.9	135.1	140.8	136.7	135.2	139.7	143.3	141.9	142.9	141.3
Banks	28.9	30.8	32.5	33.6	30.9	30.2	30.5	30.7	32.2	33.9
Other private	29.4	29.7	29.8	32.4	34.1	36.5	36.5	39.7	41.5	41.5
By external financing source										
Net debtor countries										
Total debt	**1,499.1**	**1,618.6**	**1,765.0**	**1,833.4**	**1,905.5**	**2,026.4**	**2,087.2**	**2,061.9**	**2,077.0**	**2,107.6**
By maturity										
Short-term	229.3	217.5	267.5	288.3	345.6	339.9	266.7	248.2	237.0	235.2
Long-term	1,269.8	1,401.1	1,497.5	1,545.1	1,560.0	1,686.5	1,820.6	1,813.7	1,840.0	1,872.4
By type of creditor										
Official	721.4	784.3	827.3	885.4	841.6	886.4	909.9	908.1	938.1	943.9
Banks	364.4	355.7	393.8	425.6	486.9	509.3	499.5	495.4	499.6	517.2
Other private	413.3	478.6	543.9	522.4	577.1	630.7	677.8	658.4	639.4	646.5
Official financing										
Total debt	**161.6**	**175.6**	**182.4**	**181.2**	**171.9**	**173.2**	**171.6**	**163.2**	**161.3**	**155.8**
By maturity										
Short-term	14.1	14.2	15.6	13.5	12.9	14.0	14.6	15.0	15.8	5.8
Long-term	147.5	161.4	166.9	167.7	159.0	159.2	157.1	148.2	145.5	150.0
By type of creditor										
Official	126.3	141.0	149.8	150.4	143.4	145.3	145.8	140.0	139.5	135.7
Banks	27.2	27.0	23.8	21.9	18.6	17.8	16.3	14.1	12.8	11.4
Other private	8.0	7.6	8.8	8.9	9.9	10.1	9.5	9.1	9.0	8.7

Table 40 *(concluded)*

	1993	1994	1995	1996	1997	1998	1999	2000	2001	2002
Net debtor countries by debt-servicing experience										
Countries with arrears and/or rescheduling during 1994–98										
Total debt	**683.6**	**727.4**	**767.0**	**797.8**	**826.5**	**882.0**	**914.4**	**898.5**	**900.8**	**907.1**
By maturity										
Short-term	97.6	84.0	97.1	109.3	157.1	158.9	96.1	74.8	68.4	56.0
Long-term	586.1	643.4	669.9	688.5	669.4	723.2	818.3	823.7	832.4	851.1
By type of creditor										
Official	381.6	409.2	427.6	494.7	468.4	493.8	506.6	502.1	508.2	510.3
Banks	191.6	155.6	154.7	177.4	188.3	190.3	180.5	173.9	176.2	179.5
Other private	110.4	162.5	184.7	125.6	169.8	197.9	227.4	222.4	216.4	217.3
Other groups										
Heavily indebted poor countries										
Total debt	**192.0**	**203.4**	**206.2**	**202.6**	**194.1**	**194.6**	**195.6**	**190.2**	**191.4**	**188.5**
By maturity										
Short-term	15.4	15.5	17.9	17.7	17.5	15.7	15.8	15.5	16.5	6.6
Long-term	176.6	188.0	188.4	184.9	176.6	178.9	179.8	174.7	174.9	181.9
By type of creditor										
Official	159.7	172.0	176.7	172.0	158.6	162.3	164.2	159.5	160.2	157.0
Banks	17.4	18.7	18.5	19.1	18.4	14.4	14.4	14.4	15.0	15.3
Other private	15.0	12.8	11.0	11.6	17.1	17.8	17.1	16.3	16.2	16.1
Middle East and north Africa										
Total debt	**287.8**	**303.9**	**324.4**	**329.5**	**341.4**	**363.8**	**370.0**	**368.0**	**371.4**	**378.6**
By maturity										
Short-term	55.3	36.0	33.7	34.7	40.2	46.2	46.2	43.7	44.8	46.0
Long-term	232.5	267.9	290.8	294.7	301.2	317.6	323.8	324.3	326.6	332.7
By type of creditor										
Official	174.0	187.9	205.9	207.8	199.3	203.6	202.3	201.9	203.6	208.0
Banks	90.7	93.4	92.5	108.9	121.5	136.1	142.9	142.2	143.4	144.5
Other private	23.2	22.6	26.0	12.7	20.6	24.2	24.8	23.9	24.4	26.2

Table 41. Developing Countries: Ratio of External Debt to GDP[1]

	1993	1994	1995	1996	1997	1998	1999	2000	2001	2002
Developing countries	**40.7**	**41.8**	**40.5**	**38.2**	**37.9**	**41.8**	**43.5**	**39.5**	**39.2**	**37.3**
Regional groups										
Africa	69.8	78.3	74.2	69.6	66.3	68.3	67.1	64.8	63.0	58.8
Sub-Sahara	72.5	80.8	74.7	71.1	67.5	70.6	70.0	69.2	69.3	65.3
Developing Asia	32.8	35.3	32.9	31.1	32.3	35.8	34.8	31.4	30.0	28.1
Excluding China and India	53.5	53.2	52.8	51.7	58.5	81.0	74.4	67.4	67.1	60.9
Middle East, Malta, and Turkey	47.2	52.8	49.1	46.4	48.1	54.4	54.0	50.3	51.1	52.1
Western Hemisphere	38.0	35.6	37.0	35.5	33.7	37.6	43.5	38.6	39.8	38.1
Analytical groups										
By source of export earnings										
Fuel	60.1	66.3	60.2	53.4	53.1	61.0	57.0	48.7	45.8	46.7
Nonfuel	38.0	38.7	38.0	36.3	35.9	39.5	41.6	38.2	38.1	36.0
of which, primary products	88.9	89.6	78.4	72.9	68.5	71.3	73.4	72.2	74.1	70.2
By external financing source										
Net debtor countries	42.2	43.3	41.8	39.5	38.9	42.5	44.5	40.7	40.3	38.2
of which, official financing	80.5	96.4	90.6	81.7	75.8	74.5	69.9	63.9	62.7	57.9
Net debtor countries by debt-servicing experience										
Countries with arrears and/or rescheduling during 1994–98	65.5	62.2	54.6	51.1	51.8	61.5	73.5	67.0	68.9	65.8
Other groups										
Heavily indebted poor countries	117.9	133.1	125.9	116.8	107.3	104.1	98.4	93.8	94.7	88.1
Middle East and north Africa	57.0	60.1	59.1	53.4	53.9	60.1	56.4	50.2	48.1	50.0

[1]Debt at year-end in percent of GDP in year indicated.

Table 42. Developing Countries: Debt-Service Ratios[1]

(Percent of exports of goods and services)

	1993	1994	1995	1996	1997	1998	1999	2000	2001	2002
Interest payments[2]										
Developing countries	**9.4**	**8.7**	**8.7**	**8.3**	**7.5**	**8.6**	**8.8**	**6.8**	**6.5**	**6.6**
Regional groups										
Africa	9.0	9.0	9.0	9.5	7.9	8.1	7.7	6.4	7.2	8.0
Sub-Sahara	7.2	7.7	7.8	8.6	6.8	6.8	6.8	5.7	7.0	8.2
Developing Asia	6.9	6.3	6.1	6.0	4.9	5.7	6.2	3.7	2.8	2.9
Excluding China and India	6.2	6.0	6.2	6.2	6.5	7.4	6.9	5.2	4.2	4.7
Middle East, Malta, and Turkey	5.0	4.6	4.7	3.9	3.9	4.5	4.3	3.6	4.2	4.6
Western Hemisphere	17.7	16.2	16.8	16.0	15.4	17.2	17.8	16.0	15.7	14.8
Analytical groups										
By source of export earnings										
Fuel	5.0	4.5	4.7	4.6	3.7	4.6	3.4	2.6	3.0	3.4
Nonfuel	10.7	9.7	9.7	9.3	8.4	9.4	10.0	8.0	7.5	7.3
of which, primary products	9.5	8.3	8.5	7.5	7.2	7.8	7.2	7.4	9.6	8.6
By external financing source										
Net debtor countries	10.5	9.5	9.6	9.3	8.3	9.2	9.6	7.5	7.2	7.1
of which, official financing	9.8	10.2	8.3	8.4	7.3	7.4	6.0	5.2	5.2	5.0
Net debtor countries by debt-servicing experience										
Countries with arrears and/or rescheduling during 1994–98	11.8	10.2	11.4	11.7	10.6	12.7	12.8	10.0	9.5	10.7
Other groups										
Heavily indebted poor countries	9.4	10.2	8.4	9.9	6.1	5.9	4.4	3.9	3.9	5.7
Middle East and north Africa	5.1	4.4	4.6	3.9	3.8	4.4	3.6	2.9	2.8	3.0
Amortization[2]										
Developing countries	**13.8**	**13.9**	**14.3**	**15.6**	**16.8**	**18.3**	**19.3**	**15.0**	**14.4**	**12.4**
Regional groups										
Africa	20.2	19.7	18.5	13.6	13.6	15.3	13.7	11.7	11.7	8.9
Sub-Sahara	13.6	13.3	13.1	9.8	11.0	13.4	12.0	10.8	11.1	7.4
Developing Asia	11.0	10.9	10.4	9.7	10.2	12.4	12.6	9.2	9.3	8.7
Excluding China and India	12.2	12.4	11.4	10.6	13.2	17.4	17.5	12.8	13.9	13.1
Middle East, Malta, and Turkey	7.2	9.5	10.5	13.5	10.8	13.6	11.8	8.8	9.8	8.8
Western Hemisphere	21.4	20.2	22.5	29.5	35.6	33.6	40.7	33.6	29.6	24.0
Analytical groups										
By source of export earnings										
Fuel	10.9	12.5	14.1	14.6	13.4	14.1	11.2	7.3	7.2	6.1
Nonfuel	14.7	14.2	14.3	15.9	17.6	19.0	21.2	17.2	16.3	13.9
of which, primary products	13.7	12.1	14.6	14.6	11.7	12.1	12.6	12.7	12.2	11.5
By external financing source										
Net debtor countries	15.8	15.0	15.6	16.7	18.4	19.6	21.1	16.8	15.9	13.5
of which, official financing	24.5	25.6	23.7	16.3	13.0	12.3	11.0	9.0	9.4	8.7
Net debtor countries by debt-servicing experience										
Countries with arrears and/or rescheduling during 1994–98	21.1	20.1	22.1	20.5	26.3	32.2	37.9	23.5	21.8	18.6
Other groups										
Heavily indebted poor countries	22.3	23.1	20.5	11.0	12.8	16.2	13.9	12.8	12.1	6.2
Middle East and north Africa	10.4	12.0	13.3	15.3	12.1	12.6	9.8	6.1	6.0	6.0

[1]Excludes service payments to the International Monetary Fund.
[2]Interest payments on total debt and amortization on long-term debt. Estimates through 2000 reflect debt-service payments actually made. The estimate for 2001 and 2002 take into account projected exceptional financing items, including accumulation of arrears and rescheduling agreements. In some cases, amortization on account of debt-reduction operations is included.

Table 43. IMF Charges and Repurchases to the IMF[1]

(Percent of exports of goods and services)

	1993	1994	1995	1996	1997	1998	1999	2000
Developing countries	**0.9**	**0.7**	**0.9**	**0.6**	**0.6**	**0.5**	**0.9**	**1.1**
Regional groups								
Africa	1.1	0.8	2.4	0.4	0.9	1.0	0.5	0.2
Sub-Sahara	0.7	0.5	2.8	0.2	0.6	0.7	0.2	0.1
Developing Asia	0.3	0.5	0.4	0.4	0.2	0.2	0.2	0.2
Excluding China and India	0.3	0.2	0.2	0.2	0.2	0.2	0.3	0.4
Middle East, Malta, and Turkey	—	—	0.1	0.1	—	0.1	0.2	0.1
Western Hemisphere	2.6	1.5	1.6	1.6	1.9	1.1	3.2	4.2
Analytical groups								
By source of export earnings								
Fuel	0.6	0.4	0.5	0.3	0.4	0.6	0.4	0.2
Nonfuel	1.0	0.8	1.0	0.7	0.7	0.5	1.1	1.3
By external financing source								
Net debtor countries	1.1	0.8	1.0	0.7	0.7	0.6	1.1	1.2
of which, official financing	2.0	1.0	4.9	0.6	0.9	1.3	0.9	0.4
Net debtor countries by debt-servicing experience								
Countries with arrears and/or rescheduling during 1994–98	1.4	0.6	1.4	0.4	0.4	0.5	1.3	2.2
Other groups								
Heavily indebted poor countries	1.6	1.0	5.4	0.5	0.5	0.5	0.3	0.3
Middle East and north Africa	0.4	0.3	0.3	0.2	0.3	0.4	0.3	0.1
Countries in transition	**0.4**	**1.2**	**1.4**	**0.8**	**0.6**	**1.0**	**2.4**	**1.8**
Central and eastern Europe	0.8	2.3	2.7	0.9	0.4	0.5	0.4	0.4
Commonwealth of Independent States and Mongolia	0.1	0.2	0.3	0.8	0.9	1.7	4.9	3.2
Russia	0.1	0.2	0.3	1.0	1.0	1.9	5.9	3.1
Excluding Russia	—	0.1	0.3	0.4	0.5	1.2	2.9	3.4
Memorandum								
Total, billions of U.S. dollars								
General Resources Account	7.627	8.334	12.732	9.488	9.953	8.768	18.497	22.823
Charges	2.309	1.788	2.772	2.256	2.168	2.468	2.795	2.805
Repurchases	5.319	6.546	9.960	7.231	7.786	6.300	15.702	20.017
Trust Fund	0.063	0.015	0.015	—	0.007	0.001	0.001	—
Interest	0.003	—	—	—	—	—	—	—
Repayments	0.060	0.014	0.015	—	0.007	0.001	0.001	—
PRGF[2]	0.149	0.328	0.583	0.746	0.863	0.879	0.854	0.806
Interest	0.023	0.022	0.030	0.043	0.036	0.037	0.040	0.037
Repayments	0.126	0.306	0.552	0.703	0.827	0.842	0.813	0.771

[1]Excludes advanced economies. Charges on, and repurchases (or repayments of principal) for, use of International Monetary Fund credit.
[2]Poverty Reduction and Growth Facility (formerly ESAF - Enhanced Structural Adjustment Facility).

Table 44. Summary of Sources and Uses of World Saving

(Percent of GDP)

	Averages										Average
	1979–86	1987–94	1995	1996	1997	1998	1999	2000	2001	2002	2003–2006
World											
Saving	23.0	23.0	23.6	23.4	23.9	23.0	23.1	23.7	22.8	22.9	23.7
Investment	23.7	24.1	24.2	24.1	24.2	23.3	23.1	23.5	23.1	23.1	23.9
Advanced economies											
Saving	21.9	21.7	21.4	21.4	22.0	22.0	21.6	21.6	20.5	20.9	21.9
Private	21.5	20.7	20.9	20.4	19.8	19.9	18.6	18.2	17.2	17.4	18.0
Public	0.4	1.0	0.5	1.0	2.2	2.1	3.0	3.4	3.3	3.4	3.9
Investment	23.0	22.2	21.5	21.6	21.9	21.8	21.9	22.2	21.2	21.0	21.7
Private	18.3	18.2	17.6	17.7	18.2	18.1	18.1	18.6	17.6	17.4	18.4
Public	4.4	4.1	3.9	3.9	3.7	3.6	3.7	3.6	3.6	3.5	3.3
Net lending	−1.1	−0.5	−0.2	−0.2	0.1	0.2	−0.3	−0.6	−0.7	−0.1	0.2
Private	3.2	2.5	3.3	2.7	1.6	1.7	0.4	−0.4	−0.4	—	−0.4
Public	−4.2	−3.1	−3.4	−2.9	−1.5	−1.5	−0.7	−0.2	−0.3	−0.1	0.6
Current transfers	−0.2	−0.3	−0.3	−0.3	−0.3	−0.4	−0.4	−0.4	−0.4	−0.4	−0.3
Factor income	−0.5	−0.4	−0.3	−0.3	−0.2	−0.1	0.2	0.4	0.2	0.6	0.7
Resource balance	−0.3	0.1	0.4	0.4	0.6	0.6	—	−0.6	−0.5	−0.4	−0.2
United States											
Saving	19.1	16.9	17.0	17.3	18.1	18.8	18.4	18.1	16.4	17.4	19.6
Private	19.7	17.8	17.1	16.5	16.2	15.7	14.5	13.4	11.8	12.8	15.0
Public	−0.6	−0.9	−0.1	0.8	1.9	3.1	3.9	4.7	4.6	4.6	4.6
Investment	21.0	18.6	18.7	19.1	19.9	20.7	20.9	21.1	19.6	19.3	20.9
Private	17.4	15.0	15.5	15.9	16.7	17.5	17.7	17.9	16.2	15.9	17.6
Public	3.6	3.6	3.2	3.2	3.2	3.2	3.3	3.2	3.4	3.4	3.3
Net lending	−1.9	−1.8	−1.7	−1.8	−1.8	−1.9	−2.5	−3.0	−3.3	−1.9	−1.3
Private	2.3	2.7	1.7	0.6	−0.6	−1.9	−3.1	−4.5	−4.4	−3.0	−2.6
Public	−4.2	−4.5	−3.3	−2.4	−1.3	−0.1	0.6	1.5	1.2	1.2	1.2
Current transfers	−0.4	−0.4	−0.5	−0.5	−0.5	−0.5	−0.5	−0.5	−0.4	−0.4	−0.3
Factor income	0.2	0.2	0.1	—	−0.1	0.5	0.8	1.3	0.6	1.8	2.1
Resource balance	−1.7	−1.5	−1.3	−1.3	−1.3	−1.9	−2.8	−3.8	−3.5	−3.3	−3.1
European Union											
Saving	20.5	20.6	20.8	20.4	21.0	20.9	20.7	20.9	20.6	20.7	21.5
Private	21.0	21.6	22.9	22.0	21.0	20.0	19.0	18.8	18.7	18.6	18.9
Public	−0.5	−0.9	−2.1	−1.6	−0.1	0.9	1.7	2.1	1.9	2.1	2.6
Investment	21.8	21.4	20.2	19.6	19.8	20.5	20.6	21.3	20.8	20.8	21.2
Private	17.7	18.2	17.5	17.1	17.4	18.1	18.2	18.9	18.3	18.3	18.6
Public	3.8	3.1	2.7	2.5	2.3	2.3	2.4	2.4	2.5	2.5	2.6
Net lending	−1.3	−0.7	0.6	0.8	1.2	0.5	0.1	−0.4	−0.2	−0.1	0.3
Private	3.0	3.3	5.4	4.9	3.6	1.9	0.8	−0.1	0.4	0.4	0.3
Public	−4.4	−4.1	−4.7	−4.1	−2.4	−1.4	−0.7	−0.3	−0.6	−0.5	0.1
Current transfers	−0.3	−0.4	−0.2	−0.4	−0.3	−0.4	−0.5	−0.5	−0.5	−0.5	−0.5
Factor income	−1.2	−0.9	−0.8	−0.7	−0.6	−0.8	−0.5	−0.4	−0.4	−0.5	−0.5
Resource balance	0.2	0.6	1.6	1.9	2.2	1.7	1.1	0.5	0.7	0.9	1.3
Japan											
Saving	31.3	33.0	30.2	30.6	30.9	29.9	28.6	28.5	27.5	26.9	26.8
Private	27.3	24.4	24.3	24.9	25.2	30.4	26.4	28.1	26.6	26.0	23.6
Public	4.0	8.6	5.9	5.7	5.8	−0.5	2.1	0.3	0.9	0.9	3.1
Investment	29.9	30.5	28.2	29.2	28.7	26.9	26.1	26.0	25.5	24.5	24.2
Private	21.6	23.5	19.9	20.6	21.1	19.5	18.3	18.9	18.7	18.6	19.4
Public	8.3	7.1	8.3	8.7	7.6	7.4	7.8	7.1	6.8	5.9	4.8
Net lending	1.4	2.5	2.0	1.4	2.2	3.0	2.5	2.5	2.0	2.4	2.6
Private	5.7	0.9	4.4	4.4	4.1	10.9	8.1	9.3	7.9	7.5	4.2
Public	−4.3	1.6	−2.3	−3.0	−1.9	−8.0	−5.6	−6.8	−5.9	−5.0	−1.6
Current transfers	−0.1	−0.1	−0.1	−0.2	−0.2	−0.2	−0.3	−0.2	−0.2	−0.2	−0.3
Factor income	0.2	0.8	0.8	1.1	1.3	1.3	1.3	1.2	1.4	1.4	1.4
Resource balance	1.3	1.9	1.4	0.5	1.1	1.9	1.5	1.5	0.8	1.3	1.4

Table 44 *(continued)*

		Averages										Average
		1979–86	1987–94	1995	1996	1997	1998	1999	2000	2001	2002	2003–2006
Newly industrialized Asian economies												
Saving	...	35.1	33.4	32.3	32.3	32.6	32.2	31.0	29.3	29.0	28.4
Private	...	27.1	26.3	25.4	25.2	25.4	25.6	24.3	22.7	22.3	21.6
Public	...	8.0	7.1	6.9	7.1	7.3	6.6	6.7	6.6	6.6	6.8
	...										
Investment	...	30.8	33.2	32.8	31.6	24.2	25.8	26.9	25.3	25.2	25.2
Private	...	24.6	26.5	26.2	25.1	17.5	19.5	21.3	19.5	19.7	20.0
Public	...	6.3	6.6	6.6	6.5	6.7	6.4	5.6	5.8	5.5	5.2
Net lending	...	4.3	0.2	–0.4	0.7	8.4	6.4	4.1	4.0	3.8	3.1
Private	...	2.6	–0.3	–0.8	0.1	7.9	6.1	3.0	3.2	2.7	1.6
Public	...	1.7	0.5	0.3	0.6	0.5	0.2	1.1	0.7	1.1	1.6
Current transfers	...	—	–0.4	–0.3	–0.4	0.1	–0.2	–0.4	–0.5	–0.4	–0.4
Factor income	...	0.3	0.3	0.2	0.6	—	0.3	0.5	0.8	0.8	0.5
Resource balance	...	3.9	0.3	–0.2	0.5	8.4	6.3	4.0	3.7	3.5	3.0
Developing countries												
Saving	21.8	24.1	27.2	26.8	27.3	25.7	25.7	26.5	25.9	25.7	26.1
Investment	24.0	25.9	28.7	28.0	27.9	26.2	25.4	25.8	26.0	26.3	26.7
Net lending	–2.2	–1.8	–1.5	–1.2	–0.5	–0.6	0.2	0.8	–0.2	–0.6	–0.7
Current transfers	0.8	1.0	1.1	1.1	1.1	0.9	0.9	1.1	1.3	1.2	1.1
Factor income	–1.9	–1.8	–0.6	–1.4	–1.6	–1.7	–1.9	–2.3	–2.3	–2.0	–1.5
Resource balance	–1.1	–0.9	–2.0	–0.9	–0.1	0.2	1.3	1.9	0.8	0.1	–0.3
Memorandum												
Acquisition of foreign assets	0.8	1.5	1.3	3.1	4.3	2.6	3.3	3.8	3.5	3.1	2.5
Change in reserves	0.1	1.0	1.6	2.1	1.4	0.1	0.8	1.1	1.1	1.0	0.9
Regional groups												
Africa												
Saving	19.5	16.6	15.6	17.0	16.1	14.9	15.5	18.7	18.4	18.8	19.8
Investment	22.5	19.4	19.7	19.5	19.2	20.4	20.3	19.8	20.6	21.6	21.8
Net lending	–2.9	–2.8	–4.2	–2.5	–3.1	–5.5	–4.9	–1.1	–2.1	–2.8	–2.0
Current transfers	1.4	3.0	3.1	3.0	3.1	3.2	3.2	3.5	3.4	3.4	3.0
Factor income	–2.2	–4.5	–3.9	–4.7	–4.9	–4.2	–5.0	–5.3	–4.5	–3.9	–3.4
Resource balance	–2.2	–1.4	–3.3	–0.8	–1.3	–4.5	–3.0	0.7	–1.1	–2.2	–1.6
Memorandum												
Acquisition of foreign assets	0.1	0.8	1.4	3.0	3.1	0.3	1.3	2.7	3.7	3.0	2.4
Change in reserves	0.1	0.4	0.4	2.2	2.3	–0.4	0.6	2.7	2.3	1.9	1.4
Developing Asia												
Saving	24.7	29.7	32.8	32.1	33.1	31.7	31.0	31.9	31.1	30.3	29.8
Investment	27.1	30.7	34.6	33.2	32.1	29.2	28.8	29.6	29.8	29.7	29.5
Net lending	–2.3	–1.0	–1.8	–1.0	1.0	2.5	2.2	2.3	1.3	0.7	0.3
Current transfers	1.2	0.9	1.2	1.3	1.6	1.3	1.3	1.4	1.4	1.3	1.2
Factor income	–0.8	–0.5	–1.3	–0.8	–1.0	–1.1	–1.1	–0.9	–0.9	–0.9	–0.9
Resource balance	–2.7	–1.5	–1.6	–1.6	0.4	2.4	2.0	1.7	0.7	0.2	—
Memorandum												
Acquisition of foreign assets	1.8	2.1	3.1	3.4	5.7	4.4	4.7	4.4	3.9	3.7	3.1
Change in reserves	0.2	1.2	1.9	2.1	1.6	0.8	1.3	0.9	1.0	0.9	1.0
Middle East, Malta, and Turkey												
Saving	23.1	19.5	27.5	24.7	24.9	21.1	23.8	22.7	22.8	23.4	26.5
Investment	23.7	23.4	23.3	24.2	25.2	24.8	22.9	22.0	23.0	23.9	26.8
Net lending	–0.6	–3.9	4.2	0.4	–0.3	–3.6	0.9	0.7	–0.2	–0.5	–0.2
Current transfers	0.1	–0.7	–0.8	–1.3	–2.5	–3.5	–4.2	–2.6	–0.5	–0.6	–0.5
Factor income	–0.6	–1.8	10.9	1.0	0.4	–0.4	–1.1	–6.3	–6.6	–3.9	0.2
Resource balance	–0.1	–1.3	–5.9	0.8	1.9	0.3	6.2	9.6	6.9	4.0	0.1
Memorandum												
Acquisition of foreign assets	1.8	—	–10.5	2.2	3.3	0.2	3.3	7.9	5.3	4.8	1.8
Change in reserves	0.2	0.8	2.0	2.6	0.9	–1.6	0.9	3.0	3.3	3.2	0.9

Table 44 *(continued)*

	Averages		1995	1996	1997	1998	1999	2000	2001	2002	Average 2003–2006
	1979–86	1987–94									
Western Hemisphere											
Saving	18.3	19.3	19.0	19.1	19.1	17.6	17.2	17.4	16.4	16.9	17.8
Investment	20.8	21.2	21.3	21.1	22.4	22.1	20.1	19.9	19.6	20.0	20.7
Net lending	−2.4	−1.8	−2.3	−2.0	−3.3	−4.6	−3.0	−2.4	−3.2	−3.2	−3.0
Current transfers	0.4	1.1	1.1	1.0	1.0	1.1	1.3	1.2	1.2	1.2	1.0
Factor income	−3.9	−3.3	−3.0	−2.7	−2.6	−2.6	−3.0	−3.0	−3.3	−3.3	−3.2
Resource balance	1.0	0.4	−0.5	−0.3	−1.7	−3.1	−1.2	−0.7	−1.2	−1.0	−0.8
Memorandum											
Acquisition of foreign assets	0.8	1.2	2.6	3.0	1.7	0.5	0.8	0.7	1.5	0.6	1.1
Change in reserves	−0.1	0.8	1.4	1.8	1.0	−0.6	−0.5	0.1	−0.2	0.2	0.6
Analytical groups											
By source of export earnings											
Fuel											
Saving	26.0	19.8	27.8	27.9	26.8	19.7	24.4	27.7	26.6	26.8	30.2
Investment	24.2	22.6	22.0	23.0	24.4	24.9	22.8	20.9	24.5	25.7	28.8
Net lending	1.7	−2.9	5.8	4.8	2.4	−5.3	1.6	6.8	2.1	1.2	1.4
Current transfers	−2.5	−2.8	−2.4	−3.0	−4.4	−5.6	−6.4	−4.5	−2.6	−2.2	−1.8
Factor income	−0.1	−2.3	11.5	−0.3	−1.2	−1.8	−2.6	−8.6	−7.2	−5.1	−0.6
Resource balance	4.3	2.2	−3.2	8.1	8.0	2.2	10.6	19.9	11.9	8.5	3.8
Memorandum											
Acquisition of foreign assets	2.7	−0.1	−12.7	4.7	4.8	−1.2	2.8	12.4	8.1	6.2	2.6
Change in reserves	—	—	0.2	4.2	1.8	−3.1	−0.7	6.2	4.8	4.3	1.2
Nonfuel											
Saving	21.0	24.7	27.1	26.7	27.4	26.3	25.8	26.4	25.8	25.6	25.7
Investment	23.9	26.3	29.4	28.5	28.2	26.4	25.7	26.3	26.2	26.3	26.5
Net lending	−3.0	−1.7	−2.3	−1.9	−0.9	−0.1	0.1	0.2	−0.4	−0.8	−0.8
Current transfers	1.3	1.5	1.5	1.5	1.7	1.6	1.6	1.7	1.7	1.6	1.4
Factor income	−2.2	−1.8	−1.9	−1.5	−1.6	−1.7	−1.8	−1.7	−1.8	−1.7	−1.6
Resource balance	−2.1	−1.3	−1.8	−1.9	−1.0	—	0.3	0.1	−0.3	−0.7	−0.6
Memorandum											
Acquisition of foreign assets	0.4	1.7	2.8	3.0	4.2	3.0	3.4	2.9	3.0	2.8	2.5
Change in reserves	—	1.1	1.8	1.9	1.4	0.5	0.9	0.6	0.7	0.7	0.9
By external financing source											
Net debtor countries											
Saving	21.3	24.5	27.4	26.9	27.4	26.0	25.7	26.4	25.7	25.5	26.0
Investment	24.0	26.2	28.9	28.3	28.1	26.3	25.6	26.0	26.2	26.4	26.7
Net lending	−2.7	−1.7	−1.5	−1.4	−0.7	−0.4	0.1	0.4	−0.5	−0.9	−0.7
Current transfers	1.2	1.4	1.4	1.4	1.4	1.2	1.1	1.3	1.6	1.5	1.3
Factor income	−2.1	−2.1	−0.7	−1.6	−1.7	−1.9	−2.1	−2.4	−2.5	−2.1	−1.6
Resource balance	−1.8	−0.9	−2.2	−1.2	−0.3	0.4	1.1	1.5	0.4	−0.2	−0.4
Memorandum											
Acquisition of foreign assets	0.5	1.7	1.3	3.0	4.2	2.8	3.4	3.5	3.3	2.9	2.5
Change in reserves	—	1.0	1.7	2.1	1.4	0.3	0.9	1.0	0.9	0.9	1.0
Official financing											
Saving	14.0	13.8	15.1	17.1	17.8	16.2	17.9	20.6	20.7	20.4	21.7
Investment	20.2	18.9	22.7	22.5	21.6	22.3	21.9	21.6	23.1	24.7	24.2
Net lending	−6.2	−5.0	−7.6	−5.4	−3.8	−6.1	−3.9	−1.0	−2.4	−4.3	−2.6
Current transfers	4.3	4.4	4.8	4.6	4.2	4.6	4.8	5.2	5.2	5.0	4.5
Factor income	−5.1	−3.7	−4.5	−3.5	−3.6	−4.1	−3.7	−3.7	−3.2	−2.8	−2.3
Resource balance	−5.4	−5.7	−7.9	−6.5	−4.5	−6.6	−5.0	−2.5	−4.3	−6.5	−4.8
Memorandum											
Acquisition of foreign assets	0.3	0.6	0.9	0.8	1.8	−0.5	0.8	2.9	2.9	1.8	1.3
Change in reserves	0.2	0.7	0.3	1.4	2.1	−0.5	0.5	3.1	3.0	2.1	1.3

Table 44 *(concluded)*

	Averages		1995	1996	1997	1998	1999	2000	2001	2002	Average 2003–2006
	1979–86	1987–94									
Net debtor countries by debt-servicing experience											
Countries with arrears and/or rescheduling during 1994–98											
Saving	17.6	20.0	22.3	21.5	20.9	17.4	18.5	19.7	18.1	18.4	21.1
Investment	21.0	22.6	24.1	24.4	24.6	21.4	19.7	20.1	20.9	21.4	22.6
Net lending	−3.4	−2.6	−1.8	−2.9	−3.8	−4.0	−1.1	−0.4	−2.9	−3.0	−1.5
Current transfers	0.6	1.4	1.5	1.1	0.6	0.4	—	0.7	1.4	1.4	1.4
Factor income	−2.7	−2.7	2.1	−1.6	−2.4	−3.0	−2.8	−5.2	−4.8	−4.0	−2.3
Resource balance	−1.3	−0.3	−5.4	−2.5	−2.0	−1.3	1.7	4.1	0.6	−0.4	−0.6
Memorandum											
Acquisition of foreign assets	0.3	0.8	−3.2	1.6	1.6	0.8	2.9	4.7	3.5	3.1	2.6
Change in reserves	−0.2	0.6	1.5	1.3	0.4	−0.1	0.3	2.1	1.1	1.1	0.9
Countries in transition											
Saving	...	...	23.8	22.0	21.2	17.1	22.3	27.1	25.4	24.6	24.6
Investment	...	...	24.6	24.5	24.1	21.0	20.0	21.3	22.7	23.5	25.2
Net lending	...	...	−0.7	−2.4	−3.0	−3.9	2.3	5.8	2.7	1.2	−0.6
Current transfers	...	...	0.7	0.7	0.8	0.9	1.1	1.1	1.1	1.1	1.3
Factor income	...	...	−0.7	−0.8	−1.2	−2.7	−2.6	−2.4	−2.2	−2.0	−1.9
Resource balance	...	...	−0.7	−2.3	−2.5	−2.1	3.8	7.1	3.8	2.1	—
Memorandum											
Acquisition of foreign assets	...	...	3.8	1.9	5.1	3.4	6.9	7.8	5.9	4.8	3.6
Change in reserves	...	...	3.7	0.2	1.1	−0.2	1.0	3.4	2.9	1.7	1.2

Note: The estimates in this table are based on individual countries' national accounts and balance of payments statistics. For many countries, the estimates of national saving are built up from national accounts data on gross domestic investment and from balance-of-payments-based data on net foreign investment. The latter, which is equivalent to the current account balance, comprises three components: current transfers, net factor income, and the resource balance. The mixing of data sources, which is dictated by availability, implies that the estimates for national saving that are derived incorporate the statistical discrepancies. Furthermore, errors, omissions, and asymmetries in balance of payments statistics affect the estimates for net lending; at the global level, net lending, which in theory would be zero, equals the world current account discrepancy. Notwithstanding these statistical shortcomings, flow of funds estimates, such as those presented in this table, provide a useful framework for analyzing development in saving and investment, both over time and across regions and countries. Country group composites are weighted by GDP valued at purchasing power parities (PPPs) as a share of total world GDP.

Table 45. Summary of World Medium-Term Baseline Scenario

	Eight-Year Averages		Four-Year Average					Four-Year Average
	1983–90	1991–98	1999–2002	1999	2000	2001	2002	2003–2006
Annual percent change unless otherwise noted								
World real GDP	**3.9**	**3.0**	**3.6**	**3.6**	**4.7**	**2.6**	**3.5**	**4.5**
Advanced economies	3.7	2.5	2.6	3.4	3.8	1.3	2.1	3.3
Developing countries	4.5	5.7	4.8	3.9	5.8	4.3	5.3	6.1
Countries in transition	3.0	−5.2	4.5	3.6	6.3	4.0	4.1	4.9
Memorandum								
Potential output								
Major advanced economies	2.8	2.6	2.6	2.6	2.6	2.6	2.6	2.6
World trade, volume[1]	**5.6**	**6.5**	**6.4**	**5.3**	**12.4**	**2.7**	**5.2**	**7.1**
Imports								
Advanced economies	7.1	6.2	6.3	7.6	11.5	1.7	4.7	6.7
Developing countries	1.5	9.3	8.2	2.1	16.6	6.4	8.0	8.6
Countries in transition	2.1	0.6	5.5	−7.8	12.9	10.1	7.9	7.6
Exports								
Advanced economies	5.9	6.4	5.7	5.1	11.5	1.7	4.5	6.6
Developing countries	5.2	9.2	7.8	4.6	15.1	5.0	6.6	8.3
Countries in transition	0.3	1.5	7.4	0.2	16.5	7.1	6.5	7.6
Terms of trade								
Advanced economies	1.3	0.3	−0.5	−0.2	−2.4	−0.3	0.9	0.4
Developing countries	−2.8	−1.2	2.1	4.4	6.8	−1.0	−1.7	−0.4
Countries in transition	−0.5	−1.5	1.0	0.7	6.0	−1.4	−1.2	−1.1
World prices in U.S. dollars								
Manufactures	5.3	−0.3	−2.7	−1.8	−5.1	−3.1	−0.6	1.0
Oil	−4.2	−6.8	17.0	37.5	56.9	−5.0	−8.6	−3.8
Nonfuel primary commodities	1.7	−0.5	−0.8	−7.0	2.6	−2.6	4.5	3.9
Consumer prices								
Advanced economies	4.7	2.8	2.0	1.4	2.3	2.4	1.7	2.0
Developing countries	47.3	30.0	5.9	6.8	6.0	5.9	5.1	3.9
Countries in transition	9.0	165.2	22.1	43.9	20.0	16.4	10.7	7.0
Interest rates (in percent)								
Real six-month LIBOR[2]	5.3	3.0	3.0	4.1	4.4	1.8	1.6	3.5
World real long-term interest rate[3]	5.3	3.9	2.6	3.2	2.8	2.0	2.4	3.3
Percent of GDP								
Balances on current account								
Advanced economies	−0.3	0.2	−0.8	−0.5	−1.0	−0.9	−0.8	−0.7
Developing countries	−1.7	−2.1	0.2	−0.2	1.1	0.4	−0.4	−1.1
Countries in transition	0.2	−0.6	0.6	−0.1	1.6	0.7	0.2	−0.5
Total external debt								
Developing countries	37.6	40.2	39.9	43.5	39.5	39.2	37.3	33.4
Countries in transition	8.4	18.9	19.7	20.3	20.7	19.7	18.2	15.5
Debt service								
Developing countries	4.3	5.4	6.2	7.1	6.2	6.0	5.4	4.7
Countries in transition	2.1	2.1	2.7	2.6	2.9	2.7	2.5	2.1

[1]Data refer to trade in goods and services.
[2]London interbank offered rate on U.S. dollar deposits less percent change in U.S. GDP deflator.
[3]GDP-weighted average of ten-year (or nearest maturity) government bond rates for the United States, Japan, Germany, France, Italy, the United Kingdom, and Canada.

Table 46. Developing Countries—Medium-Term Baseline Scenario: Selected Economic Indicators

	Eight-Year Averages		Four-Year Average					Four-Year Average
	1983–90	1991–98	1999–2002	1999	2000	2001	2002	2003–2006
				Annual percent change				
Developing countries								
Real GDP	4.5	5.7	4.8	3.9	5.8	4.3	5.3	6.1
Export volume[1]	5.2	9.2	7.8	4.6	15.1	5.0	6.6	8.3
Terms of trade[1]	−2.8	−1.2	2.1	4.4	6.8	−1.0	−1.7	−0.4
Import volume[1]	1.5	9.3	8.2	2.1	16.6	6.4	8.0	8.6
Regional groups								
Africa								
Real GDP	2.5	2.2	3.4	2.5	2.8	3.8	4.4	5.1
Export volume[1]	5.3	3.8	5.1	2.7	8.3	5.3	4.1	5.9
Terms of trade[1]	−1.0	−1.2	3.0	5.9	14.3	−3.8	−3.4	−0.8
Import volume[1]	2.7	4.9	4.9	2.2	7.8	6.0	3.7	5.0
Developing Asia								
Real GDP	7.2	7.8	6.2	6.1	6.8	5.8	6.2	7.0
Export volume[1]	8.1	12.5	10.3	8.1	21.8	4.3	7.7	9.9
Terms of trade[1]	−1.0	−0.2	−0.8	−1.7	−2.5	0.7	0.3	0.4
Import volume[1]	5.7	9.8	11.9	7.8	21.6	8.8	9.9	10.6
Middle East, Malta, and Turkey								
Real GDP	3.5	3.8	3.5	1.0	6.0	2.3	4.8	5.1
Export volume[1]	3.6	8.6	3.4	−1.9	7.5	4.6	3.6	4.0
Terms of trade[1]	−6.0	−3.3	8.9	20.8	28.3	−2.3	−7.2	−2.4
Import volume[1]	−2.4	9.0	5.7	−0.2	16.8	1.1	5.8	5.5
Western Hemisphere								
Real GDP	1.9	3.7	2.4	0.2	4.2	1.7	3.6	4.5
Export volume[1]	5.0	7.8	7.4	3.8	11.3	6.6	8.0	9.1
Terms of trade[1]	−1.8	−0.6	1.4	2.8	4.7	−1.9	0.1	−0.5
Import volume[1]	1.3	11.5	5.2	−4.4	11.8	6.3	8.0	8.2
Analytical groups								
Net debtor countries by debt-servicing experience								
Countries with arrears and/or rescheduling during 1994–98								
Real GDP	2.8	3.4	3.6	2.1	4.5	3.4	4.4	5.2
Export volume[1]	5.3	8.2	6.5	6.3	10.4	2.7	6.9	8.1
Terms of trade[1]	−3.5	−2.8	2.7	3.3	10.6	−0.8	−1.6	−0.6
Import volume[1]	−1.1	9.3	5.6	−3.2	10.6	8.2	7.6	7.5

Table 46 (*concluded*)

	1990	1994	1998	1999	2000	2001	2002	2006
				Percent of exports of good and services				
Developing countries								
Current account balance	−3.6	−9.9	−7.4	−0.8	3.9	1.4	−1.4	−4.1
Total external debt	191.8	191.7	180.0	172.2	138.3	136.6	131.4	105.8
Debt-service payments[2]	21.4	22.5	26.9	28.1	21.8	20.9	19.0	14.1
Interest payments	10.0	8.7	8.6	8.8	6.8	6.5	6.6	5.0
Amortization	11.4	13.9	18.3	19.3	15.0	14.4	12.4	9.2
Regional groups								
Africa								
Current account balance	−5.5	−11.6	−17.1	−12.1	1.4	−2.5	−4.0	−2.4
Total external debt	228.9	281.9	242.0	226.9	183.4	176.6	168.2	138.1
Debt-service payments[2]	15.8	28.7	23.3	21.4	18.0	18.9	16.9	14.6
Interest payments	7.2	9.0	8.1	7.7	6.4	7.2	8.0	5.7
Amortization	8.7	19.7	15.3	13.7	11.7	11.7	8.9	8.9
Developing Asia								
Current account balance	−7.6	−5.1	8.7	8.0	6.5	3.1	1.1	−0.7
Total external debt	164.4	140.1	126.4	123.5	98.9	97.1	91.5	71.2
Debt-service payments[2]	17.6	17.3	18.2	18.8	12.9	12.1	11.6	7.6
Interest payments	8.1	6.3	5.7	6.2	3.7	2.8	2.9	2.2
Amortization	9.5	10.9	12.4	12.6	9.2	9.3	8.7	5.4
Middle East, Malta, and Turkey								
Current account balance	−0.5	−1.5	−10.6	6.0	18.3	18.5	11.2	−2.5
Total external debt	131.1	154.6	174.6	158.5	123.2	123.6	129.2	123.0
Debt-service payments[2]	13.5	14.1	18.2	16.1	12.5	14.1	13.4	13.9
Interest payments	5.0	4.6	4.5	4.3	3.6	4.2	4.6	4.6
Amortization	8.5	9.5	13.6	11.8	8.8	9.8	8.8	9.3
Western Hemisphere								
Current account balance	−0.7	−25.1	−31.0	−18.7	−13.6	−15.8	−15.7	−12.5
Total external debt	266.6	272.4	257.6	254.1	209.9	208.7	196.8	153.4
Debt-service payments[2]	38.0	36.4	50.9	58.6	49.6	45.3	38.8	27.3
Interest payments	19.5	16.2	17.2	17.8	16.0	15.7	14.8	10.6
Amortization	18.6	20.2	33.6	40.7	33.6	29.6	24.0	16.6
Analytical groups								
Net debtor countries by debt-servicing experience								
Countries with arrears and/or rescheduling during 1994–98								
Current account balance	−12.9	−8.5	−20.9	−7.7	2.0	−4.2	−6.0	−5.4
Total external debt	303.4	330.4	312.7	299.2	236.6	238.9	228.7	173.9
Debt-service payments[2]	27.0	30.3	45.0	50.7	33.5	31.2	29.4	21.3
Interest payments	11.9	10.2	12.7	12.8	10.0	9.5	10.7	7.4
Amortization	15.2	20.1	32.2	37.9	23.5	21.8	18.6	13.9

[1]Data refer to trade in goods and services.
[2]Interest payments on total debt plus amortization payments on long-term debt only. Projections incorporate the impact of exceptional financing items. Excludes service payments to the International Monetary Fund.

WORLD ECONOMIC OUTLOOK AND STAFF STUDIES FOR THE WORLD ECONOMIC OUTLOOK, SELECTED TOPICS, 1992–2001

I. Methodology—Aggregation, Modeling, and Forecasting

II. Historical Surveys

III. Economic Growth—Sources and Patterns

IV. Inflation and Deflation; Commodity Markets

V. Fiscal Policy

VI. Monetary Policy; Financial Markets; Flow of Funds

VII. Labor Market Issues

VIII. Exchange Rate Issues

IX. External Payments, Trade, Capital Movements, and Foreign Debt

X. Regional Issues

XI. Country-Specific Analyses

Staff Studies for the World Economic Outlook

World Economic and Financial Surveys

This series (ISSN 0258-7440) contains biannual, annual, and periodic studies covering monetary and financial issues of importance to the global economy. The core elements of the series are the *World Economic Outlook* report, usually published in May and October, and the annual report on *International Capital Markets*. Other studies assess international trade policy, private market and official financing for developing countries, exchange and payments systems, export credit policies, and issues discussed in the *World Economic Outlook*. Please consult the IMF *Publications Catalog* for a complete listing of currently available World Economic and Financial Surveys.

World Economic Outlook: A Survey by the Staff of the International Monetary Fund

The *World Economic Outlook,* published twice a year in English, French, Spanish, and Arabic, presents IMF staff economists' analyses of global economic developments during the near and medium term. Chapters give an overview of the world economy; consider issues affecting industrial countries, developing countries, and economies in transition to the market; and address topics of pressing current interest.

ISSN 0256-6877.
$42.00 (academic rate: $35.00); paper.

2001. (Oct.). ISBN 1-58906-073-3. **Stock #WEO EA 0022001.**
2001. (May). ISBN 1-58906-032-6. **Stock #WEO EA 0012001.**
2000. (Oct.). ISBN 1-55775-975-8. **Stock #WEO EA 0022000.**
2000. (May). ISBN 1-55775-936-7. **Stock #WEO EA 012000.**
1999. (Oct.). ISBN 1-55775-839-5. **Stock #WEO EA 299.**
1999. (May). ISBN 1-55775-809-3. **Stock #WEO-199.**

Official Financing for Developing Countries
by a staff team in the IMF's Policy Development and Review Department led by Anthony R. Boote and Doris C. Ross

This study provides information on official financing for developing countries, with the focus on low-income countries. It updates the 1995 edition and reviews developments in direct financing by official and multilateral sources.

$25.00 (academic rate: $20.00); paper.

2001. ISBN 1-58906-038-5. **Stock #WEO EA 0132001.**
1998. ISBN 1-55775-702-X. **Stock #WEO-1397.**
1995. ISBN 1-55775-527-2. **Stock #WEO-1395.**

Exchange Rate Arrangements and Currency Convertibility: Developments and Issues
by a staff team led by R. Barry Johnston

A principle force driving the growth in international trade and investment has been the liberalization of financial transactions, including the liberalization of trade and exchange controls. This study reviews the developments and issues in the exchange arrangements and currency convertibility of IMF members.

$20.00 (academic rate: $12.00); paper.

1999. ISBN 1-55775-795-X. **Stock #WEO EA 0191999.**

World Economic Outlook Supporting Studies
by the IMF's Research Department

These studies, supporting analyses and scenarios of the *World Economic Outlook,* provide a detailed examination of theory and evidence on major issues currently affecting the global economy.

$25.00 (academic rate: $20.00); paper.

2000. ISBN 1-55775-893-X. **Stock #WEO EA 0032000.**

International Capital Markets: Developments, Prospects, and Key Policy Issues
by a staff team led by Donald J. Mathieson and Garry J. Schinasi

This year's *International Capital Markets* report assesses recent developments in mature and emerging financial markets and analyzes key systemic issues affecting global financial markets. The report discusses the main risks in the period ahead; identifies sources of, and possible measures to avoid, instability in OTC derivatives markets; reviews initiatives to "involve"the private sector in preventing and resolving crises, and discusses the role of foreign-owned banks in emerging markets.

$42.00 (academic rate: $35.00); paper

2001. ISBN 1-58906-056-3. **Stock #WEO EA 0062001.**
2000. (Sep.). ISBN 1-55775-949-9. **Stock #WEO EA 0062000**
1999. (Sep.). ISBN 1-55775-852-2. **Stock #WEO EA 699.**
1998. (Sep.). ISBN 1-55775-770-4. **Stock #WEO-698**

Toward a Framework for Financial Stability
by a staff team led by David Folkerts-Landau and Carl-Johan Lindgren

This study outlines the broad principles and characteristics of stable and sound financial systems, to facilitate IMF surveillance over banking sector issues of macroeconomic significance and to contribute to the general international effort to reduce the likelihood and diminish the intensity of future financial sector crises.

$25.00 (academic rate: $20.00); paper.

1998. ISBN 1-55775-706-2. **Stock #WEO-016.**

Trade Liberalization in IMF-Supported Programs
by a staff team led by Robert Sharer

This study assesses trade liberalization in programs supported by the IMF by reviewing multiyear arrangements in the 1990s and six detailed case studies. It also discusses the main economic factors affecting trade policy targets.

$25.00 (academic rate: $20.00); paper.

1998. ISBN 1-55775-707-0. **Stock #WEO-1897.**

Private Market Financing for Developing Countries
by a staff team from the IMF's Policy Development and Review Department led by Steven Dunaway

This study surveys recent trends in flows to developing countries through banking and securities markets. It also analyzes the institutional and regulatory framework for developing country finance; institutional investor behavior and pricing of developing country stocks; and progress in commercial bank debt restructuring in low-income countries.

$20.00 (academic rate: $12.00); paper.

1995. ISBN 1-55775-526-4. **Stock #WEO-1595.**

Available by series subscription or single title (including back issues); academic rate available only to full-time university faculty and students. For earlier editions please inquire about prices.

The IMF *Catalog of Publications* is available on-line at the Internet address listed below.

Please send orders and inquiries to:
International Monetary Fund, Publication Services, 700 19th Street, N.W.
Washington, D.C. 20431, U.S.A.
Tel.: (202) 623-7430 Telefax: (202) 623-7201
E-mail: publications@imf.org
Internet: http://www.imf.org